Political Patterns in America

POLITICAL patterns in america:
conflict representation and resolution

DAN NIMMO
THOMAS UNGS
University of Tennessee

W. H. Freeman and Company
San Francisco

Sponsoring Editor: Richard J. Lamb; *Project Editor:* Betsy Dilernia; *Developmental Editor:* Jeanne Martin; *Manuscript Editor:* Ruth Veres; *Designer:* Marie Carluccio; *Illustration Coordinator:* Cheryl Nufer; *Illustrator:* Tim Keenan; *Compositor:* York Graphic Services; *Printer and Binder:* The Maple-Vail Book Manufacturing Group.

Cover: Pieced quilt, c. 1900. America Hurrah Antiques, New York.

Library of Congress Cataloging in Publication Data

Nimmo, Dan D
   Political patterns in America.

   Bibliography: p.
   Includes index.
   1. United States—Politics and government—
Handbooks, manuals, etc.   I. Ungs, Thomas Dale,
1928–   joint author. II. Title.
JK274.N53   320.9'73'0924   78-11419
ISBN 0-7167-1009-9

Photo credits: p. 14, © Howard Harrison 1970; p. 35, © Howard Harrison 1968; p. 67, © Howard Harrison 1978; p. 120, © Howard Harrison 1971; p. 155, © Howard Harrison 1978; p. 174, © Howard Harrison 1971; p. 223, © Howard Harrison 1978; p. 243, © Howard Harrison 1978; p. 280, © Howard Harrison 1978; p. 328, © Stewart Brand 1977; p. 387, © Howard Harrison 1971; p. 433, © Howard Harrison 1978; p. 452, © Howard Harrison 1978; p. 466, © Howard Harrison 1978.

9 8 7 6 5 4 3 2 1

contents

Preface

Judging by the numerous texts currently available in American politics and government, one notices that the more revisions a book undergoes the bigger it gets. Such had been the case with the first three editions of *American Political Patterns.* As we contemplated the preparation of a new edition, however, we asked ourselves whether more bulk and additional detail were truly consistent with our original purpose of providing a book about the basic patterns of American politics and institutions—a book that would incorporate the most important findings and insights from the various behavioral sciences within a single coherent interpretative framework. Such a text was to be selective in its details, topics, and illustrations and straightforward in format, not overloaded with a vast array of visual devices. And, most importantly, it was to carry a common theme throughout each chapter: that politics is inherent in social life; that it is, in fact, a prerequisite of society.

As we reviewed previous editions we concluded that increased length and more details were not consistent with our original intent. Therefore, readers already familiar with *American Political Patterns* will find that in the present text we have produced a book no larger than its predecessors but one that in many respects is more selective in content, more focused in framework, and more consonant with the rule of parsimony. For example, the opening chapter is a brief exposition of our integrating framework. We discuss political conflict and consensus in conjunction with other topics rather than assigning a separate chapter to the subject. A bibliography at the end of the book removes the redundancy that end-of-chapter reference notes often provide.

The key features that marked the quality of *American Political Patterns* remain. A consistent and well-integrated teaching tool derives from a deliberate effort to link each chapter to all others, emphasizing the interrelatedness of political activity, not disparate nuts and bolts. To that end, we have woven discussions of such significant matters as civil liberties, federalism, and substantive policy decisions throughout the text rather than artificially relegating them to separate chapters. To be sure, there are points of emphasis, such as on federalism in Chapter 3 and on civil liberties in Chapter 4. Yet because such topics form the fiber of daily American political life, we continue to explore them in a variety of contexts.

In sum, we have tried not to distract the student from learning about politics and government in America. Visual devices may attract a reader's attention briefly, but if beyond that point there remain only details to memorize, then interest wanes, attention wanders, and enthusiasm dies. Moreover, exposing only the seamy side of government may have certain shock value, but learning about politics is not the same as going to a peep show, and sooner or later the less titillating dimensions must be dealt with responsibly. In short, it is our conviction that politics is too serious a subject to either trivialize or oversimplify. We have sought to avoid both pitfalls.

Many people have been of assistance in the development and preparation of this volume, most of all the students and teachers who have read and studied previous editions and offered valuable advice, comments, and suggestions. With special thanks we single out Roger Durand of the University of Houston, for his critical commentary on drafts of the present text. Paulette Acres and Eileen Cave typed the manuscript with accuracy and dispatch. And we would be truly remiss in not thanking Richard Lamb and others at W. H. Freeman for their willingness, enthusiasm, and patience in helping two authors who believe, to paraphrase a political scientist who took his readers more seriously than his sales, that students are not fools.

August 1978

Dan Nimmo
Thomas Ungs

Political Patterns in America

I

Patterns
OF CONFLICT
AND CONSENSUS:
WHAT MAKES
POLITICS
necessary
AND POSSIBLE
IN AMERICA?

CONFLICT:
THE SEEDBED
OF POLITICS

In the late summer of 1768 British troops arrived in Boston. Their mission: to uphold the authority of the Board of Customs Commissioners, a body created by the British to collect taxes, tariffs, and customs in the American colonies. The revenue would pay the salaries of colonial officials and support troops on the frontiers. Since colonial legislatures had refused to raise the needed funds, the British plan seemed a good idea—to the British. To Americans, the presence of British soldiers was a grievance, and the colonists missed no opportunity to protest. At best it was a delicate situation. To make things worse, the colonists taunted the troops to find out how much abuse the redcoats would stand in light of orders from British officers that the soldiers show stalwart restraint.

Colonists and British suffered one another's presence in the Boston community for well over a year. There were disputes, but nothing threatened the state of tense tranquillity. Then, on March 2, 1770, Boston ropemakers provoked a running skirmish with the soldiers on guard. The longer it ran, the more people the argument attracted. On March 5 a large crowd gathered, the guard contingent was increased, and the game of taunting the redcoats turned into a fight. Led by Crispus Attucks, a Black sailor, the crowd threatened one of the sentries, roughing him up so harshly that he cried for help. Captain Preston of the redcoats produced a corporal's guard. In the melee, one of the soldiers panicked and fired into the crowd; seven other soldiers followed suit. The result: five men killed, six wounded.

Instantly all of Boston was in an uproar. Samuel Adams demanded that the redcoats be withdrawn; Governor Hutchinson ordered the regiments pulled back. Captain Preston and his seven privates were tried for murder before a local court in the hostile community. Two prominent young radicals, Josiah Quincy and John Adams, were lawyers for the defendants. In spite of a situation scarcely favorable to Preston and his troops, he and five privates were acquitted. The other two soldiers were convicted of manslaughter and received a nominal penalty. The court maintained that Crispus Attucks, a victim of the redcoats' bullets, and the crowd were also responsible for the uprising.

In American folklore this incident is known as the Boston Massacre. The story is an especially pertinent introduction to a book about American politics because the Boston Massacre and its resolution illustrate several things about politics in general and about American politics in particular. The narration reminds us that society is very fragile. Because most people live their daily lives in a fairly ordered set of social surroundings, they take society for granted. They assume that social order is inevitable, the "natural" condition of things. But the conditions that prevailed in Boston in the first week of March 1770 suggest otherwise. Where there is tension between rival forces, as there often is in the lives of people, then a symbol of grievance (a redcoat), a provocation (the ropemakers' taunting), a rallying cry (Crispus Attucks), an incident (roughing up a sentry), a panicked response (shots into a crowd)—alone or in combination—can cause a tranquil social order to revert to primitive social chaos.

One premise of this volume is that conflict, not order, is the underlying condition of society. Given even the smallest opportunity, any conflict will spread to involve more and more people, just as the crowd in Boston grew larger and larger and the number of soldiers increased contingent by contingent. "The central political fact in a free society," wrote one analyst of American politics, "is the tremendous contagiousness of conflict" (Schattschneider, 1960, p. 2).

The Boston Massacre also illustrates something else. Living under conditions where conflict in social life is contagious and society itself thus problematic, people search for ways to create and recreate stable, uniform, and persistent patterns of interaction with one another. We call these ways politics. As in Boston, they can take various forms: strict orders (to British troops not to lose their poise despite the unrelenting taunts of colonists); continuing protests (of colonists about their grievances); threats to use force to restore social order (the increase in the guard contingent); government orders to reduce tensions (by removing troops); judicial proceedings to fix the responsibility (the local trial of Preston and his privates); the emergence of leaders representing diverse and conflicting interests (Adams, Quincy, Attucks, Preston, Hutchinson); and the formulation of bargains that give each party to a dispute some, but not all, of what they want (laying the responsibility for the Boston Massacre at the door of Preston's convicted troops while exonerating others; placing blame upon the mob while withdrawing troops from the community).

Governments exist to make societies possible. This is a book about American government, that is, about the political patterns that emerge as Americans strive to regulate their conduct under conditions of social conflict. The description and interpretation of American politics presented in these pages is certainly not the only way to understand how people try to fashion an answer to their most basic problem of how to live together. Other observers look at what goes on and see other patterns: efforts to bring the American soil and people under control by conquest; the irony of a nation professing government by the people when ruled instead by privileged elites; the failure of the performance of government to measure up to its promise; or the tragedy and comedy of American government today. We see instead people using politics simply to make America possible. The assumptions, categories of analysis, and perspectives we use can contribute to any reader's grasp of American political activity, not only in the colonies of the 1770s but also in a nation preparing to meet the conflicts of the late 1970s and to enter the 1980s.

Politics is people

The grammatical construction is questionable, but the point is crucial: *The common denominator of all government is people.* Throughout the world more than one hundred national governments legislate rules of conduct for billions of human beings through innumerable smaller political units, distinct in form and practice. America alone has a multitude of jurisdictions: the federal government, state governments, counties, municipalities, school districts, water districts, garbage districts, and many, many others. But strip away the diverse forms, rules, laws, and units and what remains is people. Politics is what it is because people act as they do.

NO ONE SAID IT WAS EASY: THE HUMAN SITUATION

The origins of politics lie in the human situation. That situation is a paradox: it is bounded by limitations but full of possibilities. People are limited by their physical needs and social wants, yet freed by their capacities, skills, and resources.

Sheer survival comes first. This means satisfying physical needs, including adequate food, water, clothing, and shelter. In solving the problems of survival and development, people's capacities come to the rescue. Their hands, reason, and speech enable them to invent the necessary tools and technology. But survival is not enough. People also want to be with one another: They have social as well as physical needs. However, this is where things get chancy. The same capacities that make it possible to survive and seek out one another make it hard for people to live together in harmony, that is, in society.

People who come together usually need and want different things. This diversity of desires is the basis of politics. At the simplest level, everyone must have food but people desire different foods to enjoy living. In their yearnings for respect, self-esteem, and equality, individuals differ in their social desires as well. Inevitably, it seems, they disagree over how best to gratify their desires. Moreover, they have differing capacities and resources (talents, intellectual and emotional makeups, and skills) enabling—or preventing—pursuit of those diverse desires.

In sum, people differ in their physical and social preferences and traits. To create a safe and stable social order that will enable them to get more or less what they want, people make demands upon one another. But there is rarely enough of everything they demand to go around. Disputes arise. The human situation, in all its diversity, is the source of social conflict, and a problematic social order, the very seedbed of politics.

HOW FIGHTS START: THE UNIVERSALITY OF HUMAN CONFLICT

Social conflict is universal, a normal part of the human situation. A social conflict arises when three conditions are fulfilled:

- Disputants realize that their desires differ from one another.
- Disputants act to get what they want.
- Disputants realize that their desires not only differ from those of others but also are incompatible with one another, and that limited resources make it unlikely that everybody's interests will be satisfied.

When these conditions exist, two possibilities follow: Either one disputant gains at the expense of the other, or all disputants agree to alter their demands so that none gains everything desired nor loses everything in the disagreement. In a typical conflict, the contending forces try to win as much as possible from one another, yet the parties to the dispute realize they have enough interests in common to compromise their differences. Pushed to the point of a no-compromise, nonnegotiable ultimatum, a desire can destroy the very society in which each interest seeks acceptance of its goals, as in the Civil War. Instead of rigidly adhering to extreme demands, each side in a *social* conflict resigns itself to accepting half a loaf to avoid the risk of winning nothing at all or losing everything.

The more diverse the desires and characteristics of a society's members, the greater the likelihood of social conflict. Conflicts are especially likely in pluralist societies. America is pluralist, both in its social makeup and in its governing institutions.

Social pluralism

As with any pluralist society, America has a large number of different groups, associations, and other interests. Chances are that if you are like most Americans, you are a member of a family, you associate with a few close friends, and you see fellow students or co-workers frequently. A vast array of intimate groups such as families, friends, and close associates is one aspect of a pluralist society. But this alone does not make a society pluralist. Lying between such intimate groups and the more impersonal governments that often seem far removed from your everyday life must be an intermediate layer of stable, organized group life. Again, if you are like most Americans, you may be a member of a church; you might have joined a sorority, fraternity, or other student association in college; and you may be contemplating membership in any number of occupational, military, and other voluntary organizations such as professional, civic, and recreational groups. These associations are the backbone of a socially diverse America. They provide a link between your private, daily life and your public but less frequently played role of active citizen.

What are the consequences of social pluralism? One is the generation of social conflict. Although there is often cooperation among the organizations people join, because the groups have overlapping goals, diverse groups, associations, and other interests frequently seek different things. These interests make demands upon one another and each tries to enhance its status with respect to others. The resulting tension produces social conflicts.

Moreover, there are important consequences that flow from people's affiliations with many different groups. First, people who join a variety of organizations need not be totally dependent upon any single group to satisfy all of their demands. Second, people's multiple affiliations contribute to, as well as reflect, their multiple concerns. They can pursue their interests in several groups; if a particular group does not fulfill all their aspirations, they can turn elsewhere and work to satisfy other goals, join other associations, or even form new groups to push for recognition. The variety of possibilities reduces the tendency for a person to invest all of his or her energies and emotions in any single issue tied to any single group. This is not to say that a single issue may not attract the attention of large numbers of Americans. Widespread concern over

American involvement in the Korean and Vietnam wars illustrates otherwise. Usually, however, a variety of issues cuts across the various groups a person belongs to and minimizes the likelihood of a single issue dominating public attention. Think, for instance, of the multiplicity of issues and groups currently associated with energy, housing, welfare, education, and women's rights.

Finally, because people join a variety of groups and thereby diffuse their loyalties, the various organizations must compete for the attention and support of their members. As a college graduate you will probably receive a barrage of requests for donations from civic groups, churches, alumni associations, professional associations, and clubs. Forced to woo the support of new members, groups find it difficult to control their own membership. Union members who vote against the candidate supported by their local, Democrats who vote for Gerald Ford, and Republicans who defect to Jimmy Carter all exemplify the independence from group affiliations people display in a pluralist society.

Political pluralism

America is not merely pluralist in its social composition. In addition to the many social groups, there are multiple and often conflicting governing units. Federalism enhances the development of a multiplicity of governments at the national, state, and local levels, each autonomous in a specific sphere. Separation of powers proliferates the number of governing units even more. Distinct executive, administrative, legislative, and judicial offices appear at all levels of government. Almost 90,000 governing agencies act on delegated authority that enables them to function as semiautonomous political groups. The proliferation of governing units contributes as much to the pluralist character of America as the plethora of private and nongovernmental groups that characterize social pluralism.

Political pluralism also generates social conflicts. For one thing, the governing principle of checks and balances insures a division of authority among various political units. As each tries to pursue its own interests (or the interests of the citizens it represents) it finds itself checked by others. Disputes over policies quickly develop. And, because there are so many centers of semiautonomous governing authority, conflicting social interests can lobby at a variety of points to try to influence policies. If the makers of artificial sweeteners lose out to one segment of consumer interests because the Federal Food and Drug Administration bans the sale of saccharine, the manufacturers can still turn to the courts, congressional committees, and other administrative agencies for relief.

In brief, social and political pluralism both breed conflict. A key theme of this text is that America's political and governing institutions act as participating interests in social conflicts—advancing causes of special interests—as much as they serve as arbitrators of disputes between nongovernmental interests. Imagine a baseball or football game in which the umpires and referees are not impartial, nor do they necessarily favor one team over the other; rather the officials enter the struggle against the teams (the other social groups) in order to preserve and improve their own interests in the contest. This is the character of social conflict in a pluralist society: It engages everybody—contestants, officials, and spectators.

Conflict divides people into opposing camps, but conflict can bring people together as well. When a society tolerates internal disputes, people can openly join groups that promote their personal desires. They look to the groups for goals to pursue, tactics to employ, and issues worth contesting. In the civil rights struggle of the 1950s and 1960s, for example, some Blacks followed the lead of the National Association for the Advancement of Colored People, a group that used litigation in federal courts as a means of redressing grievances. Others turned to the Southern Christian Leadership Conference of Dr. Martin Luther King, Jr., which used nonviolent protests—demonstrations, marches, sit-ins—to achieve the same goals. By joining either one or both organizations, members committed themselves to seeking equality of opportunity within the existing society. Open conflict with current social practices served both as a direct means of challenging those practices and an indirect way of remaining loyal to the society itself. Social conflict, then, derives from social divisions, but also constitutes a unifying force.

Another characteristic of conflict is that it emerges from and stimulates social change. The presence of social disputes is a reminder that "the times, they are a changin'" and that newly emergent social groups—Blacks, Chicanos, the young and the elderly, feminists, the alienated, and the impoverished—are pushing to achieve social goals that did not have a high priority in previous times. Conflict and change interlock; competing groups constantly challenge the status quo.

Just as an overly cooperative society may become stagnant, a highly competitive one may become crippled: When conflicts intensify, positions harden, and dogmatic goals are difficult to compromise. Pushed to the limit, conflict becomes *antisocial*. If a fragile social order is to avoid social chaos, there must be a widespread desire to adjust human conflict as well as a means of doing so. The desire is the presence of community; the means is politics.

FIGHTING AMONG OURSELVES:
THE UNIVERSALITY OF HUMAN COMMUNITY

No less universal than human conflict is the tendency of people to join together and share their experiences. This is the basis of human community. Communities reflect a collective disposition of human beings that cuts across regional, racial, religious, class, and other divisions.

Many scholars have tried to explain why people come together to form communities. There are many possible reasons: Humans are by nature social animals; they must associate with one another to satisfy physical needs; community is the inevitable outgrowth of the capacity to communicate; people share common beliefs and values. It is not necessary, for our discussion, to decide which explanation is the most plausible; we simply accept the fact that people do live together in community (Dewey, 1927). What does this mean in relation to the equally universal presence of human conflict?

Two considerations are uppermost. First, the fact that people live collectively does not mean that they forego disputes. Instead, the presence of community implies a willingness to tolerate conflicts, argue in the open, and adjust differences before the scope and intensity of disagreements endanger common survival. Community is an agreement to fight among ourselves, but not to annihilate each other. Sharing common territory under such an agreement means that driving one's antagonists away is not a feasible remedy for social controversies (although popular entertainment media portray this as a typical solution to the struggles between farmers and cattlemen in the days of the western frontier). Civil rights disputes cannot be adjusted by removing either segregationists or integrationists from the country, even though a dwindling number of Americans still propose it. When disputants occupy the same territory under conditions of community, they must discover solutions that make society possible.

Second, the character of whatever means people use to adjust their differences is affected by three principal aspects of the community: the personal, the social, and the constitutional.

- *Personal* considerations include individual beliefs, values, and expectations about living together in community and what people need and want from one another. Sometimes people share common ideas that constitute community ideologies or doctrines. But this is not always the case. Many times people share nothing beyond the fundamental belief in the worth of community living, disagreeing on a host of details.

- The *social* aspects of a community consist of the characteristics and relationships that draw people together in groups—groups that reach backward and forward beyond the lifetimes of the current residents of the community and include those now dead and those yet to be born. Both the socially significant attributes of individuals (age, sex, ethnicity, race, and religious affiliations) and the relations between people in a social unit (group memberships, status, privileges, occupations) define a community's social base, which is not the individuals themselves, but the aggregates of people joined by shared characteristics and activities.

- *Constitutional* arrangements exist in any community; they may be formal (written), informal (unwritten), or some combination, but in any case they constitute the arrangements, rules, and procedures for settling disputes.

Politics: making society possible by regulating human conflict

People living together, we have said, sometimes fight. The more they differ from one another in what they want and in their capacities to get it, the more likely they will be to disagree in their pursuit of scarce resources. To keep their disputes within community bounds and make society possible, they reach personal accords, social understandings, and constitutional arrangements, that is, agreements on how to disagree. In short, they turn to *politics: the most inclusive process for regulating social conflict in a community.* In the remainder of this chapter we will examine this working definition of politics and its implications for the subjects discussed in this book.

POLITICS AS PROCESS

By designating politics as a process, we focus on the *patterns* of human activities related to adjusting social disputes. To be sure, some of the things people do appear to happen in a haphazard, sporadic fashion. When, for example, Sara Jane Moore fired a pistol as President Gerald Ford was departing a San Francisco hotel in 1975, the act seemed to bear no clear relationship to other political events (although it may well have in the mind of the person committing it); it did not fit any apparent pattern. But with most political acts—expressing political opinions, campaigning, voting, protesting, policy-making—students of politics discern a pattern. More precisely, we interpret political acts in ways that make sense to us; we see a sequence in their unfolding, a regularity in their occurrence and reoccurrence, a context in which they take place, and a relationship between them. By looking for patterns we see connections between what happened yesterday, what happens today, and what will happen tomorrow. We treat acts not as isolated happenings but as events related to one another which, taken in context, form a unified whole.

There is, of course, some risk in this procedure: political scientists may see relationships between acts that have no bearing upon one another and impose a pattern where none exists. In the 1950s some Americans linked American setbacks in foreign policy to the alleged internal subversion of the U.S. government by communists; in the 1960s a few political observers insisted there was a conspiratorial pattern to the assassinations of President John Kennedy, Robert Kennedy, and Martin Luther King; and many current political analysts insist that elections, public opinion, and policymaking are all carefully orchestrated by a powerful, though not always visible, set of elites bent upon controlling government to their own selfish ends.

To avoid the pitfall of seeing ghosts, we will emphasize patterns in which connections are supported by considerable evidence. Specifically, we will analyze configurations of political participation that make policymakers aware of conflicts that require attention; we call these *patterns of conflict representation*. We will also look at the regularized ways in which policymakers go about dealing with conflicts that are brought to their attention; we label these *patterns of conflict resolution*. Taken together, patterns of representation and resolution constitute politics, a process of regulating conflict.

PATTERNS OF CONFLICT REPRESENTATION

Political activities range in variety from the simple act of marking a ballot to the physical, mental, and emotional effort that enters into making highly complex legislative decisions and controversial decisions of the Supreme Court. These activities normally reflect the pursuit of individual and group interests, the efforts of people to achieve their needs and wants through politics.

When well-defined interests confront one another and express their demands to public officials, we call this activity *conflict representation*. The critical element of conflict representation is the existence of avenues through which people can make known their shared and conflicting feelings, interests, and demands to their elected and appointed agents and governors. So defined, representation refers to the activities of any person who publicizes interest disputes for community action—whether that person be a congressman, journalist, voter, lobbyist, picket, demonstrator, bureaucrat, teacher, or student.

Conflict representation occurs in every government, but its function as a link between governors and governed is of special importance in a representative democracy. A democracy not only implements the desires of the governed but provides the means for holding governors accountable. The effectiveness of that accountability depends in large measure on communications between citizens and officials. If normal channels for presenting conflicts to officials are closed, or if officials dismiss a significant number of complaints sent through open channels and refuse to do anything about them, people will turn to other ways of voicing grievances.

In American government there are a variety of channels available to citizens who want to press demands upon officials and hold those officials accountable.

We will describe those channels and assess their contribution to conflict representation in Part II. Before analyzing these specifics, however, we will use the remaining chapters of Part I to discuss the background of conflict regulation in America: We compare the general character of conflict representation with patterns of conflict resolution in the remainder of Chapter 1; describe the liberal democratic features of American politics in Chapter 2; and explain the constitutional background of American political patterns in Chapter 3. Part II then focuses upon conflict representation: Chapter 4 looks in detail at the active and passive ways in which Americans take part in politics; Chapter 5 considers how citizens formulate and express opinions; Chapter 6 explores how Americans respond to their political leaders and how leaders try to influence followers, especially in election campaigns; Chapter 7 looks at elections and voting as one way of choosing leaders, expressing desires to them, and holding them accountable; Chapter 8 explores the vital, but perhaps diminishing, role of political parties in conflict representation; and Chapter 9 focuses upon one of the most effective ways of influencing public officials, organized pressure and protest.

PATTERNS OF CONFLICT RESOLUTION

When governing institutions decide public policies and make those decisions stick, we call this *conflict resolution*. Public policies are decisions, or courses of action, agreed upon by a variety of social interests to deal with a conflict. When people accept such policies and live in accordance with them, the policies moderate severe social disputes and thus make social order possible.

But what makes public policies stick? Political observers suggest three possibilities, and each operates in the American community.

1. Some people accept policies as binding because there are mechanisms to enforce them. Force and the threat of force are one example. People may be reluctant to break a 55 mile-per-hour speed limit if they know they will receive heavy fines, pay high court costs, lose their driving licenses, and perhaps go to jail for doing so. But if law enforcement officials look the other way, people may push down on the accelerator. Force and the threat of its use are mechanisms of *social control*, but they are not the only ones. Organized groups (for example, labor unions, business associations, farm cooperatives, and professional organizations) sometimes exert tremendous pressure upon their members to conform to policies judged to be in the group interest. In discussing the role of both the administrative bureaucracy and the courts in conflict resolution, we will see still other mechanisms of social control in American government.

2. Some people accept policies because, acting as free and independent

individuals, they find it convenient to do so. They may arrive at that choice out of a careful assessment of policies in light of the interests they pursue; they may fall into the choice out of habit; or they may have a host of private reasons of their own. When the choices of a wide variety of people, based on a wide variety of reasons, produce a common course of action, the acceptance of policies results from *social convergence*. When oil-exporting nations in the Middle East clamped an embargo on sales to this country in 1973, President Nixon announced a policy of energy conservation to enable the United States to weather the crisis. Many Americans took individual actions (lowered their thermostats in winter, consolidated automobile trips, formed car pools) for quite different reasons (to cut costs, diminish their fear of gas rationing, fulfill a sense of patriotic duty). These actions converged to reduce oil consumption for the brief period of the embargo. But, "to expect that all men for all time will go on thinking different things, and yet doing the same things, is a doubtful speculation. It is not founding society on a communion, or even on a convention, but rather on a coincidence" (Lippmann, 1922, p. 23). In Chapters 2 and 3 we explore a crucial case of problematic coincidence, the degree to which

Americans accept common beliefs and values about constitutional democracy and abide by them in their political conduct.

3. Some people accept policies because, either directly or indirectly, they have had a part in negotiating the content of those policies. In the process, they have obtained some, but rarely all, of what they demanded. For these people, the rewards of policymaking outweigh the costs, at least to the extent that the participants receive sufficient benefits from their efforts to keep on bargaining. *Social negotiation* has always been a key feature of American policymaking. Indeed, in Chapter 3 we argue that the evolution of our most fundamental policy, the Constitution of the United States, was and remains today a process of negotiation. Moreover, in Part III we explore the role of bargaining in policy formulation (Chapter 10), presidential leadership (Chapter 11), congressional adoption of laws (Chapter 12), bureaucratic applications of policies (Chapter 13), and the adjudication of the Supreme Court (Chapter 14).

For whatever reason people accept them as binding, resolutions of conflicts take two forms: (1) written laws, statutes, and decisions; and (2) unwritten customs, conventions, and ways of doing things. The federal budget, for example, is a long, detailed, and highly intricate document prepared each year to raise and expend funds for a multitude of programs and projects. By contrast, no written statute calls for quadrennial Republican and Democratic conventions to nominate candidates for President, a vital stage in the selection of our national leadership.

Although public policies resolve disputes between conflicting interests, they do not settle them for all time. Rather, it is best to think of conflict resolution in America as a method of moderating social tensions to avoid the dissolution of the community. In Chapter 10 we analyze policymaking in terms of policies devoted to exploiting America's energy resources, regulating firearms, and alleviating poverty to illustrate that instead of curing social ills or producing permanent settlements, conflict resolution is a ceaseless process.

Conflict resolution not only falls short of ending disputes, it creates new ones. No sooner is a policy that seems to placate one set of conflicting interests made than other interests challenge it. Thus, in an ambitious attempt to secure "energy independence" for the United States, executive and congressional officials in the 1970s committed large expenditures to the development of nuclear energy as a major source of power. This decision not only increased demands from the coal and petroleum interests for federal assistance in developing their resources, it also generated demands from enthusiasts for solar energy, developers of fusion techniques, and leading opponents of nuclear options, including consumer advocate Ralph Nader and his organization, Critical Mass.

In sum, to really resolve disputes, resolutions must be accepted by a large number of people; even then they resolve but do not settle, and may even generate new conflicts. Politics, therefore, produces temporary solutions that keep social disputes truly social rather than antisocial. The results are acceptable, not perfect. Governor Hutchinson withdrew British troops from the city after the Boston Massacre, but the fight went on and eventually became a war.

American political patterns: a summation

In analyzing government it is useful to think of politics as patterns of activity concerned with the regulation of social conflicts. This usage is appropriate to a view of the human situation that states: (1) people are physical beings living in societies; (2) people have different needs, wants, capacities, and resources; (3) people pursue conflicting interests because of their very diversity; (4) people associate to achieve interests that come from sharing the human experience of community; (5) people endeavor to pursue their conflicting interests but desire to do so without destroying that community; and (6) people use politics as a method of regulating social disputes.

In America, the regulation of conflict consists of the representation and resolution of social disagreements. Representation makes the conflicts known through political participation—expressing opinions, exercising and following leadership, voting, being partisan, and presenting organized demands. Resolution is a process of making policies to reach partial accommodations that keep conflicts within manageable limits. Officials make acceptable (and sometimes unacceptable) public policy through formulation, executive action, legislative adoption, bureaucratic application, and court adjudication. All of this occurs within an American community marked by varying personal beliefs and values, social diversity, and constitutional fragmentation. In short, politics is what it is because people are what they are. Bearing this in mind, let us take a closer look at American political patterns.

LIBERAL DEMOCRACY AND THE POLITICS OF CONSENSUS

Asked to define the term *democracy*, an elementary school student responded, "I don't know, but it's what we are." Despite a varied history during which some minority groups have struggled to achieve equality, voting rights, and protections against discrimination, Americans have always thought of themselves as practitioners of democracy. Despite the tolerance of slavery in the first 75 years of America's national existence, or the fact that the United States held its first nine national elections without a recorded popular vote for presidential candidates, Americans have consistently expressed belief in the "democratic values" and "rule by ballot" promised by the Declaration of Independence and the Constitution. These values, passed on from generation to generation as symbols of the "American way," shape what most Americans consider to be the proper relationship between government and citizen.

The values may vary from one time to another in meaning and importance, but they influence the conduct of American citizens. Perceptions of right and wrong in political decision-making, and even the scope of individual and group claims on society, are affected by our democratic values. Few Americans may be able to provide a sophisticated definition of democracy, nor would they be concerned about not being able to do so. Nevertheless, Americans act out a political theory that dates back to the eighteenth century. This is the theory of *liberal democracy.*

We broadly define democracy as a *system in which the governed are able to have a significant influence on public policy decisions made by those who hold formal positions of authority (the governors)* (Lipset, 1959, pp. 45–48; Schumpeter, 1942, pp. 269–273). Our definition emphasizes *representation* of those who are outside the formal structure of authority. Such representation is possible only if there are mechanisms (rules and procedures) that make access to decisionmakers possible. Access, in turn, depends upon a set of practices and attitudes that encourage political participation of individuals and organizations in conflict not only with each other but with government agencies. These practices and attitudes invoke legal and moral restraints even on a majority that is carried away by an idea or a personality of the moment.

In this chapter we examine the basic elements of democratic theory and explore their origins and development in the American experience. We also explore the extent to which Americans share ideas about the concepts of liberal democracy and the manner in which political business should be conducted. Ideas need not be held rigidly or consistently; often they are not. But they do contribute to a *community consensus, or a sharing of values and beliefs about human goals and conduct.*

The meaning of American democracy: yardsticks for measurement

Abraham Lincoln's classic phrase, "government of the people, by the people, and for the people," not only articulates an historic governing *ideal* but also refers to the basic *tools* by which the ideal of self-government is put into practice. Our discussion of democracy relies on these two basic yardsticks to assess the meaning of American democratic values. The ideals and principles supporting the political theory are the *prescriptive dimension.* The ways of putting the theory into practice and maintaining its viability are the *procedural dimension.* It is not easy to separate the prescriptive and procedural aspects of democratic theory and practice. One prescribes what liberal democracy ought to be; the other is a collection of rules, laws, and customs that define the democratic procedures of a political system.

We do not fully discuss the great *ends or goals of government*—the "general welfare," "domestic tranquility," and the "blessings of liberty," all expressly included in the Preamble to the Constitution of the United States. They *are* linked to liberal democratic theory, but primarily as the *objects* toward which democratic ideals and procedures are directed and which democracy as a system is probably capable of achieving.

THE KEY PROCEDURE OF REPRESENTATION

An element common to both the prescriptive and procedural dimensions is the idea that the governors (the policymakers) are accountable to the governed (those affected by policy decisions). This idea stems from the proposition that the only acceptable way to enforce responsibility is to assure the right of the governed to choose their governors. *Representation* is "the process by which diverse individuals and groups obtain a voice in public policy." Lack of representation can lead to frustration and violence, as the American Revolution itself attests.

The *prescriptive* ideals of accountability and participation are made meaningful by commonly accepted *procedural* rules and arrangements for representation. Thus, open, competitive, and free elections in which votes are counted honestly; widespread suffrage; and the right to criticize policy and propose alternatives without government reprisals are elements essential to any implementation of the theory of liberal democracy.

Two important qualifications should be noted here. First, although rule by the governed and representation of interests are essential to the democratic system, the particular procedural arrangements can vary greatly between different political systems. For example, Great Britain, the Federal Republic of Germany, and Israel have parliamentary systems in which the chief executive—a premier or prime minister—is chosen by a legislature elected by the voters. The United States has a presidential system in which the chief executive is chosen by an electoral college that ratifies the popular vote pluralities (*not* necessarily majorities) won by presidential candidates in the states. The government of France incorporates elements of both the parliamentary and the presidential systems: It has a premier, but because the president has the power to appoint or dismiss him, the French system is more presidential than parliamentary. Other procedural differences appear among democratic nations, and even among states in this country: voting qualifications based on literacy tests or time of residence, nomination for office by convention or direct primary, the requirement of a plurality or a majority to elect a governor.

A second qualification is that not all procedural rules and practices adhere equally to liberal democracy's prescriptive tenets. Although laws or practices that discriminate against groups of voters are, by definition, inconsistent with the right of the governed to choose their governors, truly universal suffrage is hardly ever granted and practiced anywhere. Only recently did women win the right to vote in Switzerland; and in the United States a turnout of 70 percent of the eligible voters is considered good, even in a presidential year. We can say, however, that restriction of suffrage to a specific minority—landowners, for instance, or members of the Caucasian race—is so inconsistent with the prescriptive principle as to negate democracy. But the precise line between democratic and undemocratic rules and procedures is extremely difficult to fix and may vary from system to system. A specific restriction on suffrage in one system may be considered undemocratic because it conflicts with the inherited standards or the social habits of its people; the same practice may not be inconsistent with democratic values in another system where different standards, habits, and conditions prevail.

THE KEY PRESCRIPTION OF INDIVIDUAL DIGNITY

Recognition of the basic worth of the individual is one of the hallmarks of the democratic ideal. Translated into more specifically political terms, the acknowledgment of individual dignity means that every individual should benefit from a maximum of opportunity to develop his or her intelligence, personality, and freedom of choice. People can develop fully only when they are allowed to participate in the regulation of their own conduct. John Dewey summed it up well: "The keynote of democracy as a way of life may be expressed, it seems to me, as the necessity for the participation of every mature human being in the formation of the values that regulate the living of men together" (Dewey, 1937, p. 457).

Under the democratic ideal, a sense of community and the sharing of worthwhile human experience are generated by joint participation in social choices. Democratic politics therefore has a distinct purpose: "the education of an entire people to the point where their intellectual, emotional, and moral capacities have reached their full potential and they are joined, freely and actively, in the genuine community" (Davis, 1964, p. 40). Politics, at its best or at its worst, is a distinctly human endeavor. Consequently, its contribution to human perfection determines its quality. Political institutions and procedures can be designated democratic only to the extent that they give meaning to the democratic value of individual dignity.

Individual dignity has not been fully realized in any democratic polity. Yet the *idea* remains a goal of all democratic societies. It also serves as a yardstick to measure the quality of democratic life in a political system. The moral appeal inherent in the concept of human dignity is a powerful element in public policy choices. Programs to alleviate poverty are, at least in part, a recognition that meaningful participation in a democratic society is impossible when economic deprivation is severe or social conditions deny individuals equal opportunity to employment. Similarly, most people view the right to at least a minimum of formal education as essential to meaningful participation in a democratic community.

Faced with the increasingly complex problems associated with an impersonal bureaucratic state, the growing energy crisis, and the deterioration of environmental quality, democratic societies may have to clarify and reaffirm the meaning of individual dignity. For example, they will have to decide to what extent it is necessary to restrict personal choice regarding such things as housing, transportation, and the use of natural resources in the interests of community needs. Measured in terms of individual choice, the quality of democratic life might well be increasingly defined in terms of the imperatives of community environmental and ecological needs.

The American experience has never met the democratic ideal. Participation in the choice of officeholders and access to policymakers has been denied to various groups. Women have voted in presidential elections without restriction only since 1920, and the struggle of Blacks, Chicanos, American Indians, and other minorities for political and social equality is a story known to all. However, even though equality of opportunity and participation have not been fully achieved, the democratic ideal remains strong and viable, brightening the prospect for further achievement of democratic goals.

MORE SPECIFIC YARDSTICKS

Having broadly defined democracy with an emphasis on the concepts of representation and human dignity, we now offer four more specific criteria. A political community is democratic to the extent that (1) popular control of policymakers is broadly based; (2) open discussion and criticism of policy is tolerated; (3) political liberties are protected; and (4) political equality is recognized (Mayo, 1960). In examining the historical roots of the democratic doctrine in America and the specific meaning of these four essentials, it is necessary to bear in mind that the ideals of democratic practices do not necessarily coincide with the realities. The ideals (prescriptive dimension) are measures by which to assess the quality and effectiveness of rules and procedures in the democratic system (procedural dimension).

Origins of liberal democracy in America

Political activity is shaped by both past and present. Americans generally accept democratic ideals as truth; that is, they do not consider debate on the merit of the ideals a proper area of social conflict. This kind of ideological and procedural consensus is certainly not the pattern in many other nations. There, disagreement over the basic premises upon which government ought to rest and the procedural boundaries of social conflict has historically been, and in some cases still is, the subject of divisive debate. What explains the almost total agreement on democratic ideals in America? The sources of our democratic ideas and practices account for part of the answer. The evolutionary fact that Americans accepted these ideas virtually from the beginning of their national development and have never experienced significant internal challenge to them accounts for a large part of the rest of it. We examine both of these elements in the following discussion.

SOURCES OF DEMOCRATIC IDEAS

The colonists brought to America many European concepts about the nature of people and government. Perhaps the most profound influence on colonial ideas was the theory of John Locke, the seventeenth-century British philosopher. Before analyzing Locke's ideas, we will briefly examine the impact that other thinkers and forces had on colonial ideas.

Some of the less libertarian leaders of the American revolution drew arguments from Thomas Hobbes' *Leviathan* (1651) to support their case for a strong centralized authority. The Englishman James Harrington maintained that political stability depends on the actual distribution of property; this thesis greatly influenced colonial thought. The concept of balancing power by separating the departments of government was borrowed from the early eighteenth-century writings of the French Baron de Montesquieu. Montesquieu considered the separation of powers the key to the protection of liberties. Eighteenth-century Americans quoted Montesquieu frequently and accepted his formulation of the separation of powers virtually without dissent (Rossiter, 1953, pp. 359–360).

Although political theory was of considerable importance in shaping colonial ideas, the men who took up arms in 1775 were probably more influenced by the idea that they were British subjects who had been denied their rights by a faraway government in London. They claimed the rights of British citizens everywhere, including the rights of petition and peaceful redress of grievances from Parliament. Americans defended resistance to British demands not only by referring to the ideas of political theorists but also by invoking the traditions and practices of the mother country. In the words of James Otis, a major American revolutionary figure, "every British Subject, born on the continent of America, or in any other of the British dominions, is entitled to all the natural, essential, inherent, and inseparable rights of our fellow subjects in Great Britain" (quoted in Mason, 1965, p. 96).

These notions of British and European origin soon changed. Less than fifteen months separated the battles of Lexington and Concord and the Declaration of Independence; in little more than a year what had begun as a nasty little English civil war turned into something else entirely. Moreover, both before and after independence, the old concepts were modified by the unique experience of the colonists in the new American society, which contained no feudalism, no ingrown hereditary privilege, and no radical underprivileged proletariat. Believing they had been "born free" (as Alexis de Tocqueville put it), Americans adopted a "natural liberalism" reflecting the absence of a struggle against entrenched classes (Hartz, 1955, p. 5).

"Democracy" did not finally become an acceptable word until the presidency of Andrew Jackson. Nonetheless, from the early colonial period, Americans developed a democratic liberalism based on the John Locke model. Middle class in its profile, this liberalism emphasized the virtues of hard work and the rights of the individual to acquire and hold private property. Few American leaders have ever challenged that outlook. It has characterized our nation throughout its history so intensely that Louis Hartz speaks of America as having the "moral unanimity of a liberal society" and as exhibiting the intolerance of a "dogmatic liberalism" toward any concepts not fitting into a Lockean background (1955, pp. 9–10). Thus, socialist attacks on the concept of private property have historically been considered un-American or undemocratic, whether or not they were launched within the democratic framework of free expression and debate.

The influence of Locke's thinking in the colonial and revolutionary period is amply illustrated by the charge sometimes leveled against Thomas Jefferson that, in writing the Declaration of Independence, he did little more than lift from Locke's earlier work a phrase specifying the purpose of governments: to protect "life, health, liberty, or possessions." Jefferson did make a few changes, for he spoke instead of "life, liberty, and the pursuit of happiness." But as Carl Becker shrewdly observed, "the strength of the Declaration was precisely that it said what everyone was thinking. . . . Where Jefferson got his ideas is hardly so much a question as where he could have gotten away from them" (Becker, 1922, pp. 24, 26).

Locke's political theory and democratic values

American democratic ideas are not traceable to any one single source but the political ideas of revolutionary America bear a strong resemblance to the ideas expressed by John Locke (1632–1704). His political thought is best represented in his *Two Treatises on Government*, published in 1690, which were widely read by American colonial leaders. Locke argued the truth of ideas that were revolutionary in his own time but which quickly became undebatable concepts in the lexicon of American democratic values.

Locke founded his political thought upon the concept of an initial *state of nature* preceding civil society, in which all people are "free, equal, and independent" and governed only by a *natural law* emanating from God. Although pure conjecture, the assumption of a state of nature existing before the laws of man was an important one in Locke's theory; it enabled him to argue that the origin and existence of human rights were beyond human control. By arguing that man is by nature a rational creature who uses his reason to deduce what the natural law is, Locke laid the basis for the concept of democratic equality. Additionally, he argued that the law of nature grants a person inalienable and fundamental rights of life, liberty, and property. Since these rights come from God, they are not man-made and may be neither taken away nor voluntarily given up.

THE NEED FOR A CIVIL SOCIETY.   Locke pictured human life in the original state of nature as happy and rational, not naturally antagonistic. If life became insecure or not fully satisfactory, it was because people tended to violate the fundamental moral law. In the state of nature, no one was obligated to obey man-made rules of authority, and the laws of nature could be enforced only through retaliatory action taken by each individual who suffered injury. (This is a recognizable description of the "law of nature" by which individuals once lived on the American frontier.) Locke thought that both human society and nature needed some help. In the natural state, the "want of a common judge" to protect individual rights created insecurity and brought people to recognize the need of a civil society authorized to make laws and enforce obedience. Although each person was required under the natural law to respect the natural rights of others, each was otherwise free. Any arrangement that could qualify a person's liberty would, then, require his consent. It could not be legitimately imposed in any other way, such as force.

THE SOCIAL CONTRACT.   Locke's means of providing a legitimate way to limit human freedom was the "social contract." By this device people pass from the state of nature into civil society. Each individual agrees with every other individual to a contract under which he forfeits some of his natural freedom in return for the benefits derived from man-made rules defining relationships among individuals. In short, the rights of the natural state from which people come are replaced by those of the human community. Locke held, however, that the rights of life, liberty, and property are universal and inalienable and therefore cannot be taken away by the civil society created by the social contract. The purpose of civil society is to serve the common good, but by definition the common good can never include the violation of a person's God-given rights.

THE GOVERNMENT.   Once a civil society has been created, who is to make the rules that will govern relationships within that society? Recognizing that rules could never be made if unanimous consent were required, Locke chose the practical solution of rule by the greater number, the majority.

   While the majority (more specifically, their representatives) can make rules, government exists *only as a trustee of the people who have agreed to the contract.* There is no authority independent of that granted by the people. And if such authority is claimed by one or more persons? Then, says Locke, the people may resort to revolution as the ultimate controlling weapon. Whenever governors violate the natural rights of the governed, they forfeit the authority vested in them under the social contract. Their transgressions justify public disobedience and rebellion, and free the individual of any obligation to obey civil law. But rebellion, if successful, merely returns society to the state of nature. There it remains until people agree to create another government by contract.

The Declaration of Independence

Locke's ideas found clear expression in the Declaration of Independence. Jefferson incorporated two basic Lockean themes, both of which have been built into American institutions and democratic beliefs: rational individualism and republican government.

RATIONAL INDIVIDUALISM.   The first proposition underlying the Declaration is that people are rational individuals having inalienable rights, that they are politically equal to other people and capable of rational choice between alternative courses of action. They can therefore govern themselves. This concept of individualism, which emphasizes the right of each person to make his own choices and to have that right respected and protected, is the taproot of liberal democracy. As the Declaration of Independence says, government exists "to secure these rights," and "whenever any Form of Government becomes destructive of these ends, it is the Right of the People to alter or to abolish it." This is an assertion of human dignity, founded on natural and hence inalienable rights that each individual is entitled to defend, by revolution if necessary.

The concept of individual rights and dignity has at least two important implications. One is that people are to be judged as individuals and not according to their economic or social position, or race or creed. In liberal democracy, "equality before the law" is a clear expression of individual worth. The second implication is equality of opportunity: The conditions under which a person can compete for economic, social, or political benefits must be equitable. It does not mean that all people are, or ought to be, equal in intelligence, ability, wealth, or status. It does mean that individual choices ought to be free and that arbitrary limitations on opportunity are unacceptable.

The concept of rational individualism thus provides the moral basis—the prescriptive dimension—of liberal democracy. It indicates what ought to guide the actions of people in their political relationships. It is true that the existence of natural rights and human dignity cannot be proved empirically. It is also true that real-life democratic governments dilute these moral principles in practice. Nevertheless, no American government can ignore them entirely. In American society, natural rights are presumed to exist—if only because Locke and Jefferson said so. Their triumph was to be credible when they asserted the existence of unchangeable, valid norms that were superior to man-made rules and provided the basis for judging government itself. Generations of Americans from the New England colonists on down have rallied to the Lockean standard in identifying public evils, promoting political and economic reforms, and generally insisting that any system that flouts these natural rights has forfeited its contractual right to exist.

REPUBLICAN GOVERNMENT. The second basic theme of the Declaration is that of republican or representative government. If citizens are politically equal and community authority exists only to achieve the aims of the governed, then it follows that the people must have an effective way of making their voices heard. From the Greeks through the democratic theorists of the eighteenth century, political thinkers assumed that public participation in open meetings at which community decisions were made was possible, because there were few people. It is impossible to conceive of such a system in a political community of large numbers of persons. The obvious alternative to direct democracy is representative democracy in which the people choose public officials by vote, and public officials act on their constituents' behalf and are held accountable by periodic elections.

It is also obvious that there will be conflicting goals, interests, and ideas among the people. How then is the community to decide which alternatives ought to prevail? The most practical way to operate is by majority rule. However, liberal democratic theory clearly implies that the majority may not force the minority and thereby deny them their basic human rights and freedoms which are understood to be beyond the reach of the popular will.

The relationship between majority rule and minority rights has always been an uneasy one, theoretically and practically. Ultimately majority rule rests on the ethical and moral assertion that purely private interests should not override considerations of the "public good," "public interest," "community interest," or "national interest." At the same time, the majority must not impose their will arbitrarily; in democratic theory it is morally wrong for a majority to violate the rights of minorities. Hence the problem: How to assure that the public interest will be served through majority rule while guaranteeing that minority rights will not be violated.

On the practical side, where there are serious inequalities of resources, influence, and power among the governed, the tension between majority rule and minority rights may threaten the very existence of representative government. The issue is not whether inequalities exist—they do and always have—but whether they are so great that they violate the rights of the deprived minorities. It is not easy to define the point at which minority interests are so seriously threatened by inequities that the minorities can no longer accept the laws made by the majority. In any event, inequalities and their potential consequences again raise the specter of the precarious nature of the relationship between majority rule and minority rights.

For Locke and for the framers of the U.S. Constitution the solution was to provide for limited government, that is, a government restrained from violating the rights of either majorities or minorities by rules, procedures, and laws. Less than 200 years has passed since America became an independent nation and undertook the construction of a government in accordance with Lockean principles. The events of those two centuries have altered the face of the nation—geographically, socially, and economically. The changes have put strains upon the tenets of liberal democracy and altered the degree to which Americans heed them. Let us see how.

DEMOCRATIC IDEALS AND THE AMERICAN EXPERIENCE

The ideological ties between eighteenth and twentieth century America are easy to identify. The Declaration of Independence, the Constitution, and other symbols of the democratic creed link Americans over time to a generally accepted ideology. Viewed in terms of social and economic forces, the link between the two centuries is much more difficult to understand. In the 1960s Martin Luther King appealed to the nation to "live out the true meaning of its creed: 'We hold these truths to be self-evident, that all men are created equal.'" The ideology expressed in the Declaration of Independence was as much accepted by Americans in 1776 or 1865 as during the 1960s yet their interpretation of the meaning of equality changed considerably during those two hundred years. As late as the beginning of the twentieth century President Theodore Roosevelt was severely criticized for having invited educator Booker T. Washington to lunch at the White House. U.S. Senator Theodore Bilbo expressed outrage "that Roosevelt has eaten with that nigger," and he added: "We shall have to kill a thousand niggers to get them back to their places" (L. Miller, 1966, p. 207). Such crudity and blatant racism would not be tolerated now. Equality and human rights are no longer the province of Whites only. Nevertheless, the gap between ideology and practice in the American experience did not become a salient issue until well into the twentieth century. The ideological foundation had not changed, but the social, political, and economic environment in which the meaning of democratic tenets was interpreted had changed substantially.

The eighteenth century

In its first years of independence, the United States was a nation of country dwellers. In 1790, more than 90 percent of a population of less than 4 million lived on farms. The wealth of the land was in agriculture. Manufacturing was in its early stages, and New England had most of the little that existed. By 1830, the American population had grown to 13 million, of whom more than 95 percent were native born. Many national and ethnic groups were represented in the total population, including many Germans and Scotch-Irish in Pennsylvania. But White American society in the early 1800s remained basically English and Protestant in its values and style of life. There were no large cities, even on the Eastern seaboard where the nation's people and power were concentrated. To the west lay the vast wilderness of the Louisiana Territory, purchased from France in 1803. It was hostile and largely unmapped, but it offered boundless economic opportunities to individuals dissatisfied with their surroundings. They could, if they chose, "get up and go."

The nineteenth century

As late as 1860, agriculture was still responsible for 50 percent of the nation's wealth, and by far the majority of Americans still lived on farms. But in the 1850s, 300,000 emigrants had arrived yearly, and thousands had settled not only in New York and Boston but also in the new cities farther west—Pittsburgh, St. Louis, Chicago. By 1900, about 15 percent of a population of 76 million were foreign born, and agriculture's share of the national wealth had fallen to 20 percent. The English and Protestant character of the population had been permanently altered by millions of immigrants, including a large number of Roman Catholics. After 1880, they came mostly from southern and eastern Europe rather than from the English-speaking British Isles, and they brought with them new ethnic identities and new life styles.

The "little Italys," "Germantowns," "Chinatowns," and other ethnic enclaves that developed in large cities not only served as a haven for newly arrived immigrants but also enabled the preservation of old world customs, values, and cultural ties. In contrast, Black Americans in the South experienced the institutionalization of racial barriers through Jim Crow laws that not only segregated Blacks but also denied them the right to vote, equality of economic opportunity, and the educational opportunities enjoyed by Whites.

By 1900, the industrial revolution, fueled by the Civil War and the invention of the Bessemer steel manufacturing process, was transforming America from a basically agricultural, rural nation into an industrial, urban society. The technological and demographic changes deeply affected American life. A new "gospel of wealth," fashioned out of the Protestant ethic of hard work and individual achievement and the value of individualism in the democratic creed, preached that success and affluence went to those who were most fit to survive in the economic marketplace. Government was not supposed to interfere in the marketplace; according to laissez-faire economic doctrine, artificial restraints ran counter to "natural" laws. By the beginning of the twentieth century, the businessman not only symbolized the American success story but also dominated government; the United States Senate itself was a sort of millionaires' club. The giant corporations that determined the direction of the new industrial economy were owned and controlled by a handful of people. About one-eighth of the population owned seven-eighths of the wealth, and more than 50 percent of the property belonged to 1 percent of the population. Until the presidency of Theodore Roosevelt, efforts to restore an economic balance were blocked by the United States Supreme Court, which protected laissez-faire economics by striking down laws that sought to regulate working conditions and employer-employee relationships. In 1886, the Court declared that a corporation was a "person" within the meaning of the Constitution and thus entitled to the same protections (and presumably controls) as individual citizens (*Santa Clara County* v. *Southern Pacific Railroad Co.*).

The twentieth century

As more and more wealth was concentrated in fewer and fewer hands, the distance between the top and bottom rungs of the economic ladder widened. The farmer, whose father and grandfather had prided themselves in being independent yeomen, often found himself a tenant tiller of soil because there was not enough land to go around. At best, he was a debtor businessman; the costs of new agricultural equipment and production forced him into dependency upon banking interests. Small businessmen and professionals (doctors, lawyers, professors), once at the top of the class structure, were now outranked by the industrial ruling class.

To compound their already great wealth, the industrial barons needed cheap labor, and they got it. The courts gave little support to labor unions; effective minimum-wage legislation was far in the future; and the immigration laws that existed merely discriminated against Orientals. Immigration reached high tide in the ten years preceding the outbreak of World War I; an average of nearly one million people a year entered this country between 1904 and the end of 1914. Thousands of unskilled Europeans quickly became part of an underpaid and exploited immigrant laboring class. The world of individualistic entrepreneurs like proud crafts people and skilled workers began to come unstuck; the new working class was made up of persons employed by huge industries and dependent upon them for a subsistence livelihood. Something else had disappeared from the scene: the frontier itself. Opportunities to "go West" had decreased; hardly any existed for the urban-bound immigrant who barely spoke English. With the rise of huge industrial cities came the beginning of tenement living and a social deterioration marked by poverty, substandard working and living conditions, and disease. Despite the protests of farmers, relatively weak trade unions, and various reform groups, the business ethic dominated national policy until the 1930s.

Analyzing the protests of the late nineteenth and early twentieth centuries against social, political, and economic conditions, historian Richard Hofstadter found that they were based on the old democratic ideal of equality of opportunity. "Because it was always possible to assume a remarkable measure of social equality and a fair minimum of subsistence, the goal of revolt tended to be neither social democracy nor social equality, but great opportunity" (Hofstadter, 1955, p. 10). The laissez-faire assumptions that the system was balanced by competing economic and social interests capable of checking each other found little support in reality. However, only economic collapse and the worst depression in history finally changed those assumptions.

The New Deal of Franklin D. Roosevelt in the 1930s was an attempt to restore a balance between business and other interests within the system. Roosevelt's reference to a society that was "ill clothed, ill fed, and ill housed" was a clear rejection of laissez-faire philosophy. Through legislation, the New Deal sought not only to alleviate the social and economic ills of the depression but also to create through governmental regulation a new and fairer balance of economic power. New legislation guaranteed the right of labor unions to bargain with employers over wages and working conditions; to no one's surprise, steel and automobile manufacturers refused to give in easily, and violent strikes followed. Other laws were passed to regulate securities transactions, establish a minimum wage, put ceilings on the number of hours worked, and provide social security and unemployment benefits. Such measures do not sound very revolutionary now, but they were hotly debated at the time. All reflected a belief that democratic ideals—equality, individualism, and government for the welfare of all—could be made meaningful only if government acted and intervened positively. The democratic concept of limited government did not, the New Dealers argued, mean government could not act to redress social and economic ills and an imbalance of political interests.

It took a new European war, which broke out in 1939, to end the unemployment problem, but by then the New Deal had brought about a new relationship between the corporate, industrial interests and other major economic groups like farmers and organized labor. It had also established the responsibility of government to use its powers on behalf of the individual's security and welfare. Yet the groups that benefited most from the New Deal were largely middle class. Virtually destroyed by the economic collapse of the Great Depression, they were farmers, small businessmen, white collar workers —more or less the same people who had participated in the American political marketplace since the eighteenth century. The New Deal achieved the restoration of the middle class without aborting the Constitution; its legislation left intact checks and balances and the dispersion of authority at the national and state levels of government, features which both restrain majorities and encourage governments to move slowly or not at all. In short, the New Deal brought no fundamental change in the constitutional structure; accepted the prescriptive and procedural tenets associated with it; and by restoring the middle-class basis upon which that structure had rested since its inception, reinforced the government's commitment to liberal democracy.

But neither the New Deal nor the economic changes that followed World War II made life better for all classes of American citizens. In the 1950s and 1960s, it became all too apparent that beneath the surface acceptance of institutions and processes smouldered intense dissatisfactions. These grievances erupted in the civil disobedience of the late 1950s and the nonviolent and violent protests organized by Blacks, poor people, migrant workers, Spanish Americans, American Indians, and other minority groups in the 1960s. Such interests challenged the prevailing consensus and charged that the governmental arrangement ignored (or was incapable of solving) the serious problems facing this nation in the second half of the twentieth century.

The discontent stemmed from a reinterpretation of the democratic notion of equality. Protesters argued that a nation which prescribed equality for all in fact imposed vast inequalities upon those who did not share in the economic abundance of the system; and it also denied them equal political rights. In 1968 the National Advisory Commission on Civil Disorders concluded that Black Americans were reacting to circumstances that denied them "dignity, respect, and acceptance," and this had resulted in "alienation and hostility toward institutions of law and government and the White society which controls them" (Report of the National Advisory Commission, p. 92).

The accelerating technological revolution of the twentieth century, particularly since World War II, is difficult to grasp because of its magnitude and pace. For example, more than half of the energy consumed by people during the past two thousand years (for heating, cooking, transport, making war, etc.) has been consumed in the last one hundred years. President Jimmy Carter based his 1977 proposals for a new national energy policy on the realities of limited natural resources such as oil. Carter told Americans that unless vigorous steps were taken to conserve oil and gas, the nation would be without enough energy by 1985 or before.

Alvin Toffler has described the "disease of change" or "future shock," a term he coined to describe "the shattering stress and disorientation that we induce in individuals by subjecting them to too much change in too short a time" (Toffler, 1970, p. 23). Some changes show up dramatically: The American urban population in 1900 was only 40 percent of the total; by 1950 60 percent of Americans lived in cities; only 20 years later more Americans lived in suburbs than in either the central cities or rural areas. Between 1970 and 1975 the population of metropolitan areas suffered a net decline of 31 percent. Ten of the twenty-five largest metropolitan areas in the nation have declined in population (Morrison, 1977). One more example: as late as 1940, 75 percent of American Blacks lived in the South, most of them were in rural areas. By the 1970s, seven out of ten blacks lived in metropolitan areas, and only 48 percent were residents of the South.

The composition of the American population reflects other important changes. In 1970 about 10 percent of Americans were 65 years or older, compared to 4 percent in 1900. The proportion of persons under 20 years old reached 38 percent in 1970. Finally, since 1950 women have outnumbered men.

Such changes not only affect social patterns and relationships; they also influence the subject matter of political conflict. Inner cities have decayed while middle-class Whites have fled to the suburbs to escape high taxes and high crime rates. Residents of inner cities, many of whom are black and poor, have less political power compared to their more numerous, more prosperous, and better educated suburban neighbors. As more Americans have reached retirement, the financial demands on the social security system have increased. As a result younger employed Americans will have to contribute more in social security taxes, or financing of the system will have to depend on subsidy through regular tax revenues or other new sources of funding. Women and Blacks will continue to demand equal treatment in employment and other areas, thus forcing adjustment of traditional patterns associated with a White, male-dominated economic and political system.

Americans are more likely to talk about "national priorities" now than 30 years ago. At the same time, Americans during the 1970s became disenchanted with their political leadership and the quality of their lives. In examining the trends in American public opinion from 1960 to 1973, public opinion analyst Louis Harris noted that more Americans believed America was a worse place to live than it had been ten years before, and there was a growing feeling of powerlessness combined with the suspicion that political leaders were insensitive to people's needs and opinions (1973, pp. 1–14).

The current debate over priorities has much to do with our discussion of the ideological dimensions of democracy. The decay of our cities, the deteriorating quality of our social and physical environment, White and Black racism, sex discrimination, energy resources and their consumption, population growth, the moral content of our foreign policy, honesty in government—all are part of the current national dialogue. They are there not only in the procedural context of setting priorities for actions but also in relation to the prescriptions of the democratic creed. Promoting the general welfare, securing the blessings of liberty, assuring equal protection of the laws, and other axioms of liberal democracy make up the ideological foundations that underlie most calls for reform and change.

There is no broad agreement among individuals and interests about the relative importance of each of the problems or the best way to resolve them. Can democratic ideals of equality, participation, and freedom be maintained through the procedures and institutions by which conflicts over priorities and policies are resolved? We can best analyze this question by examining the operating principles that are essential to the meaning of liberal democracy.

Democratic principles and procedures

Democratic procedures represent a distinctive style of regulating conflict. The procedures are intended to produce and protect the widest possible personal choice through *open but nonviolent conflict.* Open conflict is achieved through the application of basic rules and principles derived from the theory of democracy. The basic principles—popular control, political leadership, political equality, and political liberty—also contribute to the peaceful management of conflict by encouraging the resolution of differences through widely accepted procedural rules for making public policy decisions.

POPULAR CONTROL

The right of voters to choose their representatives and hold them accountable is essential in a liberal democracy. The heart of democracy is the peaceful management of social conflict through controlled competition for public office. If the right to choose is to be exercised effectively, there must be universal suffrage, regular periodic elections, competition between candidates, meaningful policy alternatives, and participation by all major interests. The American political system has added to its stability by broadening suffrage and eliminating property, sex, and—in recent years—racial barriers. Taking part in elections is a symbol of individual consent to the policies that are adopted and—perhaps more importantly—to the democratic way of adopting them (Edelman, 1964, pp. 2–3).

Popular control would mean little if it could be exercised only through the vote. Democratic theory assumes that human beings are fallible. Consequently, the governed must be able to exercise continuing control through public scrutiny and criticism of the actions of policymakers. There can be no sacred cows in politics: No policy or action is inherently immune to criticism. Divergent views and opinions, however abhorrent to some, must be tolerated, and there must be ways and institutions through which their proponents can express them.

In an opinion that struck down a state law compelling public school students to pledge allegiance to the flag, Supreme Court Justice Robert H. Jackson called the right of political unorthodoxy "a fixed star in our constitutional constellation" (*West Virginia Board of Education* v. *Barnette,* 1943). In practice, however, political dissidents often risk public vilification or repression by public officials on behalf of a majority that is less tolerant than it admits. Socialist Party candidates in the United States have always faced an unsympathetic and sometimes hostile public because they oppose such deeply held values as private property and limited government interference in economic matters: The Socialists polled their highest vote for President (919,000) in 1920 when their candidate, Eugene Debs, a pacifist during World War I, was in jail. In the 1960s action by local police against the Black Panther Party was criticized as an attempt to eliminate the party altogether (Fisher, 1970, pp. 18–26).

Elections are but one form of popular control. Through participation in groups organized around particular social, economic, or political interests, people can represent their interests, influence other individuals and groups, and influence the policymakers. Thus the National Organization for Women (NOW) has actively lobbied state legislators to win approval of the proposed Equal Rights Amendment. By joining forces with other groups, NOW has been able to enhance its influence on decisionmakers.

Demonstrations such as sit-ins, mass marches, petitions, and other forms of protest are another form of popular control. In 1977 west coast tuna fishermen, by refusing to fish, won changes in a federal law prohibiting the killing of porpoises. The success of civil rights demonstrations during the 1960s is well known. However, public support for demonstrations rapidly declines when they are marked by violence. The violent protests by urban Blacks in the 1960s found relatively little support among Americans who were otherwise sympathetic to the demands for social and economic change. Similarly, campus protests against the Vietnam war found little support when they led to violence.

Elections are the ultimate means by which a democratic system monitors the general mood and broad policy preferences of the governed. Although they are an imperfect device to determine public preferences on specific issues, elections nevertheless stimulate discussion between partisan groups seeking "a contract" to govern. Political parties display both similarities and differences of outlook as they mobilize popular support, woo potential followers, and encourage their sympathizers to go out and ring doorbells. By delineating the issues, parties make the act of voting meaningful and consistent with the democratic concept of popular control.

Two other major institutional vehicles for popular control are the schools and the news media. One of the strongest reasons for supporting academic freedom is that it permits the free exchange of different ideas; an educated citizen with a knowledge of unpopular views is better qualified to make a rational choice. The press justifies its existence in a democracy by the service it performs in reporting conflict and transmitting information. "Where the press is free," wrote Jefferson, "and every man able to read, all is safe." In democratic theory, the legitimate function of newspapers, magazines, and radio and television commentators is the communication of information to assist in the popular discovery of truth. This was the crux of the argument of those who defended the publication in June 1971 of the secret Pentagon Papers that exposed embarrassing and disturbing aspects of American policy in Southeast Asia during the 1960s. The oddities of this case brought about one of the

severest tests the First Amendment had ever had, but a majority of the
Supreme Court supported the right of the press to publish the papers in the
interest of free inquiry and examination. The successful effort of *Washington
Post* reporters Bob Woodward and Carl Bernstein in 1973 to expose the
cover-up of the Watergate break-in is another striking example of the relationship between a free press and the democratic principle of popular control. Like
the schools, the printed press and its electronic counterparts have a contractual responsibility to make the "marketplace of ideas" meaningful.

POLITICAL LEADERSHIP

Political leadership is a requisite of democracy because of the practical limitations inherent in the concept of popular consent and participation. In any political system the public cannot formulate policy alternatives, take rapid action in emergencies, or carry out the administrative functions of government.

Popular participation can be realized only if issues are defined for community discussion and criticism. This task is performed by political leaders. By formulating policy alternatives and mobilizing electoral groups into winning coalitions, leaders also aid in making popular control effective. Indeed, we may argue that it is conflict between political leaders that preserves free choice in a democracy. That is, individuals who participate in political affairs by formulating policy alternatives, recruiting or serving as candidates, and holding office perform the vital function of offering a choice of policy and candidates.

Political leaders in the American system are not representative of the general population. There are disproportionate numbers of males, Whites, and well-educated, middle-aged, and economically better-off citizens among those who occupy positions of power and influence. To say this is not to say that American democracy is a system in which an elite controls the rest of the citizens. A "power elite" that regularly got its way despite the contrary preferences of the governed would be inconsistent with the concept of democratic leadership. Persons outside the formal authority structure must be able to influence broad public policy. As long as there is competition among leadership elites over the content of public policy, the competing forces will seek public support. Elections, appeals to public opinion, and organized group efforts to influence policy choices are some of the means by which leadership mobilizes and represents citizens.

The separation of powers and the division of power between national and state governments in the American system aid in the development of diverse leadership interests. However, leaders in a democracy must also have a pervasive commitment to the procedural rules by which conflict is represented and resolved. "Mechanisms that undermine the democratic rules or which inhibit institutionalized conflict are destructive of democracy, in that they restrict the general population's access to, or power over, key societal decisions" (Lipset, 1963, p. 239). Not only must there be rules that help keep competition within tolerable limits, but also active minority opposition must be assured through respect for and protection of the rights of speech, press, and assembly (Key, 1961, p. 539). Leaders must not exploit public opinion by unscrupulous tactics or appeals that endanger the democratic order.

The Watergate affair caused a crisis in leadership because it revealed efforts by the nation's highest leaders to cover up violations of law and condone other illegal acts. The gravity of the offense was great enough to force a president to resign in the face of almost certain impeachment. The canons of democratic leadership had been violated so seriously that public confidence in the presidency itself could be restored only by Nixon's resignation.

POLITICAL EQUALITY AND LIBERTY

To make popular control and leadership work as intended in democratic theory, it is necessary to recognize and apply two related but separate principles. First, each voter should be *politically equal*. This means that every adult should have the franchise; each voter should cast only one vote per office; and each vote cast should be counted equally. A corollary of the principle of "one man, one vote" is that a majority of votes should count for more than a minority in the final decision.

The second principle is that each voter should enjoy the political liberty that fosters the individual participation essential to democracy. Specifically, each person should be free to exercise political choice; criticize policies (and perhaps the political-constitutional system); organize groups, parties, and associations to win converts from within the opposition; and follow alternative political leadership. In light of this principle, constitutional guarantees of freedom of speech, press, and assembly are not just prescriptions; they are procedurally essential. Each guarantee is designed to assure that (1) neither a majority nor a minority decision will block the opportunity of any community member to participate at some point in the regulation of conflict, (2) the voting community will be able to transmit preferences and opinions to leaders and receive in return proposals and action; (3) political leaders will not have a legal opportunity to destroy the opposition; and (4) individual choice and assessment of existing policies, officials, and institutions will not suffer from artificial limitations placed upon free inquiry.

All four requirements assume the tolerance of minorities. Majorities rarely need protection of their freedom to speak or write. Justice William O. Douglas, defending the rights of the minority, offered the eloquent argument that "freedom to differ is not limited to things that do not matter much. That would be a mere shadow of freedom. The test of its substance is the right to differ as to things that touch the heart of the existing order." Today's minority can never hope to become tomorrow's majority unless it has the opportunity to argue its case in the marketplace of ideas. Government "by the people" therefore demands a commitment to the procedures through which minorities can act in a meaningful fashion. Liberal democracy cannot exist without minority participation.

Democratic ideology: how much consensus?

In Chapter 1 we discussed the relationship between the regulation of conflict and the stability of the political community. Our response to the question of what makes a group of people a community was simply, "The desire to share experience." When the group achieves this aim by finding ways to settle disputes that might disrupt peaceful association, it is a political community.

Political community does not require an integrated set of beliefs accepted with the same degree of loyalty by all members. However, in each community distinctive sets of political ideas tend to develop over time. Although these ideas need not be rigidly doctrinaire, they do constitute a part of the community consensus. By community consensus we mean a sharing of values and beliefs about human goals and conduct. This chapter has so far analyzed the content of American democratic beliefs and values. In this section we will explore various aspects of consensus, examining in particular the question of whether it is possible to identify an "American ideology" shared by most Americans. If there is general agreement on a democratic ideology, does such agreement extend to all parts of the population equally? Finally, to what extent is consensus on democratic values necessary to sustain the democratic polity?

COMPONENTS OF CONSENSUS

In its broadest sense, community consensus consists in personal agreement on a variety of matters. In reaching such agreement, individuals are influenced by social and constitutional factors as well as by their beliefs. There are three main types or components of community consensus.

1. *Doctrinal consensus:* agreement on the basic values in the democratic creed.
2. *Constitutional consensus:* agreement on the rules and procedures by which conflict is regulated and policy choices are made. The general commitment to rules or procedures (due process) in the handling of criminal cases is an obvious example. Richard Nixon's conduct in the Watergate affair not only violated specific legal rules (prohibiting conspiracy to "obstruct justice") but also violated general expectations concerning the proper use of presidential power.
3. *Policy consensus:* agreement on policy choices. This type of consensus includes general support of governmental action in broad areas of policy, such as the alleviation of social and economic problems. Agreement is more probable over general policy than over specific programs or activities intended to implement general policy preferences. For example, agreement

would be greater on the need for welfare for the needy than on specific proposals such as a guaranteed annual wage.

The number of persons in agreement on each of these components may vary widely. It is possible that a very large majority of Americans may agree with the tenets of the democratic creed while fewer agree with broad policy choices in the political system. Similarly, intensity of agreement may vary. Individuals in agreement on the democratic value of free speech may differ on the application of free speech to groups of persons deemed radical or disloyal; some will hold that protections should be given regardless of the message or the background of the persons exercising free speech, while others will favor limitations. Finally, the consequences of consensus vary considerably. General agreement on the need for governmental involvement in energy and environmental matters may engender strong restrictions on the use of natural resources by private groups; it may passively permit certain actions such as bureaucratic regulation of hiring practices by corporations under affirmative action programs; or it may decisively prohibit action, as it did when public opinion turned against continued American involvement in Vietnam.

Consensus, or its absence, helps to define the type and limits of conflicts within the political system. Moreover, the nature of agreement will change in response to circumstances. We define a *working consensus* as a tentative agreement contingent on events and subject to change. The demands of civil rights groups, environmentalists, and anti Vietnam forces are clear examples of developments that challenged and refashioned the working consensus of the 1960s and 1970s. "Disagreements, often fundamental ones, arise [over any working consensus]; and citizens who stand outside the prevailing consensus often make precious contributions to democracy precisely because they do so" (Rockefeller Brothers Project, 1960, p. 20).

AN AMERICAN IDEOLOGY?

References to "Americanism" imply that U.S. citizens either do or should share some ideas. Americanism is manifested in the respect paid to our forefathers, the commemoration of great historical events, and other reminders of communal attachment. The relative absence of conflicting value symbols within the community points to a general agreement on certain fundamentals. Some commentators refer to an "underlying consensus" that enables the American polity to survive continuing and serious disputes over policy alternatives (Dahl, 1956, pp. 132–133; De Grazia, 1948, p. ix). The fact that the federal community had until the mid-1960s managed to accommodate policy differences without serious disruption (with one major exception, the Civil War), supports the notion that a basic agreement over values and procedures buttressed peaceful regulation of social conflict. It is also noteworthy that during a one-year period (1973–74) the nation saw both its president and vice-president (Nixon and Agnew) resign in a cloud of scandal; selected a new president (Ford) who had not been elected to either the presidency or the vice-presidency; and selected two vice-presidents (Ford and Rockefeller), neither of whom had been elected by the people. Yet the political system remained basically stable; few people seriously doubted the ability of the nation to make the transitions through regular political and constitutional processes.

Despite these examples of apparent consensus, the nation has experienced turbulent unrest throughout its history. Our violent past includes lynchings in the South, the relatively lawless (but romanticized) "winning of the West," the frequently brutal removal of the American Indians from land they rightly owned, violent and institutionalized intimidation of racial minorities, and, lest it be forgotten, the revolution out of which America was born. The violence and disorder in American cities in the 1950s and 1960s (which arose out of the deep frustrations of urban Blacks) and the massive and sometimes violent protests against the Vietnam war on college campuses in the 1960s and early 1970s are reminders that unqualified claims to broad consensus or peaceful resolution of conflicts must be carefully considered.

That at least some form of basic agreement exists in America is obvious to any reader of political news. Americans observe presidential campaigns in which debate is heated, invective sparkles, and each side accuses the other of "selling America short"; then on election eve, all sides remind citizens of their right and obligation to vote. Votes are cast, ballots are counted, and the winner is proclaimed and accepted by Americans as "our President."

Thus one form of constitutional consensus over who shall govern and how governors shall be chosen is reached through election campaigns that are bitterly contested, but within bounds of widely accepted ideas about what is fair and unfair, honest and dishonest.

Even on policy issues there is some degree of consensus. Presidential candidates do not seriously debate the proposition that government has no responsibility to alleviate poverty, even though they may disagree over what and how much should be done. Similarly, most people consider environmental quality a proper area for governmental action. In fact, the past decade has witnessed increasing public awareness of problems related to clean air, water, and land, and there is substantial agreement on the necessity of federal and state regulation in these areas; it is only questions about how vigorously antipollution laws should be enforced, the severity of quality standards, and whether government or private sources should finance cleanup efforts that are very much at issue.

Despite the fact that the 1960s and early 1970s were characterized by severe criticism, disruption, and even violence on college campuses across the country, most college students retained their confidence in the ability of democratic processes to resolve problems and effect social change. In the midst of the most widespread dissent in 1970, the Harris poll found that 89 percent of college students still felt they could change society from "within," 63 percent agreed "the democratic process is capable of keeping up with the pace of events and the need for action," and 89 percent agreed that "eventually governmental policy can be changed by public pressure" (Harris, 1973, pp. 220–221). However, there has been a steady decline in the number of citizens who feel that their actions to influence government will be effective (see Chapter 4). There has also been a decline in the trust that citizens place in their government.

Thus, it is possible to argue both sides of the question. On the one hand, there is evidence of deep disagreements over policy within our society, as well as signs of growing alienation from government. On the other hand, the disagreements have not seriously threatened existing institutions and procedures for resolving conflict. Community stability certainly does not mean the absence of conflict. It does mean the peaceful management of such conflict. If the polity were seriously divided over basic democratic values and procedures, then the chances for peaceful resolution of policy conflicts would be substantially reduced. But is it necessary for all citizens to accept these basic values equally and be willing to put them into practice in all situations?

AMBIVALENCE AND AGREEMENT: THE AMERICAN PUZZLE

The available evidence reveals that Americans are highly ambivalent in their attitudes toward government and politics. A noted historian has written that we approach government as a "friendly enemy, a neighbor who will probably do well enough if you keep your eye on him" (Becker, 1960, p. 7). The frequent admonition that the "public interest" is better served if "politics" is not allowed to enter into the decision process indicates not only doubt and suspicion about the motives of those who are active in politics, but also mistrust of the very exercise of political power and influence.

These attitudes may possibly be rooted in the mistrust of power inherent in the concept of limited government. Opinion surveys consistently show public suspicion of labor unions, large corporations, and government bureaucracies. Political novels often stress the seamy side of political activity: influence peddling, bribery and corruption, character assassination for political gain, and the pursuit of personal ends over the public welfare. Finally, polls indicate that a majority of Americans would disapprove of a political career for their children, believing that political careers hold comparatively little prestige and politicians are prone to corruption.

Nevertheless, when asked to reveal their feelings about their country, Americans express much greater pride in their political tradition than do citizens of other nations (Almond and Verba, 1963, p. 102). A March 1975 survey reported that 80 percent of Americans believed the American way of life is superior to that of any other country.

National pride, however, does not always carry over to widespread confidence in the institutions responsible for governing the nation. For instance, in 1977 pollster Louis Harris measured the degree of confidence people had in a number of institutions including the White House, the Supreme Court, Congress, the military, state government, and local government. He compared those measures of confidence with data gathered in 1966 on the same question. Between 1966 and 1977 confidence in all institutions dropped sharply. Moreover, nongovernmental institutions such as the press, organized religion, and higher education fared little better. We shall look more closely at the question of public confidence in political and nonpolitical institutions in Chapter 6.

Does this reveal an emerging crisis of legitimacy in which the public no longer believes its institutions are functioning in accord with basic democratic values or the "American tradition"? Everett Ladd reviewed survey research between 1966 and 1976 and concluded that although public confidence in current institutional leadership is low, this finding does not necessarily reveal a "loss of confidence in the constitutional order broadly defined—in the basic *constitutional institutions and processes*" (Ladd, 1976, p. 552). Ladd cautions that although considering public reaction to Watergate, the Vietnam war, and economic "stagflation" as dissatisfaction is quite understandable, the survey data do not answer questions regarding the depth of public dissatisfaction and its consequences for the future. Nonetheless, a continuing decline in confidence or new, highly divisive issues might bring extremely serious problems.

AN UNPHILOSOPHICAL APPROACH TO POLITICS

Americans not only have a firm belief in the superiority of the American democratic system; they are also distinctly uninterested in reflecting, speculating, and thinking about politics. Historians and other interpreters of the American experience have suggested that we are not theoreticians because our fundamental political values and philosophy have been with us from the beginning and have never been seriously challenged or questioned. Alexis de Tocqueville's classic work, *Democracy in America* (1835), concluded that even though Americans showed no interest in philosophy, they were "in possession of one, common to the whole people." De Tocqueville meant that Americans had a consensus formed out of the liberal democratic values of the seventeenth and eighteenth centuries, which had been nurtured in the new world and developed without serious competition from contrary political theories.

Historian Daniel Boorstin argues that three factors account for the unphilosophical bent of Americans:

1. Our values were "preformed" in the sense that the Founding Fathers and "certain facts of geography or history peculiar to us, supplied a set of principles to apply to all future matters." The leading example is the Constitution itself, a gift of the past, which incorporates basic principles and values that should guide the present. Although change is necessary and desirable, it is always justified as being in accord with constitutional principles. Boorstin holds that because of these preformed values, Americans are not interested in philosophical debates about whether the original principles themselves should be revised to suit contemporary problems.

2. The "American way of life" is taken for granted. Not only do most Americans see the Constitution as a nearly perfect governing arrangement, but they view their land, society, and culture as a unique combination constituting "Americanism" to be handed on to future generations.

3. The continuity of American history is unique. Europe has been racked by revolutions, ideological battles, and other cataclysmic changes. Americans are aware of the turbulence in their own short history, but they see a 200-year line of progress linking past and present. Living in a community in which the "general truths" of politics are embedded in institutions and sacred documents and transmitted from generation to generation without disfigurement, Americans simply do not need a philosophy; they live it.

The unphilosophical orientation of Americans also finds expression in contradictory political ideas and institutions. One study of the ideological outlines of the American experience argues that Americans hold "contradictory ideas simultaneously without bothering to resolve the potential conflict between them." Even those who could be classified as ideologues (persons who make choices on the basis of specific doctrines) are uncertain about the nature of democratic values (McCloskey, 1963, pp. 10–25). The great political leaders of American history have frequently been inconsistent in their political ideas. Compare Thomas Jefferson's statement that "the will of the majority in all cases [should] prevail with "the minority possess their equal rights which equal law must protect."

Inconsistencies such as these lead R. G. McCloskey to conclude that "it may be idle to seek for 'the' American tradition, for a 'consensus' in any usual sense of the word. Perhaps our only real basic quality of mind is the pragmatic spirit that can tolerate such a state of affairs and build an enduring polity upon it" (1963, p. 24).

CONSENSUS ON BASIC DEMOCRATIC VALUES?

If Americans are ambivalent toward politics, unreflective in political thinking, and contradictory in their political judgments, do they nevertheless agree on the basic democratic values that make democratic processes possible? Data concerning consensus on democratic values are scattered and too incomplete to warrant more than an educated guess.

Studies of the extent of agreement on such basic principles as majority rule and minority rights show that agreement does exist on abstract, general statements of democratic principles. However, when asked to support specific applications of the general principles, Americans are less supportive of democratic doctrine. Consensus on specific application of principles is most likely to be found among the politically active, better educated, and younger sectors of the population (Jackman, 1972; Key, 1961; McClosky, 1964; Prothro and Grigg, 1960; and Sharkansky, 1975).

Granting that Americans are more committed to some democratic principles than others and that some Americans are more committed to democracy in general than others, what are the democratic principles on which it is fair to say there is widespread consensus? Political scientist Donald Devine offers an answer (1972). He examined a variety of public opinion polls published between 1935 and 1968 to see if there was consensus on the fundamental tenets of Lockean liberal democracy. He considered a consensus to exist on any principle favored by a substantial majority that was at least 20 percentage points larger than the disagreeing minority. Here are the principles on which he found consensus:

1. Government should act in accordance with laws and rules limiting its power over citizens.
2. Government should be "government by consent."
3. The basic rule by which government operates should be popular majority rule.
4. Majorities should be restrained, as should all government.
5. The legislature should be the predominant institution of government.
6. The presidency and courts should be respected as restraints on the legislature as long as they do not violate their trust.
7. The government should have a federal structure.
8. Political parties should be decentralized.
9. Terms of officeholders should be limited.
10. The Lockean values of liberty, equality, and property plus that of religion are essential to society.

IS POLITICAL CONSENSUS NECESSARY TO POLITICAL STABILITY?

Devine's findings reflect what people tell pollsters they believe and value. It is a far different thing to carry out such tenets in political practice, especially principles pertaining to liberty and equality. For example, 63 percent of the people surveyed agreed with the statement "I believe that all public recreational facilities should be available to all people at all times," but only 38 percent said "I don't think I would mind if Negro children were to swim in the same pool as my children" (Sharkansky, 1975, p. 116).

Writers on *mass democracy* who have reviewed such inconsistencies between democratic theory and American practice argue that the democratic values Americans give lip service to are relics of an earlier and essentially rural republic. Mass democracy, they say, is "a new phenomenon . . . which it is inappropriate or misleading to consider in terms of the philosophy of Locke or the liberal democracy of the nineteenth century" (Carr, 1957, pp. 74–75). Such a view rests on the assumption that consensus on democratic tenets and their application was great through the nineteenth century but has diminished in the twentieth. That proposition is not easily tested and is probably not true.

However, the basic question is not whether Americans shared a greater commitment to democratic fundamentals in earlier periods, but rather how much consensus is necessary to sustain the democratic polity and the legitimacy of its methods for resolving conflict? The easy answer is that so long as democratic government does not collapse, there is sufficient consensus. But such an answer is too simple. It assumes that the persistence of the American democratic way of doing things flows from the widespread, popular view that government should do things that way. Yet we know that the motives and attitudes people carry into their political lives are varied. Public acceptance of the way things are is no proof of active public support for policies. The fact is that to date, research on the political values of Americans has not provided an answer to the question "How much consensus is sufficient?" Thus we can only speculate on the basis of what we know.

First, despite evidence of the ambivalence of Americans toward politics and the inconsistency between belief in fundamentals and their specific application, it may be that democracy is sustained more out of habit than out of conscious, articulate acceptance of principles. As "givens," the fundamentals are not subject to controversy. Americans feel no compulsion to explain or defend them; they merely observe them unthinkingly. In short, Americans seem to operate as if a general consensus does exist.

Second, if violence, lack of trust in political leadership, feelings of powerlessness, and discontent with the "way things are run" are interpreted as either a breakdown of consensus or an indication of a "sick society," then we have probably never had consensus on fundamentals or a "well" society. The pluralism of the American system has never given equal influence or advantages to all groups.

Contradictions between the lives of ordinary Americans and the promise of democratic equality are real and perhaps even greater than during any previous era in our history. Discontent over policy and dissatisfaction with the rate of response to demands may reveal a serious erosion of political stability. Yet the "American Dream" of Martin Luther King has activated previously silent interests—Blacks, migrant workers, the elderly, the poor, the young—and changes are occurring, though at a rate unsatisfactory to some. Thus far, protest has not become so intense that the majority of citizens have rejected the "rules of the game" through which conflicts are represented and resolved. A "sense of community over and above political differences keeps the affective attachments to political groups from challenging the stability of the system" (Almond and Verba, 1963, p. 357).

We would argue that there is considerable agreement on the worth of existing political institutions. Americans still accept such devices as federalism, the separation of powers, and the courts as legitimate instruments to resolve conflict. In light of this, the answer to the question of "How much consensus?" would be "A great deal." As one observer has stated:

> Group politics is not so much a politics without ideology as the politics of a specific ideology whose key premises are accepted by those who participate actively in the political process. These key premises [are] . . . moderation in pressing demands, respect for the claims of all groups for representation of their interests, [and] a high degree of tolerance for delay, ambiguity, and waste as the necessary price to pay for the protection of individual freedom—in short, the premises of liberalism. (Baskin, 1971, p. 131)

THE CONSTITUTION: ROOTS, PRINCIPLES, GROWTH

3

The Constitution of the United States is probably the most revered document of its kind in the world. It symbolizes both the political unification of our community and the legitimacy of its government. A court ruling that something is "constitutional" generally establishes its legitimacy in the eyes of the public. Many of the great political issues of our history have been debated within the context of their constitutionality or unconstitutionality. Although we understand that constitutional principles are subject to changing interpretation, we regard the principles as fundamental and durable.

The Constitution was written for an agricultural nation of scarcely 3 million people, but it has successfully served as the instrument for the governance of both an expanding continental state during the nineteenth century and an industrial giant of over 200 million people in the twentieth century. It has influenced the ways in which American democracy operates, but its meaning has also been shaped by the social, economic, and political changes.

American constitutionalism means not only the Constitution itself but also the basic understandings and procedures under which a community lives and regulates social conflict. We refer to these understandings and procedures as the *constitutional system*. It includes rules, customs, traditions, ideas, myths, and attitudes as well as any written constitutional documents.

The Constitution as instrument and symbol

The Constitution is a comparatively short document which grants power to government institutions (Congress, President, Supreme Court); distributes power between the national and state governments; and sets limits on the exercise of power by both levels of government. In granting and limiting power, it is a formal, legalistic set of basic rules, the "supreme law of the land" governing the behavior of those who hold and exercise political power.

A written document does not by itself create a "government of laws." By actively accepting the restraints upon their behavior, people breathe life into the formal document, constantly renewing a "living Constitution." It is this acceptance that makes the document an *instrument* for regulating social conflict as well as a *symbol* of consensus. As an instrument the Constitution is not limited simply to its original text, which is surprisingly short, and its twenty-six amendments, which are also surprisingly short, considering the length of state constitutions. Time and experience have altered American political institutions. Moreover, the actions of presidents, the decisions of the Supreme Court, and the rise of extraconstitutional agencies such as political parties and regulatory commissions have shaped the "law of the land."

Like many other symbols of American democratic values, the Constitution helps citizens to identify with the political system. In accepting the Constitution, a citizen accepts the pattern of government it contains. Furthermore, the symbolic meaning of the Constitution as the expression of both democratic values and the wisdom of the Founding Fathers makes it easier for citizens to accept the legitimacy of disputed public policy decisions held by the courts to be constitutional. Various interests may resist court decisions—such as those declaring racial school segregation unconstitutional or those requiring the busing of school children to achieve desegregation—but they usually do so by arguing that the Constitution has been misread by the judges, not that the Constitution itself is invalid.

The American Constitution, as both a symbol of consensus and an instrument of government, obtains its life and meaning from the varied activities of people. American constitutionalism is not a series of fixed rules but the product of continuing conflict and accommodation.

Making the Constitution

When the Constitution was written, fear of centralized control and a desire to limit the exercise of power were deeply rooted in the traditions and experience of the American people. John Locke and other theorists had strongly recommended the separation of powers as a tool for limiting the dangers of governmental authority. The first volume of John Adams' *The Defence of the Constitutions of the United States* (1787) was a strong reply to foreign observers who had criticized the decentralized power structure of the Articles of Confederation. Believing that the rights of property, the liberties of the people, and the welfare of all could be maintained only under a system of "balanced powers," Adams wrote:

> The majority has eternally, and without one exception, usurped over the rights of the minority. . . . Self-interest, private avidity, ambition, and avarice will exist in every state of society, and under every form of government. . . . The only remedy is to take away the power, by controlling the selfish avidity of the governor, by senate and house; and of the house, by the governor and senate. (Quoted in Scott, 1959, p. 109)

By the time the Constitutional Convention convened, many of the constitutions of the newly formed states already closely reflected the principles of the Declaration of Independence. Seven states had adopted bills of rights; and the Massachusetts constitution, which dates back to 1780, had in it a "free and equal" clause under which a Black man successfully sued for his liberty in 1781. In varying degrees, all the new state constitutions incorporated popular rule, limited government, separation of powers, and checks and balances. By the late eighteenth century, these concepts were firmly established in the American mind.

A desire for a common political community was also reflected in the political arrangements that kept the colonies united in a common endeavor. The first of these, the Continental Congress, which came into existence in 1774, adopted the Declaration of Independence, financed and prosecuted the war with England, carried on foreign relations, and submitted the Articles of Confederation to the thirteen states for ratification. Although this "first American experiment in reconciling unity with localism" did not produce a "perpetual Union" (Morison and Commager, 1950, pp. 1, 257), as the Framers had hoped, and failed to solve problems that proved to be insurmountable, the Articles of Confederation did provide the framework of American government from 1781 to 1789.

THE ARTICLES OF CONFEDERATION

The story of the "union of states," under which "each state retains its sovereignty, freedom, and independence," is one of difficulty and frustration. Under the Articles of Confederation, representation in a single-house Congress was based on the equality of the states—that is, one vote per state. Legislative, executive, and judicial functions were united in this single body. The authority to conduct foreign affairs, administer postal matters, settle disputes between states, borrow money, control the armed forces, and regulate coinage, weights, and measures was vested in the central government. But each of the thirteen states retained control over taxation, commerce, and individuals. Lacking power to tax even imports, to regulate commerce, and to enforce its mandates, the Congress was hopelessly handicapped—even though a good many citizens did fairly well economically. The states refused to amend the Articles in order to give the central government adequate enforcement authority; unanimous consent was required for amendment and this proved fatal. In 1786 a conference of states met at Annapolis to consider state problems involving commercial transactions and called for a convention to consider a general revision of the Articles.

THE CONSTITUTIONAL CONVENTION: CONSENSUS AND CONFLICT

The delegates to the Constitutional Convention faced a formidable task. Not only did they have to devise a scheme of government acceptable to themselves and to the states, but they had to take into account conflicting interests. Broadus Mitchell and Louise Mitchell (1975) have described the prevailing political circumstances:

> The colonies were differently founded and governed, had different products and habits of life, and, with poor means of travel and transport, were distant from each other. They had little experience of self-government. Their knowledge of jurisprudence was theoretical. They were insistent on "the rights of Englishmen," but did not grasp their responsibilities to themselves. Freed of irksome parental oversight, they rejoiced in liberty without much thought of how to preserve it. They fought a war of independence, but did not trouble to organize a nation as a result of it. (p. 7)

The Founding Fathers thus had to accommodate widely diverse interests and confine conflict within manageable bounds.

The delegates: profile of a leadership corps

The 55 delegates who convened in Philadelphia in May 1787 came from the elite of American politics; 7 had been governors of their states, 41 had served in Congress, and 8 had had a hand in writing their state constitutions. They formed a nucleus of the influential men of their time—merchants, bankers, gentlemen farmers, lawyers, and investors. They were also men of differing talents and accomplishments. George Washington and Benjamin Franklin lent great personal influence and prestige to the proceedings; other delegates had outstanding ability and knowledge of political affairs. Among these seasoned politicians were James Madison, who became "floor leader" of the convention, and his fellow Virginian, Edmund Randolph; John Dickenson of Delaware, who has been called the "Penman of the American Revolution"; and Alexander Hamilton of New York, the brilliant and controversial young advocate of strong government. Some delegates were men of only average ability. Others, such as New York's Robert Yates and John Lansing, were men of stature who feared the convention was about to destroy the liberty of the people and left early.

There is a long-standing argument over the question of whether the Framers were conservatives intent on stemming the tide of popular government or practical men working to fashion a constitution that would both resolve the problems of government under the Articles of Confederation and win wide popular acceptance in the states. Charles Beard's *An Economic Interpretation of the Constitution* (1913) presents the classic argument for the proposition that the Framers devised a system with a strong national government in order to resist the demands for democratic equality in the states. Beard and other historians have made much of the absence of the "common man"—the small farmer, the worker, the resident of the backcountry rural areas—supposedly resulting in a document that reflected the interests of an aristocratic, propertied minority.

More recent scholarship has attacked Beard's thesis as overemphasizing the economic element in the Framers' motives and actions (Brown, 1956). The men at Philadelphia certainly constituted an inner group who generally dominated postrevolutionary America, and they deliberated in secret—a fact that caused problems when it came time to make the argument for ratification. But these men had helped shape the revolutionary consensus on individual liberty and the right of people to govern themselves, and the original language of the Constitution testifies that they felt committed to representative government. In addition, debate in the Convention over such matters as representation and popular control was sharp, indicating that the delegates were by no means of a single mind.

Although not united in their views on specific matters, the Framers were in agreement on several important issues that provided a basis for accommodating their differences. John P. Roche has described the Founding Fathers as "first and foremost superb democratic politicians" (1961, p. 799). Although the delegates came from different states, different classes, and different economic interests, they shared an overriding goal: the desire to establish for the American community a common government that would not be limited by the parochial jurisdictions of each state. They also agreed on the necessity for an indirectly representative government and on the need to avoid putting total power in the hands of "popular majorities."

Richard Hofstadter depicts the Framers as "realists" whose political attitudes were shaped by a generally pessimistic view of human nature, a view of "reality" they believed should be translated into the legal framework of government. Unless controlled by law, people could provide neither stable government nor protection of property. The delegates also viewed an unencumbered majority as destructive of stability and liberty. In Hofstadter's opinion, the Framers' concept of liberty "was linked not to democracy but to property," and the liberties they attempted to protect were "chiefly negative." He argues that "they wanted freedom from fiscal uncertainty and irregularities in the currency, from trade wars among the states, from economic discrimination by more powerful foreign governments, from attacks on the creditor class or on property, from popular insurrection" (1958, p. 11). United in their desire for a stronger continental government and in their opposition to "mob rule," the delegates sought to devise techniques of regulating conflict that would lead to an effective but nontyrannical government acceptable to most Americans. The conflicts that did arise in the convention were about the appropriate design of a political community that would fulfill the goals of authority and would be national in scope, republican in pattern, and acceptable to those who would have to agree to it.

Writing a framework for government

The decision of American leaders to strengthen the bonds of national union carried over into framing the Constitution, but agreement upon procedural details was not easily achieved. Hence, the convention's approach combined the urgency, expediency, and cooperation characteristic of practical-minded men. The plan of union that came forth was produced by political craftsmanship rather than philosophical doctrine. The thorniest questions concerned the distribution of power: should the federal or state government have the final say? and should the people or the states have power in Congress?

The working plan of the Constitutional Convention was the Virginia Plan drafted by Edmund Randolph (*Documents*, 1927, pp. 953–956). This plan, sympathetic to the interests of the larger states, significantly increased the national government's powers and sought to ensure the supremacy of national over state authority. An opposing New Jersey Plan also favored a stronger central government but, to alleviate the fears of the smaller states, sought to preserve the equality of states.

The Virginia Plan contained a provision to give the national government power "to negate all laws passed by the several States, contravening in the opinion of the National Legislature the articles of the union." It also proposed granting the national government authority to use force against any state government "failing to fulfill its duty" to the Union—which was just what Lincoln did against the states of the Confederacy, Virginia included, 74 years later. The proposed authority to coerce state governments (also part of the New Jersey Plan) was rejected early in the convention. The delegates rejected the legislative veto power but provided, as finally approved in Article VI of the Constitution, that the "Constitution, and the Laws of the United States" are the "supreme law of the land." Although speculation about "things that never happened" is always uncertain, if Congress had been granted the power to veto state laws that it believed unconstitutional, "no stable basis for state powers would have existed" (Lockard, 1969, p. 6). The final version of the supremacy clause limited the power of the national government over the states; however, the national government did acquire the authority to operate directly against *individuals:* thus the power granted to Congress in Article 1 "to call forth the Militia to execute the Laws of the Union, suppress Insurrections and repel invasions"; thus the responsibility assigned to the President to "take Care that the Laws be faithfully executed." This language is directed to individual citizens, including, for example, governors and police chiefs who may try to disobey a school desegregation order. The principle of coercion against individuals who violate the laws of the United States is thoroughly consistent with the Framers' aim of establishing a national political community within a federal system.

The federal scheme

The desire for stronger national authority and the unwillingness of the states to submit to totally centralized power dictated the organization of the new government on the federal principle. The delegates generally believed that the liberties of the people and popular government could be secured only if the powers of government were so divided that one unit could serve as a check upon another. There was also, a widespread belief that power must be so distributed that despotic majorities would be unable to destroy or weaken the people's liberties. No serious question was raised about the need to divide power; the question was how. To get a constitution at all, the integrity of state governments had to be preserved against "centralized nationalism." This was the only way the delegates from small states could "have reasonable assurance of their continuance as efficient and effective members of an integral union" (McLaughlin, 1935, p. 180). The convention decided to grant specified powers to the national government and leave the remaining authority to the state governments.

The convention arrived at no consensus about the exact meaning of a federal division of powers. Studying what the Framers meant, Martin Diamond concluded that they, "like all other men at this time . . . regarded federalism, not as a kind of government, but as a voluntary association of states who sought certain advantages from that association." The agreement of the delegates on so loose a concept did not stop them, of course, from dividing over the practical details. Diamond asserts that a compromise between conflicting positions would have been impossible had James Madison not persuasively insisted that a large-scale republic acting directly on the people in each state would not subvert the integrity of the individual states and would better protect the liberties of the people (1963, pp. 24–41).

The Connecticut Compromise

The Virginia Plan proposed a national legislature of two houses, the lower to be based on population and elected directly by the people and the upper to be chosen by the lower house from persons nominated by state legislatures. A national executive was to be chosen by the national legislature—a reflection of the fear of direct democracy. The New Jersey Plan, carefully guarding state equality, included a single-house legislature in which states were represented as units.

Faced with the possibility of an impasse, the delegates eventually accepted a "palatable alternative to the folks at home" (Roche, 1961, p. 806). The Connecticut Compromise blended both the Virginia and the New Jersey proposals. It provided for a two-house Congress, but only in the lower house was representation to be apportioned by population. In the upper house two senators were allotted each state, regardless of population.

One object of the compromise was to achieve a balance between control of legislators by the people and control by the "aristocracy." In Madison's words, the Senate (which was elected by state legislatures until 1913) would serve as a check against the "fickleness and passion" of the people and would protect minorities by its veto over the "excesses of the first branch." Not all delegates were convinced that such an arrangement provided the necessary safeguards against reckless majorities. Some fought hard to write a property qualification for suffrage into the Constitution; others argued that a man ought not to be denied suffrage because he owned no land. A compromise finally left the determination of voting qualifications to the individual states.

Agreement upon the definition of a federal republic in America came with the Connecticut Compromise, but the issue was not settled. Both the law-of-the-land clause and the later Tenth Amendment provide the basis for a continuing dispute over the relationship between central and state jurisdictions. Controversy over "states' rights" appeared before the beginning of the nineteenth century, erupted in civil war in 1861, and remains today a subject for national debate. Where is the line between the legitimate and illegitimate exercise of state or national authority? There is no certainty about the Framers' intent. The convention's compromise over federalism was ambiguous, like its compromise over balanced government. This was the only way in which the competing interests could have been accommodated at the time.

Indirect appointment

Compromises resulting from a fear of popular democracy also produced the provisions for selecting federal judges and the method of electing the President. Judges appointed by an indirectly elected President and approved by an indirectly elected Senate were granted life tenure; the idea was to insulate the judiciary from popular pressure. As for the presidential election, the electoral college seemed an ingenious way to placate conflicting interests that wanted the President selected by Congress, by the states, or by the direct vote of the populace—a rather extreme notion in those days. According to the original terms of the Constitution, the electoral college, whose members were to be chosen in each state as its legislature provided, was to choose the President. If one candidate received a majority of electoral college votes, he was elected. It was expected, however, that after George Washington, a certain choice as first President, no person would receive an electoral college majority and that most elections would actually take place in the House of Representatives as provided in Article II. This is another aspect of state equality in the federal pattern, because the Constitution specifies that the representation from each state has only one vote if the House selects the President. A four-year term for the President was intended to reduce further the effects of popular pressure.

The role of the House of Representatives in the selection of the President did not materialize as planned because of the unforeseen rise of political parties after Washington's retirement. Article II provides that electoral votes are to be cast for two persons; the person receiving the largest number—if it constitutes a majority—is elected President, the person receiving the next largest number is chosen Vice-President. But in 1800, Thomas Jefferson and Aaron Burr ran together as a "ticket" for the Republican party, Jefferson for President, Burr for Vice-President. The problem was that all 73 electors favorable to the Republicans cast their ballots for the same two persons, 73 for Jefferson, 73 for Burr. Who was to be President? The House of Representatives had to decide and Jefferson won a narrow victory. The Twelfth Amendment, ratified before the 1804 election, corrected the constitutional flaw by mandating electors to vote separately for President and Vice-President. Since this early period, the development of competition between political parties has, with a few exceptions (to be discussed in Chapter 8), resulted in two major parties nominating candidates for President and Vice-President and one party's ticket receiving a majority of the electoral votes for both President and Vice-President. The two-party system has thus prevented the House of Representatives from acting as the elector of Presidents as originally envisioned by the Constitution's framers.

Trade, taxes, and slavery

Other disputes led to other compromises among the Founding Fathers; a key compromise resolved the issue of trade and taxes. Northern commercial interests insisted that Congress have full authority to regulate trade and navigation; to vest that authority in individual states might well lead to trade wars between the states. Southern agrarians, however, feared that granting Congress such authority might result in the imposition of export duties on agricultural products. The conflict was accommodated by the expedient of forbidding Congress to levy export taxes (thus assuaging Southern agrarians) and giving the House of Representatives exclusive power to introduce money bills (Northern commercial interests thought urban areas would be well represented in the House whereas rural interests would dominate the Senate in the early days of the Republic).

The slave trade posed both a moral and an economic problem. Several delegates, including some southerners, openly criticized slavery as immoral. Others believed slavery was disappearing and that since the slave trade would not continue much longer, it required no constitutional provision pertaining to it. However, a group of southern states considered slavery essential to their agricultural economy and would not accept the Constitution if it abolished slavery or prohibited the continued importation of slaves. The South also sought to count slaves for the purpose of determining representation in the House, but northern delegates objected to their being counted as persons when their owners legally regarded slaves as chattel property.

The South was trying to have it both ways, and the Three-fifths Compromise resolved the issue for the time being. It provided that three-fifths of the slaves would be counted for the purpose of determining representation as well as for the purpose of assessing direct taxes. The delegates agreed to prohibit the national government from interfering with the slave trade before 1808, by which time the slave population would be large enough to reproduce itself. The South came out ahead in this bargain but unwittingly set the new nation on the long road to civil war.

To understand the meaning of the Constitution in the twentieth century, we might keep in mind Roche's assertion about its origins in the eighteenth century: "The Constitution, then, was not an apotheosis of 'constitutionalism,' a triumph of architectonic genius; it was a patchwork sewn together under the pressure of both time and events by a group of extremely talented democratic politicians" (Roche, 1961, p. 815). The Constitution has endured by receiving what it required—constant reinterpretation by successive generations of political leaders and interests that are in social conflict.

The Constitution: rationale and ratification of governing doctrines

The document agreed upon at Philadelphia contained several assumptions about how government should be organized and conducted. These assumptions emerged as governing doctrines: republican government, the division of powers between states and nation and the federal principle, the separation of powers among governing institutions at the national level providing for checks and balances in policymaking. Underlying these doctrines was the common notion of balanced government. The leaders who drafted the Constitution had to describe, explain, and justify these ideas to the people in the thirteen states who would have to ratify the new Constitution; this was a formidable undertaking in several key states.

BALANCED GOVERNMENT

The Framers had created what they hoped would be the framework for a strong, effective national government with sufficient authority "to form a more perfect union, establish justice, insure domestic tranquility, provide for the common defense, promote the general welfare, and secure the blessings of liberty to ourselves and our posterity. . . ." In the struggle for ratification they had to convince Americans that they had not concentrated too much authority in the hands of this new national government. To do so they stressed that the Constitution incorporated the principle of balanced government.

The principle of balanced government affirms that the way to provide a government with adequate authority to do its job and yet avoid the risk of creating the potential for tyranny is to distribute governing powers among differing institutions and levels of government. Limits are thereby placed on government not by denying it power to act but by allocating power to separate units and balancing one against the other.

The most articulate effort to justify the Constitution as the very embodiment of the concept of balance was *The Federalist Papers*. A series of 85 letters written by James Madison, Alexander Hamilton, and John Jay, *The Federalist Papers* appealed to broad doctrinal principles and "the common sense of the situation" to build support for ratifying the Constitution.

In *Papers* No. 10 and No. 51, the authors argued that the balance provided in the constitutional structure was the most practical guarantee of the maintenance of liberty and a republican government. In No. 51, the authors made clear their conviction that the dangers to liberty and stability arose from the very nature of man himself: "But what is government itself, but the greatest of all reflections on human nature? If men were angels, no government would be necessary." Said Madison: "In framing a government which is to be administered by men over men, the great difficulty lies in this: you must first enable the governnment to control the governed; and in the next place oblige it to control itself." The problem, then, was to balance the Lockean concept of representative government with the recognized tendencies of people to abuse power.

In No. 10, Madison argued that the great danger came from what he called "factions," or groups of people united for some purpose "adverse to the rights of other citizens, or to the permanent and aggregate interests of the community." Because factions "were sewn into the nature of men," they could not be eliminated except by destroying liberty. Hence the means for controlling factions had to deal with confining their effects. The Constitution contains two such means: republican, or representative, government and the division of authority through federalism and the separation of powers.

Republican government

The institutional arrangement most suitable for controlling factions in a large and diverse country, the *Federalist* writers argued, was republican government—in other words, *representative democracy. Pure democracy,* or direct rule by an assembly of citizens who "administer the government in person," provides no protection against unreasonable majorities. Representative democracy filters and refines popular views through representatives "whose wisdom may best discern the true interest of their country." Recognizing that the elected representatives may themselves "betray the interests of the people," Madison claimed that a large republic lessens that danger. A large republic not only has a greater number of "fit characters" to serve as representatives, but the larger the area to be governed, the more difficult it is for a majority to form. As Madison wrote in No. 10, "If such a common motive exists, it will be more difficult for all who feel it to discover their own strength, and to act in unison with each other."

Division of powers

Essays No. 10 and No. 51 both viewed the division of authority between the states and the national government as an added safeguard against the destruction of liberty by a majority. The argument is explicit in No. 51: "In the compound republic of America, the power surrendered by the people is first divided between two distinct governments, and then the portion allotted to each subdivided among distinct and separate departments. Hence, a double security arises to the rights of the people. The different governments will control each other, at the same time that each will be controlled by itself." The Founding Fathers believed that federalism and the separation of powers would complement one another.

The federal principle

In principle, federalism is intended to provide a balance between the national and state governments, a balance achieved by dividing powers between the two, making each supreme within its own sphere of authority and allowing each some jurisdiction over individual citizens. Such a system produces a degree of tension between the two units. The Framers believed this tension would contribute to the protection of freedom by constraining national majorities and protecting local interests.

The impact of federalism on American politics has been profound, as our discussion of the decentralized American party system, the fragmented nature of the congressional decisionmaking processes, the organization of our electoral system, and other areas of the political system will show.

The Constitutional provisions incorporating the federal principle are scattered throughout the document—in sections specifying, for example, the system for selecting Senators and Representatives, the electoral college system for selecting the President, the granting of certain powers to Congress. The Tenth Amendment, not a part of the original document, also contains a statement regarding state power: "The powers not delegated to the United States by the Constitution, nor prohibited by it to the States, are reserved to the States respectively, or to the people."

Governing the nation was thus left to a partnership of nation and states, with power divided to prevent either complete centralization or excessive fragmentation. The built-in tension between nation and states and the ambiguity over which unit possesses the authority to act in specific areas have produced great debates over the course of our history. In every area of dispute but one, the Constitution proved adequate to contain conflict. The one exception, the Civil War, was fought over the very meaning of the federal union. The Confederates argued that the federal Constitution was merely a voluntary compact between separate states that rested on an unchanging balance between national prerogatives and "states' rights"; individual states could leave the Union should they feel their rights had been violated. Lincoln's defense of the Union held that the Constitution of 1787 had created a community of people within a federal framework that could not be dissolved by the action of any state or group of states. His supporters cited the language of the Constitution under which states agree to acknowledge a strong central authority operating directly on individual citizens.

In the twentieth century, broad court interpretations of national legislative powers have permitted the national government to enter areas once believed to be in the province of the states. The regulation of business, social legislation such as minimum wage and maximum hours laws, and civil rights legislation are examples of extensions of national government activity that were bitterly resisted.

The balance between federal and state power is sometimes uncertain. In 1977, 13 states approved legislation permitting the sale of laetrile, a highly controversial drug used in the treatment of cancer; but the U.S. Food and Drug Administration (FDA) held that the drug was worthless and ordered the seizure of supplies of apricot pits used in its manufacture. The FDA's authority stemmed from the power granted it by Congress under Article I of the Constitution. That Article gives Congress the power to "regulate commerce among the States," a power broadly construed by the Supreme Court to include the manufacture and distribution of drugs as well as other goods. At the same time that the FDA was taking action against laetrile, congressional representatives and others lobbied for strong prolaetrile interests by urging the FDA to relax its opposition to the drug.

The federal principle is deeply ingrained in American political patterns. The Framers may or may not have grasped its full significance for the future, but their general intent to decentralize power, to create a basis from which state and local interests could blunt the operation of national majorities, and to limit government by balancing competing interests has been realized.

Separation of powers

The separation of powers was another mechanism included in the Constitution to preserve balance and a republican government. In theory, allotting the functions of government to separate institutions would prevent power from falling into the hands of a single interest. Moreover, a system of checks and balances could be used to reinforce separation. Authority was assigned to three institutions—the executive, the legislature, and the judiciary—and restraints were put on the exercise of power by each.

In effect, each branch of government was given the authority to monitor the activities of the other two: The presidential veto is a restraint on legislative powers; the congressional power of the purse limits presidential action; and the courts' powers to review the constitutionality of laws or executive actions limits both the President and Congress. The provision for a bicameral legislature, in which each house can veto the actions of the other, reflects the same principle.

The argument that a distribution of the functions of government can prevent the concentration of power in a single minority or majority sounds plausible enough, but even *The Federalist* is not totally convincing on this point. Separation of powers and checks and balances can backfire. Given independence from the other two branches, the third can block policymaking and administration, and a minority may thus obstruct community action without ever capturing the whole apparatus. The refusal of a President to spend money appropriated by Congress could block the implementation of a widely supported public policy. A decision of the Supreme Court upholding legislation requiring a specific action by government officials would be ineffective if the executive branch deliberately did nothing. If a majority faction captured all policymaking positions, the simple device of separation would not serve as a safeguard against majority tyranny. But the device of periodic elections makes it difficult for one faction to control the whole government long enough to smash the constitutional crockery.

RATIFICATION

Ratification of the Constitution did not come easily. Conscious of how the unanimity requirement had made the Articles of Confederation unamendable, the Framers provided that the new document would go into effect upon approval by just 9, or two-thirds, of the 13 states. Moreover, because the delegates believed that state legislatures were less likely than the general public to approve the document, they provided for popular participation in ratification: Each state was required to ratify in conventions chosen by the voters.

Opponents attacked the proposed Constitution as a sacrifice of state autonomy, as a failure to secure the rights of Americans, as an "antirepublican" arrangement, and as a considerable overreaction to the need for strengthening the Articles of Confederation. Some convention delegates returned home to fight against ratification. But the arguments for limited government, balance, representative democracy, and federalism proved persuasive, and, by June 1788, nine states had ratified. This number did not include New York and Virginia, large and influential states whose approval was essential, both states ratified within a month of the first nine—after a hard fight.

The constitutional principles of balance, separation of powers, and federalism have become part of the American value structure. In American mythology, the Framers are viewed as men of extraordinary ability and insight into the future. The truth is that they forged a document containing both democratic ideals and political compromises, but they also gave us a document with extraordinary capacity to govern a nation that has undergone tremendous changes in its more than 200 years of existence. These social, economic, and technological changes have tested the fiber of the constitutional framework of balance, separation, and federalism. Yet the tensions inherent in American political patterns have been manageable because there has also been consensus on the basic framework. The strength of the Constitution lies not only in its symbolic appeal but also in its capacity to respond to change. Response has taken the form of both formal and informal amendment.

Constitutional change by formal amendment

A brief glance at the formal amendments to the Constitution reveals that Article V, the amending clause, has been used infrequently and that some of the 26 amendments do not significantly affect conflict regulation in the American political community. The first ten amendments—the Bill of Rights —have been described as "perhaps the best known, most cherished feature or portion of the Constitution [because they] are thought of as absolute and moral, and not—like the remainder of the Constitution—expressions of governmental policy" (Mitchell and Mitchell, 1975, p. 193). Very little discussion took place in the Constitutional Convention about a Bill of Rights; instead attention was focused on the need for a strong national government. In meeting the heavy criticism of the proposed Constitution for its lack of guarantees to protect certain basic rights of citizens, supporters of the Constitution argued that such rights were protected by bills of rights in the state constitutions. But this assertion was not enough; Massachusetts Federalists had to dangle a national Bill of Rights as bait to get their state's ratification, and the idea took hold. Widespread public demand resulted in a Bill of Rights being added to the Constitution by formal amendment shortly after the new government came into being.

AMENDMENTS ELEVEN THROUGH TWENTY-SIX

Of the remaining sixteen amendments, fewer than half have significantly affected the basic structure of government. The Eleventh and Twelfth were added as quick remedies for disruptive situations not foreseen by the Framers. The Eleventh removed the jurisdiction of federal courts in suits brought against states by private individuals. The Twelfth was aimed at eliminating the possibility of a tie in electoral votes for President, such as the one that had created the Jefferson-Burr deadlock in 1800. The Eighteenth was repealed by the Twenty-First after years of frustrated attempts to enforce prohibition. The Twentieth abolished "lame duck" sessions of Congress—the short sessions in which members of Congress defeated in the November elections continued to serve from December to the following March. The Twenty-Third Amendment granted residents of the District of Columbia a voice in presidential elections. Finally, the Twenty-Fourth abolished payment of a state poll tax as a voting qualification in federal elections; by the time it was ratified in 1964, only five states still required payment.

Three of the remaining eight Amendments (the Thirteenth, Fourteenth, and Fifteenth) are labeled the Civil War Amendments because they abolished slavery and sought to guarantee the newly won rights of the Negro. Amendments Sixteen (permitting a direct tax on personal incomes), Seventeen (providing for the popular election of senators), and Nineteen (extending the franchise to women), ratified between 1913 and 1920, reflected the Progressive Movement's efforts to extend democratic participation to all citizens. The Twenty-Second Amendment limited a President to two terms. The Twenty-Fifth, ratified in 1967, owes something to the assassination of President Kennedy in 1963; it provides for succession to a vacancy in the vice-presidency and also establishes procedures by which the Vice-President becomes acting President in case of presidential disability. The most recent amendment, the Twenty-Sixth, guarantees the vote in all state and federal elections to citizens 18 years or older; upon its ratification in 1971, 11 million Americans were added to the voting rolls.

The proposed Twenty-Seventh, the "Equal Rights Amendment," would prohibit discrimination on the basis of sex. Sent by Congress to the states in 1972, the amendment was expected to win quick approval. However, strong opposition developed over the implications of its provisions and by the end of 1978 it was still three states short of ratification. In addition, two states that had initially ratified the amendment withdrew their approval, creating an unsolved constitutional issue. If the approval of either or both of these states is needed to provide the required number (38) to finally ratify, can that approval be counted despite the state's subsequent disapproval? Or may a state withdraw its approval prior to ratification by the thirty-eighth state? If Congress declares the amendment adopted after the thirty-eighth state approves, its action may be decisive, but the U.S. Supreme Court will almost certainly become involved in the conflict.

WHY SO FEW?

It is striking that only 26 constitutional amendments have been approved, although more than 5,000 have been introduced in Congress since 1789. Relatively high procedural hurdles, which make minority opposition particularly effective, account in part for this small figure. Merely to propose an amendment for ratification by the states, the sponsors of a draft must win approval by a congressional committee and a two-thirds vote in each house of Congress. An alternative method—through a national constitutional convention—has never been used. The additional requirement that at least three-fourths of the states must *ratify* a proposed amendment further strengthens a minority's hand in blocking change. All the states except Nebraska have two-house legislatures; because both houses must approve amendments, a minority need only convince one chamber not to ratify. Amendment is not an easy process, but it was never intended to be too easy. Despite the difficulties, the states have accepted all but 6 of 31 proposed amendments. Only one, the Twenty-First, has been ratified by the alternative method of state conventions.

As Table 3.1 shows there has been a tendency to add amendments in clusters. The political temper of the American electorate may partially explain this phenomenon. The amendments added to the Constitution between 1913 and 1933 reflected the dissatisfaction with the government that had been articulated at the height of the Progressive Movement. Since that time, Congress has been more willing to use its broad legislative powers to expand federal activities; the presidency has grown in scope and status; and the Supreme Court has refrained from narrow interpretations of the constitutional powers of either Congress or the President while handing down a number of far-reaching decisions in civil rights and civil liberties that generally reflected a liberal outlook.

TABLE 3.1
The clustering pattern of constitutional amendments

Year adopted	Amendment	Clustering effect
1971	Twenty-Sixth	
1967	Twenty-Fifth	
1965	Twenty-Fourth	
1964	Twenty-Third	
1951	Twenty-Second	
1933	Twenty-First, Twentieth	
1920	Nineteenth	
1919	Eighteenth	Progressive Era Amendments
1913	Seventeenth, Sixteenth	
1870	Fifteenth	
1868	Fourteenth	Civil War Amendments
1865	Thirteenth	
1804	Twelfth	
1795	Eleventh	
1791	First through Tenth	Bill of Rights

Constitutional change by informal modification

With the exception of the Twenty-Second Amendment limiting presidential tenure, no addition to the Constitution has significantly altered the original distribution of power. To be sure, procedures for majority rule have been marginally changed by amendments extending suffrage and providing for the direct election of Senators, but other developments—judicial review, expanded presidential power, growth of the administrative branch, independent regulatory agencies, and political parties—have had a greater effect on political balance.

JUDICIAL REVIEW

Article VI declares that the Constitution, laws of Congress, and treaties of the United States must be enforced by all state and federal courts as the "supreme law of the land." But nothing clarifies which branch should decide what constitutes conflict between constitutional authority and official action. The need for a referee in disputes between states and the national government was essential if the newly created federal system was to survive. Congress gave that role to the Supreme Court when it granted the Court the power to pass upon the constitutionality of state laws in the Judiciary Act of 1789. But what about conflicts over acts of Congress or the President? And who is to arbitrate constitutional disputes involving the separate branches of the national government?

Although the question of judicial review of laws was discussed in the Constitutional Convention and was probably supported by a majority of delegates, the Constitution does not specifically provide such power (C. Beard, 1962). Instead, judicial review was asserted in 1803 by the great Chief Justice John Marshall in the case of *Marbury* v. *Madison*. For the first time, the Supreme Court struck down an act of Congress on grounds that it violated superior law, the Constitution. Marshall's decision declared that the Constitution could be changed only by constitutional amendment; therefore, "an act repugnant to the Constitution is void." The duty to declare such action unconstitutional rests with the judicial branch because the courts are the proper interpreter of the supreme law. Judicial review means that a court may examine a statute or an action by a public official to determine if it is consistent with the Constitution. Marshall's assertion of this power was a truly significant development in the constitutional framework.

From Marshall's time onward, the exercise of the power of judicial review has been considered a legitimate function of the judicial branch. However, the legitimacy of judicial review is lost if the courts overstep the boundary between defining the *legality* of an action and imposing the *political* preferences of judges. The latter is called *judicial legislating*, a term used to criticize a court on grounds that it has infringed the legitimate power of Congress to make laws. The distinction between a proper legal judgment and judicial legislating is considerably easier to draw in the abstract than in reality. Did the Supreme Court improperly invade the province of Congress when it declared racial segregation of public schools unconstitutional in its 1954 Brown decision? Or was this a proper exercise of the judicial review of state laws in terms of the Constitutional requirement that no state deny any person "equal protection of the laws"? Constitutional language is often imprecise and its meaning unclear. Such phrases as "due process of law," "necessary and proper," and "establishment of religion" permit a judge considerable judicial discretion in applying them to specific cases.

Between 1803 and 1976, the Supreme Court employed judicial review to strike down 120 provisions of federal law and 950 instances of state law or state constitutional provisions (Abraham, 1977, p. 162). Considering the fact that Congress passed over 70,000 laws in this time, judicial review was used to nullify a very small number of them; but many of the decisions implementing judicial review declared major pieces of legislation void.

Seventy-four cases concerning federal law were decided between 1865 and 1937, when the Court's influence on policymaking was steadily expanding. The peak of activity was reached in the middle 1930s when the court under Chief Justice Hughes invalidated 13 New Deal measures in four years (1933–1937). During the same period, the Court also declared 3 presidential actions unconstitutional. The frequent use of the judicial veto caused President

Roosevelt to attempt to "pack" the court in 1937—to get a majority in favor of New Deal measures; but Congress refused to approve the proposal. Since 1937, the Court has declared only 9 provisions of federal laws unconstitutional.

Given the fact that Supreme Court decisions regularly involve controversies with far-reaching consequences for the political system, one might question the "democratic" nature of judicial review. Is a nonelected group of judges with life terms, subject to removal only by impeachment or death, consistent with democratic consent? From the perspective of that part of democratic theory rooted in the concepts of representation and accountability, the Court does have an elitist, nondemocratic image. After all, the judgment of a democratically elected Congress and President can be set aside by a group of judges that voters have not elected and cannot remove. However, from the perspective of a constitutional system based upon checks and balances as a key element in limited government, the power of judicial review is an instrument of democracy. Further, the judicial branch restrains the power of legislative majorities, however representative of public opinion they might be, from violating the rights and freedoms of minorities and individual citizens. This is the side of the democratic coin that emphasizes individual freedom against majority will.

To what extent has judicial review served as an effective check on the two other policymaking branches of the American government? Although the Court has used its authority sparingly, the fact that it can invalidate laws is an effective check in itself. Congress or the President may hesitate to pursue a policy in the face of a strong expectation that the Court may rule an action unconstitutional. A potentially adverse decision does not, however, always prevent action. Once the Court declares an action unconstitutional, can it make the decision stick? Robert A. Dahl's study led him to conclude that "there is . . . no case on record where a persistent law-making majority has not, sooner or later, achieved its purposes." Dahl found that one-third of the Supreme Court decisions holding congressional legislation unconstitutional ultimately were overridden by amendment or subsequent Court decisions. Many of the remaining rulings affected minor legislation, temporary measures, or trivial sections of statutes (1956, p. 110).

We may conclude that even without frequent declarations of unconstitutionality, the possibility of judicial review serves as an important, if not precisely measurable, check. But in the long run, the Court has not been able to prevent determined legislative majorities from ultimately achieving their goal—and has not often tried.

THE PRESIDENT'S ROLE

The rise of political parties transformed the electoral college into an agency that simply reflects the popular choice in each of the states. Thus the President is the only popularly chosen official whose constituency is the whole American

political community. What he does depends upon who he is, but in the twentieth century the trend has been toward increased political leadership—the "active Presidency." The President is the leader of his party, the prodder of Congress, and a spokesman for the "national interest" as opposed to the narrow interests of congressional constituencies. The presidential role has consistently grown in scope and importance to the point where it cuts across the technical limitations that underlie the separation of powers and checks and balances.

ADMINISTRATIVE AGENCIES

The administrative branch of the government has changed greatly in both size and function since the Constitution was written. The creation of the Cabinet during Washington's first administration is an early example of change without amendment. The proliferation of executive agencies, especially in this century (about three quarters of the federal jobs have been created since the 1930s) has brought about a whole new level of policymaking not envisioned by the

Framers. A relatively new term, "bureaucratization," is used to indicate the presence of "faceless" or "depersonalized" governmental organizations in almost every aspect of American life.

Of special importance are regulatory agencies such as the Interstate Commerce Commission, the Federal Trade Commission, and the Federal Communications Commission. These agencies have the legislative discretion to make rules and regulations in highly specialized, technical areas (for example, the Securities and Exchange Commission develops and supervises regulations affecting the stock market); judicial discretion (as when the Federal Communications Commission awards a license to operate a TV station); and executive discretion (as when the Interstate Commerce Commission fixes and enforces rates for trucking companies, bus lines, railroads, and other carriers). The President appoints members of the commissions running these agencies (with the consent of the Senate) but they are not responsible to him. Given the fact that such agencies combine executive, legislative, and judicial functions, a mechanical definition of separation of powers does not adequately describe their place in the constitutional structure. We shall consider the role of the regulatory agencies in greater detail in Chapter 13.

POLITICAL PARTIES

The Constitution says nothing about parties. The Framers were fully aware that people join together to achieve common goals; they did that themselves in Philadelphia. But they had no idea that party organizations would gain power and become a significant—perhaps indispensable—element in the balance of power itself. One of the functions of political parties, although certainly not a perfectly realized one, is representation, the attempt to bridge the gap between citizens and government and translate popular desires into public policy. Since the rise of the Whigs in the 1830s (followed by the antislavery Republicans in the 1850s), dissatisfied citizens have always had an alternative through which they could work to present their demands to the party in control of the government.

Parties are organized to compete for public office and obtain positions of power. Occasionally their effect has been to reduce—but by no means eliminate—conflict among the three branches of government. The organization of American parties follows the decentralized pattern of federalism, which means that policy choices, especially in the legislative branch, tend to reflect diverse sectional and local interests. In this respect, parties have been instrumental in preserving the decentralized distribution of power desired by the Framers. Even if one party controls both the executive and the legislature, as has happened in all but 20 years of this century, the decentralized structure of the party may produce strong disagreements within the organization itself. Finally, a spin-off of partisan competition for the presidency is that it helps make citizens aware of national issues and political events.

Constitutional change by court action: applying the Bill of Rights to the states

From the time of Chief Justice Marshall, the Supreme Court has been a primary force in constitutional change. The Court's decisions extending the guarantees of the Bill of Rights against actions by state governments are among its most striking contributions. This achievement is known as the "nationalization" of the Bill of Rights.

The Bill of Rights directly limits the authority of only the national government. State constitutions similarly circumscribe state activity by a separate bill of rights or by other provisions. Presumably, therefore, citizens are protected against both units of government. In practice, the states have differed greatly in the scope and interpretation of state-guaranteed substantive and procedural rights.

Before the Fourteenth Amendment was adopted, the Supreme Court took the position that the Bill of Rights protected the citizen only against actions of the national government (*Barron* v. *Baltimore*, 1833). Following the Civil War, the question arose as to whether the Fourteenth Amendment applied the guarantees of the Bill of Rights to state governments. Legal controversy centered on the due-process clause of the Fourteenth Amendment, which provides that "no state shall deprive any person of life, liberty, or property without due process of law." Until 1890, the Supreme Court held to its pre–Civil War view that the Bill of Rights limited national action only, but in 1890 it began to interpret the Fourteenth Amendment's due-process clause as protecting property rights against state action. However, the Court held to the position that the Fourteenth Amendment did not protect other guarantees of the Bill of Rights against the actions of state governments.

The first major break in this stand came in 1925 when the Court agreed that the First Amendment guarantees of speech and press were among the "liberties" protected by the due-process clause of the Fourteenth Amendment (*Gitlow* v. *New York*, 1925). Further "nationalization" of the Bill of Rights followed. In 1937, the right to peaceful assembly was guaranteed; and in 1940 the Court extended protection against state action abridging the free exercise of religion (*DeJonge* v. *Oregon*, 1937). In 1947, the First Amendment probition against governmental establishment of religion was applied to the states when the Court ruled that a "wall of separation" must exist between church and state (*Everson* v. *Bd. of Education*, 1947).

SELECTIVE INCORPORATION VERSUS TOTAL INCORPORATION

Other provisions of the Bill of Rights remained outside the scope of the Fourteenth Amendment. Faced with the important question of which, if any, of the guarantees were to be applied to the states, the Court gave an answer in *Palko* v. *Connecticut* (1937). Palko had been convicted of second-degree murder and given a life sentence. On appeal by the state, he was tried a second time, convicted of first-degree murder, and sentenced to death. He appealed this conviction on the ground that the due-process clause of the Fourteenth Amendment, which protected individuals against action of state governments, also guaranteed the Fifth Amendment prohibition against double jeopardy (no person shall "be subject for the same offense to be twice put in jeopardy of life or limb"). Although Palko's appeal was denied, the Court, speaking through Justice Benjamin Cardozo, laid down a general formula—known as the *fair trial rule* or *selective incorporation*—for determining which of the guarantees in the first eight amendments apply to the states through the due-process clause. State actions that violate "fundamental principles of liberty and justice" were prohibited by the Fourteenth Amendment. This "natural law" doctrine of selection was contrary to the belief of Justice Hugo Black and others who argued that all the specific guarantees of the Bill of Rights were incorporated in the Fourteenth Amendment.

The *total incorporation* theory of Justice Black has never won majority support on the Supreme Court, but it has won out practically through the "absorption" of specific rights by the Court. Even *Palko* v. *Connecticut* was overruled by the 1969 decision in *Benton* v. *Maryland*. As Table 3.2 shows, only a few provisions of the Bill of Rights are not now incorporated in the Fourteenth Amendment. The Second Amendment's guarantee of the "right to keep and bear arms," and the Third Amendment's prohibition against quartering troops are of no real practical significance for state governments. Provision for indictment by a grand jury (Fifth) and the guarantee of holding trial in the district where the crime was committed (Sixth) are also not crucial. Only the Eighth Amendment's protection against excessive bail might be viewed as a right that should be brought to bear against state action.

As the Court has moved toward general application of the Bill of Rights against the states, it has also laid down more specific prescriptions for state law-enforcement officers. In *Gideon* v. *Wainwright* (1963), the Court overturned the conviction of Clarence E. Gideon, who was sentenced by a Florida court for breaking and entering. Gideon had been convicted four times before and had served prison sentences for felonies. With a five-page, handwritten petition, drafted in prison and accompanied by a pauper's affidavit, Gideon asked the Supreme Court to overturn his conviction on the ground that his request for state-appointed counsel should not have been denied by the Florida courts. Specifically, he urged that the Sixth Amendment provision of the right

TABLE 3.2
Nationalization of the Bill of Rights

Provision	Applied to states?	Important decisions
First Amendment		
Speech, press	Yes	*Gitlow* v. *New York* (1925)
Assembly and petition	Yes	*DeJonge* v. *Oregon* (1937)
Free exercise of religion	Yes	*Cantwell* v. *Connecticut* (1940)
No establishment of religion	Yes	*Everson* v. *Board of Education* (1947)
Second Amendment		
Right to keep and bear arms	No	
Third Amendment		
Quartering of troops in private homes without consent of owner	No	
Fourth Amendment		
No unreasonable searches and seizures	Yes	*Wolf* v. *Colorado* (1949) *Mapp* v. *Ohio* (1964)
Fifth Amendment		
Indictment by grand jury for serious offenses	No	
No double jeopardy	Yes	*Benton* v. *Maryland* (1969)
No self-incrimination	Yes	*Malloy* v. *Hogan* (1964)
No denial of life, liberty, or property without due process of law	Yes*	
Sixth Amendment		
Right to counsel in criminal prosecutions	Yes	*Powell* v. *Alabama* (1932)
Right of accused to confront witnesses against him	Yes	*Gideon* v. *Wainwright* (1963) *Douglas* v. *Alabama* (1965)
Right to a speedy and public trial	Yes	*Pointer* v. *Texas* (1965)
Trial in district where crime was committed	No	
Right of accused to obtain witnesses	Yes	*Washington* v. *Texas* (1967)
Trial by impartial jury	Yes	*Duncan* v. *Louisiana* (1968)
Seventh Amendment		
Trial by jury in civil suits	No	
Eighth Amendment		
No excessive bail or excessive fines	No	*Robinson* v. *California* (1962)
No cruel and unusual punishments	Yes	*Louisiana ex rel. Francis* v. *Resweber* (1947)†

*Same specific restriction in Fourteenth Amendment.
†Supreme Court assumed application against states.

to counsel is a "fundamental right" and therefore applies to the states. Gideon won his appeal. A unanimous court ruled that in all criminal cases an accused must be allowed counsel and that the court must appoint one if the accused is unable to afford his own.

One year later, the Supreme Court took another step in specifying what state courts must do to assure a fair trial. In *Escobedo* v. *Illinois* (1964), a five-to-four majority ruled that a confession obtained by police was not admissible during trial if the defendant had been denied his right to consult his attorney and had not been informed of his right to remain silent.

In June 1966, the Court went well beyond the Escobedo decision. In *Miranda* v. *Arizona* and three other cases decided at the same time, another five-to-four majority ruled that (1) a suspect taken into custody must be informed of his right to remain silent; (2) a suspect has the right to have a lawyer present during interrogation; (3) a court-appointed lawyer must be provided if the suspect requests one but is unable to pay for counsel; (4) a suspect may waive the right to counsel, but the prosecution must prove that the suspect knew his rights; and (5) if a suspect initially waives the right to counsel or starts to talk but later requests counsel or chooses to remain silent, his wishes must be complied with. Perhaps mindful of the thousands of petitions from prison inmates throughout the country who had not been accorded these protections, the Court ruled one week later that the Miranda and Escobedo decisions would not be retroactive.

THE INFLUENCE OF NONJUDICIAL ELEMENTS

Decisions on right to counsel of the Supreme Court during the tenure of Chief Justice Earl Warren stirred intense public and congressional controversy and criticism. Critics argued that the decisions created an escape for the "guilty" and an "imbalance" between the law enforcers and the "criminal." In his campaign for the Presidency in 1968, Richard Nixon charged that the Supreme Court had given the "green light to the criminal element" and pledged that he would take steps to rectify the imbalance. His appointment of Warren E. Burger in 1969 to replace retiring Chief Justice Earl Warren was seen by many as a step toward slowing down or stopping the impetus of the Warren Court of the 1960s in guaranteeing defendants' rights. Three subsequent appointments by Nixon brought to the Court justices likely to be sympathetic to the Nixon position.

Divergent views on defendants' rights between Congress and the Warren Court were revealed by two actions—one by the Supreme Court and the other by Congress—in May and June 1968. In one day, the Court overturned five convictions in criminal cases, giving more rights to defendants or convicted persons. A month later, Congress apparently responded to strong public pressures by overturning three rulings relating to the admissibility of some kinds of evidence in criminal trials in *federal* courts. The action involved only matters related to federal rules of criminal procedure. Congress cannot overrule the Court's constitutional interpretation by simply passing a statute. It does, however, have the power to alter federal court procedures based on decisions not involving constitutional requirements. In this instance, then, Congress modified only the Supreme Court's rulings affecting criminal procedures in the lower federal courts. The Court's power to interpret the Constitution was not at issue. In 1970, Congress again responded to public demands for a restoration of "law and order" by passing the Crime Control Act for the District of Columbia. Although this legislation provided for more judicial personnel and government-paid defense lawyers for indigents, it also responded to public clamor for "removing the handcuffs" from police. New rules permitted the use of wiretap and electronic sensing devices in some types of criminal investigation, search warrants for night searches, and detention of an accused if the judge concludes that such detention is necessary to ensure community safety.

By 1971 the Supreme Court's protective position seemed weaker, partly because of changes in Court personnel, especially the Chief Justice, and partly because of the increasingly complex issues raised in criminal justice. The shift appeared in decisions on cases involving guilty pleas, search and seizure, and the rights of juvenile defendants (Stephens, 1971, pp. 249–278). For instance, in 1971 the Court held that a defendant's statements during a police interrogation, even if inadmissible because police had not clearly informed him of his rights before questioning, might still be used to impeach the defendant's credibility if he made statements at his trial inconsistent with those made under police interrogation (*Harris* v. *New York*, 1971). Also in 1971, the Court held that a suspect's right to counsel was not violated, even if he had not consulted counsel, as long as the charges brought against him did not come until after he had been identified at the police station (*Kirby* v. *Illinois*, 1971).

Thus in two decisions in 1971 the Court altered earlier stands on the right against self-incrimination (announced in the Miranda case) and on the right to counsel (defined in the Escobedo decision). Whether there is "a new trend in judicial review of the criminal justice system" (Thomas, 1976, p. 74) remains unclear; although two decisions in 1975 (*Oregon* v. *Haas* and *Michigan* v. *Mosley*) further weakened protections of the right against self-incrimination, two 1976 decisions (*Doyle* v. *Ohio* and *Wood* v. *Ohio*) reaffirmed the Court's support of the Miranda doctrine.

The addition in 1975 of a new justice, John Paul Stevens, who replaced the retiring liberal Justice William O. Douglas, strengthened the moderate element on the Court. By 1978 President Carter had not yet had an opportunity to name a new justice to the Court. Although changes in personnel may again move the Supreme Court in a different direction, judicial action will continue to draw reactions from other sectors of the political system. Counterpressures may stimulate continuing constitutional change, either through formal amendments or alteration by informal means.

Changing patterns of federalism

LEGAL DIMENSIONS OF CHANGE

In 1869 the Supreme Court ruled that the states of the southern Confederacy had not ceased to be members of the Union during secession. In its decision, the Court declared that the Constitution incorporated "an indestructible union composed of indestructible states." This decision, like the Civil War itself, affirmed the durability of the federal arrangement, but the "proper" boundaries of national and state authority have always been disputed. Although the Tenth Amendment reserves to the states or the people "powers not delegated to the United States by the Constitution, nor prohibited by it to the States," federalism has undergone continuing reinterpretation.

Major factors that have enlarged the domain of national policymaking include the increase in the electorate by the removal of restrictions on suffrage; the growing sense of national community; the development of common cultural patterns; the decrease of parochialism resulting from the great mobility of the American population; and the emergence of the President as a representative of a national constituency. At one time or another all of these factors have been reflected in major Supreme Court interpretations of the federal mandate.

The case of *McCulloch* v. *Maryland,* decided in 1819, was the first major interpretation of the extent of national power under the Constitution. The issue was the creation by Congress of two national banks, the first during Washington's administration and the second in 1816. Both banks were bitterly opposed by strict constructionists of the Constitution who argued that such action went beyond the delegated powers of Congress. A number of states went so far as to impose heavy taxes on the branches of the bank within their borders. The refusal of James McCulloch, cashier of the Baltimore branch of the bank, to pay such a tax precipitated a constitutional debate over the definition of national government jurisdiction under the federal arrangement. When the issue reached the Supreme Court, Chief Justice Marshall faced two major constitutional questions: Did a state have the authority to levy a tax on a national agency and thus, by implication, threaten its very existence? and Could Congress create a bank when the Constitution did not specify its authority to do so?

The first question was answered by Marshall's assertion that "the power to tax involved the power to destroy." States could not levy a tax on a legitimate agency of the national government. But was the bank a legitimate agency? In answer to this question, Marshall cited the principle of "implied powers." The "government of the Union," wrote the Chief Justice, "though limited in its powers, is supreme within its sphere of action." Under the supremacy clause, state laws in conflict with authorized policies of Congress must give way. Was Congress, then, within its "sphere of action" in chartering a national bank? Yes, argued Marshall, even though nothing in the Constitution specifically author-izes a national bank; following the enumeration of the powers of Congress in Article I, Section 8 of the Constitution, is the clause authorizing Congress "to make all Laws which shall be necessary and proper for carrying into Execution the Foregoing Powers."

The constitutionality of the bank, therefore, hinged on how narrow or broad an interpretation was to be given to the words "necessary and proper." The Framers, argued Marshall, had deliberately written a Constitution that broadly outlined congressional jurisdiction. A constitution that listed in detail all powers flowing from generally granted powers could "scarcely be embraced by the human mind." The criterion for interpretation established by the Chief Justice was: "Let the end be legitimate, let it be within the scope of the Constitution, and all means which are plainly adapted to that end, which are not prohibited, but consist with the letter and spirit of the Constitution, are constitutional. . . ." In this case, the enumerated powers to coin and borrow money and to regulate its value implied—that is, made necessary and proper—the legitimacy of a national bank.

Marshall believed that if the Constitution was to endure, it must be adapted to fit the needs of each generation. Except in the years from about 1890 to the mid-1930s, the Supreme Court has used the implied-powers criterion to support the extension of national authority into many new areas. Moreover, it has overturned a number of state statutes that were found to be inconsistent with the Constitution in order to preserve national authority under the federal principle. Three specific grants of power to Congress formed the base for these activities: the power to regulate interstate and foreign commerce, the power to declare war, and the power to tax and spend for the general welfare. The federal laws based upon these powers today touch almost every phase of American life.

"Commerce . . . among the several states" has been interpreted as including not only the movement of goods but matters that "affect" commerce. Thus, it is a crime under federal law to transport stolen automobiles across state lines, to kidnap, to sell adulterated goods, or to discriminate in employment or the use of public accommodations. Laws establishing minimum wages, prohibiting child labor, regulating labor-management relations, and controlling the pro-duction and marketing of agricultural commodities are justified as "necessary and proper" to carry out congressional responsibility for regulating commerce. If national resources must be totally mobilized, as in time of war, congressional jurisdiction can be almost absolute. Military conscription, rationing of goods, control over production and consumption, and price control are "necessary and proper" in a concerted war effort. Finally, "to tax and spend for the general welfare" has been interpreted to include laws providing social security, unemployment compensation, subsidization of agriculture, grants to states for highway construction, and support for education. The power to tax may also be used in regulating or eliminating activities deemed harmful or undesirable. High taxes on the sale of sawed-off shotguns and narcotics are aimed not at producing revenue but at driving these activities out of existence.

Opponents of federal legislation based on the implied-powers principle have consistently charged that these statutes violate states' rights. Underlying this constitutional dispute are conflicts of interest that represent more mundane and practical considerations as well as conflicts of principle. Business interests may consider an extension of governmental regulation of labor-management relations as an undesirable limitation on practices they consider useful or necessary for economic success. A labor union official might, on the other hand, see federal activity as increasing his bargaining power with employers. One side may employ the rhetoric of "states' rights," the other that of "national needs"; yet both sides use the constitutional argument as a surface justification for achieving more immediate goals.

ECONOMIC, SOCIAL, AND TECHNOLOGICAL CATALYSTS FOR CHANGE

As technological, cultural, and economic change has altered the American style of life, it has affected the federal pattern designed by the Framers of the Constitution.

The 1970 census revealed that almost three-quarters of the American people now live in 200 standard metropolitan areas. Of these, more than 50 percent have populations exceeding one million. More than half of the population of metropolitan areas live in suburbs. The northeastern seaboard of the United States has already developed into a "megalopolis" that crosses ten states plus the District of Columbia and includes hundreds of overlapping counties, cities, and other units of local government (Gottman, 1961).

The same urban areas that produce the greatest wealth also present the nation's most pressing social, educational, economic, and environmental problems. Crime, drug addiction, poverty, unemployment, racial conflict, and environmental pollution are familiar to even the casual observer. While the large central cities in these metropolitan areas have grappled with their expanding problems, affluent citizens have moved to the suburbs. Left behind are the poor, those most in need of better living conditions. The inner city is frequently unable to support the public housing, recreation, education, and environmental programs needed by its residents. And as the suburbs become more crowded and suburban governments seek the financial resources to sustain services, their residents complain of an ever-growing tax burden.

How can government adequately respond to such needs? This is an extremely complex question. The American governmental structure was originally designed to protect its citizens through a division of power among state and federal governments, which permitted a "local autonomy" that would serve the diverse interests of the "grass roots." Today these virtues are often a barrier to attacking problems that are local in origin but national in scope. The problems have no regard for state or local governmental boundaries, and their financial and human costs may strain the federal organization. Debate over viable solutions involves not only the organizational features of the federal principle but also the political values that fostered it.

From the beginning, national and state governments have shared activities, power, and responsibilities. Morton Grodzins described the American system as a "marble cake" of mixed powers rather than a "three-layer cake" of national, state, and local governments. "In fact," he writes, "no important activity of government in the United States is the exclusive province of one of the levels, not even what may be regarded as the most national of national functions, such as foreign relations; not even the most local of local functions, such as police protection and park maintenance" (1966, pp. 7–8). Since the early 1800s, activities such as education, transportation, law enforcement, agriculture, and communications have been shared by nation and states. This sharing or collaboration, also called *co-operative federalism*, has persisted despite an opposing theory, *dual federalism*, developed in the nineteenth century. Advocates of dual federalism proposed that governmental functions be divided between state and federal jurisdictions and that the powers of each be exclusive and independent of the other. Dominant during the 70 years from 1860 to 1930, the concept lost its legal basis during the depression when greatly expanded federal participation brought general acceptance of federal-state cooperation in meeting social and economic problems.

Intergovernmental cooperation has expanded to include virtually every governmental activity, from public welfare to local police protection. Faced with the need to assist those states unable to finance essential programs, the federal government, with its larger tax resources, has assumed an increasing share of the costs of state and local government activities. In 1938 state and local governments received 7.2 percent of their total revenues from the federal government; the percentage reached 9.9 percent by 1958 and 14.6 percent by 1968 (Elazar, 1972, p. 61). The major form of federal assistance has been grants-in-aid. These are federal funds transferred to the states for specified purposes such as highway construction and social welfare. States are usually required to match the federal funds according to a prescribed formula. Since such grants are usually administered by both the state and local governments, they achieve joint government participation in meeting social and economic needs. The number of grant-in-aid programs has expanded rapidly since 1960; of the 530 programs that existed in 1970, 80 percent began within the previous ten years (Reagan, 1972, pp. 55–56).

During the 1950s and 1960s, more and more people expressed concern over the federal government's heavy use of major tax sources (especially the income tax), a trend that made it difficult for state and local governments to raise money at a time when demands for public services were rapidly increasing. The idea that the federal government could share revenues with state governments was proposed in the 1950s and considered (but not supported) during the administration of President Johnson. Revenue-sharing was strongly endorsed by national associations of state and local government officials in the 1960s and recommended by President Nixon in 1971 as a major part of his domestic program. Congress finally enacted the Revenue-Sharing Program in 1972. The major difference between revenue-sharing and grant-in-aid programs is that in revenue-sharing the money is transferred to the states without any requirement that it be used for purposes specified by the federal government; states are thus permitted more flexibility in using federal dollars. To insure that urban areas would receive their fair share of such funds, Congress required that two-thirds of the money go to local governments. In addition, the revenue-sharing law provides for some form of citizen participation in determining the use of the funds, and it also prohibits state and local governments from discriminating on the basis of race, sex, or age in programs financed in whole or part with federal funds. These requirements were strengthened in the 1976 extension of the Revenue-Sharing Program.

In the first four years of the Revenue-Sharing Program, over $30 billion were distributed to state and local governments; by 1980 the total is expected to reach about $55 billion. Whether the program will be a significant help in solving state and local government revenue problems, and whether it will strengthen the role of the states in the federal system, remains uncertain. The nation's problems belong to more than the federal government. Federal expenditures have increased steadily and dramatically since the 1930s, but so have those of state and local governments.

The accelerating change in American life makes the future of federalism uncertain. The crucial question today is not whether the states or the nation should undertake programs to meet problems, but which level can do so most effectively. Americans have valued grass-roots control and local autonomy; these traditions as well as the complex problems that overlap governmental boundaries are integral to the American pattern of conflict. At the same time, problems that are national in scope can not be solved by purely local efforts. Both the fear of "centralization" through the financial resources of the national government and the fear that broad public problems are not amenable to solution by 50 separate states reflect the political dynamics of the federal bargain. Since the 1830s federalism has been rooted in the decentralized nature of the political party system, a system that responds to both national and local interests in the processes of policy. Moreover, federalism has been defined and interpreted on a continuing basis by the Supreme Court, which responds to changing socioeconomic circumstances. Finally, citizen commitment to federalism as a constitutional principle is clearly relevant to the continued vitality of state and local governments. Since federalism is integral to the representation and regulation of conflict in the United States, short of major alterations in the system, it will continue to affect policymaking.

Constitutional politics and liberal democracy: a summation

The Constitution means different things to different people and groups. For some it is a bulwark against poorly considered change; for others it is a flexible instrument designed to enable government to adapt to the changing environment and needs of society. For virtually all Americans the Constitution is a symbol of the nation's commitment to the values of liberal democracy.

We have noted that the Framers sought to achieve a system that would control the exercise of power by balancing authority and limiting the ability of majorities to violate the rights of minorities. Federalism, separation of powers, judicial review, the electoral college, and other provisions have largely achieved these ends. Dramatic changes in public policy have been rare and American government today operates under the same basic institutional mechanisms and procedures designed by the Framers. Informal modifications such as judicial review, the growth of the Presidency, and the role of political parties have significantly affected the pattern of decisionmaking. There have been few formal amendments, but some have been of great significance in changing existing patterns.

The combination of Constitutional symbolism and the slow pace of institutional and procedural change accounts for the great stability of the Constitution. Social, technological, and economic changes have affected the style and form of American politics, but such change has been accommodated within the basic format of the document written in 1787. To cite one example: Campaign styles and techniques have changed dramatically; yet we retain the electoral college system for determining the winner of presidential elections, and the federal system still preserves the importance of localized interests in determining congressional representation.

But what of liberal democracy's substantive values? How well are they reflected in constitutional democracy? Constitutional government may be defined as limited government. Restraints and prohibitions are placed upon the exercise of power by government. Constitutional restraints can also free the individual. The Bill of Rights is a mandate against governmental interference with the exercise of free speech, press, and assembly, all essential to the people's right to determine and control their governors. Procedures underlying constitutional democracy can increase respect for human dignity, potential for human development, and freedom of intelligence. When these procedures are used to restrict the development of individual potential—by local, state, national, or *any* level of the political community—then constitutional government is a guise for bondage, not liberation.

We have seen that political differences within the American community are contained by a basic consensus on liberal-democratic ideals and procedures. Controversy seldom involves the basic features and values of the constitutional system. If one side argues that a proposal will violate a constitutional ideal, the other side usually does not condemn that ideal. The proponents of the proposal instead deny that any violation will occur, affirm the validity of the ideal, and insist that their proposed action meets that ideal better than existing provisions. Both proponents and opponents of the busing of public school children to achieve racial balance affirm the democratic ideal of political and social equality; they differ over the issue of whether busing is required to fulfill the Constitution's mandate of "equal protection of the laws" for all persons. No one questions the value of better education for an underprivileged minority or the principle of "equal protection"; but the specific policies by which they are to be achieved are highly controversial.

Our attachment to liberal democratic beliefs and practices shapes and limits disputes, but does not eliminate them. We seem to have little difficulty in supplying the political agenda with continuing controversies over the best means to approach the ends on which we agree. As Madison argued in *Federalist* No. 10, diverse and conflicting interests in our society underlie the permanency of individual and collective disagreements. Our political community is at least a partially open society that, by definition, encourages differences as well as agreement. Neither the number nor the status of groups remains static. Powerful interests lose their power (prohibition forces); relatively weak groups become stronger (labor unions, NAACP); new groups enter the political scene (National Organization of Women, National Farmers' Organization, Students for a Democratic Society); and some groups disappear entirely (Whig Party). These changes are reflected in, and affected by, constituted authority, and thereby vitally influence the determination of policy and the resolution of conflict. As long as potentially destructive conflict is thus democratically adjusted, our continuously interacting system of fundamental values and operating rules can remain viable.

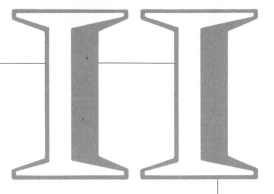

PATTERNS
OF CONFLICT
REPRESENTATION:
WHO TAKES PART
AND HOW?

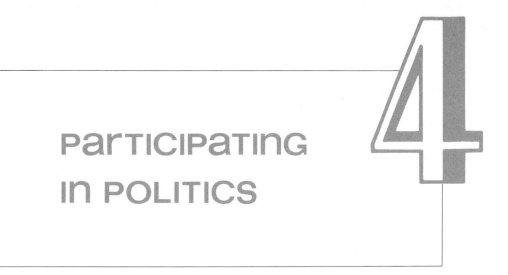

participating
in POLITICS

In a pluralist community like America there are numerous conflicts over what society's goals should be and the best ways to reach those goals. By participating in politics, people air these disagreements and thereby contribute to the representation of conflict. Do Americans believe in taking part in politics? How much participation is there? How do people participate? Who is permitted to take part and who actually does?

To take part or not?

In some respects Americans are as ambivalent about political participation as they are about liberal democratic values (see Chapter 2). On the one hand, large numbers of Americans believe that the "ordinary person" should play a part in public affairs. On the other hand, relatively few Americans do so. When asked, about eight of every ten Americans express the view that they are obligated as citizens to participate in politics even though they have many other matters that occupy their time (Milbrath and Goel, 1977, p. 49). A close inspection of such evidence suggests that this feeling of obligation extends more to passive than to active political participation. Active participation includes taking part in political parties, trying to influence government, and joining organizations interested in public affairs. About three in ten Americans feel an obligation to give up time from other pursuits to do these things. Passive participation—such as keeping politically informed and voting—requires less sacrifice. From 40 to 60 percent of Americans say they feel obligated in these passive ways.

Most Americans are interested in politics. For instance, surveys show that approximately nine of every ten respondents agree with such statements as "I like to hear what's going on in politics," "It makes a lot of difference to me who wins a presidential election," and "It makes a lot of difference to me who represents me in Congress." Less than a majority say they "find most campaigns silly and ridiculous." These expressions of interest and concern are conducive to widespread participation (Lehnen, 1976, p. 181).

Finally, there is at least one other indication of a high potential among Americans for popular participation in politics. Americans have a clear sense of the kinds of things they might do to influence government should they want to do so. Table 4.1 reports the percentages of people who would choose various courses of action to "change things they didn't like about government" (Harris, 1974, p. 21).

How much popular participation?

The ambivalent aspect of popular participation in American politics is that the general feeling of an obligation to take part, the widespread sense of involvement, and the enormous potential for a popular response to government are not always matched by actual political activity. Table 4.2 depicts a profile of American political participation in the 1960s and 1970s. It lists the estimated percentages of Americans who take part in various active and passive types of politics. Two clear patterns of participation emerge from this profile: (1) Relatively few Americans actively participate in politics on a regular, sustained basis; (2) the more passive the means, the greater the proportions of Americans who take part.

A more tidy summary of political participation in the United States appears in Table 4.3, which presents the relative proportions of Americans engaging in six types of political activity: (1) voting regularly in presidential elections, but doing nothing more; (2) voting and campaigning by persuading others how to vote, working for parties and candidates, attending political meetings, contributing money, and joining political clubs; (3) voting without campaigning, but doing such things as joining with others to work on local problems; (4) sometimes voting and maybe contacting local or national leaders for personal reasons, say about a tax problem, but doing little else; (5) voting, campaigning, and cooperating with others to solve local and national problems;

TABLE 4.1

Potential avenues of popular participation

Means of participation people would choose to "change things they didn't like about government"	Percentage selecting
Vote against a public official	94
Talk to friends and neighbors	91
Write congressional representative	84
Write U.S. Senator	81
Work through a group they belong to	79
Contact local law enforcement officials	76
Contact someone in local politics	75
Join a local citizens group	72
Join a political party and work to make changes	66
Write a letter to the newspaper	65
Send money to support a local citizens group to demand action	62
Talk to a newspaper reporter or editor	61
Vote against a public official's party at the next election	55
Take part in a demonstration	27
Take aggressive action even if someone gets hurt	27
Do nothing	17

Source: Compiled from data reported in Harris, L., Confidence and Concern: Citizens View American Government, Cleveland, Ohio: Regal Books/King's Court Communications, 1974, pp. 21–22.

and (6) taking no part whatsoever (Verba and Nie, 1972). The picture that emerges divides citizens into roughly equal percentages of active and passive participants: About 40 percent are inactive or limit their participation to voting (passive); a slightly higher percentage vote, campaign, take part in community activity, or are completely active.

In sum, a widespread sense of civic obligation, involvement, and potential for popular response results in relatively high passive participation in conflict representation, but less than one-half of our citizens actively present demands and grievances to politicians. How then do Americans most often seek to make policymakers hear their arguments? We will discuss six of the principal avenues for representing conflict in American life. In this chapter, we will provide a general description of each avenue. In the chapters that follow we will then examine each pattern of conflict representation in detail.

EXPRESSING POLITICAL OPINIONS

An easy way to represent disagreement in politics is to voice conflicting opinions on issues and personalities. This Americans are quick to do: "Americans are an articulate people and they express opinions on virtually every

TABLE 4.2

A profile of American political participation

Modes of political participation	Estimated percentage of Americans participating
Passive Participation	
Expressing political opinions:	
Normally express opinions when asked	70–90
Normally express informed opinions when asked	30–50
Possess basic "textbook" information about politics	15–40
"Very" interested in politics rather than "slightly," "somewhat," or "not at all" interested	20–25
Making voting choices:	
Register to vote in presidential election years	70–80
Identify as Republicans or Democrats (1970s)	65–70
Give "quite a lot" of thought to presidential election rather than "some," "little," or "none"	50–60
Registered and voted in recent presidential elections, 1960–1976	60–70
Registered and voted in recent congressional elections, 1960–1974	45–60
Report ever having voted in a school bond election	55–60
Register and vote consistently in all elections—federal, state, and local	60–65
Limit participation to voting	20–25
Vote occasionally or not at all	20–25
Active Participation	
Leading political opinions:	
Attempt to influence political views of others through informal discussions	25–35
Participated in school board discussion/debate	25–30
Attempt to influence political views of others by taking part in political campaigns	3–5
Campaigned or worked actively for a candidate for President	10–15
Campaigned or worked actively for a candidate for Congress	10–15
Actively defended the action of a public official in private discussion	50–55
Picketed or took part in a street demonstration	10–15
Taking part in political parties:	
Attend political meetings, rallies, dinners, etc.	15–20
Contribute financially to campaigns, parties, and/or candidates	30–33
Worked for a political party in a election	20–25
Members of a political party or organization	5–10
Regularly active as party members	2–3
Joining organized communal activity:	
Belong to an organization of any kind	60–65
Belong to more than one organization	30–40
Belong to an organization in which political discussion occurs	30–40
Belong to an organization active in community affairs	40–45
Helped form a local group to work on a community problem	10–15
Contacted public officials on a social problem	10–15
Signed a petition at least once	65–70
Active on personal behalf:	
Contacted an official about a personal problem	5–10
Visited or talked in person with own congressperson	20–25
Visited a state legislator in the state capitol	

Sources: Harris, L., *Confidence and Concern: Citizens View American Government,* Cleveland, Ohio: Regal Books/King's Court Communications, 1974; Verba, S., and Nie, N. H., *Participation in America,* New York: Harper & Row, 1972; Nie, N. H., and Verba, S., "Political Participation," in F. I. Greenstein and N. W. Polsby (Eds.), *Handbook of Political Science,* Vol. 4, Reading, Mass.: Addison-Wesley, 1975, pp. 1–74.

TABLE 4.3
Breakdown of citizen participation by type of political activity

Mode of participation	Percentage of citizens engaging in activity
Voting specialists (vote only)	21
Campaigners (vote and campaign)	15
Communalists (vote and take part in community-related projects)	20
Parochials (may vote, contact government for personal reasons)	4
Complete activists (vote, campaign, engage in community-related activity)	11
Inactives (no political participation)	22
Unclassified	7
Total	100

Source: Compiled from data reported in Verba, S., and Nie, N. H., *Participation in America*, New York: Harper & Row, 1972, pp. 73–81.

conceivable issue" (Hyman and Sheatsley, 1954, pp. 36–37). A casual reading of the numerous opinion polls published annually in American newspapers and news magazines suggests that people readily express opinions on a wide variety of matters. Typically the proportion expressing "no opinion" to a pollster is less than two in ten.

But the low percentage of persons responding "no opinion" is misleading. If given the option, many might more appropriately say "don't care" or "don't know" (Bogart, 1972). Granted that three-fourths of citizens surveyed apparently care enough about public affairs to watch news broadcasts on television every day or read a daily newspaper, far fewer take the trouble to explore issues in greater depth. In fact, eight in ten Americans report that they never read news magazines devoted mainly to politics and public affairs (Verba and Nie, 1972, pp. 368–369).

Just as a widespread willingness to express political opinions may mask general indifference to politics, so also does such willingness conceal a striking ignorance of public affairs. The proportion of "chronic know nothings" declined from about 35 percent in the 1930s to 15–20 percent in the late 1960s, yet "data from the various polling organizations clearly show that the majority of Americans have paid relatively little or no attention to most international and national issues, and only relatively small minorities have possessed even rudimentary information about those issues. . . . Accurately informed persons are few—about 5 percent of the population" (Hero, 1968, p. 24).

That voiced opinions are not necessarily informed opinions is easily illustrated. On August 10, 1977, the United States and Panama announced agreements that would give the Republic of Panama control of the Panama Canal

Zone and waterway in the year 2000 but allow the U.S. to retain the right to defend the canal against third-nation attacks. Announcement of the treaties received wide news and editorial coverage; the ensuing debate over the treaties was also widely publicized; and the formal signing of the treaties on September 7 (which attracted heads of state to Washington, D.C. from most nations in this hemisphere) was carefully orchestrated as a media event. To learn what Americans thought of the treaties, pollsters George Gallup and Louis Harris conducted separate nationwide surveys in mid-September and released their results on October 3 and October 10 respectively. Americans were quick to respond when asked about the treaties: Fewer than one-fourth said they had "no opinion" or were "not sure" about the treaties. Both polls reported majorities opposed to the treaties. The Gallup Poll, however, revealed that although Americans did not hesitate to express their views, many of them were not informed at all and only a very few were much informed. Thus, 26 percent of Gallup's sample said they had *not* even heard or read about the debate over the treaties. That there was widespread ignorance about the treaties became more apparent when Gallup asked three questions to measure the extent of popular knowledge: What year would the canal be turned over to Panama? (2000.) Did the U.S. have the right to defend the canal against third-nation attacks? (Yes.) Can current large U.S. aircraft carriers and supertankers get through the canal or are they too big? (They are not able to use the canal.) In response to the first question, 74 percent gave incorrect or "don't know" answers; to the second, 57 percent were unable to come up with the right answer; and to the third, 86 percent. Only 1 person in 14 was able to answer all three questions correctly! This in spite of wide media dissemination of information on all three matters. The "better informed" minority (the 1 in 14) favored the treaties by a 5–4 margin; those who had at least heard of the controversy opposed the treaties by a 48 to 40 percent plurality; and the unaware opposed the treaties by 39 to 23 percent. Thus the opinions of the better informed, the somewhat informed, and the uninformed differed markedly.

The conflict over the Panama Canal treaties was unusual, for relatively few issues receive such extensive media coverage over such a short period. Yet there was a relative lack of public knowledge about the controversy. On less publicized issues, expressed political opinions are probably even less informed. Policymakers are always hard pressed to draw the line between opinions that reflect active involvement and those that are simply passive, uninformed responses to political events. Nor is widespread political ignorance limited to transient political matters. It is also apparent in the public's inaccurate and insufficient information about political institutions and officeholders. Twenty percent of Americans surveyed express the view that Congress consists of the House of Representatives, the Senate, *and* the U.S. Supreme Court; another 6 percent say it is only the House, another 4 percent only the Senate, and another 8 percent have no idea about the makeup of Congress. Moreover, 40 percent of Americans surveyed do not know the name of at least one U.S. Senator from their state; 60 percent do not know the names of both senators; and only about 50 percent can correctly name the congressman from their district. But Americans do not delude themselves about their political knowledge. Asked to rate themselves on "being up-to-date about what is going on in the federal government in Washington," no more than 40 percent said they felt current with developments in the nation's capitol (Harris, 1974).

How meaningful is the representation of conflict through the expression of opinions in the face of such widespread ignorance? From the standpoint of a policymaker, it depends upon who expresses the opinions. All opinions can matter, but as we shall see in Chapter 5, the opinions of active participants rather than passive ones count most in conflict representation.

INFLUENCING POLITICAL OPINIONS

A person need not actively engage in politics to express an opinion. To express an informed opinion, however, the involvement must be greater. And to influence the opinions of others, one must have a genuine enthusiasm for public affairs. Political leaders influence opinions: They represent conflict not only by getting people to take part in politics but also by getting them to take sides.

People do many things to influence the political opinions of others. One is to engage in political talk—to debate, discuss, appeal, cajole, and persuade; to listen, deliberate, think, and respond. We saw in Table 4.2 that 25–33 percent of Americans regularly engage in such political talk. The proportion is about the same regardless of whether the nation is in the throes of a major election campaign or people are simply going through their daily routines between elections. Surveys of the election-year activities of citizens during presidential campaigns since 1952 reveal that about three in every ten report they "talk to any people and try to show them why they should vote for one of the parties or candidates" (Dreyer and Rosenbaum, 1974). Surveys in years without presidential elections reveal that about one-third of respondents "usually discuss politics and national affairs with others" at least once a week (Verba and Nie, 1972, p. 368).

There are other ways besides political discussion to influence opinions. Letters, telegrams, telephone calls, and personal contacts with officials are a few options. But again, only a minority rather than a majority of Americans engage in these political activities. Perhaps no more than one-fourth of our citizens exercise their First Amendment prerogative to "petition the government," and fewer still write letters to either public officials or to their local newspapers.

In sum, most Americans simply do not have the inclination, the time, or the knowledge to act as political leaders. In a survey conducted for the U.S. Senate

Subcommittee on Intergovernmental Relations, pollster Louis Harris asked a nationwide sample of Americans whether or not they had ever participated in 14 different activities that could influence the opinions of others. The activities included writing letters to officials, signing petitions, visiting officials, campaigning, picketing, and demonstrating. More than half of the public sampled had participated in only two such activities, namely, engaging in political discussion and signing a petition "at least once in their lives" (Harris, 1974, p. 20). Thus, most Americans are passive when it comes to influencing and leading public opinion. Some are simply apathetic; this is true of at least the 25 percent who say they have "no interest" when asked about their concern with politics and national affairs (Verba and Nie, 1972). Others, perhaps another 60 percent, are only casually interested spectators: "They watch, they cheer, they vote, but they do not battle" (Milbrath, 1965, p. 21; Milbrath and Goel, 1977).

By the most generous estimate, active leaders are the minority in American politics. Later we shall examine who they are, what they do, and how people respond to them in conflict representation.

VOTING

Liberal democratic theory, as we saw in Chapter 2, accords a high priority to voting as a way for people to influence policymakers. By voting, citizens choose between candidates competing for the authority to make public policy; by voting on constitutional amendments at the state level, referenda on taxes, bond proposals, and the like, citizens participate directly in policymaking. Because Americans declare their preferences for and against officials and policies through elections the distribution of their votes is a representation of their conflicts on selected political matters.

Regardless of its importance in liberal democratic theory, however, voting is a relatively passive means of conflict representation in American politics. Voters reach three decisions: (1) whether to qualify to vote or not, (2) whether to vote or not, and, (3) if they decide to vote, whom or what to support or oppose. To the extent that these decisions reflect efforts to seek information and actively engage in politics, they are a form of active participation. But a high percentage of Americans are too reluctant or careless about using the vote to warrant labeling it active political involvement.

Figure 4.1 provides an overview of voting turnout in U.S. presidential and congressional elections between 1868 and 1976. Between 1870 and 1920 there was a general decline in the turnout of eligible voters. The next four decades witnessed an increase in voting rates, with a peak around 1960. Since 1960 there has again been a decline in the turnout of eligible voters. Turnout in congressional elections is consistently lower in years that do not coincide with

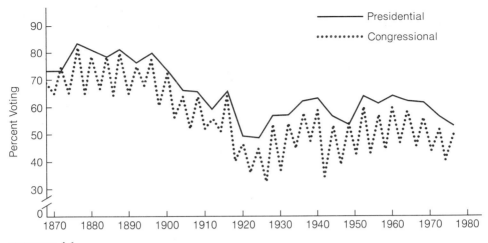

FIGURE 4.1

Participation of the Eligible Electorate in Presidential and Congressional Elections, 1868–1976. [*Sources:* Interuniversity Consortium for Political Research, The University of Michigan, Ann Arbor, 1976; U.S. Bureau of the Census, *Statistical Abstract of the United States: 1973* (94th ed.), Washington, D.C.: U.S. Government Printing Office, 1973, p. 379.]

presidential elections, and even lower in "special" congressional elections to fill a vacancy created by death or resignation.

There are two general reasons for not voting: failure to meet legal qualifications for voting (principally residence requirements and registration) and disinterest. We get some sense of the relative weight of these two factors by examining statistics from presidential and congressional elections in the 1970s. In 1972, 63 percent of the noninstitutionalized population 18 years and older in the U.S. registered and voted in the presidential election for an overall turnout (of all adults of voting age) of about 55 percent. Nine percent registered but did not vote. Of these registered nonvoters about equal proportions regarded voting as inconvenient (i.e., they could not get to the polls, were out of town, would not face long lines at the polls, etc.); or claimed they were "not interested," disliked politics and the candidates; or gave other reasons. Of the 27 percent of unregistered nonvoters, more than half expressed no interest in or a dislike for politics. All in all, about 16–20 percent of those not voting in 1972, both registered and nonregistered, failed to do so out of a lack of political involvement (U.S. Bureau of the Census, 1973). Two years later in the 1974 congressional elections, only 40 percent of eligible voters exercised their franchise. Of nonvoters, 42 percent had not registered or had not met residency requirements, 24 percent were "not interested," and 13 percent did not like any of the candidates (*Gallup Opinion Index*, No. 118, 1975). The pattern of low turnout rates in the 1970s continued in 1976 when only a slight majority (53 percent) of adults voted in the presidential election.

For a sizable proportion of Americans, then, a simple lack of interest in politics contributes significantly to nonvoting, dampening the enthusiasm either for qualifying or for going to the polls if qualified. This indifference may be a symptom of a more deep-seated malady in the political system, namely, a growing disillusion with politics and politicians. Prior to the 1976 presidential election a survey of "nonvoters"—defined as people neither registered nor likely to register to vote and having no better than a 50–50 chance of voting in 1976—found that the majority of these people were turned off by contemporary politics. Asked to express their own reasons for not voting, a majority declared "Candidates say one thing and do another," "It doesn't make any difference who is elected because things never seem to work right," and "All candidates seem pretty much the same" (*Congressional Quarterly's Guide to Congress*, 1976).

We will explore the legal and personal reasons for passive participation at greater length later in this chapter. For now, it is fair to say that only an active minority of Americans vote regularly in all federal, state, and local elections. About 30 to 40 percent vote so rarely that they can be labeled at best as passive members of the electorate; perhaps another 10 to 15 percent are so uninterested in politics as to be classified as chronic nonvoters.

WORKING THROUGH POLITICAL PARTIES

American political parties compete for the authority to govern. Citizens take part in that conflict by affiliating themselves with political parties, joining in the selection of a party's candidates, and working to get their party into office. As with expressing opinions, trying to influence others, or voting, party efforts may be passive or active. People whose efforts are passive simply have emotional loyalty or attachment to a party, a party identification. Figure 4.2 portrays the distribution of party loyalties between Democrats, Republicans, and independents as measured by answers to standardized survey questions since 1937. In the 1970s attachment to a party has been a means of passive political participation for about two-thirds of Americans. In this decade, however, the proportion of Americans declaring themselves independent of party affiliation has risen by six percentage points. As we shall see in Chapter 7, both party identification and the growing disinclination to be a party stalwart have influenced voting in the 1970s.

A slightly more active way to participate in party affairs is to join in when parties select their nominees for public office. This generally means voting in party primaries, although it may also include taking part in nominating caucuses or conventions. By and large, turnouts in party primaries have been

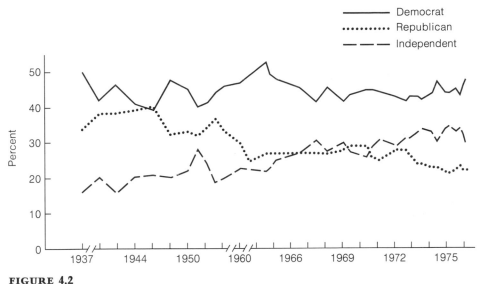

FIGURE 4.2

The Distribution of Democrats, Republicans, and Independents (1937–1976).
[*Sources: Gallup Opinion Index,* Report No. 137, 1976, p. 50.]

considerably smaller than advocates of opening the nominating process to mass participation had hoped. Although the number of presidential nominating primaries has increased, from 17 in 1968 to 23 in 1972 to 30 in 1976, this increase has not been matched by a comparable increase in the proportions of people taking part in them. The national turnout rate of 43.8 percent of registered voters in 1976 was scarcely a dramatic increase over that of 42.6 percent in 1972. Table 4.4 compares the turnout rates in selected presidential primaries for those two elections. Only four of the states listed experienced two turnouts of more than 50 percent, and turnout rates in a majority of the states declined from 1972 to 1976.

Participation in the nomination process through mass delegate selection caucuses is also low. In 1976, for example, Democrats held caucuses in 22 states and four territories to choose delegates to their presidential nominating convention. The *best* turnout rate in a caucus state (19 percent in Connecticut) was only slightly better than the worst turnout rate in a primary state (10 percent in New Jersey).

Party activities requiring even greater commitment include working in political campaigns on behalf of candidates. But as with other modes of political participation, the more demanding the effort, the smaller the proportion of Americans taking part (see Table 4.5).

The most active form of party participation is taking a stand in the partisan

TABLE 4.4

Turnout in presidential primaries, 1972 and 1976

Primary	Percentage of registered citizens voting	
	1972	1976
New Hampshire	53.3	46.1
Massachusetts	28.7	32.2
Florida	57.8	56.5
Illinois	22.6	36.2
North Carolina	52.3	35.3
Pennsylvania	30.2	43.4
District of Columbia	14.6	11.6
Indiana	43.1	42.8
Nebraska	56.5	52.1
West Virginia	50.3	47.8
Maryland	44.0	44.8
Michigan	43.7	38.7
Oregon	62.3	58.9
Tennessee	34.0	30.2
Rhode Island	9.2	14.5
South Dakota	25.5	38.9
California	68.5	70.1
New Jersey	9.4	10.1
Ohio	46.7	44.5

Source: Congressional Quarterly Weekly Report, July 10, 1976, p. 1808.

TABLE 4.5

*Relative participation in various party activities
(in percentages of survey respondents)*

Activities	1952	1956	1960	1964	1968	1972
Do you belong to any political club or organization?	2	3	3	4	3	—*
Did you give any money to buy tickets or do anything to help the campaign for one of the parties or candidates?	4	10	12	11	9	10
Did you go to any political meetings, rallies, dinners, or things like that?	7	10	8	9	9	9
Did you do other work for one of the parties or candidates?	3	3	6	5	6	5

*Question not asked in 1972 survey.
Source: Survey Research Center and Interuniversity Consortium for Political Research. The University of Michigan, Ann Arbor, 1972.

battle by working within a party organization. Active partisans include precinct leaders, party chairpersons, secretaries, fundraisers, professional organizers, campaign managers, convention delegates, and others who occupy a niche in the party hierarchy. Again, relatively few Americans are active in party politics, perhaps less than one percent of the adult population (Bone, 1952).

Although few citizens engage in party activities, those who do generally take a more active part in politics in other respects as well. For instance, more partisans than nonpartisans are regular voters. Since persons in lower social and economic circumstances are more likely than upper-status citizens to have party loyalties (Verba and Nie, 1972, p. 223), the result is to decrease the disparity between upper and lower socioeconomic classes in voting (see pp. 110–113). But when it comes to more active participation, such as campaigning, it is the upper-status partisans who are the most likely to take part. The political advantage that lower-status citizens derive from the fact that a greater proportion of their number are party loyalists is virtually cancelled out by the greater campaign participation of the relatively fewer upper-status partisans. The competition between political parties and the relative political advantages gained by members of various social classes from their partisan participation in nominations, campaigns, policies, and programs combine to make parties significant arenas of conflict representation.

JOINING VOLUNTARY ORGANIZATIONS

One way to get policymakers to heed demands and grievances is to organize and bring pressure on officials. Policymakers are sensitive to the conflicting pressures of organized interests. Strangely, however, citizens do not generally think of joining voluntary organizations as the principal means of influencing government. Recall the evidence in Table 4.1: More Americans were likely to try to "change things they didn't like about government" by individual means (voting, direct contact with an official, etc.) than by joining a citizens group. Moreover, about two-thirds of Americans belong to organizations, but only a third are members of groups in which political discussion takes place, and only about one in ten Americans has ever helped to form a local group (Table 4.2).

Generally, then, Americans are "joiners," but only a minority join distinctly political groups and an even smaller number avidly take part in organization activities. The more organizations the active person belongs to, the greater the rate of political participation of all varieties (voting, campaigning, communal activity, etc.) of that citizen: "The individual who is a *passive* member in one or more organizations is *no more likely* to be active in politics than the individual who belongs to no such association. In contrast, the active organizational member is much more likely than the nonmember to be politically active, and this rate of political activity increases as one moves from single membership to multiple membership" (Verba and Nie, 1972, p. 186, italics in original). Thus the general rule observed in opinion expression, political leadership, voting, and party work holds as well for participation in voluntary organizations: Active not passive participation exposes the citizen to the types of experiences and opportunities that foster greater involvement in conflict representation.

PROTESTING ABOUT GRIEVANCES

Americans have traditionally used the methods of political participation described above to articulate their interests and represent their differences to policymakers. When these channels have been opened to all, they have provided useful means of representing conflict despite the fact that most Americans only use them now and then. However, the conventional methods of participation have not always worked for new interests whose demands conflict with established ways of doing things: The impoverished often have not had the education to formulate informed, persuasive opinions; migrant farm laborers have been disappointed by the failure of the more established organized labor unions to improve their lot; Blacks and Chicanos have only gradually been able to take up party activity in some regions of the nation; many younger Americans have become disenchanted with the conservative and unimaginative workings of party organizations; the elderly have been disillusioned by a government too often unresponsive to their needs for medical care, housing, and an adequate retirement income; women have been frustrated in their efforts to obtain equal rights within male-dominated institutions; and citizens concerned with preserving the environment or finding safe and bountiful sources of energy have chafed at what many regard as the federal bureaucracy's mindless commitment to the development of nuclear power plants.

Upon finding their path to influencing government blocked, newly emergent interests have sometimes sought new and dramatic ways to voice their grievances. Since World War II these have included sit-ins, lie-ins, the seizure of government and university buildings, marches on city hall and the state and national capitol, the wide use of citizen's band radios to warn truckers of state troopers enforcing the 55-mile-per-hour speed limit on interstate highways, and various forms of violence—bombings of public buildings, aircraft hijackings, kidnappings, and even murder.

In the 1960s problems such as civil rights, disaffection with the war in Vietnam, poverty, and air and water pollution were placed on the agenda for national discussion and official action partly through mass protests that were widely publicized in the news media. In some cases, protest tactics have advanced the cause of those resorting to them. The civil rights movement in the early 1960s captured nationwide attention, promoted an end to discriminatory segregation, and prompted passage of a series of civil rights and voting acts (see Figure 4.3). Political observers are less certain about the success of the

1957—Civil Rights Act

1. Affirmed citizen's right to seek court injunctions to protect voting rights.
2. Authorized federal government to seek court injunctions to remove violations of voting rights.
3. Created federal Civil Rights Commission to investigate violations of voting rights.
4. Created Civil Rights Division in Department of Justice.

1960—Civil Rights Act

1. Authorized Attorney General to request court findings of patterns or practice of denial of Negro voting rights when violations warranted this.
2. Authorized courts to issue orders that Negroes were qualified to vote if voter discrimination was proved.
3. Authorized courts to appoint referees to aid Negroes in registration and voting.

1961—Twenty-Third Amendment

Extended the right to vote in presidential elections to citizens of the District of Columbia.

1964—Twenty-Fourth Amendment

Outlawed poll tax as voting requirement in federal elections.

1964—Civil Rights Act

1. Prohibited literacy tests in federal elections; prohibited unequal application of registration requirements; prohibited denial of right to vote because of voting-record errors or omissions where records were immaterial to qualification.
2. Required presumption of literacy where persons were educated through six grades in schools with instruction primarily in English.
3. Established special three-judge federal courts to hear suits on voting rights.

1965—Voting Rights Act

1. Suspended literacy test in states where fewer than 50 percent of voting-age residents were registered or voted in 1964.
2. Appointed federal voting examiners to administer registration in states and counties using literacy tests in 1964 where voter participation was below the standards established by the act (registration or turnout of less than 50 percent of the population).
3. Authorized Attorney General to seek federal court findings of voter discrimination.
4. Authorized Attorney General to proceed against discriminatory state poll taxes.

FIGURE 4.3

The Post–World War II Evolution of Voting Rights.

1968—Civil Rights Act

Prohibited the injury or intimidation of any person because he was voting or campaigning for office in a public election, serving on a federal jury, working for a federal agency, or urging others to engage in these activities (this last provision was aimed at protecting civil rights workers).

1970—Voting Rights Act

Extended the right to vote in national elections to 18-year-olds meeting normal home state requirements of citizenship, residency, and registration. (Act declared constitutional by the Supreme Court.)

1971—Twenty-Sixth Amendment

Provided that the right to vote of citizens 18 years old or older shall not be abridged by the United States or by any state on account of age.

1975—Voting Rights Act

1. Continued federal protection of voting rights in states and political subdivisions covered by 1965 Act; required these political units to submit election law changes to Attorney General for preclearance and authorized federal registrars and voting examiners to oversee election process.
2. Extended voting rights protections to Spanish-speaking Americans, American Indians, Asian Americans, and Alaskan natives (all defined as language minorities).
3. Seeks to increase voting participation among language minorities by requiring bilingual elections in areas with significant numbers of such minorities.
4. Made permanent the temporary nationwide ban on literacy tests of earlier voting rights legislation.

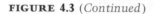

FIGURE 4.3 (*Continued*)

antiwar movement of the late 1960s. Although mass demonstrations, refusals to be drafted, and other tactics publicized a major division of opinion over the Vietnam war, American involvement continued for more than eight years, long after the peak of mass protest.

Protest movements wax or wane as conditions dictate: The strikes and violence of an earlier era and the protests that flared in the 1960s have been replaced by the relative calm of the 1970s. Whether successful or not, protest tactics and direct action will continue to be what they have always been, a vital means of representing conflict in a highly diverse, pluralist society whose various elements compete for limited benefits and resources. A traditional mode of political participation that extends back at least to the Boston Tea Party of 1773 is not likely to vanish from the political scene in the near future (Manheim, 1976).

Why so little popular participation?

Many Americans participate in politics, at least passively. The total vote in a presidential election exceeds the populations of many nations of the world; is that not mass participation? It is, and it is important. But equally important is this question: Why do so many Americans not take part in conflict representation, even in a passive way? We think there are three reasons:

- Many lack the opportunity to take part.
- Large numbers do not have the resources to participate.
- Many Americans have no desire for politics.

WHO CAN PARTICIPATE?

We have said that one of the major characteristics of any national community is its political and constitutional aspect. By political we mean the activities of people seeking settlement of disputes; by constitutional we mean the rules that govern the process of conflict regulation. Constitutional rules govern who can take part in representing conflicts and how.

Civil liberties: protections of the opportunity to participate

The opportunities to express and lead opinion (freedom of expression), become informed, organize, vote, and press demands upon government—in sum, to participate in the various ways we have already described—are protected and extended through the Constitution. A key provision pertaining to freedom of expression is the First Amendment, the ever controversial statement that "Congress shall make no law . . . abridging freedom of speech, or of the press." Neither freedom of speech nor freedom of the press is total. The amendment merely enjoins Congress from abridging either through restrictive legislation. The rest is left to the Supreme Court. The Court must answer such questions as "Should government be permitted to prohibit spoken or written words that call for the overthrow of government, even though the words themselves constitute no immediate steps to implement that goal?"

THE CLEAR-AND-PRESENT-DANGER TEST. Justice Oliver Wendell Holmes, speaking for a unanimous court in *Schenck* v. *United States* (1919), laid down the "clear-and-present-danger" test as a judicial formula for dealing with First Amendment cases involving freedom of speech and press. He wrote: "The question in every case is whether the words are used in such circumstances and are of such a nature as to create a clear and present danger that they will bring about the substantive evils that Congress has a right to prevent. It is a question of proximity and degree." In *Abrams* v. *United States* (also decided in 1919), Holmes gave a more precise definition of "present danger" in a dissenting opinion: A "present danger" is one that "imminently threatens interference with the lawful and pressing purposes of the law." Thus, danger would have to be imminent before the government could prevent people from pressing their interests through freely expressed opinions. The formula also recognizes limits to the freedom to express and lead opinions. Although the First Amendment refers specifically to Congress, the Court held in *Gitlow* v. *New York* (1925) that the "liberty" against encroachment of the states, protected by the Fourteenth Amendment, includes the freedoms of the First Amendment.

Under the clear-and-present-danger formula, any American could freely express and lead opinions as long as his or her acts did not form an imminent threat to society; however, until the mid-1930s advocates of the formula did not again command a majority on the Supreme Court. When the Court in 1931 struck down a Minnesota statute (*Near* v. *Minnesota*) that had been used to bar further publication of a newspaper that printed "malicious, scandalous, and defamatory" attacks, it did not rely on the clear-and-present-danger test. Instead the Court ruled that freedom of the press prohibits prior censorship of publications.

In 1938, Justice Harlan F. Stone breathed new life into the clear-and-present-danger test. Speaking in a footnote to *United States* v. *Carolene Products Co.*, he argued that First Amendment freedoms should be accorded a special place, a "preferred position," in the Constitution. (The Court affirmed the existence of the doctrine in *Thomas* v. *Collins* in 1945.) The preferred-position doctrine holds that because freedoms of speech, press, assembly, and religion are crucial to democratic government, government restrictions cannot be presumed constitutional: The Court must decide if a clear and present danger exists. This view found its way back into majority opinions of the Court during the early 1940s, but with the end of World War II new problems arose. Justice Felix Frankfurter repeatedly attacked both the clear-and-present-danger test and the preferred-position doctrine and called for the court to assume a more restrained position in dealing with First Amendment cases. In deciding cases about free expression, the justices now had to confront two difficult legal issues: the "hostile audience" question and the "cold war" problem of dealing with groups that, according to Congress and the state legislatures, threatened national security.

The hostile audience issue was dramatically raised in *Feiner* v. *New York* (1951). During a street-corner speech, Feiner used derogatory language about the President of the United States, other public officials, and the American Legion. He was arrested when members of the crowd became unruly and threatened him. Feiner's conviction for disorderly conduct was sustained on the grounds that "a clear danger of disorder" existed. He could deliver the speech only if there was no danger of inciting a riot. It was the first time the Supreme Court had used the clear-and-present-danger test to *uphold* an action by government, and the Court was severely criticized. Some felt strongly that those who threatened the speaker should have been punished not the speaker, because he had not advocated violence.

In cold war cases arising out of government efforts to regulate subversive activity, the Court moved toward a new position on the First Amendment. In *Dennis* v. *United States* (1951) the Court upheld the conviction of eleven leaders of the Communist Party who were charged with teaching and advocating the overthrow of the government. The defendants also were charged with conspiring to organize the United States Communist Party for the purpose of overthrowing the government by force and violence. None of the government's charges included overt activity with the immediate intention of revolution, but at the time, the United States was actively engaged in the Korean War; Americans were being killed by Soviet-manufactured bullets in the hands of Chinese soldiers, and the popular mood was ugly. In rejecting the contention that immediate and clear danger must be established to justify any abridgement of the rights of free expression, Chief Justice Fred M. Vinson laid down a new test: "Whether the gravity of the 'evil,' discounted by its improbability, justifies such invasion of free speech as necessary to avoid the danger."

The language did not sit well with the activist element on the Court. The grave-and-probable-danger test was qualified in *Yates* v. *United States* (1957) when the Warren Court distinguished between the instruction of abstract doctrine and actual incitement to dangerous action. Nevertheless the clear-and-present-danger test has not been restored to its former eminence, although in recent years the court has again moved toward it slightly. In the 1971 "Pentagon Papers" case, decided in favor of the *New York Times*, Justices Byron White and Potter Stewart in a concurring opinion for a six-to-three majority (there was no signed opinion for the whole Court) used language reminiscent of the test. They wrote that they "do not say that in no circumstances would the First Amendment permit an injunction against publishing information about government plans or operations. . . . But . . . the United States has not satisfied the very heavy burden which it must meet to warrant an injunction against publication in these cases."

RESTRAINING FREE SPEECH AND PRESS: LIBEL, OBSCENITY, AND NEWS. How free is a person to express and lead opinions if his actions constitute libel against others or are obscene? These issues have taken up a good deal of the Supreme Court's time since 1960. The most significant libel ruling came in 1964. *Sullivan* v. *The New York Times* involved libel suits filed against the *Times* because of a paid advertisement criticizing the treatment of Blacks in Alabama. The police commissioner of Montgomery, Alabama pointed out that the advertisement contained factual errors and argued that the criticisms of the police were defamatory. He and another commissioner filed separate libel suits against the *Times* and were awarded one million dollars by an Alabama court. But the Supreme Court ruled that "erroneous statements honestly made" were not punishable as libel. Proof of "actual malice" was required to recover damages; that is, proof that the facts as printed were known to be false or that there was "reckless disregard" of whether the material was false or not. The Sullivan rule has been extended to cover "public figures" as well as newspapers so that "actual malice" would have to be proved against a politician before he could be found guilty of libeling an opponent.

Restrictions on free expression will also result if spoken, printed, or other material can be banned as obscene. The Supreme Court has had considerable difficulty in defining what is protected by the First Amendment and what is not. In *Roth* v. *United States* (1957), the Court declared obscenity as "utterly without redeeming social importance" and not in the area of expression protected by the First Amendment. In the Roth decision, the Court defined obscene material as follows: "To the average person, applying contemporary community standards, the dominant theme of the material taken as a whole appeals to prurient interest." In *Manual Enterprises* v. *Day* (1962), the Court added that the material must be "patently offensive" and "self-demonstrating" in its indecency. Then in *Jacobellis* v. *Ohio* (1964), the Court exempted from its definition material "dealing with sex in a manner that advocates ideas . . ." in a literary, artistic, scientific, or other form with social importance.

The most important recent decision in this area is *Miller* v. *California* (1973). Miller was one of seven decisions handed down the same day modifying the Roth approach. The Miller ruling designates the extent of state authority in regulating obscenity; it also illustrates by its five-to-four decision how divided the Court was on the matter. Miller conducted an unsolicited mass mailing campaign advertising "adult" books (for example, *Sex Orgies Illustrated*) and a film. The campaign violated California's obscenity statutes. Finding that it would not be possible to set "uniform, fixed, national standards" of what appeals to the "prurient interest" or is "patently offensive," the Court left to the states the definition of obscenity. Miller modifies Roth in two respects: (1) The Court dropped its former standard that an "obscene" work must be "utterly without redeeming social value" and substituted "which taken as a whole, do[es] not have serious literary, artistic, political, or scientific value"; (2) the Roth guidelines of prevailing community standards are now interpreted to mean *local*, rather than national, community standards. In *Hamburg* v. *United States* (1974) the Court held that the movie "Carnal Knowledge" was not obscene, thus saying to localities that the Miller ruling was not intended to give "unbridled discretion" to juries.

The whole question of what is obscene and how to determine prevailing local standards remains a subject of considerable controversy. It is, as Justice

John Marshall Harlan remarked, the "intractable obscenity problem" (*Interstate Circuit Incorporated* v. *Dallas*, 1968).

Restrictions on the newsgathering activities of journalists can also severely limit freedom of expression by making it difficult for the news media to inform citizens about controversial matters. In the 1970s the Court has wrestled with two aspects of this question. In 1972 the Court ruled five to four that reporters had to respond to valid subpoenas and divulge information about the sources of their news reports in criminal cases (*Branzburg* v. *Hayes*). Then, in 1976 the Court ruled that a "gag order" issued against the press preventing full coverage of the trial of a mass murderer was illegal and that "high barriers" prevented such intrusions on the freedom of the press (*Nebraska Press Association* v. *Stuart*).

FREEDOM OF RELIGIOUS EXPRESSION. The First Amendment also prohibits Congress from restricting the free exercise of religious expression. The Supreme Court's position is that there can be no prior censorship on religious expression just as there can be none on free speech or press. Even during World War II, the Court used the clear-and-present-danger formula to strike down compulsory flag salutes, which Jehovah's Witnesses felt violated their freedom of expression (*West Virginia Board of Education* v. *Barnette*, 1943). The freedoms of the First Amendment, said Justice Robert Jackson, "are susceptible of restriction only to prevent grave and immediate danger," a situation that he felt refusal to salute the flag did not create. The Court has also taken a stand against the establishment of mandatory religious practices that might violate freedom of religious expression. In *Engel* v. *Vitale* (1962), it ruled against the "religious activity" in public schools of reading prayers, even though students who did not wish to participate could remain mute or leave the room. Later, in *Abington Township School District* v. *Schempp* (1963) and *Murray* v. *Curtlett* (1963), the Court declared that Bible reading in public schools—even though voluntary—violated the "no establishment" clause of the First Amendment. Since *McCollum* v. *Board of Education* (1948), the Court has held it unconstitutional for public schools to provide students with "released time" whereby they would be instructed in religious doctrines during school hours in school buildings. And in 1972 the Court resolved a long-standing controversy surrounding religion and public schools by holding that compulsory attendance at school cannot be required of Amish children beyond the eighth grade (*Wisconsin* v. *Yoder*).

In the area of "free exercise" rather than "establishment" the problem has been to define what constitutes a religious belief. Conditions surrounding the Vietnam war provoked the case of *United States* v. *Seeger* (1965), in which the Court held that the statutory exemption from military service for a conscientious objector covered more than just people expressing belief in a "Supreme

Being." Seeger, who objected to war on the basis of a "purely ethical creed," was given legal status as a conscientious objector.

THE OPPORTUNITY TO JOIN VOLUNTARY ORGANIZATIONS.   Expressing and leading opinions and joining political organizations are overlapping opportunities. In the Dennis and Yates cases, the Supreme Court dealt in part with problems raised by the freedom of association. By virtue of the Yates principle, people cannot be punished for mere membership in an organization such as the Communist Party. In *Aptheker* v. *United States* (1964) and *United Staets* v. *Robel* (1967), the Court extended this view, holding that Communists could not be forbidden to apply for passports or to work in defense plants.

The right of voluntary association, however, touches upon more than the Communist Party. Civil rights organizations, such as the National Association for the Advancement of Colored People (NAACP) are also protected. In 1958, Alabama demanded that the NAACP register as an out-of-state corporation and supply the names and addresses of its members in the state. The organization refused to disclose its membership. The Supreme Court agreed with the NAACP, arguing that to compel an organization to reveal its membership lists could interfere unconstitutionally with the right of individuals to join in legitimate association with those of common beliefs (*NAACP* v. *Alabama*). Similarly in *Gibson* v. *Florida Legislative Investigation Committee* (1963), the Court upheld the refusal of an NAACP official to reveal the organization's membership list to a committee investigating possible Communist activity in the NAACP.

It is not clear today how far government agencies can go in conducting surveillance of citizens' organizations before violating freedom of thought and association. In *Socialist Workers Party* v. *Attorney General* (1974), Justice Marshall refused to uphold a lower federal court ruling that the Federal Bureau of Investigation did not violate speech and association rights of members of the Young Socialist Alliance by conducting surveillance at their convention. Since the entire Court did not hear the case, there has been no decision on the constitutional limits of surveillance.

THE OPPORTUNITY TO PROTEST ABOUT GRIEVANCES.   Public protest, as we have seen, is an American habit older than the Constitution itself. The "right of the people peaceably to assemble, and to petition the government for a redress of grievances" is guaranteed in the First Amendment. In the decades since the Presidency of Franklin D. Roosevelt, which have seen the labor movement achieve great power, civil rights demonstrations, and antiwar protests, the opportunity to protest has become particularly important to individuals and groups desiring to take part in politics.

How far can a protest go if it threatens public order? In cases dealing with the labor movement, the Supreme Court responded to this question by applying the clear-and-present-danger yardstick. In *Thornhill* v. *Alabama* (1940), the Court ruled a state law forbidding peaceful picketing unconstitutional on the ground that the law violated freedom of speech: Peaceful picketing, said the Court, posed no "clear danger of substantive evils." Because big labor unions now hold a stronger hand than they held in the 1930s, massive strike violence has vanished from the American industrial scene. Nonetheless "peaceful picketing" may cease being peaceful if a "scab" attempts to cross a picket line.

In any event, picketing, marching, sitting-in, lying down in front of automobiles, and other protests involve more than speaking freely. They combine speech with action, and therefore, according to the Court, some restrictions are legitimate. For example, a government can require advance notification of demonstrations and can also require permits for them. But, if permit ordinances are too restrictive, they may be declared unconstitutional. In 1965 when Martin Luther King, Jr. led his famous march from Selma to Montgomery, Alabama to dramatize the demand for Black voting rights, Alabama officials denied him a march permit, but a federal judge overruled the denial.

Doubts remain about what types of restraints may be placed on the right to protest. At the 1968 Democratic national convention in Chicago, for instance, protestors were denied a parade permit, but they tried to parade anyway. Their ensuing confrontation with police illustrates how difficult it is to know how far a protest can go if it threatens public order. A legal tangle followed the violence in Chicago. Seven participants in the demonstrations were acquitted of charges that they violated the federal Anti-Riot Act, which makes it a crime to cross a state line to incite or participate in a riot. The trial of the "Chicago Seven" shed doubt on the constitutionality of such a law, but the question is still unresolved. Following the trial, members of the Chicago Seven were frequently denied a permit to speak on college campuses. Federal judges, however, issued orders restraining college officials from denying such speaking rights on grounds that the mere possibility of trouble does not constitute a threat sufficient to justify the denial.

In response to demonstrations against the Vietnam war during the 1960s, the Supreme Court distinguished between protests that are purely symbolic expressions and those that are both speech and action. In *Tinker* v. *Des Moines Community School District* (1969), the Supreme Court held that wearing a black armband to protest the war was a symbolic expression protected by the First Amendment. If, however, symbolic expression is combined with actions that challenge the constitutional authority of the government, it is not protected. In *United States* v. *O'Brien* (1968), the Court upheld a federal law making it a crime to "knowingly destroy" or "mutilate" a draft card. Congress has the constitutional power to raise and support armies; hence the symbolic expression of burning a draft card goes too far.

The distinctions drawn in *Tinker* and *O'Brien* did not easily set aside the issue of "symbolic speech," which dates back to 1943 when the Court ruled that a government could not force participation in the symbolic act of saluting the flag (*West Virginia Board of Education* v. *Barnette*). In 1969 the Court overthrew the conviction of a protestor who burned a flag to publicize his disgust with the failure of federal officials to protect civil rights advocate James Meredith against an assassination attempt while Meredith was conducting a protest march in Mississippi in 1966 (*Street* v. *New York*). And in 1971 in *Cohen* v. *California*, a five-to-four Court majority reversed—as a violation of free speech—Cohen's conviction for protesting the draft and Vietnam war by wearing a jacket with "Fuck the Draft" on the back. The Court ruled that Cohen's conduct could not be proved as invading "substantial private interests . . . in an essentially intolerable manner." The private interests cited were the persons who saw the jacket and read the words in the halls of a court house.

The Supreme Court has restricted the right of peaceful protest that disrupts the normal use of property. In *Adderley* v. *Florida* (1966) the Court upheld the conviction of a group of Florida students arrested for trespassing with malicious and mischievous intent when they assembled in front of a county jail to protest the incarceration of several classmates. Justice Hugo Black, one of the firmest defenders of civil liberties in the Court's history, held that "the state, no less than a private owner of property, has the power to preserve the property under its control for the use to which it is lawfully dedicated." Generally, among the opportunities for participating in conflict representation, those for protest are most closely restricted.

Voting rights: extending opportunities to take part in choosing rulers

Voting in America is restricted to citizens, as distinct from noncitizens of either another nationality or no nationality at all. Noncitizens must register annually with the government of the United States, may be restricted in wartime, can be deported for sufficient cause, and may suffer other limitations on personal rights.

How does a person become an American citizen? Article XIV of the Constitution and related federal statutes specify birth, naturalization, or congressional action as the means. Persons born in the United States or one of its territories or of American parents residing abroad are automatically accorded citizenship. Persons born to foreign parents outside the United States can receive the rights of citizenship by following specified procedures of naturalization. Finally, Congress can award citizenship by collective grant (as it did to American Indians in 1924).

ONLY CITIZENS ARE ELIGIBLE TO VOTE, BUT NOT ALL ARE PERMITTED TO DO SO.   Article I of the Constitution provides that the states shall establish their own voting requirements. Individual states have periodically disfranchised groups—those without property, Blacks in the South, Indians in the Southwest, women, the young, and others. The extension of the franchise to each of these groups was marked by controversy and conflict representation.

Property qualifications were the first major restrictions the states placed upon voting rights. People had to own property in order to vote. Gradually the poll tax (the payment of a nominal fee that would prove one's economic standing) supplanted property ownership as a voting requirement. Ironically, the poll tax was originally substituted for property ownership as a liberalizing measure. Ultimately, it discriminated against southern Blacks and other impoverished Americans. Beginning in the 1940s, civil rights groups representing the disfranchised minorities were pitted against southern senators in a fight to ban the poll tax. Frequently, the poll tax was defended as a source of revenue necessary to some states; in fact, its purpose was to keep some groups out of the electorate. In 1964, the Twenty-Fourth Amendment to the Constitution belatedly abolished poll tax requirements in elections for federal officials; federal court decisions also declared state poll taxes (notably in Texas, Alabama, and Virginia) unconstitutional. Despite such reforms, property tax restrictions on local voting in some school board and bond elections are reminders that the franchise may still be limited to citizens who have an economic stake in the community.

The opportunity to vote has been extended to disfranchised minorities only after prolonged conflicts. Black Americans were guaranteed the right to vote by the Fifteenth Amendment to the Constitution after the Civil War. But for a whole century they have had to fight discriminatory tactics. They waged the battle against literacy tests (see Figure 4.3) by publicizing their grievances in federal court cases, civil rights demonstrations, and Congress. Before 1965, 20 states required potential voters to prove their literacy before permitting them to cast a ballot. Some states required only a signature from the voter; others requested that applicants complete long and difficult registration forms; still others required citizens to read and explain a passage from a state constitution, statute, or other document before election judges (who were prone to make far harsher demands on Blacks than Whites). Voting rights legislation since 1957 has gradually corrected the most discriminatory aspects of literacy tests.

Women achieved the right to vote in 1919, with the adoption of the Nineteenth Amendment to the Constitution, but only after 50 years of joining voluntary associations, petitioning Congress, and engaging in marches and demonstrations. American Indians received the franchise in 1924 after a long struggle in which their interests were represented by the Association of American Indian Affairs. Residents of the District of Columbia lobbied in Congress for decades before achieving the right to vote in presidential elections in 1961, and their mayor is still appointed by the President. It would be hard to deny that the extension of the franchise to citizens 18 years old and older in 1970 and 1971 was not in part a response to the militant demands of American youth in the 1960s.

CONTEMPORARY RESTRICTIONS: RESIDENCY AND REGISTRATION.   In the early 1970s as many as 8 million Americans could not vote because they had not lived long enough in their locality; another 29 million otherwise eligible Americans could not vote because they had not registered. Aside from passage of the Twenty-Sixth Amendment in 1971 extending voting opportunities to persons 18 years old and older, the major efforts to expand suffrage in the 1970s have been through the easing of residency and registration requirements. The Supreme Court ruled in 1972 that it was unconstitutional to deny a person the vote because he or she had not lived in a locality for an extended period; although residency itself is a legitimate test, length of residence is not.

Registration requirements have not been eased so readily. By registration a person demonstrates to election officials that he or she has the necessary qualifications for voting—especially citizenship, age, and residency. It takes time and extra effort, things people with few resources or little interest are often unwilling to give up. Most states have eased the burden by adopting systems of permanent registration in which a voter establishes credentials only once and renews registration through voting itself. Periodic registration— requiring voters to reestablish qualifications, perhaps annually—is an alternative system that has lost favor. At one time, citizens in some localities were required to register as much as one year in advance of the election. Such requirements placed major obstacles in the path to voting since failure to register so far in advance denied a person the vote even if the individual grew vitally interested during the campaign. The failure of many Americans to vote may reflect inactivity during registration periods rather than a lack of interest in elections.

Several steps have been taken to remove the discriminatory effects of registration. The Voting Rights Acts of 1965 and 1975 (see Figure 4.3) enable federal examiners to register citizens in counties where literacy tests were used and fewer than 50 percent of persons were registered. The result has been a dramatic increase in the registration rates of Blacks in the South, but even by 1975 millions of Southern Blacks were still not registered to vote. To make registration easier, a dozen states adopted postcard registration by 1976, permitting registration by mail. In 1976 a postcard registration law stimulated the Democrats in California to launch a major campaign to register the 4.5–6 million unregistered California adults otherwise eligible to vote.

Registration is a partisan issue. In 1976 approximately 55 million Americans were unregistered; about 30 percent of them could have qualified if registration requirements had not existed. This proportion was higher than the 25 percent of qualified adults not registered in 1968 and 1972. The bulk of the unregistered citizens in 1976 were among the young (50 percent of those 18–29 were unregistered), Blacks (38 percent unregistered), and independents (40 percent unregistered). Looking at these figures, Democratic party leaders foresaw that increased voter registration would be to the party's benefit; perhaps, thay surmised, around 70 percent of the unregistered would turn to the Democrats. In August 1976, Democrats in the House of Representatives managed to pass a bill establishing a nationwide voter registration system that would enable persons to register to vote in federal elections by mail. Postcards were to be made available in post offices and other public buildings; registrants could pick up the cards and mail them to officials. Democrats had hoped the forms would be available before the presidential election of 1976; according to the House bill, a person would qualify to vote in a federal election if he or she fulfilled state requirements and completed registration 30 days prior to the federal election. What the House passed, however, the Senate ignored and the bill failed to win Senate approval in time for the 1976 elections.

In 1977 President Jimmy Carter proposed a form of universal voter registration for federal elections whereby people who could show proper indentification would be permitted to register when they went to the polls. This plan (dubbed "instant registration") failed to win congressional approval during its first year of consideration. Also in 1977 two states held referenda on proposals that would have made voter registration easier. However, the Ohio electorate turned down by a 2–1 margin a proposal modeled after the Carter plan, and the voters in Washington rejected by a similar margin a proposal allowing for postcard registration.

One other major federal action has helped promote American voter registration. Federal funds now help finance campaigns of Republican and Democratic nominees for president. Private contributors who once gave money to party nominees now contribute to the national party committees. This provides the committees with funds to support registration drives. Democrats in 1976 budgeted $3–$4 million for registration in 1976, twice the amount that had been available to them in 1972 before the changes in campaign finance laws. Taking advantage of computer technology, the Democrats compiled voter and resident lists; their goal was to acquire full information on the country's more than 170,000 voting precincts with particular emphasis on the 10 largest states in which more than 25 million persons were unregistered.

In addition to residency and registration requirements, the various states have other miscellaneous restrictions—denying the vote to inmates of penal institutions, to the mentally ill, etc. Moreover, even when they go to the polls, perhaps as many as four million Americans have their ballots thrown out by election judges because they are improperly marked.

The estimates are indeed rough, but it appears that one in four Americans 18 years or older does not satisfy all of the necessary requirements to vote. Thus, "universal" adult suffrage is markedly restricted in the United States.

WHO HAS THE RESOURCES TO PARTICIPATE?

Just as political and constitutional features of the American community limit the opportunity to take part in conflict representation, social factors influence the distribution of the resources to participate. By resources we refer to the social position and characteristics that enable a person to acquire the knowledge, skills, and money that make political participation relatively easy and attractive.

Social position

A person's position in society is indicated by his or her *social class*. In turn, social class results from the interplay of occupation, income, and education. As a rule, lower social class position is associated with reduced political participation.

OCCUPATION. Persons in higher-status occupations (the professions, managerial positions, business, and skilled occupations) are generally more politically active than those in lower-status occupations (the unskilled, manual workers, small farmers). Take, as an example, voting. On the average about 50–67 percent of workers in unskilled occupations vote in presidential elections. By comparison, more than 80 percent of persons in higher-status occupations vote in those elections. There are several reasons for these differences, not the least important being that participation in decisions about one's job provides experience that fosters participation in politics. People in higher-status occupations are more likely to be consulted about decisions that affect their jobs; feeling free to voice views about job decisions, they receive training in political participation as well (Almond and Verba, 1963; Greenberg, 1975). By forcing employers to negotiate on employee working hours, wages, and retirement benefits, trade unions supply training in political participation for their members, usually those in skilled and semiskilled occupations. Moreover, labor unions actively promote political participation among both skilled and unskilled workers. In general, voting rates among union workers are substantially higher than among unorganized laborers (Scoble, 1963).

The tendency of workers in higher-status occupations to participate more is not limited to voting. People in professional and managerial occupations and skilled workers actively influence the opinions of others more than do other white-collar workers, the semiskilled and unskilled, and farmers. Most leaders of political parties either are lawyers or have other professional, business, or managerial careers. Often Republican activists come from higher social class backgrounds than do Democrats, but the two parties do not differ appreciably in the fact that a higher proportion of people with professional and managerial jobs are found among their active members than among their general membership.

We should not assume that most political participants are persons of higher occupational status. Far more voting Americans perform manual, service, clerical, and sales jobs than corporate management and professional jobs. Although a smaller proportion of them vote, unskilled and semiskilled workers make up the largest part of the American national electorate. Where people of higher-status occupations do outstrip other types of workers is in their dominance of more active modes of politics—campaigning, running for office, contacting officials.

INCOME.   Closely related to a person's occupation or family inheritence, income provides the financial resources and freedom from other burdens that encourage political participation. People with higher incomes are more likely to express informed opinions, vote, support political candidates, contribute money to campaigns, and be active in political organizations.

These tendencies do not mean, however, that one must have a great deal of money to take part in politics or that income alone is an adequate indicator of whether people will take part in politics. Blacks, Chicanos, and other Americans of all ages lacking vast financial resources have sometimes been among the most politically active and militant of citizens. Yet it is clear that persons of at least modest means are far more politically active on a sustained basis than those of lower incomes. More than two-thirds of those normally voting in presidential elections, for instance, are in the middle-income bracket earning $5,000–$15,000 a year. Figure 4.4 compares the social positions and characteristics of persons classified as "complete activists" in politics (who vote, campaign, and engage in community-related activities) with the resources of those who do nothing, that is, the inactives. The horizontal bars and the numbers associated with each one report the ratio of the proportion of persons in a particular category who are inactives (or complete activists) to the proportion of that category of persons in the whole population in 1972. The bars and numbers show whether persons of a particular social position or characteristic are under- or overrepresented among inactives or complete activists. For instance, people who earned less than $4,000 per year were greatly overrepresented among inactives and greatly underrepresented among complete activists; people earning $10,000 or more were underrepresented among inactives and overrepresented among complete activists. In the 1960s an annual income of about $7,500 separated those who were likely to take part in political parties and clubs from those who were not (Milbrath, 1965, pp. 120–121). At the inflationary prices of the late 1970s, an annual income of $10,000 or higher separates the active minority from the passive majority of participants.

EDUCATION.   How much people take part in politics is also related to how much formal education they have had, a conclusion we can confirm by looking at Figure 4.4. To repeat, that figure uses an "index of representation" to illustrate how people in various social categories—Blacks, women, Catholics, the elderly,

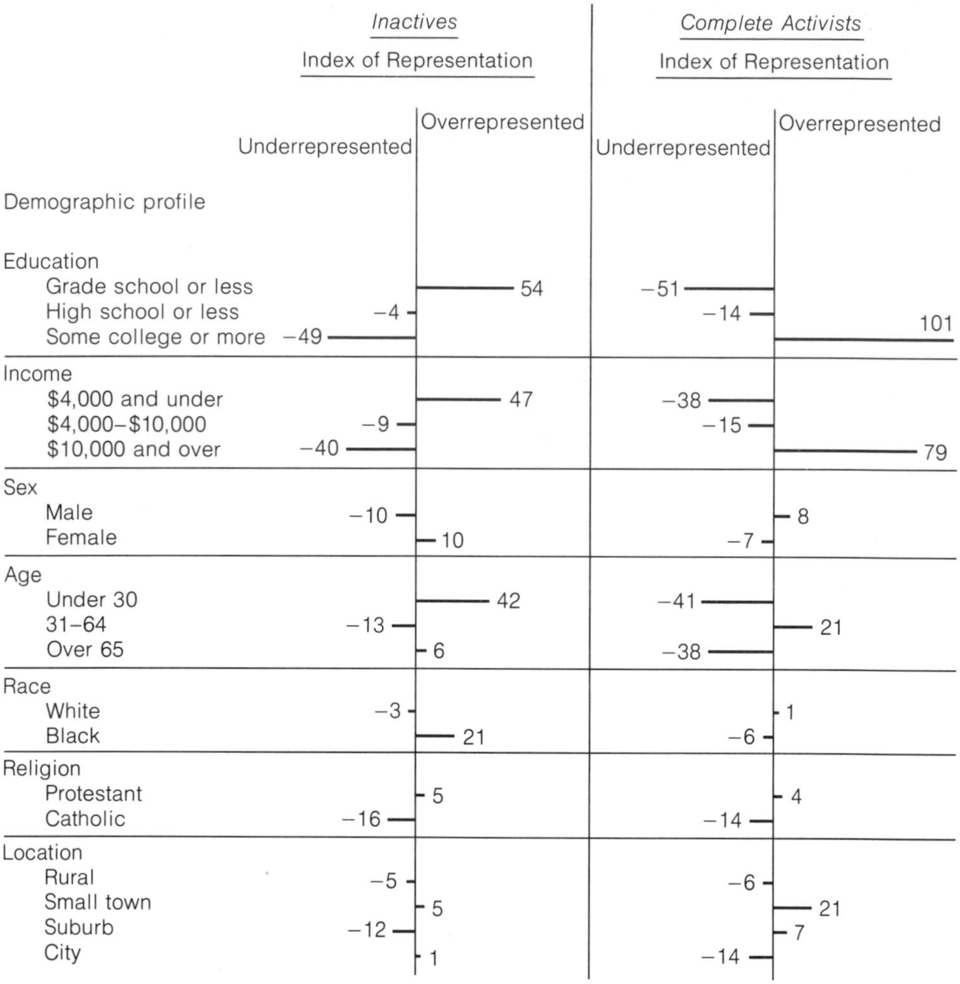

	Inactives Index of Representation		Complete Activists Index of Representation	
Demographic profile	Underrepresented	Overrepresented	Underrepresented	Overrepresented
Education				
Grade school or less		54	−51	
High school or less	−4		−14	
Some college or more	−49			101
Income				
$4,000 and under		47	−38	
$4,000–$10,000	−9		−15	
$10,000 and over	−40			79
Sex				
Male	−10			8
Female		10	−7	
Age				
Under 30		42	−41	
31–64	−13			21
Over 65		6	−38	
Race				
White	−3			1
Black		21	−6	
Religion				
Protestant		5		4
Catholic	−16		−14	
Location				
Rural	−5		−6	
Small town		5		21
Suburb	−12			7
City		1	−14	

FIGURE 4.4

A Social Position and Characteristics Profile of Inactive and Completely Active Citizens. [*Source:* Verba, S., and Nie, N. H., *Participation in America*, New York: Harper & Row, 1972, pp. 98, 100.]

etc.—are over- or underrepresented among groups of citizens who are either completely active in politics (they vote regularly, take part in election campaigns, and join with others to solve local problems) or are inactive, that is, do little beyond paying marginal attention to politics and voicing opinions. The index reflects the ratio of the proportion of people in a particular social category who are activists or inactives to the proportion of that category in the population as a whole. Assume, for instance, that 50 percent of all citizens are male but only 25 percent of political inactives are males. Males are thus underrepresented by 50 percent among inactives and receive a score in Figure 4.4 of − 50 (note that the actual score for males among inactives is − 10). If, on the other hand, males constituted 75 percent of inactives, they would have a score of + 50, indicating marked overrepresentation.

As Figure 4.4 indicates, persons with grade school educations or less are overrepresented among inactives and underrepresented among complete activists. Persons who have attended college are strikingly overrepresented in the category of complete activists.

There is other evidence that indicates how education correlates with political activity. For instance, about 90 percent of the college-educated population take part in presidential elections; this compares with 50–60 percent of those with grade school educations and about 75 percent of those with high school educations. In the total adult population, however, far fewer have gone to college than have not. As a result, although a smaller proportion of their group votes, citizens who have not received a college education cast three out of every four votes in presidential elections.

Social characteristics

A person's age, sex, race, religion, and residence (see Figure 4.4) rarely influence levels of political participation independently of social class. More frequently they work in conjunction with social position to increase or diminish participation rates.

AGE. As Figure 4.4 illustrates, Americans under 30 years of age are overrepresented among the politically inactive and greatly underrepresented among complete political activists. Persons over 65 are also underrepresented among complete activists. Generally, citizens of middle age are the most politically active. The result is an American electorate that is mostly middle-aged, neither young nor old.

Whether persons of a given age are informed about politics, care to take part, and actually do probably depends upon both how old they are and how much education they have had. Table 4.6 illustrates this point. Younger Americans are no better informed about politics than older groups. People of all ages who have not attended college have about the same amount of information. And people who have had some college education—no matter what their age—are better informed than those who have not. The college educated are also more active in electoral politics, but here age makes some difference: Those over 35 without a college education approach the youngest of the college educated in their concern about electoral outcomes and even surpass them in their belief that people have a duty to vote. Finally, when it comes to general political

TABLE 4.6

Political participation by age and education, 1972 (in percentages*)

Mode of participation	No college education			Some college education		
	18–24	25–34	35+	18–24	25–34	35+
Accurate Factual Knowledge						
Limit on presidential term	83.3	86.1	89.6	95.4	97.9	90.5
Length of senator's term	36.5	35.0	39.7	59.6	50.6	54.4
Length of congressman's term	56.8	56.7	51.9	68.0	59.5	67.2
House majority party before election	63.3	81.6	92.0	85.2	95.3	91.6
House majority party after election	71.7	80.5	87.5	78.0	85.2	83.3
Electoral Political Activity						
Have voted	46.9	61.5	72.0	81.0	85.5	89.5
Concerned about election outcome	45.9	59.7	61.6	64.7	65.0	74.2
Give money to parties	4.3	4.0	6.3	13.7	18.0	26.8
Express strong partisanship	13.0	15.5	32.5	15.6	16.8	28.7
Believe in duty to vote	36.3	48.9	56.7	39.6	57.0	65.9
General Political Activity						
Perceive lack of power	48.1	46.4	47.9	30.9	24.8	18.8
Find politics confusing	80.1	84.7	80.5	59.9	59.4	52.6
Talk to others	27.7	25.4	25.1	52.7	46.6	42.0
Write to public officials	11.7	18.7	21.5	32.9	43.4	48.9
Vote on all ballot referenda	55.2	62.6	66.5	75.7	81.6	82.5
High general interest in politics	14.9	23.1	33.9	42.5	52.9	58.2
Number of respondents	236	380	1260	162	230	389

*Entries are the percentage of each age and educational group with the designated knowledge, view, or behavior.

Source: Pomper, G., *Voters' Choice.* New York: Harper & Row, 1975, Table 5.2.

activity, education has greater significance than does age, that is, differences between age groups take a back seat to those between levels of schooling.

SEX. Differences in passive and active political participation related to sex are noticeable but not striking. In fact, women's participation in voting has been on the increase in recent years and is now equal to the voting rates of White men. The responsibilities for the care of children and lingering cultural expectations (mostly in the South) that women should take little interest in politics still depress female voting. But things have changed markedly since the 1950s when the voting rate among women was about 10 percent lower than that among men (Campbell, Converse, Miller, and Stokes, 1960, p. 484). In the 1972 presidential election, 73 percent of males registered, 64 percent voted; 72 percent of females registered, 62 percent voted (U.S. Bureau of the Census, 1972).

When it comes to participation beyond voting, women are still slightly less likely to engage in active politics. They take part less frequently in community-related activities and in campaigning; and, as indicated in Figure 4.4, women are overrepresented among inactives and marginally underrepresented among complete activists. In general, men and women with approximately the same education take part in politics in almost the equal proportions. Indeed, college-educated women are more likely to take part in some political activities than college-educated men, and high-status females are more active than high-status males. The social resources that facilitate political participation thus operate in combination with each other, and no specific resource (age, sex, class, etc.) tells the whole story of why some people participate and others do not.

RACIAL BACKGROUND.   In American elections, Black citizens register and vote in smaller proportions than Whites; moreover, Whites are more likely to know who their congresspeople and United States Senators are and what political parties those officials represent. But these differences are attributable to the low social standing (occupation, income, education) of Blacks rather than to "blackness" or "whiteness." If educational differences are taken into account, Blacks and Whites participate—beyond simply talking about politics and voting—at nearly the same rates. One study found that among college-educated southern males, a higher percentage of Blacks than Whites took part in politics (Matthews and Prothro, 1966, pp. 101–174).

Added evidence that social class differences contribute to racial differences in political participation appears in Table 4.7. The figures representing "difference" by race in the table are derived by subtracting the activity rate of Whites from the activity rate of Blacks. If the number is negative, it means that Blacks participate less than Whites; if positive, Blacks participate more. Without taking into account the effects of social class, Blacks appear to vote, campaign,

TABLE 4.7
Political participation by race and social class

Style of participation	Difference between Blacks and Whites (ignoring social class)	Difference between Blacks and Whites (considering social class)
Voting	−12	−9
Campaign activity	−7	+15
Cooperative, community-related activity	+6	+30
Citizen-initiated contact	−13	+15

Source: Adapted from Verba, S., and Nie, N. H., *Participation in America*, New York: Harper & Row, 1972, Table 10.3.

and contact officials less frequently than do Whites. But when the effects of differing occupation, income, and education are controlled for, Blacks appear to participate at a higher rate in all areas but voting, and there the difference is reduced. In fact, when we take social class into account, we find that Blacks rather than Whites tend to take part in the more active modes of politics and that Whites are more passive (see also London, 1975).

RELIGIOUS AFFILIATION.   There are differences in the political participation of Protestants and Catholics and Jews. Protestants have lower voting rates (with Episcopalians and Presbyterians slightly more active than Baptists) than do Catholics; Jews vote at higher rates than Protestants or Catholics. Bear in mind, however, that a lower rate of participation among Protestants does not alter the fact that they are the largest religious group in this nation. Two-thirds of the American electorate is Protestant. Catholics take part in campaigning, to a greater degree than do Protestants; they also exceed Protestants in contacting officials for personal gain. People involved in community-related activities are much less likely to be Catholic. Overall, as illustrated in Figure 4.4, Protestants are very slightly overrepresented among inactives and complete activists; Catholics are underrepresented in both categories.

Differences in participation among people of varying religious affiliation arise from a number of interrelated factors. Social class differences help account for contrasting levels of political involvement. For example, Jews are more active in politics than many other religious groups; they also tend to have higher incomes, better educations, and higher occupational statuses (Menendez, 1977). Moreover, Jews and Roman Catholics have been more prone to turn to politics as a means of combatting religious or ethnic discrimination. Finally, regularity of church attendance is also related to participation: Churchgoers are more likely to vote.

RESIDENCE.   Whether a person lives in a rural or an urban area, the size of the community and the region of the nation in which it is located have some bearing on his or her political habits. In general, political participation is higher in the more commercial and industrialized urban areas of America's northeast, west, and upper midwest. On the whole, people who live in the country are not as politically involved as city dwellers. The former are slightly underrepresented among inactives, yet are less likely to vote, contact public officials, and campaign than are their urban counterparts. Rural residents outdo residents of cities, however in taking part in community-related activities. Nevertheless, as indicated by Figure 4.4, neither rural or city dwellers are adequately represented in the category of complete activists, where residents of small towns and suburbanites are overrepresented.

The highest levels of political knowledge are usually found among residents of America's middle-sized communities (2,500 to 50,000), where about half of the people know the names of their state senators and representatives, how their congresspeople vote, and something of political issues. Information levels are lower among both rural residents (communities under 2,500) and persons living in cities of more than 50,000, where only about one in four is as well informed as the small-town resident (Glenn, 1972).

WHO WANTS TO PARTICIPATE?

Political and constitutional conditions create opportunities to participate in politics; social factors distribute the resources supporting varying levels of participation. But equally as vital in shaping the American pattern of participation in conflict representation is the personal element, the desire of people to engage in or avoid politics. When is a citizen motivated to act politically?

The rewards of politics

People receive a variety of benefits from taking part in politics; but there is a bill to pay as well. The costs—in time, money, and physical energy—are often too high. If the benefits outweigh the costs, however people participate.

INSTRUMENTAL GAIN.   Political participation can be used, or even avoided, to achieve specific tangible benefits. Chief among these are economic gain, neighborhood preservation, and job security. A person can use the vote to support a candidate who promises to cut taxes. A corporation magnate may contribute money to a candidate's campaign in exchange for the promise that if the politician wins, the contributor will receive a sizable government contract. A person may work for a candidate in hopes of gaining a political appointment to a job once the campaign ends. And residents of local communities often band together to protect their property and neighborhoods against rezoning, highway construction, and other proposed projects. Direct economic costs, on the other hand, may contribute to passive politics. Some persons shy away from taking public stands on political issues for fear that a boss, client, or customer will not want to do business with someone who gets involved in controversy.

Participation in politics can also satisfy intellectual curiosity. For people who want to "understand what's going on," being on the "inside" of a campaign provides enormous satisfaction. Many grass-roots volunteers of all ages worked around the clock in 1976 in the campaigns of Gerald Ford and Jimmy Carter. Some did so to put their political ideas into practice; others to learn at the most important working level of partisan politics—the bottom—what politics is all about. The politically curious try to develop informed opinions about politics; others, whose main interests lie elsewhere, find political discussion tedious and dull; still others discover a rat race that is more confusing than enlightening and turn to less demanding avocations.

SOCIAL BENEFITS AND SACRIFICES.   By taking part in politics people can associate themselves with others they like, admire, and respect. Many party precinct leaders, for example, have said they got involved in politics because of the satisfaction of making social "contacts" and the cameraderie and "fun" of involvement (Eldersveld, 1964). The desire to make or keep friends can inhibit political participation as well as foster it. Rather than get involved in a political argument that might lead to bitterness, some people avoid political discussion altogether. How many a person has turned to a companion after leaving a party and sighed, "Thank heavens, we didn't get into any arguments over politics tonight"?

Political victories and defeats also confer social status. A political battle that on the surface appears to be over the division of tangible goods may actually be waged between forces less interested in material gain or loss than in convincing others they are "number one." For instance, in 1919 the U.S. added the Eighteenth Amendment to the Constitution. Congress followed with the Volstead Act prohibiting the transportation, sale, and consumption of intoxicating beverages in interstate commerce. Did drinking and intemperance end? No. Did crime, allegedly fostered by alcoholic consumption, decrease? No. In fact, bootlegging became big business. Prohibition, it turned out, was either unenforced or unenforceable. What then did Prohibition achieve? It conferred status; it demonstrated to one and all what social groups in the country set the moral tone of the nation: "It established the victory of Protestant over Catholic, rural over urban, tradition over modernity, the middle class over both the lower and the upper strata" (Gusfield, 1966, p. 7). Ultimately the Eighteenth Amendment was repealed, an act that conferred status on the values of a lower class in the throes of economic depression.

EXPRESSIVE RELIEF.   By taking part in politics, people express themselves—who they are, who they want to be, what they value, what they abhor. A person flies the flag, sings the national anthem, votes, and thereby says to one and all, "I am an American." Another labors at the electoral grass roots to say "I am a Republican" or "I am a Democrat." Taking part in politics provides the opportunity for joining an exciting, dramatic spectacle that permits a person to vent feelings, air grievances, and identify with the glory and tradition that is one's nation, political party, ideology, or cause. To the degree that people use politics to identify with abstractions ("America," "Democracy") or to "get things off my chest," "the most cherished forms of popular participation are largely symbolic," and for most persons "most of the time politics is a series of pictures in the mind, placed there by television news, newspapers, magazines, and discussions." It is a "world the mass public never quite touches," a world, in short, of passive rather than active participation (Edelman, 1964, pp. 4–5).

Feelings about politics and government

Citizens are motivated to action when they feel politics "touches" them. Unless people think politics bears upon their lives, they seldom get involved enough to achieve the economic, intellectual, social, status, and emotional rewards that are possible. Politics touches every aspect of daily living in some fashion—economic chances, being able to walk the street in safety, what people can learn, think, and say. Do people sense this? They probably do. Asked to respond to the question: "Thinking now about the national government in Washington, about how much do you think its activities, the laws passed, and so on have on your day-to-day life?" nine of every ten people surveyed said "great" or "some" effect.

But this appraisal in response to an abstract question is not matched either by a style of daily living that continuously accentuates political involvement or by a sense that citizens can really make much difference in what the American government does. That the bulk of Americans are only passively engaged in politics on anything like a day-to-day, week-to-week, or month-to-month basis is evidence enough that very few believe the effects of the "government in Washington" (or any other for that matter) are sufficiently relevant to every-day living to worry much about. Nor do a very large number of Americans seem to think they can do all that much about what government does anyway; they have neither a strong sense of political efficacy nor trust in government.

POLITICAL EFFICACY. Citizens are more likely to take part in conflict representation if they believe that their voices will be heard and their demands will be taken seriously. People who feel this way have a sense of competence or *political efficacy*. Americans today do not feel as politically competent as they once did; recent evidence indicates that they have become disenchanted with government and what they can do about it. At the end of 1977, for example, pollster Louis Harris provided these figures reflecting how Americans perceived their political competence:

- The proportion of adults who felt largely "left out of things" going on around them stood at 35 percent, down from the 40 percent who felt that way in 1976 but well above the 9 percent who shared that sentiment in 1966.
- Sixty-one percent felt that "what I think doesn't count much anymore," an insignificant decline from the 64 percent who said this in 1976 but a monumental rise from the 37 percent who felt this way in 1966.
- Seventy-seven percent believed that "the rich get richer and the poor get poorer" in both 1976 and 1977; 58 percent felt that way in 1972, 45 percent in 1966.
- Sixty percent felt that "the people running the country don't really care what happens to me," up from the 26 percent who felt that way in 1966 and 49

percent who felt that way in 1974 and virtually the same proportion as the 61 percent with that feeling in 1976.

- About 67 percent felt "most people with power try to take advantage of people such as myself"; that was an almost twofold increase over the approximately 33 percent who were of that opinion in 1971.

- Fifty-nine percent agreed with the charge that "people in Washington, D.C. are out of touch with the rest of the country," down from the high of 68 percent who felt that way in 1976 but still strikingly high considering that President Jimmy Carter won many votes in 1976 on the platform of running against Washington as an outsider (*The Harris Survey*, December 8, 1977).

Harris combines these measures into a single figure to indicate the general level of what he calls alienation from government. Figure 4.5 illustrates the trend in the decade 1966–1976. The high of 59 percent who felt alienated in 1976 scarcely changed at all in 1977 when 58 percent still felt that way in spite of a change in presidential administrations in Washington.

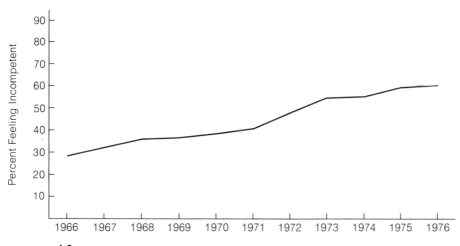

FIGURE 4.5

A Decade of Rising Perceived Political Incompetence. [*Source:* Prepared from data reported in *The Harris Survey*, March 25, 1976: "Voters Express Alienation."]

Who are the alienated? Two-thirds of each of the following categories were alienated according to the Harris measure: Blacks, the lesser educated, people in the lower-income bracket, and big city residents. Expressing almost as much alienation were union members, Catholics, Jews, Democrats, and people over 50 years of age. Least alienated were professionals, the college educated, white-collar workers, and those earning more than $15,000 per year.

POLITICAL TRUST. The loss of a sense of political competence is closely related to a decline in trust in government. One way to measure changes in levels of political trust is to create a single index based upon how people respond to five survey questions: (1) How much can you trust the government in Washington to do what is right? (2) Is the government in Washington pretty much run by a few big interests looking out for themselves or is it run for the benefit of all people? (3) Does the government waste the money we pay in taxes? (4) Are the people running the government smart people who usually know what they are doing? (5) Are the people running the government a little crooked? As Figure 4.6 illustrates, trust in government dropped dramatically in the 1960s and early 1970s.

In sum, many people have become disaffected, not just dissatisfied, with politics and politicians. A dissatisfied person does not like what politicians do but has enough faith in democratic processes to want to do something about it. A disaffected person has no such faith and believes that any form of participation is ultimately meaningless. If such a person votes, it is not to change things but to express what the protestor is against, which may be practically anything

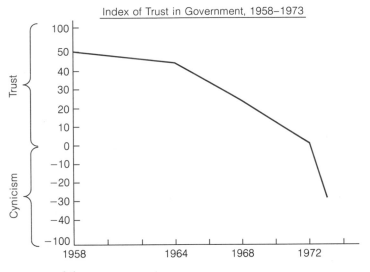

FIGURE 4.6

A Decade and a Half of Declining Political Trust. [The chart is based on five questions concerning the federal government's performance (figures represent the percentage of persons in the most trusting category minus the percentage in the most cynical category).] [*Source:* "Trust in Government Falls; Independent Voters Increase," *ISR Newsletter*, Institute for Social Research, The University of Michigan, Winter 1974, p. 5 (© King Features Syndicate Inc., 1974).]

in sight. If sufficiently estranged and angry, the disaffected may channel pent-up frustrations into outbursts of violent protest.

Who are the disaffected? Today the numbers of Americans disillusioned with politics and politicians has grown so large that alienation transcends social classes and characteristics. Whether the trend of growing political alienation will continue remains to be seen. In any event, it is a condition that governmental leaders can no longer ignore.

Conflict representation in the years ahead

Liberal democratic theory prescribes a high level of active political participation, but Americans do not measure up to the ideal. Who then will be our political participants in the future and what difference can their efforts make?

THE PROFILE OF CONTEMPORARY POLITICAL PARTICIPANTS

Today, as we have seen, there are two principal types of political participants. First, there are the active participants, that minority of Americans who not only hold political opinions and vote but also keep informed, influence others, join political organizations, and petition their officials. A social profile of this group reveals that it consists of middle-aged citizens who have attended college; have reasonably good incomes; are more likely to be males, Whites, and Protestants; and reside in middle-sized communities and suburbs. These people feel politics touches their lives. They gain personal satisfaction from political activity and feel some sense of political competence.

Contrasted with these actives is a second group, the numerous Americans who are passive participants, who express opinions, occasionally vote, but do little else. Generally Protestant and from small towns, they differ from actives in being less educated, of a lower-income bracket, younger, and slightly more likely to be female than male.

THE CONSEQUENCES OF PATTERNS OF PARTICIPATION

How do these patterns of political participation affect conflict representation? Participation does make a difference; it represents interests to policymakers and makes leaders responsive to popular concerns. It achieves this in two ways: First, participation in and of itself matters because "community leaders are more likely to concur with the problem priorities of participants than with those of nonparticipants. This is not the result of the social characteristics of participants, but appears to be an independent effect of participation" (Verba and Nie, 1972, p. 332). Apart from *who* the participants are—well or moderately educated, middle- or modest-income, male or female, etc.—political leaders listen to them simply because they are making known their demands through political action.

But second, "participants are not a representative group of the population" and "where there is a moderate amount of participation, leaders pay attention to the unrepresentative participant groups and are less responsive to the community as a whole" (Verba and Nie, 1972, p. 333). This generally means that policymakers pay closer attention to the most active of participants (and thereby the most unrepresentative segments of the population) rather than the passive. There is clearly a problem inherent in this pattern, for as long as participation is dominated by those with the resources and motivation to capitalize upon their opportunities, disputes taken to policymakers will be those that primarily serve the interest of the most consistent political activists. Hence, serious social tensions in the daily lives of passive citizens and non-participants may well go unnoticed by policymakers, at least until those tensions touch the interests of citizens who take part in active politics. Too often before that happens a crisis emerges that is beyond immediate resolution. The urban unrest and the antiwar protests of the 1960s are reminders of past crises; the problems of providing adequate living standards for the ever growing number of the elderly, of meeting the energy needs of a society whose most readily available resources (petroleum, natural gas) are being rapidly depleted, and of assuring employment in a threatened economy are all potential crises if policymakers ignore them or fail to resolve the tensions such problems produce.

TRENDS IN CONFLICT REPRESENTATION

Have the profiles of political participants changed substantially in the 1970s? What are the probabilities for the future? Answers to such questions depend upon recent and possible changes in the opportunities, resources, and desires of people to take part. Generally, the opportunity to participate expands or contracts with efforts to strike a balance between the rights of the individual and the need to maintain social order. The proper balance involves neither what the Framers of the Constitution "really" intended nor the application of abstract theories of individual liberty. Rather, the basic issue of who has the opportunity to participate is "the political one of what a certain governmental institution ought to do about a certain set of demands" (Shapiro, 1966, p. 61). As time and circumstances change, what people disagree about most, the content and meaning of constitutional guarantees, and the opportunities to take part also change. On the whole, the 1970s has produced a broadening of legal opportunities for popular participation. Notable landmarks were the enfranchisement of 18-year-old voters that swelled the potential electorate by 10 percent in 1972; Supreme Court restrictions on unreasonable requirements for length of residency for voting; changes to facilitate voter registration; requirements for bilingual elections to promote participation by language minorities; and changes in rules of political parties to broaden the base of the delegate selection process in choosing presidential nominees.

The expansion of the resources underlying popular participation have not kept pace with increases in the opportunities to take part. To be sure, more people have acquired the middle-class characteristics associated with increasing rates of participation; that is more people have gone to college, moved into higher-status occupations, increased their influence, and reached middle-age. But by the same token, there are greater numbers of Americans who have not crossed that social threshold to increased involvement. The composition and proportion of active and passive participants has shifted little in the 1970s. Yet it should be noted that Blacks have increased their rates of active participation, and that almost as high a proportion of qualified women vote in national elections as do qualified men.

It is difficult to say whether the personal desire to take part, on the whole, has changed much in recent years. Early straws in the wind—the ecology movement and women's liberation—heralded a greater sense of political involvement. But by the mid-1970s disenchantment with politics and politicians (perhaps aided and abetted by the Watergate scandals) had generated a dramatic downturn in popular interest and participation in conflict representation.

Many seemingly well-meaning authorities are critical of Americans' low rates of political participation. Politicians, political scientists, political journalists, and social reformers are quick to point to the causes and cures: Legal obstacles must be removed; there must be a drastic redistribution of the wealth so that resources for participation will be available for all; and politicians must conduct themselves in a way that will restore public trust and confidence in government. But for these political participants and observers, politics is inherently interesting. Indeed, politics is their bread and butter. Small wonder that they think it important and cannot grasp why every other American does not take politics as seriously as they do. But would any of these political enthusiasts find the livelihoods of most other Americans as interesting and important as they find politics? Would they, given the opportunity, want to devote their time, energies and psyches to working on the assembly line, driving a taxi or a big rig, walking a high scaffold, or performing any of the other countless nonpolitical occupations that fill the working day of most Americans? Would these political observers subtract from their lives the effort that they ask citizens to spend reading, campaigning, voting, and organizing?

One wonders. That wonderment suggests that more direct means will be necessary to increase Americans' interest in politics than have heretofore been employed. If they are to take part in politics, people are going to have to be convinced that political participation can produce substantial changes that will relieve their daily miseries and improve their daily routines. Appeals to abstract notions of democracy, to theoretical "duties" and "obligations" simply do not provoke the mass of Americans to take part. Nor do assurances from leaders about "honesty" and "trust." Nor do the countless strident and sometimes shrill claims that people *must* participate in order to counter the nefarious workings of "them" and "they," the faceless elites who control the "establishment." One suspects that only by becoming aware of direct, immediate payoffs worthy of personal sacrifice will citizens engage in political action. Without that, people will continue to watch the spectacle of the political drama from afar rather than walking onto the stage.

By political design, social chance, and personal choice America possesses a host of unrepresented citizens. Continued removal of discriminatory constitutional and legal barriers will correct deficiencies of design. Support of adequate living standards for all Americans will contribute to alleviating the vagaries of chance. But overcoming the "nonpolitical" persuasion that the bulk of Americans have reached through personal choice is a far greater obstacle. Passive participants, and even nonparticipants, may readily agree that "participation is good for America." Yet, each asks "What has it done for *me* lately?" Unless that question is answered to the individual's satisfaction, neither a truly pluralist America nor a working consensus arrived at by popular initiative rather than imposed by an active minority is likely to materialize in the years ahead.

5

EXPRESSING POLITICAL OPINIONS

Americans are more likely to state political opinions than to engage in any other political activity associated with conflict representation. To obtain a better understanding of this popular but passive mode of political participation, we need to consider these questions: What are political opinions and what good does it do to have them? What are their principal characteristics? What is public opinion and how is it distributed? Where do people get their opinions about politics? On what political issues are Americans most likely to express conflicting views? How does public opinion affect conflict resolution?

Representing conflict by political opinions

When people talk politics, they state their views. Sometimes they agree; sometimes they disagree. Either way, they are expressing opinions, that is, conclusions or judgments about specific matters. A *political opinion* is simply a conclusion or judgment expressed about a political matter. Taken collectively, the political opinions of people add up to *public opinion.* Widespread agreement constitutes consensus; two or more points in disagreement produce conflict.

HOW DO POLITICAL OPINIONS RELATE TO ATTITUDES AND INTERESTS?

Politics is a method for regulating conflicting interests (see Chapter 1). The relationship between attitudes, interests, and opinions in representing those conflicts is close and important.

- *Attitudes* are tendencies of our activities (Blumer, 1955) that indicate our enduring personal preferences about general matters. Feelings of pride in America, anxieties over war, concerns about the economy, a belief in universal education—all of these are personal attitudes of potential political importance.

- *Interests* are actions we take in conjunction with other people to pursue goals derived from our personal preferences, or attitudes (Bentley, 1908, Chaps. 6–7). A belief in universal education may stimulate a person to be aware of federally financed college scholarships: this reflects an interest in a general proposal.

- *Opinions* derive from the interplay of attitudes and interests, but focus upon specific topical and immediate matters (G. C. Thompson, 1886). Opinions are expressions of underlying attitudes and continuing interests sharpened in response to concrete stimuli (see Figure 5.1). Senator Procol, who has always supported federal college scholarships is up for reelection; if a person decides the senator should be reelected for that reason, that voter's ballot expresses an opinion on the matter.

The overlap of attitudes, interests, and opinions has three vital implications. First, personal attitudes and interests are building blocks of political opinions. Opinions are public statements provoked by specific political matters. People form opinions when their attitudes and interests are "turned on" by contemporary political events, personalities, and issues. To understand where opinions originate, we must therefore consider how people acquire their attitudes and interests (something we examine later in this chapter) and how politicians influence that process (a topic we discuss in Chapter 6).

Second, personal attitudes and interests influence what people see in politics. Republicans are more likely to listen to Republican politicians and agree with what they say than to listen to or sympathize with Democrats.

Third, a person reveals his attitudes or interests through his expressed

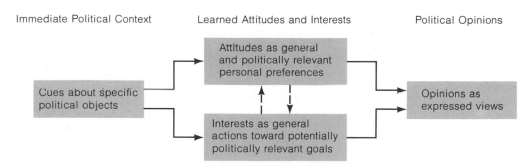

Immediate Political Context   Learned Attitudes and Interests   Political Opinions

FIGURE 5.1
The Relationship of Political Attitudes, Interests, and Opinions. (Arrows indicate
general direction of influence leading to opinion expression; one's attitudes and
cues influence one's perception of political objects as well.)

opinions. If conflicts between people's interests emerge from differing attitudes, it is possible to recognize those conflicts by listening to adversary
opinions.

Political opinions, like the personal attitudes and interests related to them,
consist of three intertwined components (Smith, 1947). The first is a *thinking* component: what people know and believe (rightly or wrongly) about a
political object. When the United States underwent a petroleum shortage in
the early 1970s, prices of gasoline and fuel oil increased sharply and long lines
of cars appeared at gasoline pumps. Many Americans believed the cause of the
shortage was an embargo against selling oil to the U.S. by the oil-producing
nations; others believed the refusal of Americans to conserve petroleum had
made a shortage inevitable; still others thought the "crisis" was manufactured
by the oil companies simply to drive up prices.

A second key aspect of political opinions is the *feeling* component: People
feel that something is either good or bad, desirable or undesirable. On the
question of whether it was necessary in the 1970s to force Americans to
conserve gasoline by imposing a 55-mile-per-hour speed limit, some Americans
backed the proposals while others objected. Here was a conflict of political
feelings.

Finally, there is an *acting* component, the things we do to realize our beliefs
and values. Many Americans in the 1970s "slowed down to 55," joined car
pools, consolidated automobile trips, and used other means to cut fuel consumption. Others, however, protested reduced speed limits, evaded them, and
continued to purchase large, gas-guzzling automobiles on grounds that "the oil
is there." This added a conflict of actions to those of beliefs and values.

The thoughts, feelings, and actions that form political opinions are generally
consistent. A person might value good roads and highways, believe government

must raise taxes to provide these services, and vote to increase those taxes. But consistency is not always the rule. Consider the range of political opinions on race relations in America. A study conducted in 15 American cities (Campbell, 1971) showed that a majority of White respondents thought Blacks were discriminated against in housing and job opportunities; a third of the White respondents thought Blacks were victims of police maltreatment. However, a smaller proportion of Whites felt sympathy with Black protests, while two-thirds felt that Blacks were "trying to push too fast." In questions designed to measure what actions Whites would accept in racial contact, a third of the Whites said they would prefer their children to have only Whites as friends and they would mind a "little" or a "lot" if a Black family moved in next door. This shows that beliefs about a practice such as discrimination need not coincide with feelings about the practice or acts to change it.

WHAT CAN POLITICAL OPINIONS DO FOR US?

We know that when asked most Americans express opinions on political matters. Even in the absence of supporting information, those expressions assist people in several ways (Katz, 1960).

Our opinions help us to understand politics

Politics is confusing to most of us; so many things in politics seem contradictory. We are told that Communist China is our enemy; then our President takes a goodwill trip there. Or a President describes himself as a "fiscal conservative" and then announces a budget to spend far more money than can be collected in revenues. Or, a Congressman says, "Washington should keep its hands out of local affairs," but urges the federal government to build a military installation in his district.

In all this confusion, we try to make sense of what is going on. Our opinions help us in the task—as political beliefs, they offer guidance for understanding. Moreover, by helping us to understand politics, our opinions also help us to realize our interests. A union member has a favorable opinion of the Democratic party if he associates that party with policies to lower taxes, keep him employed, and otherwise support his economic demands. Opinions are thus instruments people use in taking sides in conflicts that affect their interests.

Our opinions help us to relate to other people

When we state our political views we know that some people will agree with us and others will not. We can use our opinions to join with those we like, respect, and want to be with; conversely we can use them to fight or flee persons we dislike or want to avoid. Because opinions help us to adjust socially, we may tailor our expressions to conform to what persons with whom we want to get along say. Altered in this way, expressed opinions are one way of saying "I am like you," of putting into operation the old political adage that one must "go along to get along."

Our opinions reveal our personalities

A classic formulation about politics says that people project their private motives upon public objects and rationalize their actions to conform with the public interest (Lasswell, 1930). When a person states a political viewpoint, that expression reveals an inner personality—one's psychic needs, hopes, and fears. Our stated thoughts and feelings defend our egos against hostile criticism and rationalize our pursuit of narrow interests, particularly those we think are unpopular. Moreover, our stated opinions reveal a self-image we want others to accept. If it is important to someone to be a "liberal" or "conservative," that person wants others to accept that self-definition and takes every opportunity to express liberal or conservative opinions. The person's views on political issues may reflect a definition of self rather than any considered judgment of the merits of the proposals supported or condemned.

Almost any political opinion guides our understanding, helps us to adjust to others, and assists us in expressing our hidden motives. These three functions of opinion arouse parallel types of conflicts. First, there are conflicting understandings of what tangible goals to pursue and how to achieve them (such as debates over legalizing the sale of marijuana and taxing the sale to finance government services). Second, there are conflicts between social groups for political status (should alleged "pot heads" have as much to say about the matter as "respectable, straight citizens"). Third, there are conflicting private motives (as between politicians who rationalize selfish ambitions by campaigning "to end the traffic in drugs" or "let the people decide what is best for them"). When analyzing a debate on any political issue, it is wise to remember that all three types of dispute usually surround any disagreement. Conflicts of principle often mask a clash between opposing understandings, social groups, and private motives.

WHAT ARE THE CHARACTERISTICS OF POLITICAL OPINIONS?

Politicians try to find out what is on people's minds by heeding shared and conflicting opinions. Policymakers listen and respond (as we shall see later) to political thoughts, feelings, and actions. But the relationship between political opinions and public policy is complicated; people do not always want what government does nor does government faithfully do what everyone wants.

Some political opinions are easier for political leaders to take into account than others. What characteristics of political opinions affect their impact on conflict representation?

Direction is an indication of whether an opinion is favorable, unfavorable, or qualified. People's opinions are usually influenced as much by their personalities, social backgrounds, and partisan affiliation as by the merits of a proposal. Regardless of the underlying reason—the issue itself or personal predispositions—Americans usually line up clearly for or against proposals rather than giving qualified reactions.

Intensity indicates how firmly people hold opinions. Some issues excite public passion, and politicians respond quickly. When Lieutenant William L. Calley, Jr. was convicted in 1971 in a court-martial for the premeditated murder of Vietnamese civilians in the village of My Lai, the public was outraged that a "loyal American" was being used as a "scapegoat"; 80 percent of a nationwide sample disapproved of the verdict (Gallup, 1972, p. 2296). The protest was so intense that President Nixon ordered Calley removed from a military prison and returned to a comfortable apartment under house arrest. Nixon also agreed to review the case personally once all military appeals were exhausted. Eighty-three percent of Americans sampled approved Nixon's action. By contrast, policy questions that are less emotionally charged and more routine, such as the President's annual request to Congress to raise the legal limit on the national debt, stir intense feelings among far fewer Americans.

Stability is a quality that opinions acquire when their direction and intensity are fairly constant over a period of time. In the 1950s and 1960s, nationwide surveys indicated that a majority of Americans favored foreign aid, about a third were opposed, and the remainder had "no opinion." But stability in the direction and intensity of political opinions depends upon two things: consistency of underlying personal attitudes and continuity in the conditions stimulating those attitudes. Thus, when America became involved in South Vietnam in the 1960s, opinions about foreign aid changed. They were no longer clearly pro or con, but qualified. Though percentages of support and opposition to foreign aid in opinion surveys were about the same as before, three-fourths of those sampled went on to say they wanted to either "reduce" or "cut off completely" aid to any country that did not support the United States "in a major foreign decision, such as Vietnam" (Erskine, 1964, p. 168).

When opinions appear inclined to one direction, are intense, or remain stable, politicians tend to identify their stands with prevailing opinion (they "trim their sails to the winds"). We have seen how Nixon took advantage of the Calley case. Other politicians have been equally attuned to trends. For instance, in seeking the Presidency in 1976, Jimmy Carter took advantage of a widespread popular disillusionment with "Big Government" and "Washington" to convert what might have been a liability—his lack of experience in federal office—into an asset. Incumbent President Gerald Ford tried to turn the tables by claiming to have restored the integrity of the White House and administration, thus shifting the blame for popular disillusionment upon two decades of a Democrat-dominated Congress.

Representing conflict by public opinion

Public opinion consists of a collectivity of individual opinions regarding political matters that affect broad segments of the community. That collectivity possesses both organization and structure.

CONSENSUS AND CONFLICT IN THE ORGANIZATION OF POLITICAL OPINIONS

It seems that everyone in politics claims to know and speak for public opinion. Candidates vie for "the electorate's support"; a congressman professes to "know my constituency"; and the President announces "the public is behind me." Seeking to know what citizens think about political affairs, politicians, journalists, political scientists, and "persons on the street" try to measure the "public mood." Whether the measurement be sophisticated or primitive, it imposes an organization on the opinions expressed by Americans, an organization denoting patterns of consensus and conflict.

Opinion consensus

When seemingly everyone, or a very substantial portion of the population, want to do the same thing, we speak of a consensus in their opinions. There are two general ways to see if such a consensus prevails. One way is simply to observe what people do. If the bulk of the population pays income taxes then one assumes that the mass of Americans support the tax on income as a revenue-raising device. To be sure, the consensus may stem from a fear of being taken to court for failure to pay as much as from a belief in the soundness of the income tax. Whatever its source, *mass consensus* occurs when most people act in the same manner. References to a "silent majority," "the American way," "national unity" all convey the idea of large numbers of people responding to public affairs in fairly uniform ways.

Another way to estimate whether a consensus of opinion exists is through opinion surveys. If three conditions are met in such soundings, we say there is "opinion consensus": (1) large numbers of citizens are willing to express an opinion on specific issues; (2) at least two-thirds of those expressing opinions agree on a particular viewpoint; and (3) relatively few persons—less than 20 percent—support alternative views. For example, opinion polls found a consensus on proposals to register all firearms—72 percent were in favor in 1974 (*Gallup Opinion Index*, No. 113, 1974)—and on proposals to substitute direct election for the electoral college procedure of choosing the President—73 percent were in favor in 1977 (*Gallup Opinion Index*, No. 141, 1977).

There are two forms of consensus, positive and negative. When citizens express sufficient support for programs to permit officials to act in specific ways, we have *positive consensus* (Key, 1961, pp. 28–38). *Negative consensus* is widespread opposition to an action. As the U.S. approached the end of the long and bitter Vietnam war in 1975 there was evidence of both forms of consensus: 78 percent of Americans supported using U.S. troops to evacuate Americans from South Vietnam if necessary, but 79 percent opposed giving South Vietnam a proposed $722 million in military aid (*Gallup Opinion Index*, No. 119, 1975).

Actually it is difficult to discover if a consensus exists on a political question. What people say and what they do are not always the same. Between 1975 and 1977, law enforcement officers claimed that Americans were no longer obeying 55-mile-per-hour speed limits on interstate highways; the officers offered evidence of increased violations. But in opinion polls, Americans continued to give overwhelming endorsement to the law. In fact, contrary to what law enforcement officers observed, 75 percent of Americans claimed in 1975 to be adhering more closely to the limit than they had a year earlier (*The Harris Survey*, November 13, 1975); in 1977, 76 percent said they favored the 55-mile-per-hour limit, an increase over the percentage reported in earlier surveys (*Gallup Opinion Index*, No. 142, 1977).

Opinions in conflict

When substantial blocs of people (as measured in opinion polls or election results) express differing views on matters, we have *opinion conflict*. Opinion conflict typically consists of expressions on two sides of a question (generally because pollsters put issues in either/or terms); but there may be as many positions as people are willing to express. The opinions of Blacks and Whites on racial integration illustrate a variety of views. In 1976 the Harris Survey asked a nationwide sample, "Generally speaking, do you favor full racial integration, integration in some areas of life, or separation of the races?" (*The Harris Survey*, July 8, 1976). Table 5.1 shows the various clusters of responses, both for the entire sample and among Whites and Blacks.

Opinions polarize in the process of representing conflict as debate progresses; positions harden; the alternatives are reduced; or proposals get stated in simplified, emotional appeals instead of in complex, concrete terms. However, a variety of opinion clusters, rather than polarizations, are likely to develop

TABLE 5.1
Opinions regarding integration of Whites and Blacks (in percentages)

Alternative viewpoint	Total sample (n = 1671)	Whites (n = 1382)	Blacks (n = 289)
Full integration	31	28	56
Integration in some areas	46	48	29
Separation of the races	11	12	4
Not sure	12	12	11
	100	100	100

Source: The Harris Survey, July 8, 1976.

among interested, well-informed persons who discern subtle differences in alternatives, rather than among the general community.

We have so far described both opinion consensus and conflict as the distribution of opinions that emerges when individuals express their views. But people also express opinions by being members of groups that take stands on public issues. Sometimes groups support an overall consensus in opinion (e.g., in times of crisis ethnic organizations, trade unions, industrial corporations, agricultural groups, and various other interests often set aside their differences to join in a common cause). Generally, however, the expression of opinions through groups reveals social conflict.

In recognizing the role played by groups in representing conflicting opinions it is necessary to keep in mind the following: (1) A group's position on an issue is the product of internal bargaining between proponents of differing views as they try to achieve unity before contending with rival groups; (2) opinions organized through group membership frequently mask the internal strife provoked by factions or coalitions within the group; (3) although many individual opinions can be correlated with group stands, many others cannot. We shall explore the role of organized groups in reflecting opinion conflict in greater detail in Chapter 9.

Individual expressions of conflicting opinions may appear through *opinion groupings* as well as through organized groups. Opinion groupings consist of persons sharing some attribute such as residence in the same region of the country or in a distinctly urban, suburban, or rural area; the same social class; a common religion or ethnic origin. Opinion groupings are potentially as numerous as the politically relevant divisions within the population. However, the opinions people hold seldom if ever match the social divisions of which they are members. Not all urban consumers believe that farm subsidies should be abandoned nor do all farmers think such payments are desirable. Conflicts within opinion groupings and consensus across those groupings make it risky to generalize about the predominant opinion within any social category.

THE STRUCTURE OF PUBLIC OPINION
IN CONFLICT REPRESENTATION

We can better understand how the characteristics and organization of personal political opinions relate to public opinion if we extract the patterns of opinions typical of conflict representation. Let us assume that Americans face this issue: Do you or do you not agree with a bill passed by Congress requiring all industrial plants to install antipollution devices before the end of the year?

Some Americans, the nonparticipants, will express no opinion. Two groups will have opinions. First, there are those (frequently a majority) who will "approve" or "disapprove" but are otherwise indifferent. The opinions of this *indifferent majority* are likely to be uninformed, of low intensity, and unstable.

A second group of opinion-holders will take the issue more seriously. The views of this informed minority can be designated as either intense or moderate. A particularly *intense minority* will express a definite affirmative or negative response; namely, "I approve of the legislation, because America has been entirely too complacent about its pollution problems; I am writing to my congressman to say so"; or, "I disapprove; I think the cost of installing antipollution devices in such a short time will be prohibitive." The preferences of these intense "approvers" and "disapprovers" are likely to be passionate, stable (perhaps even dogmatic), and better informed than those of the indifferent nonparticipants. Those in the informed minority with less passionate views will qualify their replies: "I favor the regulation of polluting industries, but I think the bill should go further"; or "I oppose the fouling of the air that produced this bill, but I don't think that Congress should have placed so much blame on our industries." This *moderate minority*, by striving for realistic compromises between conflicting interests, frequently plays a significant role as the controversy develops.

The typical pattern of opinions in conflict representation is depicted in Figure 5.2. The triangle represents all those expressing a political opinion, excluding the "don't know" and "no opinion" groups. At the apex are the officials who must resolve the conflict by some policy. Directly below them is the informed minority, both the intense and the moderate elements. The largest area in most disputes is occupied by the indifferent majority who have opinions, express them when asked, but are generally ignorant of the details. The people in the informed minority form an active public that both influences and is influenced by public officials who strive to build support for policies.

This triangular pattern clearly shows that give-and-take in conflict representation occurs more often between policymakers and the informed minority than between policymakers and the indifferent majority (Devine, 1970).

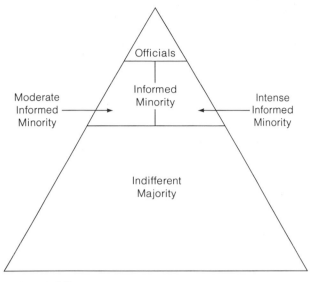

FIGURE 5.2
The Structure of Public Opinion.

Acquiring political opinions

Political opinions are a product of the interplay between personal attitudes and political stimuli. In trying to understand how Americans acquire their political opinions, a logical starting point is a discussion of how they learn their political attitudes.

Political scientists call the process of learning politically relevant attitudes *political socialization.* That process produces thoughts, feelings, and habits about the political community, the government, and political leaders; it produces both consensus and conflict. Citizens learn community loyalties that normally transcend conflicting group identifications. But they also learn loyalties to the groups they belong to, and they often identify with fellow members in disputes with other groups. Knowing more about what political attitudes people learn and how they learn them will tell us something about the sources of the agreements and disagreements that enter into conflict representation.

Like any type of learning, political socialization occurs throughout life, beginning in childhood and ending with death. Although important learning affecting later political behavior frequently occurs early in life, the early learning is usually modified in later years. If a person does not learn politically relevant attitudes early in life—say in the family or school—he or she will still have opportunities to do so in the church, on the job, from friends, through the mass media. Whenever socializing experiences take place, they need not be overtly political to have political consequences in the future. Socializing influences are cumulative so that the attitudes people learn often reinforce one another.

THE KEY POLITICAL ATTITUDES AMERICANS LEARN

The principal attitudes acquired through political socialization pertain to the political community, the political process, political leaders, civic obligation, and group identifications.

The political community

One of the first things a child learns in our society is to identify with the political community. Symbols such as the flag, the national anthem, the Statue of Liberty, and folk heroes reinforce the emotional attachment. The child of five is scarcely aware of any flag other than the Stars and Stripes. As one child put it: "God made the flag so they'd know who was the good people" (Weinstein, 1958, p. 171). Studies reveal that more than 80 percent of children in primary grades agree that "the American flag is the best flag in the world" (Hess and Torney, 1967). No less important in creating a sense of attachment to the American community is the enduring respect children acquire for selected historical personages, especially Abraham Lincoln and George Washington.

For vast numbers of Americans, at least those reared in a middle-class environment, this early link forged between child and community endures and only partially erodes when it meets the frustrations and responsibilities of adult citizenship. In the view of some authorities, "this bond is possibly the most basic and essential aspect of socialization into involvement with the political life of the nation" (Hess and Torney, 1967, p. 213). Politicians recognize this and capitalize upon it. For instance, in the 1970s as political cynicism increased and trust in government declined (see Chapter 4), one relatively unknown candidate for the presidency, Jimmy Carter, reiterated throughout his 1976 campaign in presidential primaries that America had not failed, rather its leaders had failed America: "I just want to see this country once again as pure, and honest, and decent, and truthful, and fair, and confident, and idealistic, and compassionate—as filled with love—as are the American people."

The political process

The ambivalent views about politics expressed by American adults (see Chapters 2 and 4) have traditionally been less characteristic of children. For example, studies conducted in the mid-1960s of the political attitudes of White children in the elementary grades generally found that the children displayed substantial trust in government and accepted the view that government is a necessary part of society. If Americans later develop discontent and a desire for change, their later feelings are built upon an early base of high regard for government—so went the inferences drawn from the studies (Easton and Dennis, 1965, 1969).

In the late 1960s and early 1970s the bitterness surrounding the deep divisions over the legitimacy of U.S. involvement in Vietnam produced disillusionment with government among many Americans. Moreover, the Watergate scandal of the early 1970s raised added questions about the trustworthy character of politics and politicians. Did these events leave their mark upon children as well as upon adults? There is evidence that they did. One 1974 study, for example, examined the images children in grades four through six have of government and compared the findings with the results of a similar investigation conducted in 1962. A comparison of responses across the years with respect to three statements is revealing:

- Whereas 81 percent agreed in 1962 that "what goes on in government is all for the best," only 37 percent agreed in 1974.
- A majority agreed in 1962 that government "would always (or almost always) want to help me if I needed it"; only one-fourth felt that way in 1974.
- In 1962 about six in every ten children thought government "almost never" or "rarely" makes mistakes; only about two in ten believed that in 1974.

The study noted "We can conclude at this point that Watergate and other recent political experiences of Americans have taken a substantial toll on the child's positive feelings generated toward the government" and "historical conditions thus clearly affect the levels of childhood idealization" (Dennis and Webster, 1975, p. 400).

Political leaders

The notions of both "community" and "government" are abstractions beyond the intellectual grasp of most young children. For many youngsters, these abstractions are symbolized as personal figures that the children can relate to easily. Prior to the 1970s the evidence from a variety of studies of political socialization was fairly clear on one point: The American child's image of "government" is confined mainly to the President; and the child's idea of "law" is represented by the policeman. This general pattern probably still holds; what no longer seems as clear is just how children learn to regard these two key political figures.

Studies of children in grades two through eight conducted before the 1970s generally concurred that young Americans expressed faith, respect, and warmth for the President and believed him to be a harder worker, more honest, more friendly, and more knowledgeable than most men; indeed a majority of second graders labeled him the "best" man "in the world" (Easton and Dennis, 1969, pp. 165–245). Recent studies indicate that children in elementary and high schools during the early 1970s not only responded to the events surrounding the Watergate scandal by evaluating President Richard Nixon in a very poor light, but also carried their negative outlook over to their assessments of the Presidency and of government in general. For example, one study revealed that in the 12-year period between 1962 and 1974, the proportion of positive images of the President among children in grades two through six declined sharply. In 1962, 50–67 percent of a sample of sixth graders thought that the President was "my favorite" or "almost my favorite of all" persons, that he would "always want to help me if needed" (or "almost always"), that he "knows more than anyone" or "most" people, and that he "always" or "almost always" keeps his promises. By 1974, in a comparable sample of six graders, only about 33 percent thought the President knowledgable, only 25 percent thought him reliable, and only 10 percent said he was either helpful or "my favorite" or "almost my favorite of all" (Dennis and Webster, 1975). Negative evaluations of Nixon were also related to a rise in political cynicism among school children, although it is difficult to predict what effect children's views of the Presidency will have upon their thoughts about government as they grow older (Rodgers and Lewis, 1975).

Like the President, the uniformed local policeman is one of the first political figures that enters the child's awareness. The policeman is probably the first political figure the child actually sees; most certainly it is a figure impressed upon the child by books, films, and television. Early in life both Black and White children learn to regard the policeman as dependable and trustworthy; this respect declines little among Whites over the years but erodes substantially among Black children (Greenberg, 1970).

The sources of the child's early views of political leaders are not easy to trace. Indirectly, of course, the mass media play an important role, something we shall examine later. In addition, either of two varieties of early direct experience with "nonpolitical" leaders may be important. A child who receives benevolent treatment from his parents may simply transfer his love for those figures of authority to political leaders. Alternatively, a child may be impressed with the coercive quality of authority—as with parental punishment—and learn to respect political leaders because of a fear of disobeying. Political scientists are divided on what actually happens (Greenstein, 1960, 1975; Jaros, Hirsch, and Fleron, 1968). Either way, there is a strong tendency among American children to personalize authority and to think of government as consisting of dominant political figures such as the President, governor, mayor, or policeman.

Civic obligation

American public education emphasizes citizenship training to instill civic awareness and duty. Whether it is primarily the school that gets the message across is uncertain, but the evidence is that early in life a large number of Americans acquire at least a vague sense of the civic duty to take part in politics. But young people are more apt to see the obligation as a passive rather than an active one and to focus upon their duty to participate as an individual rather than to join with others. By the eighth grade, children believe that it is every citizen's obligation to take part in politics by being interested in current events and voting; both are modes of passive, individual effort. Far fewer acquire the view that they have an obligation to join political organizations and actively try to influence government officials (Hess and Torney, 1967, p. 67). As formal education unfolds, the sense of civic obligation increases. Among college-educated persons, civic awareness is very high. But as we saw in Chapter 4, civic ideals and behavior in civics do not always coincide: As in other political arenas, more citizens feel they should participate than do.

Group identifications

Positive feelings toward the community, the government, figures of authority, and civic obligation are one source of political consensus. If time or events do not eclipse them, these sentiments help to moderate conflicts. But such consensus grows problematic, for Americans today are not as prone to acquire as positive a sense of government and politicians as they once did; moreover, by learning to identify with conflicting groups, Americans challenge political consensus by pushing their special political interests. What are the most salient group identifications that affect the political opinions of Americans?

Party identification is one form of group loyalty that many Americans learn early in life. Perhaps as early as seven years of age, a majority of American children think of themselves as having some preference for the Republicans or Democrats. And, although since 1970 relatively higher proportions of Americans have declined to identify with a political party (see Chapter 4), about 70 percent are still inclined to do so (Dennis and McCrone, 1970). Moreover, as we shall see in Chapter 7, this party identification is important to Americans as they decide who to vote for in elections; normally, well over two-thirds of those calling themselves Republicans or Democrats end up voting for their party's candidate in presidential elections.

Religious identifications also appear quite early. Nine out of every ten Americans acquire a religious preference by age 18, although many become less strongly attached to it as they grow older. Partisan and religious preferences frequently complement, or at least seldom contradict one another. But when the two do conflict, the less intense loyalty—often that of party—yields. Such was the case in the presidential election of 1960 when the Democratic candidate John Kennedy could not attract the votes of many Southern Protestants because of their reluctance to vote for a Catholic for President.

Ideological identifications are relevant political sentiments acquired by many Americans but it is hard to say just how important they are in conflict representation. There is considerable controversy among political scientists regarding the influence of ideological loyalties on political behavior. On the one side are those who argue that Americans are basically nonideological in outlook. They may classify themselves as "left," as did 27 percent in 1975, or "right," as did 36 percent (*Gallup Opinion Index*, No. 123, 1975); but these inclinations mean little to them and tell us little about how they perceive a wide range of diverse issues and novel political situations. Other political observers disagree. They point out, for example, that youthful voters have ideological orientations and are more likely than older persons to be ideological liberals regardless of party (Pomper, 1975). Advocates of this view stress the increasing ideological flavor of the response of Americans to presidential elections (A. H. Miller et al., 1976). We will not attempt to resolve this dispute here but will consider it in more detail in Chapter 7. For now it suffices to say that relatively few Americans acquire loyalty to a well-articulated ideology through political socialization.

The child learns a sense of *social status* that may produce conflict with others. Social class perspectives affect participation (as we saw in Chapter 4) as well as the direction of partisan loyalties (Chapter 7).

Finally, children learn to recognize *racial differences* along with a sense of their related social and political consequences. Although there has been a major redressing of inequities in the social and political relationships between Blacks and Whites in this country, the statement made by one young Black over a quarter of a century ago is still apt: "The people that are white, they can go up. The people that are brown, they have to go down" (Goodman, 1952, p. 28).

WHERE AMERICANS LEARN THEIR POLITICAL ATTITUDES

Where and how do people acquire their political thoughts, feelings, and habits? Most political learning results from a combination of a person's (1) genetic capacities for learning, (2) gradual physical-mental-emotional growth, and

(3) exposure to politics (Merelman, 1969). As far as a person's capacities and maturity permit, he or she reproduces in him- or herself the beliefs, feelings, and actions exhibited by real-life models (parents, friends, and others) or symbolic models (fictional persons, television figures, or well-known persons with whom one has no direct contact). Viewed as a psychological process of development, then, learning involves modeling: a person observes, compares, and either copies or tries to be different from others (Bandura, 1971; Bandura and Walters, 1963).

Many socializing agencies influence a person's political attitudes from early childhood on. The general pattern is clear: The family sets political socialization in motion; as the child grows older, parental influence decreases and school, social groups, occupation, religion, and the mass media gradually replace the family. Sometimes new experiences reinforce the political convictions acquired in childhood; but as contacts with the social environment widen, exposure to conflicting views sets up forces that often modify attitudes learned earlier in life.

The family as socializer into politics

In an earlier era when families were more closely knit, most Americans did not go to college, and the mass media were less pervasive in people's lives than they are today, the family was the most influential of socializing agencies (Gillespie and Allport, 1955, p. 8). Times have changed and family dominance has diminished. Nevertheless, parents are still important models for their children; they filter influences from the community at large and transmit political views to their offspring. Although children's political attitudes still generally conform to those of their parents, a correspondence in the political outlooks of parent and child is in no way assured. What characteristics of family socialization help determine whether a child is, or is not, merely a carbon copy of his or her parents?

PARENTAL TREATMENT.   The way parents treat their children makes a major difference in political socialization. During the late 1960s when militant students were causing major disruptions on college campuses, a provocative study explored the differences in the ways in which groups of young college students had been treated by their families in childhood (Block, Haan, and Smith, 1969). Participants in the study were classified in one of five groups: (1) inactives, who reported no participation in political or social organizations and activities; (2) conventionalists, who were members of sororities and fraternities involved in relatively little political activity—the traditional "Joe College" stereotype; (3) constructivists, who worked in social service projects but participated infrequently in organized protests; (4) activists, who protested their dissatisfaction with the status quo but also joined in social service projects to correct perceived ills; and (5) dissenters, who participated in politics primarily through organized protests. The differences in the types of treatment these students had received from their parents were clear.

- Inactives' parents were anxious about their children's health and welfare but insisted upon obedience, conformity, and docility to parental demands.
- Conventionalists' parents adhered to traditional social values (responsibility, conformity, achievement, and obedience), demanded socially appropriate behavior and achievements, and made those demands clear by invoking physical or psychological punishment.
- Constructivists' parents emphasized discipline, achievement, and dependability, restricted self-expression, and used nonphysical punishment; they were more warmly regarded by their children than the parents of conventionalists.
- Activists' parents encouraged children to be independent and responsible —as did parents of constructivists and conventionalists, encouraged self-expression short of physical aggression, and placed less emphasis on discipline; parent-child relations were considered less than good by activists.
- Dissenters' parents were inconsistent in their child-rearing practices, permissive in certain areas and highly restrictive in others; they emphasized independence and early maturity less but at the same time pressed for achievement and encouraged competition; parent-child relations were evaluated negatively by dissenters.

This study reached two major conclusions relevant to our discussion of political learning: (1) Dissenters whose parents had inconsistently combined permissive and restrictive practices were in far greater rebellion against parental attitudes than others; (2) it is a mistake to lump together all student protestors as products of a permissive upbringing (an argument made in the late 1960s by many people trying to place the blame for unrest on college campuses somewhere): Activists also protested, but not out of a need to express adolescent rebellion against all authority.

PARENTAL ROLES. The relative dominance of the mother or father within the family influences the child's political attitudes. Most children grow up in homes where the two parents share the same political views. In these families, the mother plays a key role in transmitting that consensus to the child. Where parents differ, the father *tends* to be more influential, but children do not gravitate in disproportionate numbers to his preferences. Parental roles influence how interested children get in politics as well as political preferences: Children from mother-dominated families, especially males, are less likely to be politically interested and engage in politics than those from father-dominated families (Jennings and Niemi, 1971). Children who do not develop their political interest before leaving the family nest have more opportunity to be influenced by other agencies (school, friends, etc.) whose outlooks may conflict with parental convictions.

The family is crucial in orienting children toward political parties. Most pairs of parents share partisan loyalties and most children adopt the partisan affiliation of their parents. Deviation from the party attachment of their parents is higher among children when the parents are "weak" rather than "strong" party identifiers. Where the party loyalties of the parents differ, the mother's partisanship is somewhat more influential. However, adults with only a grade school education and working class adults are more likely to have the party affiliation of their father than that of their mother.

The extent to which parents are interested in politics at all leaves a mark on the child. If politics is not important in the family, the political views of the parents are not a relevant target for juvenile protest or rebellion. If politics is important, however, the child may adopt political convictions contrary to those of his parents as a way of protesting against their authority (Langton, 1969).

SOCIAL MOBILITY.   Once children grow to adulthood and have a job and family of their own, their social interests may diverge from those of their parents because of an upward or downward change in social class. We say such people are socially mobile. Social mobility often includes the learning of political attitudes different from those acquired in the parental family. Those who improve their social position are likely to be less interested in politics, less liberal on questions of foreign policy and civil liberties, more liberal on economic questions, and more often Democrats than those above them on the social ladder. The downwardly mobile—those whose social position is lower than that of their parents—are more interested in politics, more conservative on economic questions, more liberal on foreign policy and civil liberties, and more often Republicans than persons below them on the social ladder. The socially mobile, then, change their attitudes in a direction appropriate to their new status so that their views are intermediate between those of their family and those fitting their new station in life.

THE SPIRIT AND EVENTS OF THE TIMES.   Whether a child conforms to or rebels against his or her parents' political views (that is, whether or not there is a "generation gap") also depends upon how much the political environment the child grows up in differs from the times that existed when his or her parents formed their basic political attitudes. Moreover, it is possible that at the time the child is growing up, the spirit and events of the times may reduce the possibilities of a parental-child split by affecting both generations in the same way. This is what a major study that compared the views of high school seniors with those of their parents found (Jennings and Niemi, 1975). Based upon interviews with a representative cross-section of students and their parents in 1965 and then again in 1973, the study revealed that across the eight-year span both parents and students responded to the political times in similar ways. For example, among both generations there was a marked decline in political trust and a parallel rise in political cynicism. Changes in the voting inclinations of the two generations were also very similar. The study concluded: "The flow of the two generations over time has, if anything, worked to bring them closer together now than they were eight years earlier. . . . To the extent that differences increased, they consisted of the rising generation's having emerged with slightly to moderately more liberal political views, greater independence of partisanship, and higher Democratic voting behavior. Of the other orientations . . . the pattern is either one of little change over time or of visible convergence" (p. 1335).

Regardless of how much they copy the outlook of their parents, children acquire their initial sense of political awareness in the family. The more politically active Americans have parents who voted regularly, discussed politics, were politically informed, and attempted to exert political influence.

Schools and politics

It is difficult to gauge to what degree formal education affects political attitudes. Still, it is possible to consider the effects of each level of education—primary, secondary, and college.

PRIMARY SCHOOLING.   The years of elementary education give each child the opportunity to compare personal views with those of peers. School environments that include people from diverse social classes expose students to a range of opinions different from their family's convictions. Children do not influence one another equally, however: Lower-class children tend to learn the values of children from higher-class backgrounds. The consequence is a resocializing of lower-class and working-class students in the direction of more conventional American middle-class norms, including political attitudes.

This result is cited by many who advocate racially balanced schools as a way of reshaping the motivation of children from minority groups to improve their learning and school performance. The sources and themes of disagreement with that position are many. One camp says that since home and neighborhood environments are the major determinants, the school cannot be expected to offset their influence. A counterargument is that it is wrong to assume that middle-class norms are superior or desirable; such beliefs can lead only to the alienation of the lower class, which feels rejected and despised. Readers should have no difficulty in fleshing out a list of disputants and themes for one of the most controversial domestic political issues of our day: the meaning and extent of racial desegregation in the schools and whether and how to achieve it.

SECONDARY SCHOOLING. Junior and senior high schools provide added opportunities for political socialization. Maturing includes an increasing ability to integrate diverse attitudes with consistent outlooks. Textbook knowledge and information about current events intrude upon one's political views. A systematic effort at citizenship training occurs. Finally, newly acquired secondary school friends are more likely than primary school friends to have outlooks different from those taught by the family.

The attempt to indoctrinate students with democratic values is undertaken in American high schools in "citizenship" courses, but the effect of the civics curriculum varies with the social background of the student. It is most effective for children from lower- and working-class families, who are more susceptible to political influence because of the limited political interest, information, and involvement in their family environment. Middle- and upper-class students enter high school aware of how active political participation can contribute to their lives, so that formal courses may be less important in shaping their political attitudes (Jennings and Niemi, 1974).

COLLEGE. The socializing effect of college on political attitudes, which is probably quite large for many students, results from the young adult's exposure to increasingly diverse acquaintances, more and more political information, and the opportunity—presented, by definition, to students reading this book—to compare the world "as it is" with the picture presented in the classroom. A college education increases students' tolerance for diversity of opinion and social nonconformity, heightens their sense of civic awareness and competence, improves their aptitude in expressing informed political opinions, increases the probability of voting, and lessens partisan loyalties. High school graduates who go to college already differ from schoolmates who terminate their formal education with high school graduation. Hence, differences in the political attitudes of adults with high school and college educations may be attributed both to lingering differences in social class and to the college experience itself (Langton, 1969).

To the degree that the college experience does help crystallize political attitudes, the influence is more likely to be that of the general college environment than of college teachers. At least, few college students think their views have been influenced by their teachers. In a 1975 survey of the political views of college students, three of every four replied no when asked whether college teachers had influenced their political views; of the one-fourth minority who thought they had been so influenced, 21 percent thought it was toward liberal views, 6 percent toward conservative. Interestingly enough, however, college students do not believe both liberal and conservative viewpoints are given equal treatment in the schools; a majority think conservative viewpoints are usually stressed and only one-fourth think the slant is liberal (*Gallup Opinion Index*, No. 123, 1975).

What are the political attitudes of college students? For one thing, the students are not as partisan as people in the general public. Figure 5.3 shows that the proportion of students who call themselves "independent" rather than identifying with either major party increased from the mid-1960s to the mid-1970s. Compare the 1975 statistics with the 21 percent of the general public calling themselves Republican, 44 percent Democrat, and 35 percent independent of party affiliation. Those who are college graduates, however, tend to take on some degree of partisanship; in 1975, 27 percent of the college-educated identified themselves as Republican, 29 percent as Democrat, and 44 percent as "independent."

Most college students today are also not very radical. The great majority reject far left or far right political positions. In 1975 only 6 percent classified themselves as "far left" and 3 percent classified themselves as "far right"; 36 percent saw themselves as in the "center" of the political spectrum, 19 percent as "right-of-center," and 34 percent as "left-of-center" (*Gallup Opinion Index*, No. 123, 1975). Moreover, today's college students are not very militant on the whole; two-thirds reject violence as an effective way of achieving political and social improvements.

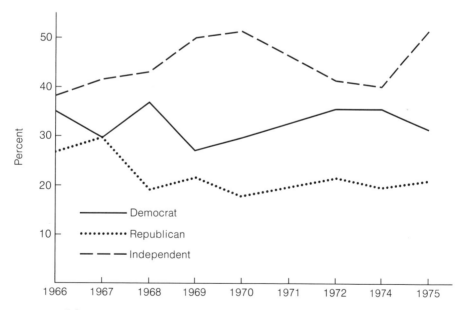

FIGURE 5.3

The Political Affiliation of College Students, 1966–1975. [*Source:* Prepared from data reported in *Gallup Opinion Index*, Report No. 123, 1975.]

The influence of social groups

A person who joins social groups encounters more diverse norms and values than are usually present in the family. A child's peer groups (the circle of friends and people he or she feels close to) are important socializing influences. Peer groups take on particular importance in the adolescent years. In some of their political views—generally those unrelated to partisan matters—students frequently resemble their friends more than their parents. This compatibility among peers is produced simply through friendship rather than because the friends come from similar social backgrounds (Sebert, 1974). Yet, social backgrounds do play a role. A middle-class child often reinforces the middle-class attitudes and values first acquired in the family. Children raised in ghetto or poverty areas do not learn such middle-class attitudes; studies indicate that they grow up with negative views toward political institutions and leaders not typical of middle-class children (Hirsh, 1971).

SECONDARY GROUPS. Voluntary associations and various civic clubs also help to create and reinforce a person's views, because one usually joins secondary groups whose aims and attitudes are congenial with learned predispositions. Frequently, however, people join particular groups to improve themselves economically or socially. When groups enforce conformity to group norms, people are reluctant to challenge the dominant views for fear of social ostracism. Generally, people adjust their attitudes to those of a group if they feel strongly about being accepted as equals and have a strong need to be liked, are in frequent contact with the group, find important issues discussed in the group, have no alternative way of gathering political information and defining political positions, and are swayed by the arguments of group leaders. If they belong to groups that hold conflicting positions on issues, people may respond to the cross-pressures on themselves by choosing one group over another, attempting to strike a compromise that permits them to stay in all of the conflicting groups, ignoring the issue in dispute, ignoring the conflict, or withdrawing from all groups if the controversy gets too intolerable.

Occupation and political attitudes

A job influences political attitudes in several ways. Work associates are a group that one wants to join; the day-to-day functions of a job therefore exercise a powerful political influence by setting the agenda for political discussion. Jobs that require a great deal of interaction with the public (sales, advertising, and service occupations) are much more likely to bring the jobholder into contact with politics than are isolated occupations like farming. In some states, some jobholders (civil servants) are prohibited by law from engaging in partisan politics.

As we saw in Chapter 4, jobs that bring opportunities to take part in decisions affecting an organization, a company, a union, or fellow workers— even though the participation may not be directly political—demonstrate favorably the usefulness of participation in civic affairs. Although such occupational influences come later in life than do the opportunities to take part in family or school affairs, they come precisely when the worker sees the connection between politics and his or her economic improvement.

Religion and political attitudes

Although more than 90 percent of the adult population identify themselves as either Protestant, Catholic, or Jewish, the number who actually go to church is much lower. Nonetheless, organized religion is still an important factor in the political socialization of Americans. The dignity of the individual and the value of moral behavior are only two examples of politically relevant teaching by organized religion. Conversely, religion may also reinforce a dogmatic attitude on some questions; a study of the relationship between Christian beliefs and anti-Semitism indicated that dogmatism, if not tempered by religious liberalism, produced intolerant attitudes toward religious minorities such as the Jews (Glock and Stark, 1967).

The conservative influence of many churches derives from absolutist doctrines that are not always congenial to democratic politics and lead to a preference for the status quo. Any social or political perspective that characterizes a religious body can affect the attitudes its members learn and influence their assessment of political issues. Evaluation of policies toward crime, the death penalty, alcoholism, gambling, divorce, birth control, abortion, communism, education, and numerous other matters is colored by religious convictions as well as other attitudes.

The mass media and political socialization

Because they are a primary source of information about the world, the mass media affect a person's outlook. No longer is a citizen limited to reading about an event or faced with only still black-and-white photographs. The same technology that brings Americans the moon and Mars from outer space provides, in vivid color on the television screen, coverage of wars, elections, assassinations, and other political matters. The mass media are agenda-setters (McCombs, 1976) and awareness of the items on the current political agenda—campaigns, presidential trips to foreign lands, riots, threats of nuclear war, hopes of peace—comes from watching television, listening to "spot" news on the radio, scanning the headlines, or reading a favorite magazine. How important is this bombardment from the communications media in political socialization?

First, it is clear that the mass media—primarily television and newspapers —are the principle source of a young person's political information. The young child first begins to use the mass media as a source of political information during the elementary school years by viewing national news programs. A survey of 700 school children showed, for example, that one-third of younger children and two-thirds of older children watched the adult-oriented national newscasts in the evening, and a majority of all children viewed the Saturday morning "In the News" segments geared especially for child audiences (Atkin, 1975).

Second, paying attention to the public affairs media increases the political knowledge of young people. A survey of a cross-section of 1300 adolescents during the 1968 presidential election campaign suggested media exposure was directly linked to political knowledge: the greater the exposure the more learned. But the kind of media exposure also makes a difference: Following public affairs through the print media (newspapers, magazines, books, etc.) probably increases knowledge of politics more than does exposure to TV and radio (Chaffee et al., 1970).

Third, young people perceive that the media have an important influence on their opinions about political matters. Researchers asked students to rate the importance of four primary socializing agents upon their political learning. They rated the mass media most important, substantially above teachers, parents, and friends (Chaffee et al., 1970). Whether the mass media are actually as influential as young people seem to think, however, depends upon what aspect of opinions we are talking about. The mass media clearly affect the political information, knowledge, and beliefs of young people. It is not as certain that media exposure influences their political values (i.e., views on issues, preferences for political candidates, and feelings of trust or cynicism about politics). Nor is it at all certain that following politics in the mass media has anything to do with how politically active young people are; in fact, there is as yet little clear evidence that the mass media affect overt political activity such as taking part in political campaigns, contacting public officials, and joining political groups.

In addition to their variable influence on political beliefs, values, and behavior, the mass media help shape people's expectations of what can and will happen in politics. In preparing the public for a major news event such as a national political convention, a series of presidential primaries, debates between presidential contenders, or the outcome of a major election, the news media give people a background against which they expect events to occur. In viewing, hearing, or reading what happens, the majority of viewers and listeners interpret events from the perspective provided by the media. Rarely do most Americans break out of the context within which the media places them, so that they can reach independent interpretations.

Television is certainly one of the most important of media technologies shaping the political socialization and opinions of Americans. If television does influence our view of the political world, then that view will be only as clear as the presentation of politics on television. But politics is scarcely as important to most citizens as professional and collegiate sports, current fashions, the amorous adventures of popular entertainers, advice to the lovelorn, or pure fantasy. Time and space limitations of the electronic and printed media reduce coverage of politics to superficiality and contrivance, accenting sensational events and controversial personalities rather than subtle details in political issues. Despite claims of objectivity, the content of the news media—notably of network news programs—simply is not and cannot be a comprehensive or impartial look at "the way it is." By defining the world outside of our personal, direct experience, the media of mass communication play a key role in how we learn the "pictures in our heads" of that political world (Lippmann, 1922).

Summary

A point made earlier warrants repeating: Although people acquire significant and politically relevant attitudes in childhood, changes in attitudes occur throughout life, and no person is destined to continue forever viewing government in ways dictated in youth. Moreover, attitudes do not dictate political opinions; they are but one element in the formation of opinions. The diverse and frequently contradictory appeals of leaders as well as the personal predispositions of followers also affect opinions. Attitudes are tendencies of human action but make no single line of action inevitable.

The big issues

Americans respond politically to those things that interest and worry them most. These are the issues they voice opinions about through conflict representation. Asked what worries them about their lives, they cite health, living standards, children, housing, and general happiness. When asked what worries them about America, they say war and peace on the international front, bread and butter on the domestic (Cantril, 1965; Free and Cantril, 1967; Watts and Free, 1973, 1975).

To examine the biggest issues on the minds of Americans in recent decades, we turn to data supplied by the *Gallup Poll* in nationwide surveys conducted since the 1930s. The pollsters asked Americans, "What do you think is the most important problem facing America today?" Figure 5.4 summarizes the proportions of Americans naming problems in five categories during each of five presidential administrations: those of Franklin D. Roosevelt, 1937–1944; Harry S. Truman, 1945–1952; Dwight D. Eisenhower, 1953–1960; John F. Kennedy and Lyndon B. Johnson, 1961–1968; and Richard M. Nixon and Gerald R. Ford, 1969–1976. What patterns emerge?

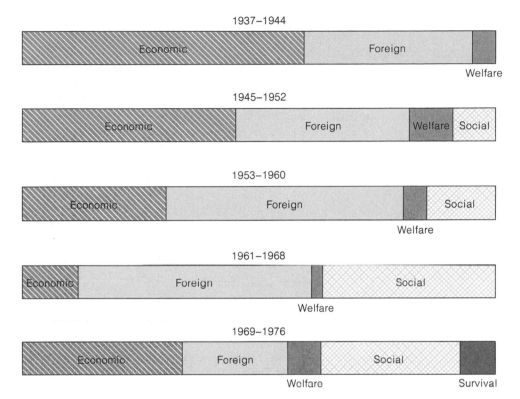

FIGURE 5.4

Salient Issues in American Political Opinion, 1937–1976. [*Source:* Constructed from data reported in Gallup, G., *The Gallup Poll: Public Opinion 1935–1971.* New York: Random House, 1972; *Gallup Opinion Index*, Report Nos. 113–137, 1972–1976; *Gallup Opinion Index*, Report No. 149, 1977.]

First, Americans are nearly always worried about economic issues. These issues include inflation, recession, and depression; whether or not a person can find work; how much money there is to spend; what it should be spent for; and how much money a person must give the government in taxes. Americans have worried about these matters often: in the economic depressions of the 1890s and again in the 1930s, in recessions like that in the 1950s, in the inflationary trends of the late 1960s and the 1970s.

Second, Americans show a continuing concern for foreign issues that rises primarily when American armed forces are directly involved in a war such as World War II, the Korean conflict, and the Vietnam war. Survey respondents considered all other foreign issues—conflicts in the Middle East, racial tensions in Africa, improvement of relations with the Soviet Union and the People's Republic of China, foreign aid, and American connections with the United

Nations—less important than "keeping out of war." Aside from concerns over war, international issues seldom touch Americans as closely as do economic and social concerns.

Third, as Figure 5.4 indicates, social issues began to play a prominent part in American thinking in the 1960s, accounting for more than one-third of the concerns voiced by Americans in surveys. Social issues include (1) the crime rate and attendant fears of threats to life and property; (2) the racial question, with some Whites resisting what they perceive as the too fast pace of integration—especially when it comes to the busing of school children—and Blacks resenting that the pace is not fast enough; (3) morality and resulting worries about the decline in public morals indicated by widespread sales of pornography, permissive sexual codes, decline in church attendance; (4) the drug culture—the use and abuse of alcohol, marijuana, and other drugs and the accompanying controversies over legalizing sales and the most effective treatment of habitual drug users; (5) and a cluster of issues surrounding changing mores—women's liberation, treatment of children, abortion, the right to life, and the right to die.

Fourth, there has been a discernible, although not major, concern over welfare issues in the past four decades. These include expenditures for public education, old-age assistance programs, medical care programs, the fight against poverty, and others. Although large portions of Americans do not express concern over these matters, interests do tend to organize around them; welfare issues have provided the basis for some of the key disputes that have captured the attention of policymakers.

Finally, in recent years Americans have displayed a growing concern with issues of survival: (1) how to protect the environment from threats of pollution and overpopulation and (2) how to conserve the nation's dwindling energy resources.

THE ROLE OF THE MEDIA AND ORGANIZED INTERESTS

In thinking about these five key areas of concern to Americans since the 1930s, we should keep a couple of points in mind. First, at any given time Americans worry most about the issues most publicized in the news. If there is widespread news coverage of urban violence or unemployment or rising prices or an oil embargo, Americans are likely to talk about it. In short, the issues on the minds of Americans are frequently those publicized by political leaders and the news media, a phenomenon we examine more closely in Chapter 6. Second, even if only a small proportion of those surveyed cite a specific worry, conflicts in that area are not necessarily unknown to policymakers. The disputes that reach policymakers depend not only upon people's interests but also upon how opinion organizes around these issues. Frequently, an opinion

expressed by a small number of Americans who form a cohesive group has influence quite out of proportion to the group's size. Minorities provoked civil rights legislation by their demonstrations in the 1950s and 1960s. To understand more fully how conflicts get represented by political opinions, we need to know more about how opinions and interests are organized, a topic we consider in detail in Chapter 9.

Public opinion and public policy

To what degree are the views expressed by people reflected in what policy-makers do? What are the "opinions held by private persons which governments find it prudent to heed" (Key, 1961, p. 14)? The answers to these questions depend ultimately upon the relationship between public opinion and policy-making. In some instances that relationship is very close; in others it is remote. "Welfare legislation concerning minimum wages, social security, medical programs are examples of issues on which public opinion has preceded and prompted government action" (Simon, 1974, p. 222). Yet, a government that has responded to public views on welfare matters has been less responsive in other areas. For instance, opinion polls consistently indicate that Americans favor strict controls on the sale and purchase of handguns and clearly approve licensing of gun carriers—77 percent of respondents favored licensing in a 1976 survey—but Congress has been reluctant to follow the dictates of public opinion and pass strict licensing and registration laws (*Gallup Opinion Index*, No. 129, 1976).

THE EFFECT OF WHO AND HOW

The fidelity of the relationship between public opinion and public policy depends upon a number of factors. Two that are particularly important are *who* expresses the opinions and the *structure* of the opinions. Generally, public policy corresponds more closely to the opinions of persons attentive to and active in politics than to those of citizens who are uninterested and passive. In part this is because the activists press their demands upon public officials; as a result, policy leaders are more likely to concur with what the active political participants define as problems requiring official action (Verba and Nie, 1972). In addition, since they are in contact with attentives, public officials may persuade them to accept their policy decisions (Devine, 1970, Ch. 7). Finally, as we shall elaborate in Chapter 9, when opinions expressed to policymakers emanate from organized interests, rather than from private persons acting alone, officials are more likely to pay attention.

But policymakers are aware of mass opinions as well as the views of activists, attentives, and organized interests. They are especially likely to respond to mass opinions when the issue involved is highly controversial and one side in the dispute mobilizes support from critical segments of the policymaker's constitutency, that is, those whose support he considers essential to staying in office. For example, in the early 1970s many members of Congress who had opposed attempts to restrict busing as a means of promoting racial integration eased their opposition in the face of opinion polls showing that three-fourths of Americans were against busing, including almost one-half of Blacks. The congresspeople were not alone in reading the public pulse: President Richard Nixon in 1972 attacked busing and proposed legislation against it; upon taking office in 1974 President Gerald Ford also outlined his opposition to busing.

THE ABSENCE OF DOMINANT ISSUES

In short, if opinion on a salient issue cuts across various population groupings, policymakers take notice. The structure of opinion can be important in another respect. Some issues divide people along social, economic, and partisan lines—the haves from the have-nots, the rich from the poor, Republicans from Democrats. Clear-cut divisions in the community provide reasonably clear-cut conflicts for officials to represent in policymaking. Any policy adopted is likely to reflect either a response to one of the contending interests or a compromise between them. In any case, conflicting views are always well enough articulated to be taken into account in fashioning policies. In contemporary American politics, however, there is evidence that no central dominant issue or series of issues exists to provide clear-cut alignments between competing groups. In the absence of dominant issues and visible structures—that is, under conditions one writer calls the "contemporary disarray" of public opinion—public officials find it difficult to discern which social disputes should take precedence and which views demand representation (Dawson, 1973).

Representing political opinions

By expressing political opinions, the most widespread form of political participation in our society, citizens let public officials know what is on their minds. However, expressed opinions do not always represent interest conflicts accurately. Several reasons lie behind this distortion.

THE COSTS OF EXPRESSING OPINIONS

Most political opinions expressed by individuals do not represent social conflicts nor are they intended to influence policymaking; instead, they represent private, personal interests flowing from the desire to relate to other people and to relieve inner tensions. Expressed opinions often have little to do with the subtleties of the issues. Opinions are uninformed; people choose to be ignorant about most political matters and to be informed about only a few. The indifferent majority generally pays little attention to politics. Is it because Americans are basically apathetic, passive, insensitive people who do not want to govern themselves? We think not. Too often those who castigate citizens for their political apathy forget that expressing informed opinions about politics is hard work. It is hard because it takes time and effort to gather and understand relevant facts about issues, especially when significant details are not readily available in the news. It takes time and energy away from private affairs to think about public issues and perhaps requires the sacrifice of financial gains, leisure activities, and more rewarding ventures. And, it is threatening. It takes courage to open our minds to information that clashes with our attitudes and is at odds with our current, secure understanding of things; it takes courage to pronounce informed views if these antagonize our friends; it takes courage to assimilate significant facts that muddy clear-cut alternatives with confusing ambiguity.

THE DISTORTING EFFECTS OF POLITICAL SOCIALIZATION

People normally learn politically relevant attitudes before they acquire the political information and knowledge to support them. Their attitudes color both their perception of government and their political judgment. Learned political attitudes can thus be a source of distortion in conflict representation. We know that the politically relevant attitudes American children learn are strongly influenced by family, schools, and peer groups. For the most part, these childhood attitudes reflect a positive acceptance of the community, the government, authority figures, and middle-class values. The child acquires a sense that he or she should influence policymaking, but primarily in passive ways—by voting, by affiliating with political parties, and by being interested in politics. Most children learn that politics involves individual effort (loyalty, obligation, responsibility), but they learn little about organized influence, how they can join with others to take part in groups. Small wonder that they retire to the relative peace of political indifference, responding to political events with their preferences for the status quo and individual action and perhaps condemning those who both dissent from the way things are and organize to change it.

Political socialization helps distort conflict representation in another way. Children are exposed not only to an overemphasis upon individual ways of expressing opinions; they may fail to learn that it is worthwhile to express opinions at all. Family background, education, and occupation encourage some citizens to take part in politics, but discourage many others. Children whose parents insisted upon conformity, docility, obedience, and punishment; the young who do not go beyond high school; the ghetto Black; the impoverished in both urban and rural America; the worker with no control over his or her destiny—these are the types of people who grow to adulthood with little interest and faith in politics and, equally important, with little respect for their own political efficacy. When opinions are counted by policymakers, the ideas of these people will probably not even have been expressed.

THE SELECTIVE CHARACTER OF OPINION REPRESENTATION

Representing conflict by political opinions is a highly selective process that covers many conflicts but overlooks or ignores many others, actual and potential. The expression of political opinions makes up the greater part of conflict representation, but not everyone participates. Some people are not called upon for opinions; others have neither the opportunity nor the resources to express their opinions; still others do not even want to express opinions, particularly informed ones. The political opinions that are voiced are only imperfectly drawn samples of all the underlying attitudes and interests on issues confronting the community.

Political leaders influence the opinions that people express through conflict representation by handpicking issues that will stimulate personal attitudes and interests. Seeking support for themselves and their causes, political leaders are selective in choosing issues and do not always choose those of deepest interest to citizens. People may feel uneasy about rising rates of divorce, suicide, or highway fatalities, but political leaders must emphasize these issues first, before the public can respond.

Once expressed, opinions are funneled into many channels (including newspaper editorials, party platforms, group stands, politicians' speeches, and opinion surveys), where it is easy to misinterpret the direction and intensity of political views. Distinguishing between the opinions of indifferent majorities and informed minorities, measuring them, and deciding which (if any) deserve greater weight is difficult. Even when political opinions are expressed, there is no assurance that all will be considered or that they will be effective in influencing policy.

POLITICAL OPINIONS AND POLITICAL CONSENSUS

As imperfect as the process may be in composing an accurate picture of the diverse social interests in this nation, the means by which political opinions are expressed to policymakers are a rich source of political consensus. It is true that loyalties to various communities and groups breed disagreements: Americans learn to be loyal to some groups and critical of others; they learn partisan loyalties that both unite and divide them; they grow acutely aware of racial and ethnic differences; and they acquire religious sentiments that are sometimes tolerant, sometimes bigoted. But can these loyalties be so intense and divisive that they endanger community consensus? Although it is possible, our political institutions have traditionally tried to moderate these disputes. Americans of many races, religions, generations, and political outlooks are often suspicious and intolerant of dissenters; rival interests are generally unwilling to compromise. But their sense of loyalty to "America," to its political institutions (the Constitution, the President, Congress, and the courts), its major political parties, and the "rules of the game"—acquired by political socialization in childhood—is vital. That loyalty promotes a politics of compromise and conciliation that permits a peaceful conflict of interests. However, if the institutional mechanisms fail to respond to groups trying to advance their interests (particularly new groups such as the young or impoverished), or if the groups think the mechanisms are useless in the struggle, then the thin consensus provided by constitutional loyalties may vanish and violent conflict may follow. For the political consensus to persevere, support for constitutional mechanisms must come from both opinion holders and opinion leaders. We now turn to a discussion of how opinion leaders fit into the representation of conflict.

EXERCISING POLITICAL LEADERSHIP

The distinction between leaders and followers is fundamental to government. As molders of opinion, political leaders take active part in conflict representation; as makers of policy, they contribute to conflict resolution. We will explore the relationships between opinion leaders and opinion-holders, specifically examining who takes the lead in representing conflicts, how public officials act as leaders, and how political leaders influence opinions.

Taking the lead in representing conflicts

Political leaders publicize social disputes—and often generate them as well—by getting people to take sides in disagreements over what goals to seek and how to achieve them. Who are our political leaders and how do they represent conflicts in American politics?

WHAT IS POLITICAL LEADERSHIP?

Leadership means mobilizing and coordinating the activities of people in the pursuit of collective goals. Political leadership consists of (1) the give-and-take of people working toward the regulation of conflicts through (2) the exercise of influence in (3) specific situations.

Underlying all political leadership is a subtle give-and-take between the interested minority and the indifferent majority that responds to leadership out of conviction, habit, fear, or the hope of personal gain. Leaders and followers depend upon one another. Leaders help fulfill popular desires, or at least leave the impression that they do, by paying attention to people's needs and wants, heeding their demands, formulating alternative ways of achieving goals, and mobilizing support for common gains. In turn, the needs, wants, and demands of followers circumscribe the leader's options. Followers bestow legitimacy upon their leaders and, in exchange, those leaders assume the responsibility to govern.

What sets the leaders off from the followers in the give-and-take between governors and governed, rulers and ruled, is the exercise of influence. A political leader exerts influence by sending messages that elicit the support of followers. Sometimes this means taking a public action that will win widespread popularity. For example, in the spring of 1975 shortly after the fall of South Vietnam and the end of the United States' long involvement in the Vietman war, Cambodians seized a U.S. merchant ship, the Mayaguez. President Gerald Ford directed U.S. forces to obtain release of the crew and the operation was completed "successfully."* Before the incident, only 40 percent of Americans approved of Ford's presidential performance in opinion polls; immediately afterward his popularity climbed to 51 percent (*Gallup Opinion Index*, No. 120, 1975). As we noted in Chapter 5, political leaders also adjust to prevailing opinions when they think it is in their interest to do so. Sensing a growing distrust of "Big Government" and the "Washington Bureaucracy" in 1976, both Ronald Reagan seeking the Republican presidential nomination and Jimmy Carter seeking the Democratic ran as former state governors, as candidates offering voters a choice from "outside" the "Washington crowd."

Whether creating or adjusting to the opinions of followers, a leader tries to modify the views of followers to conform to the leader's interests, aims, and ambitions. As situations change, so may the degree of influence exercised by the leader. In short, circumstances mold the relationship between leaders and followers. Presidential influence, for example, is easiest to exert in times of crisis—when there are threats of war against the nation, during economic depressions, or when "politics as usual" collapses. In critical times people are likely to rally around the person who can do what the scene and the times demand. After the assassination of President John Kennedy in 1963, Lyndon Johnson took immediate steps to demonstrate that he could assume the office

---

*In 1976 a report of the General Accounting Office, conducted for a Democratic controlled congressional committee, indicated that presidential actions had little to do with release of the Mayaguez crew; release had started before the U.S. Marine assault. The report produced a brief flurry of debate during the 1976 presidential campaign.

and cope with the anxieties and confusion created by the loss. After the resignation of Richard Nixon in 1974, Gerald Ford also tried to act in accordance with the unprecedented situation through a low-keyed and conciliatory address to Americans following his swearing in.

The setting influences the exercise of leadership in yet another way. Effective political leadership requires its own brand of effort—the capacity and willingness to negotiate compromises between conflicting interests. Some people who take on important public posts after only limited political experience find it hard to adjust to government service where constitutional restraints limit their activities and their behavior faces public scrutiny and criticism. The characteristics they bring to their political jobs (say outstanding records in private industry, science, or entertainment) matter less than their ability to adapt to the task, the situation, and the mood of their followers.

WHO ARE THE LEADERS?

People take part in bringing conflicts to the attention of policymakers when they have the opportunity, resources, and desire to do so (see Chapter 5). These conditions exist for those in positions of formal governmental authority, for those in responsible positions in private organizations, and for persons who enjoy the trust of their peers. Each position engenders a different kind of political leadership:

- *Public officials* exercise leadership because they occupy positions of formal authority. The prominence of their government posts ensures publicity for what they do, thus giving them a strategic advantage in influencing opinions.
- *Group leaders* exercise influence because they have important jobs in large, private organizations. Leading figures in political parties; presidents of farm organizations, large corporations, and labor unions; lobbyists; television commentators, anchormen, and newspaper columnists; and self-appointed leaders of public interest groups (such as Ralph Nader) are all group leaders.
- *Personal leaders* have influence because their fellow citizens trust them, respect their political knowledge, and turn to them for advice. Without official position in either the government or private organizations, they are likely to be influential only in their immediate environment.

Public officials

Proponents of elitist theories of American politics can marshall considerable evidence on behalf of their interpretation. To begin with, "fewer than 250 people occupy *all* of the influential posts in the combined executive, legislative, and judicial branches of the federal government" (Dye, 1976, pp. 80–81). Who are these people and what are they like? Aside from the President (who is usually someone who has either made a career of politics or has considerable experience in government), the key executive leaders come from industry, commerce, the law, higher education, and the executive bureaucracy. From one presidential administration to another they are very much alike: members of the middle and upper classes, well-educated, professionally trained, and typically male, native-born, White, Protestant, and middle-aged.

Scarcely typical of most Americans, the social backgrounds of bureaucratic, congressional, and judicial leaders are similar to the backgrounds of executive leaders. Leaders of key federal bureaucratic agencies often arise from within the bureaucracy, thus providing a continuity of background and interests. Within Congress, influence is centered in the key leaders of the Senate and the House and in the chairpersons and ranking members of standing committees. These are people of substance within their local communities and of high status compared to the social backgrounds of most Americans. Judicial authority is concentrated in the Supreme Court, where nine men rule on the legitimacy of the acts of popularly elected Presidents and legislative leaders. Here too upper-class social origins are predominant.

Group leaders

Viewed from one perspective, group leaders are more representative of American society than are public officials. The local leaders of our two major parties have varied backgrounds representative of the social and economic characteristics of their localities (Eldersveld, 1964). Many minorities inadequately represented among public officials develop spokespersons within their own associations. Leaders of Black organizations, for example, represent a variety of points of view. Other interests find in their organizations and group leaders channels for expressing their views to policymakers.

But the most influential group leaders in American politics—especially those who serve as presidents, managers, and members of the boards of directors of major corporations—have social positions and reflect interests that are far different from those of most Americans. The typical corporate leader, for instance, earns much more than $50,000 per year. Yet, only one family in a hundred in this country earns that high an annual income; indeed, only one-fifth earn more than $20,000 (Heilbroner, 1976). If business and industrial leaders make a difference in politics, and they clearly do, the interests they represent are those of the upper class, not those of "middle America."

Personal leaders

By definition, personal leaders influence opinions primarily within their immediate group. At least to the degree that each set of friends and neighbors, no matter what their backgrounds, probably has its own set of opinion leaders, personal leaders are perhaps more generally representative of Americans than other leaders. Yet personal leaders probably do not have great influence in making key policies. Moreover, social class also differentiates personal leaders from the rank-and-file. Those who have more formal education and who are in professional and managerial positions are also more likely to be personal leaders. Because formal education builds knowledge, well-educated citizens are often consulted for information and advice in political affairs. People are generally more likely to be influenced by those whose social status is the same or higher than their own than by those with a lower status.

A governing elite?

The middle and upper classes occupy most leadership positions in American politics. Social advantage makes it easier to pursue a political career and devote oneself to public service as an avocation. High social status, high income, a college education, and politically related occupations make it easier to obtain "coin of the political realm": money, social contacts, experience in dealing with people, spare time for politics, public esteem, and a reputation for success in all endeavors.

Because of such tendencies, some observers have argued that America is governed by an economic elite. They see a group of entrenched, modern aristocrats—labeled variously the "ruling elite," "power elite," "establishment," "corporate elite," or even "invisible government"—in control of all levels of government: national, state, and local (Domhoff, 1967; Dye, 1976; Mills, 1957). Some proponents of this view go on to suggest that this elite consists of a relatively small number of persons, generally those who lead the relatively few corporate enterprises that guide the nation's economic destiny. If estimates are accurate, then the number of such enterprises is indeed limited: Only 100 of more than 200,000 corporations own one-half the industrial assets in the U.S.; of more than 67,000 corporations in transportation, communications, and utilities, 33 control one-half the assets in those fields; the 50 largest banks (out of a total of 13,000) have almost one-half of all banking assets; and 18 of almost 1800 companies have two-thirds of all insurance assets (Dye, 1976, p. 20).

That economic wealth is markedly concentrated in the hands of the few is undeniable. That affluent economic interests influence policymaking is unquestionable. It cannot be proven, however, that a single elite rules the nation in its own interest and to the exclusion of others. Constructing a statistical profile of the people who exert political leadership is very different from proving that political power rests with one class united by a common interest and in control of elective and appointive officials (McConnell, 1966; Rose, 1967).

Although American political leaders are similar in social characteristics, their common interests are not strong enough to create a governing class. Leaders of corporations do have a common interest in obtaining preferential tax policies or policies regulating labor unions, but they disagree on the specifics of such policies. The interests represented by corporate managers, bank presidents, bond lawyers, and others are not always the same, despite a common preference for a capitalist economy. Their disputes are resolved by the business leaders, union leaders, popularly elected congresspeople, and officials in regulatory agencies. Faced with conflict among themselves and with others over specific policies, economic leaders are not in a position to impose their views on policymakers.

The concentration of upper-class persons in the leadership suggests we have government by the affluent even if affluent groups do differ over policy matters. Whether one believes there is an affluent elite—pluralist and divided though it may be—depends in part upon one's perspective. Blacks and Mexican-Americans, the poverty-stricken of all ethnic backgrounds, alienated youth, weary consumers, and many others feel that government is not responsive to their needs. Government certainly seems to them to be run by the affluent. But consider the following qualifications.

First, the relatively large size of the middle class (compared to the upper and lower classes) reduces, although does not prevent, sharp divisions between the wealthy and the impoverished. The American community has been able to adjust the most serious economic disputes between classes. The adjustment so urgently needed today is not prevented by a reactionary governing elite refusing to adjust to change but by (1) sharp conflicts within all classes over solutions, (2) general satisfaction with the status quo, and (3) apathy among middle-class Americans about things political.

Second, American political institutions frequently make it difficult for government to take unified action and coordinate conflicting views. The federal arrangement divides authority among local, state, and federal jurisdictions; these governments often battle over the revenue to support programs that would alleviate social injustice. The separation of powers further scatters authority among congressional committees and bureaucratic agencies that compete for support among special clienteles.

Moreover, to acquire mass support, even elites must broaden their appeals and adjust to the diversity of American political opinion. The votes of the affluent will not alone elect candidates, although the affluent are the most likely to vote.

Finally, the quest for social justice in the 1960s and 1970s has gotten somewhere. The civil rights movement has made tangible gains in racial equality; urban majorities have obtained more influence because of legislative redistricting; voting rights have been broadened by legislation and constitutional amendment; the consumer has achieved greater protection because of pricing and packaging regulations, and health and safety legislation; and various programs have helped in the struggle against poverty. However, much remains to be done—in prison and welfare reform, public education, and other areas. Current controversy concerns how it can be done, not whether it should be done.

There are many points of view. One side says the defects in our society can be corrected only at a slow, orderly pace and cautions against unrealistic hopes for massive spending of funds that simply are not available. Another feels that we must reorder our priorities, turning the money we have away from space exploration and military commitments and into social reform. Between these views are others that have provided many of the issues political leaders have dealt with in the 1970s—for instance, whether the federal government should share its tax revenues with states, so they can assume responsibility for correcting social evils. Progress in alleviating social ills suggests that government can respond to interests other than those of the affluent. But so much remains to be done that we must question the pace of reform and wonder whether future progress will dispel the notion that America is governed by an affluent elite.

We cannot yet judge whether America is run by a governing elite. We suggest that political leadership is a deck stacked in favor of some social groups, but their control is hardly absolute.

What do Americans think of their political leaders?

If they are to influence the views of their followers, public officials, group leaders, and personal leaders must have popular support. Personal leaders almost by definition have a base of support among the friends, colleagues, and neighbors whom they influence. But what of public officials and group leaders? What do Americans think of them?

THE IMAGES OF PUBLIC OFFICIALS

Like their views of democratic principles (recall the discussion in Chapter 2), Americans' opinions of politicians and politics are ambivalent. Compared to careers in business, religion, sports, or entertainment, public service has relatively little prestige as a lifetime occupation. American political folklore has always held some distrust of political power; the old slogan "the less government, the better" still strikes a responsive chord in many Americans. U.S. citizens simply do not completely trust governing officials.

Popular confidence in public officials varies in part with the government position occupied. The office of the Presidency has always been respected in its own right; anyone assuming it has fallen heir to a long tradition of public devotion. Respect for the office, however, does not imply automatic approval of the incumbent. As Figure 6.1 illustrates, recent presidents have had their ups and downs in the public eye. All received widespread approval as they began their Presidency, but their support declined as their presidential tenure wore on. Of the Presidents holding office from 1932 through 1976, only Roosevelt and Kennedy retained majority support throughout their terms.

Public approval of presidential conduct depends upon a number of factors. Time alone is of considerable importance (Stimson, 1976). The longer a President is in office the more likely his winning coalition will fragment as he is unable to meet conflicting demands. And, as a President's tenure continues, partisanship colors popular support—Democrats approve of the conduct of a Democratic president, but disapprove of a Republican, and vice versa. Short-term boosts in presidential popularity follow international crises—as when President Kennedy dealt with the removal of Soviet missiles from Cuba in 1962 and Gerald Ford responded to the Mayaguez incident in 1975—and national achievement, such as the moon landing. Chronic economic problems, pro-longed involvement in unpopular wars, or scandals seriously damage the presidential image (Mueller, 1973).

Because the President is the most visible of our public officials and his every act (be it a presidential veto or a presidential pratfall) makes news, the news media also have something to do with shifting levels of presidential popularity. As Table 6.1 suggests, being able to address people directly on television has, at least in some instances, been followed by increases in popular approval. But a public appeal is no guarantee of heightened popularity, especially if a President is in real trouble. In April 1973, Richard Nixon appeared on television to explain his part in the Watergate scandals, claiming responsibility but no blame for the affair. A nationwide survey indicated little change in public approval of Nixon: Before the talk 50 percent approved of Nixon's conduct of the presidency, following the talk 48 percent approved (Diamond, 1975).

The news also contributes to changes in presidential popularity in another way. When the news of what is going on in the world and nation is generally good, people seem to give the President credit for it. But when the news is bad, they place the blame on him as well. Even if matters are beyond the incumbent's control, citizens personify responsibility, and the President either benefits or suffers from it (Brody and Page, 1975).

One reason prestige is important for a President is that public popularity helps him to advance his proposals before Congress. More precisely, what seems to happen is that members of the President's party are more likely to support his policies in Congress if they perceive that he has widespread public approval. Public approval, however, is no guarantee that a Democratic President will mobilize Republican support or vice versa (Edwards, 1976; Wattier, 1976).

Whatever the general standing of the President in public opinion polls, it is

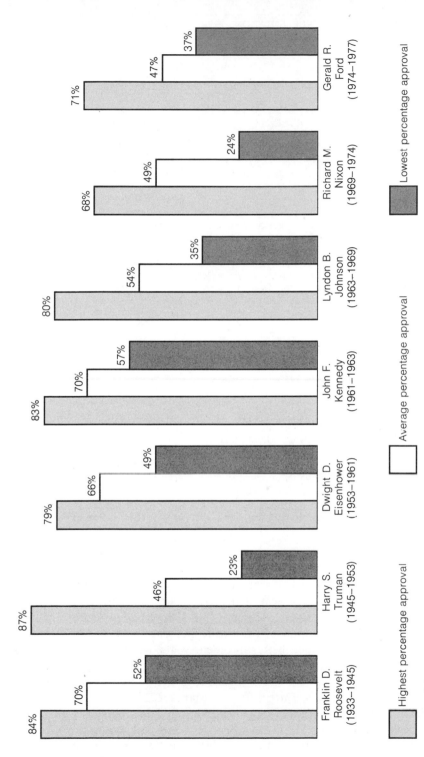

FIGURE 6.1

Presidential Popularity, 1933–1976. [*Source:* Constructed from data reported in the *Gallup Opinion Index*, Report No. 125, 1975; and Report No. 127, 1976.]

TABLE 6.1

Presidential television appearances and changes in presidential popularity,
1963–1975

Date of TV appearance	Event	Poll results
July 26, 1963	President Kennedy announces nuclear test ban treaty	Before: 72% favored treaty After: 81% favored treaty
August 1, 1965	President Johnson explains Gulf of Tonkin incident	Before: 42% positive on LBJ Vietnam policy After: 72% positive on LBJ Vietnam policy
January 31, 1966	President Johnson announces resumption of bombing on North Vietnam	Before: 61% favored resuming bombings After: 73% favored resuming bombings
May 14, 1969	President Nixon announces phased withdrawals of troops from Vietnam	Before: 49% favored phased withdrawals After: 67% favored phased withdrawals
November 3, 1969	President Nixon asks for support of Vietnam policy	Before: 46% positive on Nixon's handling of war After: 51% positive on Nixon's handling of war
April 30, 1970	President Nixon announces Cambodian strike by U.S. troops	Before: 77% favored sending U.S. troops into Cambodia After: 50% favored sending U.S. troops into Cambodia
May 27, 1970	President Nixon announces withdrawal of U.S. troops from Cambodia	Before: 47% said Cambodian move not wrong After: 56% said Cambodian move not wrong
April 30, 1973	President Nixon declares innocence of Watergate	Before: 50% positive to Nixon After: 48% positive to Nixon
May 15, 1975	President Ford announces return of Mayaguez crew	Before: 40% positive to Ford After: 50% positive to Ford

Sources: Compiled from data reported in *The Harris Survey,* September 3, 1970; May 8, 1973; June 5, 1975.

usually higher than that of Congress. (One exception was Congress' higher public support during the last year of the Watergate scandals.) In the decade 1966–1976 popular confidence in Congress fell sharply, from 42 percent who approved of Congress in 1966 to only nine percent in 1976. Other public officials have not fared much better in recent years. Between 1966 and 1976 public confidence in the "executive branch of federal government" declined from 41 percent to 11 percent and confidence in the Supreme Court from 50 percent to 22 percent (*The Harris Survey,* March 22, 1976).

Leadership images reflect the policies public officials pursue as well as the offices they hold. We would have to agree that at least one reason the Supreme Court has faced declining popular approval in recent years is that many of its decisions have been opposed by various segments of the population—segrega-tionists, antiabortionists, advocates of prayers in public schools. Further, the way an official conducts the office, that is, the official's style, makes a differ-ence in public esteem. Does a President conduct himself as a passive broker of political forces (Eisenhower) or an aggressive initiator of policies (Johnson)? Does he act as a nonpartisan, assigning many of the party-related activities of the presidency to subordinants (Nixon) or does he act as party leader as well as chief executive (Truman)? Such decisions affect who approves of the official and who disapproves.

THE IMAGES OF GROUP LEADERS

There is much less evidence on how Americans regard group leaders. Table 6.2 depicts changes in levels of confidence in the leadership of key institutions as measured by responses to the question, "As far as people in charge of running _____ are concerned, would you say you have a great deal of confidence, only some confidence, or hardly any confidence in them?" The percentages reflect those expressing a "great deal" of confidence. The pattern is clear: There has been a decline in public confidence in the leaders of private institutions generally comparable to that expressed toward public officials. The sole excep-tion is television news; about one in four Americans consistently express a great deal of confidence in TV news. A notable exception to the decline of confidence in a group leader not listed in Table 6.2 is the public esteem of

TABLE 6.2
Confidence in leadership of key institutions, 1966 and 1976

	Percentage expressing a great deal of confidence	
Institution	1966	1976
Medicine	73	42
Higher education	61	31
Television news	25	28
Organized religion	41	24
Military	62	23
The press	29	20
Major companies	55	16
Organized labor	22	10
Executive branch	41	11
Congress	42	9
Supreme Court	50	22

Source: Compiled from data reported in *The Harris Survey,* March 22, 1976.

consumer advocate Ralph Nader. In surveys conducted in 1971, 1974, and 1975, 55–60 percent of respondents gave Nader a positive rating for his "job in protecting the interests and safety of the consumer" (*The Harris Survey*, June 23, 1975).

Campaigning for office: a case of political leadership

We can get a better idea of how people in politics try to exercise leadership by examining a major conflict in American society: the competition for public office. Here political candidates and their campaign managers are the principal leaders representing conflicts between interests (including political parties) for the authority to govern.

Election campaigns are contrived, not spontaneous; every phase is designed to be reported to the public. As little as possible is left to chance. This does not always mean things go as planned. In the presidential campaign of 1976, for example, Democrat Jimmy Carter scarcely planned that an interview with *Playboy* magazine in which he presented his views on sex and morality would become a controversial topic. The focus of campaign planning is upon the candidate, especially upon managing the impressions people have of the candidate (the candidate's image) and his or her positions on salient issues. Managers stage candidates' activities for maximum exposure in the mass media: whistle-stops, airport fly-ins, televised interviews, factory tours, junkets down the Mississippi, walks through shopping centers, samplings of locally famous foods, and other "on camera" appearances. Careful efforts try to identify the candidate with the community's most revered symbols—the Constitution, the American way, justice, peace, prosperity, prudence, and trust. Simple catch phrases symbolize the candidate's intention to provide a "return to normalcy," a "new frontier," a "new prosperity," or "leadership, for a change."

Contrived though they are, campaigns are not just shams. Candidates have only so much time, money, personnel, and energy to devote to persuading people; they must budget their resources to achieve optimal publicity for themselves, their policies, and their philosophies. All this requires effective organization and communication.

CAMPAIGN ORGANIZATION AND THE ORGANIZERS

No nominee can hope to wage a successful campaign without an effective political organization working to secure funds, information, publicity, and support. Besides trusted advisors of long standing, the campaign organization of a political aspirant includes specialists in management, fundraisers, surveyors of public opinion, public relations personnel, and party leaders.

The campaign managers

Each campaign conducted on a wide scale has a manager, someone other than the candidate, whose job is to coordinate the overall strategy, tactics, and organization. Take as an example the 1976 presidential campaign. As far back as a few days after the 1972 elections, Hamilton Jordan, Jimmy Carter's campaign manager, laid out in a carefully prepared memorandum the strategy necessary for Carter to win the Democratic presidential nomination in 1976. The strategy emphasized taking advantage of the public's increasing loss of faith and trust in government (revealed in public opinion polls) and Carter's success as governor of Georgia; cultivating the good will of key political news columnists, the *Washington Post*, and the *New York Times*; and techniques for raising campaign funds. Plans were also laid for putting together a Carter "Brain Trust" composed of groups of specialists in foreign affairs, economics, social problems, etc. to advise the candidate on major issues. Jordan's task following Carter's nomination was to plan the overall campaign against Gerald Ford. Among the typical concerns that occupy a manager's time is scheduling appearances of the candidate and his key supporters. Jordan concocted an elaborate system to assure coverage of every state in the union, assigning "points" to a visit to a state by Carter, his running mate Walter Mondale, and members of the Carter family and key aides. States believed crucial to a Carter victory received greater point coverage than those considered "safe" for Carter or not likely to be won in any event.

The Jordan counterpart in Gerald Ford's prenomination efforts was former cabinet member and presidential advisor Rogers Morton, along with professional political consultant Stuart Spencer and other aides working through the President Ford Committee (PFC). Following Ford's narrow victory for the nomination over challenger Ronald Reagan, the Ford camp elevated James Baker, an experienced Texas politician and former under secretary of commerce, to the position of overall coordinator. In contrast to the Jordan plan to blanket the country with visits from Carter or the Carter family, Ford managers decided to keep their man "on the job" in the White House, limiting campaign tours to a few days in order to leave the impression of a "working President."

In formulating strategies and tactics and coordinating organizational activities, campaign managers do not work alone. They rely on key specialists who also become vital cogs in the campaign machine.

The fundraisers

Running for public office has always been expensive. As Will Rodgers remarked, "It takes lots of money to even get beat with." Assembling a competent campaign organization and managing the full range of campaign activities are costly enterprises. Figure 6.2 illustrates the striking rise in the costs of political campaigns in presidential election years in the two decades before Congress took steps to reduce those costs in the early 1970s. The cost per

vote cast in presidential campaigns increased from 19 cents in 1952 to 60 cents in 1968; even after adjusting for inflation, campaign costs increased 45 percent from 1952 to 1972.

In a series of legislative acts beginning with the Federal Election Campaign Act of 1971 and including campaign finance laws of 1974 and 1976, Congress has begun to regulate campaign spending and finance. Here are the key provisions of current regulations:

- *Public financing* The federal government provides funds for party conventions nominating the presidential candidates and for the general election campaigns; matching funds are provided to candidates in presidential primaries (if candidates raise at least $5,000 in each of 20 states through contributions of $250 or less).

- *Contribution limits* A person may give no more than $1,000 to each candidate in each federal election or primary, with an aggregate limit of $25,000 per year; no more than $5,000 a year to a political action committee and $20,000 per year to a national committee of a political party; a committee raising funds for several candidates may give no more than $15,000 per

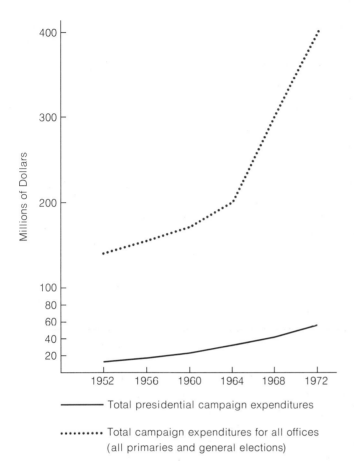

———— Total presidential campaign expenditures

·········· Total campaign expenditures for all offices
(all primaries and general elections)

FIGURE 6.2

Estimated costs of Political Campaigns in Presidential Election Years, 1952–1972. [*Sources:* Constructed from data contained in the Report of the President's Commission on
Campaign Costs, *Financing Presidential Campaigns,* Washington, D.C.: U.S. Government Printing Office, 1962; Heard,
A., *The Costs of Democracy,* Chapel Hill, N.C.: University
of North Carolina Press, 1960; and Alexander, H. E., *Financing Politics,* Washington, D.C.: Congressional Quaterly
Press, 1976, pp. 13–37.]

year to the national committee of a political party; the Democratic and
Republican senatorial campaign committees may give up to $17,500 a year to
a candidate.

- *Spending limits*   Limits on spending include $10 million per candidate
  (adjusted to inflation) for presidential primaries; $20 million (adjusted) per

candidate in presidential general elections; $2 million for each major political party's nominating conventions.

- *Reporting requirements* Candidates and political committees must keep records of contributors of $50 or more.
- *Federal Election Commission* There is now a six-member panel appointed by the President (confirmed by the Senate) to regulate campaign finance, spending, and other activities affected by federal legislation.

Public financing of presidential campaigns derives from the Revenue Act of 1971. That legislation (with some changes) set up a voluntary federal income tax checkoff which permits a person to authorize a portion of his or her income tax to a campaign fund. To stimulate participation in campaign funding by individuals, revenue laws provide that persons filing separate income tax returns may take a direct credit of an amount equal to one-half of annual political contributions up to $25 or take a regular deduction of annual political contributions up to $100; persons filing joint returns may take a direct tax credit equal to one-half of annual political contributions up to $50, or take a regular deduction of annual contributions up to $200.

States have also taken an active interest in regulating campaign finance. All but North Dakota have disclosure laws requiring reports of incomes and expenditures; 43 require disclosure before and after elections. Twenty-five states have bipartisan election commissions to enforce various statutes, and 22 limit individual contributions. Eight states have tax checkoff arrangements leading to public financing, and 14 provide tax incentives to stimulate political contributions.

The flurry of legislation passed by Congress in the early 1970s has influenced campaign fundraising in several ways. The requirement that candidates must raise money in contributions of $250 or less before receiving public funds for presidential primaries has renewed an interest in obtaining small contributions. One technique for accomplishing this is direct mail. Several firms now specialize in mailing appeals for funds to individual households. For example, one firm raised more than $800,000 on behalf of George Wallace in a three-month period in 1975 using direct mail. But direct mail itself is expensive; about 60 cents of every dollar obtained by direct mail goes to pay the expense of the mailing. Reaching small contributors through television is another technique. Ronald Reagan made an effective nationwide appeal for funds during his effort to wrest the Republican presidential nomination from Gerald Ford in 1976. Neighborhood fundraising parties, dinners, and garage sales are other means of obtaining large numbers of small contributions.

Campaign fundraisers have not forsaken sources of large contributions. Campaign funds still flow primarily from wealthy business, labor, and professional organizations as well as from key political contributors—the Rockefellers, DuPonts, Fords—who give to both Republican and Democratic candidates. Among major contributing groups are the political action committees such as the Committee on Political Education (COPE) of the AFL-CIO and the American Medical Political Action Committee (AMPAC). Nominees are also still free to pay their own way, especially if they wish to forego public financing.

Efforts to regulate campaign financing and spending have not reduced the overall cost of campaigning. For instance, the preconvention phase of the 1972 presidential campaign cost all candidates $33 million; in 1976 the amount spent by all candidates was $43 million. Of the 1976 total more than $24 million came from federal matching funds. The regulated financing of the presidential contest between Gerald Ford and Jimmy Carter suggests possible future effects of such legislation. During 1976 the Federal Election Commission approved $22 million in federal financing for each presidential candidate and his running mate. Considering that in 1972 Richard Nixon spent $60 million winning a second term and George McGovern $30 million to lose, the amount available in 1976 resulted in tight budgets for the candidates of both parties. In addition, each national party committee was authorized $3 million on behalf of its nominee, hardly enough to make up the spending deficits. Small wonder that each party's nominees were eager to take advantage of free exposure, such as the 1976 series of debates conducted between presidential and vice-presidential candidates.

The pollsters

In addition to planning and paying for a campaign, a candidate must determine what is on the voters' minds: (1) What qualities do voters believe the ideal President, congressperson, or senator should have? (2) How closely do they think the candidates match these qualities? (3) What issues are uppermost in the voters' minds? (4) Is the candidate leading or trailing his or her major opponent? (5) What is the likelihood that the candidate's supporters and opponents will actually vote? Candidates hire pollsters to survey public opinion and find answers to these questions. The answers help shape campaign tactics, identify a candidate's strengths and weaknesses, and affect fundraising.

From a candidate's perspective, there are two types of pollsters. First, there are the pollsters who take opinion soundings for corporations, newspapers, television, newsmagazines, and other institutions: George Gallup, Louis Harris, Daniel Yankelovich, Burns Roper, Albert Sindlinger, Peter Hart, and others. The results of these polls are generally available to any candidate, just as they are to any citizen, who wishes to follow the daily news. Second, there are the pollsters candidates hire to take private samplings of opinion. For example, in 1976 Ronald Reagan employed Decision Making Information, Inc. (DMI) to assess his chances in his nomination fight against Gerald Ford in 1976. The Ford camp employed Market Opinion Research, Inc. Before a candidate was even nominated, the Republican National Committee budgeted a $60,000–$70,000 survey to provide a basis for planning the campaign against Jimmy Carter for either potential Republican nominee. Carter employed pollster Pat Caddell (George McGovern's opinion analyst in 1972) not only to take regular opinion soundings but to travel with the candidate as a chief adviser. Out of data from Caddell's polls grew tactics for implementing the Carter strategy of running as an outsider against the "Washington bureaucracy" and an emphasis upon Americans' feelings of distrust and alienation from government.

The publicizers

Any election campaign requires that candidates communicate with their constituents. If the electoral district is small or sparsely populated, candidates can simply go door to door and meet each voter. But in larger constituencies, candidates must use mass communications, either getting their views covered as newsworthy or paying to advertise policy positions and personal characteristics. The candidate's publicizers are thus either press secretaries and publicity specialists bent on getting their candidate in the news or specialists in political advertising who attempt to merchandise the candidate to a mass audience.

The candidate's press secretary is a bridge between the candidate and news reporters. Jody Powell performed in this role for Jimmy Carter in 1976; Ron Nessen did so for Gerald Ford. The press secretary must respond to reporters' questions, arrange interviews and news conferences, brief and be briefed by the candidate, and shield the candidate from the press. In 1976, wearied from whirlwind campaign visits to too many parts of the country, Jimmy Carter began to fluff his lines and make errors in judgment in his news conferences. The Carter press forces immediately cut down on the number of airport news conferences. The job of the candidate's publicity specialist is to stage events for maximum favorable news coverage. In 1976 Gerald Ford's publicity people arranged a trip down the 'Mississippi river with "Steamboat Gerry" at the helm, a "happening" that received widespread television coverage in cities and towns from Memphis to New Orleans.

The advertising specialist makes certain assumptions about mass behavior: (1) A mass audience exists and is composed of individuals sharing attitudes and social characteristics; (2) the audience selects products, candidates, or policies on the basis of qualities emphasized in mass advertising; (3) an appeal will be effective if it conforms to what voters are predisposed to accept (if they believe a President should be dynamic, the candidate should appear in settings that dramatically emphasize his dynamism); (4) the candidate's image must be sufficiently colorful to attract citizen attention and stimulate voting; and (5) dramatic and sensational presentations, repetition, and saturation of the mass audience with campaign appeals will penetrate the audience's indifference and break down resistance.

The major arena of the advertising specialist in contemporary presidential politics is, of course, television. Television is an expensive medium. In 1972 all candidates for all offices in all primary and general elections spent $60 million alone on television advertising. The specialists who earn and spend such amounts are located in professional advertising firms. The Ford forces in 1976, for example, hired Malcolm MacDougall, a member of Boston's biggest ad agency, and noted for "It takes two hands to handle a whopper, the two-fisted burger from Burger King." MacDougall joined with communication consultant John Deardourff to prepare one- and five-minute TV spots around the theme of Ford's openness, post-Watergate revitalization of the presidency, and background: "President Ford. He's making us proud again." The Jimmy Carter forces relied upon Gerald Rafshoon, an ad specialist who had handled large accounts such as Sears, Roebuck and Getz Exterminators ("GETZ Gets 'Em!"). Rafshoon budgeted almost $9 million for the Carter advertising campaign, 65 percent on TV, 15 percent on radio, 5 percent on magazines, and the remainder on newspapers. Carter ads used pictures and film of the candidate in "natural, spontaneous" settings: sifting his hands through the soil of his peanut farm, stroking ears of corn, shaking hands. The theme: "A Leader, for a Change." In conjunction with the state-by-state plan of the Carter forces developed by campaign manager Hamilton Jordan, Rafshoon targeted Carter ads for four categories of states: critical, less critical, safe, and lost.

Party regulars and hangers-on

The experienced party organizer mobilizes a vigorous grass-roots organization that will complement the candidate's media-oriented efforts. The target is the individual voter and the technique is personal contact. Large numbers of people canvass neighborhoods, ring doorbells, address and lick envelopes, spend hours on the telephone, and try to explain the candidate's strengths and positions to prospective voters. The party regular's aim is to arouse interest in campaign issues, stimulate discussion, raise money, and win support (both for him- or herself and for the candidate).

In any election campaign—local, state, national—a large number of special interests linger on the fringes of each candidate's campaign organization. Local business leaders, labor leaders, government employees, college professors all feel they have something to contribute or that they have a right to be consulted. In national politics, these hangers-on include leaders of organized labor (George Meany, Leonard Woodcock), intellectual notables (John Kenneth Galbraith, William Buckley), business tycoons, and elder statesman of the political parties. Presidential candidates must cultivate the support of potential allies whose backing is critical and decide who can be ignored.

CAMPAIGN PHASES

Each political campaign has a life cycle of its own, but three phases recur in major electoral contests. First, there is the *organizing phase* when staff, information and funds are gathered, strategies and tactics laid out, and morale built. There follows the *testing phase* of the campaign when the nominee tries to hold partisans while offering a sufficiently nonpartisan, moderate stance to win voters among the undecided and the wavering opposition. In presidential contests, the acceptance speeches of the nominees generally herald the beginning of the testing phase. In accepting his party's nomination, Jimmy Carter tested before a national audience his primary theme of "trust me"; Gerald Ford's acceptance speech gave promise of a vigorous, assertive effort to take advantage of his incumbency in the face of Carter's challenge.

In addition to providing an opportunity to define major campaign themes, the testing phase also permits a candidate to prove that he or she measures up to the voters' idealized image of political leaders. The debates between presidential candidates in 1976 provided voters a rare opportunity to compare the contenders in face-to-face confrontations and decide who "won" the debates by coming closer to the voters' conceptions of what a president should be. Apparently most voters considered neither a very good fit. Surveys conducted after each debate reported about the same results: One-third declared one candidate the winner, another third declared the other candidate victorious, and the remaining third said neither candidate had won. Yet the debates gave partisans the opportunity to solidify their predebate preferences and undecideds the opportunity to gain a better impression of each candidate's personality and style.

The testing phase, finally, includes a search for issues that will inspire popular support. In some presidential contests such issues emerge early, for example, the issue of Richard Nixon's experience versus George McGovern's lack of managerial and executive experience in 1972. In other contests, however, "flash" issues dominate the testing phase for a brief period only to vanish as the day's newspaper reaches the trash can or the last light of the television tube flickers out for the evening.

The final phase of major electoral contests is the *critical phase*. Campaigns reach a point when the only voters still undecided are the nonpartisan, generally uniformed citizens who pay little attention to politics, but whose votes may mean the difference between victory and defeat. A candidate frequently tries to capture the imagination of these indifferent voters with a dramatic gesture that displays an ability to take advantage of unexpected events. In an age of closely managed and cautious campaigning, it is increasingly rare to witness such crucial events. In fact, we must go back almost two decades to find a striking example.

During the Kennedy-Nixon campaign of 1960, Martin Luther King, Jr., the prominent Black civil rights leader, was sentenced in Atlanta to four months at hard labor in the state penitentiary for sitting in at a segregated restaurant. At his campaign advisers' suggestion, Senator Kennedy telephoned the distraught wife of the imprisoned civil rights leader, expressing his concern and suggesting that he would intervene if necessary. When the press spread this dramatic news, Martin Luther King, Jr.'s father, who had come out for Nixon earlier, switched his support to Kennedy and urged all Blacks to do the same. Civil rights leaders across the nation, impressed by Kennedy's gesture (and by King's release after Robert Kennedy's plea to the judge who had pronounced sentence), followed suit. "One cannot identify in the narrowness of American voting of 1960 any one particular episode or decision as being more important than any other in the final tallies," Theodore H. White wrote later; yet

> when one reflects that Illinois was carried by only 9,000 votes and that 250,000 Negroes are estimated to have voted for Kennedy; that Michigan was carried by 67,000 votes and that an estimated 250,000 Negroes voted for Kennedy; that South Carolina was carried by 10,000 votes and that an estimated 40,000 Negroes there voted for Kennedy, the candidate's instinctive decision must be ranked among the most critical of the last few weeks. (White, 1962, p. 323)

But it is not always easy to take advantage of events quickly enough to profit by them. In 1968 President Johnson announced a halt to the bombing of North Vietnam a few days before the presidential election. It appeared that Hubert Humphrey might benefit from the move by winning the votes of antiwar dissenters. Although there was a late surge in Humphrey's support, the halt in the bombing came too late to bring him victory over Nixon. Four years later Nixon produced his own last-minute gesture when his chief foreign policy negotiator, Henry Kissinger, announced that "peace is at hand" in Vietnam. Whether the statement added to Nixon's luster or won votes in a campaign that was already running in Nixon's favor is not clear.

Political persuasion: exercising opinion leadership

A successful politician influences the opinions of followers. Americans, however, are really not very interested in politics. Hence, politicians' chances of getting their followers' attention are slim unless the political leaders are skilled at presenting attractive appeals in attention-getting ways. This means that politicians or their paid communication consultants must have talent in manipulating symbols and in mass communication.

SYMBOLIC PERSUASION IN POLITICS

In general, politicians emphasize persuasion and minimize coercion in exercising leadership and influencing opinions. Coercion and persuasion are different, albeit overlapping, forms of influence. Coercion includes the reprisals used to get people to do what they would prefer not to do; persuasion implies promises of benefits (sometimes combined with threats of deprivation) to achieve consent. Coercion involves "power talk": "If you do X, I will do Y" or "If you do not do X, I will do Y." Or more specifically, "If you do not obey, I will throw you in jail." Persuasion emphasizes not what the leader may do but what the follower will gain: "If you do X, you will do (enjoy, gain, experience, receive) Y." Persuasion is "influence talk." "If you vote for me, you will get a tax cut." In reality, of course, coercive and persuasive tactics are mingled in American politics (Bell, 1975). Some voters have been intimidated or kept from the polls; others have been guaranteed rewards if they vote as specified. Although political leaders occasionally revert to coercive tactics, they generally rely on persuasion to achieve active consent rather than on coercion to obtain reluctant compliance.

To persuade followers, a leader manipulates appropriate symbols in varying political contexts; this constitutes *symbolic persuasion.* The successful political leader identifies with popular causes (anticommunism, a balanced budget, peace, and prosperity). The goal is to convert approval of the symbolized cause into support for the politician. Similarly, the effort to devise succinct slogans that express favored symbols is commonplace in American politics: "New Deal" (Roosevelt), "Fair Deal" (Truman), "Crime, Communism, and Korea" (Eisenhower), "Get America Moving Again" (Kennedy), "War on Poverty" or "The Great Society" (Johnson), "Bring Us Together" (Nixon), "He's Made Us Proud Again" (Ford), and "A Leader, for a Change" (Carter).

Political leaders employ symbols to project qualities they think followers find attractive. The sum of the qualities projected by leaders that followers perceive constitutes the *image* of the leader. The leader's image has two sides. First are the impressions followers have of the leader's ability as a public official (training, experience, philosophy, policy preferences, etc.) and as a politician (connections with party members, relationships with group leaders and other influential people, etc.). Second is the impression of a leader's political style, which is made up of perceptions of personal qualities (appearance, personality, honesty, integrity) and skill as a public speaker, a television performer, and a person able to inspire mass confidence.

Politicians strive to manipulate the images followers have of them by carefully controlling the expressions they project as leaders (Goffman, 1959; Klapp, 1964). Some techniques of image management are easy to recognize in the public performances of politician leaders.

Dramatic encounter

It is difficult for political leaders to avoid controversy; indeed, their role in influencing and representing conflicting opinions is what makes them leaders in the first place. In confronting controversy, however, they must dramatize their ability to cope with and command every situation. Debates between political contenders provide one such opportunity. For instance, entering the first of a series of televised debates during the presidential election of 1976, Gerald Ford had the public image of a congenial, honest, but ineffectual, sometimes stumbling, President. Whether he "won" or "lost" the debate with Democrat challenger Jimmy Carter was less important than his seizure of the opportunity to appear assertive, articulate, informed, and cool under questioning of reporters and criticism by his opponent. But some of Ford's old image trouble returned in the second confrontation between the two presidential contenders. In response to a question, Ford asserted that much of Eastern Europe was no longer under the domination of the Soviet Union; this remark provoked widespread disbelief among both his opponents and many European allies who found it hard to understand how a politician could make such a statement.

Crises also offer opportunities for dramatic encounter, particularly if accompanied by mass confusion, anxiety, and uncertainty. Crises provide a setting for a leader to convey the impression of coping with an enemy force that others find hard to identify and vanquish. The outbreak of war thrusts the leader into a situation where the impression of mastery usually emerges. Natural calamaties offer dramatic opportunities on a lesser scale. A flood in the Midwest, for instance, is almost certain to produce a flight by the President over the flooded region (well publicized on television news shows) and the promise of federal relief funds for the "disaster area."

Controlled ambiguity

In earlier days it was possible for a politician to take differing, even contradictory, stands on public issues before competing interests in widely scattered parts of the country. Mass communication, however, makes it difficult for a leader to tailor positions to suit each special interest. Forced to take stands that everyone will probably hear about, leaders try to avoid alienating followers by taking ambiguous positions, commiting themselves to no specific policies and stressing "concern," continuous "study of the issue," and promises of a "forthcoming plan." The style "consists basically of the avoidance of firm positions on controversial subjects while at the same time posturing as protagonist against an evanescent enemy, thereby retaining or increasing political support from large numbers of antagonists on both sides of controversies" (Edelman, 1964, p. 81).

Campaigning for the Democratic nomination for President in 1976 Jimmy Carter capitalized on the technique of controlled ambiguity to win support from southerners and northerners, Blacks and Whites, middle and lower class, union and nonunion families, and other seemingly conflicting interests. A measure of his success in smoothing over potential contradictions emerged from opinion polls just before his nomination. One-half of Carter's supporters had no idea of his stands on issues and only about 20 percent of his followers could correctly state his views on various matters. What voters did seem to respond to was the Carter style. One reporter (Knap, 1976) found the following statements typical of those he heard about Carter: "He has the type of personality that makes me believe what he says," said one housewife. "He's very personable, attractive, charming, down to earth and stands for a different kind of government than we've had," said another. During the Carter-Ford debates of 1976, the Republican nominee endeavored to turn Carter's controlled ambiguity against the Democrat, emphasizing that Carter was "not specific on the issues." Carter thus suffered one of the possible consequences of controlled ambiguity: being stereotyped as a "waffler" and "fuzzy."

Conforming to expectations

People expect certain things of leaders and sometimes these expectations seem contradictory. Leaders must be strong-willed but flexible, decisive but not rash, efficient but sensitive and humane. The appropriate posture is a precarious balance of qualities. An incumbent seeking reelection probably has an advantage in projecting the proper amalgam of qualities. Being in office offers an impression of experience and strength; negotiating with various interests demonstrates flexibility and a willingness to listen. Thus, for an incumbent the task is to act like an incumbent is expected to act. For this reason, Gerald Ford's advisors in 1976 stressed that he should be "presidential." He strolled with visiting dignitaries through the rose garden of the White House, signed legislation and executive orders in the Oval Room, and appeared in his official capacity in appropriate places—all of these actions were staged to leave an impression on audiences of television news—these were Ford's efforts to meet public expectations of what it is to be "presidential." Contrast this with the fate of Senator Edmund Muskie of Maine campaigning for his Democratic party's presidential nomination in 1972. In New Hampshire, Muskie openly challenged a newspaper publisher who had described Muskie as allegedly making fun of Americans of French-Canadian extraction and who had criticized the Senator's wife. This dramatic encounter on the front steps of the publisher's offices displayed an angry, emotional candidate. Opinion soundings revealed that New Englanders were pleased to see the "human" side of Muskie and approved his posture; but many Americans in western states, who had witnessed the Muskie performance on televised newscasts, were astonished at the display of "weakness" in a man who wanted to be President.

MASS COMMUNICATIONS AND SYMBOLIC LEADERSHIP

Campaigns to win and hold public office have a side benefit for the community as a whole; by taking stands on issues, candidates represent social conflicts. To make their messages heard they and other political leaders need not just skill in persuasion but also publicity for their views. Political leaders rely chiefly on mass communications to publicize their views. As a result, what most Americans hear about and from politicians is a secondhand report. For most citizens, politics is a world of images mediated through mass communication.

What is the political role of mass communications?

By mass communications we mean the use of the printed word (newspapers, magazines, mailed brochures) and the electronic media (radio, television, movies, telephones) to communicate simultaneously with a relatively large, heterogeneous, and anonymous audience. In America, news organizations—the *New York Times*, the *Washington Post*, the Associated Press and United Press International wire services, and the news department of major broadcasting networks—are the largest participants in mass political communications.

The mass media expose controversy and provide a forum in which people may criticize the actions of officials. Ideally, the media perform this function on behalf of all citizens; freedom of the press is a right guaranteed by constitutional and statutory law. The basic protection of a free press, guaranteed by the First Amendment (see Chapter 4), limits interference by public officials in the operations of the news media. There are, however, some restrictions that do not violate the First Amendment: Television cameras are barred from courtrooms in the interest of impartial litigation; individuals may seek redress for libelous utterances by the press; and movies are sometimes censored by local authorities. Despite such legitimate restraints, there is still sufficient constitutional freedom for the communications media to serve as unfettered channels for political information, persuasion, and entertainment. News organizations are relatively free to interpret and comment upon public affairs as they see fit—through editorials, newspaper columns, feature articles, and TV or radio commentary. However, deliberate distortion of the news is frowned upon by reporters and politicians alike.

This ideal of a socially responsible communications network is tempered by economic and political realities. The sheer cost of media operations prevents all but the most affluent from using TV, radio, newspapers, and newsmagazines to advance their interests unless, of course, they can obtain free publicity through news stories, interview programs, televised debates, and other means. Costs also limit the capacity of the communications media to act as forums of public discussion. For instance, newspapers depend upon adequate circulation and advertising revenues for survival. To appeal to readers, many newspapers focus upon sensational fare rather than lengthy articles about continuing problems such as hunger, declining energy resources, or pollution of the environment. Similarly, TV devotes much less of its programming time to public affairs than to situation comedies, action dramas, and sports coverage. In sum, the interests of the reading and viewing audience of necessity have high priority in determining how much political information flows through the media. And even when the media do provide such information, the concerns of minority groups are less likely to be represented in the news than are the continuing interests of Americans who form a large reading or buying audience.

A political leader's capacity to influence opinions depends in large measure upon access to communication channels. A leader's position, and the social status and prestige it carries with it, is one factor governing that access. The utterances of an official of a major labor union, for example, are more likely to make news than the views of a dockworker. A local gasoline attendant may know considerably more about the pricing of gasoline at the pump than a government economist, but it is the economist's opinions that are the topic of a TV interview.

The President has automatic access to the media: Any action of his is news. In news conferences, he publicizes his stands on controversial issues; by timely releases to the press, he can dominate the headlines and ensure a few minutes of exposure on each evening's televised news (a favorite technique of President Johnson); and he can have time on radio and television, almost for the asking, to speak "directly to the people" (frequently done by President Nixon). Subordinates, rivals within the presidential party, or members of the opposition without such easy access to the news media find it more difficult to circulate their criticism of presidential policies. Access to publicity through the news media is one of the factors that makes any incumbent President and many incumbent congresspeople, governors, and big city mayors formidable opponents to challengers.

In their efforts to secure information, reporters and their parent news organizations become special interest groups in their own right. Like pressure groups, they make claims upon officials for information, demand unencumbered access to policymakers, and expect freedom from official control. Their claims generate conflicts between the media and public officials. As long as democracies cherish public disclosure of conflict, tension between the press and public officials is inevitable. Whether out of conviction, principle, or economic considerations, the communications industry is continuously at odds with policymakers, as reporters and newscasters publicize matters that officials prefer to keep secret.

This basic conflict between government and the press has been highlighted repeatedly in recent years: Vice-President Agnew in 1969 charged that public officials were subjected to "instant analysis and querulous criticism . . . by a small band of network commentators and self-appointed analysts"; the Nixon administration sought to prevent publication of a secret report of American involvement in Vietnam (the Pentagon Papers) in 1971; in the same year, a committee of the House of Representatives attempted (unsuccessfully) to cite the Columbia Broadcasting Company for contempt after the network refused to cooperate in an investigation into the background of *The Selling of the Pentagon*, a documentary film about the expensive public relations programs of the Department of Defense. The Nixon White House charged in 1974 that, by its continued reporting of events surrounding the Watergate scandals, the press was trying to "hound the President from office." But hearings before the House Judiciary Committee considering Nixon's impeachment and Nixon's resignation in August of 1974 suggested that rather than overplaying Nixon's role in the Watergate cover-up, the news media had only scratched the surface of the story.

Just as public officials are critical of the news media, reporters often charge government with "managing the news." Bureaucratic agencies have offices of public information designed primarily to control the flow of news and avoid unauthorized news leaks. As long as these offices provide reporters a convenient place for securing prepared releases covering agency events, newsmen accept them. But when such offices attempt to manipulate newsmen by concealing what is taking place or by releasing news that gives a distorted view of a controversy, reporters object. Congress also faces charges of news management from some reporters. CBS correspondent Daniel Schorr in 1976 obtained a copy of a classified report of a committee investigating alleged improprieties in the operation of the Central Intelligence Agency. Schorr leaked the report to the *Village Voice* on grounds that Americans had a right to its contents. Schorr was investigated by the House Ethics Committee, but he refused to divulge how he received the report. The committee finally ended its inquiry without taking action against Schorr. Not all of Schorr's news colleagues were as convinced of the rightness of his action as was Schorr, and the correspondent closed the incident by resigning his job as one of the chief reporters for CBS news.

Television and politics

In 1950 only about one American household in ten owned a television set; two decades later, more than nine in ten owned at least one. Americans today turn to television as their prime source of political information. Moreover, as Table 6.3 illustrates, television is not only a major news source, it is Americans' most believable news source. Because it is virtually everywhere—and believed by so many—television influences political awareness.

Television has certainly affected the style of political campaigns. In adapting television (and to a lesser degree radio) to their political needs, candidates rely on specialists in the television industry. These include not only the publicity and advertising specialists we have already described, but all manner of other experts. For example, Gerald Ford in preparing for his televised debates with Jimmy Carter in the 1976 presidential campaign received coaching from a television comic, Don Penny, who helped the President with delivery and

TABLE 6.3

Public reliance on various sources of political information in selected years,
1959–1976 (in percentages of respondents using and believing each source)

News sources	1959	1961	1963	1964	1967	1968	1971	1972	1974	1976
Most used:										
Television	51	52	55	58	64	59	60	64	65	64
Newspapers	57	57	53	56	55	49	48	50	47	49
Radio	34	34	29	26	28	25	23	21	21	19
Magazines	8	9	6	8	7	7	5	6	4	7
People	4	5	4	5	4	5	4	4	4	5
Don't know, no answer	1	3	3	3	2	3	1	1	—	—
Most believed:										
Television	29	39	36	41	41	44	49	48	51	51
Newspapers	32	24	24	23	24	21	20	21	20	22
Radio	12	12	12	8	7	8	10	8	8	7
Magazines	10	10	10	10	8	11	9	10	8	9
Don't know, no answer	17	17	18	18	20	16	12	13	13	11

Source: The Roper Organization, Inc. *What People Think of Television and Other Mass Media, 1959–1976,* New York: The Television Information Office, 1977, pp. 3–4.

presentation. Practice sessions for the President were videotaped so that Ford, Penny, and other advisers could pick out weaknesses and strengths and improve the performance.

Most television specialists bring to the political campaign the attitude that the basic task of television is not to inform but to entertain. Television viewers are not interested in devoting their leisure hours to serious programs demanding concentration and reflection. Consequently, the specialist's basic task is to present an image of the candidate that an audience accustomed to entertaining and dramatic television personalities will accept. Television viewers acquire from the mass media ideas about what is entertaining and what is dull, the exciting and the bland, the romantic and the deadening. The candidate images projected on television must conform to highly subjective evaluations that viewers make on the basis of their media predispositions (Wykcoff, 1968). A politician such as former movie actor Ronald Reagan, who can "act" the role of the candidate, makes an ideal television campaigner.

How do mass communications affect political opinions? Television specialists are probably correct in assuming that entertaining rather than informative communications are most influential in politics. The person most likely to be swayed by mass communications is the "floating voter," the person who pays little attention to politics, who does not scan the news for political information, who is influenced at the last minute of a campaign by a dramatic event or personality, and who shifts his allegiance between parties from election to election (Converse, 1962). If there is a trend away from party loyalty in America, then we might speculate that television campaigns will increase their influence on voting in the future.

The effectiveness of mass communications is limited by the characteristics of the mass audience to whom the appeals are directed. In typical political campaigns, most voters make their choice before the campaign starts (see Table 6.4). If mass communications affect voters, they probably do so between elections by providing a general impression of politics against which voters judge the adequacy of the incumbent administration. Because it is likely that the choice of the committed voters is determined by their basic party loyalties, political candidates are wise to direct their mass appeals to the uncommitted voters who can swing the vote in a close election.

In weighing the ways in which television in particular and the mass media in general affect political opinions, it is well to ask not only what the media do to people but what people do with the mass media. What uses do people make of mass communications and what gratifications do they receive from them (Blumler and Katz, 1974)? What are these possible uses and gratifications? Six are noteworthy, especially in politics: (1) to gain information about a political leader's stand on issues; (2) to help decide how to vote; (3) to find out what the candidates are like in an election; (4) to reinforce one's views about leaders and candidates; (5) to enjoy the excitement of politics and election campaigns; and (6) to acquire something to talk about in social settings. Table 6.5 illustrates how Americans used both television and newspapers for these reasons during the 1974 congressional elections campaigns. As indicated above, people use the mass media for other reasons than to reach a voting decision. Many, for instance, make up their minds early in a campaign and turn to the media to strenghten those predispositions; this helps account for the 37 percent who used newspapers "a lot" to reinforce their views about candidates in 1974 and the 45 percent who used TV to that end. And, note that in 1974 around one in

TABLE 6.4
Time of decision and voting choice in presidential elections, 1948–1972 (in percentages of respondents in each category)

Time of decision	1948	1952	1956	1960	1964	1968	1972
Before party conventions	37	35	57	30	40	35	43
During party conventions	22	30	18	30	25	24	17
During campaigns	26	31	21	36	33	41	35
Don't know, no answer	15	4	4	4	2	0	5
Total	100	100	100	100	100	100	100
Number of respondents	421	1251	1285	1445	1126	957	1119

Source: Survey Research Center and Interuniversity Consortium for Political Research, The University of Michigan, Ann Arbor, 1972.

TABLE 6.5
Uses of television and newspapers as sources of communication in electoral campaigns, 1974 (in percentages of respondents reporting each use)

	Report using source					
	A lot		A little		Not at all	
Use	TV	N*	TV	N	TV	N
To discover candidates' stands on issues	61	44	34	44	5	12
To find out what candidates are like	54	44	37	43	9	13
To reinforce views about candidates' strengths	45	37	40	43	15	20
To decide how to vote	48	42	39	35	13	23
To have something to talk about	22	18	36	38	42	44
To enjoy the excitement of the political race	23	15	38	38	39	47

* Newspapers.
Source: Compiled from data from the 1974 election survey. Center for Political Studies, The University of Michigan, Ann Arbor, available through Interuniversity Consortium for Political Research.

five said they used the mass communication to find out about politics for essentially nonpolitical reasons—to have something to talk about or to be titillated by the election drama. The 1974 data square well with a study of the 1972 presidential election which concluded that voters are not influenced simply by their exposure to the media, but in a more indirect fashion; namely, they are influenced if the media gratify desires not only for guidance on how to vote but also for reinforcing information, material for conversation and debate, and entertainment (Mendelsohn and O'Keefe, 1976).

Mass communications do not operate in isolation but in conjunction with personal communications—among friends, in the family, on the job, or elsewhere. Mass communications probably gain their effect principally from an intricate network of personal leaders, not from direct messages to citizens. Even such a shocking event as the assassination of President Kennedy was communicated to only half of the adult population through the mass media; the remainder learned about it from telephone calls and personal communications.

In determining how much mass communications influence political opinions, especially in elections, we must distinguish between the different effects the mass media can have. First, they can activate an otherwise passive voter. Second, mass communications frequently reinforce political views. People's attitudes help to determine the types of communication to which they expose themselves and which they perceive and remember; their friends and family also influence their reading, listening, and viewing habits. In short, people expose themselves to what they want and expect to read, hear, and see. Small wonder then that the messages that filter through are not likely to impose views contrary to their preferences; loyal Democrats or Republicans seek and find in mass communications reasons for voting as they intended to vote all along. Finally, mass communications can convert a voter from one position to another; but this happens infrequently. Only people without clear-cut preferences, with unstable opinions, or faced with contradictory choices are markedly influenced solely by mass communications.

Representing and influencing political conflict through leadership

Political behavior is not determined solely by the attitudes and interests people bring to politics from their political socialization. Cues from political leaders interact with these predispositions. Political leaders help to initiate disputes by stimulating mass attitudes and mobilizing diverse interests; as a result, leaders represent conflicting opinions. Moreover, relying upon the resources at their disposal—derived from their social characteristics, the esteem they have in the eyes of their constituents, and the constitutional opportunities to achieve higher office—and using many techniques, leaders influence political opinions. In representing and influencing political opinions, public officials, group leaders, and personal leaders perform a necessary task in the community.

But political leaders are not free to create and change opinions at will. For example, a call for revolution, though well publicized, is rare for good reason: It is unlikely that political leaders could get many Americans to accept a major social revolution. Since the 1960s, the status quo has been fundamentally challenged in political debate; and steps have been taken to alleviate some of the worst forms of social injustice. Yet other tasks remain, for even now the number of Americans pleading the cause of the poor, the elderly, and even the average consumer is relatively small.

The influence of political leaders in conflict representation is restricted by: (1) the repository of stable attitudes of followers that leaders must take into account; (2) the general indifference of Americans to politics; (3) the many social groups represented in the leadership despite a relative overrepresentation of the middle and upper classes; (4) limited access many leaders have to mass communications as a tool for persuasion, certainly compared with that of the President; (5) the need for leaders—certainly in this age of television—to adjust to the expectations their followers have of an ideal leader; and (6) the conflict between officials and the press in a democracy.

There are two further restrictions upon the influence of leaders. First, leaders willingly restrict themselves. American politicians, with rare exceptions, uphold the rules that make possible democratic representation and resolution of conflict. By practicing fair play—accepting defeat at the polls and looking toward the next contest—political leaders preserve free elections and enable Americans to choose between competing rulers. Politicians may still "humbug the people," but they stop short of the most extreme demagoguery (stirring animosities in religious groups, arousing class against class) that might draw support from the disaffected. Second, perhaps the greatest restriction is that political leadership is widely distributed: Official leadership is dispersed among governing branches, agencies, departments, and bureaus; group leadership is exercised by persons in competing organizations and factions; and personal leadership occurs in countless social circles, most of them isolated from one another. The concentration of leadership in a small band of influential persons is difficult in such a pluralist setting. This dispersion is inherent in the way we elect our leaders, conduct our partisan affairs, and pressure officials to do our bidding. Each of these political activities has its own distinctive pattern of conflict representation linked to political opinion and leadership.

VOTING
in ELECTIONS

Americans exhibit conflicting social interests by casting votes for leaders competing to win public office. Selecting people to govern for limited terms of office is a principal reason for having elections, but it is not the only one. People also go to the polls to accept or reject city charters, approve or reject amendments to state constitutions, grant authority to tax, vote revenue bonds, and create new governing districts. Rather than try to describe all of the varied types and purposes of elections, we will limit our account to elections of federal officeholders: the President, senators, and members of the House of Representatives.

Elections and conflict representation

Free elections help represent social conflict in America in two ways: They permit citizens to take part indirectly in policymaking by choosing between candidates; and they provide governors with an indication—if only an imperfect one—of public concerns, satisfactions, and irritations. In mobilizing support, political leaders try to attract attention to their stands on specific issues; and by voting for a candidate, citizens let public officials know their positions on these issues. But these positions are often difficult to determine because politicians modify their stands to attract as many voters with diverse interests as possible. Moreover, many voters are more interested in the personalities or party labels of the candidates than in their stands. Furthermore, when there is more than one significant political issue in the election—and there usually is—just what does the candidate's victory or defeat mean as a verdict across the whole range of issues? The choices of the electorate are only ambiguous expressions of policy preferences.

Victorious candidates like to claim they have won a "mandate." In fact, election mandates are difficult, if not impossible, to ascertain. To see why, let us examine the principal (1) constitutional, (2) social and demographic, and (3) personal influences on voting.

THE CONSTITUTION AND AMERICAN ELECTIONS

There are three ways in which the Constitution influences how American elections serve as means for representing social conflict:

- The written Constitution establishes mechanisms—notably federalism and the electoral college—that make a difference.
- Formal statutes made possible by the Constitution influence elections.
- The customs and habits of the unwritten Constitution affect voting and political parties.

How does the written Constitution affect elections?

The Constitution provides the states with considerable authority to regulate elections by leaving the determination of voting requirements to them (see Chapter 4). State authority is restricted by the constitutional amendments that prohibit the states from denying the right to vote to citizens on grounds of race, color, previous condition of servitude, sex, age, or nonpayment of a poll tax. Beyond these prohibitions, the states retain considerable authority to determine the eligibility of voters and, as we have seen, the principal device they use is voter registration.

There is little doubt that registration requirements affect electoral outcomes. This is particularly apparent in presidential contests. For example, in 1976 people who thought of themselves as Democrats outnumbered those who identified themselves as Republicans about three to one among unregistered voters. Small wonder that the Democratic party devoted considerable effort to voter registration; of the 3.5 percent increase in the number of registered voters in 34 key states from 1972 to 1976, the Democrats claimed that over 3 million of the new registrants were added because of party efforts. Given the narrowness of Jimmy Carter's victory over Gerald Ford in 1976, it is conceivable that the new registrants in New York, Ohio, Florida, and Texas (all states won by Carter) contributed to the Carter triumph.

Aside from permitting the states considerable discretion in saying who can vote, the Constitution has two other major features that affect electoral politics—federalism and the Electoral College.

THE FEDERAL SYSTEM.   As it operates in American government, the federal principle divides authority among several levels of public officials. Citizens elect the officials for each level, choosing a President, senators, and representatives for national offices; governors, legislators, and sometimes judges for state office; mayors and aldermen or councilors for city offices.

The interplay of partisanship and federalism gives rise to regional alignments that have played an important part in American electoral history. Democratic dominance in the South and Republican dominance in the Northeast were taken for granted for decades. The results of recent presidential and congressional elections, however, show a disruption of these regional patterns. Although by no means replaced, traditional regional alignments are no longer as dependable as in the past. For example, the once solid South began to turn its back on the Democratic party in presidential elections in the 1950s; in the 1960s and 1970s, Barry Goldwater and Richard Nixon captured the electoral votes of a number of southern states. It was not until 1976, when the Democrats nominated a native son of the South, Jimmy Carter, that the region again displayed solidarity (and even then Carter failed to carry Virginia). Areas outside the South that were once strongly Republican now send many Democrats to Congress, and Republicans have replaced Democrats in several southern congressional delegations (though not too many).

State patterns of partisan alignment are also changing, and these changes, in turn, cause regional patterns to shift. Because the federal system requires the citizens of each state to elect their own governing officials, it has been possible for a political party to establish itself as the dominant force in one or several states even though it has had less strength nationally. One-party domination of states—Maine and Kansas by Republicans and South Carolina, Mississippi, and Alabama by the Democrats—was an accepted political fact until the 1950s. Now one-party domination has given way in states like Maine, which has elected three Democratic governors, two Democrats to the U.S. Senate, and an independent governor since 1955, and in once strongly Democratic Missouri, which elected a Republican governor and a Republican to the U.S. Senate in the 1970s.

Several factors have contributed to shifts in partisan strength in the federal electoral system. Critical issues such as desegregation made southerners take a sharp look at the Democratic party in the 1950s and 1960s; and though unable to defeat integration, southerners expressed their opposition by turning to Republican candidates. At the same time, Blacks in both North and South—traditionally loyal Republicans since the Civil War—began to shift to the Democratic party in recent decades and formed a major source of voting support for Democrat Jimmy Carter's 1976 electoral victory. Population movement between and within states, especially Republicans migrating to the suburbs of metropolitan areas in the New South, has also changed traditional patterns. Presidential nominees bring new supporters into their party while alienating former loyalists. (Democrats in all regions found Republican Richard Nixon preferable to Democrat George McGovern in 1972; four years later many Democrats of the Catholic faith turned away from Jimmy Carter.) Whatever the source of the change, it is safe to say that regional and state strongholds of partisan strength—which owe much to the workings of federalism—are in transition.

THE ELECTORAL COLLEGE. The Electoral College, established by our Constitution, magnifies state variations in partisan support when they occur in presidential elections. The President of the United States is elected by a majority of the votes of electors chosen within the states, each state having as many electors as it has delegates in the House of Representatives and the Senate. (By constitutional amendment the District of Columbia also has three electors.) In each state a political party runs a slate of electors pledged to support the presidential candidate of that party in the electoral college; voters cast their ballots for slates of electors through their popular votes in the presidential election. The candidate receiving the plurality of popular votes receives all of the electoral votes of the state. The candidate receiving a majority of the 537 electoral votes wins the Presidency. In 1976 Jimmy Carter won popular pluralities in 23 states and the District of Columbia and 51 percent of the nationwide popular vote. Yet, by winning the electoral votes of all southern states but Virginia, and by obtaining narrow popular victories in states with large numbers of electoral votes such as New York, Pennsylvania, and Ohio, Carter obtained 55 percent of the votes of the Electoral College (see Figure 7.1).

Generally, urban America outside of the South and Southwest has voted Democratic since the New Deal. This support has given the Democrats an advantage in competition for the electoral votes of populous urban states: New York, California, Pennsylvania, Illinois, Ohio, and Michigan. Electoral majorities in a few of these states combined with support for the Democratic nominee in the South gave Democrats a clear advantage in presidential elections from 1932 to 1952. Jimmy Carter's victory repeated that pattern of electoral college voting. Republicans in 1976, and in earlier periods, were at a disadvantage because their support was strongest in states with relatively few electoral votes—midwestern, western, and the smaller northeastern states.

Although Jimmy Carter again won the electoral votes of the once solid

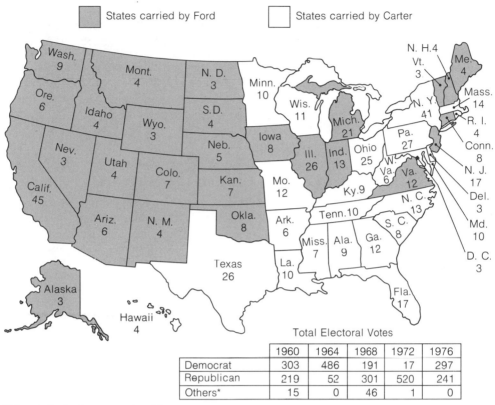

States carried by Ford   States carried by Carter

	1960	1964	1968	1972	1976
Democrat	303	486	191	17	297
Republican	219	52	301	520	241
Others*	15	0	46	1	0

Total Electoral Votes

*Other electoral votes were cast as follows:
1960—Sen. Harry Flood Byrd Sr. (D Va.) received 15 votes, including those of six of the Democratic electors in Alabama, all eight unpledged electors in Mississippi and one of the Republican electors in Oklahoma.
1968—George C. Wallace (D Ala.), candidate of the American Independent Party, carried five states having a total of 45 electoral votes: Alabama (10), Arkansas (6), Georgia (12), Louisiana (10) and Mississippi (7). In addition, one Republican elector in North Carolina voted for Wallace.
1972—John Hospers, candidate of the Libertarian Party, received one electoral vote from a Virginia Republican elector.

FIGURE 7.1
1976 Electoral Votes by States. [*Source: Congressional Quarterly Weekly Report,* 1976, 34 (45), p. 3114.]

South, neither Democrats nor Republicans can depend upon their traditional bases of support in the electoral college. Recognizing that changes are occurring, candidates for President design their strategies to appeal to new groups. Republicans in 1976 tried to appeal to an alleged "new force in American politics" (DeVries and Tarrance, 1972). This new group consisted of "ticket-splitters," people who vote for candidates of different parties for different offices (say a Republican for President and a Democrat for senator and governor). By winning the votes of these ticket-splitters, the Ford forces hoped to overcome the preponderance of Democratic loyalists in the nation and carry key states with large electoral votes, such as New York, Ohio, and Texas. Whether the outcome of the election turned on either the success or failure of such a strategy, however, is doubtful.

How do written statutes affect elections?

In addition to the state laws that set residency and registration requirements for voting, there are other statutes regulating various aspects of elections, including absentee voting, the means of tabulating votes, the placement and position of candidates' names on the ballot, ballot length, write-in voting, and which candidates names can even be listed on the ballot. These state statutes are seldom impartial in their effects upon electoral competition; each may be interpreted or manipulated to help or harm a candidate, faction, or party. Of such state regulations, three have a particularly important influence upon voting: the ballot format, the scheduling of elections, and the definition of electoral constitutencies.

BALLOTS AND VOTES.   Two major ballot formats are used in American elections (see Figure 7.2). The party-column ballot lists the candidates for each party in a separate column. It generally facilitates straight-ticket voting because a voter may select one party's entire slate merely by pulling the lever(s) for all the candidates in a column. The office-column ballot groups candidates by the office sought. Party affiliation appears next to each office seeker's name rather than at the head of a column, thus requiring the voter to do a little more thinking. Party-column ballots promote party competition by providing voters with a choice between sets of clearly labeled party candidates; office-column ballots make party label less readily available as a cue for voting. About 15 percent of persons who would vote straight-tickets if provided a party-column ballot split their votes between parties when faced with an office-column ballot (Campbell, Converse, Miller, and Stokes, 1960).

Ballots not only designate a candidate's party label, they also provide other information that a person might use as a cue for voting. When there are no party labels attached to the candidates (as in nonpartisan elections), other tidbits of information make a difference: the candidate's place on the ballot, sex, nickname, ethnic background, and occupation. Although it is not always clear that being listed first offers a vote advantage to a candidate, being listed second, third, or fourth is more disadvantageous than being listed farther down, even last. There is an advantage to having a nickname listed on the ballot and to listing one's occupation. And, in ethnic neighborhoods, it helps to have the appropriate Scandinavian, Irish, Italian, Spanish, German, or other ethnic name (see Byrne and Pueschel, 1974; Taebel, 1975).

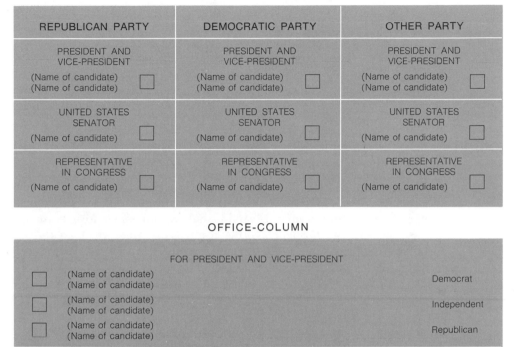

FIGURE 7.2
A Comparison of Party-Column and Office-Column Ballots.

TIMING OF ELECTIONS.   When local and statewide contests are held in conjunction with federal elections, a large number of elective offices are on the ballot. As a result, voters are unlikely to have detailed knowledge of the qualifications of more than a few of the candidates. Under such circumstances, voters base their choices on easily recognizable symbols—especially party affiliation—which simplify their task. Moreover, when several offices are voted upon at the same time, many voters concentrate on only the more important contests and simply do not vote for the offices listed farther down on the ballot; turnout may be high for the presidential election at the top of the ballot but very sparse for the coroner's race at the bottom.

When federal, state, and local elections are scheduled simultaneously, the forces producing victory for a slate of candidates at one level frequently carry over into races for other offices. Where ballot forms facilitate straight-ticket voting and federal elections coincide with state and local contests, several party candidates may ride to victory on the "coattails" of a winner at the head of the ticket. In 1976, for instance, it is likely that a few Democratic senators and governors (for example, Senator James Sasser of Tennessee and Governor Joseph Teasdale of Missouri) benefited by having a southerner, Jimmy Carter, at the head of the ballot. A presidential aspirant may also benefit from riding on a senatorial or gubernatorial candidate's coattails. Republican James ("Big Jim") Thompson's popularity in winning the governorship of Illinois in 1976 certainly assisted Gerald Ford in carrying that state in the presidential contest.

The extent and nature of "coattails" and split-ticket voting are hard to determine because they deal with voters' motivations, which are hard enough for voters themselves to disentangle and just about impossible for researchers to assess. Clearly, straight-ticket voting for reasons other than coattails— especially party identification—is very common (W. E. Miller, 1955; Campbell and Miller, 1957); and in close contests where relatively few votes may make a difference, party leaders welcome an attractive candidate at the head of the ticket, because his or her popularity may generate voter support for the party's lesser nominees. It is equally difficult to discern why voters split their tickets. Many reasons have been suggested: Ticket-splitters differ from other voters in their social and demographic characteristics, acquire their information about politics from different sources than do straight-ticket voters, are weak in their partisan loyalties, are better informed and more trusting of government, are more partisan in their choices for lesser offices than in their choices for higher ones, care more about the issue stands than the party affiliations of candidates for major offices, and make voting choices later in a campaign than other voters (DeVries and Tarrance, 1972; W. E. Miller and Levitin, 1976; Nie, Verba, and Petrocik, 1976). What all the speculation boils down to, however, is that ticket-splitting occurs because a lot of different people for a lot of different reasons decide to do the same thing in different ways.

Even the period of time that the polls are open for voting can influence an election. The reason? Different kinds of people vote at different times of the day. Most polls, of course, open early in the morning and close in the early evening. But only about 10 percent of voters go to the polls before 8:00 a.m. and only 15 percent after 6:00 p.m. About 33 percent of the electorate vote between 8 a.m. and 12 noon and the remaining 40 percent vote in about equal proportions between noon and 4:00 p.m., and between 4 p.m. and 6 p.m. Farmers, professionals, managers, and the elderly tend to vote early; craftspeople and Catholics vote later. Campaign managers, mindful of these patterns, can target their get-out-the-vote efforts (via telephone calls and radio commercials) to reach the voters most susceptible at given hours of the day (Klorman, 1976).

CONSTITUENCIES AND VOTES. Statutes regulating the boundaries, size, and composition of electoral constituencies also affect election results. When political choice is tied to such factors as party loyalties and place of residence, constituencies can be designed to make one party dominant over others. One way to do this is through gerrymandering, that is, the practice of drawing the lines of legislative districts to favor certain political interests such as the majority party, Whites, or incumbents. Because the minorities are outnumbered in the gerrymandered districts, they simply cannot win at the polls. Where this occurs, social interests usually end up competing in the primary election of the dominant party rather than aligning with lesser parties that have no chance of winning the general election. Often the votes of Blacks, Mexican-Americans, and other ethnic groups are divided into several constituencies instead of being concentrated in an electoral unit that could form a majority in the struggle for political control.

How do unwritten partisan traditions affect elections?

Constitutions not only are collections of written principles and statutes; they also reflect the political habits of a people. One of the habits of the American electorate has been an enduring loyalty to two-party competition in federal elections. The distribution of votes between Republican and Democratic parties has been remarkably stable over the years, with relatively small percentages of popular votes going to minor or third-party candidates in nationwide elections (compare George Wallace's unusually high showing of 13 percent of the presidential vote in 1968 with the 1 percent received by a scattering of minor party candidates in the 1976 election).

Recent electoral history reflects fairly clear-cut partisan voting habits. Republican majorities in presidential elections were typical from 1864 to 1932; since then Democratic majorities have been the rule. Exceptions to both patterns were Democratic popular vote majorities or pluralities in 1876, 1884, 1892, and 1916, and Republican victories in 1952, 1956, 1968, and 1972. Since 1932, Democratic control of Congress has been virtually entrenched. One-party dominance in safe districts has helped the party to maintain its congressional majority even in the face of a national landslide for the opposition. In 1972 Democrats found solace in having elected a Democratic House and Senate when Richard Nixon achieved an overwhelming victory over George McGovern.

Party voting in presidential elections since 1789 clearly reveals a cyclical trend in shifting party fortunes (Sellers, 1965). One party enters a period of ascendancy, while a minority of voters continue to favor the opposition or an occasional minor party. So long as party identifiers stick to their guns and the dominant party continues in the ascendancy, voting produces *maintaining* elections (Campbell et al., 1960). In the 1924 and 1928 elections, Republicans maintained their ascendancy; in 1964, Democrats maintained theirs.

A second stage of the cycle follows ascendancy: New voters come into the electorate and remain independent of both parties or identify with the minority opposition; a few partisans are converted; or normally indifferent citizens —attracted by a personable candidate or stimulated by a dramatic issue— vote against the ascendant party. If support for the two parties grows more evenly balanced, the close competition begins a period of two-party equilibrium. Presidential and congressional elections from 1872 to 1896 reflected such an equilibrium, and some political observers regard the period of contemporary presidential elections as one of equilibrium. In the equilibrium stage of the cycle, elections take one of two forms: In a *deviating* election, various issues, the candidates, and other influences produce temporary defections among majority party identifiers, sufficient in size to permit the minority party to win (as in 1968 or 1972), or an unusually high turnout by normally indifferent or independent voters puts the minority party over the top. The presidential elections of 1952 and 1956, for example, attracted many Democrats and independents as well as loyal Republicans to the Eisenhower cause, and he became the first Republican President in two decades. A *reinstating* election returns to power the party defeated in a deviating election; party loyalists who had defected return to the fold in sufficient numbers to provide the majority party with victory. The victory of John F. Kennedy in 1960 reinstated the Democratic majority that had been out of the Presidency for eight years; the 1976 victory of Jimmy Carter is a more recent example of a reinstating election.

But periods of equilibrium also deteriorate. When they do, a period of party realignment is in the offing, one that reflects a long-term shift in party allegiance. During this phase there is usually a *critical* election revealing that realignment and either (a) installing the opposition as the newly ascendant party or (b) reinforcing the already dominant position of the older majority party. Sometimes critical elections follow serious disturbances in American social life, disturbances resulting in permanent personal defections from one party to another. An example was the presidential election of 1932 held in the midst of the Great Depression (Key, 1955). Following a stage of realignment, the cycle begins anew with another period of party ascendancy.

Periods of party ascendancy, equilibrium, and realignment and the types of election common to each are based on the tradition of American loyalty to one of the major parties. Several indicators suggest, however, that partisan voting may be on the way out. First, although partisan identification is still a common form of political participation, the proportion of self-designated independents is rising (Table 7.1). Second, split-ticket voting is widespread, suggesting that fewer voters enter the voting booth with strong partisan convictions; indeed, many voters split their choices for President, governor, and members of Congress between parties and then do not bother to mark the remainder of the ballot. Third, deviating elections are more frequent, an indication that weak partisans and peripherally involved voters are moving back and forth across

TABLE 7.1

The distribution of partisanship in the United States, 1952–1976 (in percentages)

Question: "Generally speaking, do you usually think of yourself as a Republican, a Democrat, an Independent, or what? (If Republican or Democrat) Would you call yourself a strong (R) (D) or a not very strong (R) (D)? (If Independent) Do you think of yourself as closer to the Republican or the Democratic Party?"

	Oct. 1952	Oct. 1954	Oct. 1956	Oct. 1958	Oct. 1960	Nov. 1962	Oct. 1964	Nov. 1966	Nov. 1968	Nov. 1970	Nov. 1972	Nov. 1974	Nov. 1976
Democrat													
Strong	22	22	21	23	21	23	26	18	20	20	15	17	15
Weak	25	25	23	24	25	23	25	27	25	23	27	21	25
Independent													
Democrat	10	9	7	7	8	8	9	9	10	10	11	13	12
Independent	5	7	9	8	8	8	8	12	11	13	13	15	14
Republican	7	6	8	4	7	6	6	7	9	8	10	8	10
Republican													
Weak	14	14	14	16	13	16	13	15	14	15	13	14	14
Strong	13	13	15	13	14	12	11	10	10	10	10	8	9
Apolitical, don't know	4	4	3	5	4	4	2	2	1	1	1	4	1
Total	100	100	100	100	100	100	100	100	100	100	100	100	100
Number of respondents	1614	1139	1772	1269	3021	1289	1571	1291	1553	1802	2697	2512	2872

Source: Center for Political Studies, The University of Michigan, Ann Arbor.

party lines. Fourth, party identification is generally associated with high rates of voting in elections, that is, partisans vote more often than do independents; but turnouts in American presidential elections have dropped, which may mean that partisan attachments are weakening. Moreover, partisans are more likely than independents to vote both in presidential election years and in congressional elections in years with no presidential contest. The voting rate in off-year congressional elections is lower than in presidential years, however, which may prove that many voters who take part in presidential elections are without partisan learnings and do not vote two years later (Burnham, 1970).

SOCIAL BASES OF VOTING

Journalists, TV commentators, and other political pundits devote a great deal of time to analyzing the "youth vote," "Black vote," "blue-collar vote," "Catholic vote," and various other forms of "bloc" voting. The inference is that elections provide the opportunity for specific social and demographic groups to unite their members, turn out at the polls en masse, and by voting as a bloc represent their conflicting interests to policymakers. In fact, however, the social bases of voting in America are so shifting that it is very difficult to identify a youth vote, blue-collar vote, Catholic vote, or any other voting bloc that represents a segment of our society.

Demographics of voting

Some observers have concluded that Americans respond to elections on the basis of their sex, age, education, ethnic backgrounds, religion, residence, and social class. As Table 7.2 demonstrates, however, with a couple of notable exceptions (Blacks and party loyalists), it is rare for any single demographic group to support one party over the other consistently from one election to another. Generally, as the nationwide vote shifts from party to party between elections, so does the support of any demographic group. It is therefore misleading to claim that "demography is destiny" (Scammon and Wattenberg, 1970, p. 45).

SEX.   The voting rates of women in federal elections differ little from those of men (see Chapter 4). It is equally hard to discern differences in the partisan choices of the sexes. Although women in recent presidential and congressional contests have shown slightly greater support for the Democrats than have men (Pomper, 1975), the differences are so slight that they could reflect other social characteristics (age, residence, social class) rather than intrinsic political differences. Put simply, there is no male or female voting bloc.

AGE.   No age group shows a consistent partisan preference in voting. Claims were made in the late 1960s and early 1970s that the enfranchisement of 18-year-olds would produce a proliberal, pro-Democratic "youth" vote. The claim rested in part upon the highly publicized support of some young people for the candidacies of Eugene McCarthy and Robert Kennedy in the 1968 presidential primaries. What the claimants failed to see was that in the presidential election of 1968, young voters supported the third-party candidacy of George Wallace as strongly as they did any other candidate. Moreover, in the elections of 1972 and 1976, younger voters divided their votes fairly evenly between the two parties, again failing to produce a voting bloc of the young.

If age influences voting, it does so indirectly. As one grows older there are greater opportunities for political involvement; the habit of participation takes hold and, as we have seen in Chapter 4, middle-aged citizens are more likely to vote than are the young. Party loyalties tend to intensify with age as well. The longer one supports a party, the more inclined the person is to continue on that course—with exceptions, of course. In contrast to the 1950s, today many young people enter the voting population without strong partisan loyalties. Instead, they are politically independent, perhaps switching preferences from one party to another in the first few elections in which they take part. The decline in partisanship in the national electorate in recent years is primarily the result of adding unusually large numbers of young independents to the potential electorate rather than of movement away from partisanship among older and politically experienced voters. Between the 1964 and 1968 presidential elections, the size of the eligible electorate increased from approximately 113 million to 120 million persons (with 62 percent of those eligible voting in 1964, 61 percent voting in 1968). But between 1968 and 1972, the increase in eligible voters was from 120 million to 137 million (with 56 percent of the eligibles voting in 1972); of that 17 million increase, 11 million reflected the fact that the Twenty-Sixth Amendment had enfranchised all citizens in the 18–20-year-old age category, of whom more than 40 percent had no partisan affiliation. Only about 33 percent of the remainder of the eligible electorate declared no partisan identification. As these younger voters become politically socialized, like their elders they may also acquire partisan preferences and the decline in partisan loyalties of the 1970s may cease (W. E. Miller and Levitin, 1976).

EDUCATION. As a general rule, citizens with a grade-school education are more likely to be Democratic in their partisanship than are college-educated citizens. But this does not mean that all college graduates are Republican. Persons with postgraduate training as lawyers, medical doctors, and engineers gravitate toward Republican preferences; voters with graduate degrees in the natural sciences, social sciences, and humanities, particularly academicians, are more frequently Democrats (Ladd and Lipset, 1973).

OCCUPATION. Neither political party can count on exclusive support by any occupational group. Yet there are marginal differences: Businesspeople involved in both large and small enterprises tend to favor Republican candidates, although that depends on the type of business, the locale, and so forth; Republicans also attract the votes of white-collar, managerial, professional, and executive workers. Blue collar workers, both skilled and unskilled, lean toward the Democrats.

Such marginal differences in voting by occupation have led many political observers to attribute Republican victories to the support of businessmen, Democratic victories to the efforts of organized labor. In fact, the differences are too small to support such views. Take union membership as an example. Although the union vote is viewed as a voting bloc in many analyses, the evidence is that "in national voting patterns it is clear that the union vote has, over recent years, moved in accord with the same factors influencing the nonunion vote, *not* in accord with specifiable changes in union leadership,

TABLE 7.2
Partisan voting choices of demographic groups, 1952–1976 (in percentages)

Group	1952		1956		1960		1964	
	Stevenson	Ike	Stevenson	Ike	JFK	Nixon	LBJ	Goldwater
NATIONAL	44.6	55.4	42.2	57.8	50.1	49.9	61.3	38.7
Sex								
Male	47	53	45	55	52	48	60	40
Female	42	58	39	61	49	51	62	38
Race								
White	43	57	41	59	49	51	59	41
Non-White	79	21	61	39	68	32	94	6
Education								
College	34	66	31	69	39	61	52	48
High school	45	55	42	58	52	48	62	38
Grade school	52	48	50	50	55	45	66	34
Occupation								
Professional and business	36	64	32	68	42	58	54	46
White collar	40	60	37	63	48	52	57	43
Manual	55	45	50	50	60	40	71	29
Age								
Under 30 years	51	49	43	57	54	46	64	36
30–49 years	47	53	45	55	54	46	63	37
50 years and older	39	61	39	61	46	54	59	41
Religion								
Protestant	37	63	37	63	38	62	55	45
Catholic	56	44	51	49	78	22	76	24
Politics								
Republican	8	92	4	96	5	95	20	80
Democrat	77	23	85	15	84	16	87	13
Independent	35	65	30	70	43	57	56	44
Region								
East	45	55	40	60	53	47	68	32
Midwest	42	58	41	59	48	52	61	39
South	51	49	49	51	51	49	52	48
West	42	58	43	57	49	51	60	40
Members of labor								
Union families	61	39	57	43	65	35	73	27

Source: Gallup Opinion Index, Report No. 137, 1976, pp. 16–17.

1968			1972		1976		
Humphrey	Nixon	Wallace	McGovern	Nixon	Carter	Ford	McCarthy
43.0	43.4	13.6	38	62	50	48	1
41	43	16	37	63	53	45	1
45	43	12	38	62	48	51	*
38	47	15	32	68	46	52	1
85	12	3	87	13	85	15	*
37	54	9	37	63	42	55	2
42	43	15	34	66	54	46	*
52	33	15	49	51	58	41	1
34	56	10	31	69	42	56	1
41	47	12	36	64	50	48	2
50	35	15	43	57	58	41	1
47	38	15	48	52	53	45	1
44	41	15	33	67	48	49	2
41	47	12	36	64	52	48	*
35	49	16	30	70	46	53	*
59	33	8	48	52	57	42	1
9	86	5	5	95	9	91	*
74	12	14	67	33	82	18	*
31	44	25	31	69	38	57	4
50	43	7	42	58	51	47	1
44	47	9	40	60	48	50	1
31	36	33	29	71	54	45	*
44	49	7	41	59	46	51	1
56	29	15	46	54	63	36	1

strategy, or tactics. . . . Indeed, an analysis of the union vote between 1952 and 1972 shows almost no fluctuation that could be attributed to union leadership influence" (W. E. Miller and Levitin, 1976, pp. 28–29).

ETHNICITY/RACE. America is often described as a "melting pot" into which people of all races, national origins, and religious backgrounds have been poured; slowly ethnic traits recede and the sons and daughters of diverse immigrant groups become homogenized. There is some evidence that the melting pot theory is more myth than fact and that ethnic groups retain their individuality through many generations. Traditionally, Democrats have drawn electoral support from voters of Irish, Polish, Italian, and Slavic descent; Republicans have appealed to Americans of English, Scottish, Welsh, German, and Scandinavian ancestry. But like other alleged voting blocs, the electoral choices of ethnic groups shift from election to election and are divided between the political parties. The 1976 presidential contest witnessed such a shift: the "Italian vote," normally Democratic in inclination, was divided 55–45 percent in favor of Republican candidate Gerald Ford.

If there is such a thing as a voting bloc, it consists of Black voters. As Table 7.2 indicates, Blacks have consistently given the bulk of their support to Democratic candidates in presidential elections. Even at the low point of Black support for Democrats in 1956, two of three Blacks voted for Adlai Stevenson. Blacks were probably decisive in Jimmy Carter's narrow victory over Gerald Ford in 1976; among White voters nationwide, Ford won a majority of the popular votes, but among Black voters—turning out in some areas in record numbers—more than eight out of every ten chose Carter.

RELIGION. Although there are both Catholic Republicans and Protestant Democrats, Protestants traditionally have tended to vote for Republicans, and Catholics and Jews for Democrats. But in 1976, Baptists (who had given Richard Nixon a healthy 77 percent of their votes in 1972) gave 56 percent of their votes to fellow Baptist Jimmy Carter. Jews, however, who had given only 40 percent of their votes to Nixon in 1972, gave 45 percent to Ford in 1976, perhaps a sign of their drifting away from older habits. And Catholics—once the bulwark of the Democratic coalition—gave just over one-half of their votes to Gerald Ford in 1976.

In some campaigns, religion is a key factor. John F. Kennedy's candidacy in 1960, for instance, aroused pro- and anti-Catholic sentiments. Overall, because of Protestant Democrats who defected to Nixon in 1960 and Catholic Republicans attracted to Kennedy over the religious issue, Kennedy lost about 2 percent of the normal Democratic share of the two-party vote. This loss was more than offset, however, by the peculiarities of voting in the Electoral College. The Catholic shift to Kennedy helped him win the electoral votes of populous states; defections by Protestant Democrats occurred in states with fewer electoral votes. As a result, Kennedy's religion provided a windfall of ten electoral votes (Pool, Abelson, and Popkin, 1964; Campbell et al., 1966).

RESIDENCE.   Generally, the cities of the North have been strongholds of the Democratic party, particularly in the East and portions of the northern Midwest. Republican strength has grown appreciably in urban communities in the South, especially in the last two decades. Both parties have support in the small towns of America; southern hamlets are traditionally Democratic (aside from pockets of Republican strength in east Tennessee, Kentucky, and the southwestern section of Missouri), and Republicans receive votes in the small towns of the East and the Midwest. Rural America, especially in the Midwest and West, retains a strong Republican flavor. As Table 7.2 indicates, Jimmy Carter capitalized on his strength in the South and East in 1976 to overcome popular vote problems in the rural Midwest and West, thus recapturing his native region from two successive losses to the Republican presidential candidates in 1968 and 1972. Suburban America is neither predominantly Republican nor Democratic. Although many suburbs have distinctive class and partisan colorations, and there are thus strongly Democratic suburbs and strongly Republican ones, overall it is impossible to discern a monolithic "suburban vote."

CLASS.   As with members of other voting groups, persons sharing a common social class show certain partisan tendencies, but such inclinations alone seldom decide the outcome of elections. The influence of social class on the vote varies from election to election. "Class voting" has not been significant in recent presidential elections, but from time to time there has been evidence of it. Although class differences in voting were not apparent in 1976, four years earlier class-related appeals were a part of George McGovern's unsuccessful effort to win the White House. Bearing in mind that the ties between social class and partisan preference are loose, we can conclude that people in the upper and upper-middle classes tend to vote Republican, and people in the middle and lower classes tend to vote Democratic (Axelrod, 1972).

Social and demographic attributes alone are not the explanation

A recapitulation of what we have said about the voting tendencies of major demographic groups appears in Table 7.3. By now the reader knows not to be misled by these general profiles of support for each major party and will not conclude that any demographic category belongs exclusively or permanently to Republicans or Democrats. Neither party can stake its chances on these tendencies. Instead, if they are to win major elections both parties must build coalitions among people with different social backgrounds by blunting the conflicts between diverse interests. Viewed from the standpoint of the indi-

TABLE 7.3
Partisan tendencies of key demographic groups

Democratic	Republican
Middle- and lower-income citizens	Middle- and upper-income citizens
Organized and unskilled workers	Managerial and professional persons
First and second generation Americans: Irish, Polish, Italian, Slavic minorities	Germanic and Scottish stock
Nonwhites and whites	Whites
Farm operators	Prosperous farmers
Roman Catholics and Jews	Protestants
Citizens with both little formal education and graduate training	College educated and professionally trained
Residents of cities, lower- and middle-class suburbs, rural southerners	Residents of middle- and upper-class suburbs, small towns, rural midwesterners
Young to middle-aged	Middle-aged to elderly

vidual voter rather than the perspective of the two parties, the lesson to be drawn from this discussion of demographics and voting is that a person's social or demographic attributes do not determine his or her vote. Rather, each citizen's voting choice results from a complex intermingling of political, social, demographic, and personal factors that the person takes into account, interprets, and responds to.

PERSONAL FACTORS AND VOTING CHOICES

The personal factors underlying voting are of two principal types:

- *Political perspectives* consist of a person's view of politics in general as reflected in the attitudes he or she learns throughout life; each person views a given election from a unique political perspective.
- *Political perceptions* consists of the specific electoral objects one takes into account, that is, the candidates, parties, issues, and communications the person thinks are important in making an electoral choice.

In any election a citizen encounters a large number of appeals, claims, counterclaims, charges, and countercharges. Relatively few voters have the time or interest to ferret out all of the evidence necessary to reach a fully informed decision. Instead, the voter's decision is made under conditions of uncertainty and with imperfect information. Small wonder then that most citizens employ devices that save them time, money, and both physical and psychic energy in acquiring adequate, if not perfect, information (Popkin,

Gorman, Phillips, and Smith, 1976). A citizen's political perspectives offer one set of such devices; the selective screening out of information through the voter's political perceptions offer another.

Perspectives: partisanship, ideology, and ideals

Of the many things that color a voter's view of politics, none has been as traditionally important as the person's enduring feeling of kinship and loyalty to one or the other of our two major political parties.

As we saw in Chapter 4, identification with a political party has been one of the most widespread and consistent ways in which Americans take part in conflict representation. Although party loyalties have declined in recent years (Table 7.1), about three of every five Americans are still willing to classify themselves as "weak" or "strong" Democrats or Republicans; and of those who call themselves "independents" about as many think of themselves as close to one or the other of the major parties as regard themselves as wholly without partisan inclination.

Whatever the source of party loyalties—conscious reflection, habit, emotional satisfaction, early family socialization and subsequent reinforcement by friends and other groups—they are personally meaningful symbols that simplify the choice between candidates. Psychological attachment to a political party affects a voter's perceptions of candidates, issues, and parties (Campbell et al., 1960).

If Americans were to cast votes in federal elections *solely* in accordance with partisan sentiments, the normal distribution of the two-party vote between Democrats and Republicans would be 54–46 percent (W. E. Miller and Levitin, 1976). Although Democratic identifiers outnumber Republicans by roughly 2 to 1, Republicans tend to go to the polls more regularly than do Democrats (recall the discussion in Chapter 4). But, as illustrated in Table 7.2, in no presidential election between 1952 and 1976 has the division of the two-party vote produced the 54–46 split between Democrats and Republicans. Although deviations of the actual popular vote for Congress from the expected 54–46 vote have averaged only about 2.5 percentage points since 1952, there have been deviations of some magnitude, suggesting that factors other than party loyalties help voters reach a decision. In fact, from one-fifth to one-third of party identifiers may defect to the opposition in presidential contests because of specific forces operating in a given election.

Commitment to a political party may be weak, moderate, or strong. Weak and moderate identifiers are especially prone to defect from their party because of the attractiveness of the opposition's candidate (or lack of appeal of their own party's candidate), a striking issue, or some other factor working in the campaign. In the 1950s many Democrats voted for Republican Dwight Eisenhower, whose image as a victorious general transcended partisan loyalties

(Campbell et al., 1966); many Protestant Democrats in 1960 voted for Richard Nixon as a sign of concern over John F. Kennedy's Catholic religion; in 1964 two of every ten Republicans defected to the Johnson-Humphrey ticket out of dissatisfaction with their own party's candidate, Barry Goldwater; in 1968 many Democrats and Republicans voted for George Wallace's independent candidacy; in 1972 almost one-third of Democrats voted Republican; and in 1976 many voters of both parties crossed lines to vote for Jimmy Carter or Gerald Ford.

Even if the partisan inclinations of voters translated automatically into matching votes, the many independents in the electorate would produce some variation from the 54–46 division expected in a strictly two-party vote. True independents respond to the short-term forces of a given election rather than to the traditional appeals of candidates to party loyalty; independents are also likely to split their tickets in voting. Some political observers (DeVries and Tarrance, 1972) claim that people who split their tickets share demographic characteristics: They are younger, more educated, and more often white-collared and suburban than the average voter. Moreover, they get more of their political information from the mass media than do partisan voters and, for this reason, are more responsive to the images of candidates and issues portrayed in the media than to party appeals. Although it is questionable whether the ticket-splitter has such a distinct profile, at least as contrasted with straight-ticket voters (Atwood and Sanders, 1975; Boyd, 1972), many votors do not rely consistently upon partisanship to simplify voting decisions.

Some observers stress the importance of ideology as an alternative to partisanship. To be sure, four of every five Americans are willing to place themselves within some type of left-to-right or liberal-to-conservative spectrum of political ideology when asked to do so. Table 7.4 is one example of such a self-classification. Recent research suggests that voters may evaluate the qualities of presidential candidates from an ideological perspective (Miller, Miller, Raine, and Brown, 1976). In 1972 George McGovern was evaluated in a positive way by people on the left of the political spectrum, negatively by those on the right; he also received negative marks from liberals. Three-fourths of voters in 1972 labeled McGovern a liberal or left-of-center; to the degree that an ideological perspective counts for something, this was a bad omen from a predominantly centrist or conservative electorate. In 1976, voters' images of the ideological stances of the two candidates were not so distinct. Opinion surveys indicated that nearly 40 percent called Gerald Ford conservative, 33 percent called him moderate, 14 percent saw him as liberal, and the remainder were unsure. This general evaluation remained stable throughout the campaign. Jimmy Carter, on the other hand, started the campaign viewed as moderate by 33 percent of Americans, a conservative by about 20 percent, and a liberal by about 20 percent. As the campaign wore on, Carter came across to voters more as a liberal (36 percent) than as a moderate (28 percent) or a conservative (19

TABLE 7.4
Ideological self-classification of voters, 1976
(in percentages)

Classification	March	September
"Left"	31	31
"Middle"	10	10
"Right"	49	42
Unsure	10	17
	100	100
Number of respondents	1500	1500

Source: Gallup Opinion Index, Report No. 137, 1976, p. 41.

percent). Again, the centrist-to-conservative makeup of the American electorate—especially the independents within it—provided some observers an
explanation for why Jimmy Carter began the campaign with a substantial
popular lead in polls over Gerald Ford but won only a narrow 51–48 percent
victory (Reinhold, 1976).

Other perspectives of potential significance are the conceptions people have
of what their officeholders should be like. There is evidence (Nimmo and
Savage, 1976) that many voters formulate idealized images of the qualities they
expect to find in public officials. These images help guide the citizens' perceptions of the actual contenders in an election. Voters respond favorably to
candidates who measure up well; they evaluate in negative ways those that do
not. There are instances, of course, when neither candidate matches the voters'
ideal very closely. In 1976 a number of pollsters discovered that even up to
election day the intensity of voters' commitments to either Jimmy Carter or
Gerald Ford was very low, something not typical in presidential elections.
Public opinion analyst Louis Harris found that of those voting for Carter, only
42 percent reported feeling "very strongly for him" and of those for Ford only
40 percent felt "very strongly" (*The Harris Survey,* November 11, 1976). As a
source of political perspectives, then, idealized images of officeholders may
contribute to lukewarm feelings about all candidates if voters do not see ideal
qualities in any of the contenders.

Perceptions: candidates, parties, issues, and communications

In an election campaign, then, voters rely upon a number of perspectives to
save them time and energy as they make difficult decisions. Party identification, despite the increase in independents, remains a strong influence upon
voters' long-term perspectives on elections, although this influence is probably
greater in congressional and statewide contests than in presidential elections.
Whether a person votes according to party loyalty or defects depends upon

how that citizen responds to the short-term influences of the candidates, competing parties, political issues, and campaign communications through various media.

CANDIDATE IMAGES.   The qualities a candidate tries to impress upon voters interact with what voters actually see in the office-seeker to constitute the candidate's image. In recent presidential elections the candidates of both parties have usually emerged with positive images; two exceptions were the distinctly negative views held by substantial portions of the electorate about Republican Barry Goldwater in 1964 and Democrat George McGovern in 1972. It is relatively rare that the image of a presidential candidate remains as ambiguous and elusive to voters as did Jimmy Carter's in 1976. As the campaign began, voters attributed several assets to Carter: 69 percent of surveyed respondents thought him a "man of high integrity," 66 percent agreed he was "not part of the Washington, D.C. establishment, and that is good," and a majority said that "he has the courage not to make promises to get votes," "he would inspire confidence personally in the White House," and "he is the kind of new, fresh face that is needed in the White House." But voters saw a negative side as well; pluralities tagged him as lacking in governmental experience, as having "ducked stands on issues to avoid offending anybody," as not as independent of party bosses as he had been before winning the nomination, and too "cocksure." Summing up feelings about Carter on the eve of the campaign, a 48–41 percent plurality of respondents said "It's hard to get up real enthusiasm for him as a candidate for President" (The Harris Survey, September 16, 1976). Several weeks of campaigning and two debates with Gerald Ford did little to clarify the Carter image: a 49–41 percent plurality felt in late October that Carter "makes me uneasy because I can't tell what kind of person he really is" (The Harris Survey, October 21, 1976).

To what degree do voters take the images of candidates into account in making a voting decision? Political scientists are divided on that question, but there is growing evidence that in presidential elections, candidate images may be the most crucial short-term factor influencing the vote. One study, for example, reports that voters' images of presidential candidates probably provided the major explanation for defections from party loyalties in 1956, 1960, and 1964 (Boyd, 1969), and related research reveals that candidate images were the best single prediction of voting behavior in recent elections (Natchez and Bupp, 1968); another study claims that statistics "clearly indicate that the candidates were the most important factor in each of the elections—1960 through 1972" (RePass, 1976, p. 815). Candidate imagery has proved less important in congressional campaigns and party loyalties more so, chiefly because many voters do not know the names of the contenders and, for those who do, the incumbent's image is generally more persuasive.

Voters express more interest in candidates than in abstract programs or in issues; moreover, as long as parties do not present the electorate with clear-cut policy alternatives, voters are forced to take competing personalities into account more than other factors. The interplay between partisan loyalties and images of competing candidates is complex. Party loyalties color perceptions of of candidates (voters normally have a more positive opinion of their party's candidate), but voters frequently affiliate with parties because of the candidates nominated. If they believe that their own party has no appealing office-seekers, their partisan loyalties may weaken. And the long-term allegiance of younger voters may tip toward the party that consistently offers more attractive candidates. The lasting appeal of the major parties is tied to the images of party nominees (Kirkpatrick, Lyons, and Fitzgerald, 1975; Stokes, 1966).

PARTY IMAGES. Party images consist of the things people like and dislike about each of the major political parties. They are not the same as partisan identifications or party loyalties. A person may well identify with a party, yet not like some of the things it is doing. The content of a party image includes references to party candidates ("Gerald Ford is a decent man" or "Jimmy Carter troubles me"), evaluations of the performance of the party's officeholders ("They spend less money," "Times are just better under them"), references to the groups the party seems to favor ("They are good for the common people," or "They are good for big business"), and general expressions ("I just don't like them").

The relative evaluation of each of our major parties, as measured by surveys in presidential elections, has been fairly stable since 1952: The ratio of favorable to unfavorable comments about Republicans has been about one to one; for Democrats the ratio has been about two to one. Americans applaud Democratic efforts on the domestic scene, Republicans in international matters. Traditionally, Americans have viewed the Democrats as the party of prosperity, the Republicans as the party of peace. In 1976, however, the Grand Old Party no longer received high marks in foreign policy. Asked "which political party do you think would be more likely to keep the United States out of World War III," a cross-section of Americans surveyed arrayed themselves as follows: 33 percent said the Democrats, 28 percent the Republicans, 22 percent said it made no difference, and the remainder had no opinion. Asked "which party do you think will do the better job of keeping the country prosperous," 47 percent said the Democrats, 24 percent the Republicans, 15 percent said it made no difference, and 14 percent had no opinion (*Gallup Opinion Index*, No. 135, 1976). Two things are noteworthy about these findings: (1) Party images change according to what occurs in the political environment; on the peace and prosperity question, shifts in party fortunes may follow political events. (2) With respect to both peace and prosperity, almost one of every three Americans surveyed either could see no difference between the parties or expressed no opinion. In sum, the general images of the two political parties show that public feelings are lukewarm and mixed, but voter opinion gives the Democrats a slight edge over the Republicans (Trilling, 1975).

POLITICAL ISSUES.   Studies of American voting behavior conducted in the 1950s and early 1960s generally concluded that most voters cared little about and were unfamiliar with many of the issues in presidential elections and that in congressional contests they were even more aloof. Then, beginning with the presidential election of 1964 researchers noted a change. For one thing, in contrast to earlier election campaigns, the major party candidates took strikingly different positions on key questions: civil rights, nuclear responsibility, social welfare programs, the role of "big government," and foreign policy—especially the emerging war in Vietnam. In addition, whereas Democrats and Republicans in the past had held similar views in selected policy areas—fair employment, school integration, job guarantees—after 1964 policy views tended to coincide more with party loyalties; Democrats took slightly more "liberal" stances and Republicans slightly more "conservative" ones. And after 1964, voters began increasingly to discern clear-cut differences between the two parties on major issues—education, taxation, job guarantees, school integration, busing, medical care, and other matters. In brief, one political scientist examining the trends in voters' awareness of issues and policy differences between the two parties from 1952 to 1972 was able to conclude, "The electorate now has a clearer perception of the general ideological character of the major parties" (Pomper, 1975, p. 185).

How important are election issues to the voter trying to make up his or her mind between competing candidates and parties? That question must be answered in two parts: First, it is clear that "issue voting"—voting on the basis of where one perceives the candidates and parties stand on important issues—has increased in recent elections. For example, specialized publics spot party differences on issues that are important to them (Blacks on civil rights issues, many parents in metropolotan areas on the busing issue, the elderly on health care issues). In explanations of the voting choice of members of these specialized publics, pertinent issues have almost as much weight as party loyalties (RePass, 1971).

Issues can move the general electorate as well as special interests within it. This is particularly true if voters detect that the positions candidates take on the issues differ markedly not only from candidate to candidate but also from the views of large portions of the electorate. One explanation for the large-scale defection of Republicans from the candidacy of Barry Goldwater in 1964 was that he seemed to take more extreme positions on some issues (social welfare, civil rights, big government) than many Americans were used to hearing; similarly, George McGovern in 1972 lost the votes of many fellow Democrats because his issue stands were viewed as far to the left of those held by the bulk of Americans. Some researchers argue that Americans are moving away from the center of the issue continuum toward the extremes they were reluctant to support in 1964 and 1972: "The result is that a candidate who might have been an issue extremist in one year may be less of one in another year" (Nie, Verba, and Petrocik, 1976, p. 341). If this appraisal is accurate, then we might expect increased issue voting in future elections. However, this will happen only if contending candidates make an effort to represent the conflicting positions of the electorate in the campaign: "If the public is faced with candidates distinguished from each other on the basis of the issues, it will vote on the issues. If the public is offered a more centerist choice, the vote will depend much more heavily upon partisan identification" (Nie, Verba, and Petrocik, 1976, p. 318).

In sum, one part of the answer to the question of how important issues are to voting is that issue voting is on the increase, particularly among specialized publics. And when voters are polarized on issues and candidates appeal to the differences, widespread issue voting influences the electoral outcome. But, there is a second part to the question: Compared to other factors, how important are issues in helping voters make up their minds? On this matter there is very little agreement among political scientists. One set of researchers examined the outcome of the 1972 presidential election and noted that McGovern voters differed considerably from Nixon voters in their own issue stands, in where they thought each candidate stood on the issues, and in how far they thought their own views were from those of each of the opposing candidates. Liberals tended to vote for McGovern; centerists and conservatives for Nixon. The investigators described 1972 as an ideological election (A. H. Miller et al., 1976). Other researchers looking at the same evidence and weighing the relative influence of candidates' images, issues, and party loyalties concluded that the 1972 election was decided by the candidate factor (Nimmo and Savage, 1976; Margolis, 1977; Repass, 1976).

The problem with trying to unravel the interwined influence of candidates, issues, and parties on voters' choices is that the voters themselves cannot separate their perceptions of candidates, issues, and parties. In some elections, voter perceptions of the contenders have a heavy partisan component; in others, candidates and issues are inseparable. Sometimes voters project their own issue positions on to candidates and parties, assuming that the favored contenders agree with their own positions; at other times, voters adopt candidates' and party stands as their own.

Perhaps the best answer to what role issues play in voting lies in the voters' search for devices to assist then in reaching difficult decisions. If the images of candidates are widely publicized, clearly defined, and attractive, then they serve as convenient aids; if candidates' positions on issues are distinct, they offer voters a handle on what is happening; and if candidates stress partisan loyalties, the voters' partisan predilections come into play. One of the intriguing aspects of the 1976 presidential election was neither candidate established a clearly defined and attractive or repelling image, that issues were muted, and partisan lines were blurred. Small wonder that on the eve of the election leading pollsters in the nation found the election too close to call.

There is one other way that political issues influence voting, although here the word "issues" is less accurate than "appraisals." Voters reach general appraisals of the goodness or badness of the times they live in and of who is responsible for those conditions. If citizens are uneasy and the incumbent candidate or party seems responsible, voters may demand a change and switch their support from the "ins" to the "outs." If times are good, incumbency may reign (Key, 1966). Such general appraisals have affected the outcome of presidential elections several times in recent decades. In 1968 the uneasiness over the war in Vietnam, civil disorder, and race relations probably contributed to many Democrats and independents voting for Republican Richard Nixon or independent candidate George Wallace. In 1976 a sluggish economy, a general dissatisfaction with and loss of trust in political leaders, and a widespread uncertainty about the future with either party's candidate in the White House, may have contributed to a desire for a change in Washington officialdom for the sake of change, regardless of the consequences.

CAMPAIGN COMMUNICATION AND THE MEDIA. Voters seldom learn about the qualities of candidates, complex issues, or party activities firsthand. Instead they rely upon news and publicity, campaign propaganda and advertising, and other messages transmitted through the communications media. Candidates realize that voters use the media for information, guidance, reinforcement, and other reasons, and they plan campaigns accordingly (recall our discussion in Chapter 6).

Students of political communication are uncertain about the precise effects of political commercials on the vote. Recent research suggests that, in general, political advertising (1) makes voters aware of each candidate and mildly increases their knowledge and interest in the attributes and issue stands emphasized by the commercial messages; (2) does little to change how people feel about candidates and issues but reinforces positive or negative views of those who have already made up their minds and serves as a guide for the undecided; and (3) is therefore but one of the many factors persuading people how to vote (Atkin and Heald, 1976; Donohue, 1973–74; Patterson and McClure, 1976).

Paid political advertising is but one set of communications that may assist voters in understanding candidates and campaigns. Free publicity (such as newspaper accounts, feature articles in magazines, and television news coverage) also carries the candidates' messages. Although mere exposure to such messages is not decisive in the choices most voters make between candidates (Patterson and McClure, 1976), such publicity is important in at least two respects: First, by publicizing candidates and issues, the news media help set the agenda for public discussion of office-seekers and of major issues (McCombs, 1972); second, for voters who find it difficult to make up their minds as the campaign progresses—which may include from 5–20 percent of the electorate, depending upon the election—it "seems clear that mass media and other political information sources may be used in specific ways . . . to decrease difficulty" (Mendelsohn and O'Keefe, 1976; O'Keefe, Mendelsohn, and Liu, 1976, pp. 328–329).

A major source of free publicity in the 1976 presidential campaign (as in the 1960 contest between John Kennedy and Richard Nixon) was a series of televised debates between the presidential contenders, Democrat Jimmy Carter and Republican incumbent Gerald Ford. (There was also one televised debate between the vice-presidential candidates.) The debates occurred within a context of widespread uncertainty about the qualities of both candidates; opinion polls revealed that approximately twice as many voters were un-decided between the candidates in 1976 as in earlier presidential contests. The presidential debates, however, apparently did little to reduce the uncertainties. All in all, the debates may have done as much to reinforce uncertainty about the candidates as to alleviate it. As in the presidential debates of 1960, when John Kennedy picked up strength among voters calling themselves indepen-dents, the benefits of the 1976 debates probably went to Carter; but although some independents began to lean toward Carter, the gain was relatively small.

One other communication that voters may take into account in reaching decisions is the endorsement of candidates by the news media. In presidential elections the bulk of newspaper endorsements usually go to the Republican candidate. The presidential election of 1976 was true to form in this respect: 411 dailies endorsed Gerald Ford, 80 supported Jimmy Carter, and 168 were uncommitted. (The only exception to this pattern of endorsements came in 1964 when Lyndon Johnson received endorsements from 440 dailies, Barry Goldwater from 359.) Do such endorsements make a difference in elections? Recent research suggests they do. Because many voters perceive them as nonpartisan messages that offer a clear-cut evaluation, endorsements help wavering members of the electorate reach decisions. In close elections, such as those in 1960, 1968, and 1976, newspaper endorsements correlate with shifts in the votes of independent voters; in landslide elections—1956, 1964, and 1972 —endorsements may help determine the votes of defectors from the losing party (Robinson, 1974).

In sum, the various media participate in the evolution of a political cam-paign by "treating to a large extent the same events and responding to one another's presentations." And, "what they present is filtered and organized in diverse ways in the experience of people" (Blumer, 1959, p. 201). Ultimately, what difference communications make depends upon how voters make up their minds.

How the voters decide

During elections, voters canvass the campaign in search of readily grasped cues to assist them in transcending the contradictory and often confusing appeals aimed at them by candidates. Which of the many long-term views that shape their perspectives (i.e., partisan loyalties, ideological predilections, idealized visions of candidates) and which objects of their perceptions in a specific campaign (candidates, parties, issues, and communications) are most important depend upon a number of things. One is what the candidates choose to publicize. If the candidates' appeals are clearly partisan in tone, they will arouse the partisan loyalties of the voters; if the candidates accent key issues on which they disagree, then voters will perceive differences on policy views that will assist them in choosing between the contenders; and if there are major differences in the qualities and styles of the contenders, these will provide essential cues to simplify the choice.

A second factor in how the voter decides derives from the voter's scanning of the information available in a campaign.

> The voter canvasses his likes and dislikes of the leading candidates and major parties involved in the election. Weighing each like and dislike equally, he votes for the candidate toward whom he has the greatest number of favorable attitudes, if there is such a candidate. If no candidate has such an advantage, the voter votes consistently with his party affiliation, if he has one. If his attitudes do not incline him toward one candidate more than toward another, and if he does not identify with one of the major parties, the voter reaches a null decision. (Kelly and Mirer, 1974, p. 574)

What candidates emphasize in their appeals and what citizens choose as their priorities in scanning political communications combine with a third process to simplify the complicated business of voting. That third factor is the tendency of people confronted by contradictory influences to try to put things in order, to compose a consistent outlook that harmonizes their personal perspectives *on* and their perceptions *of* reality. Social psychologists label this effort a "strain toward consistency," a "drive toward congruity," or a "reduction of dissonance" (Bem, 1970). In a political campaign, many people try to hold consistent views of candidates, parties, and issues. Citizens who enter the campaign with consistent views are unlikely to be swayed by conflicting appeals; such persons are so convinced of their views that they simply filter out information that contradicts their convictions. Other citizens, however, formulate dissonant views and, as a result, try to change their minds to reduce the perceived inconsistencies. Some of these cross-pressured voters achieve consistency by changing a previously held view, as did numerous southern segregationists in the 1960s who foreswore their long-term Democratic loyalties rather than vote for a presidential nominee pledged to end segregation. For voters deeply committed to supporting the candidate of their party, a shift in perceptions may prove easier than a change of perspective. For example, some staunch anticommunist Republicans adjusted to President Nixon's historic trip to China in 1972 by convincing themselves that it was only a token gesture that would never lead to recognition of the Communist regime in China, despite utterances by Nixon to the contrary. Finally, a third category of voters simply find it impossible to resolve the conflicts between lifelong perspectives and perceptions of what is going on; as a result, they may choose not to vote as all, thereby neither distorting their perceptions of things nor changing their personal attitudes, but at least relieving themselves of the need to settle the contradictions between what they want to see and what they actually do see.

Voting: tangible or token representation of conflict in America?

On the surface, it seems that voting has relatively little to do with making the policies that resolve social disputes in America. After all, except for local elections (voting on constitutional Amendments, bond issues, tax increases, and the like), popular votes do not decide policies at all. Yet voting choices do help to regulate conflicts between interests.

First, to the extent that we can tell which issues helped voters make up their minds—admittedly very difficult and often impossible—popular votes roughly represent conflicting opinions on policy questions.

Second, the distribution of votes resolves the conflict over who shall govern: Because they competed for the votes, winning candidates acquire the authority to make decisions for the entire community.

Third, voting provides for participation in a vital, democratic ritual: The popular election symbolizes the liberal democratic consensus on the virtue of self-government and permits people to express and reinforce their deep emotional loyalties to political leaders, parties, and the American way of doing things.

These three ways in which voting helps regulate conflict parallel some of the ways in which citizens take part in elections. Each type of participation makes distinct demands upon the citizen. To vote on the issues, citizens must have enough interest in the election to discern salient issues, enough information to detect differences on those issues between competing candidates and parties (if there are differences), enough interest to form an opinion on those issues, and reason enough to decide which candidate represents that opinion.

In choosing to support a candidate, the voter must decide which candidates have the ability to govern. This decision is difficult because we do not always know which qualities are best suited to governing and, if we did, it would still be difficult to get a clear picture of which candidates have them, despite the vast resources devoted to campaigning.

Finally, long commitment to a political party may provide both an emotional and intellectual standard to assist voting.

In sum, American voters take part on all three levels of voting. Moreover, all voting behavior occurs within boundaries established by constitutional and statutory regulations and party traditions. Furthermore, the individual voter is influenced by social and demographic background and personal perspectives, which are greatly affected by party identifications. These are lasting, relatively stable factors that influence voting. In each election, these factors and the voting decisions themselves are affected by the citizen's impressions of the candidates, parties, and issues.

It would be easy to conclude that for most Americans, voting is only a token exercise, that their perspectives are so laden by partisan prejudices, their images of candidates, parties, and issues are so colored, and their interest in elections is so limited that they simply are not able to vote rationally on the candidates and the issues. We believe that conclusion is too harsh. It ignores the fact that party identification, although it is a screen through which people view elections, gives many Americans a rational understanding of politics. Partisanship is not simply blind; it can serve as an instrument for analyzing political facts. Candidate images, party images, and political issues have effects independent of party identification, even causing defections from old partisan loyalties. Americans do differentiate between their partisan ideas and their perceptions of short-term forces. They can and do determine which are most important in specific elections, and they represent their considered opinions by voting.

Even if party identification dictated voting choices (and we know it does not), more and more Americans are voting without firm partisan loyalties. These independents are different from those uncovered by the voting research of the 1940s and 1950s. The latter were generally uninformed about politics, apathetic, had little confidence in their ability to influence government, and were easily swayed by emotional appeals. The independent voters of the 1970s are of two kinds: the "old independents" characteristic of earlier decades and the "new independents," who identify with neither party not because they are politically passive but because they believe that neither political party represents their interests in electoral conflicts sufficiently to warrant permanent loyalty. The "new independent" is particularly prone to act on the issues and on the ability of the candidate rather than on the basis of partisanship.

The general factors affecting voting do not demonstrate that Americans are incapable of rational choices, because old loyalties and independence both contribute to rational understanding. Moreover, it is not possible to insist that extensive and continuous electoral involvement by most of the citizenry in politics is essential to the survival of American democracy. Certainly, if people are to present their disputes for public resolutions, high rates of voting are one way of representing those conflicts.

Voting choice, however, is very much like the other major patterns of conflict representation we have looked at: expressing opinions and exercising leadership. The absence of extensive and continuous involvement by the mass

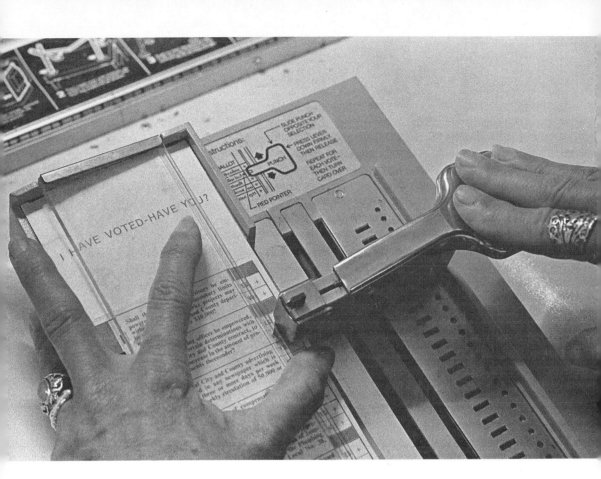

citizenry does not prove that American elections are undemocratic. Rather, as a method of representing conflicts, voting choice—like the expression of opinion and the exercise of leadership—shows America's pluralist character. People participate in voting on many levels just as they express opinion and exercise leadership (by expressing opinions as members of intense or moderate minorities or as members of indifferent majorities; by exercising official, group, or personal leadership, by voting on the basis of issues, candidate qualities, or partisanship.

The test of whether the opinion, leadership, and election processes are democratic is not simply to count the number of people who take part in them. The crucial test of democratic representation is whether those who do take part (1) permit others to do so if they want to; (2) encourage others to do so by assuring that constitutional opportunities, social resources, and personal benefits are available; and (3) respond peacefully when others join them in political participation, even if cherished interests are challenged. When these conditions prevail in the electoral arena, Americans will take part in elections on all levels and voting choices will more truly represent the interest conflicts inherent in our pluralist society.

PARTY POLITICS

Historically political parties have played an important part in revealing, creating, publicizing, and adjusting social disputes in America. In recent years, however, there has been a great deal of speculation about the declining influence of parties in American politics. Perhaps, says one observer, "the party's over" (Broder, 1972). In this chapter we will examine how parties, despite their problems, continue to contribute to conflict regulation. Specifically, we will look at what it means to be a partisan, how political parties are organized, what parties do in representing social disputes, and alternative views about the future of American parties.

Parties and partisans in conflict regulation

Political parties are vital to both aspects of what we have been calling conflict regulation: the representation and the resolution of social conflicts.

- Competing for control of government during and between election campaigns, party politicians take stands on selected issues, attack the opposition, and publicize social disagreements.

■ Party leaders in government offices formulate policies to adjust social disputes.

Before looking at how parties operate in these two significant respects, let us consider who the partisans are and what the parties are all about.

WHO ARE THE PARTISANS?

A follower of any political cause or faction is a partisan. In this broad sense, virtually anyone who takes part in politics at all is a partisan, whether it be as a party member, group affiliate, or candidate for public office. However, we will use the word partisan in a narrower sense: In our discussion the partisan is someone directly involved with an organized political party.

There are three principal categories of partisans in America: (1) Party identifiers (discussed in Chapters 4 and 7) are people who think of themselves as Democrats or Republicans and who may even vote for their party in a consistent way; (2) public officials are party members elected or appointed to public office whose policy decisions may be motivated by factors other than party loyalty, such as personal convictions, pressure groups, fellow officials; (3) party activists devote their time, money, skills, and other resources to advance a party's interests from positions in the formal party bureaucracy. This chapter is primarily about the third group of partisans, the people who operate "the machine," "the organization," or simply "the party."

A DEFINITION OF PARTY

A political party is a coalition of fairly stable, enduring, and frequently conflicting interests, organized to mobilize support in competitive elections in order to control policymaking. This definition applies to the two major American parties, Republican and Democrat, and to third parties that affect two-party politics. Each of the three principal elements in this definition—coalitions, organizations, and control of policymaking—distinguishes political parties from other political groups.

Parties as coalitions

With the exceptions to be noted later, America has always had a two-party arrangement with each party forming a coalition of diverse interests. When either party has appealed only to narrow interests, its chances for electoral victory have diminished. To build electoral majorities, both parties have recruited, represented, and mobilized a large and inclusive following instead of small, exclusive interests. Unlike factions, parties are multi- not special-interest groups. Indeed, each major party coalition contains several factions. These factions often disrupt party unity, compete for dominance, and change the balance of power within and between the parties. Intraparty disputes over platforms, programs, organization, and candidates (such as the struggle between backers of challenger Ronald Reagan and incumbent President Gerald Ford for the nomination of the Republican party in 1976) are sometimes as bitter as the campaign between the parties.

Parties as organizations

As stable organizations, political parties "exist for politics on a full-time, overt, and continuous basis" (Sindler, 1966, p. 6). Unlike pressure groups (discussed in Chapter 9) that sporadically devote their work to specific issues, parties involve themselves in *all* issues. By continuous political activity, the party does two things beyond the reach of most pressure groups: (1) It molds a durable multi-interest organization that competes in elections, and (2) it mobilizes enduring loyalty among its followers, who react with varied degrees of enthusiasm to party appeals and candidates.

Parties and policymaking

Parties also differ from other political groups in their efforts to control policymaking. Parties nominate and rally support behind candidates seeking public offices; from these bases of power they influence appointments to other executive and judicial positions. In contrast, pressure groups normally refrain from entering into direct electoral competition; they do not offer their spokespersons as group candidates for office. Instead, pressure groups try to influence the officeholders elected by party efforts and to this end offer financial aid and voting support for party candidates.

Party politics: what's it like?

The personal, social, and constitutional characteristics of America explored earlier—doctrinal inconsistency, social diversity, and constitutional fragmentation—have left their mark upon our political parties. The result is a socially and ideologically diverse two-party arrangement that spreads power through all levels of each party's organization. To describe what party politics is like, we will take a closer look at three features of American parties: two-party politics, decentralized organization, and the diverse social base of each party.

TWO-PARTY POLITICS IN THE AMERICAN SETTING

Competition for public office has traditionally been between two major political parties that have "adhered to the same basic values and sought the same basic goals in a virtually 'bipartisan' fashion even though they have differed over the best means of achieving those goals" (Wheeler, 1962, p. 304).

Origins of two-party politics

After ratifying the Constitution, American politicians faced the tough problem of making their scheme work. The Constitution had deliberately divided the governing authority among separate institutions of government, the several states, and localities on the municipal and even village level. This constitutional arrangement had to be implemented in a pluralist society. Popular demand necessitated broadened suffrage and the representation of many and diversified interests. No government had ever attempted to build and integrate a community of continental size within an entirely untested framework that had to consider the complicated terms of the constitutional bargain, the realities of a newly formed society of free people, and their visionary democratic expectations (Charles, 1961).

In this pluralist setting, a two-party arrangement developed to achieve the task. Alexander Hamilton and his colleagues needed support in Congress to enact centralizing programs in the Washington and Adams administrations. The Federalist Party filled this need: It closed the gap between the President and Congress and altered their relationship with the judiciary, making it easier for Hamilton to build support for his programs in all branches of the government. To effectively oppose the Federalists, the Democratic-Republican party was formed by the followers of Thomas Jefferson and James Madison, who recruited partisan assistance within the states.

The split between the Federalist and Republican parties in the republic's formative years laid the groundwork for the party competition that appeared in federal elections as early as 1796. Americans accepted a basic idea: Coalitions of interests could differ legitimately over policy aims and compete for the authority to advance those aims under restraints imposed by the Constitution.

That idea meant two things: Victorious partisans do not try to destroy the vanquished with far-reaching reprisals (a notion never challenged despite the Federalist-enacted Alien and Sedition Acts and Jefferson's attempted purge of federal judicial officials); and the losers in competitive elections become the "loyal opposition," criticizing the party in power and its policies, confirming their commitment to the two-party bargain by contesting the next regular election, but not attempting to overthrow the government by force (a notion of loyalty by no means accepted in many nations, then or now). Conflict over the acceptability of the Constitution was displaced by a consensus recognizing that policy and electoral differences under that Constitution were legitimate. The two-party system that has evolved, particularly since 1865, reflects a bipartisan acceptance of the Constitution but sharp partisan disagreements over who should govern, how, and for what policy goals.

The American two-party system has gone through four stages at the national level: (1) the Federalist-Republican era, from the 1790s, to the 1820s, when the Federalist party gradually went into eclipse; (2) the Democrat-Whig era from 1828 to 1860; (3) the Republican era from 1860 to 1932; and (4) the Democratic era from 1932 to the present. Each of these eras has seen periods of both one-party domination and vigorous two-party competition.

A variation on the two-party theme: one-party dominance

The two-party pattern in national politics has not been matched by equivalent competition in the states. Within the states, party competition varies by level of office. Generally, presidential elections produce closer two-party competition than contests for United States Senator or Governor, and many congressional and state legislative races are dominated by one party. Taking into account these variations in party competition by office level, we find the pattern of Democratic and Republican one-party states and competitive two-party states depicted in Figure 8.1. Because party competition at all levels is changing rapidly, such a classification has to be rough. The complex relationship among the three types of partisans—party identifiers, public officials, and party activists—shows up in the voting patterns of one-party states. Most party identifiers in one-party states side with the majority party and in local, state, and congressional elections register their party loyalties directly as votes for their party's candidates. Moreover, minority party activists in one-party states may not even bother to contest local, state, and congressional elections.

In elections for the Presidency, governorship, or United States Senate seats, however, the relationships between types of partisans in one-party states differ. Most identifiers still vote with the dominant party; but activists work for both parties, and voters frequently defect to the opposition. Such defections have recently elected the opposition candidate in several instances. Democratic control of state legislatures has not been threatened in Florida, Tennessee, Virginia, and North Carolina, yet each state has elected a Republican governor since 1965. In the same period, the legislatures of Kansas and South Dakota were heavily Republican, yet Kansas elected a Democratic governor for three successive terms and South Dakotans elected Democrat George McGovern to the Senate three times.

As a rule, then, voters in one-party states have increasingly split their tickets and followed national trends in presidential and major statewide elections while holding firmly to party loyalties in local and congressional races. By providing a locally based congressional opposition in eras of Republican or

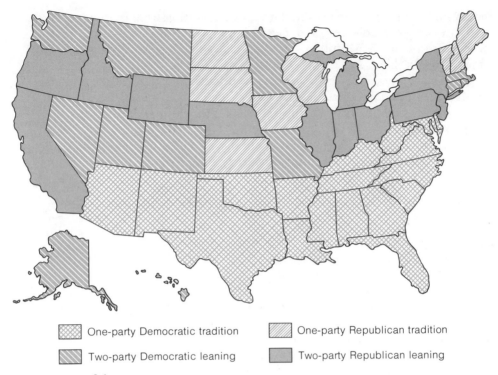

One-party Democratic tradition   One-party Republican tradition

Two-party Democratic leaning   Two-party Republican leaning

FIGURE 8.1
Patterns of Two-Party Competition in the States.

Democratic control of the Presidency, one-party states helped preserve two-party government at the federal level. But as local areas begin to respond to the same forces affecting national politics—population migrations, economic changes, urbanization, the gradual slackening of loyalties in the South since the Civil War, the reapportionment of state and congressional legislative seats—even contests for lesser offices in the one-party states will lose their insulation from national influences.

Another variation on the two-party theme: third parties

Some minor parties have been able to retain an identity and organization separate from the two major parties. Generally, minor parties reflect the claims of special interests that feel unrepresented in two-party politics. They rarely attract a large following away from the two major parties; since 1900 no minor party has won more than 10 percent of the vote except in the presidential elections of 1912, 1924, and 1968.

Minor parties are of two main types: doctrinal and splinter. Doctrinal parties push for an ideological cause, which may be narrow, like that of the Prohibition party, or broad, like that of the Socialist party. The Socialist party follows democratic procedures and strives for economic, social, and political reforms by means of propaganda, public discussion, education, and by putting up candidates for office. Early in this century, the Socialist party got broad support in elections when neither major party responded to demands from many segments of the community. In 1912, it received 6 percent of the presidential vote by appealing to populists, progressives, and reformers frustrated by the lack of innovative programs in the Republican and Democratic parties. Other doctrinal parties (the Socialist Labor party and the Communist party) run candidates from time to time, but doctrinal parties have not prospered in the diverse American social and ideological setting.

Splinter parties originate as dissident factions of a major party and reflect unresolved internal party conflicts. Whether splinter parties are parties of program, personality, or protest, they try to persuade one of the major parties to adopt their views; both success and failure in the quest facilitate their passage into political obscurity.

The Populists, a party of dissident Democrats in the Midwest and South in the late nineteenth century, advocated a specific program of economic and political reform, including public ownership of railroad, telegraph, and telephone industries, free and unlimited coinage of silver, direct election of United States Senators, and women's suffrage. After 1896, when both the Democratic and Populist parties advocated free silver coinage and nominated William Jennings Bryan for President, the Populists began to decline as a separate political force.

In contrast, the Bull Moose, or Progressive, party of 1912 had no real program but united around Theodore Roosevelt after he failed to obtain the Republican nomination for President. The party polled a larger popular vote than the Republicans; but the Democrats won the presidency with Woodrow Wilson, and the Bull Moose party quickly vanished.

The most recent splinter party effort of note was made by George Wallace's American Independent party (AIP) in 1968. Composed mainly of southern dissidents, the party articulated protests against racial integration, growing federal power, massive federal spending, crime and violence, and decisions of the Supreme Court. In 1968 it received 13 percent of the nationwide popular vote and 46 electoral votes from six states. But by 1976 the AIP was but a shell of its former self. Because of a factional split, two parties were formed from the old Wallace supporters, the American Independent party and the American party. Wallace had deserted the party four years earlier, and the success of Jimmy Carter in the South virtually ended the AIP; each of its factions received only a fraction of one percent of the nationwide popular vote in 1976.

Whether the latest doctrinal party on the scene, the Libertarian party, will have more success than previous ones remains to be seen. On some matters the Libertarians take positions generally viewed as liberal: They favor the repeal of laws against victimless crimes (those criminalizing pornography, drug use, and homosexual activities), the abolition of all federal police agencies including the Federal Bureau of Investigation and the Central Intelligence Agency, and the elimination of all government assistance to private enterprise. But there is a conservative tinge to the Libertarian party as well: Members oppose gun control, civil rights laws, controls on the price of oil and gas, laws protecting labor unions, welfare and poverty programs at the federal level, busing to achieve integration of schools, and the 55 mile-per-hour speed limit on highways. Their positions on foreign policy are isolationist: withdrawal of troops from abroad; withdrawal from international organizations; neutrality in all foreign matters; and a substantial reduction in military spending and its attendant bureaucracy. Hoping to win a million votes in the 1976 presidential elections, the scattered vote Libertarians actually won fell far short of attracting the attention they expected from their doctrinal program.

A final variation on the two-party theme: no parties

Many local elections are nonpartisan, that is, candidates appear on the ballot without party designation. The nonpartisan ballot is one way states have of shutting parties out of local elections. They make it illegal to designate the party on the ballot or for candidates to make partisan appeals, reflecting an antiparty sentiment for electoral reform. Removing the party label from elections reduces the party organization's stake in the outcome of the local races; as a result, parties make little effort to play even a covert role. The threat to the two-party tradition in state and federal elections is minor.

In 1976 Eugene McCarthy, former U.S. Senator who had been a major contender for the 1968 Democratic nomination for President, launched something of a nonparty challenge to the two-party arrangement. Filing as an independent candidate for President (and filing with a running mate for Vice-President only in those states that had laws requiring it), McCarthy was on the ballot in 30 states. Arguing that both major political parties were obstacles to democracy, that institutional reforms (such as abolishing the Vice-Presidency), should be undertaken, and that government should be more responsive to the people, McCarthy said, "We have had a bipartisan war, bipartisan economic failures, and abuse of the Bill of Rights under both parties." But his antiparty, nonparty effort fell short of the success he expected and received less than one percent of the nationwide popular vote.

Two-party persistence overall

Despite the one-party, multiparty, and nonparty variations, the basic two-party arrangement has persisted for party identifiers, officeholders, and activists. There are several reasons for the durability of two-party politics.

First, our constitutional setup reinforces two-party politics. State laws, for example, make it difficult for new parties and independent candidates to get on the ballot, requiring them either to have received a specific percentage of electoral support in past elections (unlikely if they are truly new!) or to have the support of a required percentage of the electorate, demonstrated by signatures on a petition (and petition-signing campaigns require both time and money). In 1976 many third-party and independent candidates took their cases to the courts in order to have their names placed on state ballots in the presidential election.

Second, new parties find it difficult to elect candidates under the single-member, plurality electoral system, the arrangement whereby the candidate with the most votes in the district wins the election while trailing candidates of other parties win nothing. In contrast, multimember constituencies with proportional representation guarantee seats to minority parties. Thus, whereas single-member plurality procedures discourage minor parties from entering elections, alternative arrangements that reward minorities encourage third-party efforts; under a proportional procedure a party that wins 30 percent of the popular vote in a ten-member district, say, could achieve three legislative seats in that district. But American congressional and presidential elections use single-member, plurality procedures (remember that the presidential contest is for the electoral votes of each state with the plurality winner taking all the electoral votes). The two major parties can usually muster enough loyal partisans to limit the success of the intruder. Despite third-party influences in the politics of some states—notably the Liberal and Conservative parties in New York and the Farmer-Labor party in Minnesota—most new parties get squeezed out of federal elections by the major parties.

Third, the absence of really deep and enduring social divisions in America has made it risky for new parties that base their appeals on one overriding issue. The two major parties try to win adherents from all social groups by promising rewards to each if elected. Third parties (both doctrinal and splinter) often direct their appeals to narrower social interests and thereby cannot be all things to all people. As a result they have had relatively limited success in achieving victories over the two more broadly based parties.

Fourth, the tradition of having two major parties works against the entry of new contenders. In presidential campaigns, for example, the news media publicize the candidates, programs, and policies of the two major parties but pay little attention to third-party challengers. Despite appeals to the courts and the Federal Communication Commission, third-party candidates were excluded from the highly publicized televised presidential debates in 1976. Without such a forum to promote their candidacies, third-party candidates were forced to rely upon personal appearances, occasional invitations to appear on television interview and talk shows, and whatever commercial air time they could buy.

Finally, at the personal level, voters' party commitments have supported two-party politics. In the national arena, the Republican and Democratic labels have been meaningful symbols for most Americans, and there has been a general consensus on the desirability of the two-party arrangement. Although voters frequently split their tickets, they generally do so between the two major parties. Third parties competing for statewide and local offices, but unaffiliated with the major national parties, are unable to take advantage of such widely accepted symbols as "Republican" or "Democrat" to win adherents. As a result, they find it difficult to continue as an independent force in state and local politics.

Some close observers of American politics have suggested that we are witnessing the end of two-party politics. As evidence they point to a number of things: the increased proportions of the electorate that view themselves as independents rather than party loyalists (Burnham, 1970); the failure of the two parties effectively to perform required services for the electorate—inform them on issues, organize their support for candidates, respond to their policy grievances—while other institutions supplant them in precisely these areas —the mass media (especially television), professional campaign consultants loyal to neither party, public financing of elections, federal welfare programs, mass movements (Alexander, 1976; Broder, 1972; Lowi, 1971); and the self-imposed constraints of the two parties that enable them to mask differences between one another on issues and policies so as to appear neither liberal nor conservative but middle-of-the-road (Scammon and Wattenberg, 1970).

But, the decline in the proportions of Americans willing to identify themselves as Republicans or Democrats in the early 1970s, as noted in Chapter 7, may have been the result of the enfranchisement of voters in the 18–21 age category with passage of the Twenty-Sixth Amendment in 1971. That alone added 11 million persons to the electoral rolls in 1972 who would not otherwise have been eligible to vote; 14 million more persons not over 21 years of age in the 1968 presidential election were also added. Younger members of the electorate normally do not display strong attachments to either political party. It can be demonstrated that the overall decline in party identification in the last two decades has resulted from generational change; partisanship persists among persons who entered the electorate before World War II, but among citizens becoming eligible to vote more recently the proportion of identifiers is small (Abramson, 1976). Unless new parties arise to capture the loyalties of these latter-day independents (and we have seen that forces work against that), they must choose one of the two major parties to implement their policy preferences. Doing so consistently may well serve as a socializing experience in two-party politics. Increasing numbers of independents may indeed reflect fickleness among voters who support neither of the two parties loyally, but the fact that they usually choose between the two parties simply reinforces close two-party competition. It does not portend the end of two-party politics (W. E. Miller and Levitin, 1976).

Second, recent electoral reforms could work to the advantage of the two major parties, giving them a greater, rather than lesser, role in mobilizing the electorate and increasing their responsiveness to the electorate. For example, one provision for public financing of elections allows each major party to receive funds for conducting campaigns on behalf of its candidates (the federal government and eight states had such provisions for party funding in 1976). Although third parties can also receive such funds, to do so they must have received a required percentage of the popular votes in a previous election or, if a new party, they can qualify for a share of the funds retroactively after the election in question. Clearly, however, if third parties must borrow funds in the hopes that after the election they *may* get reimbursed to pay off their debts, they are at a disadvantage. And, as we will see later, the two major parties have undertaken reforms since the late 1960s that may increase their responsiveness to the needs of their constituents.

Finally, although it is correct that neither of the major parties has had much electoral success when appealing to narrow segments of society and, hence, both parties try to capture the middle of the road, this scarcely argues for the decline of two-party politics. Rather, it reinforces two-party competition for precisely the reasons discussed in describing the origins and sources of two-party politics. That both parties compete for the votes of the same ideologically and socially diverse electorate, however, does not imply that there is not a "dime's worth of difference" between the two parties (as George Wallace charged in 1968) or every policy is "bipartisan" (as Eugene McCarthy insisted in 1976). In fact there are differences between the two parties.

- In presidential elections since 1960 there have been differences in the policy views of *partisan identifiers;* Democrats have generally been more favorable than Republicans to an increase in federal programs supporting education, medical care, job guarantees, fair employment, and racial integration (Pomper, 1975).

- There are differences in the views of the *officeholders* of the two parties. Roll-call votes in Congress, for example, reveal consistent splits between the two parties on social welfare, federal regulation of the economy, and foreign affairs. Despite divisions between southern and northern Democrats, the Democratic party has been unified in supporting major programs for social welfare, more participation by the federal government in the economy, and an active posture in foreign affairs.

- Differences also occur in the opinions of *party activists.* Among delegates to presidential nominating conventions, Democrats have been found to be more favorable than Republicans to such programs as regulation of public utilities, public ownership of natural resources, federal aid to education, taxes on corporate income, regulation of business, federal initiatives in welfare matters, expansions of civil rights, and cuts in defense spending (Kilpatrick, 1976; McClosky, Hoffmann, and O'Hara, 1960).

THE DISPERSION OF PARTISAN
POWER IN THE AMERICAN SETTING

A singular feature of the two major parties is the fragmentation of power within them. Party leaders and officeholders are controlled either by many local leaders or by their own volitions; no central power dictates the activities of subordinant units. Although the formal structures of our two major parties suggest otherwise, power in American two-party politics is dispersed.

Centralized heirarchy: a fiction

Throughout American government—national, state, and local as well as U.S. territories overseas—party organizations are at work for both parties. On paper (see Figure 8.2), each party is a hierarchial organization of committees, chairpersons, and conventions binding local parties to national party headquarters. Some organization of party activists is supplied for each voting and electoral unit: precinct, constituency, coordinating committee, and national organization.

Party organization begins with the precinct. The principal functionary is the precinct committeeperson, captain, or leader, who is elected either in the party primary or by the precinct party members assembled in convention; in some areas, he or she may be appointed by party leaders of countywide organizations. The precinct leader works to increase voter registration and achieve a respectable turnout of party identifiers on election day. Moreover, he or she preaches party doctrine, passes along information, and performs social and economic services.

The constituency is next above the precinct; it is the lowest level from which a public official is elected. In larger cities, this level is the ward; in rural areas, it is the township; in some sections of the country, it is a state legislative district; and in some states, it is the congressional district. The basic organization is the county committee, usually composed of the precinct leaders. The head of this committee is the county chairperson who is chosen either by the committee or in the party primary. He or she is charged with seeing that precinct leaders mobilize majorities in their precincts and that the party as a whole carries the constituency for local, legislative, congressional, senatorial, gubernatorial, and presidential candidates.

The coordinating level is above the precinct and constituency; it is usually composed of the state central or executive committee and includes representatives from constituency committees. The state party chairperson ordinarily is either the leader of a dominant party faction within the state or the governor's hand-picked spokesperson. Sometimes he or she is both. As at the precinct and constituency levels, conventions are regularly scheduled; at the coordinating level, they are attended by delegates from wards, counties, legislative districts,

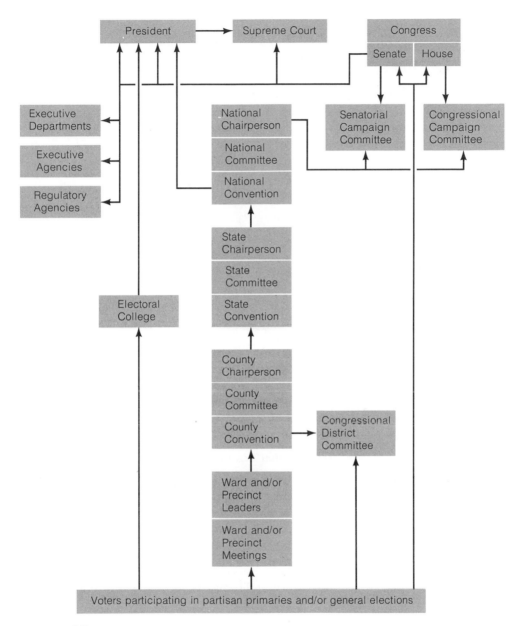

FIGURE 8.2

Formal Relations Between Public Officials, Activists, and Identifiers of the Major Political Parties. (Solid linking lines with arrows indicate formal participation in the selection of leaders through direct election, nomination, appointment, or approval of persons for positions.)

and so forth. State conventions perform tasks ranging from merely ratifying decisions made at other levels to nominating candidates for statewide office and preparing party platforms.

National organizations are at the top of the party hierarchy. Both major parties have a national committee. In the Republican party, it is composed of a man and a woman from every state and the Canal Zone, District of Columbia, Guam, Puerto Rico, and the Virgin Islands; the state chairperson of any state carried by the party's last presidential nominee or of any state that elected a Republican senator or a majority of Republicans to its House of Representatives delegation is also a member. In its 1972 presidential nominating convention, the Democratic party agreed to this makeup for its national committee: (1) the chairperson and the highest ranking officer of the opposite sex of each recognized state Democratic party; (2) additional national committee members apportioned to each state on the basis of that state's representation on the standing committees of the 1972 Democratic national convention; (3) the chairperson and two others designated by the national conference of Democratic state governors; (4) Democratic leaders in the United States Senate and House of Representatives; and (5) additional members not to exceed 25 to provide balanced representation of all Democratic voters.

The national chairperson is selected by the presidential nominee, although formal approval comes from the national committee. If the party suffers electoral defeat, a new chairperson may be chosen by dominant party interests to reintegrate and unify the party. Regardless of how he or she is selected, the chairperson's duties are extensive. With the staff, the chair administers and directs fund raising, maintains liaison between activists and officeholders, conducts public relations, criticizes the opposition, and manages the presidential candidate's campaign, if asked.

A third element of the national organization is the quadrennial national convention. Attended by party activists from states, counties and congressional districts, its tasks are to nominate a presidential and vice-presidential candidate, formulate a platform, resolve internal disputes, and conduct party business. In 1974 Democrats tried out a new element of party organization, a convention held at the midpoint of the presidential term, designated the Midterm Conference. Among other things, the conference provided an opportunity for party notables to exchange views; offered a stage for prospective presidential candidates to strut (as did Jimmy Carter in making an early bid to become known to party members); reflected a variety of conflicts over what should be the future course of party affairs; and ratified the Charter for the Democratic Party, a document that enshrined the operating procedures of the party, offered new organizational units to centralize party affairs, and elaborated principles of participation and representation in party processes (Jackson and Hitlin, 1976; Sullivan, Pressman, and Arterton, 1976).

Party fragmentation: a reality

A tight hierarchical structure describes the classic urban "machine" built of precinct workers supervised by county, ward, or district leaders who worked for the party "boss," but it was never typical of the major national parties. In fact, relations between levels of party organization are so reciprocal, loosely coordinated, and sporadic that they are at best only a modified hierarchy. Authority is diffuse within and between all levels, and lower-level activists are not generally responsible to upper-echelon members. State and local units are the influential elements of the national parties, and these lower-level organizations frequently ally with one another, with higher-level agencies, and with nonparty forces to oppose party leaders. Because committee positions at the constituency level often go unfilled or are occupied by people with no active interest in party work, the detailed work of party organizations frequently remains undone. In brief, actual party organization is decentralized and sometimes so fragmented that there is scarcely an organization at all.

Why are party organizations decentralized? There are many reasons for the lack of centralization; among the most important are the multiplicity of constituencies, the character of the electoral system, and the statutory regulation of parties.

Political parties try to win as many elections as possible by focusing their efforts on the individual constituencies that elect public officials. Elective offices are so numerous that the party inevitably shatters into many separate party units, each of which feels that it can most effectively compete for votes by maintaining its autonomy. The numerous constituency organizations are matched by a host of affiliated groups. These adjuncts to the party organization reflect many of its conflicts and compete with it for influence. Such groups include the Young Republicans, Young Democrats, and volunteer organizations that are created temporarily to handle specific problems in a campaign, raise funds, broaden the base of voting support, or even prepare policy statements.

Constituency organizations for each electoral unit respond to the basic political fact of federalism that "creates separate, self-sustaining centers of power, privilege, and profit which may be sought and defended as desirable in themselves, as means of leverage upon elements in the political structure above and below, and as bases from which individuals may move to places of greater influence and prestige in and out of government" (Truman, 1963, pp. 518–519). By following the federal pattern, however, partisans deprive the national party leadership of the means for enforcing party discipline. The local autonomy of state, county, and district party organizations assigns the fate of policy decisions to locally responsible governors, mayors, county commissioners, or congressional representatives, who are pretty much free of central control.

Pressure-group leaders understand this party fragmentation; when they want to influence Congress, they go to the congressman's local constituency and party politicians within it, not to the national party organizations. Parochial interests often have a voice in party affairs that is out of proportion to their size, particularly if the local organization depends upon pressure groups for financial aid and electoral support.

The splitting of political authority shapes the representation of social conflict by channeling disputes and demands through local party organizations. As a result, democratic responsibility is often so diffuse that parties cannot respond to broad social changes. Though civil rights was a problem in the 1930s and 1940s, southerners were able to keep civil rights statements out of Democratic platforms because they controlled local party organizations and threatened to bolt the national party. Ever since President Harry Truman was elected in 1948 despite a southern defection (when many southern Democrats formed a separate Dixiecrat party), this tactic has been less effective, but it is not yet dead.

Decentralization is further reinforced by staggered elections and single-member districts. The many offices created by the separation of powers and federalism are made even more independent of one another by provisions for nonconcurrent terms of office: The President serves four years, senators serve six years, and representatives two years; governors and state legislators serve either two or four years depending upon the state; the terms of mayors, city councillors, county commissioners, and other officials also vary. Because of the nonconcurrent terms, officials are elected at staggered intervals and voters respond to forces peculiar to each election. Local party organizations, bent upon winning their own contest, seldom have to unify their efforts to win a single national office. Only in presidential election years do they show much unity as they try to adjust to the presidential contest's effects on state and local races; even then, the national party is more a working alliance of local party organizations than a hierarchy directed from the top.

American elections are won by the candidate with a plurality of votes in single-member districts. Such a district is one from which one candidate is elected with a simple plurality of votes. There is no carry-over of votes from one district to another. Parties concentrate their efforts where they know they have enough identifiers to win a simple plurality. They restrict their efforts to constituencies in which they are dominant or at least competitive, preferring not to waste resources where they can win nothing. In districts where a party is sure to win lopsided victories because it has the most party identifiers, the party does not need strong organization. In these areas, neither party is likely to have a strong organization, the minority party because it has no chance and the majority party because it does not need to be organized.

States are more active in regulating political parties than the federal government so parties tailor their organizations to fit state regulations. Statutory regulation decentralizes party organization. The intent behind this regulation has been to promote broad participation in party affairs by the rank and file instead of tight control by party leaders. Almost three-fourths of the states require parties to hold regular conventions—city and county—of precinct members. Many also require that parties nominate candidates through primary elections, thereby removing nominations from the control of party politicians. But primary elections do not necessarily give control of nominations to party identifiers, because party lines are easily crossed in primaries. The primaries are thus but one more force weakening central organizational control within our major parties.

Centralizing tendencies in two-party politics

Although our two major parties are highly decentralized, centralizing tendencies help overcome such barriers as the separation of powers, federalism, and localism. It is in the continuing interest of partisans to stick together. Although they have no abstract belief in the merits of centralization itself, party politicians recognize that some party unity is essential for electoral victory. The dissension in the Republican party in 1964 and among Democrats in 1968 shows how disunity in presidential elections contributes to defeat.

Another tendency is clearly related to this recognition: As one-party politics declines and two-party competition spreads, more effective organizations are required for victory. Constituency-level parties, no longer assured of victory in safe districts, see an advantage in affiliating more closely with national organizations that might provide financial help or send a popular party figure to campaign for local candidates.

State and local politics is shaped more and more by national issues. The local issues (unemployment, inflation, racial integration, drug control, law and order) are now national, which makes it increasingly difficult for local and state politicians to ignore or defect from positions taken by national party leaders.

Finally, the parties themselves are slowly providing their national-level organizations with sanctions to enforce party discipline. After 1968, the Democratic party adopted guidelines making it more difficult for dissident elements to refuse to support the presidential ticket selected by the national convention.

DIVERSITY: THE COMPOSITION OF TWO-PARTY COALITIONS

By diversifying their membership, parties have made it harder to achieve organizational unity. The price they pay for a disparate following is the continuous resurgence of factional strife. The more inclusive the party, the more it reflects the same kinds of interest disputes that occur in the country at large. In their social composition and conflicts, the major parties are microcosms of America as a whole.

Instead of trying to settle their internal disputes through bitter factional warfare, party leaders normally try to bridge the differences by appealing for party unity. They pass the task of trying to resolve the social conflicts producing internal party disputes on to their elected officials. Parties are primarily channels for representing rather than resolving conflicts. When partisans are unable to live with their internal disputes, dissident factions often try to break away from the parent party, a source of splinter parties such as the American Independent party of the late 1960s and early 1970s. A political party endures in America only so long as it is able to counter the schismatic tendencies inherent in a diverse following.

The rewards of party membership

A party's clientele is diverse partly because people engage in active party work for many reasons. The social composition of each party differs from region to region, reflecting the ethnic or occupational groups that dominate each area, but the leaders of both parties are usually lawyers or have professional, managerial, or governmental jobs. Precinct leaders of both parties obtain about the same satisfactions from party activity: social contacts, patronage, privileged administrative treatment, financial rewards, career opportunities, and reinforcement of ideological convictions. The rewards and incentives for party activity are found at the local level, because local activists and elected officials, including congressional representatives, are inclined to respond to their constituency organization rather than to the national party when the two conflict.

Although party activity offers some incentives, parties have difficulty recruiting members. Unlike a business firm or football team, parties have no special staff to scout applicants for party membership. Because citizens are generally not too interested in party work and the parties have relatively few inducements to offer activists, parties must rely on means other than systematic recruitment to attract new members.

Most new activists come to the party by one of two routes. *Self-starters* seek direct rewards and incentives in party participation. Self-starters may wish to advance their careers by engaging in politics, like the many lawyers who become party activists. Governmental appointments are not the incentive they once were; the civil service, relying on competitive merit appointments, removes partisan influence from the selection of many administrative personnel. *External recruits* join parties because they have been persuaded to do so by other activists, friends, relatives, or fellow workers. By far the greatest number

of party activists are recruited through informal contacts with friends or colleagues; only 10 to 30 percent of local party ranks are self-starters (Sorauf, 1972).

Ideological diversity

Because of the extremely diverse interests represented in our two major political parties, neither is able to make narrow ideological appeals for fear of alienating potential bodies of support. There are, however, broad ideological differences between the two parties, at least as measured by the different policy views of the identifiers, activists, and officials we examined earlier. But broad policy differences rarely harden into direct ideological appeals to the electorate simply because most voters do not care about ideological conflicts. Party leaders compensate for any ideological gap between themselves and their followers by obscuring ideological stands through ambiguous campaign oratory (see Chapter 6). The disdain of most American voters for political ideology further reinforces party decentralization. The fact that party identifiers have little or no clear-cut ideological commitment leaves ideological appeals with little coordinating value.

Trends in electoral coalitions

Studies of the voting behavior of Americans underscore the conclusion that both of the major parties draw their support from a broad spectrum of the electorate. In recent decades only one demographic group, Blacks, has given more than 80 percent of its votes to either party in presidential elections. Beyond that there have been general tendencies in the composition of each party's electoral coalitions, but neither party has been able to count on the unswerving support of any group. In presidential contests the two coalitions look roughly like this: Democrats have won the votes of poor people, Blacks, union members, Catholics, the South, the people living in central cities; Republicans have attracted the nonpoor, Whites, nonunion families, Protestants, northerners, and people living outside central cities (Axelrod, 1972). To get an idea of how slight the differences are in the makeups of the electoral coalitions of the two parties, consider the data in Table 8.1. It displays where the votes came from for Democratic and Republican candidates in the congressional elections of 1974. Congressional elections held in nonpresidential election years generally offer a better measure of the electoral bases of the parties because voters are less likely to be swayed from their basic party loyalties by a particularly attractive presidential candidate, an overriding issue, or factors causing an unusually high turnout of independent voters.

Examination of the votes of demographic groups reveals that poor people, non-Whites, members of union families, Catholics, southerners, and people living in central cities do indeed make up a larger proportion of the Democratic than the Republican coalition. The key differences in the demographic composition of the two parties, however, were that non-Whites, union families, and southerners provided the bases of the Democratic coalition, whereas Whites, nonunion families, and nonsoutherners supported the Republicans.

Table 8.1 also suggests that, at least in 1974, the Democratic coalition consisted of people with high interest in the election but with low levels of political efficacy, and people who were basically distrustful of other people. To be sure the differences are small, but not simply products of chance. No significant differences prevailed between the coalitions of the two parties with respect to trust in government, belief in control over personal life, voter use of the media, and levels of information about politics. People believing government should guarantee every American a job made up a greater part of the Democratic coalition than the Republican, but the positions taken by people on other issues were not reflected in a greater proportion of one or the other party.

TABLE 8.1

Electoral coalitions of Democrats and Republicans, 1974
(*in percentages of coalition composed of each group*)

Groups	Democrats	Republicans
Demographic		
Poor	8	5
Nonpoor	92	95
White	89	97
Non-White	11	3
Union	28	18
Nonunion	72	80
Catholic	27	20
Protestant	60	72
Southern	34	24
Nonsouthern	66	76
Central-city resident	10	7
Non–central-city resident	90	93
Attitudes		
Interest in election		
High	55	47
Moderate	34	41
Low	11	12
Political efficacy		
High	54	63
Low	46	37
Trust in government		
High	54	56
Low	46	44
Trust in people		
Trusting	56	63
Distrusting	44	37
Control over personal life		
Have control by planning	66	69
It's all a matter of luck	34	31
Attention to election		
Media used		
Newspapers primarily	36	39
Newspapers and television equally	29	25
Television primarily	33	32
Level of information		
Informed	55	53
Uninformed	45	47
Views on issues		
Civil rights		
Things should stay as they are	9	7
Pace of integration too fast	40	42
Pace of integration about right	43	47
Pace of integration too slow	8	4

TABLE 8.1 (*Continued*)

Groups	Democrats	Republicans
Government should guarantee everyone a job		
Things should stay as they are	14	12
Favor job guarantees	28	15
Neutral on job guarantees	20	25
Oppose job guarantees	38	47
Dealing with urban unrest		
Things should stay as they are	16	12
Causes of urban unrest should be solved	47	48
Neutral on dealing with unrest	16	22
Greater force should be used	21	18
Rights of those accused of crimes		
Things should stay as they are	13	14
Should be greater rights protection	35	28
Neutral on rights of accused	18	16
Courts are too lenient	35	41
Busing to achieve school integration		
Things should stay as they are	9	7
Favor busing	10	6
Neutral on busing	6	5
Oppose busing	75	82
Women's rights		
Things should stay as they are	4	4
Favor greater equality for women	54	48
Neutral about advancing women's rights	19	19
Oppose greater equality for women	23	29

Source: Compiled from data from the 1974 election study, Center for Political Studies, available through Interuniversity Consortium for Political Research, University of Michigan, Ann Arbor.

In sum, the coalitions of the two parties differ, but few of those differences are substantial. Will this trend of marginal differences continue into the future? Political observers disagree. One theory, which received considerable support in the late 1960s, argued that the traditional Democratic coalition was breaking up. Specifically, voters in the South, ethnic groups in central cities, and Catholics were seen as departing the Democratic party. An "emerging Republican majority" could be forged by building an alliance between traditional areas of Republican support in the West and Midwest and new adherents to the Grand Old Party in the South and among Catholic ethnics defecting from the Democrats (Phillips, 1969). Republican victories in the presidential elections of 1968 and 1972 held out hopes to Republicans that they were indeed the "new majority," but disaffection with Republicans over the Watergate scandals in the early 1970s clouded matters. Although Democratic candidate Jimmy Carter did not attract the votes of Catholic ethnics in 1976 as successfully as had earlier Democrats, he did return the South to the Democratic coalition. For the present, the validity of the thesis of the "emerging Republican majority" is questionable.

Other political observers look at current voting trends and see a "new Democratic majority" forming (Ladd and Hadley, 1975). This new majority would include people estranged from a political arrangement they have come to think is unresponsive to their needs—the poor, Blacks, Spanish-speaking groups, youth, and the elderly. Desiring changes and reforms, these groups turn to the party of change in this century, the Democratic, and form the backbone of a new coalition (Harris, 1973). If such a scenario were to be the future of the two major parties, it would—as we have seen—be but an exaggerated version of the coalitions of the past.

Closely tied to this view about the prospects for a continuing Democratic majority is one that foresees the demise of the Republican party unless steps are taken to appeal to a new constituency. Working against the GOP are such factors as (1) a Democratic dominance of Congress (about 2–1 majorities in House and Senate) likely to extend through the 1978 elections because of the advantage incumbents have in getting elected and the efforts of organized pressure groups to support Democratic congresspeople (see Chapter 9); (2) the fact that voter registration drives qualify more new voters from groups sympathetic to Democrats (Blacks, Chicanos, and poor Whites) than from groups favoring Republicans; and (3) the fact that after the 1980 census congressional redistricting will be conducted by state legislatures, most of which are dominated by Democrats. Such prospects lead many conservative supporters of the Republican cause to argue that it is time for the Grand Old Party to strive to be the Grand New Party, a coalition of persons who in the past haven't voted because they detected no difference between the two major parties, Americans who label themselves conservative, and persons simply wanting to change from "politics as usual." Whether such a realignment is feasible remains in doubt. Moreover, the death of the Republican party as announced in 1976 may be premature. After all, following the landslide defeat of Republicans in 1964 there was much talk about the eclipse of the party, yet Republicans rebounded in the congressional elections of 1966 and won the presidency in 1968.

Yet another theory about the future of two-party politics argues that the coalitions of the major parties will fluctuate from one presidential election to another. Depending upon the candidates and the issues, either party may forge a successful coalition by winning majorities of the votes of various groups—ethnics, southerners, suburbanites, the young—with shifting loyalties. Uncertain coalitions in presidential elections will combine with an extension of the basic party coalitions maintained in congressional elections to produce Democratic dominance in Congress and close two-party competition for the presidency.

In sum, there is simply no agreement on how Democrats and Republicans will align themselves in the future. We suspect, however, that neither political party can depend totally upon any specific groups to provide victory, nor can they ignore any major groups in their appeals. An example is the problem of appealing to geographic sections of the nation. Two decades ago the major parties concentrated their campaign efforts for the presidency in the Northeast and Midwest because that was where the votes were. In 1960 the Atlantic states cast one-fourth of the nationwide votes for president and another one-fourth came from the Midwest. Less than 15 percent of the votes cast in the 1960 presidential contest were from the South. By contrast, in 1976 southern states contributed almost one-fourth of the votes cast, Atlantic states one-fifth, and the Midwest slightly less than one-fourth. Simply put, no geographic section can be written off by either party as unimportant. Put differently, in the future both major parties may have to appeal to even broader sociogeographic segments than they have appealed to in the past (Sale, 1975).

The contribution of political parties to conflict regulation

Two-party politics contributes significantly to adjusting social conflicts in America. Basic to that contribution is the part played by the parties in the conduct of elections—nominating candidates, mobilizing support through campaigns, and electing public officials. With their adherents in public office, parties go on to influence policymaking.

NOMINATING PROCEDURES

Nominating candidates to run for public office is a critical part of the parties' contribution to government; it is also vital to their own interests. Party activists can control the distribution of patronage better if victorious candidates owe their nomination and election to the party rather than to wealthy backers, a major interest group, or another power base. If successful contenders are indebted to the party for their nomination, they will be more likely to push for party programs. Controlling nominations also enables party leaders to discipline factions.

Three methods of nominating candidates have been used. The earliest was the *party caucus*, a meeting of select party leaders (often dominated by legislative officeholders) to choose the candidates for the next election. "King Caucus" expired in national politics after Andrew Jackson triumphed over John Quincy Adams in 1828. The caucus had selected Adams as the official party candidate, but the national convention nominated Jackson instead, a turning point in political history. The legend of the "smoke-filled room" persisted long afterward, however.

The *convention* spread partisan conflict by including state factional leaders as well as legislative officeholders in the nominating process. *Primary elections,* theoretically open to all party members, further enlarged the nomination process. Both Populists and Progressives justified the reform on the grounds that it would make party leaders responsive to all party members and the party's officeholders responsible to all voting citizens. Their responsiveness and responsibility were to be ensured by converting nominations from bargains arrived at by party "bosses" to victories in electoral competition.

Party primaries are of three types. In the *closed primary,* used by 43 states, only those who have registered as party members or who declare their party identification at the polling place may participate. Six states permit the *open primary,* in which the voter is given a ballot for each party at the polls; he marks only the ballot of the party of his choice. In the state of Washington, the ballot lists every party's contestants under the office they seek; in the *blanket primary* a voter may choose a Democratic candidate for one office, a Republican for another.

Primaries have opened nominating procedures to broader popular participation, but some results were not anticipated. Although the party's public officials and activists no longer control nominations, neither does the full party membership. Turnout in primaries is low, so that the party nominee is usually chosen by a small proportion of the party's members. These are the hard-core loyalists who are not necessarily representative of the diverse interests of voters in general elections. If the winning candidates were chosen because of narrow appeals to the interests of party loyalists, the candidates might handicap the party in the general election. Moreover, if a large number of candidates enter a primary—even if the turnout is large—the winner usually receives only a plurality, not a majority, of the primary vote. Where runoff primaries (a second primary to choose between the two candidates receiving the most votes in the first primary) are not provided, it is common for candidates who receive less than one-third of the votes to be nominated. Such nominees frequently owe their victories to a small band of faithful friends, relatives, neighbors, or to uninformed primary voters attracted by a popular family name. (In Massachusetts a John Kennedy was nominated for state treasurer; he was a political unknown and not related to President John F. Kennedy, yet the name drew votes.) Finally, many primary candidates are not opposed, so the voter has no choice; from a third to a half of the primary candidates for state legislative seats run unopposed.

The primary does not truly turn control of nominations over to party identifiers, but it has achieved a second aim of its advocates: to weaken the party "machine." Public competition for nominations between leaders of factions exposes the party's internal conflicts. Once publicized, such conflicts are not easily resolved by private bargaining; and the disgruntled losing factions may refuse to support the primary victor in the general election. A major Republican breakthrough in the one-party South came in the 1960s when Republican John Tower of Texas was twice elected to the United States Senate because liberal Democrats in the state voted for him rather than for the more conservative nominee selected in their own party's primary.

Parties survive by winning elections. Parties risk that survival if they field candidates with little chance of winning the general election. A reformed convention system could promote participation by minority groups such as Blacks and Chicanos (rarely achieved fully in primaries) and representation of all major factions and interests, by selecting nominees in open, give-and-take competition. Nominations by conventions of party activists might then produce candidates more representative of the party membership and therefore more likely to win the general election.

Party leaders have several tactics for restoring some bargaining to the nominations. Half a dozen states permit some form of preprimary convention that allows the party to endorse a candidate in the primary election. Some local party organizations also use screening committees of factional leaders, who meet in caucus, select the most desirable candidates from among all those who have filed (assuming that the party has tried to get desirable candidates to file in the first place), and announce a party slate. Efforts to control the nominating process by controlling the primary, however, have been only partially successful. Some interests may be disenchanted with the promises made in preprimary bargaining; they can force a primary fight and publicize the divisions within the party.

NOMINATING THE PRESIDENTIAL CANDIDATES

The primary election is the principal method for nominating candidates for Congress; it is also vital to the nominations of candidates for President. Although each party's presidential candidate is nominated by delegates meeting in a national convention, presidential primaries, along with party caucuses, play a crucial role in the selection of those delegates. In 1976, 29 states and the District of Columbia held some type of presidential primary; out of those primaries emerged three-fourths of the two major parties' national convention delegates.

Winning the Presidency is the goal of both major parties. It follows that a candidate for nomination must be able to convince the party that his qualifications and appeal to voters are superior to those of all other candidates. Specifically, he must convince a majority of the delegates to the national party convention. Winning party primaries is certainly one way to do so. Major contenders for their party's nomination jockey over which statewide primaries to enter, how to win delegates in party caucuses and conventions, and how much to promise as they bargain and accommodate the demands of opposing interests.

What qualities have candidates had that have helped them achieve their party's nomination? Of course, one obvious plus is to be the incumbent President; in this century no incumbent who wanted it has been denied his party's nomination. Some, however, have come perilously close to defeat. For example, despite all of the advantages that accrue to a campaigning President —in fundraising, publicity, staffing, appearance of being "presidential," etc. —Gerald Ford almost lost the 1976 Republican nomination to challenger Ronald Reagan. In fact, in primaries where Ford and Reagan squared off against one another, Reagan actually won a majority (51 percent) of all votes cast, although in all Republican primaries Ford piled up the greater total vote because in several he ran unopposed.

Until the 1960s, the profile of a successful candidate for his party's nomination looked like this: a governor from one of the more populous states of the North, a Protestant of Anglo-Saxon origin whose family and personal life were unimpeachable, who appealed to broad economic and political interests within the party. The nominees of the 1960s and 1970s changed the pattern. Of the presidential nominees since 1960, only one has been a governor of a state, and not of a populous northern state but of a relatively small southern state; moreover, at the time of his nomination, Jimmy Carter had been out of the Georgia governor's office for two years.

The Vice-Presidency and the Senate have been the primary seedbeds of presidential candidates since 1960. Vice-Presidents have run as incumbent presidents after succeeding to the office following the death or resignation of a predecessor (Lyndon Johnson, Gerald Ford), or they have won their party's nomination to succeed the incumbent (Richard Nixon, Hubert Humphrey). Since 1960 the Senate has produced candidates John F. Kennedy, Barry M. Goldwater, and George McGovern. Twice in recent years persons not holding public office at the time of their nomination were victorious: Richard Nixon in 1968 and Jimmy Carter in 1976.

Other changes in the characteristics of nominees have included the nomination of a Catholic, Kennedy, in 1960, despite the convictions of some Democratic party leaders that a Catholic could not be elected President; the nomination of candidates identified with liberal or conservative wings of the party (George McGovern in 1972 and Barry Goldwater in 1964) rather than with the moderate center; and the selection of candidates from states with few electoral votes: Humphrey (Minnesota), McGovern (South Dakota), Goldwater (Arizona), and Carter (Georgia).

One reason for the breakup of the older patterns of presidential nomination has been the increased influence played by presidential nominating primaries, which are a means of winning delegates not necessarily wed to the traditional views of party leaders about what kind of person should run for President. Crucial strategic decisions face candidates: how many and which presidential primaries to enter and how to maximize support for their candidacy in states that do not use the primary to select delegates or where primaries do not bind selected delegates.

Types of presidential primaries

States and territories choose their delegates to the national nominating conventions of their parties either in primaries or through meetings of party members in caucus and/or convention. There are four principal types of party primaries:

- *Preference primaries* in which people vote directly for the candidate they wish to see nominated, but choose delegates separately through local and state party caucuses; in some states the preference vote is binding on delegates, in others it is not.
- *Preference-delegate selection primaries* where voters elect delegates pledged or favorable to a candidate named on the ballot; state party organizations also run unpledged slates of delegates under this arrangement.
- *Advisory preference primary* with a *separate delegate selection* vote in which delegates are listed as pledged or favorable to a candidate or unpledged.
- *Mandatory preference primary* and *separate delegate selection* vote with delegates required to support the preference primary winner.

Further complicating the delegate selection procedures are three arrangements for allocating delegates within each state in accordance to the number of primary votes a candidate might win in the primary:

- "Winner take all" primaries in which the candidate winning a plurality of primary votes is allotted all of the delegates of the state. These primaries, a standard procedure in primary elections before the 1970s, have been abolished by Democrats but are still used minimally by Republicans.
- "Proportional representation" primaries in which candidates are allotted delegates from a state in proportion to the number of votes won in the primary.
- "Loophole" primaries permitting the election of delegates within election units no larger than a congressional district. The candidate receiving a plurality of the votes in the electoral unit receives all of the delegates apportioned to that unit, that is, "winner take all" in the district. Democrats banned such primaries after 1976.

The decision to enter a state's primary and judgments about how much time and energy to put into it may be crucial for a candidate. Jimmy Carter in 1976 endeavored to build a nationwide name by entering all of the Democratic primaries. Ronald Reagan probably made a major strategic error in his 1976 challenge to Gerald Ford when, after entering Ohio's combined winner-take-all statewide and district primaries, he did not file delegates in 8 of 23 districts, had little organization, and waited until the last minute to campaign. Thus, although Ford received only 55 percent of the primary vote, he won 91 of the 97 Ohio delegates, a victory which partially offset Reagan's victory on the same day in the California "winner take all" primary that garnered him 167 delegates.

The primaries offer candidates a chance to demonstrate vote-getting ability and to circumvent the opposition of old-line party leaders. Sometimes it is more important to do the latter than to develop the image of a proven vote-getter. For example, George McGovern in 1972 won only one-quarter of the votes in Democratic presidential primaries, yet won two-thirds of the delegates from primary states; in 1976 Jimmy Carter won less than 40 percent of the votes in all of the primaries he entered, yet wrapped up the nomination well before the Democratic convention.

How representative are presidential primaries?

The divisive struggle between Hubert Humphrey and Eugene McCarthy for the Democratic nomination in 1968 generated much criticism of the convention system for not representing the preferences and sentiments of party rank and file in the choice of a nominee. In response, the 1968 Democratic Convention created a Commission on Party Structure and Delegate Selection, chaired until early 1971 by Senator George McGovern. In its report and recommendations in 1970, the commission agreed that the 1968 convention had "exposed profound flaws in the presidential nominating process" and that "meaningful participation of Democratic voters was often difficult or costly, sometimes completely illusory, and, in not a few instances, impossible." Finding that the convention system did not fairly represent Blacks, women, and young people and that it did not accurately represent the preferences of party members on issues and candidates, the commission proposed binding "guidelines" for selection of candidates. Essentially, the rules governing the 1972 convention ensured procedures for selecting delegates that prohibited discrimination against 18- to 30-year-olds or on the basis of race, color, creed, or national origin.

Many who advocate reform of the nominating process assume that the presidential primary is the best device for achieving a more representative system of selecting presidential nominees. Austin Ranney, a member of the McGovern Commission, has raised doubts about this assumption (Ranney,

1972; 1975). Using survey data on voter opinions on issues in the 1968 New Hampshire and Wisconsin primaries, intensity of party attachments, and the extent to which voters participate in primaries, Ranney concludes that: (1) People who vote in presidential primaries do not fully represent the opinions and policy preferences of those who do not vote; (2) voters in primaries are demographically unrepresentative of party members who do not vote (participants are older, come from higher social status groups, and are more active in civic, religious, and political organizations); (3) these patterns of unrepresentation are much the same as those found among national convention delegates (at least through 1968) when delegates are compared to their parties' rank-and-file members. Although Ranney warns that these relationships need closer examination, his findings suggest that it may be wrong to assume that primaries provide a more "representative" means for nominating Presidents.

The rules governing primaries affect the calculations of prospective presidential contenders. Under winner-take-all rules, a candidate must have sufficient support in the large populous states to win pluralities that will give him large blocks of delegates. Under proportional representation, however, a candidate's advantage in a large state is minimized since he receives no more delegates than his proportion of the primary vote permits. District ("loophole") primaries also take away the advantage large, populous states have in choosing the nominee and, if anything, give an advantage to smaller, less populous states: "A presidential contender can now secure a decent minority of districts in the biggest states and then aim for all the districts in either those states which are normally Republican in the November election (mainly western or midwestern) or those states which are of the hybrid persuasion known as 'Southern-Democratic'" (Lengle and Shafer, 1976, p. 35). This view, written about prospective future trends in Democratic primaries, describes well Jimmy Carter's primary success in 1976.

Victories in early presidential primaries are an important factor in selecting party nominees through the primary system. Aside from the vote-getting ability they may demonstrate, early victories improve a presidential contenders standing in public polls. Jimmy Carter's "victory" in the first 1976 primary (he received 28 percent of the votes cast in the New Hampshire Democratic primary, a plurality widely touted as a "victory" in a heavily crowded field of candidates) helped establish his credibility as a candidate. In turn, "standing in the preference polls has a strong direct effect on success in the state primary elections," and "a strong direct effect on winning the presidential nomination" (Beniger, 1976, p. 37).

The caucus alternative

In 1976 nearly three-quarters of a million Democrats took part in mass delegate selection caucuses in 22 states and four territories. Features of the

1976 caucus system included proportional representation at all levels of the selection process to allocate delegates among all candidates receiving at least 15 percent of the vote at that level, and the requirement that participants in a caucus either label themselves formally as "uncommitted" or declare their presidential preference. For Democrats in 1980 states will be allowed to set a minimum threshold of 15–25 percent for various levels. Precinct caucuses, normally open to all voters, elect delegates to county conventions; those county conventions elect delegates to congressional district and statewide conventions, which choose delegates to the national nominating convention.

The caucus alternative has been on the decline in the face of the rising popularity of the presidential primary as a means of selecting delegates. In 1968 about one-half of Democratic national delegates came from states using the caucus; in 1976 less than one-fourth of Democratic delegates came from caucus states. The number of states and U.S. territories using the caucus alternative shrank in that period from 34 to 22. The number of primary states plus territories rose from 18 to 30. The use of primaries to select delegates apparently has the approval of at least a plurality of Americans; in a 1976 survey, 46 percent of respondents preferred a convention with primary-elected delegates to either primaries without conventions (26 percent in favor) or conventions without primaries (10 percent in favor), the remainder being undecided (*The Harris Survey*, July 12, 1976).

Winning delegate support

Because many of the delegates chosen in primaries and caucuses are uncommitted, candidates for the presidential nomination must concentrate on a careful wooing of delegates. A prospective nominee can lose several primary states and still receive the nomination if he wins the support of delegates in nonprimary states (George McGovern in 1972 and Gerald Ford in 1976 are examples).

Without an effective campaign organization these uncommitted convention votes will be lost. The interim between party conventions affords candidates time to develop and maintain party ties and to build a campaign organization throughout the nation. Normally, presidential candidates wait until about a year before the presidential election to announce their candidacy, but the formation and activity of the campaign organization begins long before that. John Kennedy began to work for the Democratic nomination in 1956 after his unsuccessful bid for the vice-presidential nomination in the 1956 convention. Senator Barry Goldwater emerged as a contender for the 1964 nomination at the 1960 Republican convention when he withdrew his name as a possible nominee and admonished conservatives to "get to work" and recapture control of the party. Senator George McGovern's campaign organization was formed about 18 months before his nomination and included key members of John F. Kennedy's 1960 campaign. And a strong and effective organization, first planned as early as 1972, was a decisive factor in Jimmy Carter's winning the Democratic nomination in 1976.

The policy goals sought by delegates and party leaders are not necessarily the same. A candidate has to build broad support for his candidacy by adjusting differences among delegates, but he must also avoid attacks on his opponents that might endanger or destroy party unity. Within this framework, delegate votes become a resource in a bargaining environment. They may be used to win platform concessions, promises for future action (or inaction), or assurances of consideration in political appointments.

The nominating convention

The nomination process culminates in the national convention. Each step of the proceedings—the report of the Credentials Committee and seating of delegates, the selection of temporary and permanent convention officers, the report of the Platform Committee, the call for nominations, floor demonstrations, and ultimately the balloting—may be crucial in the conflict over who the party's standard bearer will be.

Dramatic proof that convention rules and procedures are vital emerged at the 1972 Democratic Convention. A critical issue was exposed when the Credentials Committee ruled that California's 271 delegates—won by Senator George McGovern in a winner-take-all presidential primary—would have to be divided between McGovern and Senator Hubert Humphrey, according to the proportion of the primary vote received by each candidate. McGovern lost 151 delegates. At the same time, the Committee denied seats to 58 Illinois delegates controlled by Mayor Richard Daley of Chicago, a Humphrey supporter, mainly on the ground that the delegation did not contain an adequate proportion of youth, women, and minorities—as stipulated in the Democratic party guidelines. The Credentials Committee ruled that, although the delegates had been selected in a primary, the delegate-candidates in the primary had been chosen in a manner that violated Democratic party rules. Senator McGovern went to court but lost the legal battle when the United States Supreme Court, following a hastily called special session, ruled that the issue had to be decided by the convention and not by the judiciary. A bitter convention floor battle was resolved by seating the challenged McGovern delegates from California. The Credentials Committee decision on the 58 Illinois delegates was upheld. McGovern's victory in both struggles was crucial: Senators Humphrey and Muskie both withdrew from the race for the nomination, assuring McGovern's nomination.

Platform provisions can also cause serious disagreement; the Democratic platform statement on the Vietnam War in the 1968 convention did so. These disputes may indicate the relative strength of candidates. In 1964, the Goldwater forces in the Republican convention proved strong enough to resist all efforts by less conservative forces to alter the Goldwater-dominated platform.

If the party is to be a useful tool in supplying the presidential candidate with tactics of persuasion and command after the convention, he must be assured that his nomination has not damaged that potential. A nominating campaign filled with rancor, a convention struggle over seating delegates, and arguments about platform provisions may make partisans lukewarm, as they did for the Republicans in 1964 (Goldwater), the Democrats in 1968 (Humphrey), and the Democrats again in 1972 (McGovern).

The balloting for nomination in the convention is also part of the strategy. N. W. Polsby and A. Wildavsky (1976) point out that the front-runner at the convention must win an early victory or his chances decline rapidly. If victory does not come on the first or second ballot, opposing candidates may convince the leader's supporters that their candidate has peaked and they should therefore switch their votes to another candidate. Keeping a strong front-runner from winning on an early ballot is a slender hope. In the 12 conventions from 1928 to 1976, the Democrats nominated their candidate on the first ballot 10 times. Exceptions were in 1932 and 1952 (four and three ballots respectively) when no Democratic incumbent President was a candidate for renomination. The Republican pattern is similar: Only twice, in 1940 and 1948 (six and three ballots) did the nomination go beyond the first ballot. Even when early nomination is not assured by the time the convention meets, it seems that bargaining among party leaders produces an early selection.

If the nomination is in doubt, convention bargaining may include choosing a vice-presidential candidate: A contender promises a faction that its choice for the Vice-Presidency will be placed on the ticket in exchange for support. Normally, however, the selection of the vice-presidential running mate follows the nomination of the presidential contender. Vice-presidential candidates are sometimes chosen to heal party wounds in the hopes of winning the support of a wing of the party in the general election (Lyndon Johnson's selection by John Kennedy in 1960), to add geographical balance to a ticket and appeal to a particular section (Robert Dole's selection by Gerald Ford in 1976), to assure a "compatible" running mate who can appeal to specific interests in the party (as Walter Mondale appealed to liberal interests on behalf of Jimmy Carter in 1976), and for many other reasons the presidential candidate and his strategists view as important at the time.

Nominating conventions are thus more than instruments for choosing the party's leadership. Convention maneuvering can smooth over differences within the party and rally the party faithful to the election's struggle or, conversely, it can create as many frictions and problems as it solves and make the election campaign even harder. Conventions may also reflect the passing of party control from one party faction to another; many heralded the choice of McGovern in 1972 as a wresting of control from "old-style" Democratic liberals by reform-minded "new politics" Democrats (Sullivan et al., 1976).

CONDUCTING ELECTION CAMPAIGNS

We saw in Chapter 6 that candidates for major federal (presidential and congressional) and statewide offices rely heavily upon a campaign staff recruited more for a record of loyalty to the candidates than for long-term service as faithful party members. Despite the fact that they play a lesser role in major general elections than they once did because candidates now emphasize personal rather than party organizations in campaigns, party leaders of various stripes—local functionaries, a few bosses, and dedicated activists—still make a major contribution to the conduct of elections. Their efforts count for something in at least three respects.

Mobilizing precincts

In all elections, precinct workers are important: They urge party sympathizers to vote and reinforce partisan loyalties. Precinct canvassing, traditionally associated with the local party's campaign efforts, aims at getting a large turnout for a party's candidates by distributing literature, ringing doorbells, making telephone calls, operating car pools to get voters to the polls, and even providing babysitting on election days. These grass-roots efforts do produce higher turnouts; a party may increase its vote by about 5 percent through such activity.

In addition to winning votes in specific elections, precinct work has a long-term effect on partisan attitudes. Frequent contact by party organizers intensifies party loyalties and, in this sense, the party organization reinforces the influences of family, friends, co-workers, and the mass media on the vote. Precinct activity also recruits new adherents by performing a variety of services—especially in the poverty pockets of rural America and in urban ghettoes—providing legal counsel for constituents in trouble with the police, finding political jobs for the unemployed, taking care of the needy, and so forth. Although the service role of political parties has diminished in recent decades (in part because federal programs have supplanted party efforts), it has not vanished entirely. In more affluent suburbs, parties offer other incentives—social contacts, a boost to careers, opportunities for making friends.

As noted, the party activist shares campaign responsibilities with various specialists: public relations personnel, pollsters, mass media technicians, fundraisers, and organizers. The presence of these mercenaries raises new problems of organizational control for the party. A candidate who can successfully employ such specialists (and other paid and unpaid volunteers as well) may win elections without the support of precinct stalwarts. Opportunities abound for "outsiders" to capture control of the party through electoral victory, especially if the party needs the candidate more than the candidate needs the party.

Financing campaigns

As with mobilizing voters, new ways of doing things challenge party influence in financing political campaigns. The federal and state regulations that have been imposed on fundraising and campaign spending (see Chapter 6) have left their mark on party techniques for raising monies: fundraising dinners; appeals to the party faithful through visits, phone calls, and door-to-door canvassing; solicitation by mass mailings of letters; television, radio, newspaper, and periodical advertising; contributions from patronage appointees; special events including cocktail and theater parties; appeals to nonparty groups. How much money may be raised, how much may be allocated to which candidate, what records must be kept, provisions for making names of contributors public—all of these matters are governed by federal and state statutes that affect party fundraising and spending schemes.

As much as party leaders might like to have the money raised in a campaign go directly to the party treasury, major donors often bypass the party by contributing their money directly to a candidate, a separate fundraising committee, or some other agency. This practice has led to precisely the kinds of problems that lawmakers attempted to correct through regulatory legislation. For example, although vast sums were raised in the 1972 presidential campaign on behalf of Richard Nixon, it went to the Committee for Re-Election of the President (CREEP), not to the Republican party. Questions about the sources and distribution of those funds became a major part of the Watergate scandals. Those scandals demonstrated once again that when candidates can look elsewhere than to political parties for financing, they are not inclined to accept party discipline or respond to party needs. Unless parties can find ways of making candidates dependent upon parties rather than on large-sum donors, the major parties will be unable to control the public officials elected to key executive and legislative positions at all governmental levels. Whether provisions for the public financing of elections will alleviate the problem remains to be seen. On the one hand, public financing provides parties with federal subsidies to spend on their candidates' behalf, a step in the direction of increasing party influence; on the other hand, public financing also provides a much larger amount of monies (in presidential elections) directly to the candidates, a provision not designed to augment party control over fundraising and spending (Alexander, 1976).

Administering elections

Elections require procedures for actually casting and counting votes. These activities are performed by bipartisan precinct election boards whose members normally receive patronage appointments with the consent of party leaders. Election judges, clerks, poll watchers are all party people responsible for seeing that the election machinery operates smoothly, votes get counted accurately, recounts are made when necessary, and fraudulent practices don't occur. Although Americans would like to think that their votes are always counted as cast, this is not always true. In areas of the country where paper ballots are still employed, election judges have the discretion of throwing out, and not counting, ballots not marked in strict accordance with the law. It is a small matter, if the judges are so inclined, to give one party advantage over another by applying the rules selectively. How frequently this occurs, and with what effects, we do not know.

INFLUENCING POLICYMAKING

Political parties play a twofold role in representing social conflicts. First, party activists publicize social disputes by taking part in the election process—by nominating candidates with different views and getting them elected, they reveal interest conflicts within and between the parties. Second, partisan public officials reflect disagreements over policy goals and ways of achieving them:

- Through the Presidency, where they exercise *leadership* in making policies;
- In Congress, where they offer policy proposals and bargain in the process of *adoption*;
- By occupying appointive positions in the federal bureaucracy, where they *apply* policies;
- In judicial bodies, where they influence the *adjudication* of policy disagreements, although partisanship is less apparent here.

Parties and the Presidency

Political parties exercise policy leadership (see Chapter 11) during and between elections. A focal point of that leadership is the Presidency, occupied by the leader of one party and continuously sought by leaders of the opposition. In their efforts to win or hold the Presidency, major party leaders promote policies that publicize key social conflicts and go beyond the interests of any one group. After assuming the Presidency in 1974, Gerald Ford proposed a variety of legislative solutions to conflicts over what should be done about the economy, national defense, foreign affairs, energy, the environment, crime, welfare, transportation, and other matters. As the 1976 election year approached, leaders within the President's own party (Ronald Reagan most notably) challenged many of these proposals. Moreover, leading opposition contenders for the office—Senators Henry Jackson, Birch Bayh, Frank Church, and Lloyd Bentsen; Governors Jerry Brown of California and Milton Shapp of Pennsylvania; and one-time officeholders Jimmy Carter, Sargent Shriver, Fred

Harris and Eugene McCarthy—responded with their own proposals. In this fashion the President and his critics defined the social problems that would be on the political agenda of the late 1970s.

The political party is a base of support for a President bent upon exerting influence over policymaking. A President whose party controls Congress, such as Jimmy Carter, can use partisan loyalty as a means of getting congressional leaders to accept his legislative proposals. Sometimes it works, sometimes it doesn't, but at least partisan kinship is one more rallying cry emanating from the White House. When the President's opposition controls Congress (as it has for most of the periods of the three Republican presidencies since World War II), the President urges members of his own party to band together and tries to recruit defectors from the opposition to prevent Congress from overriding his vetoes of legislation he finds objectionable.

For the party that controls the White House, the decentralizing tendencies in two-party politics are offset in small measure by the unity spurred by the President's leadership and program. The "out party," whose presidential candidate lost, lacking such a unifying symbol has more visible factional strife. Several discordant voices claim to speak for the "opposition." The Republican party's experience following the defeat in the 1976 presidential election shows how the out-party's leadership gets fragmented. Differing—sometimes conflicting and sometimes compatible—policy positions arose from the party's spokespersons including former President Gerald Ford, his conservative challenger in 1976, Ronald Reagan, future presidential aspirants such as Senators Howard Baker and Charles Percy, former Vice-President Nelson Rockefeller, and new faces on the scene, including Governor James Thompson of Illinois, Senators John Danforth, H. John Heinz, and Richard Lugar. It is difficult enough to generate party unity behind presidential leadership; without it, a united stance on policy matters is almost impossible.

Parties in Congress

We will look in detail at the influence of political parties on congressional politics in Chapter 12. Here it is sufficient to note that most American legislative bodies, including Congress, organize along party lines: Members of the majority party control committee chairs and make up the majority of each committee, choose the presiding officer of the legislative body, and control the order of business. Other influences on legislation reflecting party biases depend upon what other efforts are made to bend the legislator's ear—ties to local constituents that transcend partisanship, the pressure exerted by the President, the legislator's sympathy for the wishes of special interests that conflict with partisan views.

Party voting in Congress on substantive issues (reflected in partisan divisions on roll-call votes) varies. Figure 8.3 displays the proportion of roll-call votes in

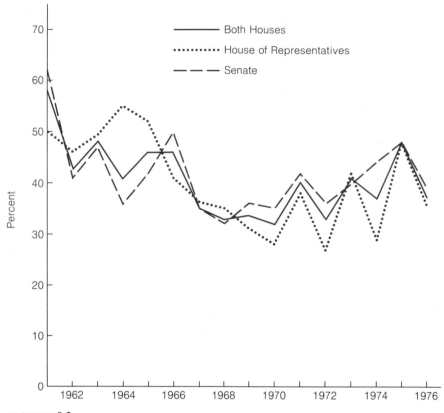

FIGURE 8.3

The Trend in Party Voting in Congress, 1961–1976. (Percentages are of roll-calls in which a majority of one party voted against a majority of the other party.) [*Source:* Compiled from *Congressional Quarterly Weekly Reports,* 1961–1976.]

both houses of Congress in recent years where majorities of Democrats voted against majorities of Republicans. It is apparent that party loyalty is but one indicator of legislative voting. Bipartisan voting (when a majority of Democrats and a majority of Republicans vote in the same way) occurs in a high percentage of roll calls. Although far from infallible, partisanship is a fairly good predictor of how the legislative party will vote in some areas. For example, partisan divisions are more likely in matters dealing with business-government relations, levels of public spending, and the public versus private development of natural resources. Democrats generally favor government activity in these areas whereas Republicans come down on the side of the private sector. Although less apparent, partisan voting also occurs on social welfare and agricultural policy questions. On matters of international and civil rights policies, voting tends to be bipartisan (Clausen, 1973).

Parties and bureaucratic politics

There was a time, following the election of Andrew Jackson to the presidency in the nineteenth century, when people generally expected that all administrative posts would be filled by members of the President's party. Today presidential discretion in making appointments extends only to top administrative and ambassadorial posts. Below these, the rules of career civil service dictate procedures of selection (see Chapter 13). Career officials develop loyalty to their agency and its established aims and programs, thus resisting many of the partisan and presidential appeals for policy changes. There have been presidential efforts to use governmental agencies for partisan ends, but such efforts have produced congressional, journalistic, and public outcries. A case in point came in the Nixon Administration. In 1969 the Nixon White House pressured the Internal Revenue Service to establish a special staff to keep tabs on "activist" and "leftist" groups. The staff compiled information—not all related solely to taxes—on more than 8,000 individuals and almost 3,000 organizations including the Americans for Democratic Action and even the National Council of Churches. Later, between 1971 and 1973, the White House provided names of 600 persons (called the "enemies list" during the Watergate investigations) whose income tax returns were to receive extra scrutiny from the IRS. Revelations that the White House had tried to use the IRS for partisan ends brought widespread indignation as well as investigations. The resulting inquiries demonstrated that the IRS did not buckle to White House efforts and managed to resist carrying out orders to harass private citizens and groups.

Parties and the courts

Partisan considerations weigh heavily in the selection process in states that elect judicial officials. In appointing persons to federal judgeships, particularly in federal district courts, the President normally selects qualified individuals from his own party. Since the 1930s, a scant 5 percent of the federal circuit and district judgeships have been filled with appointments from the opposition party. However, a President cannot automatically appoint qualified party members as he wishes to judicial positions. The tradition of "senatorial courtesy" permits a Senator of the President's party to oppose an appointment to the federal bench in his state on grounds that the nominee is "personally objectionable" to him. The rest of the Senate, regardless of party lines, is prepared to reject the nomination, not merely to please a colleague but to protect each other's power in such situations in the future. The President is thus forced to use his authority to appoint in ways that strengthen his Senate partisans, at the direct expense of his own power. Here is yet another example of the dispersion of party control.

The influence of political parties on the judiciary is restricted by the widespread belief that judges should be "nonpolitical"; that is, partisan considerations should not enter into their judicial decisions. President Franklin Roosevelt proposed in 1937 that he be allowed to appoint additional justices to the Supreme Court for each judge over the age of seventy who did not retire after ten years of service and that the maximum number of justices for the court be raised from nine to fifteen. This proposal was interpreted as an attempt to "pack" the Court with judges amenable to presidential programs previously declared unconstitutional by the justices. The proposal was criticized by many as violating the nonpartisan tradition of the judiciary, and it failed. The "Court-packing" episode shows that party leaders try to influence the appointment of federal judges; but partisanship does not then enter into the judges' decisions or result in party discipline over members of the judiciary. (See Chapter 14.)

Party politics and American democracy

Ideally the task of democracy is to organize conflict in such a way that public officials are subject to popular control and the entire political process is open for public debate. Political parties can serve that ideal by making their elected and appointed public officials responsive to social conflicts and responsible to the people.

Do American parties create a responsive and responsible officialdom? We believe that in general they do. In competing for political authority, each of our major parties appeals to and absorbs many conflicting interests. Neither party resolves these disputes, but each does unite its factions enough to contest elections. Once the elections are over, the social conflicts inherent in the two parties surface once more and are brought to the attention of public officials; in the resolving of those conflicts by government, partisanship is important but not supreme. Operating in this fashion for the past century, the Democratic and Republican parties have demonstrated to Americans that party rivalry is an acceptable way to select governing officials. Two-party politics is as much a part of the constitutional consensus as the written Constitution itself, although no provision is made for parties in the written document. And so long as partisans carry the liberal-democratic creed, the parties help bind Americans to substantive as well as procedural tenets of democracy.

But American political parties have been only partly successful in making public officials responsive and responsible to social interests. Our major parties cater primarily to interests that provide electoral majorities in localized constituencies; except in presidential elections, they seldom make nationwide appeals to Americans in all walks of life. By appealing to a majority of the voters, party candidates sometimes overlook the interests of minority groups, because the parties themselves do not adequately represent those interests. And, when party officeholders do respond to the interests of the unrepresented, the party's diverse composition makes it hard to unify behind corrective programs. Moreover, the dispersion of power within the party makes it impossible to force public officials to support legislative and executive programs.

American political parties, then, do make indispensable contributions to the democratic regulation of social conflict, even if they alone have not produced an ideally responsive and responsible government. Parties are the only large-scale, continuously active, open, and inclusive organizations in politics that represent a highly diverse clientele. Other means of bringing pressure on public officials and making them responsive may augment political parties, but they do not supplant them.

ORGANIZING
INTEREST
DEMANDS

9

We have examined in detail four of the ways in which Americans take part in conflict representation: how they express political opinions, exercise political leadership, vote, and play party politics. They also participate by joining voluntary organizations and pressing their demands and grievances directly upon government officials. These organized efforts to influence government constitute interest group politics.

Organized interests in conflict representation

How do people organize their demands through interest group politics and how do they exert organized pressure to influence government? Answers to these questions emerge from a consideration of others: What are interest groups? Who takes part in them? Which are the key organized interests in conflict representation?

THE CHARACTER OF INTEREST GROUPS

In Chapter 5 we distinguished between attitudes (tendencies that indicate enduring personal preferences), interests (actions in pursuit of general goals), and opinions (expressions of beliefs, values, and expectations about specific matters). Bearing those distinctions in mind, we say that an interest group is any organization of persons who (1) share similar attitudes, (2) make demands upon others, and (3) express group opinions to influence policies that affect the members of the group. Let us consider each element in this definition.

Shared attitudes

An interest group is not just any collection of people. The people must share some characteristic that brings them to interact and respond in a common way to social conflicts, if we are to call them an interest group (Schattschneider, 1960; Truman, 1952; Wilson, 1973). Persons of the same sex are a demographic group with a common attribute, but they are not an interest group. However, if their sex (say female) leads them to share some attitudes (like a belief in equal rights for women) and inspires some members of the same sex to make a common response to a specific question (such as seeking passage of the Equal Rights Amendment in the 1970s), then those people of the same sex constitute an interest group or groups.

When people interact because they share attitudes, they generally organize; but two things characterize organized interest. First, people need not be members of a formal organization to pursue the interests represented by it. A person can be opposed to generating electricity through the use of nuclear energy without joining an organization (say the Union of Concerned Scientists) to urge a slowdown in construction of nuclear power plants. Although we recognize the existence of such "fellow travelers," our subject here is group interests represented by formal organizations.

Second, organization is not the same as unity of purpose. Although members must share enough attitudes to make the group possible, interest groups often consist of different and competing elements or subinterests, striving to define, as well as achieve, organizational goals. Because unity promotes strength, group leaders develop lines of command and procedures to reconcile diverse elements within the organization. Internal harmony, however, is easily disrupted. Subgroups vie for control and form temporary alliances to dictate group policy. There are, for example, splits within the United Mine Workers that reflect bitter conflicts over who should lead the labor union, how the union should deal with coal mine owners and operators, and what goals should be pursued. Union leaders may forge a wage-and-hour agreement with industry managers only to have dissident elements in the union call "wildcat" strikes in protest. Also, the interests of a group's members are not always in harmony with the stated goals of the group. For instance, in recent years many physicians have grown uncomfortable with the conservative political coloring of the American Medical Association (AMA); some have even dropped out or refused to join their major professional organization. Responding to threats of declining membership, the AMA has created a membership division to examine new ways of making the association more attractive to young physicians and physicians in research, teaching hospitals, and health agencies.

Making interest demands

Demands usually begin as goals sought primarily on behalf of group members. Interest groups, however, are not inherently "selfish" or in the hip pocket of some unseen, invisible "establishment." Many of the demands of special interests ultimately benefit larger sectors of the population. The first piece of legislation signed into law in the 1970s, the National Environment Policy Act (signed January 1, 1970), established the national policy that federal, state, and local governments must act to protect the environment on behalf of all Americans. A key feature of the legislation is that any proposed construction project must take into account the environmental impact of the proposed action. This has come to mean considering not only the consequences of projects for air, water, and land quality but the economic, social, and human consequences as well. Although specialized environmental groups advanced such legislation, their demands were designed to benefit every American. The same might be said of other policies initiated by the specialized demands of narrow interests—particularly welfare policies such as those dealing with Social Security, the minimum wage, and health care.

Many interest groups are organized to advance general rather than narrow demands. Common Cause is designed to promote participation in politics, change American political institutions to make them more responsive to social needs, and produce a major reordering of national priorities; Ralph Nader's Center for the Study of Responsive Law works for consumer protection; and Saul Alinsky's Industrial Areas Foundation helped organize low-income communities for political protest in the 1960s.

To be durable and effective, interest groups must continuously adapt their demands to current political realities. When environmentalist groups got congressional legislation requiring antipollution devices for cars, the manufacturers countered by requesting that some taxes on automobile sales be dropped to free money for necessary research and development.

The goals pursued by private interests may not parallel the public interest as public officials define it. To win approval for their position, organized interests often recruit support from other groups or rationalize their narrow demands to make them acceptable to the community. The price of recruiting outside support is modification of goals to avoid conflict with groups desired as allies. An appeal to mass public opinion, claimed to be in the public interest, may require that the original position be changed. Many members of the American

Medical Association have vociferously opposed any government-sponsored medical insurance program. When almost two-thirds of the Americans surveyed in 1960 said they approved of such programs, the AMA changed its position to oppose only federal programs. It endorsed a bill providing matching federal grants to reimburse the states for medical aid to needy, aged persons. In 1965, over AMA. opposition, a medical care program for the aged, financed under the federal social security program, became law. (After losing the Medicare battle, the AMA succeeded in influencing and even controlling the program's operation.)

Influencing governmental decisions

Interest groups seek access to public officials in order to inform them of group opinions and thereby exert pressure to obtain favorable policies. Because they apply pressure on governing officials to influence policy, organized interests are often referred to as pressure groups, a term we shall consider as synonymous with interest groups. Interest groups have several avenues of access to policymakers: administrative agencies, congressional committees, and presidential advisers. Some are easier to reach than others, so interest groups plan carefully to gain whatever advantage they can get where they do gain access. A major interest may find it far easier to work through the most influential people in a congressional representative's home district (automobile manufacturers in Michigan or farming interests in the Midwest), thus reaching him by way of his constituents rather than approaching him directly as a public official.

Organized interests care less about having their own spokespersons elected or appointed to government offices (though this sometimes occurs) than about getting elective or appointive officials to recognize their claims. They do not, of course, divorce themselves from electoral politics. One avenue of access is the selection of sympathetic candidates. If party control is diffuse or party leaders are divided, interest groups significantly affect party decisions and perhaps even win nomination for their own members. But a group spokesperson who becomes a political candidate runs as a Republican or Democrat, not as a leader of the Audubon Society, the Hardwood Plywood Institute, or the Marble Industry of America. The appeal of an organized interest is too narrow to compete directly with the major parties, so group leaders prefer to work through party organizations.

Interest groups thus differ from political parties in their goals and methods. An American political party's goal is to control governmental authority; its method is to mobilize support behind candidates for office. The interest group's goal is to influence policy in a specific area; its methods include identifying with dominant community values, seeking the support of allied groups, lobbying with officials, endorsing and financing party candidates.

WHO PARTICIPATES IN INTEREST GROUPS?

Two of every three Americans belong to some formal organization, and at least half of these belong to groups that take stands on political issues. Who joins and why?

Group membership varies with social class, because members of more affluent classes have more time, money, and resources to devote to group activity. Taking occupation as an indicator of social class, we find that professional and business people almost always belong to interest groups; clerical and skilled workers are less likely to join; unskilled workers, unless required to be members of trade unions, are unlikely to join.

Education also affects group membership—more group members come from the more educated segments of society. Those with higher incomes are more likely to join interest groups; however, membership in avowedly political clubs—neighborhood groups performing both social and political functions—has little to do with income.

The politics of organized interests and interest groups do not represent all social interests. Currently, though, representation of previously unorganized sectors is increasing. Before 1965, grape workers in southern California earned a yearly pay that was scarcely above poverty level; they had no assurance of employment, no unemployment insurance, and no trade union. Cesar Chavez organized the workers well enough so that they could call a strike, march to the state capital to protest about grievances, and promote a nationwide boycott of grapes. Labor organizations and civil rights groups helped the grape workers behind Chavez get broad public support; and by the end of 1970, two-thirds of the grape growers agreed to contracts favorable to the workers. With varying degrees of success, Black Americans, Mexican-Americans, women, the elderly, and other formerly unrepresented elements have also organized to present their interest demands.

People join interest organizations for many reasons. One is their desire for political expression. Generally people do not exercise political initiative individually, but respond to group leaders who show them they have common interests, that these interests can be represented in politics, and that organized expression will influence policymakers. Martin Luther King, Jr., Cesar Chavez, Betty Friedan, Ralph Nader, and Saul Alinsky articulated for Blacks, farm laborers, women, consumers, and the poor that something can be gained by collective action. People also join groups for social and personal reasons—a need for meaningful camaraderie, to improve their social status, to enhance their sense of personal worth, or to respond to those making demands upon them. Whatever their reasons for joining, group members obtain allies in pursuing their interests that they would not have if they stuck to purely individual techniques such as voting, writing officials, keeping informed, or simply holding political opinions.

ORGANIZED SOCIAL AND ECONOMIC INTERESTS IN POLITICS

The social and economic interest groups that represent conflicting interests to policymakers are hard to count (there are well over 10,000 national associations of one variety or another, and registered lobbyists in Washington alone represent more than one-tenth that number). We can only suggest the diversity among the largest groups that organize key social and economic demands in America and describe some of their interests.

Social demands

Some of the enduring problems of our era are best reflected in the activities of interest groups in education and veterans affairs. Other significant and much-publicized interests emerging in recent decades have made policy demands in civil rights, environmental quality, and consumer protection.

EDUCATION GROUPS. A principal group interested in educational policy is the National Education Association, an organization of school teachers and administrators, which has supported federal aid to education. In particular, the NEA has advocated channeling aid directly to local school districts rather than through the states. The National Congress of Parents and Teachers (PTA), the American Council on Education, and the educational bodies of all major religious denominations have also expressed interest in federal aid and shared many of the NEA's ideas on aid to local districts. Federal aid to higher education has been a policy goal of several organizations such as the National Association for Equal Opportunity in Higher Education, which has proposed direct grants to institutions enrolling large numbers of students from low-income families to ensure that funds go to those students most in need of them. Interest groups in higher education have taken stands on proposals to allow a tax credit for the expenses of a college education, federal aid to college libraries, work-study programs, funding for construction of college classrooms, bills designed to deal with student unrest, and many others.

VETERANS' ORGANIZATIONS. Groups representing veterans have sought low-cost hospital and medical care, low-cost housing, free land, education benefits, pensions, assistance to families of prisoners of war, and privileged treatment in competing for public employment. Among the most influential groups are the American Legion, the Disabled American Veterans, and the Veterans of Foreign Wars. Like most organized interests, they do not confine themselves to seeking material benefits for members; they also take stands on issues of symbolic importance. The American Legion and the Veterans of Foreign Wars were among the chief opponents to admitting mainland China to the United

Nations. Veterans' organizations have also been some of the staunchest opponents of proposals to grant amnesty and pardons to Vietnam war deserters and draft evaders.

CIVIL RIGHTS ORGANIZATIONS.   Perhaps the most unrelenting efforts to influence policymaking on behalf of previously unrepresented interests have come from civil rights groups working on behalf of Blacks, Mexican-Americans, women, young people, the poor, and the elderly. Civil rights groups illustrate the tendency of all interest organizations to use varied techniques to publicize their cause and to influence public officials. The National Association for the Advancement of Colored People and the Mexican-American Legal Defense and Educational Fund have used nonmilitant approaches, seeking redress for grievances in the courts and Congress. The Black Muslims have advocated a separate community for their people, and the Black Panthers have urged alliance with all sympathetic minority parties to contest elections. Women's liberation groups such as the National Organization for Women, the National Women's Political Caucus, and the Women's Equity Action League have employed marches, demonstrations, and boycotts as well as court and congressional hearings to draw attention to equal rights for women and policies pertaining to abortion, employment opportunities, child care, and the draft. Young people have campaigned for political candidates, demonstrated, occupied public buildings, disrupted college campuses, and used other tactics to publicize their complaints about war, the anonymity of mass education, drug use, and the deteriorating environment. Civil rights groups working on policies toward the poor have allied with other organizations to promote the economic as well as social and political rights of members; for example, the National Welfare Rights Organization formed a coalition with the National Association of Manufacturers and the AFL-CIO to urge a major overhaul of welfare legislation and a minimum annual income for poor families. Finally, groups representing the interests of the elderly, such as the Senior Citizens Council, have employed televised rallies and television documentaries to call attention to the need for improved health programs for the aged.

Many of the civil rights organizations also illustrate the tendency of interest groups to diversify their concerns to represent fully their members. Until the mid-1960s, the Southern Christian Leadership Conference (SCLC) concentrated its efforts on obtaining federal legislation to guarantee voting rights for southern Blacks. Its leadership corps, particularly the late Martin Luther King, Jr., recognized, however, that federal policies in areas other than voting also affect Blacks. For example, the burden of the draft to provide troops for the Vietnam War fell heavily on Black youths; moreover, funds to finance that war were drained away from projects designed to alleviate Black poverty. By the close of the 1960s, the SCLC was no longer interested only in the political rights of Blacks; it had become deeply involved in urging Congress to fight poverty —as in the Poor People's March on Washington in 1968—and to cut expenditures for defense and space exploration as one means of doing so.

Although the civil rights groups mentioned above got most of the publicity in the 1960s and 1970s, other organizations were both active and influential. The Americans for Democratic Action and the American Civil Liberties Union pressed for expansion of human rights, changes in the selective service laws, fair and impartial judicial hearings, and other measures. The American Jewish Congress, the Anti-Defamation League (also Jewish), the National Council of Catholic Men, and the Protestant National Council of Churches also worked for various civil rights causes.

ENVIRONMENTALIST GROUPS.   Interest in protecting the environment from both pollution and the threat of overpopulation has grown in the 1970s. One of the main environmental interest groups is the Sierra Club, which organizes at the grass-roots level to influence congressional constituents, brings suits against major polluters, and engages extensively in publishing. In the 1970s, the Sierra Club fought the development of a supersonic aircraft transport, underground testing of nuclear devices, timber cutting in national forests, and the building of oil pipelines in the Alaskan wilderness. The Center for Law and Social Policy, the Friends of the Earth, the Conservation Foundation, and organizations for young people have staunchly battled for policies to clean up the environment. To protect the environment from overpopulation, several interest organizations, such as the Council for Planned Parenthood, the Association for the Study of Abortion Laws, and Zero Population Growth, have proposed legislation favoring birth control, liberalized abortion, and the distribution of information about contraceptives.

CONSUMER INTERESTS.   Groups have been organized to speak for consumers who are the victims of unfair sales practices, inadequate packaging, faulty products, low-quality goods, and over-the-counter sale of vitamin and food supplements of questionable effectiveness. The most vocal advocate of consumer protection has been Ralph Nader, organizer of "Nader's Raiders" (the Center for the Study of Responsive Law); his group has urged legislation to improve automobile safety, the quality of prescription and nonprescription drugs, household detergents, and numerous other products. In the mid-1970s Nader became one of the foremost opponents of the building of nuclear power plants to generate electricity, arguing that neither light water reactors nor planned liquid metal fast breeder reactors were in the interests of the health and safety of Americans and, moreover, that they would produce electricity at far greater expense to the consumer than advertised by nuclear advocates. Consumer's Union and Common Cause have also taken up the plight of the previously unrepresented consumer.

Economic demands

Some of the most influential groups in this country have been those devoted to economic matters—business, labor, agriculture, and professional interests. When allied, they are a potent force in American politics.

BUSINESS ORGANIZATIONS.   The two leading business organizations in America are the Chamber of Commerce of the United States and the National Association of Manufacturers (NAM). Both have dealt particularly with policies on foreign trade, corporation taxes, federal minimum wage, Social Security, unemployment, and government contracting. The Chamber of Commerce is an association of local chambers of commerce and thus represents many local business interests. The NAM is especially responsive to the interests of large industries. Many other groups representing small businessmen, the retail trades, the building trades, banking, transportation, and motel and hotel interests are also active in politics.

In the 1970s Americans became increasingly aware of the limited energy resources of this nation and of planet Earth. Since energy is money, it is no surprise that major economic interests organized around the supply and exploitation of our energy resources. The American Petroleum Institute, an organization of oil and gas companies as well as individual members, lobbied successfully for building the Alaska pipeline and against excess profits taxes on the petroleum industry. Also active was the Atomic Energy Forum, an organization of corporations and firms promoting nuclear energy as the best alternative to dwindling oil resources. Similarly, associations representing major mine owners and operators advocated exploitation of our nation's coal resources. Contrasting views on how to solve the energy crisis—between oil, nuclear, and coal interests, on the one hand, and environmentalists, on the other—were a continuing source of social conflict in the 1970s and will be for decades to come.

THE MILITARY-INDUSTRIAL COMPLEX.   During and after World War II, federal spending for military purposes, defense preparations, space development, and weapons technology increased immensely. Many industries relied on federal contracts for economic survival and prosperity; workers in these industries depended entirely on continued federal defense spending. In the 1950s, an alliance of interests emerged to promote ever greater defense expenditures: business firms seeking government contracts, labor unions in defense industries, government agencies urging new programs for research and development of military weapons, military officers seeking support for the armed services, and members of Congress in whose home districts the defense industries were located. For two decades industrial, labor, bureaucratic, military, and congressional interests have combined to form the most powerful national influence on defense policies.

At the top of the military-industrial complex are the Pentagon (Department of Defense), the House and Senate Armed Services Committees, and prime defense contractors. Their interests are closely allied: Two-thirds of the members of the Senate Armed Services Committee represent districts in which Pentagon expenditures are the prime source of federal funds. Though the committees in both houses reduce the Pentagon's budget request each year, the requests are often padded in anticipation of cuts. The Senate and House usually approve the budgetary recommendations for the Department of Defense the two armed services committees have made with little change. Finally, the Department of Defense now spends considerably more than many other key federal agencies.

Despite one of the severest challenges to its influence, the alliance demonstrated its power by winning approval in 1969 and 1970 of an elaborate research and development program for an antiballistic missle system (ABM) to deter Chinese or Soviet missile threats. Environmentalist, scientific, antiwar, religious, and other groups opposed it; even opinion polls indicated a gradual increase in general public opposition during the controversy. Opponents of the program argued that the ABM would be unworkable and excessively expensive (its cost perhaps amounting to a total of $400 billion), that it would be a threat to communities near ABM sites which would be targets of enemy missiles, and that it would make world disarmament impossible. But the military-industrial interests were able to convince enough members of Congress of the need for such a deterrent and of the economic benefits to their constituencies; they received substantial approval in the House of Representatives and a one-vote victory in the Senate.

It is necessary to keep the role of the military-industrial alliance in perspective. Although important in American politics, it is not all-controlling nor does it always get its way. Military contracts account for about 10 percent of the sales of our largest corporations, indicating that industries do not depend solely upon the fate of the military. Moreover, the proportion of the total national budget devoted to defense spending declined from about half in 1960 to less than one-third by the mid-1970s. The military-industrial complex now competes with other forces for a portion of the federal dollar, especially with the "school lobby" (an alliance of interests in the U.S. Office of Education and various education-promoting organizations) and the "welfare lobby" composed of interests from large metropolitan areas and the Departments of Health, Education, and Welfare and of Housing and Urban Development seeking federal support for welfare programs.

LABOR ORGANIZATIONS.   Labor organizations have greatly expanded their involvement with policy since the 1930s when legislation on minimum wages and maximum hours were their big interests. Unions are still deeply interested in such bread-and-butter matters as labor-management relations, wage-and-hour legislation, Social Security, and income tax legislation, but other issues —federally sponsored health insurance programs, legislation dealing with problems raised by automation, foreign aid, federal aid to education, a guaranteed annual wage, policies dealing with housing and government contracts —also occupy their attention. Among the most influential labor organizations are the AFL-CIO, the United Mine Workers, the International Teamsters Union, the United Automobile Workers, the International Ladies Garment Workers' Union, and the International Telecommunications Union. Government employees are also represented in the labor movement by such organizations as the American Federation of Government Employees (an AFL-CIO affiliate), the National Alliance of Postal and Federal Employees, and the National Postal Union.

Like other organized interests, the labor lobby has had its share of success and defeat. For example, in 1977 President Carter asked Congress for a 20-cent-an-hour increase in the minimum wage paid to workers in this country. Organized labor sought a more substantial increase, despite arguments by business groups that such an increase in the minimum wage would result in massive inflation and economic disruption. Labor prevailed and Congress passed legislation to increase the minimum wage from $2.30 an hour in 1977 to $3.35 an hour by 1982, an average 25-cent-an-hour increase in each of four years. But the labor lobby suffered defeat in 1977 on a proposal for common-site picketing. That legislation would have allowed unions to protest the actions of a single contractor by setting up picket lines around an entire construction site, thus holding all contractors responsible for the actions of but one. The House of Representatives defeated the proposal by a vote of 217–205, a setback labor leaders attributed to their own "sloppy lobbying" (*Congressional Quarterly Weekly Report*, December 17, 1977, p. 2590).

THE FARM BLOC. Before farmers began to migrate from the land to urban areas, farm groups were among the most influential in American politics. They still exert great pressure, particularly over programs that set farm subsidies and crop allotments and deal with farm laborers. The American Farm Bureau Federation has generally opposed strict production controls and favored high price supports; the National Farmers Union has supported both programs; and the National Grange has varied its position. The National Farmers Organization was organized mostly to force food processors to pay higher prices for agricultural products.

One of the most highly publicized of organized interests in the agricultural sector in recent years has been the American Milk Producers, Inc. This dairy cooperative seeks higher federal support prices for milk on behalf of more than 40,000 members. One of its basic tactics is to subsidize the electoral campaigns of sympathetic officeholders. The organization figured prominently in a case against former Secretary of Treasury John B. Connally, who was indicted in

1974 for allegedly taking bribes from the organization's lawyer in exchange for working to increase federal milk price supports. Connally was later found innocent of all charges, but the incident revealed the dairy co-op's tactics and was a major setback to Connally's political aspirations.

PROFESSIONAL GROUPS. The interests of major professional groups encompass both social and economic demands. Among professional groups with much influence are the American Bar Association and the American Medical Association. The National Association of Realtors and the National Association of Home Builders are professional and business groups that take stands on such issues as federal subsidies for home building, urban redevelopment, open-housing legislation designed to end racial discrimination in sales of homes, and even drug abuse (local organizations of realtors developed the "Turn in a Pusher" program to encourage citizens to report to local authorities anyone suspected of illegally selling drugs).

Organizations of scientists have become increasingly active in politics since the 1940s. An informal group of nuclear scientists was instrumental in persuading Congress to establish a civilian agency, the Atomic Energy Commission, to control the development of nuclear power after World War II instead of letting the military manage it. More recently, many scientists have opposed the increasing reliance of nations on the use of nuclear energy to generate electricity and pressed this opposition through the Union of Concerned Scientists and the Natural Resources Defense Council. In 1969 and 1970, the American Federation of Scientists was one of the most active anti-ABM groups; it was unable to keep the ABM on the ground, but it did reduce the funds committed to the project.

Techniques of organized interests in conflict representation

Each social and economic interest takes stands on issues affecting its membership. Organized interests thus represent diverse and frequently conflicting points of view to executive, legislative, and judicial officials. In representing social conflict to policymakers, interest groups engage in two general activities: First, to win support and to counter claims made by opposing interests, groups *publicize* their demands and thus influence political opinion; second, to inform government of their members' interests, groups *present* their demands directly to public officials and thereby influence public policy.

PUBLICIZING GROUP INTERESTS

Organized interests use varied tools to influence political opinions. Among the principal ones are organizing opinions among their own members, socializing members, exercising leadership in calling attention to issues, electioneering, and protesting grievances.

Organizing group opinion

Before interest groups can recruit outside aid in pursuit of their goals, they must mobilize internal support for those goals and for the means and strategies to realize them. Because large social and economic organizations (such as education groups or large labor unions) have many interests, they must often work hard to reconcile divergent opinions. When the techniques they use to achieve those adjustments are democratic, members are more likely to support democratic ways of settling disputes within the larger community, including the occasional need to accept compromise on their own position (Lipset, 1959).

Internal democracy in private interest organizations, however, is not the rule. Many organized interests are governed by oligarchic controls; most members participate relatively little in running the organization while an active minority makes decisions and speaks for the group. The opinions of group leaders about issues on which their group has taken a stand may differ substantially from those of the rank and file. Oligarchic and nondemocratic though it may be, rule by an active minority is necessary to the organization. The active minority is usually a stable, experienced leadership core that sees to the necessary day-to-day detailed operations about which most members do not care. In the group's conflict with other interests, a small core of leaders can respond more quickly and effectively to outside pressures than can the mass membership; and concentrating the responsibility for making public statements in group leaders leaves the impression of organizational unity in making demands on public officials, in spite of internal rifts. (George Meany, head of the AFL-CIO, could say that he speaks for all his members despite internal dissension about his political ideas.)

Socializing members

People who share attitudes join interest groups that respond as they do to problems, but simply being in the group also reinforces one's own attitudes. Group membership thus helps socialize members. In general, taking part in an organization makes members more aware of politics, reinforces their awareness of political competence, and stimulates them to be politically active. The closer a person's affiliation with a group, the more the organization affects one's thinking.

Exercising leadership

When interest groups and group leaders identify problems and alert a larger public to them, they influence opinions outside their own organizations. Ralph

Nader wrote *Unsafe at Any Speed* (1965) in which he called attention to the problem of automobile safety. The issue was not new or ignored by public officials, yet the public was not worried about it until Nader's revelations prompted General Motors to investigate him with the intent of discrediting both him and his book. The publicity generated by the Nader-General Motors controversy focused the public's attention on the real problem, safety in automobiles, providing an impetus for Congress to legislate more stringent safety requirements.

Electioneering

Interest organizations advance their aims during election campaigns by mobilizing their members to support candidates, by endorsing candidates, and by making financial and other contributions. Up until the 1970s, organized labor, particularly the AFL-CIO, was effective in mobilizing votes on behalf of candidates it favored, generally Democratic candidates. For example, during the 1968 presidential campaign, George Wallace, candidate of the American Independent Party, had considerable support among organized labor's rank and file. He threatened to siphon votes away from Hubert Humphrey, the preferred candidate of union leadership. To offset the Wallace appeal, the AFL-CIO's Committee on Political Education (COPE) distributed a brochure to union members entitled *George Wallace's Alabama*. Alabama, it said, had one of the worst records of any state in supporting policies favorable to organized labor. It is doubtful that the COPE effort alone was the cause, but in the last weeks of the campaign Wallace's support among union workers decreased substantially. He ended up with 15 percent of the vote of members of union families in contrast to Humphrey's 56 and Nixon's 29 percent.

In the 1970s, however, organized labor has found it increasingly difficult to mobilize as a voting bloc. In a key 1976 presidential primary in Pennsylvania, for example, union leaders threw their support to Senator Henry Jackson, but Jimmy Carter came away with an "upset" victory that demonstrated a southerner running for president could win votes in heavily industrialized and unionized northern states. In the 1972 presidential campaign, Richard Nixon won 54 percent of the two-party votes among members of union families over George McGovern, perhaps reflecting the declining electoral impact of "Big Labor," but more likely the lukewarm support of union leaders for McGovern. The efforts of organized labor in the 1976 presidential election on behalf of Democrat Jimmy Carter were more successful; through direct mailings, voter registration drives, computerized targeting of voters, and other techniques, organized labor helped provide margins of victory in key industrialized states.

Many interest groups endorse candidates for public office, thus informing their members and nonmembers of their preferences. The National Committee for an Effective Congress (NCEC), composed of leaders of both political parties, operates partially by making endorsements. The NCEC seeks congressional reform and election of liberals to Congress. Although this interest has little formal organization, the efforts of its members have brought notable successes in selected congressional elections (Scoble, 1967). In 1976 the NCEC provided $350,000 worth of "in-kind" services to 100 candidates for Congress and 75 were victorious. These services included 64 polls, computerized precinct targeting in 40 districts, provision of television and radio materials, and—in some cases—campaign supervision. Once its candidates get elected, the NCEC teaches the new members of Congress how to provide fast, efficient service to their constituents, how to conduct press relations, and how to learn their way around Congress. A measure of the success of such efforts is that all of the 35 congressional representatives the NCEC helped elect in 1974 were reelected in 1976.

A principal channel for the financial contributions of major organized interests has been the "political action committee" (PAC), designed to solicit funds from members and dispense them to favored candidates. Big contributors include the National Association of Manufacturer's Business-Industry Political Action Committee (BIPAC), the Bankers' Political Action Committee, the American Medical Political Action Committee (AMPAC), and the AFL-CIO's Committee on Political Education (COPE). In the 1970 congressional elections, political action committees collected and disbursed almost 40 percent of the contributions reported by candidates for the House of Representatives. In 1972 the top 10 political action committees in funds available for campaign expenditures had more than $10 million to dispense to candidates (see Table 9.1).

Through the Campaign Finance Law of 1976, Congress placed restrictions on political action committees. First, Congress limited the number of PACs a corporation, union, or other organization might have by legislating that all such committees established by a company or union would be treated as a single committee for contribution purposes. This limited the contributions the PACs of a company or union could make to no more than $5,000 overall to the same candidate in any election. Second, Congress restricted the fundraising activities of political action committees. Company committees can solicit funds regularly only from stockholders and executive and administrative personnel and their families (not from employees). Union committees can

TABLE 9.1
Top ten political action committees, 1972

Committee	Total expenditures and cash on hand
1. Committee for Thorough Agricultural Political Education (C-TAPE) of the Associated Milk Producers, Inc.	$1,876,678
2. American Medical Political Action Committee (AMPAC) of the American Medical Association	1,759,715
3. MEBA Retirees Group Fund of the Marine Engineers' Beneficial Association, AFL-CIO	1,254,656
4. National Education Association	1,094,849
5. AFL-CIO COPE Political Contributions Committee	1,063,090
6. United Auto Workers Voluntary Community Action Program (UAW-V-CAP)	921,371
7. Laborers Political League of the Laborers' International Union of North America, AFL-CIO	624,079
8. United Steelworkers of America Political Action Fund	513,061
9. Trust for Special Political Agriculture Community Education (SPACE)	511,338
10. Machinists nonpartisan Political League of the International Association of Machinists, AFL-CIO	506,788

Source: Constructed from data reported in *Dollar Politics*, Vol. 2., Washington, D.C.: Congressional Quarterly, Inc., 1974, p. 56.

raise funds regularly only from union members and their families. However, twice a year corporate PACs may seek, by mail, contributions from employees other than executive and administrative personnel; and trade union PACs may likewise solicit contributions from the stockholders and executive and administrative personnel (and their families) of member companies twice per year.

The money supplied to political candidates by interest organizations is only part of the story. Interest groups also contribute the "free time" of paid secretarial and administrative staffs, postage and stationery, private airplanes, and other items. On election day, interest organizations provide message services, car pools, and babysitting for voters. These tactics are significant when directed at the local precinct organizations of the two major parties. They augment party efforts, and the interest groups hope to receive sympathetic consideration from the party's elected public officials in return.

Public protests

Most people associate protest activity with the civil rights movement, but public protests have a long history. Protest tactics are designed to publicize the grievances and demands of both economic and social interests. The tactics include strikes, boycotts, peaceful demonstrations, picketing, sit-ins, lie-ins, mass moratoriums, and violence. Many of these tactics constitute civil disobedience.

STRIKES.   The strike is a tactic employed most often by organized labor, although it has been used by other groups as well. (In the nationwide Vietnam Moratorium of October 15, 1969, students on many college campuses refused to attend classes as a protest against the war.) As a technique in labor-management disputes, the strike is regulated by federal law. Under specified circumstances, the President may seek a court injunction enjoining a labor union from striking if in his opinion the work stoppage would imperil the national health or safety. In March 1978, President Carter sought a temporary court order to send coal miners, who had been on strike for three months, back to work. Although a Federal District Court issued a temporary one-week injunction ordering miners back to work, the order was widely ignored and the court refused to grant an extension. Without additional judicial action, mine owners and union officials reached agreement on a new contract by the end of the month, thus ending the strike.

BOYCOTTS.   A boycott is a collective refusal to purchase commodities or services from a manufacturer, merchant, firm, or utility whose economic or social policies are considered unfair. Boycotts have been used primarily as a form of economic reprisal by labor unions and consumers to force changes in wages, prices, and the like. One of the most famous boycotts, however, publicized a social demand: The boycott of buses in 1955 was organized by Martin Luther King, Jr. in Montgomery, Alabama, to give force to a demand for racial equality. Similarly, women's liberation groups have sometimes refused to purchase cosmetics, undergarments, laundry soaps, or other products, not to force price changes but to demonstrate their dissatisfaction with what they regard as a demeaning image of women in the advertising of such products.

PEACEFUL DEMONSTRATIONS.   Nonviolent protests proved an effective attention-getting device in the 1960s and 1970s, especially for civil rights groups, environmental interests, and antiwar protestors. In general, civil rights advocates selected a policy they considered unjust, such as the practice then widely accepted in the South of refusing to serve Blacks and Whites together in restaurants, and they protested by disobeying the policy (Black and White civil rights workers would occupy restaurant seats for hours). Mass marches and rallies, like the civil rights march on Washington in 1963 and the "Poor People's" march in 1968, dramatically demonstrated minority grievances.

Opponents of legislation designed to hasten racial integration have also turned to peaceful demonstrations to publicize their positions. In 1972, mass caravans of cars and school buses moved along highways in some states of both the North and the South to protest the busing of school children to achieve racial balance in public schools. And groups interested in cleaning up the environment have worn gas masks to publicize the dangers of air pollution, organized the nationwide appeal that culminated in Earth Day in 1970, held cleanup campaigns, and established collection points for recycling bottles, cans, and newspapers.

Protesters sometimes use peaceful demonstrations to test the legitimacy of laws by disobeying them, being arrested, and arguing the case in court. When Congress passed a law in 1965 forbidding men to burn their draft cards, several youths protested both the Vietnam War and the law by holding public burnings. David P. O'Brien burned his draft card in 1966, was arrested, tried, and convicted. He appealed the decision on the grounds that the 1965 law was an unconstitutional abridgment of freedom of speech. Although the Supreme Court ruled against O'Brien, the publicity given the case effectively demonstrated the antiwar point he wished to make.

VIOLENT ACTION.   Violence, said a protest leader of the 1960s, is as American as cherry pie. To be sure, violence has been used many times in American history to protest grievances: the Whiskey rebellions of the 1790s, the use of terrorism in the post–Civil War South by such groups as the Ku Klux Klan, violent conflict in labor-management disputes in the 1890s, assassinations of public figures, periodic riots in urban areas, and student disruptions on college campuses in the 1960s. Violence, however, is not a preferred tactic for publicizing group interests. Few people approve of violence, even when they support a group's goals. Dissident groups have only a limited capacity to mount an open revolt so long as governing authorities have the guns, planes, tanks, and manpower to repress it. Moreover, violence, whether used by protesters or enforcers of the law, raises the moral question of whether the end justifies the means. The moral dilemma applies to civil disobedience as well as to violence.

Civil disobedience

Many of the tactics, both peaceful and violent, that have been employed to publicize interest demands have been justified by dissident groups as legitimate forms of civil disobedience; that is, as deliberate, public infractions of the law aimed at changing policies. Agreement on just what civil disobedience is has been anything but universal. Protesters, politicians, lawyers, judges, philosophers, and interested citizens disagree on several important points.

Civil disobedience involves illegal acts; is it thereby inherently violent? Infractions of the law do not in themselves constitute violence as long as they do not involve physical injury to persons and are carried out with consideration for the rights of others. Much political rhetoric, however, has equated violations with violence and thereby urged repression of all civil disobedience.

Does the illegality of civil disobedience imply that the people using it must willingly suffer the consequences of violating the law? One side says yes, because this willingness demonstrates that the disobedients are sincere; proponents of this view suggest that objectionable laws should be reconsidered in the courts. Another side says that it is the citizen's duty to disobey in order to make an extraordinary appeal to the community's conscience; as an act of political obligation, civil disobedience entitles the disobedient person to legal immunity or lenient punishment. Following this reasoning, some militant students in the 1960s who occupied campus buildings, denied military or industrial recruiters access to college campuses, and performed similar acts were not willing to be arrested or stand trial. And, claiming that it takes political courage to disobey, Senator Edward Kennedy in 1972 urged amnesty for all young men who fled the country in protest against compulsory military service in a war that they and he considered immoral. Neither President Ford nor President Carter was willing to go that far. In 1974–1975 the Ford Administration followed an "earned re-entry" clemency program whereby after a deserter or draft evader had undertaken up to 24 months of low-paid service in schools, hospitals, and other public institutions, he was freed of all charges against him. Although more than 21,000 applications for presidential pardons and clemency discharges were processed, another 100,000 eligible for clemency did not apply. In seeking the Presidency in 1976, Carter promised when elected to grant a presidential pardon to draft evaders and to consider desserters on a case by case basis, an action he subsequently took as President.

Is civil disobedience not justified until all other legal means of protest have been exhausted? Some advocates of the tactic argue that it should be a last resort against injustice; others argue that infractions of the law are necessary precisely because the system against which they protest is unresponsive and provides no legitimate means other than disobedience to redress grievances.

Which laws are subject to protest? Some civil rights leaders argue that disobedience is civil only when it challenges laws of doubtful constitutionality; they do not condone the breaking of laws such as traffic regulations or laws against murder. Other leaders believe that all laws of a corrupt government are subject to civil disobedience.

Is civil disobedience justified if it is not intended to test a law or change a policy? Responsible dissent is assumed to have a reformist end, to alleviate ills within the established system. Yet the dissenter who is more interested in revolution than reform, more concerned with overthrowing the government than with improving its policies, often practices agitation for its own sake.

These questions about civil disobedience as a technique used by interest groups will not be quickly or easily resolved. It is best that they should not be. They are the very heart of democratic government—part of the issue of how minority dissent works under popular majority rule—and deserve continued public debate.

Two functions of civil disobedience conflict with established ways of doing things. First, civil disobedience strikingly demonstrates to established regimes that grievances about the status quo have been overlooked or ignored by governmental leaders but that they must be alleviated. When civil rights, women's liberation, and antiwar groups in the 1960s turned to civil disobedience, it was no longer possible for political leaders to return to business as usual without trying to meet some of the demands. Second, civil disobedience stimulates interest organizations and elected officials to reexamine their popular followings and political institutions to find out why they failed to represent dissident interests. It forces them to reform both themselves and those institutions to regain the confidence they have lost. The franchise was extended to young people not long after the campus demonstrations. Civil disobedience has resulted in some functional benefits that cannot be discounted in organizing interest demands.

PRESENTING GROUP INTERESTS

Many techniques by which organized interests publicize their demands are also used to present those demands to policymakers. Occupying government office buildings is a direct confrontation with officials as well as an effort to call public attention to grievances. Other techniques, such as lobbying, influencing the appointment of public officials, working within government, and litigation are designed solely to influence public officials, not public opinion.

Lobbying

A lobbyist is a paid representative of an interest group whose principal function is to link organized interests with public officials. He does his work by contacting public officials, performing services for them, and giving services to the organization.

Lobbyists work for enactment, alteration, or defeat of policies by personal contact with governing officials. They present testimony to administrative officials and legislative committees, stimulate group members and sympathizers to write letters to policymakers, make financial contributions to election campaigns, become personal friends with lawmakers, and so forth. Lobbyists usually try to contact officials already sympathetic to their views. Officials return the favor. The stereotype of special interests dictating policy to lawmakers is unrealistic; instead, lobbyists and officials are brought together because they have the same interests and can help each other work toward the same goals.

By their services to governing officials, lobbyists try to keep open the channels of communication between groups and government, to establish mutual respect between themselves and policymakers, and to build personal reputations for honesty, expertise, and efficiency. They supply specialized information to legislators and administrators and encourage officials to solicit their opinions. In a survey of Washington lobbyists, only 14 percent said that their views were solicited regularly by officials (Milbrath, 1963), but another study of congressional representatives' feelings about lobbyists (see Table 9.2) shows that they do make some use of the lobbyists' services even if they rarely solicit their views.

Many lobbyists inform their organizations of policy developments, assist the organization in inquiries, discover loopholes in the laws, and negotiate with other interests. Some spend far more time trying, often without success, to warn about the implications of policies than working to influence the policies themselves.

The popular idea of the lobbyist portrays him as a shady character getting officials to do his bidding by bribery if all else fails. Actually, both lobbyists and members of Congress condemn bribery as a method of securing influence. In 1968, both the Senate and the House of Representatives, as a guard against unethical tactics, passed resolutions calling for limited disclosure of honorariums received by legislators for performing any service (such as addressing a convention) for organized interests. In recent years, a few congressmen have engaged in blatantly unethical conduct (Representative John Dowdy of Texas

TABLE 9.2
How members of Congress perceive lobbyists

View	Percentage (of 122 respondents)
Personal Aid	
"Most lobbyists are helpful to me because they supply detailed facts on complicated legislative questions."	62
"Some lobbyists are helpful to me because they supply detailed facts on complicated legislative questions."	7
"Most lobbyists confuse the issue because they distort the facts."	3
"Lobbyists neither help nor hinder me in my work."	17
No response	11
Aid to Congress	
"Lobbyists help Congress to legislate with maximum intelligence."	41
"Congress would be better off without lobbyists."	5
No Response	54
Pressure	
"I have often felt unreasonable pressure from lobbyists."	11
"I sometimes have felt unreasonable pressure from lobbyists."	21
"I have never felt unreasonable pressure from lobbyists."	33
No response	35

Source: Data taken from a *Congressional Quarterly* survey conducted in 1957, reported in *Congress and the Nation, 1945–1964,* Washington, D.C.: Congressional Quarterly Service, 1965, p. 1554.

was convicted in 1972 of accepting a $25,000 bribe to prevent a federal investigation of a Maryland home improvement company), keeping public suspicion alive despite Congress' steps to deal with it.

Influencing government appointments and removals

In their attempts to influence policy, organized interests support and oppose nominees and incumbents in appointive offices. The American Bar Association, for example, has made it a practice to comment on the legal background and qualifications of anyone selected for a judicial position. Environmentalists endorse or protest nominees to a variety of government units dealing with the ecology, such as appointments to the Tennessee Valley Authority, a government corporation providing electricity for a major region of the country by the operation of dams, coal burning plants, and nuclear power plants. Similarly, organized labor worries about who will head the Department of Labor, farmers and agribusiness leaders want a sympathetic Secretary of Agriculture, and so forth.

Interest groups are also sensitive to what officeholders do; any objectionable behavior is likely to raise the wrath of some interests. During the 1976 Presidential campaign when the media publicized that President Ford's Secretary of Agriculture, Earl Butz, had related a racist joke in the presence of newsmen, Blacks and others troubled by racial slurs demanded that Butz be fired. Ford left the decision to Butz, who resigned. Although as agriculture secretary, Butz had the support of major farming groups, some farmers—notably those in the National Farmers' Organization—thought that he should have been removed from office far earlier, not for any racial feelings but for his policies favoring the "big" and "corporate" rather than family farm.

Working within government

Political interest groups are not just private interests trying to pressure public officials. Officeholders also try to advance their own interests by applying pressure on both their colleagues and private organizations. At least three varieties of organized interests operate within the governmental structure:

- Government agencies work in consort and in conflict with other agencies to serve a special clientele. The Veterans Administration promotes the interests of veterans, frequently joining with veterans organizations in urging Congress to provide more money for programs to aid veterans.

- Private interest organizations achieve representation within government when interest group leaders are appointed to government positions. If a labor lawyer is appointed Secretary of Labor or a railroad executive is appointed to the Interstate Commerce Commission (the agency charged with regulating the railway industry), those interests acquire appointed administrative lobbyists.

- Many government agencies and legislative bodies develop their own specialized interests, which they pursue in competition with others. The publicity surrounding the Watergate scandals of the early 1970s revealed, for example, that an intense rivalry existed between elements in the Justice Department, Federal Bureau of Investigation, and Central Intelligence Agency regarding who should have the dominant role in conducting surveillance programs.

Litigation

The courts provide another avenue for organized interests to reach officials. Interests have won notable successes through litigation: The National Association for the Advancement of Colored People won a ruling against segregation in the public schools through appeals to the Supreme Court in 1954 (*Brown* v. *Board of Education*); *Baker* v. *Carr*, decided in 1962, was a judical victory for interests who believed they were unfairly represented in malapportioned state legislatures; and such strange bedfellows as liberal Eugene McCarthy, conservative Senator James L. Buckley, and the citizens' lobby Common Cause used litigation to overturn portions of the Federal Election Law of 1974 that they found objectionable.

In spite of such successes, there are clear disadvantages to litigation. It is usually expensive—in money for attorneys, court costs, research, and being available. Moreover, it is not a quick resolution of a conflicting situation; it sometimes takes years to appeal a case through the tiers of the court system. Finally, there is of course no guarantee of victory; as we will discuss in Chapter 14, a number of conflicting forces impinge upon judges as they approach their decisionmaking and it is not always easy to predict which interests a judge will honor.

Group effectiveness in a competitive setting

Because there are many interest groups in our pluralist society competing for the attention, support, and loyalty of citizens and public officials, it is hard for any one organization, working by itself and in competition with all the others, to mobilize the people's interests into an effective majority. What organized interests do, of course, is negotiate alliances with one another on behalf of the specialized interests of each group. The effectiveness of interest groups in representing conflicting demands this way depends upon a variety of factors associated with the personal, social, and politico-constitutional aspects of the American political community. Three factors of particular importance are citizens' views of the proper role of interest groups in society, the internal characteristics of various groups, and legal provisions for regulating interest activity.

POPULAR VIEWS OF INTEREST GROUPS

Political groups can organize popular support for their demands if citizens regard collective action as a useful way of approaching lawmakers. As with so many things in politics (recall our discussion in Chapters 2 and 4), Americans have an ambivalent view about political organizations: They believe collective action is an effective way to influence policy but they do not in general choose to participate in organized activity to influence government. As we saw in Chapter 5, citizens learn early during their socialization to emphasize individual over collective efforts in politics. Asked to say what they would do if Congress were considering a law they believed would be unjust or harmful, Americans talk first about contacting officials as individuals, voting, arousing friends and neighbors, or doing nothing. Working through a political organization ranks low on the list of preferred actions (Almond and Verba, 1963). And, keep in mind that although Americans are generally joiners, relatively few belong to specifically *political* organizations.

Why are Americans reluctant to take part? The reasons are probably not very

complex. Most people simply prefer to spend their leisure time doing something other than joining political organizations. Many distrust organized
activity because they stereotype political groups as serving "selfish" interests.
And, of course, American indifference to politics generally makes it hard for
groups to arouse interest in special causes. Political groups thus appeal primarily to an already participating and intensely involved minority.

Whether people will support group activity also depends upon their views of
the goals of organized interests. Some groups find their goals acceptable, others
do not. For example, the most effective groups representing Blacks in the civil
rights movement were those whose moderate goals received the support of both
Blacks and Whites. The Black Panthers had limited popular support (see Table
9.3), because Blacks did not believe militant organizations like the Panthers
represented their views as well as did more moderate Black interest groups
such as the NAACP, the Urban League, and others.

Many organized interests sacrifice popular support because their techniques
for publicizing and presenting demands do not have public approval. During
the student protests of the late 1960s and early 1970s, opinion surveys indicated that one-third of adults generally agreed with the goals of student
protesters, but only about one in ten approved of the students' tactics—
occupying offices of university administrators, disrupting classes, etc. (Harris,
1971, p. 274).

In some instances, popular opinion supports a way of protesting against
grievances only if it approves the group using it. Asked if workers should have
the right to strike, two-thirds of Americans say yes. But, when asked about
specific types of workers, a majority say that air traffic controllers, school-
teachers, and hospital employees should not have that right (Harris, 1971, pp.
74–75).

TABLE 9.3
Popular respect for Black civil rights organizations

Organization	Amount and degree of respect (in percentages)			
	A great deal	Some, but not a great deal	Hardly at all	Not sure
National Association for the Advancement of Colored People	75	18	3	4
Congress of Racial Equality	42	28	6	24
Southern Christian Leadership Conference	73	18	3	6
Urban League	53	24	5	18
Black Panthers	25	24	36	15

Source: Harris, L. and Associates, *The Harris Survey Yearbook of Public Opinion, 1970,* New York: Louis Harris and Associates, Inc., 1971, p. 255.

GROUP COMPOSITION AND EFFECTIVENESS

The size, motivations of members, goals, quality of leadership, politically relevant resources, and capacity to act in concert help to determine how well organized interests do in influencing government.

Size

Sheer numbers always mean a great deal in a democracy: The spokesperson for 16 million union workers gets more deference from public officials than the president of a neighborhood civic club. But bigness may be offset by the difficulty of achieving solidarity. The disputes that racked the Students for a Democratic Society (SDS) at the close of the 1960s threw that organization into a decline that just about made it vanish. Formed in 1962 to promote individual participation in decisionmaking and to encourage an independent spirit in citizens, SDS sharply criticized rampant materialism, the loss of individual identity in mass institutions, racism, and militarism in American life. As the group expanded, members disputed goals and tactics: Moderate members favored reforming American institutions from within; more militant elements such as the Weathermen urged drastic challenges to the institutions themselves—challenges such as the "days of rage" in Chicago in 1969 which resulted in destruction of property. Another faction, the National Officer Collective, dedicated itself to class warfare in the Communist tradition. By 1970, the extremist tactics of the most militant members had so alienated the moderates that no compromise was possible. The moderates withdrew, the national headquarters closed, and the militants went underground.

Motivations of members

The commitment of members is often as important to effectiveness as group size. Intensely committed members in small organizations can recruit broader support. The women's liberation movement began with a relatively small number of women in organizations scattered throughout the country. Their loyalty and dedication were so great that, even though they were ignored by many men and women, they were able to publicize their demands, expand their membership, and by 1972 win approval of Congress to submit a constitutional amendment forbidding discrimination based on sex.

Goals

Group effectiveness also depends on how salient a group's goals are to people generally and, if the goals are not salient, on the ability to obtain ends through other means than winning broad popular support. Group members may be intense about an issue but have a difficult time winning support if the populace at large is indifferent to their cause. There is, for example, an endangered species of fish, the snail darter, whose only habitat is in a single river in Tennessee. When the Tennessee Valley Authority (TVA), a federal government corporation, built a major dam on the river, the snail darter faced extinction for it could not survive in the vast lake to be formed by the project. An environmentalist group organized to save the snail darter had little success in gaining the attention, let alone support, of people in the region or the nation. Unable to obtain public support (and thereby catch the eye of congressional officials who vote funds for the TVA), the group turned to the courts and obtained injunctions to prevent the closing of the locks on the dam that would have formed the lake. Ultimately the TVA tried to develop a means of moving the snail darters to another portion of the river not affected by the formation of the lake in hopes of adjusting to a 1978 Supreme Court decision favoring the fish.

If groups are not sufficiently flexible in defining their goals and evolving their tactics to attract popular attention and support, their influence may wane, and this ebb may threaten their very survival. Such a decline can occur when group goals become obsolete because of changing times or even when a group succeeds in obtaining its ends (Greenwald, 1977, p. 55). After World War II when mainland China became the communist People's Republic and nationalist forces established a government on the island of Formosa (now Taiwan), a group organized in this country to deny recognition to "Red China." The group retained great influence in foreign policy circles until 1972 when President Nixon undertook his trip to the People's Republic. There are now signs that the China lobby is losing its campaign; it is unable to appeal for public support solely on the basis of the recognition issue. Other groups, faced with the consequences not of defeat but of success, find they must adjust to events as well. The March of Dimes originated as an organization to end infantile paralysis; it sought support through private contributions and public funds. When a vaccine against the disease was discovered, the organization did not vanish but turned its attention to other problems, notably the battle against birth defects.

Leadership

Group leaders influence the effectiveness of their organizations by their ability to define group goals, mobilize support among both members and nonmembers, contest and negotiate with other groups, and present group demands to policymakers. In doing these things, many group leaders develop specialized interests that may not reflect those of other group members. For several years, some miners argued that the leaders of the United Mine Workers had lost touch with the union membership's interests and above all had failed to press for improvement in mining safety and treatment for black lung disease caused by inhaling coal dust. After a West Virginia mine explosion in 1968 trapped and killed 78 miners, protesting miners took their grievances not just to the federal government but to their own union by forming the West Virginia Black Lung Association, demanding that the United Mine Workers seek better health and safety standards. The union's leadership responded favorably, and the miners ultimately were rewarded with the Federal Coal Mine and Safety Act in 1969, which acceded to their principal demands.

Resources

An organized interest's politically relevant resources also contribute to its ability to influence policymakers. Material resources are money, workers, permanent office space near legislative and administrative halls, facilities for regular meetings, and perhaps even ownership of a popular newspaper. Because many groups are not involved in politics full time, however, they lack financing, skilled personnel, information, and time to do an effective job of pressuring policymakers. Although great sums of money are spent by interest groups to influence officials, the overall expenditure is divided among uncoordinated, sometimes even conflicting, organizations. Most organizations can afford to spend relatively little on political activities. Swiss watch manufacturers budget more than $2 million annually for advertising and public relations, but only about one-eighth of this amount is spent campaigning against United States tariff increases. Less tangible resources also have their value. Among these are personal "contact" and friendships with public officials and knowledge of how the decisionmaking machinery works.

Any group fares better in a policy struggle if it has public respectability. The American Medical Association used the medical profession's positive image (some of it deliberately created, including the homely appeal of the doctor-patient relationship) as a weapon in combating legislative proposals on medical care until its stand became too intransigent and it was forced to accept the Medicare program.

Capacity to act in concert

To strengthen their specific claims, groups often form alliances for common action. To achieve cooperation, however, they must bargain and perhaps accept positions they did not originally intend to take. Varied groups reconciled their differences in the battle to obtain federal aid to education and won in the Elementary and Secondary Education Act of 1965. The principal interest groups were the National Education Association, the American Federation of Teachers (affiliated with the AFL-CIO), and the Americans for Democratic Action. They sought support from religious organizations such as the National

Council of the Churches of Christ and the National Association of Evangelicals, and other groups that favored federal aid to public schools. They also had to oppose such groups as the National Catholic Welfare Conference, the Council of Catholic Men, and others that strongly favored aid to parochial schools. Representatives of all these groups met with officials of the Johnson administration and approved an arrangement giving aid to school districts with many children from low-income families and permitting private schools to share in some of the federally aided services through special programs. Only after the administration got organized interests to approve the proposal did it submit the bill to Congress, where it won rapid approval. Thus, a major religious conflict over education policy was resolved by negotiating with contending interests before Congress began handling the bill.

POLITICAL AND CONSTITUTIONAL CONSIDERATIONS

Guarantees granted by the Constitution, the governmental structure provided by that document, and various policies made in pursuance of of the Constitution affect the way organized interests operate in our society.

Constitutional guarantees

It is a commonplace in American political rhetoric to belabor the "special interests" that are thought to be responsible for undesirable community conditions and policies. The crowds enjoying President Truman's attacks on "the interests" in the 1948 campaign urged "Give 'em hell, Harry." Yet interest group politics has its utility—whatever its defects—because it represents social conflict to public officials and provides ingredients essential for resolving these conflicts. Though some activities of interest groups shock us, a healthy democracy could not operate without them. The Founding Fathers fretted over the "mischievousness of faction," but they provided specific constitutional guarantees giving interests the opportunity to organize, publicize, and present their demands (see Chapter 4). James Madison wrote in *Federalist* No. 10: "Liberty is to faction what air is to fire, an ailment without which it instantly expires." The First Amendment guarantees of freedom of speech, association, and petition provide the liberty that makes interest group politics possible.

Governmental structure

Like all large organizations in the political arena (such as political parties), interest groups are affected by constitutional features that structure the governmental process and determine the access of organized interests to policymakers. These include separation of powers, the system of checks and balances, and federalism. The United States Chamber of Commerce, with its dispersed local units, matches the federal structure of government. This feature has greatly helped the organization by affording access to members of Congress who depend, in part, on the type of business support represented by the local chambers. Many other interests are similarly organized to work not only through lobbyists in Washington but also through local congressional representatives and the field offices of federal agencies.

It is much easier to keep legislation from being passed than to get it passed, because policymaking authority is scattered among many semiautonomous agencies. The chance that a proposal will die increases directly in proportion to the number of official agencies that must agree before a policy is adopted. Separation of powers, checks and balances, federalism, and other forces dispersing power thus work against groups seeking significant alterations of the status quo and favor groups trying to prevent change.

Federalism frequently sharpens conflict between interests. Groups that have favorable access to officials in state governments seek support there; those that can best obtain their goals through federal action concentrate their energies at that level. In the conflicts over civil rights, segregationist and integrationist forces had different points of access in the federal structure. Segregationists often found that state and local officials, local courts, and local school boards were sympathetic; through them they could delay or dilute school desegregation, the integration of public facilities, or the removal of literacy tests for voting. Integrationists successfully took their case to federal officials, particularly the President and Congress, who passed civil rights acts in the 1960s. Moreover, they asked the Department of Justice to investigate cases of discrimination and appealed judicial decisions of state courts to federal courts. The quarrel over the principals of "states' rights" versus "national authority" was more rhetoric than reality; the dispute simply reflected the disputants' different leverage points within the federal structure.

In this century there have been substantial changes in the design of our governing structure. One change that affects organized interest has been the proliferation of bureaucratic agencies charged with specialized functions in policymaking. A pluralist bureaucracy now complements the social pluralism reflected in the multiplicity of organized interests (see Chapter 13). Some agencies operate with a minimum of close supervision from either President or Congress. Agencies at all levels of the administrative establishment have developed close relationships with constituent interests, the very groups the agencies were designed to regulate: the Federal Communications Commission with the radio and television broadcasting networks, the Federal Trade Commission with business interests, the Securities and Exchange Commission with financial interests, agencies within the Department of Energy with major energy-producing corporations, and the military-industrial complex described earlier. The favored access of these organized interests to other policymakers is not only permitted but promoted by the dispersion of governing authority which is inherent in the contemporary bureaucratic structure.

Policies affecting organized interests

The tactics that organized interests may use and their access to public officials are regulated by legislation and administrative rules. The Federal Regulation of Lobbying Act, part of the Legislative Reorganization Act of 1946, was designed to publicize the lobbying activities of interest organizations. It requires any person who hires out as a lobbyist on behalf of someone else to register with the clerk of the House of Representatives and the secretary of the Senate, to file quarterly reports of receipts and expenditures, and to list the bills in which his or her organization was interested. Other statutes forbid bribery (making it a crime to offer a congressperson "anything of value" to influence him or her), prevent corporations and labor unions from making direct contributions to finance candidates' election campaigns, require congresspersons to disclose their sources of outside income and restrict the amount of that income. Administrative rules define the legitimate channels of communication between group leaders and officials. Many administrative agencies specifically restrict congenial informal contacts between their officials and parties interested in agency decisions. The owner of a television station who seeks access to federal communications commissioners by offering them trips on a yacht may lose an operating license because the commission forbids such tactics.

Most of these legislative and administrative requirements and restrictions contain loopholes that free organized interests from close scrutiny. Interest organizations must report their lobbying expenditures, but they can determine what portion of those expenditures should be reported; corporations are prohibited from contributing to political campaigns, but officers of corporations are not. Policies directly regulating interest activities still provide ample opportunity for groups to exercise political influence.

Acts of Congress, administrative rules, and judicial decisions also determine the influence of pressure groups in a less obvious way. Policies specify which officials are responsible for decisions that apply to particular interests. Laws authorizing special programs serve as a road map—informing groups about access routes and, more importantly, about residences of key officials—and thus make it easier to concentrate pressure rather than disperse it. In bidding for federal contracts, a potential contractor may be asked to submit a design of the missile guidance system under development. More than a dozen agencies, departments, and administrative bureaus make recommendations on this subject, each with a specialized function and numerous personnel dealing with the details of the proposal. A potential contractor must be selective; it is not possible to get to each responsible official. Other firms are seeking such contracts, so one goes for support to the officials authorized to recommend a project. A contractor has to know just who makes the decisions and learns it by studying authorizing legislation and by experience in negotiating the administrative labyrinth in Washington.

Organized interests and democratic representation

Judging by the tenets of procedural democracy—the procedures designed to implement popular control, political leadership, political equality, and political liberty—we must conclude that interest group politics decidedly contributes to democratic government, but the representation of social conflict by way of organized interests has its defects. Interest groups advance popular control and political leadership in several ways: They organize and express political opinions on public issues; they stimulate their members to active participation by urging them to vote, to take stands on issues, and to support group leaders; they provide a means for collective political action supplementing individual political efforts; and they inform policymakers about demands made by people who might otherwise be ignored. Interest groups that have organized in recent years have publicized and presented to governing officials for reconciliation the demands of many previously unrepresented "have-nots" in our society. These contributions help democratic government in its task "not to express an imaginary popular will, but to effect adjustments among the various special wills and purposes which at any given time are pressing for realization" (Dickenson, 1930, p. 293).

But even as they advance social interests, some of the characteristics of interest group politics raise doubt about whether they conform to the ideals of political equality and liberty. Not everyone fares equally well in the give-and-take of interest group politics. Although the have-nots are more effectively organized and policymakers are more responsive to their demands than in the past, most of the politically organized are well-educated people from the upper and middle classes. The most influential interests are the ones that can afford expensive techniques (contributions to election campaigns, mass advertising, lobbying) for publicizing and presenting their views. The advantage in interest group conflicts still lies with the more affluent.

A second problem in interest group politics is a structural conflict with democratic theory: In their internal organization, interest groups do not always promote the freedom of members to take part in organizing demands. Many are oligarchic, are run by an active, elitist minority, and do not always represent the interests of their rank-and-file members. They are controlled by active minorities for strong reasons—the indifference of their members, the tactical advantages of having disciplined workers, and the flexibility offered by centralized decisionmaking. But group leaders can lose touch with the rank and file and act on their own behalf, and then the organization does not promote democratic representation.

The politics of organized interests is the essence of government by a pluralist elite: Group leaders represent diverse interests vying to influence policymaking. Its deficiencies reveal a large defect in the American pluralist way of representing social conflict: Representation is very selective. Only a few social disputes and problems get enough public attention to be resolved by policymakers.

Perhaps a method of representation that fixes only the most pressing problems is not all bad because it keeps the policymakers' task of reconciling differences within manageable bounds. But it also fails to reflect the plurality of American interests and is, instead, biased, favoring some and penalizing others. Does the selectivity in conflict representation so distort reality that policymakers ignore major social problems—environmental pollution, hunger, overpopulation, mass disaffection from government—until they have reached a critical, perhaps unresolvable, stage? That question demands that we examine the implications for presenting conflict inherent in our pluralist society and the effects of social and governmental pluralism on our way of resolving social disputes by formulating policy.

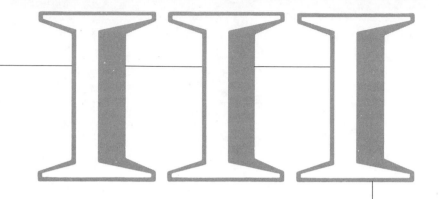

patterns
OF COnFLICT
ResOLUTION:
WHO makes
PUBLIC POLICIes
anD HOW?

FOrMULaTInG POLICieS

We saw in Chapter 1 that public policies rarely end disputes for all time, nor do they solve social problems. But properly made policies do keep social tensions from destroying the community. In this respect the method of formulating policies is often as important as their content. To see why this is so, we now look into the characteristics of public policies, their formulation, and the strengths and weaknesses of policymaking in our pluralist society.

Public policies: key characteristics

To understand what policymaking contributes to conflict resolution we need to answer some vital questions: What is public policy? What is policy formulation, and who does the formulating? What types of policies are formulated? What features of our society and government influence how policies get made?

WHAT PUBLIC POLICY IS

Public policies are legitimate decisions made by political institutions that resolve disputes affecting the general community. Consider the distinctive qualities implied by this definition; the policies are:

- *Public*   People facing problems try to cope with them. So long as their efforts affect only one another—the parties immediately involved—the problems and acts are private. (A marital quarrel and its settlement are usually private matters.) But if the steps people take to cope with their difficulties affect others and these other persons think those effects important, then the problem and consequent actions are public. (If a husband and wife decide to dissolve their marriage in the courts, the divorce is a public matter.) Problems and actions affecting people beyond the immediate parties to a dispute are public.

- *Legitimate*   When people affected by a policy accept it as binding, we say it is legitimate. As noted in Chapter 1, acceptance may result from threats and promises of punishments or rewards (mechanisms of social control), from a coincidence in personal views (social convergence or consensus), or from the give-and-take of bargaining (negotiated acceptance). In any case, legitimacy requires that people accept public decisions as binding on their own behavior as well as on that of others affected by the policies.

- *Political*   Policies are made by governments, but policymaking is not limited to people acting in official capacities. Public policies generally result from coalitions of diverse interests that have something to gain by associating instead of acting alone. Such an alliance usually consists of both official and private interests working to achieve legislative majorities, favorable administrative treatment, or judicial support for their proposed courses of action.

POLICY FORMULATION AND THE FORMULATORS

Policy formulation consists of developing acceptable courses of action to resolve social disputes. There are several reasons why this is easier said than done. First, policymakers do not know all the problems. For example, the idea of helping to solve energy shortages by extracting petroleum from deposits of shale located in western states is very attractive until policymakers begin to wrestle with the costs of extraction and processing, the environmental consequences of stripping the shale from the surface layers of the earth, and the problems of transporting the product over long distances.

Second, policymakers may know about a problem, yet not think it pressing enough to require action. It took more than a decade for government officials to recognize that automobile exhausts contribute to air pollution and, hence, require corrective action. Third, even if they agree that a problem requires action, policymakers may not be able to agree on the action. Throughout the early 1970s policymakers agreed that something would need to be done to prepare for the time when abundant supplies of petroleum would no longer be available to Americans, but Congress could not agree upon a comprehensive energy program for the future.

Fourth, a relevant course of action is not always the passage of a law or the issuance of an administrative edict or a court decision. Policymakers sometimes react to public problems, even though they are aware of them and their inportance, by doing nothing or by taking halfway measures that don't correct the situation. For instance, the quality of passenger service on American railways has declined steadily since the end of World War II. In 1970 Congress passed the Rail Passenger Service Act, creating Amtrak, a government-funded company, to run the nation's passenger trains at a profit. Amtrak was a compromise between interests advocating a nationwide, interconnected system of rail service (such as the consumer group, National Association of Railroad Passengers), private railroad companies (such as Missouri Pacific), and transportation interests opposed to any subsidies for railways (notably the nation's airlines). Amtrak did not solve the problem: After five years the corporation's operating deficits totaled over $1 billion, its advocates sought greater federal subsidies, and its opponents sought Amtrak's demise.

In sum, policy formulation is only that action thought relevant by key policymakers, and their decisions may or may not respond to the underlying sources of public problems. Who then are these key policy formulators? In democratic theory, policy is supposed to be formulated by officials freely chosen and authorized to act for the community. In practice, however, both public officials and the leaders of private groups formulate policy, sometimes acting separately but more often in concert and conflict with one another. Specifically these formulators include:

1. *The President* and his chief advisers, at least in this century, have become primary initiators of action on public problems.

2. *Appointed and career public officials* in the administrative bureaucracy help to formulate policies by keeping abreast of problems within their responsibility, developing proposals to cope with them and to respond to special interests, and submitting these to presidential and congressional scrutiny.

3. *Legislators* identify problems, solicit suggestions, and formulate courses of action in congressional hearings and by informal contact with organized interests and administrative officials.

4. *Judges* are often the first officials to deal directly with pressing problems, particularly in lower courts where cases originate. Federal district court judges have helped resolve disputes on racial integration, apportionment of legislative bodies, opportunities for citizens to vote, rights of people who

objected to the Vietnam war, abortion, the death penalty, and other questions.

5. *State and local government officials* formulate policy within their own governing units; they also bring problems to the attention of federal officials, seek financial assistance, and make other demands. Scores of federal policies have provided money to deal with the problems of urban America in response to the pleas of mayors and other local officials.

6. *Leaders of private interest organizations* also formulate policy, sometimes acting on the government's behalf. For example, in efforts to combat inflation and unemployment at the beginning of the 1970s, President Richard Nixon appointed boards composed of labor, business, and consumer interests to administer guidelines for wage and price increases affecting any major sector of the economy. As we shall see later, leaders of private interest organizations are key members of policymaking coalitions at the federal level. In this capacity group leaders present to government proposals that their organizations have formulated—as alternatives to the courses of action requested by executive, administrative, legislative, or judicial formulators.

TYPES OF POLICIES

Three varieties of public policies can be distinguished by their general effects (Lowi, 1966):

- *Distributive policies* take natural, social, and economic resources and award them to specific interests. In the nineteenth century, for instance, the federal government provided tracts of land to farmers, ranchers, railroaders, speculators, and others settling the frontier.

- *Regulatory policies* try to ensure that specific activities (such as operating an airline, a bank, a public school, or even one's automobile) are in the public interest, not for selfish advantage. It is characteristic of regulatory policies, however, that public officials and representatives of organized interests cooperate in their formulation, and the latter sacrifice little of their prerogative to decide how best to utilize resources to their own advantage.

- *Redistributive policies* reallocate resources, taking from the "haves" and benefiting the "have-nots": Prime examples are taxation policies to provide financing for welfare, antipoverty, educational, public health, and similar programs.

To clarify how these three types of policies differ, especially in formulation, we will look at three cases of policy formulation. Each pertains to a problem not only relevant to the 1970s but also spanning several decades.

Distributing economic benefits:
the development of breeder technology

Long before oil-producing states in the Middle East imposed their short-lived embargo on petroleum shipments to the United States in 1973, energy experts were aware that this country was approaching an energy shortage. Despite construction of a major pipeline to transport oil from Alaska's northern slopes, America is rapidly depleting its oil and gas reserves. Even if foreign sources of oil were reliable, estimates are that the entire world's oil reserves will be gone in 50 to 80 years.

Faced with depletion of the energy resource that has been the driving force of this nation's industrial economy since World War II, energy engineers have turned to other possibilities—fossil fuels, of which coal is in abundance in this country but costly to mine; solar energy, which has yet to be adapted to widespread use; nuclear fission relying upon high-grade uranium; undeveloped nuclear fusion technology; and even the movement of wind and ocean currents. Major energy companies (such as General Electric, Consolidated Edison, and the Tennessee Valley Authority—a government corporation) have promoted the use of uranium-based fission as a source of energy for generating electricity. But, like oil reserves, high-grade uranium resources are not abundant. Estimates vary but there is no guarantee that nuclear reactors built after the year 2000 can be fueled by relatively inexpensive, high-grade uranium.

The nuclear reactors in operation in the United States in the 1960s and 1970s, called light-water reactors, use no more than 1–2 percent of the energy content of uranium; in the process they produce small amounts of plutonium. To take advantage of the abundant supplies of low-grade uranium and of the by-product plutonium, technologists have concentrated upon developing the liquid metal fast breeder reactor (LMFBR). Simply put, in a breeder reactor, neutrons moving at very high speeds sustain a chain reaction that converts uranium into plutonium; liquid sodium (a metal) carries off the heat produced by the fission, and the heat is used to make steam to drive turbines generating electricity. The breeder uses 60–70 percent of the energy available in uranium as well as producing plutonium that can be used to fuel other breeder reactors and, with modification, light-water reactors, as well. The key to the breeder is that it produces more fuel than it consumes. However, estimates are that it will take the first commercial breeders 25 years to produce twice as much fuel as they consume; later generations of breeders will have a "doubling time" of a decade.

All in all, then, breeder technology sounds like a panacea, a veritable perpetual motion machine. Small wonder that at the behest of energy companies, utilities, and technical advisers, President Richard Nixon made the LMFBR the nation's top energy research priority in a 1971 message to Congress: "Our best hope today for meeting the nation's growing demand for economical, clean energy lies with the fast breeder reactor." He called for completion of a demonstration plant by 1980 (experimental models existed in the 1950s and small breeders successfully generated electricity in the 1960s) and the introduction of commercial plants in the 1990s.

The ensuing development of breeder technology provides an excellent example of how the federal government, local interests, and private corporations cooperate in distributing economic benefits to favored groups. It also illustrates how a technology becomes a political controversy. In 1972 the Atomic Energy Commission (AEC) accepted a proposal from private energy concerns as a basis for negotiating a contract for construction of a demonstration breeder reactor. The proposal called for a cooperative arrangement between the AEC (which would provide basic research and administration for the project), the Breeder Reactor Corporation (a coordinating corporation for the special interests of various private electric utilities), Project Management Corporation (the overall coordinator of construction), Commonwealth Edison Company (the firm selected to provide personnel and services for the management corporation), Tennessee Valley Authority (which would eventually operate the plant), and Westinghouse Electric Corporation (selected as the principal reactor manufacturer). The site selected for the demonstration plant was on the Clinch River near Oak Ridge, Tennessee, an area in which considerable research on the uses of nuclear energy has taken place since World War II. The project was to cost $700 million; electric utilities would provide $250 million, the federal government the remainder. If costs rose above estimates, the AEC would seek the additional funds from Congress.

By 1972, then, a project existed for development of a demonstration breeder reactor. That project, if executed, would result not only in the development of a technology but in the distribution of sizeable economic benefits to private corporations and a single region of the country. The Joint Committee on Atomic Energy (made up of members of the U.S. Senate and House of Representatives) held hearings on the proposed project in 1973, made slight modifications in the proposed arrangement, and supported the program. Since that time the breeder program has been a source of continuing social conflict over what benefits were to be derived from the project and who is to receive them.

Arrayed on the side of the advocates of breeder technology (and supporting construction of a demonstration facility) have been private utilities, electric companies, construction firms, local government leaders who see economic windfalls for their constituences from construction of the demonstration plant, pronuclear forces in Congress, and the Energy Research and Development Administration (an agency created following the reorganization and demise of the Atomic Energy Commission and charged with promoting various federally supported energy related projects). The proponents' argument is simple: The breeder will provide safe, efficient energy and save perhaps $50 billion in power generation costs by the year 2020.

A variety of interests oppose breeder technology. First, there is congressional opposition. In the early 1970s this was minimal: Congress rejected efforts to kill funding for the demonstration plant in 1972 and no such efforts were made in 1973 and 1974. In the mid-1970s, however, congressional opposition grew. Opponents made two points: (1) Cost overruns on the demonstration plant were high and (2) the Nixon-Ford administration was emphasizing the development of nuclear energy at the expense of other resources. The cost overrun was substantial: The 1972 $700 million estimated cost for the demonstration breeder reactor rose to $1.7 billion in 1974 and to $2 billion in the late 1970s. Critics blamed the open-ended funding arrangement whereby the federal government rather than private utilities would pick up the tab for breeder development; defenders of the program countered that overruns were inevitable in any long-term research and development program for a new technology. Despite rising opposition to cost overruns, Congress refused to cut the breeder reactor funds substantially, thus providing an even larger economic pie to be divided than originally planned. With respect to the overemphasis upon nuclear technology, congressional opponents have been more successful. Congress has increased funding for the development of synthetic fuels, solar energy, and other alternatives—thus distributing economic benefits to a wider set of private energy concerns working on research and development.

A second set of opponents of the breeder program comes from groups concerned with the safety, environmental, social, and economic costs of the new technology. Among the concerned groups have been the Natural Resources Defense Council, Sierra Club, Friends of the Earth, and Ralph Nader's Critical Mass. Safety and environmental concerns have revolved about the hazardous consequences of an accident or structural failure that would release radioactive materials; what to do with nuclear waste by-products; the increasing reliance upon plutonium (a toxic substance) as the fuel of the future; how to safeguard the recycling of plutonium to keep it out of the hands of persons or nations intent upon nuclear blackmail; and how to lessen the likelihood of the proliferation of nuclear weapons under a plutonium economy (plutonium is used to make nuclear bombs). Some opponents argue that the social costs are too great: reliance upon nuclear energy requires plans to protect nuclear facilities and the transportation of nuclear fuels from sabotage, plans so restrictive as to herald the emergence of a police state. Those concerned with the economic aspects argue that the energy requirements of this nation will not grow so rapidly in the future as to require a major commitment to nuclear energy, that conservation measures should be employed, and that there is no basis for concluding that the breeder will actually provide economical electricity.

Although opponents of breeder technology have tried to win allies in Congress, their principal efforts have been devoted to fighting the LMFBR program in the courts and regulatory agencies. In 1973, for instance, opponents were successful in obtaining a ruling in the U.S. Court of Appeals in the District of Columbia that there must be an environmental impact statement prepared for the entire breeder program, not just the Clinch River demonstration plant. And, opponents of the breeder program actively intervened in hearings before a licensing board of the Nuclear Regulatory Commission in 1975–1977, the body charged with reviewing the technical, safety, and environmental aspects of the program.

Two outcomes of the 1976 elections alerted both proponents and opponents of the LMFBR that the fight over breeder technology was not yet over. First, the election of Jimmy Carter (a nuclear engineer during his career in the U.S. Navy) placed in the White House a President with professed reservations about LMFBR technology. Not only did he object to the amount of money to be spent on developing a demonstration plant, he was particularly concerned that the LMFBR's production of plutonium would increase the threat of nuclear warfare by making this weapons-grade fuel readily available. In 1977 he took two steps opposing the LMFBR: (1) He called for major cuts in the funding of the proposed demonstration plant, using his first veto of congressional legislation to reject a bill calling for higher funding than he desired; and (2) he took steps to redirect research to the development of breeders that would produce only nonweapons-grade fuel. The second development following the 1976 elections was the reelection to Congress of reformist legislators along with the election of new representatives favoring reforms. In 1977 the 95th Congress stripped the Joint Committee on Atomic Energy of authority to initiate legislation, leaving the committee with only advisory functions. The committee had long been a staunch advocate of the LMFBR program.

In sum, when first conceived, the LMFBR program was a classic example of how a project justified in the name of a broader public interest by proponents would ultimately allocate economic resources to specific interests—government agencies, geographic regions, private utilities, major corporations, construction firms, and others. The project moved ahead with the support of two Presidents, Nixon and Ford, as well with that of Congress and influential lobbies. But this case also shows how an organized opposition can take advantage of available channels—Congress, courts, lobbying before government agencies, and a newly elected President—to express disagreement with an on-going program. Finally, the LMFBR program illustrates that conflicts over policymaking are ceaseless. Advocates of the program suffered crucial setbacks in 1977, yet they continue to seek funding to sustain a scaled-down version of the project in order to keep "a foot in the door."

In 1978 they encountered some success. The comptoller general of the United States ruled against President Carter's proposal to use $80 million in federal LMFBR funds to kill the program. The comptroller general wrote Carter that funds allocated for the project by Congress had been authorized only for construction of the project, not for its termination; if the President sought to end the project with the funds, he would be breaking the law and any officials ordering the funds spent to kill the breeder would be held personally liable for the money. The President then turned to Congress, requesting $13 million specifically to phase out the project. A subcommittee of the House Science and Technology Committee refused to abide by Carter's wishes, voting instead for $172 million to continue the LMFBR program. Thus, although the prospects of a commercial breeder industry by the 1990s are remote, the conflict over the distribution of economic benefits through breeder technology will undoubtedly continue until at least the end of this century.

Regulating a social problem: the sale of firearms

In 1961 a study by the Senate Judiciary Subcommittee on Juvenile Delinquency, headed by Democratic Senator Thomas J. Dodd of Connecticut, found that neither federal nor state laws effectively restrained mail-order sale of firearms to juveniles, felons, and narcotics addicts. Dodd introduced a bill to restrict the mail-order sales of handguns and to prohibit interstate sales to persons under 18. Then, the assassination of President Kennedy in 1963 stimulated intense interest in gun-control legislation. Because the assassination was carried out with a mail-order, military surplus rifle, Dodd proposed an amendment to his bill to cover rifles and shotguns as well as handguns. Congressional advocates of stricter controls included Dodd, Democratic Senator Joseph Tydings of Maryland, Senator Edward Kennedy of Massachusetts, and Senator Robert Kennedy of New York. In 1965, President Lyndon Johnson also proposed legislation to prohibit the interstate mail-order sale of all firearms to private individuals and the over-the-counter sales of handguns to persons not living in the dealer's state. He also called for limitations on the importation of firearms to the United States and asked for a minimum age for purchasers of guns.

The opposition to strict regulation, led by the National Rifle Association (representing 900,000 members), was well organized. The NRA's principal tactic was to encourage its members to write to members of Congress protesting against regulation as an infringement on the "right to bear arms." The NRA was assisted by its close ties with military officials. The Department of the Army supported its national rifle matches and even provided ammunition; moreover, since 1903, NRA members had been able to purchase surplus firearms and ammunition from the army at a discount, because such privileges encouraged civilian training, which supposedly improved marksmanship in the armed forces. Opponents of the NRA's lobbying activities, however, claimed that only 3 percent of the army's trainees were members of the NRA and that the average age of NRA members was 39, well beyond the draft age.

The NRA's position drew support in Congress from Senator Strom Thurmond, Republican of South Carolina, Senator Frank Church, Democrat of

Idaho, and Senator Bourke Hickenlooper, Republican of Iowa. The Wildlife Management Institute and the Issac Walton League also opposed strong federal regulation. Such organizations are supported financially by excise taxes on the manufacture of sporting arms and ammunition to aid state fish and game agencies, which then lend financial support to the organizations' wildlife and conservation efforts. Gun manufacturers themselves, of course, also opposed regulation of firearms, particularly through such trade associations as the Sporting Arms and Ammunition Manufacturers' Institute (SAAMI), which consists of the nine largest gun and ammunition manufacturers.

Between 1963 and 1967, efforts to pass federal legislation placing strict controls on the sale of firearms were unsuccessful. During that time, however, events continually brought to public attention what gun-control advocates called the consequences of unregulated sales. Among these they cited the summer riots in major cities in which some law enforcement officers claimed mail-order guns had been confiscated. Investigations revealing that 100–200 Americans die every week from gunshot wounds reinforced the case of the gun-control advocates. In early 1968, a nationwide survey revealed that more than eight out of every ten Americans favored some type of federal regulation.

The impetus for strict regulation grew in 1968. Dr. Martin Luther King, Jr. was assassinated in April. An amendment was added to the Omnibus Crime Control and Safe Streets Act of 1968 prohibiting the interstate shipment of pistols and revolvers to individuals and the over-the-counter purchase of handguns by individuals not residing in the dealer's state. The bill, however, specifically exempted rifles and shotguns from regulation. During the formulation of this measure, the combined efforts of the NRA and independent gun owners produced a massive amount of mail opposing strict regulation. Senator Charles Percy, Republican of Illinois, received 3,500 letters, most of them against gun controls; Senator James Eastland, Democrat of Mississippi, reported his mail ran 5 to 1 against controls.

Then, three months after the King assassination, Senator Robert Kennedy was slain with a .22 caliber pistol that cost $30.95. After that assassination, advocates of strict gun control organized their own campaign in response to that of the "gun lobby." The Council for a Responsible Firearms Policy sought 10 million signatures on a petition favoring registration of all firearms; former astronaut John Glenn announced that he was forming a nationwide group to stimulate a letter-writing campaign aimed at swaying Congress, and President Johnson proposed banning the mail-order and out-of-state sale of rifles, shotguns, and ammunition, and requiring registration of all firearms and licensing of all gun owners.

We cannot know how much public officials and group leaders were influenced by the Kennedy assassination and the campaign for strict gun controls that followed, but some actions were clearly related: (1) On the day of Kennedy's death, Congress passed the Omnibus Crime Control Act with its gun-control provisions. (2) After the assassination, congressmen began to report a new trend in their mail and on June 10, Senator Percy's office received 1,300 letters favoring stronger regulations. Representative G. Elliot Hagan of Georgia reported that, whereas his mail had been overwhelmingly against gun controls before the assassination, it now ran 50–50. (3) A number of congressmen shifted their positions on gun control. Senator George McGovern, Democrat of South Dakota, worked against strict legislation in May, but said in June he would support restrictive legislation; Senate Majority Leader Mike Mansfield of Montana had been cool toward regulation but declared in June that he would support proposals for strict regulation. (4) Other governing officials moved to restrict the shipment and use of firearms. The Postmaster General announced new regulations requiring all firearms sent through the mail to be clearly identified, and he instructed local postmasters to notify police before delivering guns. (5) The Department of the Army, acting on a recommendation by the National Board for the Promotion of Rifle Practice (a group composed of both military and civilian officials), announced that it would limit its support to rifle clubs whose members still had their service obligations ahead of them, would limit the sale of rifles to clubs specifically designed for rifle competition, would sell only to clubs affiliated with the army's program, and would hold to its earlier decision not to supply men or ammunition for the 1968 national rifle matches. (6) The heads of such firearms manufacturing firms as Remington, Savage, and Winchester-Western urged Congress to prohibit the sale of shotguns and rifles by mail to individuals. (7) Finally, on October 10, 1968, Congress extended the restrictions placed on handguns by the Omnibus Crime Control Act to long guns and ammunition. Specifically, it banned mail-order sales and interstate shipments, set licensing standards for parts of the firearms and ammunition business, and established minimum ages for the purchasers of various types of firearms and ammunition.

This policy conflict illustrates many typical features in policy formulation, especially the way in which regulatory policies are formulated. Like many policy disputes, the controversy over gun-control legislation cut across party lines, placing Republicans and Democrats on both sides of the issue; party lines did not vanish, of course, for there was still party division over the recommendations of a Democratic President. Second, the conflict pitted informal coalitions of major interest groups against each other. Alliances of political leaders may shift when opposed by counterpressure; the Department of the Army, firearms manufacturers, and many members of Congress sympathetic to the NRA changed their ideas when popular support for gun-control spread—such popular interest is not typical of all legislative disputes. Like many regulatory policies, the 1968 legislation contained loopholes to protect the prerogatives of organized interests. On the surface, it made small caliber handguns unavailable by banning their importation from abroad, but manufacturers and dealers were able to get around the law by importing gun parts, and attaching them to frames made in the United States. Moreover, the act did not require that firearms be registered or the owners licensed. Finally, the legislation neither laid the dispute to rest nor solved the problem.

In 1971, Senator Birch Bayh proposed a ban on the transfer or sale by any federally licensed dealer of any firearm other than rifles or shotguns to anyone except law enforcement officers; the "Saturday night special" (a handgun costing $10–$20), he said, accounted for most of the country's murders, and 22 people die in America each day from wounds inflicted with such weapons. The attempted assassination of Governor George Wallace of Alabama while campaigning in Maryland in the 1972 presidential primaries stimulated renewed interest in firearms control. Again a coalition of interests, headed by the NRA, opposed legislation and once more the controversy over regulation of firearms was resumed. A bill passed by the Senate forbade the sale of "Saturday night specials," but the House failed to act on the measure. Had it done so, inexpensive Saturday night specials would no longer have been available for legitimate sale and sales of any easily concealed firearm whatever its cost would have been regulated. As a result, the weapon Sara Jane Moore used to shoot at President Gerald Ford in 1975 (which cost $145) would have been banned for sale. Taking these thoughts into account and recognizing that two-thirds of Americans surveyed in opinion polls favor stricter gun controls, it is small wonder that advocates insist that the regulation of the sale and possession of firearms is a policy whose time has come.

Redistributing resources: the lost war on poverty

In 1964, President Lyndon Johnson launched a "national war on poverty," an innovative program designed to accomplish something unusual in American life: the redistribution of basic resources to solve a chronic social problem. Poverty had been a plague for many generations, but only modest policies to alleviate it had been tried, most of them for the aged, the handicapped, the orphaned, and similar groups. But it became apparent that poverty was not limited to the aged or otherwise dependent population; poverty was widespread among residents of urban ghettos, rural areas such as Appalachia, Blacks in the North and South, Mexican-Americans in the Southwest, and American Indians. Born into poverty, children of impoverished parents lacked the resources to leave their environment, get an education, and acquire the skills that could "break the poverty cycle"; instead the children of poverty grew up to beget more poverty-stricken children.

Because awareness of the severity of poverty was growing, Presidents Kennedy and Johnson gave executive agencies responsibility for formulating a policy to deal with chronic poverty. Among these were the President's Council of Economic Advisers, the Bureau of the Budget, the White House Staff, the

Peace Corps, the Small Business Administration, and the agency that later became the Department of Housing and Urban Development. Private citizens complemented their efforts through the Ford Foundation and the President's Committee on Juvenile Delinquency and Youth Crimes.

Officials and citizens in these agencies and groups formulated this policy: (1) A Job Corps with centers in rural and urban areas would provide young men and women aged 16 through 21 with education, vocational training, and work experience; (2) federal assistance for state and local programs would provide local work experience; (3) grants to institutions of higher education would enable students from low-income families to obtain part-time work to support their schooling—the work-study program; (4) federal grants to community action programs conducted by state or local public and private non-profit agencies—with a maximum of participation of local residents—would develop job opportunities and improve working, learning, and living conditions; (5) federal grants would support adult education programs; (6) financial assistance would be given needy children; (7) money would be provided for loans to low-income rural families, assistance to migrant workers, business incentives for small business in poverty areas, and various work experience programs. The Office of Economic Opportunity was created to recruit, select, and train volunteers in cooperation with state and local agencies to assist such groups as Indians, migratory workers, the mentally ill and retarded, and the poor of the District of Columbia and of United States territories.

The Economic Opportunity Act, formulated mostly by executive leaders, was sent to Congress, although there had been little prior consultation with members of that body. The Senate acted quickly on the bill after the Democrats narrowly defeated a "states' rights" amendment that would have required state governors to approve all federal-local community action projects. The Chairman of the House Committee on Education and Labor moved the bill quickly through committee despite Republican protests; it then passed the House quickly (with a southern conservative as its chief sponsor). President Johnson had declared the war on poverty in March of 1964; by August, the Congress had adopted the necessary legislation, a remarkably quick response to an executive proposal.

The Economic Opportunity Act of 1964 illustrates successful formulation and passage of a redistributive policy. Relevant and acceptable courses of action were clearly facilitated by consensus among the formulators (primarily executive officials) that the problem was real and that sweeping, innovative action had to be taken to allocate resources and deal with it. The policy was formulated without consulting the interests most affected by it: the poor. Perhaps things would not have gone so smoothly if the affected interests had been consulted; the rivalry that developed between Blacks and Puerto Ricans for control of local action programs in New York City strongly suggests that some intense conflicts would have come about.

Nevertheless, broad redistributive legislation was proposed and adopted, a new agency was created, and large sums were appropriated. Carrying out the program then became the job of officials and group leaders at all levels of government, who had not been privy to the formulation. Conflicts soon divided these interests, especially in community action programs. Interest rivalries produced criticism of the program that quickly reached members of Congress from their constituents. Congressional enthusiasm began to wane and appropriations declined.

But the blow that crippled the antipoverty program was the channeling of funds to support the Vietnam War. A decade before the War on Poverty was dreamed of, President Dwight Eisenhower had said: "Every gun that is made, every warship launched, every rocket fired signifies, in the final sense, a theft from those who hunger and are not fed, from those who are cold and are not clothed."

President Lyndon Johnson, the architect of the Great Society, foresaw the dangers of a two-front war, one in Vietnam, one on poverty. Using a metaphor typical of the LBJ style, he said:

> I knew from the start that I was bound to be crucified either way I moved. If I left the woman I really loved—the Great Society—in order to get involved with that bitch of a war on the other side of the world, then I would lose everything at home. All my programs. All my hopes to feed the hungry and shelter the homeless. All my dreams to provide education and medical care to the browns and the blacks and the lame and the poor. (Kearns, 1976, p. 73)

And shortly before his death, Johnson accepted the defeat, the death of the Great Society: "She's getting thinner and thinner and uglier and uglier all the time; now her bones are beginning to stick out and her wrinkles are beginning to show. Soon she'll be so ugly that the American people will refuse to look at her; they'll stick her in a closet to hide her away there she'll die. And when she dies, I too will die" (Kearns, p. 73). And he was correct: The struggle to break the poverty cycle—an innovative effort to allocate resources and solve a chronic social problem—lost most of its redistributive strength and, like Johnson, was dead in 1973.

Policy types and policy conflict

The LMFBR program, firearms control, and the War on Poverty illustrate the differences in distributive, regulatory, and redistributive policies and the conflicts associated with them. As with the LMFBR program, distributory policies offer the "haves" in society the opportunity to improve their economic lot in the name of the greater public interest. If approved, distributory policies take some national resource (in the case of the LMFBR, federal tax dollars) and use it to the advantage of special interests possessing the affluence and influence to win policy approval. The opposition to these distributory efforts comes from several sources: "have nots" protesting a government "give away"; those who oppose federal subsidies to private interests as a matter of principle; groups opposed to the substance of such programs as the LMFBR or to projects to land earthlings on Mars or to fund a city to host the Olympics. The policy's fate then rests on the struggle between conflicting interests, with the likely outcome for one side to win and the other to lose but for neither to give up the fight until it has lost all hope of victory.

Actions to limit the benefits that accrue to special interests give rise to regulatory policies. There are many: to control firearms sales, regulate airline rates, regulate prices for natural gas, limit over-the-counter sales of drugs, and so forth. The justification for such regulation is to assure that special interests will operate in the public interest rather than reap high profits at the expense of consumers' health, wealth, safety, welfare, or morals. Proposals for regulation come from many groups including consumers, producers unable to compete with advantaged interests, citizens concerned with a particular social problem, executive agencies, and congressional officials. The opposition arises from the interests the policies seek to regulate. The ensuing conflict is not settled in absolute terms with clear-cut victors and vanquished. Instead, the policies passed and enforced are products of compromises struck by conflicting interests. Those policies do not end the dispute; rather they provide the legal framework within which disagreements over regulation continue.

If distributory policies work more to the advantage of "haves" than "have nots," and regulatory policies try to assure that "haves" will not take advantage of "have nots," then redistributory policies seek to balance the advantages of "haves" and "have nots" by alleviating the plight of the latter. The passage of a redistributory policy requires a unity of purpose and action exemplified in the early days of the War on Poverty. But to remain successful it must receive the support not only of those it benefits but also of those who must give up something as well. That support (again illustrated by the War on Poverty) is hard to sustain. Opposition mounts to cut back the redistribution on grounds that it is not solving the problem in question, is a "handout," breeds federal interference and bureaucracy to administer it, is wrong in principle, and so forth. New conflicts soon fuel the on-going formulation and reformulation of policies, often cutting back the proposed redistribution substantially, as in the War on Poverty, or raising questions about funding the redistribution, as in the case of the continuing problems associated with providing retirement and other benefits under the Old Age and Survivors Insurance program known as Social Security.

Regardless of type or of the politics associated with it, no policy is final. Policies are tentative simply because their outcomes stimulate new social conflicts and problems as well as accommodating existing ones. This effect of policies flows in part from the influence of pluralism on policy formulation.

Pluralism and policy formulation

In each of the three cases of policymaking outlined above, many interests took part; the diversity of interests involved in formulating policies reflects our pluralist social and political context.

THE PLURALIST SOCIETY

Those who advocate high tariff rates on imported raw materials, industrial goods, and agricultural products are in a difficult position. They may try to broaden their appeal by urging that all major economic interests in America can benefit from high tariff policies. But high tariffs do not benefit all economic interests. A large building contractor wants low-priced steel, whether purchased domestically or from European or Asian producers. This contractor would oppose a high tariff on imported steel, however pleasing that tariff would be to an American steel producer.

Conflicting group interests in a pluralist society thus compel any group to choose between holding fast to a narrow, uncompromising position, and moderating its demands to attract allies. Relationships between a group and its constituency generate similar choices. A trade association for an industry made up of many "Mom and Pop" retail stores and a few large chain stores may find that it either has to straddle many industry issues on which its members are divided or elect to narrow its membership to one of the other group.

In a pluralist society, groups also compete for the attention of officials. A politician has a choice of which groups to listen to and may listen to more than one side. A congressman considering a proposal to eliminate discrimination in the sale and rental of houses and apartments can draw information from opponents and supporters of such legislation, including realtors, civil rights groups, mayors of large cities, and congressional colleagues. The many groups seeking his vote give him a chance to take a more independent stance toward each and to legitimize whatever position he does take, on the basis that some groups have pushed for that view.

Because claims made by interests are channeled through group leaders, contacts between them and public officials are vital. In a pluralist society, influence is spread widely among leaders both inside and outside of formal government. In formulating policy, citizens acting as members of organized interests control their leaders and are controlled by them; their leaders, in turn, influence other group leaders and public officials are influenced by them. Because of this relationship among citizens and private and public leaders, popular control over policymaking is at best exerted indirectly, as in our examples showing how distributive, regulatory, and redistributive policies are formulated.

THE PLURALIST GOVERNMENT: FEDERALISM

Over the years, governments at the various levels of our federal system have grown stronger, and the national government has gained power much faster than the states. Responding to demands that it regulate business, alleviate social and economic ills, improve education at all levels, and preserve and restore the environment, the federal government has expanded its influence.

This tendency toward centralized power still leaves protection for state autonomy in both the party system (see Chapter 8) and the Constitution (see Chapter 3). The states have been beneficiaries, as well as victims, of the federal government's growing dominance; programs of cooperative federalism enable the states to prosper too. The network of interstate highways on which we now drive grew from this cooperation. Congress authorized the federal government to pay 90 percent of the cost of the interstate system, yet the states retained authority over construction. Compliance by all states made it possible for the federal government to initiate construction of this highway network that benefits interstate commerce and national defense. In return, the states profited from the money poured into local economies and from increased tourist travel. Moreover, the automotive industry, tire manufacturers, petroleum companies, trucking firms, motels and restaurants, and others gained indirectly.

Although the federal arrangement has changed since 1789 because the national government is more powerful and federal-state programs have been developed, federalism still influences policy formulation. The federal arrangement and the separation of powers increase conflict between governing officials at different levels or in different political institutions, who seek to advance or safeguard their interests and authority at the expense of others. State officials see their authority threatened by federal expenditures for schools, highways, and other facilities within the state; often they demand control over federal money spent in their states.

By providing separate national and state governing authorities, federalism gives interests many chances to try to influence policymaking. Failing to gain satisfaction at the local level, an interest can take its demands to Washington; or, if it is dissatisfied with federal policies, it can attempt to block them by appealing to state and local officials. Organized interests frequently advance their demands by promoting conflicts over who has the authority to make a decision affecting them. The interests that opposed strict gun controls argued that only the states had the authority to set regulations. They took this position because of their strong influence with state officials and because the states have no authority to prohibit the interstate sale of firearms. Arguing that the Constitution prohibits federal regulation—"the right of the people to keep and bear arms, shall not be infringed"—the gun lobby really hoped to avoid any regulation at all. Advocates of gun control aimed at the national government, arguing that the right to bear arms was intended only to assure "a well-regulated Militia," which surely involved the federal government. But federal officials were not completely successful in overcoming objections by state agencies to gun-control legislation.

THE PLURALIST GOVERNMENT: SEPARATION OF POWERS

Again, although American government has changed a great deal since 1789, the separation of powers, and its corollary principle, checks and balances, also still strongly influence policy formulation. Figure 10.1 shows how constitutional authority is distributed among selected key bodies in the legislative, executive, and judicial branches. Each branch now has several divisions, such as the General Accounting Office under congressional authority, the various offices, departments, and agencies linked to the executive, and the several levels of the judicial system.

The mere presence of separate institutions that restrain and balance one another in the exercise of authority makes conflicts inevitable between the institutions, their divisions, and the political subunits—such as bureaus and committees—attached to each. To settle these conflicts, political subunits forge coalitions that perform crucial functions in formulating policy.

Conflicts between policymakers

Built into the provision for three branches of government and the division of governmental functions among them, conflict requires that the President win legislative approval for his appointments, proposed legislation, and financial requests. Yet, between 1953 and 1976 (Eisenhower through Ford), Congress accepted less than half of the President's proposed programs. Both the House and the Senate have institutional interests or prerogatives that their members try to protect against encroachment by the President, the courts, or the other legislative body. These may take the form of Senate resentment of undue presidential control over foreign policy and the war and treaty powers (as the Senate was dissatisfied over President Johnson's and President Nixon's conduct of the Vietnam War). Another type of prerogative is that a member of Congress can be disciplined only by his or her colleagues and has immunity from many forms of legal action. Controversies between the courts and either the President or the Congress also dot our history. President Roosevelt's attempt to enlarge the Supreme Court in the 1930s and the late Senator Everett Dirksen's attempt in 1965 to override the Supreme Court's decision that both houses of state legislative bodies must be apportioned according to population clearly show conflict between the major branches of government.

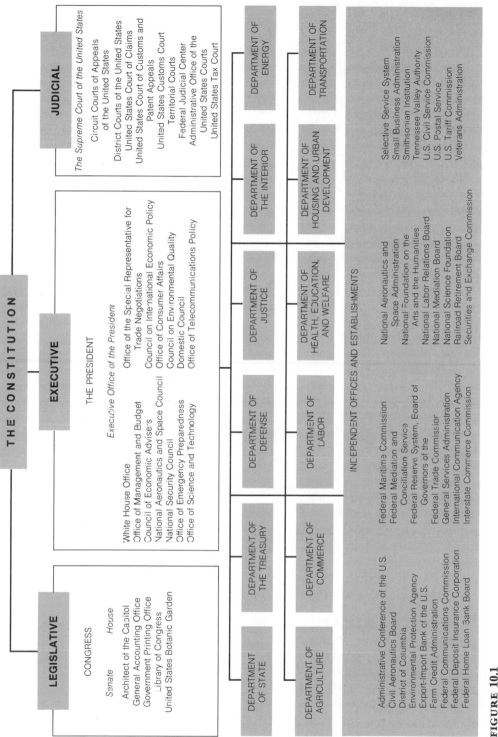

FIGURE 10.1

The Government of the United States. [*Source:* This is an adapted, updated version of the organizational chart of the same title appearing in the *United States Government Manual, 1977–1978*, Washington, D.C.: U.S. Government Printing Office, 1977, p. 28.]

Policymaking fiefdoms

Units within each major institution of government (particularly legislative committees and executive agencies and bureaus) have considerable autonomy over their own affairs and discretion over policymaking. Policy decisions therefore often reflect compromises between interests represented through these governing subunits.

Interests diversify in Congress as committees and subcommittees in each chamber get authority of their own and win the deference of the rest of the chamber. Committees gain autonomy because legislators assume that committee members are expert in the committee's specialized areas, from which it follows that the committee's judgment on bills should be given great weight by the rest of the chamber: The Armed Services Committees of the House and Senate have seldom had their recommendations for the defense budget overridden by their chambers. Tenure on committees automatically confers status and respect for the competence of members and increases as veteran legislators remain with their committees despite changes in party control. Longevity, specialization, and congressional acquiescence promote the development of semiautonomous policymaking committees or subcommittees.

The chairpersons of congressional committees are key leaders in inviting or blocking policy in the legislature. They often compete with the President and his legislative leaders. The Chairman of the House Ways and Means Committee is an example. Traditionally the committee—charged with reviewing legislation in such areas as taxation—has been one of the most powerful in Congress. With a Democratic majority in Congress the committee was a thorn in the side of Republican Presidents Nixon and Ford. Even after reforms in the 94th Congress that strengthened House leadership at the expense of committee chairpersons (such as enlarging the membership of the committee and establishing subcommittees) and the demise of once powerful chairman Wilbur Mills, Ways and Means retains considerable autonomy in clashes with the President. For example, in 1975 President Ford proposed taxes on imported oil, which he said would raise the cost of gasoline to the consumer, reduce consumption, and thus curtail the rising dependence of America upon foreign oil. Ways and Means, under the chairmanship of Al Ullman (Democrat of Oregon) balked at the measures and ultimately reported a compromise which neither Ford nor the entire House, for quite different reasons, found suitable. Through the mid-1970s much of the inability of policymakers to furnish a comprehensive energy program derived from the wrangling of various such autonomous subunits charged with making energy policy.

In theory, the administrative branch simply applies and enforces the laws adopted by negotiations among legislators and other officials. In practice, administration involves so much discretion that it gives lawmaking authority in fact, and at times in form, to that branch as well. A regulatory agency charged by Congress with providing "a fair rate of return" for the firms it regulates has plenty of leeway in determining what the criterion means and how to apply it. So, too, did the Office of Economic Opportunity have considerable leeway in figuring out how the congressional instruction to provide for "maximum feasible participation of the poor" at local levels could be worked out. Even when a statute is more precise, "gray areas" of interpretation remain, meaning that the administrative unit's handling of them makes the law on that point.

Finally, no sizable administrative unit can hope to enforce with equal energy all of its statutory obligations and rules. In choosing which to enforce and to what extent, the bureaucracy in practice determines what is effective law and what is not; for example, the incidence of categories of crime in a community depends partly on which categories of crime the police enforce.

Administrative discretion continuously reshapes policies, especially when regulatory agencies are empowered to make, apply, and interpret rules. A quasi-judicial regulatory agency such as the Interstate Commerce Commission is a subgovernment in that it combines executive, legislative, and judicial tasks. It sets railroad rates, sees that they are enforced, and decides when rules have been violated by railroad companies. The National Labor Relations Board not only applies labor legislation aimed at eliminating unfair labor practices but also investigates complaints from labor and management, promotes collective bargaining, and may prescribe rules and regulations advancing the purposes of major labor statutes.

Each administrative department, such as the Department of Health, Education and Welfare, is made up of many subunits, which are administrative bureaus with considerable autonomy. Bureau leaders can often circumvent the direct control of their superior department heads by developing their own links to Congress and interest group supporters. By developing political "clout" in their own right and combining it with their technical knowledge and protected civil service status, they insulate themselves from presidential or departmental control. Bureaucratic leaders can thus be significant formulators of policy.

Coalitions of policymakers

Separation of powers, which contributes to policy conflicts and subunit autonomy, also promotes the formation of coalitions by those who formulate policy. Such coalitions contain both public officials (from relevant executive bureaus and congressional committees) and leaders of powerful organized interests. These coalitions operate as subgovernments, each developing an exclusive and autonomous sphere of policy on matters important to the members of the coalition.

Among examples are the military-industrial complex of congressional leaders, military and bureaucratic officials in the Department of Defense, and major defense contractors; the National Rifle Association's alliance with state officials, members of Congress, and officials in the Department of the Army; the alliance of the House Committee on Government Information with public information officers in administrative agencies and Washington journalists trying to find out what is going on; the alliance of the House Agriculture Committee, the Sugar Division of the Agriculture Department, leaders of the sugar industry formed to determine the prices and quotas of imported sugar; and the coalition of the Bureau of Indian Affairs, the Association on American Indian Affairs, and the House and Senate Committees on Indian Affairs.

A specific case will show how coalitions of policy formulators form. In the early 1960s, some consumers complained that food products were packaged and priced so that purchasers could not compare prices, make a reasonable choice, and obtain the full value of their dollar. Packaging in "regular," "family," or "jumbo" sizes, odd package shapes, not filling packages to capacity, and offering goods at "cents-off" the regular prices were typical packaging and pricing techniques that consumers found confusing and misleading. Senator Philip Hart, Democrat of Michigan, introduced a bill in 1961 which prohibited deceptive packaging. This bill came under the jurisdiction of the Senate Antitrust and Monopoly Subcommittee of the Senate Judiciary Committee. Food industry spokespersons had much influence with the Judiciary Committee, but advocates of consumer legislation, despite the support of President Kennedy and his 12-member Consumer Advisory Council, had little. Through 1964, the coalition of opponents of truth-in-packaging legislation prevailed, chiefly because the Senate Judiciary Committee failed to report a bill.

In 1965, Hart introduced a new bill to authorize the Food and Drug Administration and the Federal Trade Commission to issue regulations requiring clear statements of net quantity in packages. It also provided standards for weights, quantities, sizes, and shapes of packages; and it prohibited offering a product at less than the customary retail price. Hart attempted to give jurisdiction over the bill to the Senate Commerce Committee rather than to the unresponsive Judiciary Committee by designating the new bill an attempt to prohibit deceptive packaging and labeling in interstate commerce. By voice vote, the Senate sent the bill to the Commerce Committee over the objections of Minority leader Everett Dirksen, Republican of Illinois. The Senate Commerce Committee held hearings; and in 1966 Congress passed a truth-in-packaging law, but only after a coalition of interests (lobbyists for the food industry, several southern Democrats, and the Republican members of the House Interstate and Foreign Commerce Committee, together with officials in the Department of Commerce) won deletion of the key provision that authorized officials to establish standard package sizes. Instead manufacturers were required to develop their own standards. The House Committee said it had substituted the voluntary procedure to meet the "recurrent objections raised by industry that mandatory standards would result in greatly increased cost to the consumer and would stifle package innovations." The Commerce Department also agreed with the substitution in order to placate the food industry. In the words of Representative Leonor Sullivan, Democrat of Missouri and supporter of consumer legislation, the final legislation that proved acceptable to the food industry and its allies in the Congress and executive agencies was so far removed from what had been sought by consumers that "we can all voice a very mild cheer—for very little."

Partial autonomy characterizes the operations of the two legislative houses and their subcommittees and committees, agencies and bureaus within agencies, and interest groups and factions within them. Diversification of interests at every level of authority generates give-and-take that results in two types of policy formulation: in specialized areas (regulation of the railroad industry, or the setting of quotas for the importation of sugar) and in general areas (energy policies, regulation of firearms, or the War on Poverty). Because of the pluralist influence, select minorities rule in specialized areas and a collection of diverse minorities rules in more general policy matters; popular majorities are rare in either type of policy formulation.

Forging policy agreements

In American government there are distinctive styles of policy formulation (i.e., distinctive methods used to reach decisions on courses of action and to obtain compliance) and distinctive traditions of policymaking (i.e., distinctive habits, expectations, conventions, and guidelines customarily involved in the formulation of agreements).

STYLES OF POLICY FORMULATION

The policy style most used in reaching decisions and achieving compliance is bargaining. By bargaining, conflicting leaders reach a common policy position; they explore and accept mutually beneficial adjustments of their differences. Policy formulators adjust conflicts by modifying their own demands and persuading their opponents to modify theirs. In America, mutual adjustment is inescapable because of constitutional features as well as social pluralism. The separation of powers requires that policy decisions receive the approval of executive, legislative, and, at times, judicial branches to be legitimized. Legal separation but actual interdependence underlies all political bargaining.

In order to bargain, both sides must be willing to negotiate and must have something to negotiate about; they must be able to offer something others want and they must want something others have. Some problems are easy to negotiate; others, very difficult. On the issue of minimum wages, it is easier to find a compromise between those who urge a $2.50 minimum and those who want a $3.00 minimum than it is to negotiate the question of whether there should be any minimum wage at all.

Two broad types of bargaining can be distinguished. In *explicit bargaining*, the policy formulators minimize the chances of misunderstanding by clearly formalizing their agreement. Treaties are explicit bargains in international affairs; wage contracts and government defense contracts, in domestic affairs. *Implicit* or *tacit bargaining* is more significant for most American policymaking. At times, ambiguity is desirable and the responsibilities of formulators to one another are purposely couched in such vague notions as "future support," "good will," or "favorable disposition." The most common implicit bargain is an exchange of support between legislators whereby one legislator agrees to go along with another on a bill in exchange for cooperation at some unspecified future time. The convertibility of such political IOUs into actual support when requested rests more on mutual respect for playing by the rules than on the clarity of the terms in any formal agreement.

At the heart of either type of political bargaining is an exploration for mutual advantages: Bargains are made by pleasing everyone somewhat. If one accepts that bargaining is the principal style of policy formulation, then politics is the art of compromise. Compromise is one way in which agreements can be reached, because if disputants hold to their initial claims, none is likely to profit; impasse or total defeat are the more likely outcomes. If all sides decide to give in a little, none is completely satisfied but none is completely unhappy with the result.

Bargaining may have other consequences. For example, elected leaders may find after a while that the people they have appointed to regulate groups are finding bases of support within those groups; the appointees then become difficult to control and make regulation of the groups very difficult. Popular control over the policymakers is diluted as well. Another effect is that bargaining extends the time it takes to make policy. Bargaining also often makes it impossible to fix responsibility for public policy on any individual, group, party, or legislative body. Moreover, policymaking is usually costly in wasted effort and resources as well as in uncoordinated and inefficient policies.

Finally, the issues resolved by political bargaining are necessarily only a small part of the almost limitless number of social conflicts facing policymakers. The political circuits would be grossly overloaded if all actual and potential conflicts had to be attended to. Political bargainers must therefore conserve their resources and efforts for issues of most importance to them. The bargainer's need to pick and choose his issues complements the need of the political system to filter social conflicts. However, the items that do not get on the political agenda may be just as vital for the continued health of the community as the ones that do.

Bargaining is the principal style of policy formulation in America, but others sometimes replace or underpin it. Through persuasion, formulators influence one another by holding out promises of gratification and reward. Recent Presidents, for example have made a practice of holding occasional "White House breakfasts" with congressional leaders. These are sometimes negotiating sessions designed to forge policies, but more often they permit the President to outline his already set program, point out its advantages for members of Congress and their constituents, and ask for their support in obtaining congressional approval, which he hopes will result from the merits of his persuasive arguments.

If a policy leader regularly threatens reprisal as well as promising rewards, his style is one of command. A policy leader commands as much support as he has sanctions to apply. The formal sanctions that the President holds over administrative subordinates include his authority to review their budget requests, appoint administrative personnel, clear their legislative proposals, and limit the information they may release to the press.

The authority to review and cut agency budget requests is of particular importance. Because agencies and bureaus cannot formally request more funds from Congress than are authorized in the President's budget, their autonomy is limited. Bureaucratic leaders are often able to circumvent such formal restrictions, however, by testifying before sympathetic legislators on congressional committees. President Nixon regularly requested less federal spending for public education than some education interests, both in Congress and in the executive, wanted. Although instructed to support the President's requests publicly, a few administrators in the Office of Education expressed their desire for more funds before congressional committees. Congress responded by budgeting more federal aid to education than requested by the President, prompting him to veto several education measures.

Within administrative agencies, conflicts arise between administrators seeking to command support and their subordinates who have outside help in refusing to obey. In the late 1960s, Secretary of Defense Robert S. McNamara announced that the United States would begin developing a limited antiballistic missile system costing $5 billion to defend against a possible nuclear attack by Communist China. The dissatisfaction of portions of the army and air force, who wanted a more elaborate program costing $40 billion, was shared by members of the House Armed Services Committee who criticized the "austerity" of the McNamara plan. The military and congressional proponents of a major antiballistic missile system thus remained free to lobby against the secretary's decision.

Bargaining, persuasion, command, and competition as styles of policy formulation seldom appear alone in policymaking. They overlap and supplement one another, although bargaining predominates. The words used to

describe the political style of Mayor Richard Lee, an energetic leader dedicated to urban renewal and other policies to invigorate New Haven, Connecticut, typify the American style of policy formulation:

> The mayor was not at the peak of a pyramid but rather at the center of intersecting circles. He rarely commanded. He negotiated, cajoled, exhorted, beguiled, charmed, pressed, appealed, reasoned, promised, insisted, demanded, even threatened, but he most needed support and acquiescence from other leaders who simply could not be commanded. Because the mayor could not command, he had to bargain. (Dahl, 1961, p. 204)

TRADITIONS OF POLICY FORMULATION

In formulating policies various habits, expectations, conventions, and guidelines develop. Three such traditions stand out as policymakers work to resolve conflicts in the American setting: reciprocity, the custom of "you scratch my back and I'll scratch yours"; incrementalism, or "muddling through"; and symbolizing "the public interest."

Reciprocity: going along to get along

Perhaps no activity sets apart the politician as much as bargaining. One's selection and subsequent success as a policymaker depends upon skills at negotiating. Once chosen, a politician's life and energy are devoted to continuously reshaping coalitions of policy formulators. In arranging political bargains, the politician cares only about finding solutions that work, not perfect ones. All policymakers are committed to mutual accommodation, even when they are spokespersons for divergent interests, so they are willing to adjust to each other's demands rather than push their differences beyond reconciliation.

The give-and-take of the politician's job has its good side. We often think of reciprocal influence as the shady side of politics, though we should realize that, however implicit and subtle, compromise and bargaining are part of our day-to-day relationships. (When was the last time you refrained from arguing because to do so would have jeopardized your relations with a friend or group?) Bargaining is just as vital in the welter of social interests making legitimate claims on government and policy.

Incrementalism: a little bit at a time

Many critics argue that bargaining is not a rational way to formulate policies; the bargains usually work to the advantage of the bargainers and seldom solve social problems. They advocate a more rational and comprehensive approach to policy formulation. (1) Clarify policy goals before considering alternative courses of action to reach those goals. (2) Search for all alternative means of achieving the agreed-on policy objectives. (3) Comprehensively test each alternative course of action against the criterion that the most rational (and hence, "best") policy will be the most appropriate and efficient means of reaching agreed-on ends. Finally, (4) select this most rational policy (Lindblom, 1959).

A rational, comprehensive procedure of formulating policies may seem desirable, but its requirements contradict all that we know about how human beings reach decisions, particularly in American politics. It is rarely easy, and usually impossible, to get people to clarify and agree on policy goals. Our pluralist society and government restrict political consensus to the most vaguely defined and abstract goals—"government by the people," "justice," "freedom," "a better standard of living." Policymakers cannot comprehensively analyze alternative ways of achieving goals if those goals are not agreed on in advance. Comprehensive policy analysis also requires knowing what courses of action are available. Seldom, however, do policymakers know all the options. Finally, the comprehensive approach requires politicians to anticipate the consequences of each conceivable option in order to select the policy most apt to advance their goals. But it is unrealistic to believe that even the most knowledgeable person can correctly predict what will happen if he or she adopts any possible course of action. (Let the reader, for instance, think of how many times he or she has chosen the right course of action and then found that the expected result did not follow.) Unanticipated consequences have a way of frustrating even the best laid plans.

Political scientists call the behavior of American politicians in formulating policy the incremental approach to change, or "muddling through." In this approach, policymakers do not agree on goals before considering how best to achieve them; instead they examine various means that will help achieve each goal—the contrary of the first step under "rational" policymaking. The true meaning of the goal, and a better way of knowing how much support it has, appears only in the reactions to each of the proposed means. When a goal, racial integration, is cast in the form of school integration, one set of pro and con forces develops; when the means is open housing, another set comes forth; equal voting rights produces still another configuration of forces, and so on.

The alignment of interests on the various proposed means will, of course, overlap, but significant differences will emerge as well. The "rational" model assumes that policy goals are clear and independent of proposed means, and that dispassionate and technical analysis can determine the best (most efficient) means to agreed-on ends. As our example indicates, however, it is only in the conflict over means that goals become clarified. Public policy, therefore, is not simply a matter of devising effective means to reach known and shared ends; it is a simultaneous search for means and ends on which disagreement is widespread.

Following the incremental approach, the parties to a dispute frequently agree on a "good" policy without agreeing on what it is good for; although unable to agree on ends, conflicting interests still agree on means. For example, congressional liberals want to extend old-age benefits through Social Security as a means of having the federal government provide equal welfare opportunities to all elderly Americans (to achieve the principle of equality). Conservatives support the same policy, but for a different reason; they see it as a way of reducing labor demands on private corporations for support of union pension plans (to protect private enterprise). In the rational-comprehensive approach to formulating policy, it is assumed that a "good" policy is one that achieves agreed-on goals; the incremental approach has no criterion for a "good" policy apart from saying that it serves the separate, perhaps conflicting, goals of specialized interests.

In selecting an appropriate policy through the incremental approach, policymakers usually neglect to analyze in detail the consequences of adopting the policy. When officials formulated the policies leading to the development of the breeder reactor, they did not ignore the consequences for the environment of operating large numbers of breeder plants. However, they chose to analyze only relevant consequences first: the stimulus the reactor would give business and employment. In the incremental approach, alternative policies that might accomplish a specified goal in a better way than the proposed policy are seldom considered initially. After a time, such alternative policies are offered: The all-volunteer army was offered as an alternative to selective service in sustaining a defense force; the Nixon administration offered a comprehensive alternative to current welfare programs for the needy. Nevertheless, in initial policy conflicts, relatively few proposals are considered and they look very much alike; fresh approaches to old problems are therefore rare.

In the incremental approach, policies are changed by successive comparison. Instead of examining policies to see if they have been successful, retaining the ones that accomplish stated goals and scrapping the ineffective ones to start anew, policies already chosen are periodically adapted to changing conditions to patch up obvious mistakes. In the budgetary process, for instance, last year's appropriation for an agency is typically considered the base for change, which the Office of Management and Budget or Congress questions all too seldom. Only the size of the increase comes under attack.

The disadvantage of incrementalism is that programs and agencies are seldom allowed to die or be severely cut back (Carter's decision on the LMFBR was an obvious exception); that coordination of policy is made much more difficult; and that the President can control only a small fraction of the total budget to implement his own priorities and policies. The advantages are that the reduction in review efforts and conflicts assures stability and continuity in policies and agency programs and activities. To be sure, some programs, such as many associated with the War on Poverty, lose support and end; but the general rule is program survival. If government activities were continuously open to basic reconsideration, the burden on officials, groups, and citizens would be intolerable. The adjustment of social conflicts by traditional, incremental change means that policies are allowed to evolve and that great basic shifts in policy are the exception.

The incrementalists' way of formulating policy appears chaotic. It reveals no deliberate effort to coordinate the disparate efforts of policy leaders. But such procedures do simplify the complex business of making policy. Instead of considering all alternative policies in a conflict, leaders limit themselves to those which differ little from current policies. Policymakers measure the worth of each policy by what diverse interests demand, insulating themselves from more demanding interests.

Incrementalism simplifies policymaking in yet another way. The "best" policy is the one on which bargained agreement has been achieved. The complex task of estimating how specific policies will affect distant goals gives way to a more simplified accounting: which immediate interests are pleased and displeased, whose support is won and whose lost. Policymaking thus develops into a search for workable solutions that satisfy although they do not maximize the demands of interests, rather than into the more difficult, and perhaps impossible, search for perfect solutions to public problems.

Incrementalism has been the leading tradition in conflict resolution, but this is not to say that all policy formulation reflects solely that pattern. Some policies reflect considerable planning conducted on a large scale rather than piecemeal adjustments to changing situations. America's program for manned space flights, which placed men on the moon in the late 1960s and early 1970s, was such a large-scale effort; it was not accomplished by simply living from day to day without considering alternate designs and carefully weighing costs and benefits (Schulman, 1975). And two of the policymaking areas we discussed earlier—the development of breeder technology and the War on Poverty—reflected a mixture of both incremental and nonincremental approaches.

Moreover, recent efforts in Congress suggest that many policymakers desire to move away from the tradition of incrementalism or at least to modify it. For instance, in 1974 Congress created a Congressional Budget Office and a Budget Committee in each house. The aim was to plan, coordinate, and review the consequences of revenue and spending policies rather than adopt them as the piecemeal by-products of efforts to conciliate conflicting interests. Congress has also established an Office of Technology Assessment as a research arm to review the potential social, economic, and environmental consequences of new technologies—such as the breeder reactor, nuclear fusion, and the liquification and pumping of coal across vast distances.

In sum, the picture we have drawn of the tradition of incrementalism is but a description of how most—but not all—policies are made. Nor is that description intended to be a prescription of how policies should be made. It is too early to tell what changes will result in the incremental mode of resolving conflict from the efforts of its critics to reform it by introducing either greater coordination in policy formulation (as in the space program) or a more comprehensive weighing of possible outcomes of proposed policies (as with the Office of Technology Assessment).

The public interest, or, what about the rest of us?

But if bargaining and incremental policy formulation are attempts to satisfy diverse private interests, what happens to the general interest? The public interest has a history of being many things to many people. Most often it is thought of as substantive ideals—goals—against which all policy proposals should be judged: "equality of opportunity," "equal justice," "fairness to all." As symbols or norms, such goals spell out the aspirations of a society. Special interests tie their claims to these symbols to rationalize their desires and to increase support for their position.

It would be misleading, however, to suggest that organized interests cynically manipulate the definition of the public interest to suit their selfish aims. Is it so clear or obvious, after all, what "the public interest" requires in any major social conflict? In public welfare policies? In taxation? In education? In defense spending? In relations with other nations? Because "the public interest" is an ambiguous idea, special interests are often genuinely persuaded that their demands are indeed in the public interest.

We can look at the public interest in another way: Public interest is not some external and autonomous standard "out there," but the result of bargaining by group interests seeking to resolve their conflicts. The public interest, like substantive policy itself, constantly evolves in the continuing adjustment caused by social conflicts; it is not a fixed, permanent entity. Procedurally, however, the public interest may be said to require viable decisionmaking by the community to facilitate the conciliation of clashing interests. Bargaining and incrementalism facilitate this conciliation and so promote the public interest. This is not to say that any policy decision is by definition in the public interest. Rather, it is to adopt the argument of the authors of the *Federalist Papers* that the public interest is not something to be given in advance of policymaking but to be continuously discovered and reformulated through institutionalized procedures that guarantee restraints on both self-seeking majority and minority interests—federalism, separated powers, checks and balances, and popular elections. But is "the American way" sufficient?

Conflict resolution: pros and cons of the American way

In making public policy within our pluralist society and constitutional arrangement, policy formulators are greatly influenced by a bargaining style and the tradition of incrementalism. Critics of American democracy have suggested major defects in this method of resolving social disputes. What are their criticisms?

Our pluralist system consists of innumerable semiautonomous fiefdoms— coalitions of policymakers protecting their own interests and beyond control by any central authority. Rarely is a leader under our fragmented constitutional arrangement able to call attention to the many social problems in need of resolution, to formulate adequate responses, and to mobilize widespread public interest and effort. Instead, government is more prone to formulate policies that distribute resources to favored interests and permit special clienteles to regulate affairs on their own behalf than to try to devise redistributive policies directed at removing the causes of pressing social tensions.

Incremental change is very slow and often stifles or delays the search for solutions to deep problems. All too often the delay is long; and social evils are allowed to grow so intense that it becomes difficult, perhaps impossible, to formulate workable responses. Bargaining and incremental change can be quite unreceptive to innovative policies; as a result, formulation descends into a routine, unimaginative, conservative approach that sustains the status quo for its own sake. The real threat may be not a government quick to act in a tyrannical way but a government unable to act at all, immobilized by its tendency to reach negotiated settlements in response to the demands of privileged interests. The government does respond to the challenges of the discontented, but often the responsive is symbolic, giving such interests the illusion that their voices are heard in formulating policies, but seldom responding to the substance of their demands.

The above criticisms are representative of those that have been leveled against the process of formulating policies described in this chapter. A good deal of controversy rages over the validity of these criticisms. Many critics point to crises in race relations, disaffection among youth, intensification of poverty, and deterioration in the environment as evidence that our way of making policy has been tried and found wanting. Some call for moderate reforms to compensate for weaknesses, others say the whole system is faulty and demand that it be discarded.

By contrast, many citizens argue that the pluralist-bargaining-incrementalist system can resolve social conflicts and has done so. They point to civil rights legislation passed in the 1950s and 1960s as fruitful incremental change; they cite antipoverty and medicare legislation as indicative of innovative though defective programs that affect the redistribution of resources. They deny that social ills are ignored, pointing to major proposals calling for welfare reform, national health insurance, environmental improvement, tax reform, and other basic policy changes that Congress is considering. They point to examples of policy formulation (the antipoverty program) in which initiative for program development was centralized, not dispersed among conflicting interests. Nor are they willing to accept the charge that our way of formulating policy is beyond repair; they cite new techniques of budgeting that reform the conventions of incremental change by involving the President in the early stages of policy development, providing for him to scrutinize existing programs, and giving him authority to do more than simply cut some agency requests and add a few items of his own.

This controversy reflects a basic tension always found in American government: It opposes coordination and fragmentation, centralization and decentralization, majority rule and minority rights. Each of the major policymaking institutions reflects this tension. In weighing the defects of policymaking, their consequences, what can be done and is being done about them, and their origin in the pluralist character of American society and government, it is well to keep in mind that for all its faults, its defenders say, it does manage conflict by building a consensus stronger than any we could imagine if every group received precisely what it demanded of the community.

POLICY Leadership: THE Presidency

11

The first three articles of the Constitution set forth the governmental framework for resolving social conflicts: The legislature passes laws, the executive administers and enforces them, and the judiciary interprets them. But our discussion has shown that the resolution of conflict is not as simple as that. Authority and influence are so dispersed throughout the complex constitutional structure that it is difficult to trace the origins of public policy and fix responsibility for its implementation. Within this complicated set of relationships, the Presidency occupies a key role. In fact, the influence of the chief executive is so great that in many respects his office dominates the American political structure.

Writers on the Presidency during the 1960s debated whether the office was too powerful. The use of secrecy and occasional deliberate deception regarding American operations in Vietnam during the Johnson administration, and the revelations surrounding Watergate in the early 1970s produced serious reassessment of the role of the President. Secrecy, credibility gaps, conviction and imprisonment of powerful presidential aides, and the near impeachment of a President all contributed to grave misgivings or deep concern about the extent of presidential power.

The power of the Presidency is not, of course, a product of the 1960s and 1970s alone. Primarily a development of the twentieth century, the consolidation of presidential power gained momentum particularly in the three and a half decades from the administration of Franklin D. Roosevelt in the 1930s to the present. To assess and understand the impact and scope of the office in the American political system we must view it within the perspective of history, analyzing the personalities and ambitions of Presidents; the role of Congress and the courts in relation to the office of President; the party system; and the economic and technological changes of the twentieth century. Only within this framework can we evaluate questions concerning a "crisis of the Presidency," or proposals to limit its power.

The President and policy leadership

Policy leadership defines the community's goals, initiates proposals to achieve those goals, and obtains both official and popular compliance in their execution. Even the most severe critics of presidential power and influence do not dispute the President's status as the nation's primary policy leader. Beyond this broad consensus on the need for leadership from the White House, Americans have seemingly contradictory expectations about how a President should perform this role. One scholar of the Presidency, Thomas E. Cronin, has described the office as a set of paradoxes and dilemmas (1975, pp. 2–10). Americans expect the President to reconcile diverse interests but also to be an innovative leader; they want a "common man" in the White House yet they also want a person of "uncommon" leadership; they recognize the necessity of a strong chief executive who is able to act decisively in foreign affairs, yet they fear that his use of such power might take them to unnecessary war and deprive them of civil liberties under the guise of acts to protect the nation; they want their President to be "above politics" yet fail to recognize the necessity for compromise and accommodation that is the essence of democratic leadership; finally, they expect their President to use his power in the solution of problems yet they frequently decry decisive action as "dictatorial" and "unconstitutional." Despite the absence of any known solutions to problems

> a President is expected to generate hope, confidence, and a sense of national purpose: to "bring us together," to "let us reason together," to remind the people of past greatness and future glories, or to "bring America home again." . . . Presidents must act as moral leaders or teachers, provide assurance and inspiration to the people, and summon society to high achievement. In this role of political folk hero, a President sustains the people's sense of direction and reaffirms the nation's credibility and legitimacy. (Cronin, 1975, p. 10)

DEVELOPMENT OF THE PRESIDENCY

The dominant Presidency was not foreseen by the Founding Fathers and was achieved only after a long and sometimes bitter struggle between the governing institutions. The men who wrote the Constitution focused on the legislative branch, but they nevertheless wanted an executive with great independence and potential. They therefore rejected selection of the President by Congress except in extraordinary circumstances (the House of Representatives selects the President when no candidate receives a majority of electoral votes) and provided a fixed term of office, subject only to removal by impeachment. The Framers gave the President control over foreign relations, made him chief of the administrative branch, and granted him a veto over legislation. These formal powers assigned by Article II have not been changed by amendment.

The nature of the Presidency cannot be understood by studying its legal status only. "The executive Power shall be vested in a President of the United States of America" are the opening words of Article II. But the extent of "executive Power" is left undefined. A renowned student of the development of the Presidency, Edward S. Corwin, remarked that for those who seek certainty in the Constitution the phrase is a "nightmare" and for those who prefer broad language it "should be a vision realized" (1948, p. 2). Every President has been charged with the constitutional responsibility to "take care that the Laws be faithfully executed," but the meaning of the obligation has undergone marked changes.

Under the leadership of James Wilson, James Madison, and Alexander Hamilton, the Framers decided on a single executive rather than a collegiate body and gave to the President prerogatives independent of the other branches. We are not sure how much authority they intended to give the President. At least one of the Framers, Alexander Hamilton, foresaw a strong chief executive. In *Federalist* No. 70, he argued: "Energy in the executive is a leading character in the definition of good government. . . . A feeble executive implies a feeble execution of the government . . . and a government ill executed, whatever it may be in theory, must be, in practice, a bad government." He urged that Article II laid the foundation for strong leadership: "that the executive power of the nation is vested in the President; subject only to the exceptions and qualifications which are expressed in the instrument."

Hamilton saw the office as the fulcrum of leadership in the American system, drawing its legal foundations from the specific grants of power in the Constitution and its vitality from the person who occupies the office and puts his powers to use. Hamilton urged President Washington to pursue vigorous executive action both in foreign affairs and in organizing the administrative branch of the new government. The Presidency today is Hamilton's hope fulfilled.

Concern over the extent of presidential power arose early in our history. During the administration of Andrew Jackson, Daniel Webster charged that "the President carries on the government; all the rest are subcontractors." The power of the Presidency grew steadily until 1865, but during the several decades that followed the Civil War it went into eclipse. The trend was reversed in this century, so that Harry S. Truman could say in the 1940s that the Presidency is "the greatest and most important office in the history of the world." The great power and prestige of the twentieth-century Presidency is attributable less to his powers under the Constitution than to other factors that have centered public attention and the major source of policy leadership in the office. However, the Presidency is not a single person. It is the entire set of relationships, expectations, and limitations that constitute the executive branch of government, which together both limit and expand the policy choices of the man who occupies the White House.

THE PRESIDENT AND OTHER POLICYMAKERS

The modern President, by definition of his office, cannot be a neutral force in conflicts of interest. Problems that were once purely local matters—race relations, urban blight, education, finance of governmental services and activities, crime—are now among the national government's most urgent problems. Political conflict tends more and more to reflect the clash of national social and economic interests, and national programs and goals now clearly influence even congressional contests. Although members of Congress can claim collectively to represent all the people, the President is the only single individual who can claim a national constituency.

Congress

Congressional constituencies are local, and congressional policy leadership is dispersed within each house; thus the pressure members of Congress respond to are different from those affecting the President. Moreover, legislative policy goals often differ from those of the President, a fact which frequently results in conflict between the two branches. For example, while both branches agree on the need for a national energy policy, President Carter has clashed with the legislature over how best to reduce the consumption of gasoline by Americans. Yet the two branches do have incentives for cooperating: party ties and the need to respond to both pressing domestic problems and crises in foreign policy. Cooperation, not command, characterizes relations between the President and congressional leaders, involving them in the mutual negotiation and accommodation so characteristic of the entire political system. A President, then, must reconcile the autonomous interest claims of congressional leaders with his overall policy.

The courts

Viewed historically, judicial interpretations of presidential power have generally expanded the scope of the Presidency. However, the judiciary also stands as a strong potential check on presidential leadership and power. The Supreme Court's restrictive interpretation of national power in economic regulation before 1937 severely hampered President Roosevelt's attempts to meet the problems of the depression. A subsequent change in the Court's position opened the way for new policies and further extension of federal programs by 1940.

In matters of foreign policy, the courts have substantially supported presidential initiatives and prerogatives. Repeated efforts to bring judicial power to bear against President Johnson's prosecution of the Vietnam war generally failed.

The courts can make policy as well as block it, and Presidents are sometimes unwilling enforcers of court-mandated policy. In *Brown* v. *Board of Education* (1954), the Supreme Court made policy by overturning the legality of racial segregation in public school systems. That action created important problems of policy leadership for Presidents from Eisenhower to Nixon, who had to enforce the decision in parts of the South where both state governments and community sentiment were hostile to integration. President Eisenhower had to use federal troops to achieve integration in Little Rock, Arkansas and at the University of Mississippi. The precedents set by the Brown decision and others that followed made it necessary to bus public school children across school district boundaries in order to achieve racial integration. In sum, the Court forced presidential initiatives in the area of civil rights; in implementing the busing of school children, President Nixon was unable to prevent the legitimization of a policy he personally opposed.

The most striking illustration of court checks on presidential power and initiatives is the record of the Nixon administration. The Supreme Court effectively blocked Nixon's preferences regarding several highly controversial policy issues. He lost the celebrated "Pentagon Papers" case when the Court denied the government's claim that it could stop publication by the *New York Times* and the *Washington Post* of classified material on the U.S. role in Indochina, after the material had been released by Department of Defense employee Daniel Ellsberg. The Nixon Administration also lost cases that struck down the death penalty (1972); declared unconstitutional tax benefits to parents of parochial school children (1973); and upheld the right of a woman to an abortion during the first three months of pregnancy (1973). The President's most damaging defeat occurred in the Watergate tapes case, *United States* v. *Richard M. Nixon* (1974). Judge John J. Sirica, the presiding judge in the trials of Watergate defendants, directed the President to produce, for Sirica's review, 64 tapes of conversations that were considered relevant to the trial of Attorney General John Mitchell. Nixon refused, arguing that the principle of separation of powers gives the President an "absolute privilege of confidentiality" for all presidential communications. The U.S. Supreme Court unanimously ruled against Nixon, holding that while the President may legitimately claim executive privilege in such matters as national security and diplomatic affairs, there is no "absolute privilege." Nixon was ordered to submit the tapes so that Sirica could review them to determine which portions were evidence relevant to the Mitchell trial. One of the tapes contained conversations that established the President's involvement in the Watergate cover-up, an involvement that Nixon had repeatedly denied. Their release was probably the single most important factor in forcing Nixon's resignation in August 1974.

The bureaucracy

One student of the Presidency has noted that the executive branch does not operate as a unit moving in a single direction with the President at the top and subordinates following his wishes; rather "presidential authority is constantly leaking away" (Cronin, 1975, p. 19). The President must leave specific decisions to subordinates, who often do not follow general directives or wishes. Leadership is further complicated by regulatory agencies with policymaking authority that are not directly responsible to the President. Coordination is hampered by multiple layers of decisionmaking and decentralized administrative structures, even in executive agencies that are legally responsible to the chief executive. By yielding to external groups or allying with them, administrative bureaus develop independent support for their goals, weakening the President's control over the executive hierarchy. The strong influence on Congress of the Army Corps of Engineers is one important example. Presidents have had little success in preventing congressional approval of flood control and other projects urged by the Corps but contrary to presidential programs.

The President's capacity to lead policy depends on a set of relationships—formal and informal—between competing interests and institutions in the political community. A close adviser to President Kennedy, Theodore Sorenson, described that interaction as follows:

> The one quality which characterizes most issues likely to be brought to the President [is] . . . conflict between departments, between the views of various advisers, between the administration and Congress, between the United States and another nation, or between groups within the country: labor versus management, or race versus race, or state versus nation. (Sorenson, 1963, p. 28)

The manner in which the President leads is heavily influenced by the style and personality of the man himself, by the environment in which he finds himself, and by the demands that flow from that environment. The Presidency, however, is also a continuing force in defining and translating national goals into specific policy choices. A significant aspect of that role is the symbolic nature of the office itself.

SYMBOLISM AND THE PRESIDENCY

President Taft's description of the President as "the personal embodiment and representative of [the people's] dignity and majesty" pinpoints, albeit somewhat pompously, an inherent function of the President as a community leader. No other leader in the American system can rival him in status or command the immediate attention of the public through the mass media. In fact, no President can escape the responsibilities thrust upon him by a public that looks to the Presidency to resolve problems, to handle crises, successfully and to personify American values at home and abroad. When he lights the Christmas tree on the White House lawn, throws out the first ball to open the baseball season, receives Miss America, congratulates an Olympic champion, visits the site of a flood-ravaged community, or participates in countless other similar activities, he is acting *for* Americans. Through the President we can express our own emotions about "America," focus attention on national problems, find reassurance and comfort that crisis situations are being taken care of, and join with other Americans in expressing our unified sentiments about international affairs.

As the center of attention, the President has the opportunity to use the prestige of the office to strengthen his position in relation to other decision-makers and the public. At a moment's notice he can command the attention of the communications media and speak directly to the public. The contemporary Presidency has been characterized by constant efforts to create a favorable image of the President in the minds of the public. The earliest and perhaps most effective technique in building a coalition of political support through the mass media was initiated by Franklin Delano Roosevelt. In the midst of the worst years of the Great Depression of the 1930s, Roosevelt employed radio "Fireside Chats" to generate public support for his New Deal programs by speaking directly to the American public. Using the first person plural in his messages—"we cannot fail," "our plan"—Roosevelt made Americans feel that he cared. The close relationship with the people that FDR developed through this technique not only built great personal support but also reduced opposition to his programs.

The effectiveness of symbolic acts and symbolic appeals is clearly enhanced by the fact that the President is *the* focal point of the political system. The image of the resolute and forceful leader who is confident in a crisis not only reassures the public but also creates and reinforces his political support in conflicts with other decisionmakers. Surveys consistently show that presidential popularity rises after dramatic actions. For example, President Kennedy's handling of the Cuban missile crisis in 1962 and Richard Nixon's dramatic visit to the People's Republic of China in 1971 increased their popularity with the American public.

Symbolic efforts to build political support can, however, create difficulties for Presidents as well as enhance their position. President Ford's repeated reassurances to the public in 1975 and 1976 that the economy would perform better left the impression that nothing was being done to alleviate unemployment and inflation. President Lyndon Johnson's assurances that the war in Vietnam was being won were ultimately destroyed by television cameras and newspaper stories that revealed the other side of the war effort. President Nixon employed the technique of identifying "enemies" and "friends," a practice that was not only an insidious effort to destroy political opposition but which also contributed to his own political destruction. Finally, President Carter was confronted with his own image as a "moral model" for the nation when it was revealed that his Director of the Office of Management and Budget, Bert Lance, had participated in questionable banking practices prior to joining the Carter administration. In the face of criticism that in defending the retention of Lance he was not practicing what he preached, Carter accepted Lance's resignation. Carter's popularity fell dramatically as a result of the Lance affair and critics viewed his announcement of an extended trip abroad—which followed closely upon the resignation of Lance—as an effort to turn public attention away from the questions raised by the Lance affair.

The President must respond when a major problem confronts him. Whatever his response, he will have an attentive national audience that listens closely because it views him as the nation's leader, not just as the chief spokesman for his party or other interests. By capitalizing on this unique position, a skillful President can modify our pluralistic and fragmented system of policymaking. Thus, President Kennedy as the symbol and representative of the larger community in 1962 forced the steel industry to revoke its increase in prices; and President Nixon in March 1972 signed a bill ending a west coast dock strike. The strike was already over, but the legislation was important as "a symbolic gesture" that emphasized the need for legislation that would set up permanent machinery to avert crippling strikes.

The constitutional basis of presidential power

Article II of the Constitution provides the President with broad but ambiguously defined powers in domestic and foreign affairs. Supplemented by statutes, court interpretations, and the actions of persons who have occupied the office, the Presidency is undoubtedly more powerful than the Framers envisioned.

Four clauses in Article II provide the broad basis for his power: "The executive Power shall be vested in a President"; "he shall take care that the Laws be faithfully executed"; he is "Commander in Chief of the Army and Navy"; and he shall "appoint Ambassadors and other Ministers and Consuls . . . and . . . receive Ambassadors and other Ministers." Together these clauses form the basis for presidential dominance of domestic and foreign affairs.

Limitations on his power are relatively few. The checks and balances provided in the Constitution include the power of Congress to legislate, approve treaties, tax and spend, investigate, and pass bills over a presidential veto. The ultimate sanction of the President rests in the power of Congress to remove him through the process of impeachment. Impeachment, which is the action of bringing charges against a President by a majority vote of the House of Representatives, is followed by trial and conviction by a two-thirds vote of the Senate. Only one President, Andrew Johnson (in 1867), has been impeached, but the Senate failed to convict by one vote. In 1974, the House Judiciary Committee recommended the impeachment of President Richard Nixon, but Nixon resigned before the full House could act on the charges, which would almost certainly have been approved. In a television interview with David Frost in May 1977, Nixon described his resignation as a "voluntary impeachment." The nation could not stand having a President "spend six months in the dock of the Senate" defending himself, a spectacle Nixon believed he had prevented by his resignation.

Article IV of the Constitution specifies that the House may impeach for "treason, bribery or other high crimes and misdemeanors." Whether the meaning of "high crimes and misdemeanors" is to be narrowly interpreted, whether the actions of persons responsible to the President justify his impeachment (Nixon argued they did not), and whether Congress can impeach for purely political or partisan reasons (as was probably true in Johnson's impeachment) are unresolved questions that most probably only Congress itself can answer.

The Nixon case indicates that impeachment is a realistic weapon in controlling the abuse of presidential power. However, it cannot prevent either the exercise of presidential power or its growth, if such actions do not go beyond acceptable legal and personal behavior. The great powers and resources that the President derives from the Constitution and the statutes are not without other important limits, of course. The President cannot force solutions unacceptable to other sources of power in the system; and it sometimes seems that his responsibilities are too great for the resources granted him. However, he has other powers than those outlined in the Constitution; these are based on interpretations of presidential authority by incumbents and by the courts, and the development of the office by custom and usage. Although the Constitution draws seemingly distinct boundaries between the symbolic, administrative, strategic, international, and legislative dimensions of the Presidency, the

President can coalesce these forces when he chooses to act. The "seamless unity" uncovered by students of the Presidency makes distinctions of this kind meaningless (Rossiter, 1960, p. 41).

Administrative leadership

The constitutional mandate that the President faithfully execute the laws is a responsibility that is often difficult to meet. His administrative subordinates, legally subject to presidential control, often operate outside it; many of his orders therefore fail to elicit an obedient response and his line of command is often tenuous. Louis Koenig, a frequent contributor to literature on the Presidency, distinguishes between an "imagined Presidency," which is vested in our minds with more power than the President really has, and the "real Presidency," which is "what the Presidency effectively is in the present, what it can do in a given situation" (Koenig, 1975, p. 3).

As leader of the administrative bureaucracy, the President must consolidate policy activity taking place in thousands of administrative units around the nation and involving three million civilian employees. Programs range from efforts to alleviate poverty to confining criminals in federal prisons. In 1800, nonmilitary federal employees numbered around 3,000; when the Capitol was moved in that year to the District of Columbia, the complete files of the executive branch were shipped in seven packing cases. In 1977, about 5,000 people worked in President Carter's Executive Office alone, only one of hundreds of agencies. Directing, controlling, and coordinating the executive branch of government as well as responsibility for anything that goes wrong with it, constitutionally fall to the President.

POWER TO APPOINT AND REMOVE

How much control over the bureaucracy does the President's power of appointment and removal give him? The Constitution and statutes grant him broad appointment power, subject to Senate approval. He appoints high-ranking officials such as department heads, executive office personnel, and members of regulatory agencies. But more than 90 percent of federal employees are under the merit system of the Civil Service, which establishes entrance requirements, conditions of work, and grounds for dismissal.

The Constitution says nothing about his removing executive branch officers and employees, but the Supreme Court has ruled that his removal power extends to all "purely executive officials"; it does not include members of quasi-judicial or quasi-legislative agencies such as the Interstate Commerce Commission, delegated by Congress to carry out duties not a part of the executive function.

Despite his legal authority to hire and fire, the President is under strong political restrictions in exercising that authority. One study of how sub-Cabinet officials are appointed observes that "practice and expediency dictate that presidential control over appointments has to be shared with others who also have a stake in the administrative branch of government." In choosing appointees for important posts, the President cannot ignore party leaders, members of Congress, interest group representatives, and agency and department heads. Appointments to high executive posts may be exchanged for political support of major groups or in payment for political debts incurred during a campaign.

Political considerations similarly limit the President's power to fire. J. Edgar Hoover's position as chief of the FBI was impregnable for many years because of his strong support from Congress and the public. The political cost of removing an official such as Mr. Hoover, even after he passed the age of retirement, was greater than any President was willing to pay. By removing important appointees a President may lose support for his programs. "The ends of bureaucratic control and of acquiring political support are often mutually exclusive" (McConnell, 1967, p. 58).

MANAGING THE EXECUTIVE BRANCH:
THE EXECUTIVE OFFICE OF THE PRESIDENT

A President cannot possibly meet all the demands made on his time and resources. He is responsible for the activities of an immense bureaucracy, yet there is little chance that he can fully control it. Direction of the executive branch thus depends upon his ability and capacity to provide general administrative directions, set an overall tone for his administration, and compose a staff to assist him in formulating, articulating, defining, and achieving his program and goals (see Figure 11.1).

George Washington had one full-time aide, his nephew, who was paid out of Washington's own pocket. Nineteenth-century Presidents had few aides, and even in the twentieth century, Woodrow Wilson was said to have typed his own speeches. But in 1937 a Presidential Committee on Administrative Management studying the executive branch characterized the problem bluntly: "The President needs help. His immediate staff assistance is inadequate." At the urging of President Roosevelt, Congress passed the Reorganization Act of 1939. Roosevelt used the authority granted by this legislation to create the Executive Office of the President (EOP), a unit that consisted of five major offices designed to assist him in managing his administration and policymaking. By executive order, subsequent Presidents have increased or reduced the number of EOP subunits, but it remains the center of executive branch management. President Carter reorganized the EOP in 1977, reducing

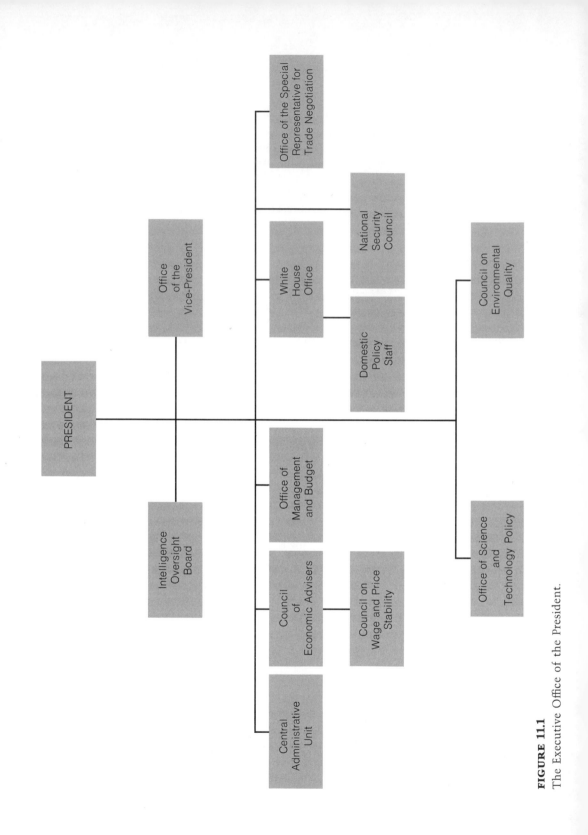

FIGURE 11.1
The Executive Office of the President.

the number of units from 17 to 12 and the number of full-time staff from 485 to 351.

Included in the Executive Office are the Vice-President's Office, the White House Office, the Office of Management and Budget, the Council of Economic Advisers, and seven other units.

The office of management and budget

The budget not only represents the President's overall program for action; it is also a key instrument for controlling and coordinating the administrative structure. The chief executive exercises these controls through the Office of Management and Budget (OBM), one of the most powerful units in the Executive Office. Created by President Nixon in 1970, the OMB was the successor to the Bureau of the Budget which had been created by the Budget and Accounting Act of 1921 and transferred to the Executive Office from the Treasury Department in 1939. The director of the OMB advises the President on budgetary matters and reviews the budget requests of agencies to determine if they are consistent with the program and spending objectives of the President. The OMB also clears and coordinates legislative proposals coming from executive branch agencies. Responsibilities in evaluating programs and reviewing the organizational structure and management of the Executive Branch augment the OMB's broad functions of management and coordination.

From Harry Truman to the present, Presidents have used the OMB (or its predecessors) as a crucial arm of executive policymaking. Truman had his budget director prepare an integrated legislative program, and succeeding Presidents have all utilized the office in a similar way. The OMB's review of budget requests is an invaluable aid in coordinating administrative interests and programs. The office thus provides a centralizing influence to counter the separation built into the semiautonomous policy coalitions that form around executive bureaus and congressional committees.

The President must share with Congress the power to shape policy through the purse strings. Presidents can propose budgets, but only Congress can appropriate funds. As a result, executive agencies are not easily subjected to control by the OMB. Any agency will respond most readily to the institutional device best able to control its economic life. Through budgetary control the President can vitally affect an agency's growth, programs, and importance in relation to the goals and priorities of other agencies. Yet in reviewing the President's proposed budget, Congress can restore to an agency what has been lost at the executive stage of the budgetary process. Agencies with strong supportive clientele, especially if that clientele is influential in many states and districts, will receive support from congressional representatives responsive to constituent interests. Because the OMB wants to retain control over executive agencies, it will attempt to win congressional endorsement of its recommendations for the various agencies or at least to prevent Congress from increasing recommended spending. The political effect of this orientation is that politically strong agencies can "force" the OMB to endorse their requests, but politically weaker units are heavily dependent on the OMB because they lack access to congressional appropriations subcommittees. A President may therefore find it almost impossible to control the expansion of agency programs he believes are less important to his goals; he may also find it hard to muster congressional support for programs he considers very important.

Mindful of the efforts of the OMB to reduce and control the semiautonomous policy coalitions that form around executive bureaus and congressional committees, congressional leaders have periodically charged the OMB with attempting to obstruct policy innovation within executive agencies. Moreover, Congress has reacted strongly against presidential strategy to undo the policy choices of Congress by refusing to authorize the spending of funds appropriated by Congress. For example, Congress complained in 1971 that the Nixon administration's refusal to spend $13 billion for domestic programs (the funds had been impounded by President Nixon) violated the principle of separation of powers. Members of Congress felt, and a series of 1973 court decisions tended to confirm, that impoundment—a practice also used by previous Presidents—negated or modified laws of Congress. Congress also responded by passing legislation in 1974 that requires congressional review of a President's proposals to delay or cancel spending. If a President wishes simply to delay spending until a later date, he may do so provided that either the Senate of the House does not overturn the decision. Presidential proposals to not spend funds at all must be approved by both houses within 45 days. It would appear that Congress did not react to the impoundment of funds for reasons of managerial efficiency; rather, the issue was over control of policy, that is, Presidential refusal to spend funds for programs he disapproved. Whether the 1974 legislation will seriously affect the President's powers of the budget is not clear. Early indications are that it may generate a mountain of paper work, made necessary by the requirement to submit all spending delays or cancellations to Congress for review, even those involving only a few thousand dollars.

Presidential control of the budget is thus limited by the realities of competing political forces, but his power to reward and punish or to support or not support programs assures substantial compliance by administrative agencies with OMB decisions.

The White House office

As the complexity and size of the bureaucracy have increased, problems of administration have also intensified. Confronted by difficult issues but limited in power by the decentralized and fractured nature of American policy processes, Presidents have had to rely on close and trusted aides to help them formulate their responses to issues, get information, communicate with the public, and keep the bureaucratic structure moving in desired directions. Although a President may include other persons, in or outside government, in his "inner circle," the staff of the White House Office provides not only close aides but also a host of other services that make his job manageable. The appointment secretary, press secretary, special assistants for foreign and domestic affairs, speech writers, legislative liaison staff, and other specialized personnel work here. Unlike Cabinet members and other political appointees, White House staff are chosen for their ability and loyalty to the President. They are his "team" and serve him alone.

The influence of White House staff has increased substantially in the contemporary Presidency, probably because Presidents since Franklin Roosevelt have come to depend on staff as their eyes and ears in understanding, anticipating, and acting upon the environment of leadership. But Presidents have reacted differently to organizational needs. Bringing different expectations and experience to his job, and possessing different personal traits, each President has a different style of management. Richard Neustadt compared the styles of the five presidents preceding Richard Nixon and found that "no continuity of pattern, no stability of doctrine, and precious little lore survives from one administration to the next . . ." (Neustadt, 1976, p. 59).

Franklin Roosevelt preferred informality to tight organizational patterns, a style also preferred by John F. Kennedy. Roosevelt deliberately created situations in which one adviser was pitted against another, a device that FDR felt maximized his opportunities for information and influence. By contrast, Dwight Eisenhower brought the hierarchical pattern of his military background to the White house, choosing to allow key staff members wide authority to handle all but the most important policy matters. President Truman was attracted to the sharp organizational lines of a hierarchically organized staff, yet his frequent alteration of procedures created a Roosevelt-like informality in his staff relationships. Kennedy designated policy assignments to several different key staff members, preferring not to be constrained by a closely organized staff chain of command. During the first two years of his administration Lyndon Johnson accepted a pattern of organization that allowed wide access to him, but increasing problems associated with his Vietnam policy led to an organizational pattern that made the President less accessible and staff lines more rigid.

The power given by President Nixon to two of his aides, John Erlichman and H. R. Haldeman, established a pattern that invited and encouraged the Watergate cover-up. As chief of staff, Haldeman screened virtually anything of importance before it reached the President. Having reduced experienced staff to lesser roles (Erlichman and Haldeman had no previous Washington experience), Nixon became increasingly isolated; by shutting out advice from experienced Washington hands that could have prevented grievous errors in judgment, he encouraged a trail of cover-up laid on cover-up. The result politically destroyed not only the President but also those around him. Erlich-man and Haldeman, 13 other lesser White House aides, and 4 Cabinet officials were ultimately indicted. Seventeen were convicted, a staggering statistic that helps explain the growing concern over the power of the Presidency.

The Executive Office of the President was created for the purpose of giving the President tools to manage and control the executive branch. In a very real sense its organization reflects presidential style, showing how he wishes to manage the problems he faces and the manner in which he prefers to reach his choice among alternatives. The number of units in the EOP and the number of staff are less important than *how* they function. The team's access to the President (open or restricted); the scope and format of the information the President receives, including the presentation of controversial views; and the organization that directs staff activities are all crucial elements in the "how" of administration. The style of a Johnson, a Nixon, a Ford, or a Carter varies according to personality, perceptions of how to achieve organizational control, policy priorities, and experience prior to, and in, office. Formal reorganization may not be necessary to effect their ends, although some Presidents believe it is. A President utilizes staff, advice, organizational change, and other adminis-trative directives to gain and retain control.

To alter structure is to change points of influence and power. As James W. Davis writes:

> To organize means to allocate power and responsibility and to reorganize means to change the existing pattern of allocation. Certainly, just who exercises power may have little to do with who has what powers on paper. But even though there have been weak or ineffective Presidents, no one would argue that the formal powers of the President are meaningless. Formal powers give the man who has them an advantage in seeking actual power. They provide stepping stones to actual power. (1970, p. 196)

Clearly, organizational and political conflict are reflected in structure. On the one hand, an administrator may find that the prospect of losing his authority or influence because of organizational change is an incentive to comply with presidential wishes. On the other hand, congressional, bureaucratic, party, and private interests always scrutinize proposals for organizational change or shifts in personnel heading major offices and agencies to discover what effect the moves will have on their goals and policy preferences. Considering potential gains and losses for his goals, a President seeks to achieve command over the administrative structure.

THE CABINET

The Cabinet developed as an extraconstitutional body to "consult" with the President. Some Presidents have treated it as an important policymaking body;

others have used it as a means of gathering information by means of reports, discussions, and debates on major issues. The common view that the Cabinet is the nation's board of directors or the President's major source of advice on policy formulation is mistaken. Twenty years ago Richard F. Fenno concluded that the Cabinet does not coordinate relations between executive departments and that it is an ineffective forum for "well-informed, well-organized discussion of policy alternatives." Its principal uses include advising the President and serving as a sounding board for the variety of alternatives suggested by competing interests (Fenno, 1959, p. 20). The role of the Cabinet has remained basically unchanged since Fenno wrote.

From George Washington's presidency to the present, the Cabinet has never been a major policymaking body. Some Presidents have given it greater importance than others, but none have utilized it as a closely knit policy group. President Eisenhower took the role of his Cabinet more seriously than any President in the twentieth century, holding frequent meetings to discuss matters of great importance, but the Cabinet did not decide policy.

Thomas E. Cronin offers a useful classification for understanding the role of the contemporary Cabinet. He differentiates the "inner" and the "outer" Cabinet. The inner cabinet includes the four Cabinet secretaries—State, Defense, Treasury, Justice—who carry broad and high priority responsibilities. These four department heads hold a special relationship to the President as counselors. Other Cabinet departments—Interior; Health, Education, and Welfare; Labor; Agriculture; Commerce; Housing and Urban Development; and Transportation—constitute the outer cabinet. They "deal with strongly organized and more particularistic clientele, an involvement that helps to produce an advocate or adversary relationship to the White House." In selecting the heads of inner cabinet departments, the President frequently uses the same criterion as in selecting White House aides: personal loyalty to the President. Considerations of political, racial, ethnic, and geographical balance influence the selection of outer cabinet members. Because these departments are particularly susceptible to pressures from the clientele and interests they serve as well as from congressional committees who deal with policy associated with departmental functions, their loyalty to the President is less strong or reliable (Cronin, 1975, pp. 188–192).

Jimmy Carter's selection of his Cabinet fit Cronin's classification. He named life-time associate and friend Griffin Bell as his Attorney General; a weapons scientist and experienced national security policy expert, Harold Brown, as Secretary of Defense; a highly respected finance and banking expert, W. Morris Blumenthal, as Treasury Secretary; and Cyrus Vance, an experienced foreign-affairs expert, as Secretary of State. A new Department of Energy was created by Congress in 1977; its first head, James Schlesinger, was already a close adviser to President Carter and thus may be included as part of his "inner" cabinet. Carter's "outer" cabinet appointments reflected attention to geographical, racial, and interest-group considerations: He named a Black woman to head HUD; a woman educator with business associations to head Commerce; a conservationist to head Interior; an economist with appeal to organized labor for Secretary of Labor; and a congressman and farmer as Secretary of Agriculture.

Writers on the Presidency frequently stress the need to revitalize the Cabinet as a management arm of the Presidency. Some also argue that a strengthened Cabinet would provide a check on the abuses of presidential power by bringing highly talented persons to the administration of the executive branch. Appointments based on appeals to geographic, racial, or political interests would be displaced by appointments based on merit in which ability would be the sole criterion of choice. Presumably, cabinet members chosen in this manner would be of high caliber and would also have the strength of character and the stature to speak out against any efforts a President might make to go beyond his powers. Whatever the appeal of this argument, it is doubtful that the pluralistic pulls of American politics will permit either an early or an easy change in traditional patterns of selection. Moreover, it is not likely that the Cabinet will ever be able to function as a collective body with collective responsibility. As the head of a major executive department, each Cabinet member inevitably concentrates on the special needs and quasiautonomous politics of his own department. The Secretary of a "service" department, such as Commerce, Labor, or Agriculture, is caught among conflicting interests. His departmental bureaucracy and the outside interests his department serves expect him to represent them, but the President expects him (according to the model of collective Cabinet responsibility) to rise above such parochialism. If he comes too close to the latter, he will alienate his own constituency and soon become an ineffective department head. No occupant of the White House could bear such a cost. Little wonder, then, that Presidents are both unable and unwilling to rely on the Cabinet, and instead selectively use individual Cabinet members and a variety of non-Cabinet personnel for continuing advice and counsel.

Leadership in military affairs

COMMANDER IN CHIEF

The Constitution names the President "Commander in Chief of the Army and Navy . . . and of the Militia of the several states, when called into the actual Service of the United States." May he, then, employ armed forces whenever he wishes? Although Congress alone is constitutionally empowered to declare war, the President may precipitate conflict by using troops, leaving Congress no choice but to appropriate funds to bring the conflict to a successful conclusion. In 1907, when relations with Japan were strained, Theodore Roosevelt ordered the navy to sail around the world to show our peaceful intentions and to assert the right of the American Navy to sail in Pacific waters. Roosevelt had funds enough for only half the trip, so Congress was forced to appropriate money to bring the fleet home.

American involvements abroad since the end of World War II have raised more serious questions about the extent of the President's powers as Commander in Chief. Since that war ended, no American military involvement has been based on a formal declaration of war. Presidents have acted either when authorized by congressional resolutions to use troops if necessary or on their own initiative. Using the argument that Russia and China had violated post–World War II agreements on Korea, and supported by a United Nations resolution, President Truman ordered troops to defend South Korea. A congressional resolution empowered President Kennedy to take military action in the Cuban missile crisis in 1962. But President Eisenhower sent troops to Lebanon in 1958 and President Johnson sent troops to the Dominican Republic in 1965, both on their own authority, with the justification that such action was necessary to prevent communist takeovers.

Johnson relied heavily upon the congressional action embodied in the Gulf of Tonkin Resolution to expand American action in the Vietnam war. Following two incidents involving the alleged attack by North Vietnamese naval craft on U.S. destroyers, Congress declared that the U.S. "is prepared, as the President determines, to take all necessary steps, including the use of armed force" to defend the "freedom" of any member nation included in the Southeast Asia Collective Defense Treaty.

Public and congressional dissatisfaction with the war brought Congress to try to control presidential actions involving the United States in armed conflicts. In the early 1970s it became increasingly apparent that the administration had passed on to Congress and the public distorted information concerning incidents in the Gulf of Tonkin and had even omitted some information entirely. Had the full and accurate story been reported to Congress in 1964, it might well have acted differently; at least the opposition to the Gulf of Tonkin Resolution would have been considerably greater. Senator William Fulbright and others charged that the President had turned the Resolution into an authorization for a major war, contrary to the intentions and the expectations of Congress. The term "credibility gap" was widely used by the press to refer to the Johnson administration's deceptiveness and sometimes deliberate manipulations in reporting the continued prosecution of the war. As public support declined— from 48 percent in 1965 to 36 percent in favor immediately after a major North Vietnamese offensive in 1968—Johnson did alter the course of continued escalation. He restricted bombing of North Vietnam and refused the urgings of the military to commit 200,000 more troops to the conflict. He also announced that he would not seek another term in office.

Congressional efforts to restrict the discretionary powers of the President to use of armed forces arose not only because of opposition to the Vietnam war but also because of concern over the power of the President to commit the nation to conflict without congressional approval. Congress repealed the Gulf of Tonkin Resolution in 1971, but Nixon indicated that the Resolution was not the basis for American intervention anyway—he justified the action on the basis of other American commitments to defend Southeast Asian nations and the President's constitutional power as Commander in Chief. Congress also threatened, with very little success, to use its appropriations power to control the use of American troops overseas. After Nixon ordered American troops into Cambodia in April 1970, both houses approved a measure forbidding expenditures to support these operations after July 1, 1970. The troops were withdrawn by that date, so the effectiveness of such legislative power remained untested.

The War Powers Act of 1973 reflects the effort of Congress to gain some measure of control over presidential use of troops. Passed over President Nixon's veto, the Act provides that, lacking a declaration of war, the President must notify Congress within 48 hours following emergency military action. Combat must end within 60 days unless Congress approves it, or Congress may order immediate withdrawal of troops. Despite such legislation, President Ford ordered the bombing of Cambodia in 1975 in response to the seizure of an American ship, the Mayaquez. Rescue of the vessel and its crew was accomplished in a few days, thus the War Powers Act was not really tested by this incident. Further, there was virtually no congressional criticism of Ford's action, and the American public strongly supported it.

Although the unpopularity of the Vietnam war was a major policy issue, the basic constitutional issue goes deeper. How far can the President go with his power as Commander in Chief to involve the nation in war? The experience in Vietnam has sharpened congressional efforts to limit his power, but the United States is committed by treaties and other agreements to defend more than 40 nations and maintains military bases in about 30 countries. Even the constitutionality of the War Powers Act of 1973 has been questioned on grounds that Congress lacks authority to interfere with the President's constitutional power as Commander in Chief (Koenig, 1975, pp. 220–221). And, as a practical matter, can troops really be withdrawn once they have been committed by the President? One student of executive-congressional relations has pointed out that legislative action aimed at checking the President is either unlikely or ineffective during crises (Burns, 1972, pp. 169–170), because the public will tend to rally around the President, the focal point of the political system.

Wartime emergency powers

As a strategic commander in time of war, the President has authority to do much more than issue military orders. Presidents Wilson and Franklin Roosevelt extended wartime controls over the American economy, the labor force, and transportation, and approved government seizure of strike-bound or strike-threatened plants and industries. In February 1942, the army, acting in the name of the Commander in Chief, evacuated 100,000 Japanese-Americans from areas in three west coast states and part of Arizona on the grounds that a danger of espionage and sabotage existed. This action must be considered one of the most deplorable deprivations of civil liberties in American history.

During the Civil War, President Lincoln combined the powers of Commander in Chief with his constitutional duty to faithfully execute the laws and formulated the "war power" with which he justified unprecedented measures, including suspension of the writ of habeas corpus in designated areas and the spending of unauthorized funds from the federal treasury. Moreover, using powers granted under Article II and by congressional statute, Presidents since Lincoln have been able to use force to compel compliance with federal law and to prevent domestic disorder and violence. In 1894, Grover Cleveland broke the Pullman strike by ordering federal troops to protect the movement of the United States mails. Both Presidents Eisenhower and Kennedy used federal troops to quell disorders arising from resistance to court orders to integrate public schools.

Although the courts have recognized and upheld presidential "emergency powers" in wartime, the Supreme Court in *Youngstown Sheet and Tube Co.* v. *Sawyer* (1952) denied President Truman's assertion that "inherent" emergency powers of the presidency justified his seizure of the steel mills to avoid a crippling strike. How well does this decision fit the realities of cold war politics? Because twentieth-century life has been one long crisis in which foreign and domestic problems are closely related, permissible action by a President probably hinges more upon circumstances than upon legal distinctions under the Constitution. Increased concern over the exercise of presidential power in general and the experience of Vietnam in particular, have heightened congressional and public sensitivity to presidential assertions of authority. The scope of his prerogatives in future emergency situations will depend upon both the particular circumstances and the limitations imposed on presidential discretion by the current political environment.

International leadership

The increasing involvement of the United States in world affairs during this century and the grave risks inherent in foreign policy decisions in the nuclear age place the President in a crucial position as an international leader. He cannot avoid the task.

FORMAL LIMITATIONS ON CONTROL OVER FOREIGN AFFAIRS

President Truman affirmed presidential dominance of foreign affairs when he said in 1948, "I make American foreign policy." In 1799, John Marshall, then a member of the House of Representatives, described the Presidency as "the sole organ of the nation in its external relations, and its sole representative with foreign nations." Marshall's statement accurately describes the President's role. The Supreme Court has repeatedly affirmed his primacy in foreign affairs. In a 1936 decision, *U.S.* v. *Curtis-Wright Export Corporation*, Justice George Sutherland commented that the President has not only specific constitutional and statutory authority in these matters but also "the very delicate plenary and exclusive power of the President as the sole organ of the federal government in the field of international relations."

The President has the top job in foreign affairs because he is Commander in Chief and has constitutional authority to make treaties, appoint diplomatic representatives, and recognize foreign governments. Checks on these formal powers are not very significant. The Senate must confirm his major appointments and the House retains the power of the purse. Congress may also pass laws that affect foreign policy.

These checks have not substantially interfered with presidential actions. Although the Senate may withhold or qualify its concurrence in treaties, it has ratified without change about 80 percent of more than 1200 proposed treaties since 1789. It has completely rejected only 11. The most famous was the Treaty of Versailles, rejected in 1920 mostly because of fears about United States entry into the League of Nations. The Senate may alter or amend provisions of proposed treaties, thus requiring resubmission to other parties to the agreement. It has taken many actions in this capacity since the end of World War II. For example, in 1946 the Senate added reservations to its approval of United States participation in the International Court of Justice.

In 1978, the Senate debated the Panama Canal treaties for 38 days, making this the longest treaty debate since that over the Versailles treaty. The treaties won approval by a one-vote margin only after the Senate inserted a reservation giving the United States the right to intervene to insure that the Panama Canal remains "open, neutral, secure, and accessible." Panama will become the owner and operator of the Canal in the year 2000.

The *executive agreement* provides Presidents a means to conclude agreements with foreign nations without consulting Congress. Based on his authority as Chief of State and Commander in Chief, or upon statutory authority granted by Congress, the President can conclude agreements with other nations which, because they are not classified as treaties, do not require the concurrence of either house of Congress. The vast majority of executive agreements have pertained to routine matters such as postal agreements or the settlement of private claims against another government, but some have been major foreign policy decisions. In 1940, President Franklin Roosevelt used the executive agreement to transfer 50 United States destroyers to Great Britain in exchange for long-term naval bases on British territory. American participation in a number of international associations is also based upon executive agreements. Over 7,800 executive agreements were concluded between 1789 and 1974, more than 80 percent of these since World War II.

During the late 1960s President Nixon reached agreements with several foreign nations about the use of military bases and other commitments that were not made public until 1972. Reacting to these disclosures, Congress enacted legislation in 1972 that requires the Secretary of State to file with Congress within 60 days copies of any executive agreements concluded by the President. Further efforts by Congress to require congressional approval of executive agreements have been strongly resisted by the executive branch on grounds that such approval would infringe upon the President's constitutional authority in the area of foreign affairs and adversely affect his ability to negotiate with other nations. Although Congress has not succeeded in requiring its concurrence with executive agreements, its efforts in this direction illustrate a growing unwillingness to allow the President to operate in the field of foreign affairs without the restraints of greater legislative surveillance.

Since World War II, large appropriations for foreign aid and defense have increased the President's power of the purse. Presidents have defended requests for foreign aid, consisting primarily of economic and military assistance programs, as "essential" to American foreign policy. Congress has supported these requests but not without close scrutiny. The President must mobilize bipartisan support for foreign aid and military appropriations by bargaining with powerful members of Congress.

FOREIGN POLICYMAKING: THE POLITICAL CONTEXT

The President's political importance in foreign affairs overshadows his formal, legal status as chief arbiter of foreign policy. Pursuit of the "national interest" sets the tone for his leadership, more so here than in domestic policy. His control of information and communications with other nations and his symbolic position as representative of the nation enable him to define the "national interest" for both the nation and the international community. By recognizing the President as the sole spokesman of American interests, other nations enable him to set the pattern of foreign policy at home. He is *the* authoritative spokesman for the nation, a position that assures his status as the initiator of foreign policy and the person who sets the agenda for debate in Congress and the community.

Developments over the past two decades, especially in relation to the Vietnam war, have clearly shown that the presidential role in foreign affairs is limited more by the realities of political relationships than by constitutional restraints. Legal challenges to continued prosecution of the war met with no success in the courts, but determined congressional and public opposition ultimately forced the withdrawal of American forces from Vietnam. Indeed,

President Johnson's inability to achieve consensus in support of his Vietnam policies was a crucial factor in his decision not to seek reelection in 1968.

When a President defines the "national interest," he must do no more than the community will accept. Through his control of information he can significantly influence public attitudes, but he does not always succeed. President Roosevelt tried in the late 1930s to get American opinion to support the British against Nazi Germany, but he failed to overcome strong isolationist sentiments throughout the nation. Only the Japanese attack on Pearl Harbor in 1941 solidified public opinion behind American military involvement against both Japan and Germany. Revelations that the Johnson Administration distorted and withheld information concerning the Vietnam conflict—presumably to defuse opposition and strengthen existing public support—destroyed the credibility of the President's efforts. It is doubtful whether any President can involve the nation in future conflicts without careful assessment of public attitudes and without building and maintaining congressional support through consultation with key leaders.

Each President inherits his predecessors' policies and finds that changing their direction is a very difficult and slow process. Commitments made to other nations are not easily broken. Dwight Eisenhower's campaign promise in 1952 to shift American policy from "negative" containment of communist advances to "positive" emphasis on the "liberation" of areas behind the iron curtain failed to materialize. President Nixon's visit to the People's Republic of China in 1972, aimed at reducing tensions between the two nations, was carefully reported by the White House to avoid suggesting that America was abandoning its support of Taiwan.

President Truman's remark "I make foreign policy" is, then, still an accurate statement of the presidential role, if the political limits of his choices are understood. The President will be effective in foreign affairs, as in his other duties, only if he gets and keeps the support of many interests. Congress has control of appropriations, the power to investigate, and the right to criticize and thereby commands the President's respect as he chooses between alternatives. The chief executive must also weigh the opinions of other national leaders—friendly, unfriendly, or neutral—in assessing American goals and actions in international matters. He deals with international treaty organizations—the North American Treaty Organization, the Southeast Asia Treaty Organization, and the United Nations—and he heads a nation whose domestic programs are closely related to foreign affairs. Economic or social crises at home may shake the confidence leaders of other nations have in his ability to lead the free world. Conversely, whatever he does in exercising his international leadership may well affect his ability to maintain his support at home.

The President's alternatives in dealing with other nations are conditioned by long-standing domestic ideology as well as by public opinion. The American experience has produced ideological public support for political and moral ideals based on liberal democratic concepts such as the right to self-government and basic individual rights and freedoms. Americans have felt comfortable in claiming leadership of the "free world" and in accepting a foreign policy aimed at combating communism. Although American involvement in Southeast Asia was defended as an obligation to meet our "moral commitments" to noncommunist nations, *opposition* to this involvement was based on the belief that traditional American democratic and moral values were being ignored.

Further public disapproval of tactics emerged when a 1975 Senate investigation revealed that the Central Intelligence Agency had been involved in assassination attempts against five foreign leaders in South American and Africa. Moreover, after failing to prevent the 1970 election of Marxist Salvatore Allende as President of Chile, the CIA was implicated in the military coup that overthrew Allende in 1973. The generally negative public reaction to these revelations indicated that anticommunism does not excuse tactics that violate American moral and political values. Although Americans remain anticommunist, the Vietnam experience and the revelations of CIA activities impose limitations on the extent to which Presidents may use American power abroad.

Just how public opinion reacts to foreign policy decisions and issues is difficult to assess. The general public's views on international affairs are generally less firm than on domestic issues and the public vacillates between total apathy and intense but often short-term interest. Only 20 to 30 percent of Americans surveyed are classified as "attentive," meaning well-informed, articulate, and interested (Rainey, 1975, pp. 83–85). Gabriel Almond has found, however, that the public as a whole has a foreign policy "mood"; that is, a combination of very general attitudes or predispositions (Almond, 1950, pp. 26–28). The predominantly isolationist mood in the 1930s, the fear and hostility toward communism in the 1950s, and the thawing of cold war attitudes during the 1970s have certainly limited the policy alternatives available to Presidents. The scope of public involvement in foreign affairs enlarges during crises and tends to produce opinion consensus, a fact that also reduces the options available to the President.

Managing all these interests and arriving at a long-range foreign policy depend more on a President's ability to persuade and to bargain than on his ability to command a course of action. Above all, his control over the nation's foreign affairs is political, not constitutional.

Legislative leadership

The President gets his power in legislative affairs more from the evolving political scope of his office than from constitutional grants. Article II enjoins him to provide Congress with information in a State of the Union Address and special messages, authorizes him to call special sessions of Congress "on extraordinary occasions," and permits him to set an adjournment date when-ever the two houses cannot agree on one. He also has the power to veto legislation. Within ten days of receiving a bill, he may sign it into law, allow it to become law without his signature, or return it to Congress with a message stating his reasons for vetoing it. If Congress adjourns within the ten days, he may exercise the so-called pocket veto by simply failing to sign the bill. (Congress cannot override this type of veto by a two-thirds vote of both houses.) From Washington through Gerald Ford, Presidents have vetoed 2,342 bills, over half of these since Franklin Roosevelt's administration. Congress has succeeded in overriding less than 4 percent of all vetoes since Washington, and the record of overrides from Roosevelt onward is even poorer than that (*Congressional Quarterly's Guide to Congress*, 1976, p. 628). We do not know how many times a presidential *threat* of veto has prevented congressional action on legislation, but this threat has often induced Congress to comply with presidential wishes.

Formal powers do not, however, indicate the scope of presidential influence in legislative matters. That influence has been formed by the development of the office, especially during this century, and by the inability of Congress to operate as a major initiating force for policy change. Speaking and acting as representatives of a national constituency, Presidents have seized the initiative in proposing legislative policy and focusing national attention on their legisla-tive programs. Woodrow Wilson broke tradition by delivering a special message asking for currency-reform legislation. Franklin D. Roosevelt responded to the economic depression of the 1930s by proposing sweeping changes in social and economic policy, which Congress enacted with record speed. The concept of an official presidential legislative program was developed during the Roosevelt administration and institutionalized when President Truman established a legislative liaison office in the Executive Office. Every president has a legislative program which is the object of countless articles by journalists and commen-tators. In short, the President is the "chief legislator" in the American system.

Legislative leadership is not synonymous with dominance of Congress. The "box scores" of congressional approval of legislative requests by the President show that Congress frequently does not give him what he wants. Of the five Presidents between 1954 and 1976, only Eisenhower (1954) and Johnson (1964–1968) were able to get more than 50 percent of their legislative requests enacted, and both experienced declines in their congressional support scores in later years of their terms. In 1971 President Nixon achieved the least success (20 percent) of any President during this period.

High scores do not reveal the accommodations and compromises forced upon a President by the political environment. In fact, the President may decide not to propose a piece of legislation at all, because he knows that he cannot win approval for it. Or he may postpone a legislative recommendation until the time is more propitious to success or make neccessary concessions to congressional and other interests before submitting the recommendation. Further, much of the President's program may not be initiated or formulated in the White House, contrary to widely held beliefs that Congress simply responds to legislative programs initiated and written in the White House. Presidents expand upon or modify the policies of previous Presidents, support the traditional priorities of their party, and claim as part of their program congressional proposals that have drawn interest and support within and outside Congress. Political scientist James L. Sundquist's study of President Kennedy's legislative program shows that Kennedy drew substantially upon programs the Democratic party had formulated during the eight years preceding his administration (1968, pp. 412–416). A study of Johnson's Great Society program also shows that Congress played a significant role in initiating, formulating, and publicizing proposals that were subsequently incorporated in Johnson's legislative proposals (Price, 1972).

The President's prestige and powers of persuasion, his sense of knowing when to act, and his formal powers as chief executive all enhance his role as the primary influence in the legislative process. But the institutional, social, and constitutional pluralism of the system limit his authority. Congress is not only jealous of its constitutional mandate to legislate but is less willing now than in previous decades to follow presidential initiatives. Presidents must therefore bargain within these limits; their success depends on their tactics and the strength of their party in Congress.

Partisan leadership

Unlike his other leadership responsibilities, the President's leadership of his political party is not imposed by the Constitution. Political parties were the conscious creations of such politicians as Hamilton, Madison, and Jefferson and they were designed specifically to support presidential efforts of command and persuasion. Yet the organization of American parties does not accommodate a direct line of command. The national chairman and national committees remain relatively inactive between presidential campaigns; their role is largely to build support for the party in presidential elections. Further, the decentralization of the party structure among fifty state and countless local party organizations, each structured around state and local campaigns for office, prohibits presidential command of party leaders. The growth of the primary election as a nominating mechanism has also contributed to the inability of the President to influence the choice of his party's congressional candidates. The attempt by Franklin Roosevelt in 1938 to prevent the nomination of Democratic congressmen who opposed his program not only failed but also set a strong precedent for future Presidents not to attempt such direct interference.

If the President's role as chief of his party does not stem from organizational command, what is the major source of his leadership? Lacking a national organization to define party policy and programs and decentralized in structure, the two national parties are divided by issues largely defined and symbolized by the President. The actions and programs of Jimmy Carter define the Democratic party at the national level for the electorate. He cannot command his party's members of Congress to support his program, but the fact that he symbolizes his party in the minds of the electorate substantially means that he can define his party's position on issues. Congressional representatives may and often do disagree with specific aspects of a President's program but there is no dispute over his role as party chief. A popular President can help elect a congressperson, a governor, or a mayor; an unpopular chief can diminish candidates' chances of winning.

Finally, the same decentralized party structure that limits the command function of the President in relation to his party also enhances it. Controls on a President are difficult to impose when no alternative force for party leadership exists. His fate is therefore very much the fate of the national party.

PARTISANSHIP AND PRESIDENTIAL GOALS

A President can carry out his foreign or domestic programs only if he wins and keeps the support of the coalition that elected him to office. His party's nationwide success depends on the quality of his leadership and the support his programs get in Congress and the electorate. A highly popular President is a distinct asset to party candidates at other levels, and party fortunes rise and fall with his success. Thus, congressional representatives of his party have a significant stake in strengthening the public's favorable image of the President; it is a good way of improving their own chances of electoral success.

A President wields partisan controls of his own, some overt and others created by changing patterns in party politics that enhance his bargaining position. The overt type stems from the President's power to dispense patronage and political favors of all kinds. The second type results from the strategic power of the President as the national leader. The nationalization of politics is reflected in the presidential technique of appealing to the public at large to mobilize opinion on behalf of his program and to pressure members of both parties in Congress. Thus, presidential leadership can counteract the localism of legislators and the recalcitrance of local party leaders and organizations.

The President has yet another resource for exercising party leadership: the "presidential party," the group of people who help him shape and execute his program. Its nucleus is usually made up of the President's staff and several Cabinet heads, most of whom have been highly active in his nomination and campaign efforts. Members of Franklin Roosevelt's "brain trust" occupied key positions in his administration and helped to formulate New Deal policy. Lyndon Johnson surrounded himself with advisers and Cabinet members sympathetic to his Great Society program. President Carter brought with him to the White House close associates who had served in his administration when he was Governor of Georgia and who composed the core of his presidential campaign staff; a few close advisers, such as James Schlesinger, had substantial experience in previous administrations.

As we have noted, because the political party the President leads is fragmented in organization and leadership, his ability to provide direction for the congressional party and command support from it is limited. Legislative alignments typically reflect party lines and presidential partisanship, but they do so imperfectly, so that it is commonplace for some legislators of the President's party to refuse to vote for some of his major programs. Legislators have found their problems with their local constituency modified, but by no means displaced, by the nationalizing trend in politics.

To get his programs through, a President often has to depend on the votes of opposition party members in Congress. If he appears to be an extreme partisan, he risks solidifying the opposition and defeating his program. When he does pursue partisan ends, he is expected to refrain from putting too much pressure on his own party's congressional representatives and to recognize that congressional constituency interests must sometimes be given preference over presidential demands.

The President, in short, must balance the interests of the major party groups that make demands upon him. He must satisfy interests both as party leader and as President of all the people. He cannot look like a blind partisan who seeks narrow goals, nor can he be indifferent to partisan demands. He must adjust his use of the great resources available to him to the decentralized and diverse American party system, but he must also keep the support of the coalition of voter groups that put him into office.

Conceptions of the presidency

SOME PRESIDENTIAL VIEWS

The President who is aware of the varied and conflicting demands made upon him considers those demands in the light of his own image of the office. Richard Neustadt, adviser to Presidents and student of presidential politics, identifies five major presidential constituencies, each of which makes different claims upon the President's time, energy, and influence: the administrative bureaucracy, Congress, fellow partisans, the general citizenry, and foreign groups. Each depends on him for benefits but does not always support him in exchange. His bureaucratic clients and congressional allies have their own constituencies and interests to represent. The demands his partisan friends present are usually narrower than he can accept without compromise. Community leaders may go somewhere other than Washington for help. And, Neustadt concludes, "friends abroad are not compelled to run in our elections" (Neustadt, 1976, p. 76). Each President must define his own part in our diversified political community. In building support for a policy that reflects his own goals, he gradually moves closer to some constituents while alienating others. He will respond to some community conflicts and pay little attention to others. Many of the pressures he encounters are of his own making to the extent that, in defining his role, he chooses the areas of conflict from which demands will come.

Knowing what he ought to do and can do depends on the President's concept of the office. Professor Corwin, describing the background of the presidency as "a history of aggrandizement," shows how the office developed under five major personalities: Jackson, Lincoln, Wilson, and the two Roosevelts. These men all used well a keen sense of history, circumstances, and timing to achieve their goals; and each had a clear idea of the presidential role. Theodore Roosevelt's theory of presidential powers provides a useful description of the "strong" President; he called it the "residuum of powers" theory.

> I insisted upon the theory that the executive power was limited only by specific restrictions and prohibitions appearing in the Constitution or imposed by Congress under its Constitutional powers. My view was that every executive officer, and above all, every executive officer in high position, was a steward of the people bound actively and affirmatively to do all he could for the people, and not content himself with the negative merit of keeping his talents undamaged in a napkin. I did not care a rap for the mere form and show of power; I cared immensely for the use that could be made of the substance. (T. Roosevelt, 1946, p. 35)

President Hoover's contrasting approach was more in harmony with strict constitutional edict. Although he modified his views toward the end of his term, Hoover's style reflected a strong moral and legal commitment to formal limits on power, buttressed by an equally strong belief in "American individualism." He felt that the "executive" must not encroach on the "independence of the legislative army," and he confessed that he had "little taste for forcing Congressional action or engaging in battles of criticism" (Hoover, 1952, p. 217). Although he exercised the veto, he disapproved of using it to defeat congressional will or to force legislative action into desired channels; rather, he used the veto to protect the fundamentals of the Constitution.

Hoover's perspective and that of Franklin Roosevelt contrast strikingly. Roosevelt believed that a President must be "alert and sensitive to change." He forcefully used the prerogatives and prestige of the Presidency to lead the nation to ends he thought desirable. Roosevelt's biographers have agreed that he thoroughly enjoyed exercising leadership. According to Neustadt, "he saw the job of being President as being F.D.R. He wanted mastery, projected that desire on the office, and fulfilled it there with every sign of feeling he had come into his own" (1976, p. 230).

President Kennedy brought to the White House a firm conviction that the Presidency is the focal point of the political system. He cited Lincoln, Jackson, Wilson, Truman, and both Roosevelts as models of what the Presidency should be. Recognizing early in his term that the powers of the Presidency were limited, he generally followed a policy of persuasion rather than pressure in his dealings with Congress.

Lyndon Johnson's long service in Congress and his experience as Senate majority leader provided him with a background of skills and experience that he readily used as President. Early in his administration he stressed the need and displayed the techniques for obtaining consensus; this approach led him to emphasize a highly personalized Presidency in which competing interests were balanced in order to achieve the widest possible support for policies. The Vietnam debate brought out another side of Johnson. As criticism against his policies mounted, he refused to confront adverse opinion, publicly holding to the position that the President must act in the best interests of the nation even in the face of mounting popular belief to the contrary. Unable to unify the nation around the continuing pursuit of the war, Johnson chose to retire rather than seek another term.

The style of Jimmy Carter was slow to become clear. He carefully chose key members of his Cabinet and announced that he intended to rely heavily on the Cabinet in matters of general administration and would not permit the White House staff to run the departments. Carter also announced that Vice-President Walter Mondale would be his "top staff person," an unusual and probably unprecedented role for a Vice-President. However, this designation of Mondale's role did not mean that Carter assigned him a status similar to that of Haldeman in the Nixon administration. In fact, Mondale has not emerged as a Vice-President with a role uniquely different from that of his predecessors.

T. M. Simpson carefully studied Carter's style as Governor of Georgia and predicted that Carter's style as President would follow somewhat similar patterns. Possessing an enormous span of attention to the work of departments, Carter preferred "a circle of assistance" to "points of influence" in his Georgia administration. Simpson thus projected that Carter would not permit small cliques, coalitions or party and interest group leaders, or even the Georgians he brought with him to the White House to monopolize his attention. Department heads would run their own departments, stimulated and directed by the President through the OMB (Simpson, 1977).

A full assessment of Carter's style must await completion of at least his first term in office, but he has so far left considerable administrative discretion to department heads. Believing that the proper timing of legislative proposals and open relations with Congress are more productive than a politics of executive-legislative confrontation, Carter has also carefully cultivated good relations with Congress. No single adviser has emerged as a dominant force in the Executive Office, a pattern consistent with Carter's policy as Governor. Like other Presidents, Carter is a complex personality whose view of the Presidency will take on sharper focus in the years ahead.

PRESIDENTIAL PERSONALITY

Recent studies of the Presidency have analyzed the relationship between the personality and behavior of various Presidents. Our understanding of the strengths and weaknesses of a President should be enhanced by any insight into the way in which he relates to his constituency, advisers, critics, and others. Probably the best known of such studies is James Barber's *The Presidential Character* (1972). Barber classifies Presidential personalities and styles into four categories: active-positive; active-negative; passive-positive; passive-negative. The active-positive President shows "confidence, flexibility, and a focus on producing results through rational mastery." Active-negative executives "emphasize ambitious striving, aggressiveness, and the focus on the struggle for power against a hostile environment." The passive-positive personality is a "receptive, compliant, other directed" person who enjoys the routines of his office but is filled with inner doubt. The fourth type, the passive-negative President, tends to become frustrated with the duties of office, to be inactive, and "to withdraw from conflict and uncertainty." Under Barber's classification, Harry Truman was an active-positive President, Wilson, Hoover, Johnson, and Nixon were active-negative presidential personalities; and Dwight Eisenhower displayed passive-negative qualities. Although no past Presidents exactly fit any one category, Barber's analysis points to tendencies that bear upon broad behavior and increase our understanding of why a President may have acted as he did in a particular instance. Herbert Hoover's almost unyielding defense of his noninterference economic policies in the early years of the depression and Lyndon Johnson's refusal to listen to advice contrary to his Vietnam war policies might have been rooted in their personality traits and style (active-negative). Response to events, public opinion, and other aspects of the political process are therefore important in evaluating the overall effectiveness of Presidents as leaders. Of equal concern are questions related to personality traits that encourage Presidents to be open, tolerant, and democratic in responding to crises. Whether or not Nixon's response to Watergate could have been predicted (as Barber suggests), questions regarding the linkage of personality and performance in office do have a significant bearing on the achievement of democratic goals in a political system heavily influenced by the power of the Presidency.

The President and policy choices

Whether a President is thrust into policy conflict by force of circumstance or whether he deliberately initiates policy disputes, he "must always be setting priorities and measuring costs" (Sorenson, 1963, p. 28). His choices are limited by the resources he can command as opposed to those of the interests in conflict. The decision he finally makes will be based on the data he has, immeasurable factors such as hunches, and sheer conviction that one alternative is "right" and others "wrong."

FLOW OF INFORMATION AND POLICY CHOICE

As representative of all the people, a President must be sensitive to demands that reach the White House from all sectors of the electorate. But the breadth of the interests that seek access to him means that a policy acceptable to some groups will be anathema to others; these may seek access to policymaking through Congress or the courts and sometimes get there what a reluctant or opposing President has refused to give. In short, the President's power to initiate policy is no guarantee that he will have his way.

A President is not master of all around him. He depends on those closest to him for information and advice; and although he can seek it whenever he wishes, both time and his style of leadership limit how far he can go in search of information. Moreover, the President communicates information as well as receiving it. How he communicates, to whom, and when are of great importance. His decisions, reflecting broad or particular interests, can produce confidence and support among other decisionmakers and the public.

Many people thought of the Pentagon Papers controversy of 1971 as a crisis of confidence, because the information revealed by these documents raised questions about where several Presidents had gotten their advice, how much information had been kept from Congress and the public, and whether Congress and the President had been deliberately deceived. Although a President must make choices, he does so in part as a leader limited by both the need to decide and the isolation resulting from dependency on those with whom he chooses to consult. The Pentagon Papers controversy also revealed the potential hazards faced by a President who ignores the public's right to know by withholding or distorting information of critical importance.

SOURCES OF INFORMATION AND POLICY CHOICE

Pressure groups seldom present their goals and demands directly to the President. He listens carefully to selected legislators, especially those in key positions, and to Cabinet heads and other major executive officials, who may act as a channel for various social interests. Party leaders and the press also provide contacts for the President and put pressure on him too.

Conflicts may arise within the President's own circle of advisers or within the bureaucracy, forcing him to decide between the interests represented. The State and Treasury Departments sometimes fundamentally disagree on the proper approach to world trade; the Defense Department and the State Department may see matters affecting foreign policy quite differently; and the Agriculture Department and the Bureau of the Budget may look on farm subsidy programs from entirely different perspectives. The President must bridge all such conflicts, which extend far beyond the boundaries of the administrative hierarchy to interest groups at all levels of the political structure.

Presidential decisionmaking is continuous, ranging from the routine to decisions carrying profound consequences. Some are "programmed" in that they cannot be avoided or delayed, such as nominations of Supreme Court justices, Cabinet officers, and other officials. The schedules for preparing and presenting the budget and the State of the Union Address are fixed by the Constitution and statutes. But most decisions are not on this kind of timetable. Some are initiated by the President himself: President Kennedy pressed the attack on poverty during the campaign of 1960 and proposed extensive legislation to deal with it after he entered the White House. Others are responses to situations that demand immediate action, such as Kennedy's threat to bomb or invade Cuba when the Soviet Union established missile bases there in 1962. President Carter entered office in the midst of a serious fuel shortage brought on by the hard winter of 1977. The closing of schools and industries because of lack of heating fuel highlighted the need for a long-range federal energy policy. Carter's response, which necessarily required complicated and far-reaching proposals to deal with energy problems, forced the formulation of major legislation within only a few months. Subsequent criticism by members of Congress, environmentalists, and other interest groups that some of the President's proposals were not well thought through before submission to Congress shows that preferred time tables do not always fit the demands for action. The President does not have a free choice in selecting the conflicts that he will attend to nor can he avoid acting upon them.

The vice-presidency

Many political observers consider the office of Vice-President to be superfluous. The first occupant of the office, John Adams, called it the "most insignificant office that ever the invention of man contrived." John Nance Garner, Vice-President during Franklin Roosevelt's first term described the office with the ascerbic comment that the position "isn't worth a pitcher of warm spit." Yet this is the same office that is "a heartbeat away from the Presidency." In all, 9 Vice-Presidents have succeeded to the Presidency, 8 because the President died and 1 (Gerald Ford) because the President resigned. Six of the last 14 Vice-Presidents have become President. Why then have we paid relatively little attention to the choice of vice-presidential candidates and why have Vice-Presidents played such insignificant roles in the administrations of Presidents?

The answers to these questions lie in the nature of the American party system and in the status of the duties assigned to the office under the Constitution. The Vice-President was an early victim of the American party system. By the early 1800s, vice-presidential candidates were selected less for their presidential potential than for their usefulness in winning sectional or factional support for the presidential candidate. John Nance Garner was chosen by FDR as his 1932 running mate as part of a bargain to win the support of the Texas and California delegations for his nomination as presidential candidate. John Kennedy chose Lyndon Johnson in 1960 to counter the opposition of the South to a liberal Northern Catholic. Walter Mondale was named Jimmy Carter's running mate because, among the other qualities he possessed, he was a midwesterner and a popular figure with liberal elements in the Democratic party. Richard Nixon hardly knew Spiro Agnew in 1968 but selected him because Agnew could provide geographical balance to the ticket.

The resignation from the Democratic ticket of vice-presidential candidate Thomas Eagleton in 1972 after revelations that he had been treated for mental illness, and the resignation of Vice-President Spiro Agnew in 1973 after disclosures of income tax evasion placed greater attention on the process by which vice-presidential candidates are chosen. Carter engaged in a long deliberate process before selecting Walter Mondale as his running mate and President Ford employed a long investigative process before selecting Robert Dole. Yet a major contender for the Republican presidential nomination, Ronald Reagan, announced his vice-presidential selection in advance of the Republican convention in order to win support from moderate Republicans for the nomination. Reagan's action shows that the traditional pattern of haste in selecting a running mate has not been laid to rest even though Ford and Carter have established a precedent for more careful examination of the qualifications of vice-presidential nominees in the future.

Constitutionally, the job of the Vice-President is to preside over the Senate, a far less significant role than the speakership of the House of Representatives. Other than to be available in the event of the death, resignation, disability, or removal of the President, the Vice-President has no assigned Constitutional duties. The Twenty-fifth Amendment (1967) established procedures under which the President is empowered to name a Vice-President, subject to majority approval of both Houses of Congress, if that office becomes vacant. Gerald Ford and Nelson Rockefeller both became Vice-President through this procedure.

Historically, Presidents have infrequently given their Vice-Presidents a significant role. Franklin Roosevelt delegated considerable authority to Vice-President Henry Wallace for a short period during war, but removed the responsibilities when Wallace clashed with several department heads. Eisenhower sent Richard Nixon on important foreign-policy missions, and Lyndon Johnson was appointed chairman of President Kennedy's Committee on Equal Employment Opportunities, which increased his contacts with Black interests and enhanced his political image with minority groups. Nixon used Vice-President Agnew as a purely partisan tool in attacking the press and critics of Nixon's policies. Because the Vice-President can do little by himself to develop his importance, he depends on the President to determine the meaningfulness, if any, of his role. President Carter announced prior to his inauguration that Vice-President Mondale's role "will be unprecedented in American history for a Vice-President. I look on [him] as my top staff person." Mondale was given wide responsibilities in the administration, including a special role in relations between Congress and the White House, but as we have indicated, his role has not been truly different from that of previous active Vice-Presidents.

In Paul David's phrase, the "life of the Crown Prince is likely to be hard" (1967, p. 74). The political aspirations of a Vice-President in the second term of a President may be bouyed by the prospect of winning the presidential nomination for himself, but the possibility of developing his own image outside the President's shadow is not great. Lyndon Johnson's characterization of the Vice-President's role remains accurate: "He's in a difficult place. He has no troops; he has no real power; he's at the mercy of the President."

Closer public attention to the need for parties to nominate highly qualified vice-presidential candidates and the increased stature of some recent Vice-Presidents have enhanced the office, but it nevertheless remains captive to the Presidency. There has been more discussion of the Vice-Presidency in recent years than ever before, with the greatest attention being paid to strengthening the office through better selection procedures for vice-presidential candidates. Presumably, if the presidential candidate were to select a running mate before the presidential primaries, the caliber of the choice would be higher. Some critics of the present selection system point out that choosing a vice-presidential nominee immediately after the nomination of the presidential candidate prevents careful consideration of qualifications and encourages selection for purely political reasons. Others have urged that the office of Vice-President be abolished and in the event of a vacancy in the Presidency a special election be held to choose a new President (Schlesinger, 1973, pp. 493–494). A constitutional amendment to effect such a change is highly improbable. Whatever upgrading of the office is to be achieved rests largely with the President, because the Vice-Presidency is a "visible, vulnerable, and for the most part powerless" office (Polsby, 1974, p. 159).

Is the Presidency too powerful?

Watergate and the Nixon Presidency focused attention on the power of the Presidency to a greater extent than at any time in modern history. Until the 1960s most scholars viewed the rise of strong Presidents as both desirable and necessary to meet the needs of a crisis-prone and increasingly complex political system. They argued that only the Presidency could provide the focus of leadership and organization for action needed to respond to new and pressing demands in the political system. The "strong" Presidencies of the two Roosevelts, Harry Truman, and John Kennedy were favorably compared to the "weak" Presidencies of Harding, Coolidge, Hoover, and even Eisenhower. Generally, sympathies for a strong Presidency followed partisan lines: Liberal Democrats welcomed the growth in presidential power, and conservative Republicans decried the record of growth illustrated by Franklin Roosevelt's 13 years in office. Watergate and Vietnam forced supporters of a strong Presidency to reappraise their position. One of these, Arthur Schlesinger, termed the office the "imperial Presidency," marked particularly by almost unlimited power in foreign affairs and possessing resources in all areas so far superior to other institutions as to pose a serious danger to the principles of democratic government itself (Schlesinger, 1973).

Presidential power did not, of course, begin with Johnson and Nixon. It developed and grew as a twentieth-century response to social, economic, and political forces. Presidents such as Franklin Roosevelt used the resources at their command to fashion a leadership role that reduced Congress to more of a reactive than an active agent in the initiation and formulation of policy. Further, the constitutional authority granted to the President in foreign affairs and the broad nature of his "executive power" in domestic matters have clearly been supplemented by the impact of the personalities who have occupied the office. Presidents who sought to develop and expand their role have generally succeeded; those who viewed the Presidency in narrower terms were "weaker" political men.

The late 1960s and the 1970s have been marked by congressional efforts to impose controls on presidential power in both foreign and domestic affairs. Supported by a broad range of forces—academic, public interest groups, and public opinion—Congress has succeeded in forcing the President to recognize the need for closer consultation with the legislature in formulating broad policy. Nevertheless, the Presidency is a powerful office because there is no alternative to it. As long as Americans look to the President for leadership, and because it is unlikely that either Congress or the courts can provide an alternative focus for policy initiation, the President will remain the dominant force in the American system.

congress and
the adoption
of policy

It has been commonplace to criticize Congress as unresponsive to majority preferences, incapable of responding to new needs, dominated by the President, and too restricted by its rules and procedures to become an effective and efficient branch of government. Supporters of a strong Presidency used the weaknesses of Congress to defend the growth of presidential power in a world where crises, especially in foreign relations, frequently confronted the nation.

As the dangers of a powerful Presidency were revealed in Watergate and the conduct of the war in Vietnam, attention turned to the role of the legislative branch in the system of checks and balances. The near impeachment of President Nixon, the reclaiming of the congressional role in foreign affairs, efforts to establish a congressional budgetary process independent of the executive budget, and reforms of congressional procedures all signal an improvement in the image of Congress in the eyes of its critics. Whether the legislative branch will be able to reclaim a stronger role in policymaking is an open question. In this chapter we will examine the structure, procedures, and functions of Congress, which define its role in the representation and resolution of conflict in the American system.

Neither the President nor Congress makes decisions independently of other forces in the political system. Public policy is a continuing series of decisions, an interplay of interests operating inside and among the three branches. Throughout the system, both formal and informal power relationships reflect the pluralism of the American structure and sustain bargaining and compromise among conflicting social interests. This interaction is nowhere better illustrated than in the functioning of the legislature.

The authority of Congress

Legislatures and representation are closely linked in democratic theory. The Framers of the Constitution provided for an executive removed from the direct control of the people and a judiciary that would be independent and insulated. Congress, the most representative branch within the constitutional structure, was to be the major institutional symbol of the democratic creed.

Congress gives legitimacy to public policy by passing bills and carrying out its other legislative functions of representation, control, oversight, and so forth. Part of the executive's role in adjudicating disputes is based on authority granted by Congress. The President's power to initiate the national budget is based on the Budget and Accounting Act of 1921; the independent regulatory agencies in the administrative branch make rules under authority granted by Congress; and the right of courts to hear appeals is to a large extent based on congressional action creating appellate courts and regulating their jurisdiction.

FORMAL POWERS

Article I, Section 8 of the Constitution gives Congress broad legislative authority to raise and support an army and navy, tax and spend for the general welfare, borrow money, regulate commerce, coin money, establish courts, declare war, establish post offices, and govern the capital district. This section also contains the "necessary and proper" clause, which laid the basis for the doctrine of implied powers that John Marshall voiced in *McCulloch* v. *Maryland*. We have seen in Chapter 3 how this doctrine became the foundation for the extension of national legislative authority into almost every corner of community affairs.

The power of Congress is nevertheless limited by the working principle of balanced government. The presidential veto and judicial review are major potential limitations. The separation-of-powers doctrine also prohibits legislative encroachment on the jurisdiction of the other two branches by limiting the legislative matters that Congress may delegate to administrative or judicial agencies. Finally, eight *specific* limitations are imposed by Article I, Section 9 of the Constitution: Two are of minor importance; four limit the taxing and appropriations powers; and two—prohibiting bills of attainder and ex post facto laws and limiting suspension of the writ of habeas corpus—are protections of individual rights. Individual rights and liberties are more completely protected against legislative violation by the Bill of Rights: The First Amendment prohibits Congress from abridging the rights of free speech, freedom of the press, assembly, petition, and the free exercise of religion.

Four other constitutional provisions govern legislative authority. Congress may propose constitutional amendments by a two-thirds vote in both houses and may admit new states to the Union. Its power to investigate and hold hearings enables the legislature to educate and inform the public, as well as itself, on social and economic problems and other important public matters. It also has an elective function: if no candidate wins a majority of electoral votes, the House selects the President from among the leading three candidates and the Senate selects the Vice-President from among the top two candidates. Vacancies in the office of Vice-President are filled by nomination of the President and confirmation by a majority vote of both houses of Congress.

CONTROLLING ITS OWN HOUSE: DISQUALIFICATION, CENSURE, EXPULSION

The Constitution specifies the minimum qualifications of members of Congress: minimum age (30 in the Senate, 25 in the House); United States citizenship (at least seven years for the House and nine years for the Senate); residency in the state from which a Senator or Representative is elected; and the holding of no other "Office under the United States" during service as a member of Congress. Under the last provision, a congressman would be required to resign his seat if he were appointed to a position in the executive or judicial branches.

Article I grants each house the power to "be judge of the elections, returns, and qualifications of its Members," and to "punish its Members for disorderly behavior and with the concurrence of two thirds, expel a Member."

Qualifications of members

Until at least 1969, Congress apparently assumed that its power to judge the qualifications of its members extended to the right to add qualifications beyond those specified in the Constitution. Since 1789, 14 Senators-elect and 31 Representatives-elect have been challenged as unqualified to serve. Of these, the Senate has voted to exclude 3 (the last in 1867) and the House has excluded 10, 4 since 1900. Grounds for denying a seat have included failure to meet the constitutional requirements on citizenship, age, or residence as well as such matters as misconduct before election, polygamy (Mormons in the nineteenth century), and charges of sedition.

The House denied Representative Adam Clayton Powell his seat after his reelection in 1966 on grounds that he had misused both committee funds and his power as chairman of the Education and Labor Committee. However, the Supreme Court upheld Powell's claim that Congress lacked the power to refuse him his seat, because he met the age, citizenship, and residency requirements. The Court ruled that the courts may intervene if Congress imposes qualifications beyond those listed in the Constitution (*Powell* v. *McCormick*, 1969). This decision raises doubts as to whether Congress may exclude a properly elected person who meets minimum constitutional qualifications, regardless of whether he or she meets expected moral or political norms for membership. Nonetheless, the decision may not prevent a future confrontation between the Supreme Court and a Congress determined to have its way.

Censure and expulsion

For serious offenses, each house of Congress can impose censure or expel a member. Since 1789, 18 representatives and 7 senators have been censured. Most recently, Senator Joseph McCarthy was censured in 1954 for his conduct in investigating an alleged "communist conspiracy," and Senator Joseph Dodd of Connecticut was censured in 1967 for misconduct in diverting campaign funds to his own use.

Expulsions are rare: Only 18 members of Congress have ever been expelled and all but one (in 1797) were southern congressmen expelled in the early 1860s for their support of secession from the Union.

THE FUNCTIONS OF CONGRESS

Legislation

The principal function of Congress is to legislate. Legislation is a process characterized by defined procedures and formal and informal relationships of power among the three branches of government as well as between Congress and private interests. The structural setting within which legislation is enacted plays an important role in defining the way conflicts are managed and resolved.

Representation

Much legislative activity does not directly concern the passage of bills. Three other important functions of Congress can be identified. When a member of Congress votes on legislation, that action is "representative" of interests in the political community. Although his or her vote is supportive of some interests and not supportive of others, it is nevertheless an act that represents broad opinion on issues. Members of Congress perform the representative function in other ways as well. When they mediate conflicts between the bureaucracy and their constituents they are performing a representative function. Assisting a constituent in establishing eligibility for veterans benefits, aiding a business executive with a problem related to a regulatory agency, or offering assistance in obtaining information about a federal program are all forms of representation. In providing such services, which are sometimes referred to as "errand boy" activities, a congressperson helps to bring government closer to the people, make it more understandable, and generate support for public policies.

Imparting legitimacy

Related to the representative role is a third function: legitimizing the policies of the national government. The procedures and rules under which policy decisions are made help to build public consensus on the legitimacy of policy choices. Decisions are made within the context of conflict and compromise between competing interests. An environment in which differences can be debated and many groups can be heard serves to reinforce public acceptance of policies. This is not to say that all interests are equally represented or that all groups possess equal resources to pursue their influence. Most policies reflect an accommodation between dominant interests; yet because the minority can make its voice heard and thereby influence the shape of policy, public consensus can evolve and conflict can be managed.

Control and oversight

A fourth function of Congress is the *control* and *oversight* of bureaucracy. Legislative control refers to actions that *precede* administrative activity, including instructions from the legislature regulating agency practices and the consideration of administrative proposals for approval or veto. Legislative oversight takes place *after* administrative action has occurred. Some forms of oversight are committee reports criticizing the operation of an agency, full-scale investigations of a particular policy or the operations of an agency, and the cutting of appropriations to indicate disapproval of agency actions. Recent congressional investigations into such areas as campaign finance, energy pricing and distribution policies, concentration of economic power, and the operations of the Central Intelligence Agency reveal the scope of the oversight functions of Congress.

To say that Congress can exercise control and oversight over administration is not to say that it can effectively regulate it. As the most representative branch in the system, its claim—on the basis of both constitutional and democratic principles—to have a voice in the policies and operations of the administrative branch can hardly be contested. How it should exercise its legitimate role in this regard is, however, a matter for debate. Whether Congress is equipped in available time, information, organization, and procedures to do more than deal in broad policy areas is questionable.

Patterns of representation

BIAS IN CONGRESSIONAL REPRESENTATION

No method for apportioning representatives is neutral; any arrangement will favor some interests and slight others. Our discussion of political participation and influence in previous chapters has revealed that the level and nature of political interest, skills, and resources varies widely among the electorate; money, education, social standing, and position skew political influence in the direction of the "haves" and reduce access to decisionmakers for the "have-nots" in the system. The structural features of representation under the Constitution are thus only one element in developing an understanding of the full meaning of "to represent."

The federal bargain of 1787 provided for representation by states in the Senate and by population in the House of Representatives. Behind this bargain lay an assumption that the interests of the majority of the people in all the states were different from the more particular interests of the people in each of the states. The Senate and House were designed to balance the interests of different sets of people. Overlapping six-year terms for Senators (one-third elected each two years) and indirect election by state legislatures were meant to be a conservative check on the popularly elected House. All members in the House would reflect the popular will more directly. The Seventeenth Amendment, ratified in 1913, finally provided for the direct election of Senators, but the Senate remained the more conservative body through the 1930s. Then, from World War II until the mid-1960s the House took on the more conservative image. Legislative proposals on federal aid to education, aid to economically depressed areas, housing, and unemployment were more likely to receive favorable treatment in the Senate. However, the solid opposition of Southern Senators, aided by the filibuster, made the Senate the more conservative body in civil rights (Froman, 1963, pp. 71–84). The Senate's willingness to look more favorably on social legislation was probably a function of differences between House and Senate constituencies. Urban residents now make up about 75 percent of the total U.S. population; although reapportionment of House districts and the trend toward urbanization have probably made both houses of Congress more receptive to federal social programs, Senate constituencies reflect a larger number of social interests than the more homogeneous constituencies of House districts.

The differences between constituencies also show up in the degree of competitiveness of House and Senate elections. Table 12.1 illustrates the pattern of competition in the 1976 elections to the House. More than one-half of the seats in the House were won by candidates who received 65 percent or more of the total vote. Less than one-third of the House elections were lost by candidates receiving 40 percent or more of the vote. The large majority of House districts are therefore considered "safe" for one or the other major party. In contrast, of 33 elections to the Senate in 1976, only 6 were won with 65 percent or more of the vote. Almost two-thirds of these elections were lost by candidates who received 40 percent or more of the vote, a reversal of the pattern in House contests.

Party strength and allegiance certainly provide one explanation for the large number of "safe" seats in the House. For years Democrats have enjoyed the advantage of strong Democratic allegiance in the South and in northern central city constituencies, and Republicans have benefited from the support of traditionally Republican voters in rural districts in other parts of the nation. From 1952 to 1960, 168 House districts (two-thirds of them Democratic) were won by the same party with 60 percent or more of the vote. Only 95 of all House districts changed party representation during this period (*Congressional Quarterly Weekly Report*, March 10, 1961, pp. 1–2).

The advantages of incumbency may contribute as much to making a district safe as party affiliation. Members of Congress are rarely defeated in their efforts to win renomination in primary elections. Defeat in the general election occurs more frequently but not often. Between 1956 and 1974, only 6 percent

TABLE 12.1
Competition for House seats, 1976
(by percentage of vote of winning candidates in geographical regions)

Region*	No. of seats won by 40–49% of vote	No. of seats won by 50–54% of vote	No. of seats won by 55–59% of vote	No. of seats won by 60–64% of vote	No. of seats won by 65 + % of vote	Total seats won	Percentage of total seats in House	Percentage of all "safe" districts†
Northeast	1	10	18	14	61	104	23.9	24.5
Northcentral	1	18	16	19	67	121	27.8	26.9
South	3	18	18	11	84	134	30.8	33.7
West	3	11	16	9	37	76	17.5	14.9
Total number and percent of all seats	8(1.9%)	57(13.1%)	68(15.6%)	53(12.2%)	249(57.2%)	435	100.0%	100.0%

Northeast: Pennsylvania, New Jersey, New York, Connecticut, Rhode Island, Massachusetts, Vermont, New Hampshire, Maine. *Northcentral:* North Dakota, South Dakota, Nebraska, Kansas, Minnesota, Iowa, Missouri, Wisconsin, Illinois, Indiana, Michigan, Ohio. *South:* Arkansas, West Virginia, Maryland, Delaware, Virginia, North Carolina, Kentucky, Tennessee, South Carolina, Georgia, Florida, Alabama, Mississippi, Louisiana, Texas, Oklahoma. *West:* Washington, Oregon, Idaho, Montana, Wyoming, Colorado, Utah, Nevada, California, Arizona, New Mexico, Alaska, Hawaii.
† "Safe" districts are defined as those in which the winning candidate received at least 65 percent of the vote.

of incumbent House members lost in the general election. However, one-third of those defeated were first-term members, a figure which indicates that length of service relates to the likelihood of reelection (Jewell and Patterson, 1977, pp. 92–94).

Incumbents are better known to their constituents than their opponents, are able to build and maintain voter support by providing services, and benefit from visibility through the news media. Also, incumbents are rarely obligated to national or local party organizations for their reelection. Usually geared to their own reelection, their campaigns are organized around local coalitions built through careful attention to representing and serving local interests. Defeat may result from changes in national political trends, the redrawing of legislative districts, the popularity of the opposing party's presidential candidate which carries that party's congressional candidate into office, or a failure to attend to the needs of constituents. Nevertheless, reelection is the norm, and the longer the service the greater the advantages of incumbency. The margin of victory in an election is frequently attributable to the incumbent's own efforts, a point illustrated by the opposing party's capture of a "safe" seat when the incumbent retires (Mayhew, 1974, pp. 33–35).

The more heterogeneous and larger constituencies of senators and the more competitive nature of Senate elections reduce the advantages of incumbency in comparison with House elections. Nevertheless, studies of congressional elections during the past 30 years have shown that the importance of incumbency in both House and Senate elections has increased compared to the influence of party loyalty, national political trends, and the strength of winning presidential candidates (Cummings, 1966; Erikson, 1971; Kostroski, 1973).

What are the implications of the high rate of electoral success by incumbents? A representative or senator who has built support through careful attention to constituent interests and who relies on a campaign organization built with little help from the national party is obviously in a position to resist the pressures of congressional party leaders or a president of his or her party. The local voters and political interests that put him or her into office are his or her political lifeline, and if these interests do not coincide with party or presidential positions the congressional representative is likely to vote with his constituency.

The pattern of congressional elections also has a bearing on the nature of policy choices and change in Congress. Members of Congress able to win reelection on the basis of a proven pattern of votes and positions on issues rarely propose or support new and controversial legislation. Because the possibility of a large number of seats changing hands is small, the likelihood of a predominance of new ideas from new members that could force policy changes of a dramatic and far-reaching nature is remote. As a result, congressional agendas and procedures remain stable, producing only relatively small changes in policy over time. A significant change in party balance could, of course, quickly move Congress to make major alterations in general policy, but as in other parts of the American system, such changes are infrequent. A relatively stable Congress means that new interests or long-standing minorities have less chance of increasing their access to the legislative process. One may speculate that only strong shifts in policy preferences within the constituencies of large numbers of incumbents will significantly alter the direction of congressional policy.

Despite the "safe" nature of a majority of House districts—a pattern that has generally meant a lower rate of turnover in the House than in the Senate—recent trends indicate that the composition of both houses is changing. About half the House membership at the beginning of the 1970s had been elected during the 1960s. By 1976, 82 percent of Representatives had come to Congress since 1960; 61 percent since 1967. Fully one-third of the 1977 House were first- or second-term congresspersons. Thus a large majority were new and less committed to old methods and rules.

Lawrence Dodd and Bruce Oppenheimer compared voting patterns of House members in the 86th Congress (1959–1960) with those of members in the 94th (1975–1976) and found that there were fewer "conservative" southern Democrats in the 94th (59 percent compared to 85 percent), a change that resulted in an increase of "liberals" and "moderates" among Democrats from 64 percent in 1959 to 81 percent in 1975. The ideological pattern among Republicans remained substantially the same (about 80 percent classified as "conservative"), but the large majority of Democrats in both the 86th and 94th Congresses may anticipate a greater receptivity of the House to liberal programs in the future (Dodd and Oppenheimer, 1977, pp. 21–26).

During the same period, the Senate also moved toward a more "liberal" profile. In the 85th Congress (1957–58), 54 percent of senators were "conservative." By 1975, because of a decline in the number of conservative Republicans and southern Democrats, 45 percent of senators were classified as "liberals" and another 20 percent as "moderates." The Republicans and Democrats in the Senate both showed greater ideological heterogeneity in 1975 than they did 20 years earlier (Dodd and Oppenheimer, 1977, pp. 4–6).

LEGISLATIVE APPORTIONMENT: THE STRUGGLE FOR NUMERICAL EQUALITY

Since 1939, the 435 seats in the House have been automatically redistributed among the states according to the latest population count. The responsibility to redraw district lines has traditionally rested with state legislatures, but a few states now use special commissions to perform this task. The intent of the commission arrangement (usually a nonpartisan group) is to reduce the partisanship inherent in legislative efforts. Majority parties in state legislatures have historically drawn districts to the advantage of their party. The resulting distortions have been either unequal district populations (*malapportionment*) or strangely shaped districts (*gerrymandering*), both designed to inflate the electoral strength of the majority party in the state legislature and minimize that of the minority party. As a result of malapportionment over the past three or four decades, suburban and, to a lesser extent, urban sectors of America have been underrepresented. Rural districts, generally smaller in population, are often drawn so as to make the district "safe" for the incumbent congressperson.

In 1963 Andrew Hacker found that 41 percent of the congressional districts varied more than 15 percent from the number of people that would have been included if each state were apportioned strictly according to population (p. 104). In 1964 the United States Supreme Court ruled in *Wesberry* v. *Sanders* that wide discrepancies in the number of persons living in each congressional district violated the requirement (Article I, Section 2) that congresspersons be chosen "by the People of the several states." A 1969 Supreme Court decision, *Kirkpatrick* v. *Preisler*, declared that any variation, "no matter how small," must be justified. By 1972 the variance in population in 385 of 435 House districts was less than 1 percent from the average state district population, a sharp contrast with ten years earlier when only 9 districts deviated less than 1 percent from the state average. Although federal courts have not insisted on absolute equality among congressional districts, as late as 1973 (*White* v. *Weiser*), the Supreme Court struck down a Texas redistricting plan that varied 4.9 percent between the largest and smallest districts.

The end of malapportioned legislative districts does not, of course, insure either majority rule or an accurate reflection of party strength. Representatives are elected on the single-member district, plurality-vote system. By carefully drawing district lines, state legislatures can insure numerical equality of districts while also manipulating the electoral strength of the parties. Gerrymandering, already practiced in the eighteenth century, is the drawing of district lines by the majority party in the state legislature so as to create a maximum number of districts expected to elect candidates of that party. For example, in 1961 the North Carolina legislature drew congressional district lines in a way that forced the sole Republican congressman into an election with a strong Democratic opponent. Gerrymandering is not affected by the Supreme Court decisions on apportionment, and the Court has shown no inclination to deal with the practice.

In 1946, the South accounted for 79 percent of all "safe" Democratic party districts, but by 1964 this proportion had been reduced to only 36 percent (Wolfinger and Heifetz, 1965, p. 347). In 1976 about 33 percent of all "safe" Democratic seats in the House were held by southern representatives. We have also seen that the rate of membership turnover has increased and ideological voting patterns in the House have become more "liberal." A reduction in the number of long-tenured conservative Democrats from the South and the increasing number of newer members of Congress, many of whom represent urban interests, should produce a rise in leadership positions held by non-southern, urban-oriented, more liberal congresspersons.

Can we attribute the changes that have occurred to the end of malapportionment? Reapportionment of congressional districts has most benefited the growing suburban population, not the inner cities of metropolitan America. The social, political, and economic problems and interests of these two demographic areas are significantly different, in many respects as different as the traditional contrast between rural and urban interests. Over the past three decades the population of inner cities has shifted from a more heterogeneous pattern to one dominated by Blacks and the poor. This trend, quite independent of legal disputes over malapportioned congressional districts, has resulted in a greater number of safe, urban Democratic seats. However, political interests cannot be defined purely in terms of geographical factors. The pluralism of interests within the electorate works to define electoral cleavages along lines more complex than geography. Further, it is extremely difficult to attribute changes in the direction of public policy to alterations in the way district lines are drawn for electoral purposes. The exploitation of issues by political parties, the nationalization of issues that divide the parties, the influence of a popular or unpopular President, and the softening of regional loyalties (such as in the South) may play an equally important or greater role in determining the outcome of Congressional elections.

Political conflict and members of Congress

Members of Congress bring to their office values and attitudes acquired from many sources: their political socialization, their social and political environment. They also bring their own expectations of how a congressperson ought to behave as well as expectations about their colleagues and the public. The pattern of expectations—of others and of the individual member of Congress —define the representative's *role*.

SOCIAL BACKGROUND: WHO ARE THEY?

If representation were to be measured by the extent to which the members of the legislature are characteristic of the population at large, then Congress is clearly unrepresentative. Legally any person meeting the age, residency, and citizenship requirements under Article I of the Constitution is eligible to serve, but in practice eligibility is more narrowly defined. Members of Congress are better educated than the average American, and about three-fourths have had prior experience in public office. Commonly, 55 to 60 percent are lawyers, another 25 to 30 percent list business or banking as their profession, and the rest come from occupations such as journalism, education, and agriculture. In 1976 there were only three labor leaders in the House, none in the Senate, and no member of Congress listed the occupation of student, factory employee, secretary, common laborer, sales clerk, or any other type of employment characteristic of the population as a whole.

By age, representatives and senators are 10 to 20 years above the average age of Americans (49 in the House and 55 in the Senate in 1977). Women are in the majority in the electorate, yet in 1977 only 17 women served in the House and there were none in the Senate.

These patterns suggest that certain characteristics are necessary for success in seeking legislative office. For example, in large northern urban areas with large concentrations of Black or Catholic voters, successful candidates for House seats reflect the characteristics of these minority groups. Although senatorial constituencies are larger and include a larger number and variety of social groups, these patterns still apply. A Catholic is more likely to be elected in Massachusetts or Maryland than in Mississippi or Tennessee, which are predominantly Protestant. As Blacks enter the electorate in larger numbers in the South, it is likely that more Black candidates will be recruited and elected there.

Social background and experience also affect policy but it is difficult to determine how much. Public opinion on issues is frequently correlated with socioeconomic groups in the population but individual members of groups often deviate from majority opinion within the group (Dye, Jacob, and Vines, 1971, p. 176). Studies of the social background of decisionmakers do not justify firm statements regarding the relationship between background and decisions. The social and economic backgrounds of members of Congress make them an elite among the American population. But do they promote some interests over others because of this background? Although legislators are drawn from occupational groups particularly suited for legislative jobs, that trend does not necessarily invalidate the principle of the representative system. That parties recruit more politically active members from some social and economic groups as candidates for office does not mean that these candidates are insensitive to constituency demands. Indeed, our discussion of consensus on democratic values and practice in Chapter 2 indicated that the better-educated, higher-income, and more politically active groups in the population are the "carriers of the democratic creed."

CAREER PATTERNS AND PROFESSIONALISM IN CONGRESS

Unlike the patterns in most state legislatures, service in Congress is not a part-time job. Few state legislators pursue a career in the legislature as a full-time occupation. Legislative sessions in most states are relatively short compared to those of Congress, and in 13 states the legislature meets biennially rather than annually. Staff assistance is minimal in most states and nonexistent in some. Turnover rates of membership in state legislatures are persistently high, a pattern usually attributed primarily to low pay. By comparison, members of Congress are better paid ($57,500 per year, with future cost of living increases provided by statute); enjoy a liberal congressional pension system; receive generous budgets to hire staff ($238,584 per year in the House; $413,082 to $844,608 per year in the Senate, depending upon the size of the state population); have the franking privilege under which official mail is free; and receive special allowances for travel, telephone service, and other office expenses. The pay, perquisites, and prestige of representatives and senators is thus fully consistent with the needs of a full-time career employment.

By comparing the "pre-modern" to the "modern" Congress, Randall Ripley has traced the development of Congress from a legislative body with little sense of professionalism to the modern, professionalized, highly organized body it is today (1975, pp. 33–56). Pre-modern Congresses—from 1789 to about 1870—were characterized by short sessions and light workloads; chaotic and disorderly procedures for the conduct of business; high turnover on committees and no clear criteria for determining their membership; and a party structure marked by little formal organization or leadership, with party membership having little influence on voting behavior compared to the influence of regional or other interests. The post-1870 "modern" Congress has well-developed party structures and procedures, a clearly identified leadership structure, and is marked by heavy workloads and long sessions. From 1789 to about 1880 the average service of a representative was two years and senators averaged about four years; midterm resignations were common. Almost one-half of House members and one-third of senators in each Congress were freshmen. In contrast, modern Congresses have low turnover rates. The average number of freshmen is about 12 to 14 percent, and the average length of service of members is about 12 years in the Senate and 10 years in the House. Ripley concludes that "the modern Congress has become both professional and stable. The professionalism has allowed Congress to cope with its increasing workload and also to face the fact of a powerful executive branch in such a way as to keep a considerable amount of legislative influence" (p. 56).

THE JOB OF A CONGRESSPERSON

A member of Congress performs his or her job, not only in relation to personal goals and beliefs but also in response to other demands and interests. First, there are the demands of the legislative body itself, including rules and procedures that must be observed, norms of legislative behavior, and the patterns of legislative leadership that cannot be ignored. Second, retention in office depends on the continued support of voters, or at the very least the backing of those parts of the constituency whose support is necessary for reelection. If a member of the House is ambitious and looks to other offices such as the Senate or even the Presidency, he or she must serve a constituency and other interests that are much broader in scope and much more complex than those of his or her district. As a member of a legislative committee, a member of Congress acquires knowledge, and perhaps great expertise, in particular areas of legislative policy, yet he or she must also keep informed about other issues of concern to constituents. Service to constituents is a necessary part of maintaining good relationships with the people back home. Pressured by party, constituents, and other interests on a regular basis, a representative or senator must make choices that satisfy the expectations of not only personal values and goals but also those he is expected to serve.

WHAT INTERESTS SHOULD A CONGRESSPERSON REPRESENT?

After a meeting with President Carter to discuss support for the President's energy legislation, a freshman Democratic representative commented that he supported the President's program but was also sensitive to views of his constituents that challenged certain features of the program. The congressman had to determine how to resolve a conflict of roles. Should he respond to the desires of his constituents even though these ran contrary to those of the President or even his own? And what ought he to do if, as might very well be the case, his constituency was divided on specific energy policies?

A classic answer to the question of what interests a legislator should represent was offered in 1744 by Edmund Burke who, following his election to the British House of Commons from Bristol, told his constituents that "Parliament is a *deliberative* assembly of *one* nation, with one interest, that of the whole—where local purpose, not local prejudices, ought to guide, but the general good, resulting from the general reason of the whole. You choose a member, indeed; but when you have chosen him, he is not a member of Bristol, but he is a member of Parliament" (1886, pp. 95–96). This assertion infers that constituents may not know the legislative facts or may fail to understand them. Consequently, according to the Burkean view, the representative acting on the basis of his knowledge "represents" his constituents well even when his view is at odds with what the people in his district say they want. Where Burke emphasized conscience and independent judgment, others believe that representatives should give constituents what they want. They argue that public policy issues are rarely reducible to a "right" side and a "wrong" side that can be determined by the representative's own judgment. Thus, democratic representatives must pay special attention to the desires of their constituents; a representative may attempt to influence or change the judgments of his constituents, but he must not override them.

Which of these positions best describes how legislators see their jobs in relationship to their constituencies? In a 1959 study of the members of four state legislatures, researchers classified each legislator according to his views about how he should make decisions: The *trustee* sees himself as a free agent, "votes as he sees it" after appraising all sides of an issue, and bases his decisions on what he thinks is morally right or just. The *delegate* sees himself as a "servant of the people" and defers to the instructions of his constituents. The *politico* is more flexible in behavior, at times acting like a trustee and at others like a delegate or a combination of the two. The authors concluded that the trustee may be a "functional necessity" because modern government is so complex. People who cannot understand the problems of government are likely to entrust decisions to their better informed representatives (Eulau, Wahlke, and Buchanan, pp. 742–756). Moreover, the fact that a legislator often finds it difficult to discover what his constituents think about issues reinforces the basis for trusteeship.

How much do constituencies influence congressional behavior?

No matter how he views his proper role, a senator or representative would probably not oppose the wishes of his constituency if he were convinced that such opposition would cause his defeat in the next election. Also, a congress-person who represents a relatively homogeneous district or state tends to view issues in much the same manner as his or her constituents. Thus, because of both personal conviction and district preferences, a representative from a predominantly rural, small-town district would tend to favor agricultural policies that benefit farmers and farm-related interests. One student of Congress, Aage Clausen, suggests that constituency influences members of Congress in two general ways. First, representation "comes through the congressman's internalization of the political orientations of the constituency . . . in which he now resides and probably has resided for many years. . . . Representation . . . is involuntary in that it occurs without a conscious effort by the representative. . . . The constituency orientations are an integral part of his being." Second, constituency influence "is exerted both through the sending of signals from the constituency to the attentive congressman and through the existence of the constituency, and all its properties, as objective facts of the congressman's environment." Letters, telegrams, press comments, visits to the congressman's office are "signals" of constituent policy preferences. The constituency also

> exerts its influence by simply being there. . . . The legislator is the active agent, seeking information about changes in the constituency, utilizing information on the major societal groups (occupation, region, religion, ethnicity, race) that he has stored up during his tenure as a member and representative of his constituency—in general, making sure he understands his constituency and that it doesn't "slip away from him." (Clausen, 1969, pp. 131–133)

The links between the actual behavior of congressmen and constituency attitudes and opinions or constituency characteristics such as socioeconomic makeup are difficult to determine. Generally, districts represented by Democrats are more urban, have higher proportions of non-White voters, and have more people in the lower socioeconomic groups. Republicans tend to represent districts with suburban populations, fewer non-White voters, and citizens of a higher socioeconomic status. However, this pattern does not hold for the South, where Republican districts are more urban than those of Democrats (Flinn and Wolman, 1966; Froman, 1963; Shannon, 1968). Although differences occur within each party, Democrats are more likely than Republicans to support "liberal" policy measures in civil rights, social welfare, and government regulation of the economy. Thus there is a rough linkage between the "ideology" of members of Congress, party affiliation, and type of constituency.

In a 1969 study of 87 members of the House of Representatives, Roger Davidson found that House members from "safe" districts tended to classify themselves as "trustees" rather than as delegates by a margin of three to one. Representatives holding marginal seats were more likely to see themselves as delegates rather than as trustees (44 percent as compared to 19 percent). In addition, Davidson found that as the congressional district became more competitive between the two parties, the Representative paid more attention to issues reflecting local rather than national concerns. Members from safe districts emphasized local and national concerns about equally, paying slightly more attention to local matters (1969, pp. 117, 128, 140–141).

Systematic studies of the relationship between voter attitudes and congressional behavior are rare. Warren Miller and Donald Stokes (1963) compared the policy preferences of constituents (determined by interviews) in 116 congressional districts with the views and voting record of their representatives. The views of constituents and members of Congress correlated closely in social welfare and civil rights matters (especially civil rights), but there was a low correlation between constituency attitudes and congressional behavior in foreign policy. Despite the finding that the views of constituents and congressmen were closely related in key areas, Miller and Stokes also found that "the Representative has very imperfect information about the issue preferences of his constituency, and the constituency's awareness of the policy stands of the Representative ordinarily is slight" (p. 56).

The majority of voters are unaware of how their representatives actually vote on issues. A 1970 Gallup Poll found that less than 25 percent of constituents with incomes of less than $7,000 knew how their representative had voted on major bills, and even among those with incomes of $15,000 or more (who would also be the better educated and generally more informed politically), less than 50 percent indicated awareness. It is quite possible that even with knowledge, citizens may not really care how their congressperson votes. Like some nonvoters, they are simply uninterested. Lack of constituency interest or awareness may give members of Congress greater latitude in deciding how to vote on issues, especially in those areas where there is little voter sentiment on either side of the issue. In making his choice, the legislator may represent "what he hears from the district as he interprets it" (Dexter, 1963, p. 12). What he hears is likely to be the voices of interests with a special stake in the outcome of particular conflicts, many of which may not be salient to the majority of voters.

The extent of constituency influences on congressional behavior is difficult to determine in part because such influences are not uniform among representatives and senators. Moreover, as we have noted elsewhere in this chapter, party affiliation and other factors also play an important role, perhaps a dominant one, in the policy choices of members of Congress.

NORMS OF BEHAVIOR

Legislators pursue policy decisions according to behavioral norms set by both the public and the legislative body. The public expects a member of Congress to observe—at least openly—standards of conduct: avoiding relationships and associations that raise questions about his honesty or ability to weigh evidence impartially, defending orderly procedures so that the opposition gets its day in court, and observing generally accepted norms of personal behavior. The legislative body itself expects conformity to its informal standards of behavior. These traditions of behavior, important in both chambers, are especially so in the Senate. There they govern participation in debate, specialization in a particular area of legislative interest, the observation of rules of courtesy, loyalty to the Senate as an institution, and the serving of an "apprenticeship" before assuming full status in the Senate (Matthews, 1960). There is some evidence, however, that the "apprenticeship" norm is no longer a significant restriction on junior members in either house. Senator Robert Kennedy, already nationally known before his election to the Senate in 1964, waited six months before delivering a major address on the floor of the Senate. Even then, some of his colleagues thought he had spoken too soon. Junior senators in the 1960s (most of whom were liberal northern Democrats) came to view the apprenticeship norm as a means for senior conservative senators of both parties to dominate the Senate. As the liberal class of the 1960s acquired seniority, the apprenticeship norm assumed less importance for newly elected members. "Today, not only do junior members not want to or feel the need to serve an apprenticeship, but also the senior members do not expect them to do so. . . . The Senate of the 1970s is a more egalitarian institution when considered along seniority lines" (Ornstein, Peabody, and Rohde, 1977, p. 8).

A similar decline in the apprenticeship norm has occurred in the House. Herbert Asher's study (1973) of the attitudes of freshmen members in the 91st Congress (1969–1970) toward House norms showed that almost half rejected the apprenticeship norm. Perhaps of even greater importance to the strength of the norm itself was the finding that almost two-thirds of a sample of nonfreshmen members viewed apprenticeship as unnecessary. In fact, the more senior members of the House supported it less than incumbents with fewer years of service.

A congressperson's opinions about his job, his party's programs and proposals, and himself as a member of a congressional committee are relevant to the legislative process. Informal groups—so-called because they operate outside regular procedures—may help members of Congress to define their jobs and increase their influence in the decision processes. Informal groups have had significant success over the past 20 years in achieving their goals. The Democratic Study Group (DSG), formally organized in 1959, began as an effort by liberal members of the House to reduce the effects of the more cautious and conservative Democratic House leadership. It raised money for the campaigns of liberal Democrats in marginal districts, served as a fact-finding group, and coordinated congressional support for liberal measures (Ripley, 1967, pp. 176–179). In 1974 and 1975 the DSG led successful efforts to reduce the power of the traditional seniority system which dominated committees in the House. Similar, but smaller and less successful groups are the Republican Wednesday Club and the House Black Caucus. The Wednesday Club was formed in 1963 and includes moderate and liberal Republican members opposed to the conservative positions of their fellow Republicans. The Black Caucus, formed in 1971, works in the interest of legislation of particular benefit to low-income and minority groups.

CONGRESSIONAL ETHICS: THE SEARCH FOR ORDER IN THE HOUSE

As has been noted, Congress has always faced the question of where to draw the line between unethical conduct and proper legislative behavior. The Watergate scandals in the executive branch heightened public attention to standards of ethics for the legislative branch as well. The revelation that Representative Wayne Hays, powerful chairman of the House Administration Committee had employed his mistress, who testified "I can't type, I can't file, I can't even answer the phone," produced a furor that ultimately forced the resignation of Hays from Congress. Sex scandals involving other congressmen, congressional junkets abroad (officially labeled "fact-finding trips"), the use of congressional position for financial gains, and large campaign contributions to congressmen by corporations resulted in widespread public cynicism about the integrity of Congress itself. Throughout 1977 and 1978 both the Justice Department and congressional ethnics committees studied the operations (including cash payments to congressmen) of Korean "businessman" Tongsun Park, an apparent agent of the South Korean government.

Ethics committees to investigate the conduct of members have existed since the 1960s, but until 1977 members of Congress did little either to provide a strong code of ethics or to seriously investigate alleged abuses. Although a permanent House Committee on Standards of Official Conduct was established in 1968 the committee launched no investigation of a member until 1976.

Stung by public criticism and reacting to the scandals of 1976 and 1977, Congress adopted a new code of ethics in 1977; the code strengthened rules requiring financial disclosures of sources of income, gifts, official foreign travel, and the use of the franking privilege.

The extent to which Congress will put its houses in order probably depends upon whether public dissatisfaction with clear violations of ethical standards remains intense. A 1975 study of congressional ethics concluded that

> the atmosphere surrounding a heavily publicized scandal is conducive to the reordering of old standards; indeed it appears to be vital for such change to take place. . . . Although for the moment self-interest and political realism in the House are serving to encourage reform measures, the reverse was true in the past. In the absence of continued public pressure, the past may overtake the present again. (Beard and Horn, 1975, p. 83)

Structure and procedures of Congress

Figure 12.1 illustrates the formal process by which Congress considers bills. Thousands of bills are introduced during each session of Congress, and although only a very small number are enacted into law, each one receives consideration through some stage of the legislative process. The initial step after introduction is referral to a standing committee. Subcommittees of each standing committee sort out the bills referred to them and eliminate all but a few for further consideration. The rest are simply allowed to die. The sub-committee holds hearings on those bills that pass its initial screening.

Although the positions of various interests are frequently known in advance of hearings, controversial bills will generate testimony from interest groups, which use the opportunity to publicize their opposition or support and to mobilize support of both the group membership and the larger public. Hearings also help to identify particular wording or sections in bills that could produce problems in the administration of the legislation or that carry special conse-quences for the interests affected. During the hearings, committee members become aware of those parts of the bill that will determine its chances for success or failure, which enables them to map out the accommodations and compromises necessary for passage.

After the hearings, the committee or subcommittee considers the bill in detail (in the "mark-up" stage), deleting, amending, or rewriting as it sees fit. The final draft of the bill is voted on by the full standing committee.

If approved in committee, the bill is reported for consideration on the floor. In the House, the Rules Committee determines the conditions for debate of the bill; in the Senate, bills are scheduled for debate by the majority leader, usually in consultation with minority party leaders.

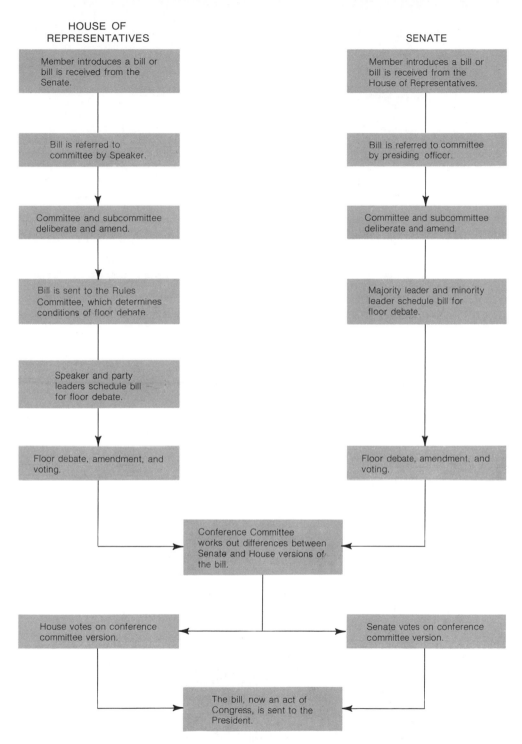

HOUSE OF REPRESENTATIVES

SENATE

Member introduces a bill or bill is received from the Senate.

Member introduces a bill or bill is received from the House of Representatives.

Bill is referred to committee by Speaker.

Bill is referred to committee by presiding officer.

Committee and subcommittee deliberate and amend.

Committee and subcommittee deliberate and amend.

Bill is sent to the Rules Committee, which determines conditions of floor debate.

Majority leader and minority leader schedule bill for floor debate.

Speaker and party leaders schedule bill for floor debate.

Floor debate, amendment, and voting.

Floor debate, amendment, and voting.

Conference Committee works out differences between Senate and House versions of the bill.

House votes on conference committee version.

Senate votes on conference committee version.

The bill, now an act of Congress, is sent to the President.

FIGURE 12.1
The Path of Major Legislation Through Congress.

CONSIDERATION ON THE FLOOR
AND FINAL PASSAGE OF BILLS

Floor debate on bills reported from standing committees in the House is rigidly controlled by time limits and other procedural rules set by the Rules Committee. However, the whole House may name itself a committee—the Committee of the Whole—whose members can discuss a proposal without being subjected to all the formal rules of parliamentary procedure. In this way, the House can reach important decisions and compromises that could not be so easily negotiated under more rigid conditions.

The smaller Senate does not have the restrictive schedules and controls of the House. Control of floor debate rests mainly with the majority leader, but he lacks the power to limit debate. Once a senator has the floor, he may talk as long as he pleases and he may yield the floor to whomever he chooses. A group of senators can prevent a bill from coming to a vote by exploiting this "free and unlimited speech" to kill time, a tactic known as the *filibuster.* As a weapon of the minority, the filibuster has had many dramatic successes, and the threat of resorting to this tactic has won many concessions from the majority. Although conservatives have frequently used the filibuster to prevent the passage of civil rights legislation, liberals have employed it too. In 1970 they used it to prevent Senate votes on the supersonic transport, and in 1972 to block passage of an antibusing bill.

It is possible to limit debate in the Senate by invoking *cloture,* otherwise known as Rule 22. Cloture restricts each senator to one hour of speech on a bill, but it must be passed by a three-fifths vote (60) of the membership of the Senate. Of 79 votes on cloture between 1960 and 1975, only 18 succeeded.

Methods of voting in Congress

Four methods of voting on measures are used in the House and three in the Senate. In the House, the *voice vote* is the most common: Members simply respond to the call for "aye" or "nay," and no individual votes are recorded. If there is doubt about the outcome of a voice vote, a *division (standing) vote* may be ordered in which members stand and are counted, but individual votes are not recorded. Standing votes may be challenged by demanding a *teller vote;* one-fifth of a quorum (44 members) must back the demand. Teller votes and *roll-call* votes are recorded by electronic voting machines. A roll-call vote is taken if one-fifth of those present demand it. Roll-call votes are recorded and published in the *Congressional Record,* the official proceedings of Congress.

The Senate uses the same voting methods as the House except for the teller vote. Roll-call votes are easier to obtain (usually by the request of one senator) and employed more often than in the House, probably because it is easier to handle roll-calls in the smaller Senate. The votes of individual senators are recorded only when roll calls are taken.

Conference committees

When the House and Senate pass a legislative proposal but disagree on some features, an ad hoc joint committee called a *conference committee* is created. Members are appointed by the presiding officers of each house and are usually drawn from the two standing committees that handled the bill on the floor. Each house may instruct its conference members. Because conference committees freely ignore the procedural rules prohibiting them from making major changes in the legislation and because their report must be voted on without change by both houses, they represent "committee power in its most concentrated form" (Gross, 1953, p. 317).

PARTY LEADERSHIP AND POLICY ADOPTION

As in elections, political parties are crucial in determining the outcome of legislative policy conflicts, but they are by no means the only elements in the policy adoption process. We have already noted that regional and local interests produce substantial differences in the policy orientations of members of the same party. The President's position on legislative issues may not be supported by a member of his party in Congress if that representative's constituency has expressed different preferences. Even within Congress, a senator and a representative of the same party from the same state may vote differently because of conflicting constituency pressures and loyalties.

Differences between the British and American systems help clarify the role of parties in policy adoption in Congress. The party that wins a majority of seats in the British House of Commons selects the prime minister, who then chooses his cabinet. The highly unified and more disciplined British party structure assures that policies proposed by the Prime Minister and his cabinet will be supported by the party's members in the House of Commons. In the highly unlikely event that a very important proposal is not supported, the cabinet resigns and new elections are held. The voting discretion of individual members of the House of Commons is thus substantially less than that of a member of Congress. Intraparty conflicts exist, but they are not usually manifest in party splits on votes in Parliament. Votes reflect differences between the majority and minority parties, not between the Prime Minister and his majority party members or between various members of the majority party. Under this system, the constituencies of all members of the House of Commons are oriented to the differences between the "in" majority party and the "out" minority party in Commons, and party candidates are elected or defeated on the basis of the policy positions of the national party organization.

Biennial American congressional elections produce a majority and a minority party, but about the only time all Republicans vote in opposition to all

Democrats is at the beginning of each session. The first item of business for each chamber is to "organize": to select the Speaker of the House, the President Pro Tempore of the Senate, and members of the standing committees. The candidates previously selected by the majority party are elected by the House, of course, and the majority party gains the chairmanship and a majority in all committees. Once the key posts are safely in the hands of the majority party, partisanship fragments.

Party leadership is crucial to the organization and functioning of the legislative process. Leaders help organize their parties in the conduct of business; among other duties, they arrange for participation in the appointment of committee members, schedule business for consideration on the House or Senate floor, and see that party members are in attendance when votes are taken on the floor. The organization of a party effort also requires the collection and distribution of information to members. Party positions on legislative issues must be communicated to party members, and there must be a formal party leadership corps through which members can express their attitudes and preferences. In addition, party leaders maintain liaison with the White House on policy matters, a function that enhances their influence over the legislative process.

In dispensing or withholding favors to members, controlling the conduct of business on the floor, and collecting and distributing information, congressional party leaders help shape the working environment of individual members. Yet their influence depends more upon their skill and ability to persuade than upon formal powers or direct commands. Lyndon Johnson, one of the most effective Senate majority leaders during his tenure in the Senate commented: "The only real power available to the leader is the power of persuasion. There is no patronage; no power to discipline; no authority to fire Senators" ("Leadership: An Interview," 1960, p. 88). Although both parties have formal party caucuses in the Senate and the House, these groups meet infrequently and rarely attempt to bind their members. Party leadership is somewhat tighter in the House than in the Senate, because the Speaker of the House has greater influence over committee assignments and over the choice of new leaders. But overall, coercion is rare, and bargaining, persuasion, and exchanges of favors are the norm.

The majority party has trouble guiding a program through Congress because congressmen in key legislative posts are often jealous of their prerogatives and responsible to neither the leadership in Congress nor influential party spokesmen outside Congress. It is very hard to weld a coalition of semi-independent congressmen, even of the same party. Further, party leaders cannot and will not insist on a legislator's support when his constituency's preferences are contrary to the party's position. All representatives understand and tolerate a legislator's defection from his party majority's vote to represent his constituency; in fact, they consider it necessary. When party leadership is effective in winning the support of party members, legislators are less likely to operate autonomously and the access of interest groups to legislative policymaking is reduced.

The elected legislator comes to Congress as a developed personality with his own personal attitudes and relationships. His social background, group associations, and convictions help define his relationship to his constituency, his relations with colleagues, and his attitudes toward the political community itself. His membership in the House or Senate adds one more group loyalty to his web of relationships. Some pressure groups have special influence because many congressmen are among their members. For example, because one-third to one-half of the members of Congress are members of the American Legion, that organization has a considerable influence on policymaking. Similarly, on the state level, it presumably helps a state's law school if a high proportion of legislators are its alumni.

Speaker of the House

The majority party in each house controls the selection of legislative officers, and each party chooses its own leaders. The presiding officer in the House, the Speaker, is more pivotal in getting policies adopted than either of his counterparts in the Senate—the Vice-President or the President Pro Tempore. During the nineteenth century, the Speaker gained almost unlimited power over House proceedings and policymaking. In 1910, his powers were severely restricted by the House so that until recently, the power of the Speaker depended heavily on the skills of the man himself (Ripley, 1967, pp. 16–24). However, in 1975 the House Democratic Caucus gave the Speaker power to appoint Democratic members of the powerful Rules Committee. The Speaker also appoints members of select committees (nonpermanent committees established for a particular purpose). The choice of other standing committee members rests with the Democratic Steering Committee and the Democratic Caucus, but the Speaker, as party leader, can exercise strong influence on the choice of committee members.

Because House leadership is diffuse, perhaps the Speaker's most important function is to facilitate the making of policy. The Speaker can use his influence to move legislation through the House by mediating between interests and between the two parties. Also, when both the President and the House are controlled by the same party, the Speaker is usually the main contact between them. This position encourages a sense of independence from the President and also builds the Speaker's prestige in the House. Sam Rayburn, who occupied the speakership for 18 years during four administrations, used the power of his position to great advantage in the formulation of legislative policy. Members who "went along" with the Speaker were rewarded with favors; Rayburn appointed to standing committees representatives who could be counted on to support his policy preferences (MacNeil, 1963, pp. 129–132).

Majority and minority leaders and party whips

The major partisan spokesmen in both houses are the majority and minority floor leaders, who are chosen by their party caucuses. They have little formal authority, but they have persuasive influence on the legislative process. The House majority floor leader works with the Speaker, the minority floor leader, and the Rules Committee to set the schedule for debate. As chief strategist and tactician, he must negotiate as well as harmonize diverse interests within his own party while cooperating with the opposition to ensure legislative action on policy proposals. Majority and minority leaders also present to the press and public their party's position on policy issues.

Party whips, or assistant floor leaders, keep party members informed of the weekly legislative schedule and see that they are on the floor for important votes. The whip cannot command members to follow the party position, but tries to persuade them to do so while communicating partisan strategy and position on specific measures.

The President as legislative party leader

The most significant unifying force in legislative party leadership is the President. Although his influence is greater when his party controls either or both houses, decentralized legislative leadership limits presidential influence under any circumstances. When the President's party is in the majority, the President speaks for his party, but he still bargains more than he commands. The pull of presidential preferences is, of course, considerably lessened when legislative control rests in the hands of the opposition party. Leadership is then scattered among several party leaders, committee chairpersons, and influential legislators, making the initiation and formulation of a distinctly "legislative" program unlikely. The scattering of legislative leadership shows even more clearly within the legislative minority party when that party does not control the Presidency. "Divided leadership hurts the minority party's functioning as an 'alternate government,' [and] is a defect in the party system that merits more attention than the absence of tight party lines on many roll-call votes" (Truman, 1959, pp. 106–116).

PARTY AFFILIATION AND VOTING BEHAVIOR

Despite other influences, party ties remain the most important factor in congressional votes. However, the influence of party varies with the policy area. A study of congressional voting from 1921 to 1964 concluded that party influence was strongest in foreign trade, health and welfare, government economic intervention, housing, education, and labor; and weaker in foreign affairs, veterans affairs, taxation, and public works (Turner, 1970, pp. 103–104). In a more recent study, Clausen classified House and Senate votes over an 11-year period (1953 to 1964) into five general policy areas—civil liberties, international involvement, social welfare, agricultural assistance, and government management—and found that the correlation between party affiliation and voting was highest on issues of government management, agricultural assistance, and social welfare. The reliability of party affiliation in predicting votes was considerably lower in international and civil rights matters. These patterns held for voting in both houses of Congress, an indication that despite constituency differences both the House and the Senate react to the same forces in the *national* constituency. The long-term differences between southern Democrats and other Democrats on civil rights issues explains the low rate of intraparty agreement in this area. In the international arena, the tradition of bipartisanship in foreign policy matters probably explains the lesser influence of party in determining voting perferences within both parties (Clausen, 1973, pp. 91–100).

For many years *Congressional Quarterly* has computed an index of the relative influence of party and constituency on voting patterns as these factors relate to the "conservative coalition" between Republicans and southern Democrats and splits between the North and the South within the Democratic party. Table 12.2 shows these two traditional voting alignments at work over a 20-year period (1958 through 1977). North-South Democratic splits are frequent. These two wings of the party differed on roll-call votes from 21 per cent of the time in 1962 to a high of 40 percent in 1960. The proportion of conservative coalition votes in both houses ranged from 14 percent in 1962 to a high of 30 percent in 1971. Although these votes constituted a minority of all roll calls, it is significant that when the coalition operated it usually got its way. The percentage of coalition victories ranged from 33 percent in 1965 to 83 percent in 1971.

The Democrats controlled both the House and the Senate during the entire 20-year period, although Republican Presidents served for 11 of the 20 years (1958 through 1960 and 1969 through 1976). The conservative coalition was relatively successful from 1958 to 1960 and from 1969 to 1972. This pattern of success is attributable in part to the appeal the more conservative domestic programs of Republican Presidents Eisenhower and Nixon had for conservatives of both parties. The relatively small Democratic majorities in Congress during these years also enhanced the coalition's effect. However, the lowest percentages of coalition victories (35 and 45 percent) occurred in 1965 and 1966, even though the number of coalition and North-South Democratic splits were among the *highest* during the 15-year period from 1958 to 1972. The overwhelming victory of President Johnson in 1964 was accompanied by very large Democratic majorities in both houses—a margin of 155 seats in the House and 36 in the Senate. The strong resistance of conservatives to Johnson's

TABLE 12.2
Constituency influences and party cohesion, 1958–1977

Year	Total roll calls	Percentage of Republican-Democratic conservative coalition votes*	Percentage of coalition victories	Percentage of North-South Democratic splits†
1958	293	15	79	29
1959	302	17	71	27
1960	300	22	56	40
1961	320	28	55	33
1962	348	14	62	21
1963	348	17	50	24
1964	306	15	51	24
1965	459	24	33	35
1966	428	25	45	29
1967	560	20	63	26
1968	514	24	73	34
1969	422	27	68	36
1970	684	22	66	34
1971	743	30	83	38
1972	861	27	69	38
1973	1,135	23	61	28
1974	1,081	24	59	30
1975	1,214	28	50	34
1976	1,349	24	58	28
1977	1,341	26	68	28

* Roll calls on which the majority of voting southern Democrats and the majority of voting Republicans opposed the stand taken by the majority of voting northern Democrats.
† Roll calls on which a majority of voting southern Democrats took a position opposite to that of a majority of voting northern Democrats.
Source: Congressional Quarterly Almanac, 1970, 26, pp. 1145 and 1156; Congressional Quarterly Weekly Report, January 7, 1978, p. 3; January 14, 1978, p. 76.

Great Society program was no match for this oversized Democratic majority. The hands of the conservatives were similarly tied in 1975 and 1976, when the Democrats also had large majorities in both houses.

In our earlier discussion of the linkage between constituency characteristics and voting patterns, we stressed the difficulty of measuring these and other factors as determinants of roll-call votes. Just as loyalty to the constituency may cause a legislator to defect from the party line, it may also promote party cohesion if the wishes of the constituency and the party coincide (Froman, 1963, pp. 710–784). Although party affiliation does help greatly to predict congressional voting, it is not the whole explanation, because (unlike the British system) other things affect a legislator's vote: sectionalism, constituency, the intensity of group demands, legislative norms and customs, personal attitudes, reciprocal relations with administrative officials, and congressional leadership. All of these limit the effect of partisanship on congressional voting.

THE COMMITTEES: ARCHITECTS OF LEGISLATION

The work of Congress is done primarily by its committees. There are four types of committees: (1) *Standing committees* are the workhorses of Congress and are permanently provided for by House and Senate rules; (2) a *special* or *select committee* is appointed by the Speaker of the House or the President of the Senate for a specific task, usually an investigation, and is dissolved when its task is completed; (3) a *conference committee*, consisting of members of both houses appointed by the presiding officers, irons out differences in Senate and House versions of a bill; and (4) a *joint committee*, with members of both houses appointed by the presiding officer in each, usually conducts investigations, research, or supervisory activities of Congress. There were four joint committees in 1977.

Standing committees

In *Congressional Government* (1885) Woodrow Wilson described American politics as "government by the Standing Committees of Congress," and said the fate of all legislation lay in the hands of these "little legislatures." Standing committees do the work of Congress itself, and they have not changed much in this century. Every legislative matter is covered by one or more of the standing committees in each house, and the adoption of every bill lies in the hands of committee members. Only 10 to 15 percent of bills referred to committees are reported out for further consideration. Administration-sponsored legislation is usually considered and reported, but a committee or one of its subcommittees may amend or change a bill to suit its own purposes.

The number of standing committees has varied; the House now has 22 and the Senate 18. Some are very important—Appropriations, Ways and Means, Agriculture, Foreign Relations—and membership on them is sought more than service on less significant committees such as House Administration, Government Operations, and District of Columbia.

To expedite business, each standing committee creates subcommittees that handle work within its jurisdiction. This division is necessary, but it further splinters legislative leadership. Since the full committee customarily accepts subcommittee recommendations, subcommittees and particularly their chairpersons are powerful. In 1976, there were 139 standing subcommittees in the Senate and 146 in the House. Appropriations subcommittees in areas such as foreign operations (which control foreign aid spending), defense, and public works exercise great influence over expenditures in crucial areas of public policy.

Before the 1970s, committee chairpersons in the House tended to dominate subcommittees through control of their memberships and staff resources and by designating legislation to be considered. Recent reforms in the House included new rules that reduce the power of committee chairpersons to control subcommittee work. The new rules increase subcommittee operating budgets and staffs, give committee members authority to select chairpersons of sub-committees and fix their jurisdictions, and require chairpersons to refer bills to subcommittees.

Proposed legislation must go through the committee stage in both the House and Senate. After a bill is introduced, it is referred to a standing committee, which subjects it to review (including hearings on major bills). The committee may recommend the bill for adoption as submitted, or as changed—sometimes a little, sometimes extensively. Or it may kill the bill. If a House committee refuses to report a bill to the floor, a discharge petition signed by a majority of the House membership (218) can force the bill out of the committee. The discharge method is not often successful; used 860 times, it has succeeded only 25 times since the discharge rule was adopted in 1910, but party leaders may threaten to use it to speed up committee action.

Committees also investigate. They may request or subpoena witnesses as they look into the operations of executive agencies, the effects of a law, conflicts requiring new legislation, and other problems. Hearings by the Senate Committee on Foreign Relations, many of whose members were highly critical of administration policies, prompted wide public interest in a review of Vietnam policies. Disagreement between the executive branch and Congress over "executive privilege"—the President's refusal to provide Congress information on grounds that such information was privileged for reasons of national security or constitutional prerogatives—produced wide debate during the 1970s. Clashes with the Johnson administration over information about Vietnam and with President Nixon over Watergate documents highlighted attempts by Congress to investigate. Again in 1975, House and Senate select committees investigated the operations of United States intelligence and law enforcement agencies (Central Intelligence Agency and the Federal Bureau of Investigation) and revealed startling abuses of governmental power in the field of individual rights: illegal surveillance and invasions of personal privacy.

Whatever its basis, the selection of both members and chairpersons of standing committees clearly affects the ability of groups to influence policy choices. Committees are autonomous centers of power and their chairpersons are often in competition with party leaders for legislative leadership. This further diffusion of leadership in the formulation and adoption of policy increases the opportunity for delay, amendment, or defeat of legislative proposals.

Committees in action: public hearings

Standing committees and their subcommittees do their crucial work in closed sessions with much bargaining among interests. Yet all major committees spend many hours holding public hearings, supposedly to take evidence from all interested parties. What purpose do hearings serve if the real decisions turn on other considerations?

Through hearings, committees perform their expected function as fact-finding bodies. While the committees gather information, they give interest groups and individuals a formal opportunity to present their own versions of the facts and their positions on proposed policies. This procedure accords with the democratic principle of representation, but committee members are not always impartial judges. A chairman may give priority to witnesses sympathetic to his own ideas, or he may not give opposing groups a chance to be heard. Furthermore, a committee member may put his or her questions in such a way as to show a group in its most favorable light.

Some proceedings are intended to persuade other committee members or to generate public support (or the appearance of support) for the committee's position. Hearings may, however, perform an important democratic function: providing information and an official medium for raising dissent to current or proposed policies. The widely publicized hearings on American policy in Southeast Asia conducted by the Senate Committee on Foreign Relations beginning in the late 1960s gave opponents of the administration's policy opportunities publicly to oppose decisions on the Vietnam War. Committee chairman Senator J. William Fulbright also used the hearings to suggest alternative policies.

The most dramatic and publicized hearings over the past decade were the 1973 Senate Watergate Committee hearings conducted under the chairmanship of Senator Sam Ervin of North Carolina. The live audience at the hearings were overtly anti-Nixon, showing their sentiments by laughter and applause during the appearances of Nixon administration officials. Ervin, who liked to characterize himself as "just a plain old country lawyer," became a national hero to the public television and radio audience. The testimony of John Dean, Nixon's White House counsel, that Nixon participated in the Watergate cover-up was profoundly damaging to Nixon's assertion that he was not aware of the cover-up.

THE HOUSE RULES COMMITTEE

One of the most critical committees in the legislative process in either house of Congress is the House Rules Committee. The bulk of legislation passed by the House is routine and noncontroversial in nature. These bills, as well as appropriations bills, go to the floor of the House through procedures that do not involve the Rules Committee. However, in the event of major legislation, the Rules Committee must report a "rule" before the bill can be considered on the floor of the House. A rule usually specifies how long the bill may be debated, how the time will be divided between opponents and supporters of the legislation, and whether amendments may be offered. If the Rules Committee refuses to hear a request for a rule or denies a rule after hearing a request, it can delay or defeat legislation. House membership is so large that careful management and control of the flow of legislation is clearly necessary. It is also obvious that the Rules Committee can be a powerful force favoring or opposing particular legislative interests.

Before the 1960s, the Rules Committee was dominated by a coalition of Republicans and southern Democrats who consistently blocked domestic legislation favored by more liberal forces in the House. This conflict reached a head in 1961 when the committee posed a threat to programs supported by President Kennedy and Speaker of the House Sam Rayburn. To break the power of the conservative majority on the committee, the House increased the size of the committee and gave liberal forces a one-vote majority. Subsequent reforms in the procedures of the committee and replacement of retiring committee members have removed the threat that legislation would be blocked by conservative forces. Additional changes during the 1970s have placed the Rules Committee under the control of majority party leadership. The Speaker of the House appoints all Democratic members of the committee, which means that the Democratic members selected will support the party leadership in the House.

Although the Rules Committee no longer obstructs legislation supported by the leadership, it still functions as a "traffic cop" of legislation. However, it is "a traffic cop that serves the leadership instead of one that serves the chairman of the committee" (Oppenheimer, 1977, p. 114). Thus the advantages of this major organizational and procedural feature of the legislative process in the House have passed from conservative forces to forces representing party leadership and broader party interests.

Assignment of members to standing committees

The majority party in each house fills a majority of the seats on all standing committees, a practice intended to ensure partisan control. The seats on each committee are generally allocated to the parties in proportion to their numerical strength in the chamber as a whole. However, to ensure control of some of the most important committees, such as the House Rules Committee, the majority party claims a disproportionate number of their seats. Each party determines the assignments of its partisans, limited only by the Legislative Reorganization Act of 1970, which says that each senator may serve on no more than two major and one minor committee and that he may serve on only one of the following: Armed Services, Appropriations, Finance, Foreign Relations. Representatives rarely serve on more than two standing committees.

A freshman representative must sometimes serve on a less important committee before winning a more important assignment, but each party assigns freshmen senators to some major committees. A new congressman will naturally seek a major committee assignment that is congenial to his own or his constituency's interests. Transfers between committees may be made when vacancies occur, or when members agree (with party approval) to switch committee assignments.

Assignments to three major House committees—Appropriations, Rules, and Ways and Means—are usually based on factors such as representing a fairly "safe" district, geographical balance of committee representation, and the representative's reputation as a "responsible" member of the House. Assignments to other House committees are based on such factors as the desire to place each party member on a committee that will help him or her win reelection (the most important consideration), the congressperson's interest group support, his or her professional background, and the geographical area he or she represents (Masters, 1961, pp. 345–357). In the Senate, the major committees do not accurately reflect either geographical or ideological balance, but regional representation is considered. A vacancy is normally filled with a member from the same state, if the senator wants membership on that committee.

Some standing committees—Agriculture, Education and Labor, Interior and Insular Affairs, Judiciary—reflect specific interests. Members of Congress from farm states control the Agriculture Committees; western senators dominate Interior and Insular Affairs; congresspersons from urban and industrial states compose the Education and Labor Committee; and lawyers dominate the Judiciary Committees. Pressure groups are deeply interested in which committee obtains jurisdiction over legislation. Although most bills fall clearly within one committee's jurisdiction, some major legislation could be assigned to either of two committees. If the attitudes of the committee majorities differ markedly on the bill, then its fate can be determined by which committee gets the bill.

Given the power of standing committees, it follows that special interest groups will concentrate their efforts on committees that handle legislation of particular concern to the group. The linkage between interest group campaign contributions and congressional committees has drawn increasing attention from public interest groups. One such group, Common Cause, reported that in 1976 the National Education Association contributed a total of $54,080 to 25 of the 37 members of the House Education and Labor Committee; the American Medical Association gave $74,503 to the campaigns of 29 of the 37 members of the House Ways and Means Committee, which has jurisdiction over national health insurance legislation; and dairy interests contributed $205,986 to 23 of the 46 members of the House Agriculture Committee, which handles dairy product price support legislation. The Common Cause report also mentioned that special interest groups contributed two-thirds of the campaign expenses of 15 major House committee chairmen ("Report to the American People," 1977). These patterns not only illustrate the strategic importance of standing committees in the legislative policy process but also raise serious questions about the larger issue of congressional ethics. Proposals to extend public financing of elections to include congressional as well as presidential campaigns are based in part on the argument that limiting interest group contributions to members of Congress will reduce or eliminate conflicts of interest brought about by large campaign contributions to key congresspersons.

THE SENIORITY SYSTEM

The seniority system is of great importance because of the power of standing committee chairpersons. A chairperson has power over setting the committee's agenda, appointing its staff (the administrative specialists who serve the committee), presiding over meetings and deciding when hearings will be held on a bill, choosing subcommittee members and chairpersons, representing the committee in negotiations, and designating who will handle a bill once it reaches the floor. Although the reforms of the 1970s resulted in greater controls over their prerogatives, chairpersons still remain key figures in the legislative process.

Simply put, the seniority rule awards chairmanships to those members of the majority party who can acquire the longest uninterrupted committee service, a feat accomplished by winning repeated reelection to Congress. The member of the minority party with the longest continuous service becomes chairperson when his or her party gains a majority. High seniority may also be acquired through the death, transfer, or resignation of one or more senior members from a committee. Building seniority through reelection is considerably easier for members of Congress in states and districts dominated by one party. Because representatives from areas where party competition is close rarely survive long in Congress, most committee chairmanships and ranking minority positions have been controlled by congressmen from a few states. Between the 80th and 89th Congresses (1947 to 1966), southern Democrats controlled 53 percent of the chairmanships and ranking minority positions in the Senate and 61 percent in the House (Democrats were in the majority in both houses in all but four years during this period). Midwestern Republicans held 51 percent of these positions in the House and 46 percent in the Senate (Hinckley, 1971, p. 27). The seniority rule has tended to enthrone conservative chairpersons, since safe districts are frequently represented by conservatives and most safe districts are in the South and Midwest. Although the hold of southern Democrats on committee chairmanships has diminished since 1966, 6 of the 22 standing committee chairmanships in the House and 7 of 18 in the Senate were held by southerners in 1977.

Nevertheless, as Table 12.3 indicates, the longtime advantage enjoyed by southern Democrats relative to other regions in the nation has weakened. Of 33 members of the House with 20 years or more of seniority in 1977, 17 were nonsouthern Democrats. In the 10- to 20-year seniority category, the South is considerably weaker; nonsoutherners hold 47 of 65 of these seniority positions. The pattern in the Senate is even more striking. Senators from outside the South already occupy a majority of committee chairmanships and are building a sizeable advantage in terms of seniority. Over the next ten years even more nonsouthern senators and representatives will assume committee chairmanships.

Because key committee positions are determined by party label and the ability to be reelected, and not by the record of party loyalty, legislative party leadership is weakened. Legislators who build their seniority "on their own" have little incentive to be grateful to or dependent on the party leadership. Similarly, a recalcitrant chairman whose policy interests differ substantially from those of the President and whose reelection is quite independent of presidential influence may weaken the policy proposals of the President, even if he is of the same party as the President.

Political analysts and commentators have long held that the seniority rule not only weakens the parties but also enthrones unrepresentative, minority interests from safe districts. One rebuttal to this negative criticism is that continuous committee service of high-seniority legislators gives them experience in their committee's specialties that makes it possible for Congress to exercise effectively the powers assigned to it by the Constitution. That argument seems questionable at best, if only because a rigid seniority formula is not the only way to create experts.

TABLE 12.3
Democratic chairpersons and seniority in the Senate and the House, 1977

| | | | Number of members in two categories of seniority | | | |
| | Number of chairpersons | | 20 years or more | | 10–19 Years | |
Region	House	Senate	House	Senate	House	Senate
Non-South	6	11	17	4	47	13
South*	16	7	16	6	18	4

*Includes states listed in Table 12.1.

The real utility of the seniority rule and the reason that Congress quietly and stubbornly retains the rule despite nearly universal criticism is its secure fit with the legislative party's character. A centralized party's major source of power would be control over the distribution of key committee posts among its partisans; and if committee posts were assigned by the party leadership, a party caucus, or according to criteria such as party loyalty in voting, these measures would describe a centralized party system. But American legislative parties— like the national parties themselves—are too weak and decentralized to perform in that manner. Parties might also assign committee positions according to personal attributes and talents. Yet, could we find a better guarantee of enfeebling conflict within each legislative party than to equate committee assignments with judgments of the personal qualities of individual legislators? Conversely, if we wish to minimize conflict, could we find any better guarantee of continual trading of support for personal advancement, unrelated to any interest in "fairer," "better," or "more effective" chairpersons than those produced by the present seniority rule?

The seniority rule, then, is an impersonal formula for distributing power among legislators who operate within a fragmented party system and who are generally equal in legal and political standing as elected representatives. Reforms would change the nature of the party system as well as the way of choosing chairmen. Changes in the way committee positions are allotted, in short, are not a matter of insulated tinkering but a question of altering the central characteristics of the legislative and party process.

THE TWO HOUSES: SIMILARITIES AND DIFFERENCES

Similarities

With two exceptions, the legal authority of both branches of Congress is about the same. The exceptions are the special prerogatives of the Senate in foreign affairs and presidential appointments, and the constitutional requirement that all revenue bills originate in the House. Because both houses must concur on legislation, either can block a bill passed by the other. The overall procedures and organization of the two houses operate in much the same way, with some significant exceptions. The activities of both chambers are highly decentralized by the committee system, which gives great power to committee and subcommittee chairmen. Reinforced by a weak party structure, this decentralization has produced a policymaking system based on compromise among diverse local interests.

The Senate's smaller size enhances the visibility and prestige of each senator; rarely, and certainly not in recent years, have senators aspired to membership in the House. By contrast, representatives often seek the greater prestige and longer term of a Senate seat. Nonetheless, influence in the legislative process does not necessarily depend on which house a member serves in; his legislative perspective and importance are also governed by his position within the House of Representatives or the Senate.

Differences

The bargain of 1787 that produced a two-chamber legislature built into the policy-adoption process a tension that has never been relieved despite partisanship, presidential coordination, and policy coalitions. Different constituencies give senators and representatives different perspectives on legislation, and it is a rare piece of legislation that is not a compromise between the two houses.

SIZE. From the point of view of House and Senate members, the two houses differ in several important features. The great difference in size of the two houses significantly affects procedural rules and the effectiveness of leadership. The House needs rigid procedures and a hierarchical leadership more than the Senate. Furthermore, because the House is larger, its leadership has more power over its members. The House leadership schedules legislation with little or no consideration of House members other than committee or subcommittee chairpersons, which makes the House a more impersonal body and isolates leaders from the rank and file. The Senate's smaller size enhances the power and prestige of each senator: Because of more committee assignments and the greater importance of his one vote, a senator can exert greater influence over more issues than a member of the House.

CONSTITUENCY. The differences in constituencies between House and Senate members are also significant. A senator represents a whole state and must listen to a greater number of more diverse interests than a member of the House, who necessarily concentrates on fewer, more local interests

SPECIALIZATION AND ITS CONSEQUENCES. The workload of Congress has increased as the size and scope of federal programs has grown. National problems generate new issues that Congress must attempt to resolve. No single member of Congress can possibly keep abreast of the evolution of all legislation. The response of Congress to twentieth-century growth has been to rely on party leadership for coordination and management of legislative business; to decentralize the workload by placing the job of formulating and writing legislation in a highly professionalized committee system; and, as a consequence of this decentralization, to foster the development of individual expertise in specific areas of policy.

Although specialization characterizes the work of both houses, the larger size of the House increases the necessity for representatives to specialize. Both houses have about the same number of committees but the larger House memberships permits fewer committee and subcommittee assignments for each representative. In 1977 there were 18 standing committees, 5 special committees, and 92 subcommittees in the Senate; the House had 22 standing committees, 7 select (special) committees, and 149 subcommittees. It should be clear that each senator must serve on a larger number of committees and subcommittees, and that senators must also divide their time among more policy areas. A representative not only has fewer committee assignments but also has more time to specialize in the one or two policy areas associated with his particular assignments.

One consequence of the greater specialization in the House is that power is both widely dispersed and also exercised by a smaller portion of the total House membership. Since the workload is shared by a larger number of members, each of which tends to direct his attention to a small number of policy interests, a chairperson of a committee or subcommittee can wield great influence over particular legislation. The total workload of the Senate is equal to that of the House but is distributed among only 100 persons compared to 435 in the House. Consequently, power in the Senate is shared more equally; each senator serves on several major committees and three or four subcommittees and each is therefore familiar with a larger part of the Senate's workload. The wider, more equitable distribution of power in the Senate permits a greater degree of individualistic behavior. Even maverick Senators can acquire subcommittee chairmanships more quickly than can new House members, and Senators can use the opportunity of multiple committee memberships to develop a range of individualized interests and expertise (Ripley, 1969, pp. 151–154).

Congressional reform

The organization and procedures in both houses are closely related to the party organizations. As has been noted, key reforms in the House and the Senate were generated by dissatisfaction among newer, more liberal majority party members. The majority party in each house basically controls the procedures and appointments to standing committees, and can thereby modify the power of senior members in key positions. Leadership positions are also party controlled, but support of the leadership is essential to change, a point clearly demonstrated during the efforts toward reform of the 1960s.

REFORM IN THE HOUSE

Beginning in the 1950s and continuing into the 1960s, the Democratic Study Group pressed for changes in procedures and party organization that would improve the chances for passage of liberal proposals. It achieved many of its goals with the passage of the 1970 Legislative Reorganization Act, which liberalized procedures in committees, required publication of all committee roll-call votes, reduced the power of committee chairmen to block clearance of bills for floor action, and required the recording of teller votes of members when the House is considering amendments to bills.

As a result of pressure for reforms within the House Democratic party organization during the late 1960s, Majority Leader Carl Albert and Speaker John McCormick supported changes in party rules that permitted more frequent meetings of the Democratic Caucus, a unit that had little power before the 1970s. The caucus had only met infrequently to formally ratify the nominations for standing committee and party leaders made by the Democratic Committee on Committees; this group was dominated by senior conservative members of the House who also served on the House Ways and Means Committee. In 1971 the revitalized party caucus enacted new rules that permitted consideration of committee nominations by the full Democratic House membership one committee at a time (in contrast to approval or disapproval of all committee nominations) and allowed debate and a caucus vote on any committee nomination. At the same time, House Republicans changed their procedures for the selection of ranking committee members, allowing all members of the Republican Conference (the equivalent of the Democratic Caucus) to vote by secret ballot on each such nomination (Dodd and Oppenheimer, 1977, pp. 26–32).

Further major changes were made by the House Democratic Caucus in 1974. The power to nominate standing committee members was taken from the Democratic members of the Ways and Means Committee and given to the Democratic Steering and Policy Committee. Also, nomination of standing committee chairpersons can now be made from the floor of the caucus if the recommendation of the Steering and Policy Committee is rejected by the full membership. In addition, chairpersons of Appropriations Committee subcommittees—among the most powerful groups in the House—must now be approved in the same manner as standing committee chairpersons.

The impact of these changes on the power of committee chairpersons, the seat of conservative power in the House, became evident in 1975 when the Democratic Caucus removed three major standing committee chairmen (two of them southern conservatives) and replaced them with liberal, northern Democrats.

It should be noted that the seniority rule for choosing committee chairpersons has not been scrapped, nor has the great power of chairpersons been removed. To review, seniority means that the member of a standing committee of the majority party who has the longest continuous service on that committee will become chairperson when a vacancy occurs. The seniority rule still prevails and will probably continue to be the most important consideration in ascendancy to committee leadership posts. However, the resurgence of the Democratic Caucus signals an end to the dominance of members with long service and a record of persistent opposition to the desires of committee colleagues or a majority of party members. This development was strengthened by the House Democratic Caucus' adoption in 1973 of a "subcommittee Bill of Rights" giving subcommittees greater freedom from domination by committee chairpersons. Committee members now vote on subcommittee memberships as well as for subcommittee chairpersons, and they also determine the number of subcommittees and their jurisdictions. All of these functions were once carried out by standing committee chairpersons.

REFORM IN THE SENATE

The relatively small size of the Senate has traditionally permitted more flexible procedures and a less hierarchically organized structure for decisionmaking. We have previously noted that the apprenticeship norm in the Senate carries considerably less influence than it once did, a mark of the growing sense of egalitarianism and a modification of the privileges of seniority. Since the early 1970s other developments have also contributed to a more open process and a lessening of the influence of senators with long tenure. As mentioned above, senators are now permitted to serve on only one of the four major committees (Appropriations, Armed Services, Finance, Foreign Relations); this stricture reduces the relative power of senior members who frequently used to serve on more than one of these committees. In addition, both the Republicans and the Democrats have provided for greater participation of the caucus and conference memberships in the selection of committee chairpersons. Finally, Senate rules for ending filibusters have been modified so that fewer Senators are required to vote to end debate (three-fifths of the entire membership compared to the previous rule of two-thirds of those present and voting).

EFFORTS TOWARD FISCAL CONTROL:
THE CONGRESSIONAL BUDGET

Until 1974, Congress appropriated funds and enacted revenue measures by acting on the federal budget proposed by the President. Initiation of the budget and the gathering of information upon which it was based thus lay almost totally in the hands of the President acting through the Office of Management and Budget. Further, the budgetary process in Congress lacked coordination. A relatively large number of committees and subcommittees in each house worked on parts of the proposed budget and no central coordinating unit was able to monitor the spending process. The inadequate congressional control over the budgetary process combined with concern over accelerating federal spending generated reforms that increased the active participation of Congress in both establishing fiscal goals and monitoring expenditures and revenues.

The most important review of executive requests for specific appropriations takes place in the Appropriations Committee of each house. More precisely, appropriations subcommittees (13 in each House with the same title and jurisdictions) operate in a highly independent and uncoordinated fashion. Each subcommittee exercises jurisdiction over specific categories of appropriations (defense, foreign aid, agriculture, military construction, public works, independent agencies, etc.), and the full committee rarely overrules or interferes with the work of its subcommittees. Further, the House and Senate regularly accept the appropriations recommendations of the two Appropriations Committees (Fenno, 1966, pp. 131–135).

Executive agencies naturally concentrate on building support and gaining the confidence of the Appropriations Committees and subcommittees. Agency staff carefully prepare materials for hearings, respond to committee requests for information, and maintain contacts throughout the year, developing strategies that will maximize their chances for increased funding and approval of their programs. Appropriations subcommittees in turn oversee federal expenditures and scrutinize agency operations. The result of this give-and-take is incremental budgeting; that is, slight changes in appropriations that are usually increases (Sharkansky, 1965). Since the House acts first on appropriations, Senate subcommittees hear appeals from agencies whose budgets the House has cut in the process of approving them.

The decentralized and uncoordinated nature of the congressional budgetary process has been unable to curb the rapid growth of federal spending and ever-increasing federal deficits. For example, total federal expenditures in 1960 were $92.2 billion. By 1970 they had reached $196.5 billion, and in 1976 they reached $350 billion. During the same period (1960 to 1976) there were deficits in all but two years, with the deficit in 1976 reaching $52 billion. By the end of 1974 the national debt had risen to $475 billion, about twice what it had been 20 years earlier.

To what extent has Congress been able to control government spending? The answer to this question is largely revealed in the fact that only about 65 percent of federal spending has been subject to annual appropriations. The remaining 30 to 40 percent falls under practices known as "backdoor spending," which effectively deny congressional control over appropriations. Devices such as executive agency powers to borrow or enter contracts that require appropriations have contributed substantially to noncontrollable expenditures. Congress has also permitted expenditures for programs that do not require continued appropriation funds, such as interest payments on the public debt. In addition, programs such as veterans benefits, social security, and welfare are based on legislation that requires the appropriation of funds into the indefinite future.

Since the early 1960s, both supporters and opponents of old and new spending programs have voiced concern about decreasing congressional control over expenditures. As growth in the national economy began to slow in the late 1960s and early 1970s, it became apparent that revenues would not permit ever increasing expenditures for all programs. Choices had to be made among programs and within existing programs. Conservatives and liberals had different priorities for such choices, but both sides could agree that Congress lacked the organization and the information to exert effective control over the budgetary process.

Within this context Congress passed the Budget and Impoundment Act of 1974, its first major effort to exert a strong, organized influence on fiscal policy. Basically, the act created a budget committee in each house and established the Congressional Budget Office (CBO) staffed with professional analysts. The staff of CBO consists of about 200 persons, most of whom are professionals who monitor economic trends, estimate the impact of changes in the economy on the federal budget, provide information to Congress on budgetary matters, and present Congress with alternate budgetary choices.

The Senate and House Budget Committees are charged with two major responsibilities: (a) to establish expenditure and revenue targets for each fiscal year; and (b) to set a ceiling on expenditures and a minimum on revenues for each fiscal year. The committees are also expected to monitor on a regular basis expenditure and revenue measures approved in the House and Senate to determine if these conform to the guidelines previously approved by each of the two houses.

Although the reformed congressional budget system is still too new to judge its success in influencing fiscal policy, it seems that the new system provides Congress with an organizational and procedural basis by which it can debate and decide policy priorities and their relation to expenditures and revenue. The reforms cannot eliminate backdoor spending, but Congress can exert greater long-term control over its extent and development. Fiscal policy will, of course, remain a crucial area of conflict. Agreement among conflicting interests over the desirability of an increased congressional role in budgetary matters does not resolve questions such as how to balance the budget and how to bring down the unemployment rate. Nor will it resolve differences over the relative value of defense spending compared with the financing of domestic programs. However, the new budget system can make the choices more meaningful to both Congress and the public by designating the alternatives more sharply than was possible under the old, chaotic processes.

Congress in the 1970s

We began this chapter with a discussion of common criticisms of Congress and some of the developments that indicate a strengthening of the legislature relative to executive power. Efforts at reform during the 1970s certainly blunted the argument that Congress is unable to reform itself as one means of balancing the power of the Presidency. Yet it must be remembered that the nature of legislative power precludes a centralized organization. Representation grants distinct advantages to some interests because of single-member districts, safe seats, and gerrymandering. Legislative procedures provide multiple points of decision so that exclusive interests, official and nonofficial, can block, delay, frustrate, and sometimes force through legislative policy. The causes and effects are the same as in other parts of the system: limited coordination, ineffective parties, negotiated decisions, difficulty in fixing responsibility for policy, and incremental decisionmaking.

But legislative decentralization also gives the average congressperson much freedom to choose alternative policies. On the surface, fragmentation seems to provide perfect conditions for pressure groups to dictate policy and use legislators as mere pawns of exclusive interests; yet each legislator filters out or misperceives the pressures he does not want to bear and recognizes those that support him in his work. Consequently, pressure groups succeed by exploiting the common ground they share with some legislators, not by overt pressure. A congressperson whose constituency is mostly agricultural does not have to be "pressured" by farm groups: His goals are already compatible with theirs. He considers "sound" or "in the public interest" demands that parallel or support his own views. Pressure organizations, in turn, nurture mutually beneficial relations with legislators on whom they can rely.

To a significant extent, the very autonomy of congressional representatives prevents Congress from being able to assert greater control over policymaking. Scattered power and points of influence do not easily lend themselves to coordinated policy leadership. Policy initiation still remains substantially outside Congress. Despite important internal changes Congress legislates less than it ratifies; formulates less than it adopts; and leads less than it responds. Legitimate community policies require that congressional majorities be mobilized behind them, but the policies are usually inititated elsewhere.

The trend in the twentieth century has been toward the growth of executive power in response to the needs of a crisis-oriented, increasingly technical, and complex society. Presidential leadership has been aggressive in relation to Congress, and Congress has surrendered to the executive conflicts it could not resolve, delegating much of its policy leadership and altering its function of representing conflict. We hear little about a congressional policy program, but much about the President's program.

Congress has expressed its concern over the erosion of its power relative to that of the President in several ways. The War Powers Act of 1973, the Budget and Impoundment Control Act of 1974, and the investigations of the conduct of agencies such as the CIA and FBI are efforts to bring better balance between the two branches, a balance badly skewed by the misuse and abuse of executive power. The Budget Act of 1974 might be viewed as a long-range positive effort toward joint legislative-executive program development. If Congress can develop an effective alternative to the fiscal programs of the President then it will have strongly reasserted its constitutional authority to tax and spend. A second type of action that will have an impact on executive-legislative balance relates to the internal matters of Congress. The demands of party members for a greater voice in standing committees and in the appointment and retention of committee members and chairpersons are a move in the direction of a more responsive Congress. Reducing the power of conservative members with long seniority has provided a greater voice for opposing forces in the legislative process. Similarly, the enhanced role of Democratic majority party leadership signals better coordination of the legislative process, which could augment the effectiveness of the House as a representative institution. However, an increase in the power of subcommittees has decentralized power and weakened party control, thus pitting against presidential power a congressional structure of power that speaks in many, diverse voices. To be sure, no President can act without reckoning with the power of Congress, which can deny his initiatives or force compromises he is reluctant to make; but the representative process in Congress is nevertheless the representation of disparate and often fragmented interests.

A more cohesive and centralized congressional party structure would be better able to resist pressures from the executive and encourage the initiation of alternative policies to those of the President. An expansion of the number of congressional veto points has provided multiple barriers to presidential efforts to force congressional action, but has also made it almost impossible for Congress to press alternatives to presidential initiatives. If a coequal legislative branch depends on the ability of Congress to seize the function of formulating policy, then Congress is probably not coequal with the executive and judicial branches. Fragmented leadership, decentralized power, and localized interests characterize Congress; they do not add up to a body that can easily initiate policy.

To acknowledge that Congress cannot effectively challenge executive initiative is not to relegate it to a subordinate status. It retains its claim as the most representative institution in our constitutional system. Representation in Congress is fostered by the pluralism of constituencies and the access they provide to decision processes; by the bargaining and compromise that result from the decentralized legislative structure, procedures, and patterns of leadership; and by the role of Congress as overseer and investigator of executive programs and budgets.

Advocates of congressional reform do not usually propose changes that are inconsistent with its decentralized structure and the style of compromise and accommodation of pluralistic interests. Whether the procedural, organizational, and leadership changes we have discussed in this chapter will improve congressional responsiveness to national needs in such areas as transportation, energy, the environment, and human welfare, and whether these changes will better equip Congress to share power with the President, remain to be seen.

THE FEDERAL BUREAUCRACY AND POLICY APPLICATION

13

When the Constitution of the United States was written, no one imagined the great bureaucracy that would some day be required to govern the country. Articles I and II, however, lay the foundation for the development of an administrative bureaucracy: Article I grants Congress the right to create administrative agencies, and Article II authorizes the President to appoint public officials, including "all other Officers of the United States, whose Appointments are not herein otherwise provided for, all which shall be established by Law." Today the federal government alone employs 2.9 million persons in a national civilian work force of approximately 65 million. State governments employ 3.3 million and local governments employ over 4 million employees, excluding teachers. The bureaucracy has been called the "fourth branch of American government" not only because it reaches into the lives of every citizen but also because of its role in shaping public policy decisions.

"Everywhere," wrote the well-known sociologist Max Weber in *Date Koming*, "the modern state is undergoing bureaucratization." Weber saw that as society evolved, a stable foundation for exercising authority became necessary; consequently routine and systematic forms of organization gradually developed. The technological revolution and its accompanying demands for specialization finally produced the highly rational, legalistic, and technical organizations that Weber called "bureaucracies." Without an administrative bureaucracy to carry out policy, government could not function. Even absolute rulers "are powerless to oppose the superior knowledge of the bureaucratic expert" (Gerth and Mills, 1946, pp. 232, 234).

The term bureaucracy brings negative images to the minds of citizens. Washington has been characterized as "Disneyland East," the "Marble Jungle," and the "Citadel of Nonresponsiveness." Candidates for public office find attacks on the bureaucracy a safe campaign issue and make frequent assertions about "cutting red tape" and the need for "greater efficiency and economy." Jimmy Carter made administrative reorganization of the federal government a major part of his campaign for the Presidency in 1976. President Ford referred to "the deadweight and impudence of bureaucracy" in his nomination acceptance speech.

Obviously, governments cannot operate without bureaucracies, "the late bloomers of modern political structure. They grew silently, inexorably in the underbrush—seldom noticed, little analyzed. Convenience and necessity, not ideology and legitimacy, are their life-blood; they are not loved and respected, but rather tolerated and depended upon" (Krislov, 1974, pp. 40–41). Concerns over the modern bureaucracy relate primarily to its growing size and complexity, its unresponsiveness, and the problems posed by an increasingly professionalized and highly organized staff with knowledge and technical skills that are powerful influences on public policy. This chapter focuses on the aspects of bureaucracy that are particularly relevant to the process of policy application in the American system.

What is policy application?

The notion that under the system of separated powers, Congress enacts policy and the administrative branch implements it oversimplifies the reality of the policy process. If the will of the community is to be reflected in public policies, someone must insure compliance with them. One way is to gain public acceptance of the legitimacy of legislative decisions and their subsequent implementation by the administrative branch. An element of coercion, either potential or actual, must also be there. But bureaucrats go beyond that narrow activity and take part in the broader work of setting community goals.

The executive branch has activities and responsibilities almost beyond counting. Legally and technically they cover two broad functions: the application of policy decisions made by Congress, the courts, and the President; and the adjudication of disputes between individuals, groups, and organizations under authority granted by Congress. The laws of Congress and court decisions on taxes, narcotics, welfare, corporations, and civil rights are defined and interpreted by the administrator responsible for their application. Hundreds of rules and regulations come from administrative—not purely legislative—action. Choice and discretion are inherent in all these activities: when and if to prosecute a violator of law; whether to spend money appropriated and for which purposes; whether to centralize or decentralize the administration of a program.

Like legislators and judges, administrators formulate and adjudicate policy. When administrators develop rules or guidelines for carrying out the broad intent of Congress as expressed in statutes, they are formulating policy. When a regulatory agency such as the Federal Trade Commission or the Interstate Commerce Commission issues an order to a broadcaster or a trucking company to "cease and desist" from an activity, it is adjudicating policy. Because administrators participate in the resolution of conflict, they are subject to many of the same pressures as a legislator or a judge.

POLICY APPLICATION AND COMMUNITY GOALS

Much legislation is written in broad language, merely outlining what an administrative agency can and cannot do. The missing details are filled in by the agency itself. In fact, some administrators distinguish between their agency's programs and the policies that the executive and the legislature entrust to them to apply. To be sure, the programs are intended to effect the application, but the administrators have much room to use their discretion. Their choices are, in effect, acts of policymaking that directly affect the distribution of advantages and disadvantages among conflicting interests, as two examples will show.

Since 1914, the Federal Trade Commission (FTC) has been responsible for administering and enforcing laws aimed at protecting consumers. The commission writes and enforces regulations affecting packaging standards, advertising claims, and credit. The message on packages of cigarettes, "Caution: Cigarette Smoking May Be Hazardous to Your Health" (and later ". . . is dangerous to your health") is an effort to protect consumers against cancer. The stronger warnings proposed initially were vigorously opposed by tobacco interests, which felt that any message would be economically injurious.

The Food and Drug Administration (FDA), with a budget of about $245 million, is charged with administering federal laws controlling the purity of food and the safety of drugs. The FDA has faced increasing problems arising from cancer-causing substances (carcinogens) in food and the environment. The agency has been caught between interests that want all foods containing carcinogens banned and food industry spokespersons and others who are critical of proposals to ban substances that cannot be clearly shown to cause cancer. Upon leaving office in November 1976, Food and Drug Administrator Dr. Alexander Schmidt complained that "we build highways, we build bridges, knowing full well what the statistical probability [is] of people being killed in doing those things. So it is not reasonable to believe the use of chemicals in our society can be totally without risk" ("FDA: Government Can't Ban All Carcinogens," p. 1). Schmidt also complained that the hours spent "responding to Congress, responding to critics" made it impossible "to accomplish or even to work at what I came here to work at." Whatever choices are made regarding such sensitive issues, there is no way that totally "nonpolitical" decisions can be reached. Policy application is essentially an aspect of conflict resolution.

Administrators take part in representing social conflict as well as in its resolution. Norton Long (1962), has written that in some ways the bureaucracy represents interests better than Congress does. Its varied composition compensates for congressional representation (see Chapter 12), which results in large numbers of "unrepresented, underrepresented, or malrepresented" citizens (p. 68). The head of the bureaucracy, the President, works toward broader public goals than congresspersons do. Because Congress does not accept responsibility for the success of legislation after it takes administrative form, the bureaucracy provides a continuing structure and constitutional medium through which a changing political and social environment can be reflected in new policies that meet new needs and new group demands.

Who are the bureaucrats?

There are two basic ways in which civil servants are selected: by political appointment and election or through a system that stresses objective standards of merit. Each relates to democratic theory through basic assumptions about the role of public servants and their relationship to the governed. The system of merit rests on the assumption that the public is best served by administrators who are competent to perform the tasks of administration; in fact, administrators are expected to be politically "neutral" in the performance of their responsibilities. This perspective projects a separation, either implied or asserted, of "administration" and "politics." By contrast, appointment for political reasons is based on the belief that all or part of the civil service should be relegated to political control under elected officials; loyalty to officials and ultimate democratic responsibility can be better secured through political selection. Competence and political appointment are not viewed as contradictory qualities; rather, proponents of political selection argue that it is possible to achieve both administrative competence and democratic responsibility through political appointment.

Historically, the federal government has operated under both systems of selection; political appointment was the dominant mode of selection until the early twentieth century, and a merit system has predominated since then. However, at the upper levels of federal administration, political appointment has always prevailed, from George Washington on.

THE RISE OF THE MERIT SYSTEM

Until the election of Andrew Jackson in 1828, Presidents emphasized continuity in government personnel, and government employees were an elite group of men of stature and long service (White, 1954). In his first annual message to Congress, Jackson said that "the duties of federal employees are so plain and simple that men of intelligence may readily qualify themselves for their performance." He brought the "spoils system" to federal employment, rewarding the party faithful with government jobs. Jacksonian democracy extended participation to the "common man," using rotation in office as a safeguard against elitism. For most of the nineteenth century, partisan supporters of new Presidents were installed in government posts from the highest to the lowest levels.

Not until after President James Garfield was assassinated in 1881 by a rejected office-seeker was the spoils system reformed. The Pendleton Act of 1883 created a federal civil service based on merit, to be established by competitive examination and administered by a bipartisan Civil Service Commission. This system, known as the classified service, has grown steadily: It covered 10.5 percent of federal employees in 1884; 41.5 percent in 1901; 79.6 percent in 1930; and more than 83 percent by 1970. Most executive branch agencies now select their employees through the merit system, but some agencies with specialized functions have systems of selection separate from the Civil Service Commission—for example, the Federal Bureau of Investigation, the Atomic Energy Commission, the Tennessee Valley Authority, and the Central Intelligence Agency.

POLITICAL NEUTRALITY: THE HATCH ACT

The merit system is supposed to reduce political pressure on government employees. It provides for job security and fair treatment by procedures and regulations governing dismissals, compensation, and promotions. Because of alleged abuses of the system during the rapid expansion of the federal bureaucracy in the 1930s, Congress enacted the Hatch Act of 1939 to remove civil servants from political influence even further. The law prohibits the coercion of federal employees for political reasons, the soliciting of campaign funds from federal workers, and the active participation of federal employees in political campaigns. Originally it also applied to state employees whose salaries were paid in whole or in part by federal grants or loans, but in 1974 Congress lifted most of the restrictions on this group of employees.

Administered and enforced by the Civil Service Commission, the regulations have confused public employees about what they may and may not do. A 1968 Commission study found that almost 65 percent of federal employees understood fewer than six of the ten restrictions under the Hatch Act (J. W.

Davis, 1970, pp. 69–71). Although the Commission recommended lifting most restrictions other than those controlling the coercion of employees by superiors, Congress took no action. In 1972, a federal district court held that the act was excessively vague about what types of action were prohibited, but the Supreme Court reversed the lower court decision on the grounds that Congress has the constitutional power to prohibit activities that may endanger the job security of federal employees under the merit system (*Civil Service Commission* v. *National Association of Letter Carriers, AFL–CIO,* 1973). The issue became a partisan struggle in Congress in 1976 when Republicans charged that Democrats supported the proposed changes in the law because they would benefit most from the partisan activities of civil servants (the majority of whom were Democrats). Proponents of the legislation argued that the changes would grant to federal workers the same political rights enjoyed by other Americans. Congress approved a bill permitting partisan activities by civil service employees, including running for office and soliciting campaign contributions from fellow workers, but President Ford vetoed the bill, charging that it would "politicize" the civil service.

A PROFESSIONALIZED BUREAUCRACY

Because the bureaucracy's need for professional and technical employees has grown, President Jackson's "plain and simple" description of government jobs no longer applies. About 1 in every 14 civil servants is engaged in engineering and scientific work. Of the top 5,000 career employees about one-third are program managers (bureau chiefs, division directors, office heads); another one-third are involved in budget management, personnel management, administration, and management analysis; and about one-third are professionals (economists, lawyers, engineers, scientists, accountants) (Corson and Paul, 1966, pp. 15–19).

Growth and organization of the bureaucracy

Legislation is often a response to demands by interests that have sought government help in reaching their goals. Before this century, federal activity in community life was limited because of a prevailing attitude that economic and social life should be as free of government as possible. An expanding frontier, where land was easy to get and towns were isolated and sparsely populated, encouraged the self-reliance that made Americans suspicious of government interference. This spirit was reinforced by laissez-faire social and economic theories: Government was mostly a policing operation. Politics and economics were separate spheres of activity. The U.S. government did not become involved in economic regulation until late in the nineteenth century.

American government first intervened in the economy at the state level when agricultural groups in the Midwest began to agitate for the regulation of railroads and other economic reforms. As the nation experienced the industrial revolution and the accompanying social and economic adjustments, the demand for federal regulatory action increased. The new federal agencies created by Congress after the turn of the century were justified by reform groups as necessary to control "private interests" whose activities interfered with the "national interest." But the groups that fought the creation of these agencies believed that the government's new regulatory role interfered with free enterprise.

The creation of all major agencies has parallelled the development of new problems and issues, and government recognition of new groups organized to promote and protect the needs of their members. The Department of Labor was created in 1913, following the formation of mass-member labor unions. More recently, the Departments of Health, Education and Welfare (1953), Housing and Urban Development (1965), Tansportation (1966), and Energy (1977) resulted from the consolidation of existing agencies already administering government programs in response to changing needs and new problems. The emergence of new departments reflects new priorities in meeting group demands for programs promoting civil rights, urban renewal, the alleviation of poverty, the improvement of education, mass transit, and the development of energy resources.

In creating administrative agencies, Congress establishes public policy, but the policies are broad. The tasks assigned to the new agencies are too technical to allow for detailed direction by either Congress or the courts. As a result, congressional directives stipulate that in fulfilling their responsibilities agencies should act in a "just" and "reasonable" fashion and in the "public interest." The main burden of reconciling group conflict has thus shifted from Congress to the administrative bureaucracy, which has consequently become the new target for pressure groups seeking to influence the policy choices of administrators. In brief, administrative agencies have become the focal points for disputes and decisions on policy, as well as for policy application.

THE EXECUTIVE DEPARTMENTS

The organization of a large federal agency such as the Department of Interior (see Figure 13.1) reveals how massive and complex the federal administration is. Generally speaking, the administrative branch is organized by departments for specialized areas. The pattern is hierarchical with authority and responsibility—the chain of command—based on superior-subordinate relationships. At the top of this hierarchy, and in formal command of the entire administrative structure (except as discussed below), is the President. Immediately below him are the executive departments headed by secretaries who are also mem-

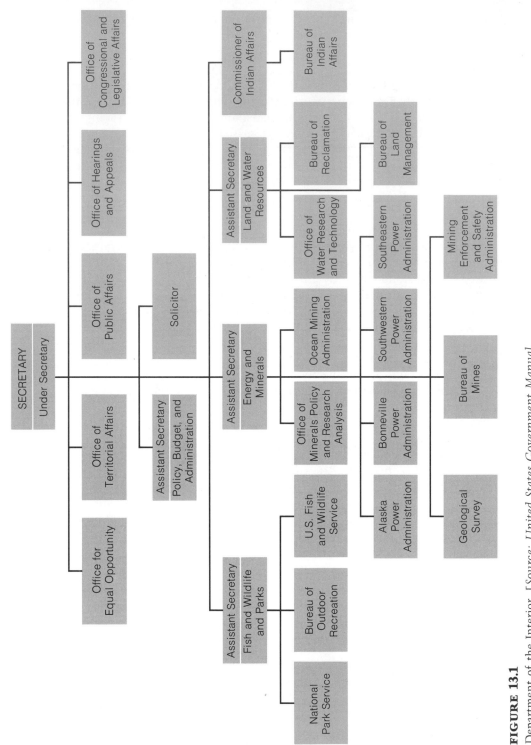

FIGURE 13.1

Department of the Interior. [*Source: United States Government Manual,
1977–1978* Washington D.C.: U.S. Government Printing Office, 1977, p. 303.]

bers of the Cabinet. These departments include the Departments of State; the Treasury; Defense; Justice; the Interior; Agriculture; Commerce; Labor; Health, Education, and Welfare; Housing and Urban Development; Transportation; and Energy. Each department is formally divided into bureaus, divisions, sections, and even desks.

Many executive departments have semiautonomous subagencies. The Federal Bureau of Investigation in the Department of Justice and the Office of Education in the Department of Health, Education, and Welfare are only nominally administered by the Attorney General and the Secretary of Health, Education, and Welfare. Administrators who try to coordinate the activities of these subagencies are often caught up in conflict between semiautonomous agencies and their administrative superiors. The same kind of conflict has hindered coordination of the Army, Air Force, and Navy under the Department of Defense.

INDEPENDENT AGENCIES

About 60 federal agencies are not part of any executive department. Some of these are largely unknown, relatively unimportant units such as the American Battle Monuments Commission and the Commission of Fine Arts. Others are responsible for important governmental services and regulations. The National Science Foundation, for example, awards millions of dollars of research funds to colleges and universities. Among the most important independent agencies are the regulatory boards and commissions.

The regulatory commissions

The size of various regulatory commissions and boards and the length of their members' terms differ, but the groups all function independently of direct presidential control. Appointed by the President, members may be removed only for causes specified by Congress. Because regulatory commissions exercise some judicial and legislative power, they are sometimes referred to as "quasi-judicial" or "quasi-legislative" bodies. The "Big Five"—the Interstate Commerce Commission, Federal Trade Commission, Federal Communications Commission, Securities and Exchange Commission, and Civil Aeronautics Board—exercise extensive regulatory authority over such matters as rail and truck transportation, oil pipelines, advertising, telephone rates, the sale of securities, stock transactions, air fares, and airline routes.

The oldest of the major regulatory commissions is the Interstate Commerce Commission, created in 1887 in response to public pressures to prevent railroads from charging exorbitant rates and discriminating against some users. The Federal Trade Commission was created in 1914, and the remaining three came into existence in the 1930s when the federal government expanded its regulatory role to broad sectors of the economy.

Another major regulatory commission, the Federal Power Commission (FPC) was abolished in 1977 as part of President Carter's reorganization of energy-related agencies. The President recommended that the new Department of Energy be given responsibility for all energy functions, including the FPC's regulatory authority over the sale and pricing of natural gas and electricity. Congress rejected this part of Carter's plan, basically on the grounds that it would place excessive power in the hands of the Secretary of Energy and thus "politicize" government decisions on energy pricing and sales. Instead, the legislature created a new, independent Federal Energy Regulatory Commission (FERC) to be housed in the Department of Energy; the five members of the commission are appointed by the President with Senate approval for four-year staggered terms of office. The FERC regulates the prices and sale of natural gas and electricity, and thus makes its regulatory decisions outside the direct control of the Secretary of Energy. In fact, the new agency functions quite similarly to the former Federal Power Commission.

Given the rule-making and judicial functions of regulatory agencies, Congress has sought to organize them in a way that assures their independence from both the President and the interests they are supposed to regulate. To what extent have these agencies retained their independence?

HOW INDEPENDENT? It should come as no surprise that Presidents have appointed members to regulatory commissions whose "ideologies" are compatible with presidential policy preferences. As with federal judges, Presidents usually choose members of their own party and commissioners often divide along party lines in voting. Thus while Presidents do not exercise direct control over independent commissions, they influence their policy decisions through the indirect means of political appointment.

CAPTIVES OF THOSE THEY REGULATE? The independence of regulatory commissions is also questionable because the backgrounds of many commissioners include employment in the industries they are expected to regulate. A 1976 House Investigations subcommittee concluded that eight of the nine regulatory agencies it examined were guilty of a "common defect"—their actions favored the regulated industries more than the public. The subcommittee found that consumer participation in decisions was infrequent, and the mechanisms for such participation were inadequate. These charges reflected a growing criticism of regulatory agencies by a variety of public interest groups.

A 1969 Ralph Nader investigation of the Federal Trade Commission documented the close association between a regulatory agency and its clientele groups. Nader charged that the FTC was guilty of a "colossal default" in protecting consumers against harmful products and fraudulent services. Special interests and business lobbyists took precedence over the "unrepresented consumer" and the Commission often failed to enforce its orders against companies to stop illegal or harmful practices (Cox, Fillmeth, and Schultz, 1969, pp. viii, xi, 14–32). Nader's findings reinforced other evidence on regulatory agencies. For many years, the Interstate Commerce Commission favored the railroads over other forms of transportation, such as trucking, and thus defended the status quo against new developments in transportation.

As critics have attacked the regulatory commissions for failure to represent consumer interests and enforce existing rules, business and other interests have charged that government regulations are unnecessarily burdensome and costly to both consumers and business. In 1975 and 1976 Congress considered several proposals for reorganizing regulatory procedures, but no major legislation emerged.

Economic regulation by the federal government will undoubtedly continue indefinitely. But increasing pressures from consumer advocate groups might well lead to changes in the policy positions of regulatory units; and Presidents may try to alter the image and performance of regulatory agencies by their appointments.

Oversight or service agencies

Some administrative agencies serve other government agencies. The General Services Administration is the purchasing agent, storage agent, documents clerk, and builder of federal offices. The Office of Management and Budget aids the President in fiscal control and policy coordination. The Civil Service Commission recruits employees and manages public personnel policies.

Government corporations

Government corporations extend credit to farmers, produce electric power, insure bank deposits, provide loans for home buyers, and operate terminal and port facilities. Organized much like private businesses, the corporations, such as the Federal Deposit Insurance Corporation and the Tennessee Valley Authority, were created to carry out primarily economic operations not provided by private enterprise. The U.S. Postal Service was a Cabinet department until 1970 when Congress made it a government-owned corporation. In 1970 Congress also created the National Railroad Passenger Corporation, known as Amtrak, to operate railroad passenger service.

AGENCIES AND THEIR CLIENTELE

An administrative agency that provides a special voice for a particular set of community interests is called a clientele agency. All agencies are expected to serve the larger public interest, but as we have already noted some were brought into being by Congress to provide services and a voice inside government for particular groups. The Department of Agriculture promotes farm interests, the Labor Department those of workers, and the Commerce Department the interests of the business community. Some governmental units are even more closely associated with clientele groups. The Veterans Administration dispenses about $5 billion per year in benefits to veterans; the Defense Department is closely associated with defense-related industries which depend on military contracts; and the Interior Department's Bureau of Land Management has a special client in western state ranchers who graze their livestock on federally owned land.

Agencies not only serve but also rely on the support of their clientele interests. These interests support budgetary requests and defend the agency against attacks that threaten programs of benefit to them. A large membership, wide geographic dispersal, and good organization all enhance a group's influence. Thus veterans groups exert a powerful influence on the policies of the Veterans Administration, as well as Congress, in matters pertaining to veterans benefits.

Groups are clearly at a disadvantage if they lack access to administrative agencies. Although the Department of Agriculture serves agricultural interests, all agricultural groups do not get equal representation. The powerful Farm Bureau Federation usually reflects the interests of larger and more prosperous farmers. Other agricultural interest groups, such as the Farmers Union, have shown more interest in preserving the family farm, but the small and economically marginal farmer has lost more and more ground in the conflict over farm policies. Migrant farm laborers are even worse off; they have virtually no access to the Agriculture Department. Both the marginal farmer and the migrant farm laborer are "orphaned," with no government agency representing their interests.

Sometimes agencies pay a price for their close ties with interest groups. Such ties may inhibit or prevent change and thereby reduce the agency's flexibility in responding to changes in the environment or to the demands of new interests. In 1977 the Food and Drug Administration announced that it would permit ice-cream makers to use a European product, sodium caseinate, in place of nonfat dry milk in the production of ice cream. In addition to lowering the cost of ice cream, the new product was judged to be as nutritious as dry milk and to have no effect on the taste of ice cream. Dairy industry interests reacted strongly to the proposal, arguing that the use of the European product would adversely affect the income of dairy farmers and force the Agriculture Department to increase by $300 million the cost of dairy price support programs. Under pressure from the dairy industry and the Agricultural Department, the FDA reversed its decision.

Interest groups are, of course, a part of the political process at all levels of government. Where clientele groups are closely related to the programs and interests of an agency, they limit the independence of the agency and its ability to represent other publics. As we noted earlier, the close association between regulatory agencies and the groups they regulate has been of special concern to public interest and consumer groups. The process of applying policy is as much a part of group conflict as other parts of the political system. Administration is never neutral.

The Tennessee Valley Authority (TVA)

The origins, growth, and development of the TVA illustrate how shifting support for agency programs among clientele groups can change the thrust of an agency. The TVA was established as a government corporation by Congress in 1933 to develop the water, electric power, and agricultural resources of a vast seven-state region. Congress chose the grass-roots approach because it would be more efficient and democratic than imposing an administrative hierarchy on top of already existing federal structures. Local and state governments and private interests would carry out the tasks of the Authority. Although this approach accomplished much that it was intended to accomplish, some un-intended effects were detrimental to TVA goals. Philip Selznick wrote that the TVA, by "a process of informal cooptation," absorbed spokespersons for interest groups into its policymaking structure "as a means of averting threats to its stability or existence" (1953, p. 13). Farmers and other agricultural interests in the TVA region considered TVA agricultural improvement and planning programs "socialistic." To overcome opposition and suspicion, the Authority reached an agreement under which the seven land-grant colleges in the region were integrated into TVA's Agricultural Relations Department. This move assured agricultural interests that the TVA would view them as partners in agricultural development, and that radical farm programs would not be pursued. By making the Agricultural Relations Department the sole contact between TVA and the colleges (which represented agricultural interests), the Authority informally brought the farm interests in the region into the structure of the TVA itself.

The Agricultural Relations Department succeeded in getting the TVA to change its initial goal of achieving soil conservation by public ownership of land (Selznick, pp. 111–116, 190–213). The confidence and support built by the close association of the Authority and its agricultural clientele paid off in 1937 when the TVA faced a Senate investigation of charges of corruption and mismanagement. It was the farmers in the region who defended the organization as a government program that had "turned on the lights in Tennessee" and brought prosperity to a poor seven-state region. In turn, the TVA fought the introduction into the valley of legislatively mandated farm programs viewed as undesirable by farm interests. The TVA's efforts gained strong regional support for its power policies against critics who viewed them as "socialistic." However, the Authority's refusal to encourage new farm programs represented a "perversion of policy determined through representative institutions" (Selznick, p. 265).

More recently, the TVA has come into conflict with environmental and other groups that consider it a conservative organization no longer willing to serve the interests of the larger public. The Authority has relied heavily on strip-mined coal to fire its power-producing steam plants, thereby not only contributing to the devastation of thousands of acres but also producing polluted rivers. Ecologists attacked a TVA proposal to build a new dam (Tellico), primarily for recreation, on the Little Tennessee River. They brought a court suit to halt construction of the dam on the grounds that the project would needlessly flood thousands of acres of land and destroy the beauty of one of the few remaining natural streams of the region; and when a small fish, the snail darter, was found in the Little Tennessee, the ecologists strengthened their case by having the fish declared an endangered species under the Environmental Protection Act and then arguing that since the fish cannot survive in other habitats and Tellico dam would destroy its habitat, the dam should not be completed.

As this brief discussion reveals, the TVA grew and prospered as an organization with the support of regional groups who became closely tied to its economic and social goals and policies. But in the 1970s, some groups who once supported the Authority depicted it as an overly conservative organization no longer in harmony with the best interests of the region.

CONTROLLING AND REORGANIZING THE BUREAUCRACY

Sheer size prevents the heads of large departments, much less the President, from dominating the bureaucracy even though their authority to control is clearly mandated. Controlling a constantly expanding and changing "fourth branch" is so difficult that the administrative branch has undergone three comprehensive reviews in 40 years, and President Carter went to the White House promising a fourth. Major reorganization efforts occurred under Franklin D. Roosevelt's Committee on Administrative Management (Brownlow Committee) in 1937; the Truman-appointed Hoover Commission, headed by former President Herbert Hoover, which reported in 1949; and a second Hoover Commission in 1955. All plans for reorganization emphasized the "integrative principles" of organization of the executive branch by recommending a hierarchical arrangement with a central superior, a relatively small number of subordinates (usually between 3 and 15), and clear lines of authority and responsibility. Of the 97 reorganization plans submitted to Congress by Presidents from 1939 through 1966, Congress approved 75 (Mansfield, 1969, p. 339). President Nixon proposed substantial changes, including the consolidation of 11 Cabinet departments into 8, but achieved only limited success, most of it by executive order. President Carter formed several special study units inside the executive branch to review various aspects of administrative organization. His campaign pledge to substantially reduce the number of executive branch agencies and to deal with "the complicated and confused and overlapping and wasteful federal bureaucracy" remained a major goal of his administration after his election.

Proposals for reorganization are likely to surface when a new administration takes office and views change as necessary to achieve its programs; when an existing program or structure is subjected to strong criticism (as regulatory agencies and the Selective Service System were in the 1960s); or when an administrator feels that reorganization would help him achieve his goals or satisfy new demands. No matter how rational and wise an attempt at reorganization may seem, it is bound to cause conflict. Power and access are affected by change; despite the conventional symbols used to justify change (among them "efficiency" and "economy"), agencies and interests generally support or oppose reorganization depending on whether they expect to lose or gain by it. The same "cozy little triangles"—coalitions of interest groups, bureaucratic forces, and congressional committees—that operate in the legislative process are also effective in negating or modifying proposals for organizational change (James, 1974, p. 212).

The interests fighting over reorganization are often many and varied. Congresspersons (and the interests they support) are unlikely to favor changes that would reduce their access and influence. Conversely, a President may seek such changes to enhance his own control and reduce the influence of competing interests over agency policies. In spite of claims supporting its efficiency and economy, centralized control over administration is inconsistent with a political system characterized by decentralized and fragmented power.

Bureaucratic behavior and the politics of administration

Administrators are part of the political system; but they also belong to an organization formally tied together by a hierarchy of management, rules of procedure, standards of conduct, and the technical and professional tasks of administration. These organizational elements make the bureaucrat something more than the automaton buried in a forest of red tape that caricaturists portray.

FORMAL RELATIONSHIPS

A stable and predictable environment is a natural goal for any highly formal, continuing organization. Bureaucratic organization is at least partly achieved by a structural arrangement of the various units within the agency into a hierarchy of command and responsibility. Details of organization vary from agency to agency. Some strive for unity of command, making one official ultimately responsible for all policy decisions; others have a co-executive or a set of officials who share responsibility.

PROCEDURES AND CONDUCT

Agencies establish routine procedures for the handling of appeals by interests, office communications, personnel matters, and the release of information. The procedures reduce as much as possible ambiguity in the agency's relations with outside groups as well as in superior-subordinate relationships within the organization. Nevertheless, the structure and rules restricting those who make decisions are anything but static.

The impersonality and hierarchic structure of a large organization determine the individual administrator's status. Each person is superior to some and subordinate to others, and each position has specified rights and duties. The administrator's perspective is shaped by his understanding of the prerogatives of his position and his ability to command or require obedience. Several features distinguish the "boss" from his subordinates: He has a final say on policy measures that is often not subject to appeal; he may have absolute discretion in decisions affecting the goals of employees, such as raises and promotions; he has coercive tools that define his decisions as commands; and he can monopolize organizational communications both internally and with the public (V. Thompson, 1961, pp. 60–68).

Although structure and rules give a superior control over his subordinates, they also limit that control. Civil service regulations protect employees against arbitrary treatment or dismissal. Procedures and grounds for dismissal may be so technical and cumbersome as to make firing an incompetent employee unrealistic. A manager expected to be responsive to the needs of both his agency and his employees may be unable to meet his responsibilities to either while struggling with overly restrictive regulations.

The subordinate's status can nevertheless be threatened by both his chief and the continuing possibility of congressional investigation or cutbacks of personnel. In a study of the way in which organizational activity has affected American life, Robert Presthus (1962) calls this characteristic "status anxiety"; the underling is never really secure in his position. His actions are influenced by the desire to equate his personal interests with those of his organization. He may prefer to show caution and remain anonymous rather than risk his status by innovative or unorthodox behavior.

The desire to enhance their status and protect their positions from adverse action by superiors may lead administrative subordinates to try to modify the

superior-subordinate relationship. Special skills, strong public support, alliances with influential congressmen, or long career service can insulate bureau chiefs from control by superiors. Control of an agency may rest with administrators who are officially subordinate but actually autonomous. For example, widespread public and congressional support have traditionally given the heads of the FBI in the Justice Department and the head of the Army Corps of Engineers in the Department of Defense special status.

HIERARCHY AND THE POLICY PROCESS

The President controls the bureaucracy mostly by his power to appoint and remove major department heads. These political executives are his "first team" and share his political responsibility for policies. But to succeed, a political executive must work within the bureaucratic structure he heads. It is impossible to distinguish clearly between the job of the political executive and that of the career bureaucrat in bureaucratic policymaking. Each depends on the other. The bureaucrat depends on the department head to represent him at the highest administrative level, and the department head depends on his subordinates for the information and technical knowledge necessary to reach policy goals and formulate new programs. Because the career bureaucrat will be a part of the structure long after the department head has departed, he serves to administer and help develop the policies of each new administration. Increasing administrative specialization helps the bureaucrat protect his status against threats from political executives at the top of the hierarchy.

Proposals for administrative reorganization consistently stress that the increasing scope and complexity of the tasks of government require better coordination of policy priorities and greater control of the bureaucracy. An emphasis on hierarchy validates command as a style of policy formulation and the success of a clear chain of command rests on sanctions that can be applied against subordinates to achieve compliance. The power to appoint and remove personnel, review budget requests and monitor expenditures, and control information within the organization are the most important sanctions available. As hierarchical control succeeds, the effect of bargaining as a style of policy formulation diminishes.

The bureaucrat's idea of his place in the organization influences his outlook on policy application. Performing duties by routine rather than reflection limits the sense of personal discretion in policy affairs, organizational goals, and ultimately in serving community interest. An administrator who feels his discretionary authority is narrow will be less accessible to interests who want to change his point of view than an administrator who believes he has broad discretionary powers. The administrator with little discretion may choose to "play it safe" instead of risking loss of status (or job) by new approaches or techniques advocated by interests outside the organization.

Not only are tasks specialized within bureaucratic organizations but individuals also become specialists. Task specialization is illustrated by an employee of the Federal Home Loan Bank Board who becomes highly competent in handling a particular type of loan application. Specialization in a particular subject-matter also characterizes large-scale organizational life. A chemical engineer may specialize in environmental quality controls and become an expert in the broad field of ecology. The power and influence he gains by long experience on the job make his agency dependent on him for information and administrative know-how; this type of dependency creates semiautonomous pockets of power within the organization.

The limits of hierarchy

Except for partisan appointees, most government administrators come through the ranks of the civil service. A professional outlook colors their conceptions; as career civil servants, they are on the inside of policymaking and their tenure transcends that of partisan appointees, pressure-group leaders, and a community that becomes aware of their existence sporadically. Professional specialization sets bureaucratic administrators apart from superiors who may be less informed about matters in the agency's jurisdiction or who may be short-term political appointees.

Professionalism is part of modern administration, but it carries risks as well as advantages for the public. The risks have been described as "inertness, separation, and specialization." Inert bureaucrats are "sluggish, self-satisfied, and interested in the survival of their existing habits and thought patterns" (Redford, 1958, pp. 63–67). They adapt slowly to changing times and circumstances and have little initiative. The second danger—separation—arises when a bureaucrat becomes so self-centered that he loses contact with public opinion or gets suspicious of outside forces. Specialization, which may be the "most persistent cause of separateness and the greatest danger of bureaucracy," occurs when administrators see only their own or their clientele's position as valid in a controversy over policy.

Coordinating highly specialized personnel and agencies into a unified, coherent organization is a formidable job. To protect its status within the administrative structure, "each functional organization develops its own self-centered attitudes," as well as close ties with private groups and key committees and individuals in Congress (Redford, 1958, p. 66). A bureau in the Department of Agriculture would have little sympathy for consumer interests that oppose agricultural price-support programs. The military establishment does not appreciate domestic and foreign policy needs that compete with military demands for congressional support. Both the agricultural and the military interests have supporters in key congressional positions who help them resist pressures for changes in policy.

Administrative perspective differs from the executive and the legislative perspectives examined earlier. Administrators depend on each other's skills and cooperation in striving to achieve administrative goals, but conflict arises over how much influence on policy decisions the technical skills of specialists should have (V. Thompson, 1962, pp. 108–110). One source of disagreement is the refusal to accept new administrative specialists, such as computer experts, as legitimate participants in the application of policy. It took some time for the computer specialist to be admitted to the ranks of public administration; but despite continuing resistance, he now occupies positions of high status in the Internal Revenue Service, the Census Bureau, and the Social Security Administration.

Most bureaucratic conflict is caused by differences between the viewpoints of specialists and those of employees whose administrative skills lie in managing general goals. The specialist is more likely to emphasize innovation in procedures and new approaches to problems, whereas the nonspecialist will probably consider consolidation of current tasks and the resolution of conflict between interests as more important. A specialist highly trained in the disposal of industrial waste might find his proposals for regulating disposal vetoed or modified by a nonspecialist superior who is sensitive to the political effects of promoting a new policy. Efforts to resolve such conflicts might include formal reorganization of authority; but simply reorganizing lines of command (changing staff and line functions, and modifying organization charts) does not get to the source of the disputes. Hence, administrators look outside the organization for support. They form informal policy alliances with partisan appointees, members of Congress, and pressure-group leaders; and they supplement internal conflict resolution with external bargaining.

BARGAINING AND INCREMENTAL CHANGE

Policy application is generally characterized by two basic features of the American political community: The formal organization of a bureaucracy suggests that it is directed by formal hierarchical controls, but both the Constitution and extraconstitutional procedures make it highly decentralized. Consequently, the bureaucracy works through bargaining, not command— particularly when agency leaders get their own political support from legislators and pressure groups.

The practice of incrementalism in policymaking (see Chapter 10), buttressed by the need to bargain and compromise, obstructs the efforts of the administration to secure consistent programs and pursue long-range goals. Consequently, administrators most often try to effect piecemeal but workable solutions to immediate problems regardless of the long-term effectiveness of the solutions. Federal programs of the 1960s and 1970s that aimed at fighting the "war on crime" and restoring "safe streets" are considered a massive and expensive failure by many, but powerful interests such as local and state law enforcement agencies, with the strong support by public opinion, have kept the programs going. Annual congressional and administrative tinkering with the amount of funding for such programs is likely to put off a frontal assault on the policy itself until the programs become intensely and widely discredited.

Congress and the bureaucracy

The view from the bureaucrat's desk is shaped not only by personal and organizational factors, but also by the pressures that the legislative branch imposes on him or her.

Article I of the Constitution empowers Congress to exercise control over the administrative branch by its authority to create administrative agencies, to advise and consent to presidential appointments, and to exercise the power of the purse. Implicit in such delegations are other powers. Congress derives its right to investigate the operations of the executive from its authority to make laws and to reorganize the bureaucracy as well as from its power to authorize new programs and departments. Ever since 1789, Congress has prescribed the organization of the executive branch, shaped the government's functions by appropriations, investigated practices and policies, and regulated federal employees.

CONGRESS AND THE CIVIL SERVICE

Students of public administration agree that the personnel policies of the civil service covering retirement, salary schedules, organization, public employee organizations, and employee participation in party activities are the province of Congress but that Congress should leave the formulation and application of detailed rules and regulations to the President and the Civil Service Commission. Congress has pretty much done so, although it has bowed to pressure from veteran's organizations that have sought hiring preference for veterans.

CONGRESS AND THE BUDGET

Budgets are the financial mirrors of what government is doing or plans to do. Because resources are limited, appropriations reflect the outcomes of conflicts among interests, supporting or opposing new programs, altering or retaining existing programs, or eliminating an activity entirely. For the administrator, the appropriations process consists of several stages of review during which the programs and proposals of his agency are at stake. The first is review by the Office of Management and Budget, which seeks to protect the President's interests in achieving his overall directives on the national budget.

Once an agency's request for appropriations has been incorporated in the President's budget, it is considered by Congress. The first step in the congressional review of an agency's request takes place in one of the subcommittees of the House Appropriations Committee. These subcommittees usually approach their review with an eye to cutting the requested appropriations. Sometimes, however, an agency has to accept unwanted programs that are especially important to the constituency of a powerful congressperson. A bureau chief called to testify before a subcommittee is subjected to intense questioning about the general goals and purposes for which the money has been requested, and sometimes to grilling about minor but embarrassing matters, such as a complaint about the agency that a subcommittee member may have had from one of his constituents. Above all, an agency must prevent the appropriations subcommittee from developing a hostile or unsympathetic attitude toward its programs. It will, therefore, try to build support for its programs among interests outside Congress by associating its own goals with those of its clientele and by maintaining close communications with appropriations subcommittees.

The House Appropriations Committee usually accepts the recommendations of its subcommittees, which normally propose cuts in agency requests. The Senate Appropriations Committee is a kind of appeals court for the agencies; it frequently restores some or all of the cuts made by the House. Most members of the Senate Appropriations Committee see their role as that of the "responsible legislator" who rectifies the wrongs done by "the irrepressible lower House." Conversely, members of the House Appropriations Committee consider it their duty to balance the action of Senate "dilettants who swap favors and do not care what happens to the public purse" (Wildavsky, 1974, p. 51). The bureaucrat must predict as best he can the reactions of the various committees in the two chambers, which means assessing what his agency can obtain in the political environment of each committee's attitudes as well as administrative constituency support and his own ability to convince congresspersons of the rightness of his agency's request for support.

The Office of Management and Budget (see Chapter 12) is less effective in controlling the budgets of agencies with special access to Congress than those of politically weaker agencies. Other stages in the appropriations process also reveal the politics of the budgetary process. In short, an agency must participate in the bargaining, persuasion, and compromise that mark the other policy processes.

As we have noted in Chapter 12, the effect of the new Congressional Budget Office in assisting Congress to exert greater long-term control over expenditures is as yet uncertain. Congress now has a professional staff and improved procedures for influencing general fiscal policies, but the alliances between some administrative agencies and key committees may be unaffected by the new process. However, if Congress can develop an effective review of general executive budgetary requests, the process could very well affect the fate of some agencies.

INFORMAL CONGRESSIONAL SUPERVISION

Congress obtains informal control over agencies from the relationship between executive officials and individual legislators. In committee hearings, legislators ask questions and make statements from which administrators can gather important clues about the preferences of congresspersons. Both administrators and interest groups know that the statements made by legislators at committee hearings are important, because the major decisions made in standing committees are rarely rejected by the whole Congress. Skillful administrators can use hearings to resist pressure from the President, private groups, and other administrative agencies.

Congressional-administrative relationships are an important informal means of control, because congresspersons act as administrative "lobbyists" for their constituents. Inquiries that a representative or senator addresses to an agency on behalf of a constituent or interest group usually get special attention, especially if the legislator is in a position to assist or block the agency's program. Most administrators will try not to antagonize a legislator; they may not comply with legislator's demands, but they will usually try hard to conciliate them.

Recognizing the powers of congressional committees, pressure groups and administrators often attempt to work out clearance for significant policies in advance. Relationships between an agency and the influential members of a committee, especially its chairman, are sometimes very close. During World War II, Representative Carl Vinson of Georgia, Chairman of the House Naval Affairs Committee, and the Navy Department were intimate because of Vinson's extensive knowledge of naval affairs. Because Vinson had served more than 20 years on the committee and because he was chairman, the Navy Department frequently consulted with him about policy. After the war, when unification of the armed services had been achieved, Vinson became Chairman of the House Armed Services Committee, a position he used to develop much the same relationship with the Army and Air Force as he already had with the Navy.

LIMITS ON CONGRESSIONAL CONTROL

The powers to investigate, legislate, reorganize, and control appropriations are powerful weapons in limiting the bureaucracy's influence in policymaking. Yet these controls are only nominally exercised by Congress.

The most important control is appropriations, but congressional control over spending has been marked by restraint. A study of the budgetary requests of 39 agencies handling domestic policy from 1947 to 1962 found that during this period 27 of the agencies received congressional appropriations within an average of 5 percent of what the President had requested and 35 were within 10 percent of these requests. It also found that at the administrative stage of budgetary review (the OMB), 24 of the 36 agencies had requested increases over the previous year of at least 10 percent; 11 had requested an increase of 20 percent; and 2 had requested an increase of at least 75 percent (Fenno, 1966). Congress does not cut back funds dramatically, at least not in the domestic area. Once the budgetary process has been completed by the President, Congress makes only small changes. This "incremental budgeting" means that "the budgets of most agencies inch upward over the years. Nothing short of a major social or economic crisis seems able to cause a major alteration" (Fenno, 1966, p. 143).

The pattern of congressional response to requests for appropriations is a result mostly of the congressional environment. A congressperson has neither the time nor the information to review such requests thoroughly. He must divide his attention among many legislative matters, and he must also service the many requests of his constituents. It is almost impossible for him to learn enough to review the operations and programs of all units in the executive branch. Some representatives, such as Appropriations subcommittee chairpersons, become highly knowledgeable experts in particular areas, but, on the whole, Congress must rely on the presidential budget and on the knowledge of his staff.

The fragmented congressional organization, bicameral system, and difficulties of coordinated leadership also reduce congressional control over the bureaucracy to a nominal level. Because congressional leadership has limited control in either of the two houses, bureaucratic interests (and the private interests that support them) have access to many veto points in the legislative process. The incrementalism that generally characterizes the legislative process protects and insulates the bureaucracy from more than nominal control by Congress. Reorganization of the executive branch, major changes in policy direction, and dramatic budget cuts are inconsistent with incremental change. Congress can review the administration, but it cannot effectively regulate it. Its influence over the bureaucracy consists of broad policy choices that, once made, are administered with limited legislative control.

The President and the bureaucracy

Although the bureaucracy looks to the President for policy leadership and initiative, a President's control over his administration is far from complete. Agencies with quasi-legislative and quasi-judicial functions are largely independent of direct presidential control because their governing executives are not subject to the President's power of removal and the agencies were deliberately established to operate outside the President's chain of command. Moreover, the President lacks the time and resources to supervise and direct the administrative structure over which he has formal authority. Instead, he deals with matters that he considers of greatest importance and leaves much of the bureaucracy free to operate at the discretion of career administrators. The ability of pressure groups to influence policy is enhanced by administrative discretion, especially if the clientele interests of an agency can readily turn to Congress. Even a department head or bureau chief who is loyal to the President may be put in a position where his support of his chief arouses the wrath of clientele groups and allied legislators.

THE POWER OF THE BUREAUCRACY

Certainly crisis situations reduce resistance to presidential initiative. But crisis is not the norm. Presidents must achieve their goals within the limits set by the two other branches of government, and they must also contend with a bureaucracy not geared to rapid or dramatic changes. When partisan control of the White House changes but Congress remains under the control of the opposition party, the President's problems increase. This was the situation Richard Nixon faced in 1969.

A case study of the clash between a conservative Republican President committed to reversing liberal social programs and a bureaucracy resistant to change reveals the power of the bureaucracy (Aberbach and Rockman, 1976, pp. 456–468). Nixon entered the White House in 1969 after eight years of Democratic "War on Poverty" programs that he wished to either curtail or eliminate. The new administration not only faced a Democratic-controlled Congress but also inherited high-level civil servants from the previous administration who occupied key positions in departments and agencies associated with domestic social service programs. Furthermore, Nixon was suspicious of some of his own political appointees. The authors of the case study interviewed 126 top-level administrators from 18 federal agencies with primary responsibilities in domestic policy to determine their attitudes about what role government should play in providing social services and their views on whether the political system provides equality of access and consideration to all groups ("representational equity"). Their findings "document a career bureaucracy with very little Republican representation but even more pointedly portray a social service bureaucracy dominated by administrators ideologically hostile to many of the directions pursued by the Nixon administration in the realm of social policy" (Aberbach and Rockman, pp. 466–467).

Party affiliation and the type of agency in which the administrators worked were the key factors in explaining their attitudes and beliefs. Democrats in social service agencies (OEO, HEW, HUD) were the most supportive of an active government role in meeting social problems and were most likely to express the beliefs that opportunities for some groups to influence government were not equal to those of other groups and that reform was needed. Republicans in nonsocial service agencies, (Interior, Treasury, ICC, Transportation) did not support an active and expanded government role in social services and thought groups were more equally represented than did Democrats. Although Republicans in social service agencies believed there were more representational inequities and a greater need for a strong government role in social affairs than their partisan counterparts in nonsocial service agencies saw, Democrats and Independents expressed those beliefs more than Republicans.

What might these findings reveal about future ideological clashes between Presidents and the bureaucracy? Certainly conservative or moderate Republican Presidents facing a more liberal bureaucracy and a Democratic Congress are the most likely to experience serious problems of bureaucratic control. Nixon did succeed in cutting and altering the antipoverty programs of the Johnson administration, but the changes reflected compromises forced by a Democratic Congress ideologically linked to key officials in the bureaucracy. However, even a Democratic President who is more centrist in social policy than the bureaucracy could also have problems (Aberbach and Rockman, p. 468).

When a President does choose to intervene in a dispute within the executive branch, he may not get his way. The classic example (others are less publicized) is the friction between the President and the Army Corps of Engineers. By statute, the corps is in the Department of Defense under the Commander in Chief, but in practice it considers itself responsible to Congress (Maas, 1950, pp. 576–593). Originally designed to handle federal flood control and harbor projects, the Corps began to expand its activities in the 1930s to include land reclamation, power production, land irrigation, and other matters. The resulting conflict with the Bureau of Reclamation in the Department of Interior caused President Roosevelt, and later President Truman, to intervene on behalf of the bureau. The corps used its close association with Congress to resist presidential directives and policy statements submitted to congressional committees handling water projects. Because Corps projects are of special interest to congresspersons and their constituencies, the President has been unable to develop a coordinated water-resources and flood-control policy.

THE EFFECT OF CONSTITUENCY

Administrative agencies are interested in their own survival and expansion; their activities must therefore have political support. Service agencies must keep the support of the groups most directly affected by their functions and services. The larger the number of states or congressional districts that an agency can serve, the greater will be its effectiveness in building a supportive clientele and influencing Congress. The Corps of Engineers' constituency has for many years included states and districts throughout the nation, since its operations include navigation, flood control, the dredging of harbors, and other water-resource projects. Similarly, the Department of Defense builds support by linking the interests of local and state governments, labor organizations, and business interests, all of which receive economic advantages from defense contracts and military bases in their area.

By comparison, the President represents a larger public, and his policies and decisions must accommodate a more diversified clientele. The compromises he negotiates in pursuing his goals are likely to differ from those shaped by administrative agencies. The President is only one source of bureaucratic vitality; other sources become, in effect, his rivals for control over the administrative branch. Despite these limitations the President is a very powerful force. He is the center of national attention and can use that position to mobilize support for his goals. He sets the tone and style of his administration, and appoints and dismisses department heads. Congress takes its budgetary cues from the President; and although he cannot prevent some agency requests from winning congressional approval without his support, the budget remains a significant weapon of presidential control.

Popular control and policy application

Liberal democracy requires that policymakers be responsible to the governed. But how can the bureaucracy be held responsible to the citizens in a democratic system?

Until about the time of the New Deal, Americans were generally more interested in increasing the professionalism of the public servants than in controlling the power of bureaucracy. The reforms of the late nineteenth century emphasized merit and knowledge as the basis for government employment and paved the way for eliminating the spoils system in the federal service. Since the 1930s, the public administrator's part in policymaking and his relationship to the whole political system have received greater attention.

STRUCTURAL CONTROL OF BUREAUCRATIC POWER

The bureaucracy is deeply involved in formulating public policy and therefore has great power. Control over bureaucratic activity results from direct intervention by the President and Congress and from the limits its own environment imposes on it. Limits on bureaucratic action flow from the system itself, especially from the two basic features of a pluralist community and the fragmentation of policymaking authority.

Separation of powers and checks and balances prevent any branch of government and any combination of interests from controlling the whole of the policymaking process. Federalism also divides governing authority and contributes to the fragmentation of power. Fragmented policymaking is more likely to produce an inefficient administrative organization than a system that is tyrannical or uncontrollable. Multiple sources of power and multiple veto points are more likely to produce incremental change and limited central authority than dramatic departures in policy or a unified source of policy. The problem is not one of a bureaucracy intent on moving an unwilling public toward dramatic change. On the contrary it is more a problem of moving the system rapidly enough to accommodate the demands arising from both a rapidly changing environment and the traditional, deep-seated pluralistic distribution of power.

Does fragmented policymaking in a pluralist community encourage the development of an autonomous and unresponsive bureaucracy? On the whole, the pattern of decisionmaking does not reveal an autonomous bureaucracy. It is true that the independence of some agencies within the bureaucratic structure is promoted by close associations between the agencies and congressional committees, the support of agency programs by clientele groups, the ability of an agency to mobilize clientele and employee support in achieving its goals, the possession of technical and specialized knowledge by agency personnel, and bureaucratic lobbying of Congress on behalf of an agency's programs.

Two counterforces are important, however. First, the President, Congress, and the courts all have the power to mold policy. The President can and does demand action from the agencies under his control. Congress can and does legislate changes and impose restrictions. The courts can and do rule against administrative action. Further, competition within and between agencies fosters pluralist administrative decisionmaking, another barrier to bureaucratic autonomy.

Second, pressure flows in several directions. Interests are opposed by competing interests. Access to one committee or one house of Congress is balanced by the opposition's access to other points in the legislative process. Executive agencies trying to block presidential policy are opposed by other agencies that support him. Moreover, the setting or implementation of policy may be blocked by interests within an agency. Faced with pressures exerted by competing forces, an administrator may choose not to act, or his choice may represent the point of least resistance.

When we refer to limitations imposed by multiple competing interests we do not mean that there is equality of access, resources, or influence among groups. As in other aspects of the policy process, differences in resources and skills advantage some interests and hurt others. For example, until recently, consumers were poorly organized and were consequently at a disadvantage in comparison with traditionally strong and well-organized clientele groups. Public interest groups such as Common Cause and groups in support of Ralph Nader now provide active and influential spokespersons for consumers. Aided by consumer and environmental legislation, by new agencies concerned with environmental protection, and by public demands for more consumer-oriented actions by regulatory agencies, these groups should be able to increase their influence relative to competing interests in and outside government.

Public interest groups are, however, financed and supported primarily by the middle and upper classes. Citizens at the lowest levels of the socioeconomic ladder remain generally unorganized and are forced to depend on the support of better organized and financed groups. They are represented only to the extent that other interests, including the bureaucracy, continue to speak and act for them.

IMPROVING THE REFLEXES OF THE BUREAUCRACY

The very size and complexity of the bureaucracy hinder its responsiveness to the public, especially to the individual citizen. The faceless, impersonal, seemingly immovable bureaucrat is too often a reality for many citizens. Some organizations in the federal administrative structure, such as the Office of Management and Budget and the Civil Rights Commission, monitor the activities of agencies to see that they conform to defined policy goals. The OMB acts on behalf of the President to see that agencies follow his general directives in financial matters. The Civil Rights Commission reviews the hiring practices of agencies to prevent discrimination against minority groups and women in personnel practices. These are examples of controls *within* the bueaucracy that are aimed at assuring compliance and responsiveness to internal rules, regulations, and expectations. But what arrangements protect citizens against the behavior of arbitrary or unresponsive officials?

In many other countries, as well as in about ten states and some local governments in the United States, an officially designated person serves as the representative of the citizen in his or her interactions with the bureaucracy. Called an ombudsman, this official and his staff handle complaints and try to resolve disputes. Proposals for a federal ombudsman have received support as one means of bringing greater responsiveness to the bureaucracy. In campaigning for the Presidency, President Carter promised to bring about a more responsive bureaucracy through both administrative reorganization and a study of how to improve the effectiveness of the process whereby citizens communicate their complaints and the bureaucracy acts upon them.

A bureaucracy that is responsive to citizens is vitally important to the concept of democratic representation; it is also important to the representation of that part of society not well represented through organized interests in possession of political resources that can achieve access to the bureaucracy and thus achieve action on group goals and grievances.

THE DANGER OF IMMOBILIZATION

Viewed from the perspective of response to broad social change, the changes of an arbitrary, unresponsive, or irresponsible bureaucracy is probably less real than the danger of a bureaucracy immobilized by fragmentation. The pluralism of the American policy process clearly affects the direction, extent, and pace of change. How can a large bureaucracy, subject to the pulls and pressures of competing forces both from within and without, be effectively mobilized and coordinated to meet the challenges of a rapidly changing social, economic, and political environment? Fragmentation does not prevent change, but it does highlight the tension between pressures for change and the politics of compromise and accommodation of competing interests that ordinarily allows only incremental change. The bureaucracy is less a master than it is an instrument for action or inaction; it is limited by the same multiple interests that set the agenda for action in other parts of the political system. Thus it is difficult to answer our question about bureaucratic mobilization. Historically, major changes have been infrequent and have resulted from the entry of new groups making new demands. The last major administrative change occurred in the 1930's in response to major shifts in public attitudes that increased support for vastly expanding the role of government in economic and social affairs. Today, the demands and pressures for change lie in such areas as consumer rights, environmental protection, and a more responsive government. We can expect the bureaucracy to respond to basically the same forces that move the Presidency and Congress. The pace and direction of change will be closely related to the strength of new forces in the political system.

THE COURTS AND POLICY ADJUDICATION

The meaning of "the rule of law" was never more dramatically demonstrated than during the 1970s when a President was forced to resign and the attorney general of the United States and several other of the most powerful persons in the nation were sent to prison for violations of the law. The determination to force the revelation of Watergate evidence, including an order that President Nixon turn the White House Watergate tapes over to the court, made Federal District Judge John J. Sirica a celebrated figure.

The law and the courts mean different things to different people. For most Americans they symbolize the commitment of a democratic society to a system of justice based on equality before the law and protection of the individual against arbitrary behavior by government in criminal trials. The threat to "go to court" implies that grievances can be redressed in a fair hearing by an impartial judge or jury. Ultimately, it is possible to appeal to the U.S. Supreme Court itself. The Supreme Court is generally held in awe as the ultimate protector of the rights of the people against "unconstitutional" actions by Congress, the executive branch, or other levels of government in the federal system.

For some Americans, however, the law and the courts represent unequal and differential justice. The charge that the poor go to jail and the rich go free or receive light sentences has some basis in fact. As one author has commented, "Poor people are prone to legal trouble. They are often defendants, rarely plaintiffs" (Wald, 1965, p. 6). The socially and economically disadvantaged frequently lack the financial resources necessary to obtain legal assistance; they are also less aware of their legal rights, particularly in matters such as consumer fraud, rental housing, and debtors rights. James Eisenstein (1973) has effectively summarized a growing body of evidence that the system of justice reflects a reality different from the theory that underlies it:

> The poor, the young, the very old (especially if poor), and disadvantaged minority group members receive a disproportionately large share of the sanctions and a correspondingly small share of the benefits allocated by the legal process in comparison to other individuals in society. . . . The inescapable conclusion is that these outcomes [of the legal process] reflect the same values and balance of interests that characterize other components of the political system. (pp. 323 and 338)

A contrasting view of the role of law in American society is offered by Federal District Judge Leon Higgenbotham. Although he is sensitive to the need for courts to respond to contemporary problems, Higgenbotham argues that "the greatest legacy of our legal and judicial institutions [in this century] has been their role in helping to secure the rights of racial minorities, women, the voter, working people, and others" (Higgenbotham, 1976, p. 140).

Whether the courts are doing an acceptable job depends upon one's expectations of the judicial system in the resolution of social conflict. Social conflicts of all kinds often grow into legal controversies. Illustrating this range of issues, the following decisions were among those handed down by the Supreme Court in 1977. The Court ruled that spanking a junior high student with a paddle does not constitute "cruel and unusual punishment"; that the State of Connecticut could limit medicaid payments to persons undergoing "medically necessary" abortions; that a suburban government's refusal to allow a low-income, integrated housing project to be built, even though it had a "racially disproportionate" impact in the community, was not a violation of any person's civil rights; that an Oklahoma law prohibiting the sale of 3.2 percent beer to males under the age of 21, while permitting its sale to females at age 18, constituted sex discrimination; that Arizona could not prohibit lawyers from advertising competitive prices for certain legal services; and that freedom of the press under the First Amendment did not give a TV station the right to broadcast the performance of a "human cannonball" shot 200 feet through the air into a net, because the performer's money-making activities would be injured (that is, people would not pay to see him if they could watch the act on television).

The procedures, organization, constitutional authority, and environment within these controversies were decided are clearly different from those affecting executive or legislative conflict resolution. Nevertheless, judicial policymaking is shaped by the same broad features that affect policymaking in the other branches of government: federalism, the separation of powers, and checks and balances.

Policy adjudication

A DUAL SYSTEM OF COURTS

Federalism imposes on Americans a dual system of courts: state and national. The Constitution speaks only of national jurisdiction and assigns to federal courts the authority to hear only specific kinds of cases. The jurisdiction of state courts is fixed by the constitution and laws of each state, subject to the supremacy of the national Constitution. The two systems come together in those instances where the parties to a suit are able to raise points involving "federal questions." Ultimately, the Supreme Court of the United States determines when a federal question is "substantial" enough to be heard. In most instances, however, the two jurisdictions remain separate, each operating on the same persons within a state, sometimes using different legal procedures. Because federal and state courts apply the law of their respective jurisdictions, it is possible to be tried twice for the same offense; the double jeopardy provision of the Constitution protects only against trial twice for the same offense by one level of government (*Bartkus* v. *Illinois*, 1959; *Abbate* v. *U.S.*, 1959). The vast majority of cases decided in American courts begin and end at the state level. The decisions of the U.S. Supreme Court receive wide publicity because they rule on controversial issues whose resolution requires interpretation of the Constitution or federal law.

CONSTITUTIONAL AUTHORITY

The judicial power of the federal government is spelled out by Article III, Section 2 of the Constitution. This power extends "to all Cases in Law and Equity, arising under this Constitution, the Laws of the United States and Treaties made, or which shall be made, under their Authority." Specifically, Article III extends federal jurisdiction to cases involving admiralty and maritime laws, federal law, treaties, or the Constitution, and to suits to which the United States is a party, suits between citizens of different states, suits in which one state sues another, and suits involving foreign ambassadors or other official foreign representatives. State courts are not barred from hearing cases involving these matters because Article III also grants Congress authority to assign jurisdiction to state courts to hear some cases concurrently or even exclusively. Congress has provided that suits between citizens of different states involving more than $10,000 may be heard in either state or federal courts but those involving lesser amounts must be heard in state courts.

All cases not authorized by the Constitution to federal courts fall within the exclusive jurisdiction of state courts. A violator of state law may under specified conditions appeal to a federal court, but his case must first be heard in a state court. A person convicted of a crime in a state court may appeal to a federal court if he feels that the procedures in his trial violated his constitutional rights.

FEDERAL JUDICIAL ORGANIZATION

Unable to resolve the dispute over creating a separate system of federal courts or allowing state courts to decide federal cases subject to a review by a Supreme Court, the Framers provided in Article III for a Supreme Court and granted to Congress the authority to establish lower federal courts. The Judiciary Act of 1789 established a Supreme Court with one chief justice and five associate justices and provided for 13 federal district courts. It also created 3 circuit courts, each consisting of any two justices of the Supreme Court and a judge from the district in which a case was heard. In 1891, Congress substituted a separate system of 10 circuit courts of appeals. The number of justices on the Supreme Court has varied from five in 1801 to as many as ten in 1863; it has remained at nine since 1869. Congress established three other courts—the Court of Customs and Patent Appeals, the Customs Court, and the Court of Claims—to complete the system of courts required by Article III (see Figure 14.1).

The national court system reflects the federal pattern. Judicial districts generally follow state boundaries, and the circuit system divides the nation into ten geographical units or circuits. Each state has its own judicial system beneath the national system. The Supreme Court supervises state courts through the supremacy clause of the Constitution, which empowers the Court to declare void any state actions that conflict with the "supreme law of the land": the Constitution, valid acts of Congress, and the treaties of the United States.

All the courts established under Article III are called constitutional courts to distinguish them from the legislative courts created by Congress under authority drawn from other clauses in the Constitution. The United States Tax Court is a legislative court established in accordance with congressional authority to levy and collect taxes. The Court of Military Appeals and the system of territorial courts are derived from the congressional authority to regulate land and naval forces and to acquire and govern territories. Legislative courts are not created under Article III, so Congress does not have to adhere to

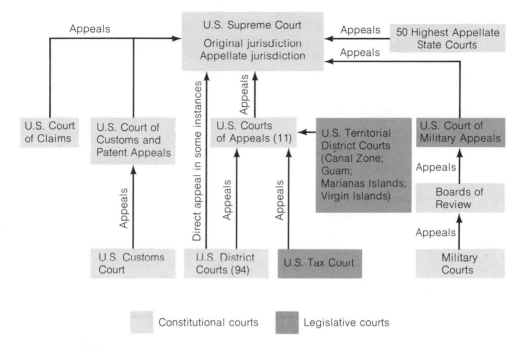

FIGURE 14.1

The Federal Court Structure.

the requirement that judges be given life terms or to restrictions on the salary and the removal of federal judges.

Federal courts exercise original jurisdiction, appellate jurisdiction, or both. A court exercising original jurisdiction is the first to hear and decide a case; a court with appellate jurisdiction hears appeals on cases already decided at a lower level. Article III requires the Supreme Court to exercise original jurisdiction "in all Cases affecting Ambassadors, other public Ministers and Consuls, and those in which a State shall be a Party." Except for this requirement, Congress may assign original or appellate jurisdiction to district courts and courts of appeals as it sees fit.

Federal district courts

Most federal cases are decided by district courts; each year about 100,000 cases are initiated in these lowest federal courts. District courts exercise only original jurisdiction, handling matters ranging from criminal trials to the review and enforcement of orders issued by federal administrative agencies. The 94 district courts are distributed so that at least one is located in each of the 50 states, the District of Columbia, Puerto Rico, the Canal Zone, and the

Virgin Islands. Almost half of the cases heard at this level are filed in the 12 district courts in the larger metropolitan areas. Each district has at least one judge but many have several; in 1977 there were 398 district judges. Normally, one district judge presides over a case, although the law requires a panel of three judges to hear some types of disputes, the most important of which involve the constitutionality of federal or state statutes.

The classic image of an adversary system of justice, characterized by the confrontation of competing parties in open court, does not apply to the vast majority of cases filed in federal district courts (and state trial courts, as well). Only about 10 percent of civil suits and about 15 percent of criminal cases are resolved by trial. Civil suits are usually settled out of court through negotiations between the contending parties. The great majority of criminal cases are dismissed before trial or the accused pleads guilty or does not contest the charge.

It is clear that the judicial process involves participants outside the courtroom. Lawyers often negotiate out-of-court settlements of civil suits for their clients through bargaining with the opposing party. In criminal cases, defendants engage in "plea bargaining" with prosecuting attorneys; in return for a plea of guilty to a lesser charge or promise of a light sentence or both, a defendant agrees to plead guilty without going to trial. Such "bargain justice" reduces the work load of courts, but it also means that "the norms of production may conflict with the norms of law," that these arrangements may be inconsistent with protection of the right to trial by jury (Klonoski and Mendelsohn, 1970, p. 76).

United States courts of appeals

There are ten circuit courts and one District of Columbia circuit court. Circuit courts have from 3 to 15 members and include from three to nine states within their circuits. About 80 percent of all circuit court cases involve appeals from district courts; the remainder are original proceedings and appeals from administrative regulatory agencies. Original jurisdiction cases account for only about 2 percent of all cases. About half the cases filed with courts of appeals are disposed of with formal decisions after a hearing. The remainder are dismissed without a hearing or consolidated with other cases. Of the cases appealed and decided by formal decision, about one in five reverse federal district court or administrative agency decisions (Goldman and Jahnige, 1971, pp. 105–107).

The Supreme Court

The Supreme Court exercises both original and appellate jurisdiction, but original jurisdiction covers only a small fraction of the Court's work; between 1789 and 1976, it rendered only 127 decisions under its original jurisdiction. Article III gives Congress the power to regulate the appellate jurisdiction of the Supreme Court. The Court gets its work load as well as its influence in policymaking from its authority to review the decisions of lower federal courts and to hear appeals from state courts in matters that involve "federal questions."

Appeals reach the Court on the basis of a *writ of certiorari*, a *writ of appeal*, or by *certification*. Certification, which is very rarely used, is a method by which lower federal courts request instruction on questions of law from the Supreme Court. A writ of *certiorari*—meaning "made more certain"—is an order issued by the Court directing a lower court to send the records of a case to the Supreme Court for review. The Court usually denies about 95 percent of petitions for such writs, which means that it will not hear oral arguments or accept written arguments by the petitioning party. However, about 90 percent of all cases accepted by the Court each year reach it through writs of certiorari. At least four justices must vote to grant a writ, and their decision is limited to cases on legal issues that go beyond the immediate interests of the litigants.

The writ of appeal is granted by statute. Congress has directed that a case may be appealed by the losing party to the Supreme Court under any of these circumstances: (1) if a state court declares a federal statute or treaty unconstitutional; (2) if a state court upholds a state statute in opposition to a challenge that the statute conflicts with the federal Constitution, federal law, or a federal treaty; (3) if a district court declares a federal statute unconstitutional in a suit to which the United States is a party; (4) if a district court issues an injunction against the enforcement of a state statute; or (5) if a court of appeals declares that a state statute is void because it is contrary to federal law or treaty.

In practice, the Supreme Court may refuse to hear an appeal on the grounds that a "substantial federal question" is lacking or because it has no jurisdiction over the legal issue involved. In a typical annual term—from October to the end of June—the Court dismisses more than 50 percent of the appeals based on statutory rights. The Court does not explain why it accepts some appeals and rejects others. It has full discretion on whether to issue a writ, and therefore, within the bounds of the cases on appeal coming its way, the Court selects the issues it will decide.

WORK LOAD OF THE COURT.   The number of appeals brought to the Supreme Court has steadily increased over the past several decades. Even though the Court retains substantial control over the cases it will fully consider, the number of appeals imposes a growing burden on the nine justices. Table 14.1 shows the total number of cases brought to the Court from 1966 through the 1976 term. Obviously, it would be impossible for the Court to hear oral arguments on over 4,000 cases per year, but the Court must review each case and every justice participates in any action taken by the Court.

Of the 4,730 cases filed in the 1976 term, 85 percent were disposed of and the remainder carried over to the next term. Table 14.2 shows the disposition of

TABLE 14.1
U.S. Supreme Court caseload,
1966–1975 terms

Term	Number of cases
1966	3356
1967	3586
1968	3918
1969	4150
1970	4212
1971	4533
1972	4640
1973	5079
1974	4668
1975	4761
1976	4730

TABLE 14.2
Disposition of cases by the U.S. Supreme Court, 1976 term

Docket	Number of cases	Number and percent disposed of on merits	Number and percent denied or dismissed
Original	2	2 (100.0)	0
Appellate	1,929	309 (16.0)	1,620 (84.0)
Miscellaneous	2,075	62 (2.9)	2,013 (97.1)
Total	4,006	373 (9.3)	3,633 (90.7)

Source: Harvard Law Review, 1977, 91, p. 298. (Copyright 1977 by the Harvard Law Review Association.)

the cases on each of the Court's dockets during this typical term. Overall, the Court denied or dismissed almost nine out of ten of all appeals and petitions. The appellate docket includes writs of appeals and petitions for *certiorari*. The miscellaneous docket contains *in forma pauperis* petitions, which are usually handwritten or typed papers submitted by indigent persons—frequently in prison—that do not follow the required form for other types of petitions for review. As Table 14.2 indicates, the large majority of miscellaneous docket cases were dismissed by the Court (97.1 percent) and most petitions under appellate review were also denied or dismissed (84 percent).

Of the 373 cases disposed of "on merits," 142 were decided by full written opinions, the remainder being "affirmed," "denied," "dismissed," or disposed of with *per curiam* ("for the court") opinions. The latter are unsigned and usually short statements through which the Court decides cases considered simple enough not to require long statements to justify its decision.

A NEW NATIONAL COURT OF APPEALS? The increasing work load and growing backlogs of cases in both federal and state courts has been the object of concern and substantial written commentary. Chief Justice Warren Burger of the Supreme Court is a leading proponent of "court reform" to not only improve the efficiency of courts in handling cases but also enhance the quality of justice rendered at all levels of the court structure by, for example, reducing delays between the arrest and trial of criminal defendants. In an address to the American Bar Association in 1970, Burger emphasized that the increasing case loads are due to the economic and social changes that have occurred during the middle decades of the twentieth century. The automobile alone has resulted in thousands of lawsuits each year; legislative and judicial decisions regarding the rights of defendants in criminal cases require greater care by trial courts in procedural matters; and the congestion and problems in our large cities have produced conflicts that have found their way into the courts as well as into the other branches of government. The chief justice has advocated better methods and machinery for handling growing case loads, as well as better financing and more judges for federal courts.

As the number of cases in lower federal courts has increased, so too have the appeals coming to the Supreme Court. One proposed solution for handling the burden faced by the justices is a National Court of Appeals. A distinguished study group on the work load of the Supreme Court proposed in 1973 that a new National Court of Appeals be established immediately below the Supreme Court. The new seven-member court would consist of judges from the 11 courts of appeals who would serve three-year staggered terms. This court would screen appeals coming to the Supreme Court and could deny, review, or pass the case on to the Supreme Court for final disposition. The proposal mentioned the expectation that about 400 hundred cases would be passed on to the Supreme Court each year. The presumption is that this system would eliminate the need for the Court to review all cases coming to it on appeal, thereby allowing more time for the Supreme Court to consider the cases before it and improving the overall quality of decisions.

Introduced in Congress in 1975, the plan received strong criticism from legal circles, which argued that the new court would only create another layer in the federal court hierarchy and would reduce the prestige of the Supreme Court. While the new court concept was endorsed by five of the current Supreme Court justices, other present and former justices disagreed that the Court's review of appeals imposed an excessive burden on the Court. Congress has not acted on legislation to create the new court, although it is still being proposed by many who see it as a major means to relieve the case load burden of the Supreme Court.

CONSTITUTIONAL AUTHORITY AND FEDERAL ORGANIZATION

The court that has jurisdiction in a case is very significant for the parties involved in litigation as well as for the public affected by judicial decisions. Differences in decisions on civil rights and liberties between some of the state supreme courts and the United States Supreme Court are extensive. District and circuit courts in some parts of the nation show similar differences.

District and circuit courts encompass different geographical areas. District courts may include only parts of one state, whereas circuit courts are regional. As a result, they reflect different social and cultural influences: "Policies are formulated by [district] judges with strong local connections, are administered by a locally appointed and sanctioned court staff, and serve a clientele usually drawn from the district" (Richardson and Vines, 1970, p. 46).

Courts of appeals have a larger geographical constituency and are therefore more free of the localism that restricts district courts; however, the effects of regional associations are also evident. The pull of regional ties was revealed by the findings of J. Richardson and K. N. Vines (1967), who studied the frequency with which lower court decisions in civil liberties cases were reversed by higher courts from 1956 to 1961. Courts of appeals agreed with district court decisions more than the Supreme Court agreed with courts of appeals decisions. Richardson and Vines concluded that "the remnants of parochialism which are maintained in the judicial system by the courts of appeals—the fact that judges are appointed from the circuit, often with district court experience and values, and adjudicating in circuit boundaries along state lines—made the courts of appeals responsive to the district courts" (p. 605).

The effect of localism is lessened, however, by a number of factors: The life tenure of federal judges insulates them from the pressures and demands of local interests; judges are united by experience and values drawn from similar legal educations; the federal courts are subject to common rules of procedure and legal concepts, and their actions are subject to review and veto by established patterns of appeal. Even so, the localism of federal court organization reduces the centralizing tendencies of a hierarchic organization, headed by the Supreme Court, that responds to a national constituency.

The hierarchical judicial system, coupled with the Supreme Court's authority to hear appeals from both state and federal courts, heightens the Court's influence in policymaking. The Court is the final judicial voice in resolving conflicts over such matters as school segregation, legislative reapportionment, and freedom of expression; all have great political and social consequences. Although final decisions in the vast majority of cases are reached in state and lower federal courts, the Supreme Court is the ultimate arbiter of disputes.

SELECTION OF JUDGES

District and courts of appeals appointments

A general summary by Richardson and Vines (1970) of how lower federal court appointments are made reveals that a few individuals control such appointments.

> Senator(s) of the presidential party, and/or [the] local presidential party and the President and his advisers interact to produce a nominee who is then affirmed by the acquiescence of the Senate Judiciary Committee and a majority of the Senate. (p. 64)

Although the Constitution gives the President the power to appoint and leaves the power to "advise and consent" to the Senate, in practice the roles have been reversed. Senators of the President's party and state party organizations have the most influence over these appointments. In selecting judges for district and appeals courts, the President must adhere to the custom of senatorial courtesy. This custom, which the Senate is willing to sustain should the President violate it, permits a senator of the President's party to block confirmation of appointees to lower court positions in his home state. The President also finds that senators must be consulted on prospective nominations and that they are not bashful in sponsoring candidates for judicial appointment.

Of 920 persons appointed to the federal district bench from 1908 through 1960, 811 (88 percent) were of the same party as the President (*House Judiciary Subcommittee Hearings, 87th Congress, 1961,* pp. 402–403). Table 14.3 presents data on appointments to both district and appeals courts from Franklin Roosevelt through the first year of the Carter administration. It is clear that lower appointments reflect the control of the party in the White House.

Presidents can substantially affect the partisan profile of lower courts through the appointment process. In five years Nixon appointed about half of the total number of judges serving on district and circuit court benches. Appointments are given usually to party activists, but the relative influence of party, compared to factors such as localism, the norms of judicial behavior, and personal ideology, is extremely difficult to measure. Judges, like other public officials, bring to the bench preferences and predilections which are the product of socializing experiences prior to assuming office. Partisanship is but one of these experiences.

The prestige, relatively high salaries, and life tenure of judicial appointments guarantee that senators and state party organizations will be deeply interested in influencing the choice of appointees. This influence is obviously enhanced by the localized nature of the federal judicial organization. The federal pattern has required that district and appeals judges be drawn from the state or circuit in which the vacancy opens. Richardson and Vines found that most district and appeals judges on the bench in 1963 were born and attended law school in

TABLE 14.3
Party affiliation of federal judicial appointments, 1933–1977
(district courts and courts of appeals)

President	Total	Democrat	Republican	Percent of President's party
Roosevelt (D)	194	188	6	96.9
Truman (D)	125	116	9	92.8
Eisenhower (R)	174	9	165	94.8
Kennedy (D)	123*	111	11	90.2
Johnson (D)	168	159	9	94.6
Nixon (R)	214†	15	192	92.7
Ford (R)	64	12	52	81.3
Carter (D)	27	27	0	100.0
Totals	1,089	637	444	93.4

*Includes one New York Liberal.
†Includes six nominees for whom no party affiliation was available and one independent
Source: Adapted from *Congressional Quarterly Weekly Report,* November 19, 1977, pp. 2443–2444.

the state of the district or circuit they served. Those not born or educated there were residents at the time of appointment.

In response to the growing number of cases filed in lower federal courts, Congress considered expanding the number of federal district and circuit judges. Since 1970 the number of case filings in district courts has increased by 36 percent and in courts of appeals by 140 percent. Prior to 1977, the Democratic-controlled Congress refused to authorize additional judgeships, most probably because the new appointments would have been made by a Republican President. The election of Jimmy Carter facilitated passage of a bill in 1978 that increased the number of district and appeals court judges. As a result, President Carter will appoint more than 150 new judges, most of them at the district level, in addition to filling vacancies caused by the resignation or death of incumbent judges. During the 1976 campaign Carter pledged that he would appoint federal judges "strictly on the basis of merit, without consideration of political . . . influence." However, the new President only suggested to Democratic senators that voluntary "merit selection commissions" be appointed in their states to serve as advisory units. In addition, the President issued a carefully worded executive order establishing a U.S. Circuit Judge Nominating Commission. Senators from a few states did devise advisory panels for recommending district judges, but it remains doubtful whether these steps have basically altered the traditional system of selecting lower court appointees.

Supreme Court appointments

Historically, Presidents have had the opportunity to nominate one justice about every two years. If the Court is closely divided on issues, one or two appointments can tip the balance in the direction of the minority or strengthen the position of a weak majority. Most of the 100 justices who have sat on the Supreme Court were selected by Presidents more interested in their "ideological partisanship"—that is, their positions on the socioeconomic issues of the day—than in their scholarly knowledge or prior experience on the bench. Presidents have appointed only 13 candidates not of their own party to the Supreme Court, preferring to choose those whose views are similar to their own.

David Rohde and Harold Spaeth (1976, pp. 107–109) have estimated the extent to which Presidents from Taft through Nixon were "ideologically" successful in their choice of nominees. Based on their assumption that Republican Presidents would prefer justices whose decisions reflected moderate to conservative voting preferences and Democratic Presidents would prefer justices with moderate to liberal voting patterns, the investigators found that: (1) about three-fourths of the nominees of both Republican and Democratic Presidents supported presidential views; and (2) Presidents were most successful in choosing justices consistent with their policy views when the appointees had prior service on the bench.

Of course, some Presidents emphasize the policy views of nominees more than others. This was certainly true with Franklin Roosevelt during the 1930s when he chose nominees he could expect to counter the conservative posture of a Supreme Court that blocked major New Deal programs. Richard Nixon campaigned for the Presidency in 1968 on the issue of law and order, attributing part of the problem of crime and lawlessness to Warren Court decisions that strengthened the rights of defendants in criminal cases. Nixon was clearly satisfied with the performance of the four Justices confirmed during his first term in office—Burger, Blackmun, Powell, and Rehnquist. In accepting renomination as President he pledged that he would continue to make appointments "to strengthen the peace forces in the United States," a reference to the Burger court's modification of the Warren court decisions in cases involving defendant's rights.

Measured by their educations, family backgrounds, and political and professional careers, Supreme Court justices are an elite group. John R. Schmidhauser (1960) studied the social backgrounds of 92 Supreme Court Justices who served between 1789 and 1959: One-third came from families with a tradition of judicial service; all but 9 of the 92 were from socially and economically advantaged families; almost 90 percent were of British ancestry; 88 percent were Protestant; almost all came from politically active families and were themselves politically active; and 80 percent had been educated in prestigious law schools or had studied law under a prominent lawyer or judge. If the Supreme Court is the guardian of the American conscience, says Schmidhauser, "it is essentially the conscience of the American upper-middle class sharpened by the imperative of individual social responsibility and political activism, and conditioned by the conservative impact of legal training and professional legal attitudes and associations" (p. 59).

The Supreme Court frequently decides major issues of public policy, so the attitudes of the justices are crucial, and interest groups are deeply interested in the choice of a nominee to the Supreme Court. The Senate rejected two of President Nixon's nominations to the Court, dramatizing the clash of interests over the Supreme Court. Following Justice Abe Fortas' resignation from the Court in 1969, Nixon nominated Clement Haynsworth of South Carolina, chief justice of the Fourth Circuit Court of Appeals. The Senate Judiciary Committee approved the nomination, but Haynsworth was strongly opposed by labor and civil rights leaders who attacked his voting record on the lower federal court bench. Haynsworth was also accused of impropriety and poor judgment in participating in cases before the Fourth Circuit Court of Appeals in which he was said to have a financial involvement. Despite strong pressure from the White House, the Senate rejected Haynsworth's nomination.

In early 1970, President Nixon nominated another southerner, also an appeals court judge, G. Harrold Carswell of Florida. Carswell's nomination was opposed on grounds that he had given a "White supremacy" speech while campaigning for state office in 1948, that his voting record as a federal judge revealed "racist" tones, and that his ability was mediocre. Again, labor and civil rights interests fought the nomination, and despite the President's vigorous efforts to win approval, the nomination was rejected by the Senate. With the nomination of Harry A. Blackmun of Minnesota, another court of appeals judge, the President finally won by unanimous vote Senate confirmation of a conservative justice.

The American Bar Association (ABA) has long sought, with some success, to serve as a consultant to the President in the appointment of judges. President Eisenhower asked the opinion of the ABA's Committee on the Federal Judiciary before submitting the nomination of William J. Brennan, Jr., to the Senate. But President Kennedy appointed Arthur Goldberg without seeking the committee's opinion. Early in his administration, President Nixon indicated that any candidate for a lower federal court appointment rated "not qualified" by the ABA Committee would not be nominated. After the Haynsworth and Carswell nominations were rejected, the President took the unprecedented action of announcing through Attorney General John Mitchell that prospective Supreme Court nominees would be submitted to the ABA Committee for consideration. The implication was that any such nominee who failed to receive a rating of "qualified" or better would not be nominated (Weaver, 1970, p. 1). Although President Ford did not repeat Nixon's pledge, he asked the ABA to review his nomination of John Paul Stevens, which it strongly endorsed.

The ABA has consistently urged Presidents to select judges who demonstrate diligence, legal scholarship, and honesty rather than appointing them for political reasons. Beyond these qualifications, the Bar Association has never offered more explicit criteria on the qualities of a good judge; and despite its support for nonpolitical appointments, its stands on social and economic policies over the years have had a strong conservative bias. In this respect, it is no different from other groups that seek to influence judicial policymaking by urging that justices with views similar to their own be appointed. Joel Grossman's 1965 study of the role of the ABA's Committee on the Federal Judiciary demonstrated that the committee was composed largely of older, more experienced lawyers who were partners in big-city law firms. Although this "legal establishment" bias has been modified to some extent, the committee tends to reflect the more conservative image of the ABA itself (pp. 83–91). Because it is the major representative of the legal profession, the ABA's views carry a prestige not accorded other interests. Whether any private group, notwithstanding its close professional relationship to the judicial function, should have a special role in the appointment of judges is a debatable question.

Although the background and political orientation of judges must affect judicial policymaking, becoming a judge probably counters class or personal bias. Justice Felix Frankfurter argued that "on the whole judges do lay aside private views in discharging their judicial functions" (*Public Utilities Commission* v. *Pollack*, 1952). It is hard to distinguish between private views and judicial objectivity, however. Judicial decisions cannot be ascribed precisely to political and social background, but the influence of background cannot be ignored.

LIMITATIONS ON THE IMPLEMENTATION OF DECISIONS

Federal court limitations

The federal system often impedes federal or state court compliance with Supreme Court rulings. With fifty separate state systems involved, some ignore the mandates of the Court or interpret them so as to avoid compliance. Of 175 cases reversed by the Supreme Court and returned to state courts for litigation between 1941 and 1951, 46 were reheard at the state level. In almost half of these, according to one survey, "the winner at the Supreme Court level lost his victory in the state court" ("Evasion of Supreme Court Mandates," 1954).

Compliance with Supreme Court decisions by lower federal courts is also by no means assured. In *Brown* v. *Board of Education* (1954), a unanimous Supreme Court found that racial segregation in public schools violated the equal protection clause of the Fourteenth Amendment. Because of the decision's great impact and differences in local conditions, and perhaps to provide a cooling-off period, the Court postponed considering how its decision should be implemented. It invited all who were interested to submit their views. One year later the Court ordered "full compliance . . . with all deliberate speed." The task of implementing these orders fell to the federal district courts and circuit court judges whose jurisdictions contained segregated public schools. Federal judges in the South, whose courts became the arena for litigation following the 1954 decision, frequently acted under the influence of local values and pressures by ordering desegregation of public schools but only vaguely specifying the time and manner of implementing it (Peltason, 1961).

The extent to which local officials and private citizens comply with a Supreme Court decision depends on the type of issue decided by the Court and the resources available to groups who wish to comply or oppose enforcement. Many southern states fought enforcement of *Brown* v. *Board of Education* with their full legal and political resources, in spite of public support for the decision in other parts of the nation. By contrast, the legislative reapportionment decisions of the 1960s were vigorously supported by urban interests that had suffered under previous schemes of apportionment; consequently, compliance came relatively quickly and change was extensive.

In the 1960s Supreme Court decisions against the reading of the Bible and recitation of religious prayers in public schools faced widespread public opposition. In Tennessee, a "Bible-belt" state, only one of 152 public school districts had ceased all such devotional exercises by 1965 (Birkby, 1966, pp. 304–319). Official pressures to comply were not vigorous, which encouraged and tacitly condoned noncompliance with Court decisions.

Presidential and congressional limitations

Executive and legislative prerogatives also limit the courts. As Alexander Hamilton wrote in *Federalist* No. 78, "In a government in which [departments] are separated from each other, the judiciary, from the nature of its functions, will always be the least dangerous." It has "neither force nor will, but merely judgment, and must ultimately depend upon the aid of the executive arm even for the efficacy of its judgments." Presidents have sometimes heeded the apocryphal remark of President Andrew Jackson: "[Chief Justice] John Marshall has made his decision, now let him enforce it." Lincoln bitterly criticized the Court for its decision in *Dred Scott* v. *Sanford* (1857) which declared the Missouri Compromise unconstitutional and also held that Negroes could not be citizens and were the property of their masters even if they escaped to states that did not permit slavery; Franklin D. Roosevelt was reportedly prepared to disobey a Court ruling if it invalidated his decision to go off the gold standard; President Truman might have kept control of the steel mills in 1952 despite the Court's decision in *Youngtown Sheet and Tube* v. *Sawyer* (1952) that declared his seizure of the mills unconstitutional; and President Eisenhower supported district courts belatedly in the Little Rock desegregation crisis of 1957. The possibility of presidential resistance or constitutional crises are therefore potential restraints on judicial decisions.

Congress also maintains control over the judiciary. Its extensive formal controls include the authority to alter or abolish the jurisdiction of federal courts, except for the Supreme Court's original jurisdiction; to control judges' salaries and provide funds for operating the federal court system; to increase or decrease the number of judges; to remove judges by impeachment; and to determine when the Supreme Court will sit. The Senate has the authority to confirm judicial appointments. Along with these formal controls, Congress may nullify Supreme Court decisions by initiating constitutional amendments. The Fourteenth, Sixteenth, and Twenty-Sixth Amendments all overturned previous interpretations of the Constitution by the Court.

Most decisions of the Court, however, are based not on constitutional interpretation but on statutory interpretation. Congress may nullify a decision based upon statutory interpretation by either changing the law or passing new legislation, but it rarely does this if congressional sentiment on an issue created by a Supreme Court decision is mixed. Professor C. Herman Pritchett's analysis of 21 instances of congressional reversal between 1947 and 1957 revealed that most Court decisions provoke mixed congressional reaction and are successfully reversed only under special circumstances, such as an intense, nationwide lobbying campaign (1961).

THE SCHOOL BUSING ISSUE. The reaction in southern states to the 1954 school desegregation decision (*Brown* v. *Board of Education*) produced a series of confrontations between state and federal authority in the 1950s and 1960s. Generally, northern states were less directly affected by the decision since public schools there were not segregated by state law or action, as they were in the south. However, a 1971 unanimous Burger Court decision, *Swann* v. *Charlotte-Mecklenburg Board of Education*, ordered a North Carolina school system to bus public school children to schools other than those closest to their homes on grounds that a governmentally sponsored segregation pattern existed that could not be remedied in any other manner. *De facto* segregation is that which results not from any state law or action (*de jure* segregation) but from other factual patterns such as the location of residential housing. De jure segregation had been the pattern in southern states. Northern states did not require segregation of schools by law, but de facto segregation has nevertheless been a common pattern in metropolitan areas. Many residential neighborhoods in cities are segregated along racial lines. This pattern, plus the traditional pattern of neighborhood schools, has meant that Black children attend predominantly Black schools and White children attend predominantly White schools. As Whites have moved to the suburbs, inner city schools have become more Black and suburban schools have remained almost totally White.

Following the 1971 Swann decision, federal district judges required the busing of children away from neighborhood schools to other schools within their school district. In Detroit, the district court went one step further. A district judge ruled that racial desegregation could be achieved only if the White suburban school districts surrounding Detroit were included in a cross-district busing plan. In 1974 the Supreme Court, by a five-to-four majority vote, overturned the district court order, ruling that even though Detroit was guilty of de jure segregation, the surrounding suburban school districts were not. Consequently, school children outside Detroit could not be bused, nor could the court require that Detroit district children be bused into suburban school areas (*Milliken* v. *Bradley*, 1974).

Although the 1974 ruling made it appear that busing across district lines could not be constitutionally required as a remedy for de facto segregated schools, doubts still existed as to the circumstances under which busing could be ordered. These doubts led President Ford to order Attorney General Leonard Levy to find a "test case" that would determine the extent to which the Fourteenth Amendment required busing as a remedy for de facto segregation. Boston was chosen as the test case. Demonstrations and violence followed the order of a federal district judge to bus Black children to predominantly White neighborhoods in that city. Resistance in Louisville and other parts of the nation was equally strong, and sometimes violent.

Prodded by constituents opposed to busing (this time primarily northern), the declared opposition of President Nixon to the practice, and general public debate over its educational and social merits, Congress made several efforts in the early 1970s to intervene against busing. For example, a 1975 rider to an appropriations bill, passed by Congress over President Ford's veto, prohibited the busing of any student beyond the school closest to his home that offered courses desired by the student. The legislation raised questions about the constitutionality and effectiveness of such congressional action, because the Supreme Court's school desegregation decisions have rested squarely on the belief that racial segregation violates the Fourteenth Amendment. District courts had ordered busing presumably to comply with the constitutional requirement; and civil rights leaders charged that Congress could not, therefore, override busing orders without violating the principle of separation of powers.

The constitutional issue posed by the antibusing legislation might have arisen earlier had other attempts to limit the Court's jurisdiction succeeded. An attempt in 1958 to withdraw the Court's appellate jurisdiction in some national security matters was overwhelmingly approved in the House but failed by one vote in the Senate. In 1964, the House approved a measure to strip the federal courts of jurisdiction in state reapportionment cases. The bill did not pass the Senate, but a substitute motion jointly sponsored by Democratic Majority Leader Mike Mansfield and Republican Minority Leader Everett Dirkson would have deferred the execution of court-ordered reapportionment of state legislatures until Congress could submit a constitutional amendment prohibiting the judiciary from applying the "one man, one vote" principle to the upper houses of state legislatures. A filibuster that followed introduction of the substitute motion was ended when Congress resolved that the Supreme Court should not disrupt forthcoming state elections by requiring prior reapportionment.

These congressional efforts grew out of widespread dissatisfaction with the Supreme Court's decisions under Chief Justice Earl Warren. Southerners, police chiefs, the American Bar Association, church organizations, and even the chief justices of state supreme courts were among the many interests that charged the Court had gone "too far" in protecting civil rights and liberties, assuring equitable legislative apportionment, and securing religious freedom.

The Court has suffered comparatively little direct interference or retribution from the other branches of government during this century. Yet the antibusing legislation shows the judiciary may not be immune to direct intervention.

The four Nixon appointments to the Court (including a new chief justice)

were clearly intended to provide "conservative" replacements for "liberal" Warren Court justices. Changes in the ideological orientation of the Supreme Court make conflict with Congress short-lived. An active Court in one generation may give way to a more restrained judiciary in the next.

The politics of judicial choice

Courts are one instrument used by a political community to regulate conflict. As the arbiter of disputes between interests, courts give interests another way of trying to reach their goals. Judicial decisions are therefore a way of effecting social change. Courts define rules or norms of permissible behavior and apply sanctions when these rules are violated. By negating laws or formulating new law, courts also legitimize changes that have already taken place in society. Supreme Court decisions liberalizing the rules defining obscenity, for example, may have begun to legitimize changing attitudes toward sex in American society.

The line between "legal" decisions and "political" decisions is unclear because "law" cannot be separated from "policy." Judicial authority is more structured, less ambiguous, and more limited than legislative or executive authority. Legal arguments in the form of briefs, the judiciary's procedural and jurisdictional rules, and the formal atmosphere of the courtroom distinguish policy adjudication from other forms of policymaking. However, these features, together with the myth that judges are impartial in their judgments, obscure the judiciary's real place in the resolution of conflict. The public usually views a judge as a decisionmaker who applies a more or less fixed set of rules to cases, permitting him little discretion and insulating him from external pressures. That popular view is a misreading of the adjudication of policy.

The parties involved in a judicial controversy, including the judges themselves, seek a favorable resolution of the dispute by utilizing whatever resources they can command within the framework of the judicial arena. The immediate parties to a suit and other interested parties who may become involved, the strategies employed by both sides, the legal precedents that apply to the issues at hand, public opinion, changing social patterns, and the personal values and biases of the judge all affect decisions. Bargaining takes place within the judicial realm just as it does within the legislative and executive realms, because the resolution of conflict often depends upon the accommodation of several interests. In the following section, we concentrate on the Supreme Court's role in the resolution of social conflict.

THE SUPREME COURT AND JUDICIAL POLICYMAKING

The judicial branch was designed as the instrument for realizing the rule of law. Granting federal judges life terms and protecting their salaries from reduction by Congress helped to insulate them from the demands of popular majorities. Chief Justice John Marshall's decision in *Marbury* v. *Madison* (1803) emphasized their responsibility to uphold the Constitution against legislative actions. In the event of conflict between a law and the Constitution, said Marshall, "the court must determine which of these conflicting rules governs the case: this is the very essence of judicial duty." Marshall's assertion of the power of judicial review and its exercise by subsequent Supreme Courts contrasts sharply with the role of courts in Great Britain. Although the English system of law was the most significant influence on the development of American law, English courts have never held the power to declare unconstitutional acts of the legislative branch. They may interpret legislation, but Parliament is supreme and its will always prevails. Parliamentary power is checked by the party system, the executive branch (Prime Minister), and the great weight of English consensus on the protection of individual rights and liberties.

The U.S. Constitution does not, of course, explicitly give the Supreme Court the power to limit actions of Congress and the executive through judicial review or the authority to arbitrate relations between the states and the national government. The acceptance of the Supreme Court's role has depended on the cooperation by the other two branches of government and on the public itself. Public acceptance of the Court's actions rests on the notion that judges are not as interested in political conflict as Congress and the President are and reflects a deep commitment to insulating the administration of justice from popular pressure.

Some of the Supreme Court's decisions have provoked considerable criticism, but Americans still support the institution. Table 14.4 shows the findings of one study that measured *specific support* by the amount of praise or criticism people gave decisions and individual justices, and *diffuse support* by how much people believed the Supreme Court was impartial and competent. These data show that diffuse support is significantly stronger than specific support: 37 percent of respondents gave positive general responses about the court, but only 12.5 percent offered positive responses indicating specific support. The authors of the study also found that 53.8 percent of the respondents could not identify any specific likes or dislikes about the Court ("don't know, no response"), and 29.4 percent did not offer general opinions about the Court as an institution. The data suggest that the Supreme Court retains its image as an institution that legitimizes changes in the political system, even

TABLE 14.4
Specific and diffuse support of the Supreme Court
by the American public, 1966 (in percentages)

Level of support	Specific	Diffuse
Strong positive*	2.5	19.9
Moderate positive	7.0	17.1
Pro/con†	5.0	11.9
Moderate negative	19.2	11.4
Strong negative‡	12.5	10.3
Don't know, no response	53.8	
Unclassified		29.4
Total	100.0	100.0
(N = 1,291)		

* Very strong and strong positive categories combined for specific support data.
† Pro/con category refers to responses in which positive and negative comments were about evenly balanced.
‡ Very strong and strong negative categories combined for specific support data.
Source: From Murphy W. F., and Tannenhaus, J., "Public Opinion and the United States Supreme Court," *Law and Society Review* May 1968, *2*, pp. 370, 372.

though its specific decisions often are criticized by many members of the public.

Figure 14.2 illustrates shifts in public confidence in the Supreme Court between 1966 and 1977, as compared with patterns of confidence in Congress and the President. The Court has generally fared better in maintaining a high level of confidence than the other two branches, but public satisfaction has declined significantly from a high of 50 percent in 1966.

Clearly, public confidence in the Supreme Court has declined along with confidence in all government institutions. However, the data reported by Harris might also reveal dissatisfaction with the Warren Court's activities in criminal procedures, civil rights, and religion during the 1960s. Nevertheless, lack of support for specific decisions or a specific court is not synonymous with

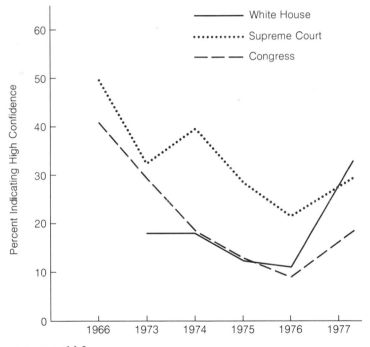

FIGURE 14.2

Public Confidence in the Supreme Court, the White House, and Congress, 1966–1977. A sample of 1522 adults were asked: "As far as people in charge of running [the White House; U.S. Supreme Court; Congress] are concerned, would you say you have a great deal of confidence, only some confidence, or hardly any confidence at all in them?" The question was not asked about the White House in 1966. [*Source:* Based on data reported in *The Harris Survey*, March 14, 1977.]

lack of support for the Supreme Court as an institution. That is, the public may support the legitimacy of the Court's role as the ultimate arbiter of constitutional disputes while expressing dissatisfaction with particular attempts to resolve such conflict.

LEGAL RULES AND COURT RESPONSE TO SOCIAL CONFLICT

How do legal rules and norms limit the judiciary in choosing among alternatives and responding to new demands? Judicial choice is limited by a fundamental principle of English and American jurisprudence: Decisions on law by a higher court having jurisdiction must be followed in similar cases in the future. This rule of *stare decisis*—"stand by the things decided"—lays the stable and predictable foundation of the law. The rule limits the lower state and federal courts much more than it limits appellate courts. Although appellate judges are also expected to exhibit consistency and certainty in policy choices, they are sometimes unable or unwilling to follow precedent, because changing conditions may demand changing law. A new case often differs enough from previous cases to enable the Supreme Court to depart from precedent without specifically contradicting it. When precedents conflict, the judge's opportunity to follow one precedent and neglect another leaves him much discretion. The validity of federal aid to parochial schools might be determined by several precedents—some supporting such aid, others not. Precedents impose a limiting but not unalterable restraint on a justice: "He has free choice, but only among limited alternatives and only after he has satisfied himself that he has met the obligations of consistency and respect for settled principles which his responsibility to the Court imposes upon him" (Pritchett and Westin, 1963, p. 17).

The Court must also be sensitive to policy goals expressed by the other two branches of the government and by the public. The need for understanding and restraint is visible in the Supreme Court's activity in economic matters before the 1930s and in its reaction to the New Deal.

From 1870 until the 1930s, the Supreme Court regularly held state and national regulatory statutes unconstitutional on many grounds. By the mid-1930s, it was clear that the Court looked upon itself as the "protector" of "all the 'common callings' (the grocer, the dairyman, the butcher) from the peril of public rate control" (McCloskey, 1968, p. 168). That is, the Court used the "contract" and "due process" clauses of the Constitution to strike down government efforts to regulate economic affairs.

Economic individualism was the philosophic basis of the great economic interests built during the 1870s and 1880s. But Court decisions equating the small entrepreneur's need of protection from the government with the need to protect the great power and wealth of big business were unrealistic. In 1905, the

Court struck down a New York statute that limited the hours of bakers to 60 per week to protect their health (*Lochner* v. *New York*, 1905). The Court ruled that such legislation interfered with the liberty of workers to contract to work more hours if they wished to do so. It ignored the economic fact that the bargaining power between employer and individual employee so favored the employer that the freedom of contract was a mockery.

In *Adair* v. *U.S.* (1908), the Court invalidated labor legislation designed to protect the union activity of employees against interference by employers. Such legislation by Congress, the Court said, by its very content violated the liberty of employees to quit their employment and the employer's right to fire workers. The Adair decision illustrates the doctrine of "substantive due process" which held that in addition to procedural violations of individual liberties, property and liberty could be denied by government regulation itself. The doctrine was devised and used to grant powerful economic interests immunity from government regulation of working conditions, minimum wages, and standards of health. In short, the Supreme Court made the right of government to intervene in social and economic problems subordinate to the rights of property.

The Court also narrowly construed the power of Congress to regulate business by the "commerce" clause of the Constitution. A federal law outlawing shipment in interstate commerce of goods produced by child labor was struck down because the manufacturing of goods was not commerce; commerce began only after the goods were produced, and Congress had authority to regulate only production. This interpretation of the commerce clause blunted the efforts of Congress to end the employment and exploitation of children. Thus, dominant economic interests used the Supreme Court's role as "protector" of the "small businessman" to block governmental response to social and economic needs.

The great depression of the 1930s altered American attitudes toward government, a shift symbolized by Franklin D. Roosevelt's New Deal. Acting under its commerce and taxing powers, Congress enacted laws establishing economic controls and social welfare programs; but between 1933 and 1937, a series of Supreme Court decisions negated some of these and threatened to invalidate the entire New Deal program.

The landslide reelection of Franklin Roosevelt in 1936 and large Democratic majorities in Congress showed that the public approved of the New Deal. To change the negative attitude of the Supreme Court, Roosevelt proposed that one additional Justice be appointed to the Court for every Justice who had served at least ten years and had failed to retire at the age of 70. These conditions were met, not coincidentally, by six of the nine members of the Court. Roosevelt called it "reorganization," but his opponents dubbed it "court packing." The Senate rejected the proposal as "political tampering" and thus saved a Supreme Court that a few months before had been labeled reactionary.

"No issue so great or so deep," wrote Walter Lippmann, "has been raised in America since secession" (quoted in Mason, 1952, p. 706).

Roosevelt lost the battle, but in the end he won the war. Justice Owen Roberts subsequently switched sides on the constitutionality of the New Deal laws and turned a five-to-four majority against these measures into a favorable majority. Robert H. Jackson, then attorney general and later a Supreme Court justice, commented that "this paradoxical outcome is accounted for by the recognition on the part of some justices—belated but vigorous—of the validity of the complaints against their course of decision. They subdued the rebellion against their constitutional dogma by joining it" (1941, p. vi). By the late 1930s, President Roosevelt had been able to appoint seven new justices to the Court, and the threat posed by the pre–New Deal Court was ended.

LIMITING DEMANDS: RULES AND JUDICIAL "GATEKEEPING"

A legal controversy represents demands made upon the political system. Those demands may be limited to a controversy between two private parties or a small number of people, or they may represent broad social conflicts involving large numbers of people and interests. Not all conflicts are resolvable by a court, a limitation recognized by the judiciary itself in the form of rules that define the types of issues or controversies that may be taken to court. Developed and imposed by the Supreme Court, these rules enable the Court to control the issues it will decide and thus serve the function of "gatekeeping."

Cases in controversy

The Supreme Court has refused to render advisory opinions on constitutional questions; a case must represent a real conflict, not a hypothetical question. This rule applies to all federal constitutional courts. In 1793, the Court declined to advise President Washington concerning how far his authority extended on the policy of neutrality in foreign conflicts. In the opinion of the justices, Washington was simply asking for legal advice and the Court had no authority to render advice. The Court has historically insisted that issues brought before it must be an actual "case" or "controversy." In *Muskrat* v. *United States* (1911), it refused to hear an appeal that had been brought on the basis of a law that authorized legal suits to test the validity of certain acts of Congress; the case was not heard on grounds that the suit was not a genuine controversy between two parties and the courts could not issue what amounted to an advisory opinion.

Standing to sue

Federal courts have long held that before a court will decide an issue, the person bringing the suit must be able to show that a personal interest is at stake to the extent that personal and substantial injury will result from a law or government action. This rule also bars suits brought on behalf of the public at large. The meaning of "standing" can best be illustrated by reference to specific cases decided by the Supreme Court.

In *Poe* v. *Ullman* (1961) the plaintiffs, a doctor and his patients, challenged an 1889 Connecticut law that banned the use of contraceptives and giving medical advice about their use. Although the state had made no effort to enforce the law against the plaintiffs, they contended that it violated the Fourteenth Amendment because it deprived them of liberty without due process of law. The Supreme Court held that since none of the plaintiffs had been arrested, jailed, or fined, no injury could be shown. Thus, there was an absence of "standing."

In 1970 the State of Massachusetts enacted legislation that authorized its attorney general to file suit in federal court asking that the Vietnam War be declared unconstitutional because Congress had not authorized it. Although three justices dissented, the Court refused to hear the case, *Massachusetts* v. *Laird* (1970), partly on grounds that the state lacked standing to sue and partly on grounds that the issue was a "political question" to be resolved by the other two branches of government.

In cases where courts hold that "standing" has not been established they do not rule on the "merits" of the issue, such as whether the sale of contraceptives can be prohibited. The standing-to-sue doctrine heightens Court control over hearing only issues it wants to hear. The difference between hearing and not hearing a suit may depend more on what the Court deems it *politically* feasible to decide than upon properly brought action. If the justices accepted a case challenging the constitutionality of an undeclared war, they might be unable to get Congress or the President or the public to accept a decision affirming the illegality of the war. Such a confrontation not only might provoke a constitutional crisis but also might weaken or imperil the Supreme Court's authority to decide other controversial cases.

In the view of one observer, Karen Orren (1976), the Supreme Court has since 1970 been more receptive to allowing interest groups to establish standing in order to challenge the actions of corporate business or other private institutions. According to Orren, the Court has liberalized the standing rules by insisting less strongly on "legalistic" definitions of standing and being willing to recognize that injuries other than property loss or direct personal injury can occur to plaintiffs. Under this more liberalized view, environmentalists, consumer groups, and minority racial groups, acting on behalf of a "public interest," can probably acquire greater access to the courts and thus perhaps achieve at the judicial level what they are unable to win in Congress or the executive branch.

Doctrine of "political questions"

The Supreme Court has declined to decide issues that it defines as "political questions": conflicts that the Court says lie within the proper decision arena of Congress or the President and are therefore not subject to judicial remedy. Admittedly, this is a vague distinction, but the Supreme Court itself has been no more precise in defining the doctrine. The doctrine was employed as early as 1849, when the Court refused to decide which of two governments claiming legitimacy was the lawful government of Rhode Island. The question, said the Court, was "political" and must be decided by Congress and the executive. The Court has refused to decide when a constitutional amendment has been legally ratified, what constitutes a "republican form of government" under the guarantee clause of the Constitution, the dates of the duration of a war, questions about the conduct of foreign relations, and the status of Indian tribes (*Coleman* v. *Miller, 1939; Pacific States Telephone and Telegraph Co.* v. *Oregon, 1939; Rudecke* v. *Watkins, 1948; The Cherokee Nation* v. *Georgia,* 1831).

In a broad sense, all questions decided by the Court are "political." John P. Roche (1955) has said the word "can be expanded or contracted in accordion-like fashion to meet the exigencies of the times . . . for at root the logic that supports it is circular; political questions are matters not soluble by the judicial process; matters not soluble by the judicial process are political questions. As an early dictionary explained, violins are small cellos, and cellos are large violins" (p. 766). Conflicts that no one is willing to resolve are sometimes passed from branch to branch.

ACCESS TO POLICYMAKING

Litigation represents a campaign. Cases that reach the Supreme Court are the result of the carefully executed efforts of interested parties to achieve their goals by legal means. Most interest groups rarely go to court to further their interests, preferring to operate at other levels of the political process. Some, however, have used the courts as a primary means of influencing public policy.

Amicus curiae briefs

The *amicus curiae* ("friend of the court") brief enables parties not directly involved in a case but with a vested interest in it to present their position before the Court. Under Supreme Court rules, amicus briefs require the

Court's consent. The Court generally permits such briefs if a group shows a vital interest in the case and if it offers arguments that may not otherwise be presented.

Most amicus briefs are filed by private interest groups, but federal and state governments also contribute them. For example, the attorneys general of 22 states filed supporting briefs for nondenominational prayers in public schools in the case of *Engel* v. *Vitale* (1962), which held such prayers to be a violation of the First Amendment's "no establishment" clause. Among private groups frequently using this form of access to the Supreme Court are the National Association for the Advancement of Colored People (NAACP), the American Jewish Congress, the American Civil Liberties Union, and more recently, consumer and environmental groups.

The test case

The test case is a prearranged controversy between two parties who are in "conflict" for the purpose of bringing a legal question to court. It enables an interest group to link broad social problems to a specific case. The most widely known organization that has used test cases to achieve its ends is the National Association for the Advancement of Colored People. Because the cause of racial equality received little support from the executive and legislative branches of the national government before the 1940s, the NAACP turned to litigation. Many racial cases decided in this century by the Supreme Court in housing, transportation, voting, and education were test cases initiated by the NAACP. The organization has supplied the financial resources and the legal talent needed for victory in the courts.

The class action suit

As defined in the *Federal Rules of Civil Procedure*, the class action suit permits a group of people to bring suit in the names of persons "constituting a class" so as to ensure "the adequate representation of all" before the courts. The class action is especially appropriate for civil rights cases because it permits large numbers of people in a jurisdiction to protest practices without requiring them to seek redress of grievances individually. Cases challenging de facto segregation in public schools have been filed in behalf of both the parties bringing the suit and all others similarly affected. The class action suit may also be used by environmental and consumer groups to bring suit on behalf of large numbers of persons.

Government as an interest group

We have already noted that government itself—federal, state, and local—can be an advocate for its own causes in the judicial arena. Through the attorney general and the solicitor general of the United States, the federal government decides which cases will be appealed by the government as well as which issues will be stressed in arguing a case. The solicitor general, a subcabinet-level position in the Justice Department, is the government's lawyer. He clears cases for appeal after assessing the government's chances of winning the appeal, the consequences of defeat, and the policy significance of the case. His decisions affect the degree of access interest groups have to the courts, because through those decisions government itself voices support or opposition to policy alternatives. Early in 1972, a group of young lawyers in the Civil Rights Division of the Department of Justice resigned in angry protest over what they considered the Department's policy not to investigate vigorously and prosecute violations of the civil rights law.

The devices we have considered under Access to Policymaking expand conflict representation in the courts and make possible the reconciliation of potentially explosive conflict. The increasing use of these devices may, however, alter the judiciary's traditional insulation from the political arena.

DECISIONMAKING WITHIN THE COURT

The public sessions of the Supreme Court are conducted in a formal atmosphere with procedural rules, protocol, and dignity. The bargaining, compromises, and negotiations characteristic of the legislative and executive branches are not as visible in the Supreme Court, yet these styles of decisionmaking are nevertheless present.

The Court determines the cases it will rule on by utilizing its power to hear or not to hear an appeal. Only about 140 cases a year reach the formal decision stage. Although each decision determines a "winner" and a "loser" among parties to the dispute, the division of opinion among the justices and the reasoning of the Court have broader implications. Unanimous opinions are handed down in only about one in four cases. Concurring opinions (agreeing with the opinion of the majority of the Court but on different grounds) and dissenting opinions (presenting the views of the minority) are the most common. Any justice may write or join his fellow justices in writing a concurring or dissenting opinion.

Traditional judicial scholars have closely examined Court opinions for what they reveal about the development of the law, the philosophy of the Court, the views of individual justices, and the Court's position compared with that of the other branches of the government. Students of the Supreme Court over the past 30 years have also developed techniques to measure the how and why of judicial decisions. Efforts to relate the social backgrounds of justices to decision patterns (Goldman, 1969; Schmidhauser, 1961) have proved of limited value in understanding judicial behavior. Studies employing more sophisticated techniques have explored the influence of values on judicial decisions (Rohde and Spaeth, 1976; Schubert, 1959; Tannenhaus, 1966; Ulmer, 1969).

To illustrate briefly the nature of these studies we refer to the work of Glendon Schubert (1965). Using a technique called "cumulative scaling," Schubert found patterns among votes on judicial issues that he inferred were measures of attitudes. He analyzed two attitudes closely connected to votes on civil liberties and economic matters by developing the C scale (including cases in which individual rights and liberties conflict with government authorities) and the E scale (including cases in which the economically privileged conflict with the economically underprivileged). Schubert used the C and E scales to study the 1968 term of the Supreme Court and found that in the 47 C-scale cases, five justices—Douglas, Fortas, Marshall, Warren, and Brennan—formed a group in opposition to the four other justices—White, Stewart, Harlan, and Black. The E-scale issues in 14 cases during the 1968 term also divided the Court, but only two justices—Harlan and Stewart—responded favorably to the economically affluent instead of the underprivileged. Schubert's findings revealed a clear and consistent division of attitudes among the justices and also indicated that the division was more visible in the civil liberties cases.

No one can enter the mind of a justice, and analytic tools are not good enough to specify cause-and-effect relationships in explaining judicial behavior. Moreover, the Court as an institution is less accessible than other parts of government. Court norms prohibit justices from publicly criticizing decisions with which they have formally disagreed. Personal antagonisms between justices are usually not aired in public, although they may be known. Only members of the Court can sit in on the conference, the meetings held at least once a week during the Court's term (October to June), in which the business of the Court takes place. Conferences are formal: Justices are seated around the table in order of seniority, and the chief justice always speaks first. The Court discusses, considers, and decides upon which cases it will hear; takes formal votes; and assigns justices the task of writing opinions.

Intra-court relationships: bargaining and persuasion

Decisionmaking on a multiple-member court is a group process. Individual justices with different personalities, goals, and backgrounds must work together to fashion court decisions. If his position on an issue is to prevail, a justice must get at least four fellow justices to support him. Persuasion, bargaining, and personal relationships mold decisionmaking and behavior on the Supreme Court.

A fascinating glimpse of persuasion is given by J. Woodford Howard's account (based on notes taken in conference by Justice Frank Murphy) of the way in which a major issue on separation of church and state was decided in 1947 (Howard, 1968). The case was *Everson* v. *Board of Education*, and the issue was a New Jersey statute that authorized payment of subsidies to parents of parochial school children for transporting them to school. Justices Wiley Rutledge and Frankfurter argued for a strong decision against the statute on grounds that the Court should put an end to subsidies of parochial education. Justice Hugo Black agreed that there should be absolute separation of church and state, but argued that the New Jersey subsidy did not violate that principle. In the end, Black succeeded in winning four other justices to his side and the decision reflected his position.

The Court's history reveals that some justices have been better able than others to persuade and influence their fellows. However, although some justices may fail to convince a majority, their positions can become majority policy in subsequent Courts. The lone dissenting opinion of Justice John Marshall Harlan against the Court's "separate but equal" doctrine in *Plessy* v. *Ferguson* in 1897 became the unanimous opinion in *Brown* v. *Board of Education* in 1954. The language and arguments used in Court opinions often reflect the bargaining that took place inside the Court. If the justice writing the opinion of the Court ignores the suggestions of other justices in the majority, he risks losing his majority. A note to Justice Frankfurter from Chief Justice Harlan Stone about a proposed opinion said: "If you wish to write, placing the case on the ground which I think tenable and desirable, I shall cheerfully join you. If not, I will add a few observations for myself" (quoted in Murphy, 1964, p. 59).

When the Court is divided on an issue, the losing interests outside the Court have an incentive to exploit this division with further litigation, and the Court may lose public support for its decision. Severe public criticism is more likely when the Court is divided or uncertain. The unanimous opinion in *Brown* v. *Board of Education* (1954) and the subsequent unanimity in segregation cases reinforced the Court's authority to make policy in these matters. But frequent five-to-four decisions during the 1960s in cases on the procedural rights ("due process") of accused persons under the Fifth and Fourteenth Amendments brought severe criticism of the Court and great uncertainty among public prosecutors about the standards required by the Court.

The chief justice

The status and authority of the chief justice enhance his capacity to lead a unified and productive Court. He presides over sessions of the Court and the conference. When in the majority, he assigns the writing of the opinion of the Court to one of the justices in the majority or he may write the opinion himself. The senior justice in the minority assigns the writing of the minority opinion. The chief justice is also responsible for the administration of the Court's docket of cases, and he controls the timetable of each conference.

David Danelski (1974) has used a concept of dual leadership—task leadership and social leadership—to evaluate leadership within the Court. The task leader is highly esteemed by his colleagues but reserved in his personal relations. He presents his views forcefully in conference, leads the discussion, and provides guidance on difficult questions. The social leader has a warm and responsive personality and concentrates on the "emotional needs of his associates by affirming their value as individuals and as Court members" (p. 526). His primary aim is unity and cohesion within the Court. Frequently the chief justice exercises either task or social leadership, but not both; he thus shares leadership with one of his associates. In Danelski's opinion, Chief Justice Charles Evans Hughes exercised both roles; his successor, Harlan F. Stone, neither.

The leadership abilities of the chief justice depend upon many factors, including his personality, his view of his role, and the personalities of other members of the Court. Strong chief justices, such as Marshall, Taft, and Hughes, have maintained unity and cohesion in spite of drastic intra-Court differences over policy and strong personality conflicts, but others have failed. "The chief justiceship supplies numerous opportunities to exert influence," wrote Walter F. Murphy, but "it offers no guaranty that the incumbent can utilize these opportunities to achieve his policy goals" (1964, p. 89).

ACTIVISM OR SELF-RESTRAINT: WHICH ROLE FOR THE COURT?

Debate over what the Supreme Court's job ought to be has gone on since the Marshall Court. The controversy has intensified since the 1950s, because Court decisions have profoundly affected broad areas of social and economic policy. There are no set definitions of judicial activism and judicial self-restraint. They are sometimes defined in relation to the principle of checks and balances: Each branch has powers to check the other, but each must exercise restraint to avoid going beyond constitutional boundaries.

The activist position is that the Supreme Court has never overstepped its boundaries because, along with the formal checks that Congress and the President may exercise, public opinion is a major restraining force. Definitions differ, but the underlying denominator of judicial activism is assuring the Court's role as a major architect of policy to promote social and political goals. The judicial activist may or may not be in accord with legislative or public opinion and policy choices, but from this point of view such accord is subordinate to other values required by the Constitution's broad directives. Thus the activist Courts of the late nineteenth and early twentieth centuries read economic rights as predominant values over competing social and political claims. The Warren Court of the 1950s and 1960s emphasized other rights and liberties and extended the protection of the individual against government to states as well as the national government. Justice Black, one of the staunchest supporters of judicial activism in First Amendment controversies, argued that the Bill of Rights contains "absolutes" in that government "was denied all power to do some things under any and all circumstances" (Black, 1963, p. 45).

Those who advocate judicial self-restraint emphasize the Court's duty not to intervene in policy matters unless such intervention is clearly necessary to correct violations of the Constitution. Like Justice Harlan, they consider maintaining a constitutional balance between governing branches more important than achieving the social or personal values of judges or courts. Judicial policymaking is unavoidable, but advocates of self-restraint would keep it to a minimum. The Supreme Court of the late 1930s and the 1940s was a self-restraining Court in that it accepted the broad congressional interpretations of the "commerce and tax" clauses of the Constitution that Congress had used to enact major social and economic legislation. The Warren Court was self-restrained in economic matters, but it was also the most active in history in defining and protecting civil rights and liberties.

The foremost advocate of judicial self-restraint was Justice Felix Frankfurter, who died in 1965. Frankfurter's view was clearly expressed in his dissenting opinion in *Baker* v. *Carr*, the 1962 decision that held for the first time that federal courts could hear and decide cases challenging state legislative apportionment. Arguing that the Court should not get itself involved in this "political thicket," the justice stressed that courts are "ill-adapted" to handle such matters. Courts, he said, should not be "arbiters of the broad issues of political organization historically committed to other institutions and for whose adjustment the judicial process is ill-adapted."

Arguments over self-restraint versus activism are heavily influenced by the extent to which the protagonists agree or disagree with the decisions or policy directions of the Court. Those who criticized the Warren Court for "going too far" will support the more restrained position of the Burger Court in its view of the rights of the defendant. Whether it follows the pattern of self-restraint or activism, no Court can avoid being a major policymaker in the American system. And whichever policy alternative is chosen in specific areas of law, some interests will benefit and others will be hurt.

The Supreme Court and public policy

When Congress was considering a proposal by Senator William E. Jenner in 1958 to strip the Supreme Court of jurisdiction in cases dealing with contempt of Congress and the federal loyalty and security program, Senator Thomas Hennings labeled it a "kill the umpire" proposal. The Court enforces the rules, and it is sometimes the object of abuse as it meets its responsibilities. An institution able to veto the actions of other branches of government, to act contrary to public opinion, and to formulate new policies on its own is by definition controversial. It seems paradoxical that the Court—especially over the last two decades—has been subjected to bitter and frequently widespread criticism, and yet has weathered almost all efforts to alter its jurisdiction or reverse its decisions by legislative action or constitutional amendment. How can this strength be explained?

Beliefs about court power and its relationship to other forces in policy-making provide part of the answer. Is the Court a "democratic" institution? If democratic is defined as "chosen by election by the governed," the Court obviously does not qualify. Justices are appointed for life and their social, educational, and economic backgrounds make them probably the most elite group of governors in the American system. Nine men who are intentionally insulated from public pressure control the destiny of millions—that is scarcely democratic.

If, however, we define democracy as the rights of the individual against arbitrary government power, or the principle of political and social equality, then it may seem that the Supreme Court in the past three decades has been more democratic than the other branches of government. Supreme Court decisions have protected and advanced the rights to dissent, a fair trial, social and educational equality, and political equality in casting a ballot as well as in having it count equally. They have also produced criticisms against the exercise of judicial power ("usurpation," "irresponsibility," "coddling the criminal").

Historically, of course, the Supreme Court has supported different interests and has fostered different causes at different periods. The philosophy of laissez-faire economics dominated Court decisions from the 1890s to the mid-1930s, and finally gave way to a Court that endorsed the social and economic reforms of the New Deal. The Warren Court of the 1950s emphasized both individual rights and the goal of equality, the first Court in American history to foster both of these attributes of democracy (Schubert, 1970, p. 52). The Court has enjoyed majority support among the public for only part of these periods, yet it has consistently survived criticism and efforts to curb its activities. We suggest that because the Court has assisted in realizing and protecting fundamental democratic norms, even though its membership and organization are overtly undemocratic, its position as "guardian of the Constitution" protects it against its most vehement critics. In short, the Supreme Court symbolizes the values built into the Constitution itself, and efforts to alter its jurisdiction or its structure are viewed with suspicion.

Yet we have not fully answered the original question: How does the Court survive under the stress of severe criticism? The rest of the answer may lie in the nature of the majorities in pluralist America.

Majorities are coalitions of interests that elect Presidents, articulate opinion, and translate demands into public policy. Americans normally look to the party system and elections as the instruments through which majorities act. Wallace Mendelson (1959) has argued that the courts have been unsuccessful in determining national policy in times when cohesion within dominant partisan alliances was great. Mendelson's data show that between 1790 and 1864 the Supreme Court declared only two congressional measures unconstitutional, in *Marbury* v. *Madison* and *Dred Scott* v. *Sanford.* From 1865 to 1937, the Court vetoed congressional legislation in 76 instances. According to Mendelson, the use of judicial review grew substantially because of disagreement between the interests forming the dominant Republican coalition—businessmen, grain farmers, and laborers—which left the Court free to exercise a veto without united opposition. Business interests in the coalition were victorious, not because of legislative victories but because the Supreme Court exercised its judicial veto over legislative economic policy. The probusiness, laissez-faire leaning of the Court lasted until the New Deal. Since 1937, the Court has exercised restraint in cases dealing with economic legislation, Mendelson concludes that "judicial 'legislation' apparently feeds on defects in the political structure" (p. 454).

Whether Mendelson's thesis can explain the success of the activistic Warren Court is difficult to assess. That Court spent far less time blocking the actions of Congress than extending the scope of constitutional provisions to areas where legislative majorities were unable to accept Court influence. The antibusing legislation of the 1970s followed federal district court interpretations of Supreme Court mandates in school desegregation that neither Congress nor the public could support. And of course many Warren Court decisions were applied against state government practices in racial equality and individual rights.

The Court activism of the 1960s may, however, be giving way to an era of Court restraint in balancing the rights of the individual and the rights of society as defined by legislatures. Four new justices appointed by President Nixon swung the balance of the Court toward such restraint in interpreting defendants' rights. Thus the Nixon administration, avowedly on the side of Court restraint in this area of law, by the power of appointment moved the Court toward moderation. Carter appointments may, however, shift the balance in yet another direction.

Robert Dahl (1957) holds that current evidence does not support the common assumption that the Supreme Court protects minorities against majorities. The Court can delay, but not permanently block, a majority in Congress. Dahl based his analysis on a study of 78 cases decided between 1789 and 1957 in which the Court declared 86 provisions of federal law unconstitutional. Half of these decisions came within four years of enactment of the legislation and most of the rulings were subsequently overturned by the Court itself or through other congressional action. Thus the Court is not able to block the actions of an alliance of President and Congress for more than a short period. In fact, the Court has often served to legitimize the policy of the dominant national political alliance. Yet, says Dahl, the Court is more than simply an "agent" of a party; it is an essential part of political leadership and possesses "bases of power of its own, the most important of which is the unique legitimacy attributed to its interpretation of the Constitution." Thus, "the Court operates to confer legitimacy, not simply on the particular and parochial policies of the dominant political alliance, but upon the basic patterns of behavior required for the operation of democracy" (pp. 293, 294).

A recent study by Jonathan Casper (1976) extended Dahl's study to include the 28 cases from 1957 to 1974 in which the Supreme Court declared legislation invalid. Six of these cases invalidated legislation that had been enacted during the previous four years, but only one of the six decisions was subsequently overturned. No court decisions declaring invalid actions of Congress that were more than four years old were overturned.

Caspers' findings suggest that the Court has been more successful in blocking policies in recent years than during the period reviewed by Dahl. However, he supports Dahl's position that the Court cannot permanently block majority preferences and that it is more successful in asserting its authority when Congress, the President, and the public are divided over policy issues. He also cautions that too much emphasis on the Court versus Congress or the Court versus the President and Congress may lead to a "winner"-"loser" view of the Supreme Court's ability to influence and make public policy. The Court is not only able to affect the implementation of policy through judicial review; it can also limit policy application or expand its meaning through its power to interpret statutes. For example, policies excusing conscientious objectors from military service, setting residency requirements to qualify for welfare, and permitting radio and television broadcasters to refuse editorial commercials are court-created policies based on interpretations of federal legislation.

Finally, Casper notes that even if a Court-made policy is overturned or significantly changed, future social change away from that policy may be difficult to achieve. If the Supreme Court were to alter its position regarding the extent to which the Constitution protects "obscene" material or a constitutional amendment were to grant state governments greater authority to restrict such material, such restrictions would be difficult to enforce. Supreme Court decisions since 1957 have given wide protection to the sale and distribution of pornographic material and some groups do not believe that it is socially harmful. In addition, there are substantial economic interests involved that would resist enforcement of restrictive measures. Consequently, a policy choice to return to pre-1957 restrictions on pornography might be difficult or impossible to implement.

The judiciary legitimizes policy formulated by administrators, congresspersons, and pressure-group leaders; moreover, it protects the political rights and freedoms that make democracy work. At the same time, it mirrors the ambivalence of liberal ideology: the emphasis upon both individual rights and majority rule. The judiciary's ability to make policy rests upon its official role as umpire of the system, but it is limited and conditioned by the realities of pluralistic power in the American political system. History shows that the Court cannot stray too far from the limits of public acceptance of new doctrine.

BIBLIOGraPHY

Aberbach, D., and Rockman, B. A. "Clashing Beliefs Within the Executive Branch: The Nixon Administration Bureaucracy." *American Political Science Review*, 1976, 70, pp. 456–468.

Abraham, H. *The Judiciary: The Supreme Court in the Governmental Process*, 4th ed. Boston: Allyn & Bacon, 1977.

Abramson, P. R. "Generational Change and the Decline of Party Identification in America: 1952–1974." *American Political Science Review*, 1976, 70, pp. 469–478.

Alexander, H. E. *Financing Politics: Money, Elections, and Political Reform*. Washington, D.C.: Congressional Quarterly Press, 1976.

Almond, G. *The American People and Foreign Policy*. New York: Harcourt Brace Jovanovich, 1950.

Almond, G. A., and Verba, S. *The Civic Culture*. Princeton, N.J.: Princeton University Press, 1963.

Asher, H. B. "The Learning of Legislative Norms." *American Political Science Review*, 1973, 67, pp. 499–513.

Atkin, C. "Communication and Political Socialization." *Political Communication Review*, 1975, 1, pp. 2–6.

Atkin, C., and Heald, G. "Effects of Political Advertising." *Public Opinion Quarterly*, 1976, *40* (2), pp. 216–228.

Atwood, L. E., and Sanders, K. R. "Perception of Information Sources and Likelihood of Split Ticket Voting. *Journalism Quarterly*, 1975, 52, pp. 421–428.

Axelrod, R. "Where the Voters Come From: An Analysis of Electoral Coalitions, 1952–1968." *American Political Science Review*, 1972, 66, pp. 11–20.

Bandura, A. *Social Learning Theory.* Morristown, N.J.: General Learning Press, 1971.

Bandura, A., and Walters, R. H. *Social Learning and Personality Development.* New York: Holt, Rinehart and Winston, 1963.

Barber, J. *The Presidential Character.* Englewood Cliffs, N.J.: Prentice-Hall, 1972.

Baskin, D. *American Pluralist Democracy: A Critique.* New York: Van Nostrand Reinhold, 1971.

Beard, C. *The Supreme Court and the Constitution,* rev. ed. Englewood Cliffs, N.J.: Prentice-Hall, 1962.

Beard, C. A. *An Economic Interpretation of the Constitution of the United States.* New York: Macmillan, 1914.

Beard, E., and Horn, S. *Congressional Ethnics: The View from the House.* Washington, D.C.: The Brookings Institution, 1975.

Becker, C. L. *The Declaration of Independence.* New York: Harcourt Brace Jovanovich, 1922.

Becker, C. L. *Freedom and Responsibility in the American Way of Life.* New York: Vintage Books, 1960.

Bell, D. V. J. *Power, Influence, Authority.* New York: Oxford University Press, 1975.

Bem, D. *Beliefs, Attitudes, and Human Affairs.* Belmont, Calif.: Brooks/Cole, 1970.

Beniger, J. R. "Winning the Presidential Nomination: National Polls and State Primary Elections, 1936–1972." *Public Opinion Quarterly*, 1976, 40, pp. 22–38.

Bentley, A. F. *The Process of Government.* Chicago: University of Chicago Press, 1908.

Birkby, R. "The Supreme Court and the Bible Belt: Tennessee Reaction to the Schempp Decision." *Midwest Journal of Political Science*, 1966, 10, pp. 304–319.

Black, H. L. "The Bill of Rights and the Federal Government." In E. Cahn (Ed.), *The Great Rights.* New York: Macmillan, 1963, pp. 43–63.

Block, J. H., Haan, N., and Smith, M. B. "Socialization Correlates of Student Activism. *Journal of Social Issues*, 1969, 25, pp. 143–177.

Blumer, H. "Attitudes and the Social Act." *Social Problems*, 1955, 3, pp. 59–65.

Blumer, H. "Suggestions for the Study of Mass-Media Effects." In E. Burdick and A. J. Brodbeck (Eds.), *American Voting Behavior.* Glencoe, Ill.: The Free Press, 1959, pp. 197–298.

Blumler, J. G., and Katz, E. (Eds). *The Uses of Mass Communications.* Beverly Hills, Calif.: Sage Publications, 1974.

Bogart, L. *Silent Politics.* New York: Wiley, 1972.

Bone, H. A. *Grass Roots Party Leadership.* Seattle, Wash.: University of Washington Press, 1952.

Boorstin, D. *The Genius of American Politics.* Chicago: University of Chicago Press, Phoenix Books, 1960.

Boyd, R. W. "Presidential Elections: An Explanation of Voting Defection." *American Political Science Review*, 1969, 63, pp. 498–514.

Boyd, R. W. "Review: *The Ticket Splitter.*" *American Political Science Review*, 1972, 66, pp. 1361–1363.

Broder, D. S. *The Party's Over.* New York: Harper & Row, 1972.

Brody, R. A., and Page, B. I. "The Impact of Events on Presidential Popularity: The

Johnson and Nixon Administrations." In A. Wildavsky (Ed.), *Perspectives on the Presidency*. Boston: Little, Brown, 1975, pp. 136–148.

Brown, R. *Charles Beard and the Constitution*. Princeton, N.J.: Princeton University Press, 1956.

Burke, E. *Works* (Vol. 2). Boston: Little, Brown, 1886.

Burnham, W. D. *Critical Elections and the Mainsprings of American Politics*. New York: Norton, 1970.

Burns, J. M. *Uncommon Sense*. New York: Harper & Row, 1972.

Byrne, G. C., and Pueschel, J. K. "But Who Should I Vote for for County Coroner?" *Journal of Politics*, 1974, *36*, pp. 778–784.

Campbell, A. *White Attitudes Toward Black People*. Ann Arbor, Mich.: Institute for Social Research, 1971.

Campbell, A., Converse, P. E., Miller, W. E., and Stokes, D. E. *The American Voter*. New York: Wiley, 1960.

Campbell, A., Converse, P. E., Miller, W. E., and Stokes, D. E. *Elections and the Political Order*. New York: Wiley, 1966.

Campbell, A., and Miller, W. E. "The Motivational Basis of Straight and Split Ticket Voting." *American Political Science Review*, 1957, *51*, pp. 293–312.

Cantril, H. *The Pattern of Human Concerns*. New Brunswick, N.J.: Rutgers University Press, 1965.

Carr, E. H. *The New Society*. Boston: Beacon Press, 1957.

Casper, J. D. "The Supreme Court and National Policy Making." *American Political Science Review*, 1976, *70*, pp. 50–63.

Chaffee, S., Ward, S., and Tipton, L. "Mass Communication and Political Socialization." *Journalism Quarterly*, 1970, *47*, pp. 647–659.

Charles, J. *The Origins of the American Party System*. New York: Harper & Row, 1961.

Chase, H. *Federal Judges: The Appointing Process*. Minneapolis: University of Minnesota Press, 1972.

Clausen, A. R. *How Congressmen Decide*. New York: St. Martin's Press, 1973.

Congressional Quarterly's Guide to Congress, 2nd ed. Washington, D.C.: Congressional Quarterly, Inc., 1976.

Congressional Quarterly Weekly Report, March 10, 1961; December 17, 1977.

Converse, P. E. "Information Flow and the Stability of Partisan Attitudes." *Public Opinion Quarterly*, 1962, *26*, pp. 578–599.

Corson, J., and Paul, R. *Men Near the Top*. Baltimore, Md.: Johns Hopkins Press, 1966.

Corwin, E. S. *The President: Office and Powers*. New York: New York University Press, 1948.

Cox, E. F., Fillmeth, R. C., and Schultz, J. E. *'The Nader Report' on the Federal Trade Commission*. New York: Richard W. Bacon, 1969.

Cronin, T. E. *The State of the Presidency*. Boston: Little, Brown, 1975.

Crotty, W. J. "Party Efforts and Its Impact on the Vote." *American Political Science Review*, 1971, *65*, pp. 439–450.

Cummings, M. C., Jr. *Congress and the Electorate*. New York: The Free Press, 1966.

Dahl, R. A. *A Preface to Democratic Theory*. Chicago: University of Chicago Press, 1956.

Dahl, R. A. "Decision-Making in a Democracy: The Supreme Court as a National Policy-Maker." *Journal of the Public Law*, 1957, 6, pp. 279–295.

Dahl, R. A. *Who Governs?* New Haven, Conn.: Yale University Press, 1961.

Danelski, D. "The Influence of the Chief Justice in the Decisional Process of the Supreme Court." In W. F. Murphy and C. H. Pritchett (Eds.), *Courts, Judges, and Politics*, 2nd ed. New York: Random House, 1974, pp. 525–534.

David, P. T. "The Vice-Presidency: Its Institutional Evolution and Contemporary Status." *Journal of Politics*, 1967, 26, pp. 721–748.

Davidson, R. *The Role of the Congressman.* New York: Pegasus, 1969.

Davis, J. W., Jr. *The National Executive Branch.* New York: The Free Press, 1970.

Davis, L. "The Cost of Realism: Contemporary Restatements of Democracy." *Western Political Quarterly*, 1964, 18, pp. 37–46.

Dawson, R. E. *Public Opinion and Contemporary Disarray.* New York: Harper & Row, 1973.

De Grazia, S. *The Political Community.* Chicago: University of Chicago Press, 1948.

Dennis, J., and McCrone, D. J. "Preadult Development of Political Party Identification in Western Democracies." *Comparative Political Studies*, 1970, 3, pp. 243–263.

Dennis, J., and Webster, C. "Children's Images of the President and of Government in 1962 and 1974." *American Politics Quarterly*, 1975, 3, pp. 386–406.

De Tocqueville, A. *Democracy in America.* New York: Oxford University Press (Galaxy ed.), 1947.

Devine, D. J. *The Attentive Public.* Chicago: Rand McNally, 1970.

Devine, D. J. *The Political Culture of the United States.* Boston: Little, Brown, 1972.

DeVries, W., and Tarrance, V. L. *The Ticket-Splitter: A New Force in American Politics.* Grand Rapids, Mich.: William B. Erdamns, 1972.

Dewey, J. *The Public and Its Problems.* Denver: Alan Swallow, 1927.

Dewey, J. "Democracy and Educational Administration." *School and Society*, 1937, 45, pp. 457–462.

Dexter, L. "The Representative and His District." In R. L. Peabody and N. W. Polsby (Eds.), *New Perspectives on the House of Representatives.* Chicago: Rand McNally, 1963.

Diamond, E. *The Tin Kazoo.* Cambridge, Mass.: MIT Press, 1975.

Diamond, M. "What the Framers Meant by Federalism." In R. A. Goldwin (Ed.), *A Nations of States.* Chicago: Rand McNally, 1963.

Dickenson, J. "Democratic Realities and Democratic Dogma." *American Political Science Review*, 1930, 29, pp. 291–293.

Documents Illustrative of the Formulation of the Union of the American States. Washington, D.C.: Government Printing Office, 1927.

Dodd, L. C., and Oppenheimer, B. *Congress Reconsidered.* New York: Praeger, 1977.

Domhoff, G. W. *Who Rules America?* Englewood Cliffs, N.J.: Prentice-Hall, 1967.

Donohue, T. R. "Impact of Voter Predisposition on Political Commercials." *Journal of Broadcasting*, 1973–1974, 18, pp. 3–15.

Dreyer, E. C., and Rosenbaum, W. A. (Eds.). *Public Opinion and Behavior*, 3rd ed. Belmont, Calif.: Wadsworth, 1974.

Dye, T. R. *Who's Running America?* Englewood Cliffs, N.J.: Prentice-Hall, 1976.

Dye, T. R., Jacob, H., and Vines, K. (Eds.). *Politics in the American States*, 2nd ed. Boston: Little, Brown, 1971.

Easton, D., and Dennis, J. "The Child's Image of Government." in R. Sigel (Ed.), *Political Socialization: Its Role in the Political Process. The Annals of the American Academy of Political and Social Science*, 1965, *261*, pp. 40–57.

Easton, D., and Dennis, J. *Children in the Political System.* New York: McGraw-Hill, 1969.

Edelman, M. *The Symbolic Uses of Politics.* Urbana: University of Illinois Press, 1964.

Edwards, G. C., III. Presidential Influence in the House: Presidential Prestige as a Source of Presidential Power. *American Political Science Review*, 1976, *70*, pp. 80–113.

Eisenstein, J. *Politics and the Legal Process.* New York: Harper & Row, 1973.

Elazar, D. *American Federalism: A View from the States*, 2nd ed. New York: T. Y. Crowell, 1972.

Eldersveld, S. *Political Parties.* Chicago: Rand McNally, 1964.

Erikson, R. S. "The Advantage of Incumbency in Congressional Elections." *Polity*, 1971, *3*, pp. 395–405.

Erskine, H. G. "The Polls: Some Guages of Conservatism." *Public Opinion Quarterly*, 1964, *28*, p. 168.

Eulau, H., Wahlke, J. C., and Buchanan, W. "The Role of the Representative: Some Empirical Observations on the Theory of Edmund Burke." *American Political Science Review*, 1959, *52*, pp. 742–756.

"Evasion of Supreme Court Mandates." *Harvard Law Review*, 1954, *67*, pp. 1251–1259.

"FDA: Government Can't Ban All Carcinogens." *UT Daily Beacon*, Knoxville, Tenn., November 15, 1976, p. 1.

Fenno, R. F., Jr. *The Power of the Purse: Appropriations Politics in Congress.* Boston: Little, Brown, 1966.

Fenno, R. F., Jr. *The President's Cabinet.* Cambridge, Mass.: Harvard University Press, 1959.

Fisher, J. "Black Panthers and Their White Hero-Worshippers." *Harper's*, 1970, *241*, pp. 18–26.

Flinn, J., and Wolman, H. L. "Constituency and Roll Call Voting: The Case of the Southern Democratic Congressman." *Midwest Journal of Political Science*, 1966, *10*, pp. 192–199.

Free, L. A., and Cantril, H. *The Political Beliefs of Americans.* New Brunswick, N.J.: Rutgers University Press, 1967.

Froman, L. A., Jr. *Congressmen and Their Constituencies.* Chicago: Rand McNally, 1963.

Gallup, G. *The Gallup Poll: Public Opinion 1935–1971.* New York: Random House, 1972.

Gallup Opinion Index, Report No. 113, 1974.

Gallup Opinion Index, Report No. 118, pp. 24–26, 1975.

Gallup Opinion Index, Report No. 119, 1975.

Gallup Opinion Index, Report No. 120, 1975.

Gallup Opinion Index, Report No. 123, 1975.

Gallup Opinion Index, Report No. 125, 1975.

Gallup Opinion Index, Report No. 127, 1976.

Gallup Opinion Index, Report No. 129, 1976.

Gallup Opinion Index, Report No. 131, 1976.

Gallup Opinion Index, Report No. 135, 1976.

Gallup Opinion Index, Report No. 137, 1976.

Gallup Opinion Index, Report No. 141, 1977.

Gallup Opinion Index, Report No. 142, 1977.

Gallup Opinion Index, Report No. 149, 1977.

Gerth, H. H., and Mills, C. W. (Eds.). *From Max Weber: Essays in Sociology.* New York: Oxford University Press, 1946.

Gillespie, J., and Allport, G. *Youth's Outlook on the Future.* New York: Doubleday, 1955.

Glenn, N. D. "The Distribution of Political Knowledge in the United States." In D. Nimmo and C. Bonjean (Eds.), *Political Attitudes and Public Opinion.* New York: David McKay, 1972, pp. 273–283.

Glock, C. Y., and Stark, R. *Christian Beliefs and Anti-Semitism.* New York: Harper & Row, 1967.

Goffman, E. *The Presentation of Self in Everyday Life.* Garden City, N.Y.: Anchor, 1959.

Goldman, S. "Voting Behavior on the United States Courts of Appeals, 1961–1964." *American Political Science Review,* 1966, *60,* pp. 374–383.

Goldman, S. "Background, Attitudes, and the Voting Behavior of Judges: A Comment on Joel Grossman's 'Social Backgrounds and Judicial Decisions.'" *Journal of Politics,* 1969, *11,* pp. 214–222.

Goldman, S., and Jahnige, T. P. *The Federal Courts as a Political System.* New York: Harper & Row, 1971.

Goldman, S. Voting Behavior on the United States Courts of Appeals Revisited. *American Political Science Review,* 1975, *69,* pp. 491–506.

Golembiewski, R., and Cohen, M. *People in the Public Service.* Itasca, Ill.: F. E. Peacock, 1970.

Goodman, M. E. *Race Awareness in Young Children.* Cambridge, Mass.: Addison-Wesley, 1952.

Gottman, J. *Megalopolis.* Cambridge, Mass.: MIT Press, 1961.

Greenberg, E. S. "Orientations of Black and White Children to Political Authority Figures." *Social Science Quarterly,* 1970, *51,* pp. 561–571.

Greenberg, E. S. "The Consequences of Worker Participation: A Clarification of the Theoretical Literature." *Social Science Quarterly,* 1975, *56,* pp. 191–209.

Greenstein, F. I. "The Benevolent Leader: Children's Images of Political Authority." *American Political Science Review,* 1960, *54,* pp. 934–943.

Greenstein, F. I. "The Benevolent Leader Revisited: Children's Images of Political Leaders in Three Democracies." *American Political Science Review,* 1975, *69,* pp. 1371–1398.

Greenwald, C. S. *Group Power.* New York: Praeger, 1977.

Grodzins, M. *The American System* (Ed. by D. Elazar). Chicago: Rand McNally, 1966.

Gross, B. *The Legislative Struggle.* New York: McGraw-Hill, 1953.

Grossman, J. *Lawyers and Judges: The Politics of Judicial Selection.* New York: Wiley, 1965.

Grossman, J. "Social Backgrounds and Judicial Decision-making." *Harvard Law Review,* 1966, *79,* pp. 1551–1572.

Gusfield, J. R. *Symbolic Crusade.* Urbana: University of Illinois Press, 1966.

Hacker, A. *Congressional Districting: The Issue of Equal Representation*. Washington, D.C.: The Brookings Institution, 1963.

Harris, L. *The Harris Survey Yearbook of Public Opinion, 1970*. New York: Louis Harris and Associates, 1971.

Harris, L. *The Anguish of Change*. New York: Norton, 1973.

Harris, L. *Confidence and Concern: Citizens View American Government*. Cleveland, Ohio: Regal Books/King's Court Communications, 1974.

The Harris Survey, June 23, 1975: "Public Approves Job Nader is Doing."

The Harris Survey, November 13, 1975: "Energy Conservation: Fewer Do It."

The Harris Survey, March 22, 1976: "Confidence in Leadership Down Again."

The Harris Survey, March 25, 1976: "Voters Express Alienation."

The Harris Survey, July 8, 1976: "Public Willing to Obey Courts on Busing."

The Harris Survey, July 12, 1976: "Public Rates the Primaries."

The Harris Survey, September 16, 1976: "Carter's Ratings Slip."

The Harris Survey, October 21, 1976: "Doubts Grow about Carter."

The Harris Survey, November 11, 1976: "Voter Turnout Dismal Showing."

The Harris Survey, October 10, 1977: "Carter Rating Down."

The Harris Survey, December 8, 1977: "Alienation Index."

Hartz, L. *The Liberal Tradition in America*. New York: Harcourt Brace Jovanovich, 1955.

Heilbroner, R. L. "Middle-Class Myths, Middle-Class Realities." *The Atlantic*, October 1976, pp. 37–42.

Hero, A. "Public Reaction to Government Policy." In J. P. Robinson, J. G. Rusk, and K. B. Head (Eds.), *Measures of Political Attitudes*. Ann Arbor, Mich.: Institute for Social Research, 1968, pp. 23–89.

Hess, R. D., and Torney, J. V. *The Development of Political Attitudes*. Chicago: Aldine, 1967.

Higgenbotham, A. L., Jr. "The Priority of Human Rights in Court Reform." *Federal Rules Decisions*, 1976, 70, pp. 134–159.

Hinckley, B. *The Seniority System in Congress*. Bloomington: Indiana University Press, 1971.

Hirsch, H. *Poverty and Politicization*. New York: The Free Press, 1971.

Hofstadter, R. *The Age of Reform*. New York: Knopf, 1955.

Hofstadter, R. *The American Political Tradition*. New York: Vintage, 1958.

Hoover, H. C. *Memoirs, the Cabinet and the Presidency, 1920–1933*. New York: Macmillan, 1952.

House Judiciary Subcommittee Hearings, 87th Congress, March 1 and 2, 1961. Washington, D.C.: Government Printing Office, 1961.

Howard, J. W., Jr. "On the Fluidity of Judicial Choice." *American Political Science Review*, 1968, 62, pp. 43–56.

Huntington, S. P. "Congressional Responses to the Twentieth Century." In D. B. Truman (Ed.), *Congress and America's Future*. New York: American Assembly, 1964.

Hyman, H. H., and Sheatsley, P. B. "The Current Status of American Public Opinion." In D. Katz, D. Cartwright, S. Eldersveld, and A. M. Lee (Eds.), *Public Opinion and Propaganda*. New York: Holt, Rinehart and Winston, 1954, pp. 36–37.

Jackman, R. W. "Political Elites, Mass Publics, and Support for Democratic Principles." *Journal of Politics*, 1972, *34*, pp. 753–773.

Jackson, J. S., III, and Hitlin, R. A. "A Comparison of Party Elites: The Sanford Commission and the Delegates to the Democratic Mid-term Conference." *American Politics Quarterly*, 1976, *4*, pp. 441–482.

Jackson, R. H. *The Struggle for Judicial Supramacy*. New York: Knopf, 1941.

James, D. *The Contemporary Presidency*, 2nd ed. New York: Pegasus, 1974.

Jaros, D., Hirsch, H., and Fleron, F. J. "The Malevolent Leader: Political Socialization in an American Sub-culture." *American Political Science Review*, 1968, *62*, pp. 564–575.

Jennings, M. K., and Niemi, R. G. "The Transmission of Political Values from Parent to Child." *American Political Science Review*, 1968 *62*, pp. 169–184.

Jennings, M. K., and Niemi, R. G. "The Division of Political Labor Between Mothers and Fathers." *American Political Science Review*, 1971, *65*, pp. 69–82.

Jennings, M. K., and Niemi, R. G. *The Political Character of Adolescence: The Influence of Families and Schools*. Princeton, N.J.: Princeton University Press, 1974.

Jennings, M. K., and Niemi, R. G. "Continuity and Change in Political Orientations: A Longitudinal Study of Two Generations." *American Political Science Review*, 1975, *69*, pp. 1316–1335.

Jewell, M., and Patterson, S. C. *The Legislative Process in the United States*, 3rd ed. New York: Random House, 1977.

Katz, D. "The Functional Approach to the Study of Attitudes." *Public Opinion Quarterly*, 1960, *24*, pp. 163–176.

Katz, D., and Eldersveld, S. J. "The Impact of Local Party Activity on the Electorate." *Public Opinion Quarterly*, 1961, *25*, pp. 1–24.

Kearns, D. "Who *Was* Lyndon Baines Johnson? Part II: The Great Society, the Bitter End." *The Atlantic*, 1976, *237*, pp. 65–90.

Kelley, S., Jr., and Mirer, T. W. "The Simple Act of Voting." *American Political Science Review*, 1974, *68*, pp. 572–591.

Key, V. O., Jr. "A Theory of Critical Elections." *Journal of Politics*, 1955, *17*, pp. 3–18.

Key, V. O., Jr. *Public Opinion and American Democracy*. New York: Knopf, 1961.

Key, V. O, Jr. *The Responsible Electorate*. Cambridge, Mass.: Belknap Press, 1966.

Kirkpatrick, J. *The New Presidential Elite*. New York: Russell Sage, 1976.

Kirkpatrick, S. A., Lyons, W., and Fitzgerald, M. R. "Candidates, Parties, and Issues in the American Electorate." *American Politics Quarterly*, 1975, *3*, pp. 247–283.

Klapp, O. E. *Symbolic Leaders*. Chicago: Aldine, 1964.

Klonoski, J., and Mendelsohn, R. *The Politics of Local Justice*. Boston: Little, Brown, 1970.

Klorman, R. "Chronopolitics: What Time Do People Vote?" *Public Opinion Quarterly*, 1976, *40*, pp. 182–193.

Knap, T. "Carter's Popularity Based on Appearance, Personality." *Knoxville News-Sentinel*, February, 26, 1976, p. 1.

Koenig, L. *The Chief Executive*, 3rd ed. New York: Harcourt Brace Jovanovich, 1975.

Kostroski, W. L. "Party and Incumbency in Postwar Senate Elections: Trends, Patterns, Models." *American Political Science Review*, 1973, *67*, pp. 1213–1234.

Kramer, G. H. "The Effects of Precinct-level Canvassing on Voter Behavior." *Public Opinion Quarterly*, 1970–1971, *34*, pp. 560–572.

Krislov, S. *Representative Bureaucracy*. Englewood Cliffs, N.J.: Prentice-Hall, 1974.

Ladd, E. C., Jr. "The Polls: The Question of Confidence." *Public Opinion Quarterly*, 1976, *40*, pp. 552–554.

Ladd, E. C., Jr., and Hadley, C. D. *Transformation of the American Party System*. New York: Norton, 1975.

Ladd, E. C., Jr., and Lipset, S. M. *Academics, Politics, and the 1972 Election*. Washington, D.C.: American Enterprise Institute for Public Policy Research, 1973.

Langton, K. P. *Political Socialization*. New York: Oxford University Press, 1969.

Lasswell, H. D. *Psychopathology and Politics*. Chicago: University of Chicago Press, 1930.

"Leadership: An Interview with Senate Leader Lyndon Johnson." *U.S. News and World Report*, June 27, 1960, pp. 88–93.

Lehnen, R. G. *American Institutions: Political Opinion, and Public Policy*. Hinsdale, Ill.: Dryden Press, 1976.

Lengle, J. I., and Shafer, B. "Primary Rules, Political Power, and Social Change." *American Political Science Review*, 1976, *70*, pp. 25–41.

Lindblom, C. E. "The Science of Muddling Through." *Public Administration Review*, 1959, *19*, pp. 79–88.

Lippman, W. *Public Opinion*. New York: Macmillan, 1922.

Lipset, S. M. *Political Man*. Garden City, N.Y.: Doubleday, 1959.

Lipset, S. M. *The First New Nation*. Garden City, N.Y.: Doubleday, 1963.

Lockard, D. *American Federalism*. New York: McGraw-Hill, 1969.

London, B. "Racial Differences in Social and Political Participation: It's Not Simply a Matter of Black and White." *Social Science Quarterly*, 1975, *56*, pp. 274–286.

Long, N. *The Polity*. Chicago: Rand McNally, 1962.

Lowi, T. J. "American Business, Public Policy, Case Studies, and Political Theory." *World Politics*, 1966, *18*, pp. 677–715.

Lowi, T. J. *The Politics of Disorder*. New York: Basic Books, 1971.

Lupfer, M., and Price, D. E. "On the Merits of Face-to-Face Campaigning." *Social Science Quarterly*, 1972, *53*, pp. 534–543.

Lyman, S. M., and Scott, M. B. *A Sociology of the Absurd*. New York: Appleton-Century-Crofts, 1970.

Maas, A. A. "Congress and Water Resources." *American Political Science Review*, 1950, *44*, pp. 576–593.

MacNeil, N. *Forge of Democracy: The House of Representatives*. New York: David McKay, 1963.

Madison, J., Hamilton, A., and Jay, J. *The Federalist*. New York: Modern Library, 1937.

Manheim, J. B. *Deja Vu: American Political Problems in Historical Perspective*. New York: St. Martin's Press, 1976.

Mansfield, H. *Federal Executive Reorganization: Thirty Years of Experience*. Washington, D.C.: The Brookings Institution, 1969.

Margolis, M. "From Confusion to Confusion: Issues and the American Voter (1956–1972)." *American Political Science Review*, 1977, *71*, pp. 31–43.

Mason, A. T. "Harlan Fiske Stone and FDR's Court Plan." *Yale Law Review*, 1952, *61*, pp. 791–817.

Mason, A. T. *Free Government in the Making*, 3rd ed. New York: Oxford University Press, 1965.

Masters, N. A. "Committee Assignments in the House of Representatives." *American Political Science Review*, 1961, *55*, pp. 345–357.

Matthews, D. B. *U.S. Senators and Their World*. Chapel Hill: University of North Carolina Press, 1960.

Matthews, D. R., and Prothro, J. W. *Negroes and the New Southern Politics*. New York: Harcourt Brace Jovanovich, 1966.

Mayhew, D. R. *Congress: The Electoral Connection*. New Haven, Conn.: Yale University Press, 1974.

Mayo, H. B. *An Introduction to Democratic Theory*. New York: Oxford University Press, 1960.

McClosky, H. "Consensus and Ideology in American Politics." *American Political Science Review*, 1964, *58*, pp. 361–382.

McClosky, H., Hoffman, P. J., and O'Hara, R. "Issue Conflict and Consensus among Party Leaders and Followers." *American Political Science Review*, 1960, *54*, (2), pp. 406–427.

McCloskey, R. G. "The American Ideology." In M. Irish (Ed.), *Continuing Crises in American Politics*. Englewood Cliffs, N.J.: Prentice-Hall, 1963, pp. 10–25.

McCloskey, R. G. *The American Supreme Court*. Chicago: University of Chicago Press, 1968.

McCombs, M. E. "Mass Communication in Political Campaigns: Information Gratification, or Persuasion." In F. G. Kline and P. J. Tichenor (Eds.), *Current Perspectives on Mass Communication Research*. Beverly Hills, Calif.: Sage Publications, 1972, pp. 169–194.

McCombs, M. "Agenda-Setting Research: A Bibliographic Essay." *Political Communication Review*, 1976, *1*, pp. 1–7.

McConnell, G. *Private Power and American Democracy*. New York: Knopf, 1966.

McConnell, G. *The Modern Presidency*. New York: St. Martin's Press, 1967.

McLaughlin, A. A. *Constitutional History of the United States*. New York: Appleton-Century-Crofts, 1935.

Mendelsohn, H., and O'Keefe, G. J. *The People Choose a President*. New York: Praeger, 1976.

Mendelsohn, W. "Judicial Review and Party Politics." *Vanderbilt Law Review*, 1959, *12*, pp. 447–457.

Menendez, A. J. *Religion at the Polls*. Philadelphia: Westminster Press, 1977.

Merelman, R. M. "The Development of Political Ideology: A Framework for Analysis of Political Socialization." *American Political Science Review*, 1969, *63*, pp. 750–767.

Milbrath, L. W. *The Washington Lobbyists*. Chicago: Rand McNally, 1965.

Milbrath, L. W., and Goel, M. L. *Political Participation*. Chicago: Rand McNally, 1977.

Miller, A. H., Miller, W. E., Raine, A. S., and Brown, T. A. "A Majority Party in Disarray: Policy Polarization in the 1972 Election." *American Political Science Review*, 1976, *70*, pp. 753–778.

Miller, L. *The Petitioners: The Story of the Supreme Court of the United States and the Negro.* New York: Pantheon, 1966.

Miller, W. E. "Presidential Coattails: A Study in Political Myth and Methology." *Public Opinion Quarterly,* 1955, 19, pp. 26–39.

Miller, W. E., and Levitin, T. E. *Leadership and Change: The New Politics of the American Electorate.* Cambridge, Mass.: Winthrop Publishers, 1976.

Miller, W. E., and Stokes, D. "Constituency Influence in Congress." *American Political Science Review,* 1963, 57, pp. 45–56.

Mills, C. W. *The Power Elite.* New York: Oxford University Press, 1957.

Mitchell, B., and Mitchell, L. *A Biography of the Constitution,* 2nd ed. New York: Oxford University Press, 1975.

Morison, S. E., and Commager, H. S. *The Growth of the American Republic.* New York: Oxford University Press, 1950.

Morrison, P. A. "Migration and Access: New Public Concerns in the 1970s." Paper cited in *Current Public Policy Research,* 1977, 1, p. 1.

Mueller, J. E. *War, Presidents, and Public Opinion.* New York: Wiley, 1973.

Murphy, W. F. *Elements of Judicial Strategy.* Chicago: University of Chicago Press, 1964.

Murphy, W. F., and Tannenhaus, J. *The Study of Public Law.* New York: Random House, 1972.

Nader, R. *Unsafe at Any Speed.* New York: Grossman, 1965.

Natchez, P. B., and Bupp, I. C. "Candidates, Issues, and Voters." *Public Policy,* 1968, 17, pp. 409–437.

Neustadt, R. E. *Presidential Power: The Politics of Leadership, with Reflections on Johnson and Nixon.* New York: Wiley, 1976.

Nie, N. H., and Verba, S. "Political Participation." In F. I. Greenstein and N. W. Polsby (Eds.), *Handbook of Political Science,* Vol. 4. Reading, Mass: Addison-Wesley, 1975, pp. 1–74.

Nie, N. H., Verba, S., and Pretrocik, J. R. *The Changing American Voter.* Cambridge, Mass.: Harvard University Press, 1976.

Nimmo, D., and Savage, R. L. *Candidates and Their Images.* Pacific Palisades, Cal.: Goodyear, 1976.

"Nonvoters on the Rise." *Congressional Quarterly Almanac,* 1976, 34, p. 2466.

O'Keefe, G. J., Mendelsohn, H., and Liu, J. "Voter Decision Making, 1972 and 1974." *Public Opinion Quarterly,* 1976, 40, pp. 320–330.

Oppenheimer, B. "The Rules Committee in a Decentralized House." In L. C. Dodd and B. Oppenheimer, *Congress Reconsidered.* New York: Prager, 1977.

Ornstein, N. J., Peabody, R. L., and Rohde, D. "The Changing Senate: From the 1950s to the 1970s." In L. C. Dodd and B. Oppenheimer (Eds.), *Congress Reconsidered.* New York: Praeger, 1977.

Orren, K. "Standing to Sue: Interest Group Conflict in the Federal Courts." *American Political Science Review,* 1976, 70, pp. 723–741.

Patterson, T. W., and McClure, R. D. *The Unseeing Eye: The Myth of Television Power in National Politics.* New York: G. P. Putnam, 1976.

Peltason, J. *Fifty-eight Lonely Men.* New York: Harcourt Brace Jovanovich, 1961.

Phillips, K. *The Emerging Republican Majority.* New Rochelle, N.Y.: Arlington House, 1969.

Polsby, N. W. "Dilemmas of the Vice-Presidency." In N. W. Polsby (Ed.), *Political Promises*. New York: Oxford University Press, 1974.

Polsby, N. W., and Wildavsky, A. *Presidential Elections* 4th ed. New York: Scribner's, 1976.

Pomper, G. *Voters' Choice*. New York: Harper & Row, 1975.

Pool, I., Abelson, R., and Popkin, S. *Candidates, Issues, and Strategies*. Cambridge, Mass.: MIT Press, 1964.

Popkin, S., Gorman, J. W., Phillips, C., and Smith, J. A. "Comment: What Have You Done for Me Lately?" *American Political Science Review*, 1976, 70, pp. 779–805.

Presthus, R. *The Organizational Society*. New York: Knopf, 1962.

Price, D. *Who Makes the Laws?* New York: Schenken, 1972.

Price, D. E., and Lupfer, M. "Volunteers for Gore: The Impact of a Precinct-Level Canvas in Three Tennessee Cities." *Journal of Politics*, 1973, 35, pp. 410–438.

Pritchett, C. H. *Congress Versus the Supreme Court*. Minneapolis: University of Minnesota Press, 1961.

Pritchett, C. H., and Westin, A. F. *The Third Branch of Government*. New York: Harcourt Brace Jovanovich, 1963.

Prothro, J. W., and Grigg, C. M. "Fundamental Principles of Democracy: Basis of Agreement and Disagreement." *Journal of Politics*, 1960, 22, pp. 276–294.

Rainey, G. E. *Patterns of American Foreign Policy*. Boston: Allyn & Bacon, 1975.

Ranney, A. "Turnout and Representation in Presidential Primary Elections." *American Political Science Review*, 1972, 66; pp. 21–37.

Ranney, A. *Curing the Mischiefs of Faction: Party Reform in America*. Berkeley: University of California Press, 1975.

Reagan, M. *The New Federalism*. New York: Oxford University Press, 1972.

Redford, E. S. *Ideal and Practice in Public Administration*. Birmingham: University of Alabama Press, 1958.

Reinhold, R. "Moderate Image Helping Carter Stay Ahead." *Knoxville News Sentinel*, October 20, 1976.

RePass, D. E. "Issue Salience and Party Choice." *American Political Science Review*, 1971, 65, pp. 389–400.

RePass, D. E. "Comment: Political Methodologies in Disarray: Some Alternative Interpretations of the 1972 Election." *American Political Science Review*, 1976, 70, pp. 814–831.

Report of the National Advisory Commission on Civil Disorders. Washington, D.C.: Government Printing Office, 1968.

"Report to the American People on the Financing of Congressional Election Campaigns." *Frontline*, April–May 1977, pp. 3–15.

Richardson, R. J., and Vines, K. R. "Review, Dissent, and the Appellate Process: A Political Interpretation." *Journal of Politics*, 1967, 29, pp. 597–616.

Richardson, J., and Vines, K. N. *The Politics of Federal Courts*. Boston: Little, Brown, 1970.

Ripley, R. B. *Party Leaders in the House of Representatives*. Washington, D.C.: The Brookings Institution, 1967.

Ripley, R. B. *Power in the Senate*. New York: St. Martin's Press, 1969.

Ripley, R. B. *Congress: Process and Policy*. New York: Norton, 1975.

Robinson, J. P. "The Press as King-Maker: What Surveys from Last Five Campaigns Show." *Journalism Quarterly*, 1974, *51*, pp. 587–594.

Roche, J. P. "Judicial Self-Restraint." *American Political Science Review*, 1955, *49*, pp. 762–776.

Roche, J. P. "The Founding Fathers: A Reform Caucus in Action." *American Political Science Review*, 1961, *55*, pp. 799–816.

Rockefeller Brothers Special Studies Project. *The Power of the Democratic Idea.* Garden City, N.Y.: Doubleday, 1960.

Rodgers, H. R., Jr., and Lewis, E. B. "Student Attitudes Toward Mr. Nixon." *American Politics Quarterly*, 1975, *3*, pp. 423–436.

Rohde, D., and Spaeth, H. *Supreme Court Decision Making.* San Francisco: W. H. Freeman and Company, 1976.

Roosevelt, T. *An Autobiography.* New York: Scribner's, 1946.

Rose, A. M. *The Power Structure: Political Process in American Life.* New York: Oxford University Press, 1967.

Rossiter, C. *Seedtime of the Republic.* New York: Harcourt Brace Jovanovich, 1953.

Rossiter, C. *The American Presidency*, rev. ed. New York: Harcourt Bracc Jovanovich, 1960.

Rourke, F. *Bureaucracy, Politics, and Public Policy*, 2nd ed. Boston: Little, Brown, 1976.

Sale, K. *Power Shift: The Rise of the Southern Rim and Its Challenge to the Eastern Establishment.* New York: Vintage, 1975.

Scammon, R. M., and Wattenberg, B. J. *The Real Majority.* New York: Coward-McCann, 1970.

Schattschncidcr, E. E. *The Semisovereign People.* New York: Holt, Rinehart and Winston, 1960.

Schlesinger, A. M., Jr. *The Imperial Presidency.* Boston: Houghton Mifflin, 1973.

Schmidhauser, J. R. *The Supreme Court.* New York: Holt, Rinchart and Winston, 1960.

Schmidhauser, J. R. "Judicial Behavior and the Sectional Crises of 1837–1860." *Journal of Politics*, 1961, *23*, pp. 615–633.

Schubert, G. *Quantitative Analysis of Judicial Behavior.* New York: The Free Press, 1959.

Schubert, G. *The Constitutional Polity.* Boston: Boston University Press, 1970.

Schubert, G. *The Judicial Mind Revisited.* New York: Oxford University Press, 1974.

Schulman, P. R. "Nonincremental Policy Making: Notes Toward an Alternative Pardigm." *American Political Science Review*, 1975, *69*, pp. 1354–1370.

Schumpeter, J. *Capitalism, Socialism, and Democracy.* New York: Harper & Row, 1942.

Scoble, H. M. "Organized Labor in Electoral Politics." *Western Political Quarterly*, 1963, *16*, pp. 666–685.

Scoble, H. M. *Ideology and Electoral Action.* San Francisco: Chandler, 1967.

Scott, A. M. *Political Thought in America.* New York: Holt, Rinehart and Winston, 1959.

Sebert, S. K. "The Political Texture of Peer Groups." In M. R. Jennings and R. G. Niemi (Eds.), *The Political Character of Adolescence.* Princeton, N.J.: Princeton University Press, 1974, pp. 229–248.

Sellers, C. "The Equilibrium Cycle in Two-Party Politics." *Public Opinion Quarterly*, 1965, *29*, pp. 16–37.

Selznick, P. *TVA and the Grass Roots*. Berkeley: University of California Press, 1953.

Shannon, W. W. *Party, Constituency and Congressional Voting*. Baton Rouge: Louisiana State University Press, 1968.

Shapiro, M. *Freedom of Speech: The Supreme Court and Judicial Review*. Englewood Cliffs, N.J.: Prentice-Hall, 1966.

Sharkansky, I. *The United States: A Study of a Developing Country*. New York: David McKay, 1975.

Simon, R. J. *Public Opinion in America: 1936–1970*. Chicago: Markham, 1974.

Simpson, T. M. *Jimmy Carter: Governor of Georgia*. In preparation, 1977.

Sindler, A. P. *Political Parties in the United States*. New York: St. Martin's Press, 1966.

Smith, M. B. "The Personal Setting of Public Opinions: A Study of Attitudes Toward Russia." *Public Opinion Quarterly*, 1947, *11*, pp. 507–523.

Sorauf, F. J. *Party Politics in America*, 2nd ed. Boston: Little, Brown, 1972.

Sorenson, T. C. *Decision-Making in the White House*. New York: Columbia University Press, 1963.

Stanley, D. T., Mann, D. E., and Doig, J. W. *Men Who Govern: A Biographical Profile of Federal Political Executives*. Washington, D.C.: The Brookings Institution, 1967.

Stephens, O. H., Jr. "The Burger Court: New Dimensions in Criminal Justice." *Georgetown Law Journal*, 1971, *60*, pp. 249–278.

Stimson, J. A. "Public Support for American Presidents: A Cyclical Model." *Public Opinion Quarterly*, 1976, *40*, pp. 1–21.

Stokes, D. E. "Some Dynamic Elements of Contests for the Presidency." *American Political Science Review*, 1966, *61*, pp. 19–28.

Stouffer, S. *Communism, Conformity, and Civil Liberties*. New York: Doubleday, 1955.

Sullivan, D. G., Pressman, J. L., and Arterton, F. C. *Explorations in Convention Decision Making: The Democratic Party in the 1970s*. San Francisco: W. H. Freeman and Company, 1976.

Sundquist, J. *Politics and Policy*. Washington, D.C.: The Brookings Institution, 1968.

Taebel, D. A. "The Effect of Ballot Position on Electoral Success." *American Journal of Political Science*, 1975, *19*, pp. 519–527.

Tannenhaus, J. "The Cumulative Scaling of Judicial Decisions." *Harvard Law Review*, 1966, *79*, pp. 1583–1594.

Thomas, W. R. *The Burger Court and Civil Liberties*. Brunswick, Ohio: Regal Books/King's Court Communications, 1976.

Thompson, G. C. *Public Opinion and Lord Beaconsfield*. New York: Macmillan, 1886.

Thompson, V. *Modern Organization*. New York: Knopf, 1961.

Toffler, A. *Future Shock*. New York: Bantam, 1970.

Trilling, R. J. "Party Image and Electoral Behavior." *American Politics Quarterly*, 1975, *3*, pp. 284–314.

Truman, D. B. *The Governmental Process*. New York: Knopf, 1952.

Truman, D. B. *The Congressional Party*. New York: Wiley, 1959.

Truman, D. B. "Federalism and the Party System." In N. W. Polsby, R. A. Dentler, and

P. A. Smith (Eds.), *Politics and Social Life.* Boston: Houghton Mifflin, 1963, pp. 513–526.

Turner, J. *Party and Constituency: Pressures on Congress* (revised by E. V. Schneier, Jr.). Baltimore: Johns Hopkins Press, 1970.

Ulmer, S. S. "Dimensions of Judicial Voting." *Midwest Journal of Political Science,* 1969, *13*, pp. 471–484.

U.S. Bureau of the Census. "Voter Participation in November, 1972." In *Current Population Reports,* Series P-20, No. 244. Washington, D.C.: Government Printing Office, 1972.

U.S. Bureau of the Census. "Voting and Registration in the Election of 1972." In *Current Population Reports.* Series P-20, No. 253. Washington, D.C.: Government Printing Office, 1973.

Verba, S., and Nie, N. H. *Participation in America.* New York: Harper & Row, 1972.

Wald, P. *Law and Poverty.* Washington, D.C.: Government Printing Office, 1965.

Warner, W. L., Van Riper, P., Martin, N. H., and Collins, O. *The American Federal Executive.* New Haven, Conn.: Yale University Press, 1963.

Wattier, M. J., Jr. "Presidential Popularity and the Political Process: Public Opinion Polls as Linkage." Paper presented at the annual meeting of the Southern Political Science Association, Atlanta, Georgia, November 4–6, 1976.

Watts, W., and Free, L. A. *State of the Nation.* New York: Universe Books, 1973.

Watts, W., and Free, L. A. *State of the Nation 1974.* Washington, D.C.: Potomac Associates, 1975.

Weaver, W., Jr. "Mitchell Yields on Court Choices." *New York Times,* July 28, 1970, p. 1.

Weinstein, E. A. "Development of the Concept of Flag and the Sense of National Security." *Child Development,* 1958, *28*, pp. 167–174.

Wheeler, H. " 'Duocracy' or the Imperfect Competition in Our Party System." In J. R. Fiszman (Ed.), *The American Political Arena.* Boston: Little, Brown, 1962.

White, L. D. *The Jeffersonians.* New York: Macmillan, 1951.

White, L. D. *The Jacksonians.* New York: Macmillan, 1954.

White, T. H. *The Making of the President, 1960.* New York: Atheneum, 1961.

Wildavsky, A. "Political Implications of Budgetary Reform." *Public Administration Review,* 1961, *21*, pp. 183–190.

Wildavsky, A. *The Politics of the Budgetary Process,* 2nd ed. Boston: Little, Brown, 1974.

Wilson, J. Q. *Political Organizations.* New York: Basic Books, 1973.

Wolfinger, R. W., and Heifetz, J. "Safe Seats, Seniority, and Power in Congress." *American Political Science Review,* 1965, *59*, pp. 337–349.

Wycoff, G. *The Image Candidates.* New York: Macmillan, 1968.

THE

CONSTITUTION

OF THE

UNITED STATES

Proposed by Convention September 17, 1787. Effective March 4, 1789.

PREAMBLE

We, the people of the United States, in order to form a more perfect union, establish justice, insure domestic tranquillity, provide for the common defense, promote the general welfare, and secure the blessings of liberty to ourselves and our posterity, do ordain and establish this Constitution for the United States of America.

ARTICLE I

SECTION 1

All legislative powers herein granted shall be vested in a Congress of the United States, which shall consist of a Senate and House of Representatives.

SECTION 2

[1] The House of Representatives shall be composed of members chosen every second year by the people of the several States, and the electors in each State shall have the qualifications requisite for electors of the most numerous branch of the State legislature.

[2] No person shall be a Representative who shall not have attained to the age of twenty-five years, and been seven years a citizen of the United States, and who shall not, when elected, be an inhabitant of that State in which he shall be chosen.

[3] Representatives and direct taxes shall be apportioned among the several States which may be included within this Union, according to their respective numbers, which shall be determined by adding to the whole number of free persons, including those bound to service for a term of years, and excluding Indians not taxed, three-fifths of all other persons. The actual enumeration shall be made within three years after the first meeting of the Congress of the United States, and within every subsequent term of ten years, in such manner as they shall by law direct. The number of Representatives shall not exceed one for every thirty thousand, but each State shall have at least one Representative; and until such enumeration shall be made, the State of New Hampshire shall be entitled to choose three; Massachusetts, eight; Rhode Island and Providence Plantations, one; Connecticut, five; New York, six; New Jersey, four; Pennsylvania, eight; Delaware, one; Maryland, six; Virginia, ten; North Carolina, five; South Carolina, five; and Georgia, three.

[4] When vacancies happen in the representation from any State, the executive authority thereof shall issue writs of election to fill such vacancies.

[5] The House of Representatives shall choose their Speaker and other officers, and shall have the sole power of impeachment.

SECTION 3

[1] The Senate of the United States shall be composed of two Senators from each State, chosen by the legislature thereof for six years; and each Senator shall have one vote.

[2] Immediately after they shall be assembled in consequence of the first election, they shall be divided as equally as may be into three classes. The seats of the Senators of the first class shall be vacated at the expiration of the second year, of the second class at the expiration of the fourth year, and of the third class at the expiration of the sixth year, so that one-third may be chosen every second year; and if vacancies happen by resignation or otherwise during the recess of the legislature of any State, the executive thereof may make temporary appointments until the next meeting of the legislature, which shall then fill such vacancies.

[3] No person shall be a Senator who shall not have attained to the age of thirty years, and been nine years a citizen of the United States, and who shall not, when elected, be an inhabitant of that State for which he shall be chosen.

[4] The Vice-President of the United States shall be President of the Senate, but shall have no vote, unless they be equally divided.

[5] The Senate shall choose their other officers and also a President *pro tempore* in the absence of the Vice-President, or when he shall exercise the office of President of the United States.

[6] The Senate shall have the sole power to try all impeachments. When sitting for that purpose, they shall be on oath or affirmation. When the President of the United States is tried, the Chief Justice shall preside; and no person shall be convicted without the concurrence of two-thirds of the members present.

[7] Judgment in cases of impeachment shall not extend further than to removal from office, and disqualification to hold and enjoy any office of honor, trust, or profit under the United States; but the party convicted shall, nevertheless, be liable and subject to indictment, trial, judgment, and punishment, according to law.

SECTION 4

[1] The times, places, and manner of holding elections for Senators and Representatives shall be prescribed in each State by the legislature thereof; but the Congress may at any time by law make or alter such regulations, except as to the places of choosing Senators.

[2] The Congress shall assemble at least once in every year, and such meeting shall be on the first Monday in December, unless they shall by law appoint a different day.

SECTION 5

[1] Each House shall be the judge of the elections, returns, and qualifications of its own members, and a majority of each shall constitute a quorum to do business; but a smaller number may adjourn from day to day, and may be authorized to compel the attendance of absent members, in such manner, and under such penalties, as each House may provide.

[2] Each House may determine the rules of its proceedings, punish its members for disorderly behavior, and with the concurrence of two-thirds, expel a member.

[3] Each House shall keep a journal of its proceedings, and from time to time publish the same, excepting such parts as may in their judgment require secrecy, and the yeas and nays of the members of either House on any question shall, at the desire of one-fifth of those present, be entered on the journal.

[4] Neither House, during the session of Congress, shall, without the consent of the other, adjourn for more than three days, nor to any other place than that in which the two Houses shall be sitting.

SECTION 6

[1] The Senators and Representatives shall receive a compensation for their services, to be ascertained by law and paid out of the Treasury of the United States. They shall, in all cases except treason, felony, and breach of the peace, be privileged from arrest during their attendance at the session of their respective Houses, and in going to and returning from the same; and for any speech or debate in either House they shall not be questioned in any other place.

[2] No Senator or Representative shall, during the time for which he was elected, be appointed to any civil office under the authority of the United States, which shall have been created, or the emoluments whereof shall have been increased during such time; and no person holding any office under the United States shall be a member of either House during his continuance in office.

SECTION 7

[1] All bills for raising revenue shall originate in the House of Representatives; but the Senate may propose or concur with amendments as on other bills.

[2] Every bill which shall have passed the House of Representatives and the Senate shall, before it become a law, be presented to the President of the United States; if he approve he shall sign it, but if not he shall return it, with his objections, to that House in which it shall have originated, who shall enter the objections at large on their journal and proceed to reconsider it. If after such reconsideration two-thirds of that House shall agree to pass the bill, it shall be sent, together with the objections, to the other House, by which it shall likewise be reconsidered, and if approved by two-thirds of that House it shall become a law. But in all such cases the vote of both Houses shall be determined by yeas and nays, and the names of the persons voting for and against the bill shall be entered on the journal of each House respectively. If any bill shall not be returned by the President within ten days (Sundays excepted) after it shall have been presented to him, the same shall be a law, in like manner as if he had signed it, unless the Congress by their adjournment prevent its return, in which case it shall not be a law.

[3] Every order, resolution or vote to which the concurrence of the Senate and House of Representatives may be necessary (except on a question of adjournment) shall be presented to the President of the United States; and before the same shall take effect shall be approved by him, or being disapproved by him, shall be repassed by two-thirds of the Senate and House of Representatives, according to the rules and limitations prescribed in the case of a bill.

SECTION 8

[1] The Congress shall have power to lay and collect taxes, duties, imposts and excises, to pay the debts and provide for the common defense and general welfare of the United States; but all duties, imposts and excises shall be uniform throughout the United States;

[2] To borrow money on the credit of the United States;

[3] To regulate commerce with foreign nations, and among the several States, and with the Indian tribes;

[4] To establish an uniform rule of naturalization, and uniform laws on the subject of bankruptcies throughout the United States;

[5] To coin money, regulate the value thereof, and of foreign coin, and fix the standard of weights and measures;

[6] To provide for the punishment of counterfeiting the securities and current coin of the United States;

[7] To establish post offices and post roads;

[8] To promote the progress of science and useful arts by securing for limited times to authors and inventors the exclusive right to their respective writings and discoveries;

[9] To constitute tribunals inferior to the Supreme Court;

[10] To define and punish piracies and felonies committed on the high seas and offenses against the law of nations;

[11] To declare war, grant letters of marque and reprisal, and make rules concerning captures on land and water;

[12] To raise and support armies, but no appropriation of money to that use shall be for a longer term than two years;

[13] To provide and maintain a navy;

[14] To make rules for the government and regulation of the land and naval forces;

[15] To provide for calling forth the militia to execute the laws of the Union, suppress insurrections, and repel invasions;

[16] To provide for organizing, arming and disciplining the militia, and for governing such part of them as may be employed in the service of the United States, reserving to the States respectively the appointment of the officers, and the authority of training the militia according to the discipline prescribed by Congress;

[17] To exercise exclusive legislation in all cases whatsoever over such district (not exceeding ten miles square) as may, by cession of particular States and the acceptance of Congress, become the seat of the Government of the United States, and to exercise like authority over all places purchased by the consent of the legislature of the State in which the same shall be, for the erection of forts, magazines, arsenals, dockyards, and other needful buildings;

[18] To make all laws which shall be necessary and proper for carrying into execution the foregoing powers, and all other powers vested by this Constitution in the Government of the United States, or in any department or officer thereof.

SECTION 9

[1] The migration or importation of such persons as any of the States now existing shall think proper to admit shall not be prohibited by the Congress prior to the year one thousand eight hundred and eight, but a tax or duty may be imposed on such importation, not exceeding ten dollars for each person.

[2] The privilege of the writ of habeas corpus shall not be suspended, unless when in cases of rebellion or invasion the public safety may require it.

[3] No bill of attainder or ex post facto law shall be passed.

[4] No capitation or other direct tax shall be laid, unless in proportion to the census or enumeration hereinbefore directed to be taken.

[5] No tax or duty shall be laid on articles exported from any State.

[6] No preference shall be given by any regulation of commerce or revenue to the ports of one State over those of another; nor shall vessels bound to or from one State be obliged to enter, clear or pay duties in another.

[7] No money shall be drawn from the Treasury but in consequence of appropriations made by law; and a regular statement and account of the receipts and expenditures of all public money shall be published from time to time.

[8] No title of nobility shall be granted by the United States; and no person holding any office of profit or trust under them shall, without the consent of Congress, accept of any present, emolument, office, or title of any kind whatever from any king, prince, or foreign state.

SECTION 10

[1] No State shall enter into any treaty, alliance, or confederation; grant letters of marque and reprisal; coin money, emit bills of credit; make anything but gold and silver coin a tender in payment of debts; pass any bill of attainder, ex post facto law or law impairing the obligation of contracts, or grant any title of nobility.

[2] No State shall, without the consent of the Congress, lay any imposts or duties on imports or exports, except what may be absolutely necessary for executing its inspection laws; and the net produce of all duties and imposts, laid by any State on imports or exports, shall be for the use of

the Treasury of the United States; and all such laws shall be subject to the revision and control of the Congress.

[3] No State shall, without the consent of Congress, lay any duty of tonnage, keep troops and ships of war in time of peace, enter into any agreement or compact with another State or with a foreign power, or engage in war, unless actually invaded or in such imminent danger as will not admit of delay.

ARTICLE II

SECTION 1

[1] The executive power shall be vested in a President of the United States of America. He shall hold his office during the term of four years, and together with the Vice-President, chosen for the same term, be elected as follows:

[2] Each State shall appoint, in such manner as the legislature thereof may direct, a number of Electors, equal to the whole number of Senators and Representatives to which the State may be entitled in the Congress; but no Senator or Representative, or person holding an office of trust or profit under the United States, shall be appointed an Elector.

[3] The Electors shall meet in their respective States and vote by ballot for two persons, of whom one at least shall not be an inhabitant of the same State with themselves. And they shall make a list of all the persons voted for, and of the number of votes for each; which list they shall sign and certify, and transmit sealed to the seat of government of the United States, directed to the President of the Senate. The President of the Senate shall, in the presence of the Senate and House of Representatives, open all the certificates, and the votes shall then be counted. The person having the greatest number of votes shall be the President, if such number be a majority of the whole number of Electors appointed; and if there be more than one who have such majority, and have an equal number of votes, then the House of Representatives shall immediately choose by ballot one of them for President; and if no person have a majority, then from the five highest on the list the said House shall in like manner choose the President. But in choosing the President the votes shall be taken by States, the representation from each State having one vote; a quorum for this purpose shall consist of a member or members from two-thirds of the States, and a majority of all the States shall be necessary to a choice. In every case, after the choice of the President, the person having the greatest number of votes of the Electors shall be the Vice-President. But if there should remain two or more who have equal votes, the Senate shall choose from them by ballot the Vice-President.

[4] The Congress may determine the time of choosing the Electors and the day on which they shall give their votes, which day shall be the same throughout the United States.

[5] No person except a natural-born citizen, or citizen of the United States at the time of the adoption of this Constitution, shall be eligible to the office of President; neither shall any person be eligible to that office who shall not have attained to the age of thirty-five years, and been fourteen years a resident within the United States.

[6] In case of the removal of the President from office, or of his death, resignation, or inability to discharge the powers and duties of the said office, the same shall devolve on the Vice-President, and the Congress may by law provide for the case of removal, death, resignation, or inability, both of the President and Vice-President, declaring what officer shall then act as President, and such officer shall act accordingly until the disability be removed or a President shall be elected.

[7] The President shall, at stated times, receive for his services a compensation, which shall neither be increased nor diminished during the period for which he shall have been elected, and he shall not receive within that period any other emolument from the United States or any of them.

[8] Before he enter on the execution of his office he shall take the following oath or affirmation:

"I do solemnly swear (or affirm) that I will faithfully execute the office of President of the United States, and will to the best of my ability preserve, protect, and defend the Constitution of the United States."

SECTION 2

[1] The President shall be Commander-in-Chief of the Army and Navy of the United States, and of the militia of the several States when called into the actual service of the United States; he may require the opinion, in writing, of the principal officer in each of the executive departments, upon any subject relating to the duties of their respective offices, and he shall have power to grant reprieves and pardons for offenses against the United States, except in cases of impeachment.

[2] He shall have power, by and with the advice and consent of the Senate, to make treaties, provided two-thirds of the Senators present concur; and he shall nominate, and, by and with the advice and consent of the Senate, shall appoint ambassadors, other public ministers and consuls, judges of the Supreme Court, and all other officers of the United States whose appointments are not herein otherwise provided for, and which shall be established by law; but the Congress may by law vest the appointment of such inferior officers, as they think proper, in the President alone, in the courts of law, or in the heads of departments.

[3] The President shall have power to fill up all vacancies that may happen during the recess of the Senate, by granting commissions which shall expire at the end of their next session.

SECTION 3

He shall from time to time give to the Congress information of the state of the Union, and recommend to their consideration such measures as he shall judge necessary and expedient; he may, on extraordinary occasions, convene both Houses, or either of them, and in case of disagreement between them with respect to the time of adjournment, he may adjourn them to such time as he shall think proper; he shall receive ambassadors and other public ministers; he shall take care that the laws be faithfully executed, and shall commission all the officers of the United States.

SECTION 4

The President, Vice-President and all civil officers of the United States shall be removed from office on impeachment for and conviction of treason, bribery, or other high crimes and misdemeanors.

ARTICLE III

SECTION 1

The judicial power of the United States shall be vested in one Supreme Court, and in such inferior courts as the Congress may from time to time ordain and establish. The judges, both of the Supreme and inferior courts, shall hold their offices during good behavior, and shall, at stated times, receive for their services a compensation which shall not be diminished during their continuance in office.

SECTION 2

[1] The judicial power shall extend to all cases, in law and equity, arising under this Constitution, the laws of the United States, and treaties made, or which shall be made, under their authority; to all cases affecting ambassadors, other public ministers, and consuls; to all cases of admiralty and maritime jurisdiction; to controversies to which the United States shall be a party; to controversies between two or more States; between a State and citizens of another State; between citizens of different States; between citizens of the same State claiming lands under grants of different States, and between a State, or the citizens thereof, and foreign states, citizens, or subjects.

[2] In all cases affecting ambassadors, other public ministers and consuls, and those in which a State shall be party, the Supreme Court shall have original jurisdiction. In all the other cases before mentioned the Supreme Court shall have appellate jurisdiction, both as to law and fact, with such exceptions and under such regulations as the Congress shall make.

[3] The trial of all crimes, except in cases of impeachment, shall be by jury; and such trial shall be held in the State where the said crimes shall have been committed; but when not committed

within any State, the trial shall be at such place or places as the Congress may by law have directed.

SECTION 3

[1] Treason against the United States shall consist only in levying war against them, or in adhering to their enemies, giving them aid and comfort. No person shall be convicted of treason unless on the testimony of two witnesses to the same overt act, or on confession in open court.

[2] The Congress shall have power to declare the punishment of treason, but no attainder of treason shall work corruption of blood or forfeiture except during the life of the person attained.

ARTICLE IV

SECTION 1

Full faith and credit shall be given in each State to the public acts, records, and judicial proceedings of every other State. And the Congress may by general laws prescribe the manner in which such acts, records, and proceedings shall be proved, and the effect thereof.

SECTION 2

[1] The citizens of each State shall be entitled to all privileges and immunities of citizens in the several States.

[2] A person charged in any State with treason, felony, or other crime, who shall flee from justice, and be found in another State, shall, on demand of the executive authority of the State from which he fled, be delivered up, to be removed to the State having jurisdiction of the crime.

[3] No person held to service or labor in one State, under the laws thereof, escaping into another, shall, in consequence of any law or regulation therein, be discharged from such service or labor, but shall be delivered up on claim to the party to whom such service or labor may be due.

SECTION 3

[1] New States may be admitted by the Congress into this Union; but no new State shall be formed or erected within the jurisdiction of any other State; nor any State be formed by the junction of two or more States or parts of States, without the consent of the legislatures of the States concerned as well as of the Congress.

[2] The Congress shall have power to dispose of and make all needful rules and regulations respecting the territory or other property belonging to the United States; and nothing in this Constitution shall be so construed as to prejudice any claims of the United States or of any particular State.

SECTION 4

The United States shall guarantee to every State in this Union a republican form of government, and shall protect each of them against invasion, and on application of the legislature, or of the executive (when the legislature cannot be convened), against domestic violence.

ARTICLE V

The Congress, whenever two-thirds of both Houses shall deem it necessary, shall propose amendments to this Constitution, or, on the application of the legislatures of two-thirds of the several States, shall call a convention for proposing amendments, which in either case shall be valid to all intents and purposes as part of this Constitution, when ratified by the legislatures of three-fourths of the several States, or by conventions in three-fourths thereof, as the one or the other mode of ratification may be proposed by the Congress; provided that no amendment which may be made prior to the year one thousand eight hundred and eight shall in any manner affect the first and fourth clauses in the Ninth Section of the First Article; and that no State, without its consent shall be deprived of its equal suffrage in the Senate.

ARTICLE VI

[1] All debts contracted and engagements entered into, before the adoption of this Constitution, shall be as valid against the United States under this Constitution as under the Confederation.

[2] This Constitution, and the laws of the United States which shall be made in pursuance thereof, and all treaties made, or which shall be made, under the authority of the United States, shall be the supreme law of the land; and the judges in every State shall be bound thereby, anything in the Constitution or laws of any State to the contrary notwithstanding.

[3] The Senators and Representatives before mentioned and the members of the several State legislatures, and all executive and judicial officers both of the United States and of the several States, shall be bound by oath or affirmation to support this Constitution; but no religious test shall ever be required as a qualification to any office or public trust under the United States.

ARTICLE VII

The ratification of the conventions of nine States shall be sufficent for the establishment of this Constitution between the States so ratifying the same.

AMENDMENTS

AMENDMENT I

Congress shall make no law respecting an establishment of religion, or prohibiting the free exercise thereof; or abridging the freedom of speech or of the press; or the right of the people peaceably to assemble, and to petition the government for a redress of grievances.

AMENDMENT II

A well-regulated militia being necessary to the security of a free State, the right of the people to keep and bear arms shall not be infringed.

AMENDMENT III

No soldier shall, in time of peace, be quartered in any house without the consent of the owner; nor in time of war; but in a manner to be prescribed by law.

AMENDMENT IV

The right of the people to be secure in their persons, houses, papers, and effects, against unreasonable searches and seizures, shall not be violated, and no warrants shall issue but upon probable cause, supported by oath or affirmation, and particularly describing the place to be searched, and the persons or things to be seized.

AMENDMENT V

No person shall be held to answer for a capital, or otherwise infamous crime, unless on a presentment or indictment of a grand jury, except in cases arising in the land or naval forces, or in the militia, when in actual service in time of war or public danger; nor shall any person be subject for the same offense to be twice put in jeopardy of life or limb; nor shall be compelled in any criminal case to be a witness against himself, nor be deprived of life, liberty or property, without due process of law; nor shall private property be taken for public use without just compensation.

AMENDMENT VI

In all criminal prosecutions, the accused shall enjoy the right to a speedy and public trial, by an impartial jury of the State and district wherein the crime shall have been committed, which district shall have been previously ascertained by law, and to be informed of the nature and cause of the accusation; to be confronted with the witnesses against him; to have compulsory process for obtaining witnesses in his favor, and to have the assistance of counsel for his defense.

AMENDMENT VII

In suits at common law, where the value in controversy shall exceed twenty dollars, the right of trial by jury shall be preserved, and no fact tried by a jury shall be otherwise re-examined in any court of the United States, than according to the rules of the common law.

AMENDMENT VIII

Excessive bail shall not be required, nor excessive fines imposed, nor cruel and unusual punishments inflicted.

AMENDMENT IX

The enumeration in the Constitution of certain rights shall not be construed to deny or disparage others retained by the people.

AMENDMENT X

The powers not delegated to the United States by the Constitution, nor prohibited by it to the States, are reserved to the States respectively, or to the people.

First Ten Amendments passed by Congress September 25, 1789.
Ratified by three-fourths of the states December 15, 1791.

AMENDMENT XI

The judicial power of the United States shall not be construed to extend to any suit in law or equity, commenced or prosecuted against one of the United States by citizens of another State, or by citizens or subjects of any foreign state.

Passed by Congress March 4, 1794.
Ratified February 7, 1795.

AMENDMENT XII

[1] The Electors shall meet in their respective States and vote by ballot for President and Vice-President, one of whom, at least, shall not be an inhabitant of the same State with themselves; they shall name in their ballots the person voted for as President, and in distinct ballots the person voted for as Vice-President, and they shall make distinct lists of all persons voted for as President and of all persons voted for as Vice-President, and of the number of votes for each; which lists they shall sign and certify, and transmit sealed to the seat of the government of the United States, directed to the President of the Senate. The President of the Senate shall in the presence of the Senate and House of Representatives, open all the certificates and the votes shall then be counted. The person having the greatest number of votes for President shall be the

President, if such number be a majority of the whole number of Electors appointed; and if no person have such majority, then from the persons having the highest numbers not exceeding three on the list of those voted for as President, the House of Representatives shall choose immediately, by ballot, the President. But in choosing the President the votes shall be taken by States, the representation from each State having one vote; a quorum for this purpose shall consist of a member or members from two-thirds of the States, and a majority of all the States shall be necessary to a choice. And if the House of Representatives shall not choose a President whenever the right of choice shall devolve upon them, before the fourth day of March next following, then the Vice-President shall act as President, as in the case of the death or other constitutional disability of the President.

[2] The person having the greatest number of votes as Vice-President shall be the Vice-President, if such number be a majority of the whole number of Electors appointed; and if no person have a majority, then from the two highest numbers on the list the Senate shall choose the Vice-President; a quorum for the purpose shall consist of two-thirds of the whole number of Senators, and a majority of the whole number shall be necessary to a choice. But no person constitutionally ineligible to the office of President shall be eligible to that of Vice-President of the United States.

Passed by Congress December 9, 1803.
Ratified July 27, 1804.

AMENDMENT XIII

SECTION 1

Neither slavery nor involuntary servitude, except as a punishment for crime whereof the party shall have been duly convicted, shall exist within the United States, or any place subject to their jurisdiction.

SECTION 2

Congress shall have power to enforce this article by appropriate legislation.

Passed by Congress January 31, 1865.
Ratified December 6, 1865.

AMENDMENT XIV

SECTION 1

All persons born or naturalized in the United States, and subject to the jurisdiction thereof, are citizens of the United States and of the State wherein they reside. No State shall make or enforce any law which shall abridge the privileges or immunities of citizens of the United States; nor shall any State deprive any person of life, liberty or property, without due process of law; nor deny to any person within its jurisdiction the equal protection of the laws.

SECTION 2

Representatives shall be apportioned among the several States according to their respective numbers, counting the whole number of persons in each State, excluding Indians not taxed. But when the right to vote at any election for the choice of Electors for President and Vice-President of the United States, Representatives in Congress, the executive and judicial officers of a State, or the members of the legislature thereof, is denied to any of the male inhabitants of such State, being twenty-one years of age, and citizens of the United States, or in any way abridged except for participation in rebellion or other crime, the basis of representation therein shall be reduced in the proportion which the number of such male citizens shall bear to the whole number of male citizens twenty-one years of age in such State.

SECTION 3

No person shall be a Senator or Representative in Congress, or elector of President and Vice-President, or hold any office, civil or military, under the United States or under any State, who, having previously taken an oath as a member of Congress, or as an officer of the United States, or as a member of any State legislature, or as an executive or judicial officer of any State, to support the Constitution of the United States, shall have engaged in insurrection or rebellion against the same, or given aid or comfort to the enemies thereof. But Congress may, by a vote of two-thirds of each House, remove such disability.

SECTION 4

The validity of the public debt of the United States, authorized by law, including debts incurred for payment of pensions and bounties for services in suppressing insurrection or rebellion, shall not be questioned. But neither the United States nor any State shall assume or pay any debt or obligation incurred in aid of insurrection or rebellion against the United States, or any claim for the loss or emancipation of any slave; but all such debts, obligations, and claims shall be held illegal and void.

SECTION 5

The Congress shall have power to enforce, by appropriate legislation, the provisions of this article.

Passed by Congress June 13, 1866.
Ratified July 9, 1868.

AMENDMENT XV

SECTION 1

The right of citizens of the United States to vote shall not be denied or abridged by the United States or by any State on account of race, color, or previous condition of servitude.

SECTION 2

The Congress shall have power to enforce this article by appropriate legislation.

Passed by Congress February 26, 1869.
Ratified February 3, 1870.

AMENDMENT XVI

The Congress shall have power to lay and collect taxes on incomes, from whatever source derived, without apportionment among the several States, and without regard to any census or enumeration.

Passed by Congress July 2, 1909.
Ratified February 3, 1913.

AMENDMENT XVII

SECTION 1

The Senate of the United States shall be composed of two Senators from each State, elected by the people thereof, for six years; and each Senator shall have one vote. The electors in each State shall have the qualifications requisite for electors of the most numerous branch of the State legislatures.

SECTION 2

When vacancies happen in the representation of any State in the Senate, the executive authority of such State shall issue writs of election to fill such vacancies: Provided, that the legislature of any State may empower the executive thereof to make temporary appointments until the people fill the vacancies by election as the legislature may direct.

SECTION 3

This amendment shall not be construed as to affect the election or term of any Senator chosen before it becomes valid as part of the Constitution.

Passed by Congress May 13, 1912.
Ratified April 8, 1913.

AMENDMENT XVIII

SECTION 1

After one year from the ratification of this article the manufacture, sale or transportation of intoxicating liquors within, the importation thereof into, or the exportation thereof from the United States and all territory subject to the jurisdiction thereof, for beverage purposes, is hereby prohibited.

SECTION 2

The Congress and the several States shall have concurrent power to enforce this article by appropriate legislation.

SECTION 3

This article shall be inoperative unless it shall have been ratified as an amendment to the Constitution by the legislatures of the several States, as provided in the Constitution, within seven years from the date of the submission hereof to the States by the Congress.

Passed by Congress December 18, 1917.
Ratified January 16, 1919.

AMENDMENT XIX

SECTION 1

The right of citizens of the United States to vote shall not be denied or abridged by the United States or by any State on account of sex.

SECTION 2

Congress shall have power to enforce this article by appropriate legislation.

Passed by Congress June 4, 1919.
Ratified August 18, 1920.

AMENDMENT XX

SECTION 1

The terms of the President and Vice-President shall end at noon on the 20th day of January, and the terms of Senators and Representatives at noon on the 3d day of January, of the years in which such terms would have ended if this article had not been ratified; and the terms of their successors shall then begin.

SECTION 2

The Congress shall assemble at least once in every year, and such meetings shall begin at noon on the 3d day of January, unless they shall by law appoint a different day.

SECTION 3

If, at the time fixed for the beginning of the term of the President, the President-elect shall have died, the Vice-President-elect shall become President. If a President shall not have been chosen before the time fixed for the beginning of his term or if the President-elect shall have failed to qualify, then the Vice-President-elect shall act as President until a President shall have qualified; and the Congress may by law provide for the case wherein neither a President-elect nor a Vice-President-elect shall have qualified, declaring who shall then act as President, or the manner in which one who is to act shall be selected, and such person shall act accordingly until a President or Vice-President shall have qualified.

SECTION 4

The Congress may by law provide for the case of the death of any of the persons from whom the House of Representatives may choose a President whenever the right of choice shall have devolved upon them, and for the case of death of any of the persons from whom the Senate may choose a Vice-President whenever the right of choice shall have devolved upon them.

SECTION 5

Sections I and II shall take effect on the 15th day of October following the ratification of this article.

SECTION 6

This article shall be inoperative unless it shall have been ratified as an amendment to the Constitution by the legislatures of three-fourths of the several States within seven years from the date of its submission.

Passed by Congress March 2, 1932.
Ratified January 23, 1933.

AMENDMENT XXI

SECTION 1

The eighteenth article of amendment to the Constitution of the United States is hereby repealed.

SECTION 2

The transportation or importation into any State, territory, or possession of the United States for delivery or use therein of intoxicating liquors, in violation of the laws thereof, is hereby prohibited.

SECTION 3

This article shall be inoperative unless it shall have been ratified as an amendment to the Constitution by conventions in the several States, as provided in the Constitution, within seven years from the date of the submission hereof to the States by the Congress.

Passed by Congress February 20, 1933.
Ratified December 5, 1933.

AMENDMENT XXII

No person shall be elected to the office of President more than twice, and no person who has held the office of President, or acted as President, for more than two years of a term to which some other person was elected President shall be elected to the office of President more than once. But this Article shall not apply to any person holding the office of President when this Article was proposed by the Congress, and shall not prevent any person who may be holding the office of

President, or acting as President, during the term within which this Article becomes operative from holding the office of President or acting as President during the remainder of such term.

SECTION 2

This article shall be inoperative unless it shall have been ratified as an amendment to the Constitution by the legislatures of three-fourths of the several States within seven years from the date of its submission to the States by the Congress.

Passed by Congress March 21, 1947.
Ratified February 27, 1951.

AMENDMENT XXIII

SECTION 1

The District constituting the seat of Government of the United States shall appoint in such manner as the Congress may direct:
A number of electors of President and Vice-President equal to the whole number of Senators and Representatives in Congress to which the District would be entitled if it were a State, but in no event more than the least populous State; they shall be in addition to those appointed by the States, but they shall be considered, for the purposes of the election of President and Vice-President, to be electors appointed by a State; and they shall meet in the District and perform such duties as provided by the twelfth article of amendment.

SECTION 2

The Congress shall have power to enforce this article by appropriate legislation.

Passed by Congress June 16, 1960.
Ratified March 29, 1961.

AMENDMENT XXIV

SECTION 1

The right of citizens of the United States to vote in any primary or other election for President or Vice-President, for electors for President or Vice-President, or for Senator or Representative in Congress, shall not be denied or abridged by the United States or any State by reason of failure to pay any poll tax or other tax.

SECTION 2

The Congress shall have power to enforce this article by appropriate legislation.

Passed by Congress August 27, 1962.
Ratified January 23, 1964.

AMENDMENT XXV

SECTION 1

In case of the removal of the President from office or of his death or resignation, the Vice-President shall become President.

SECTION 2

Whenever there is a vacancy in the office of the Vice-President, the President shall nominate a Vice-President who shall take office upon confirmation by a majority vote of both Houses of Congress.

SECTION 3

Whenever the President transmits to the President pro tempore of the Senate and the Speaker of the House of Representatives has written declaration that he is unable to discharge the powers and duties of his office, and until he transmits to them a written declaration to the contrary, such powers and duties shall be discharged by the Vice-President as Acting President.

SECTION 4

Whenever the Vice-President and a majority of either the principal officers of the executive departments or of such other body as Congress may by law provide, transmit to the President pro tempore of the Senate and the Speaker of the House of Representatives their written declaration that the President is unable to discharge the powers and duties of his office, the Vice-President shall immediately assume the powers and duties of the office as Acting President.

Thereafter, when the President transmits to the President pro tempore of the Senate and the Speaker of the House of Representatives his written declaration that no inability exists, he shall resume the powers and duties of his office unless the Vice-President and a majority of either the principal officers of the executive department or of such other body as Congress may by law provide, transmit within four days to the President pro tempore of the Senate and the Speaker of the House of Representatives their written declaration that the President is unable to discharge the powers and duties of his office. Thereupon Congress shall decide the issue, assembling within forty-eight hours for that purpose if not in session. If the Congress, within twenty-one days after receipt of the latter written declaration, or, if Congress is not in session, within twenty-one days after Congress is required to assemble, determines by two-thirds vote of both Houses that the President is unable to discharge the powers and duties of his office, the Vice-President shall continue to discharge the same as Acting President; otherwise, the President shall resume the powers and duties of his office.

Passed by Congress July 6, 1965.
Ratified February 10, 1967.

AMENDMENT XXVI

SECTION 1

The right of citizens of the United States, who are eighteen years of age or older, to vote shall not be denied or abridged by the United States or by any State on account of age.

SECTION 2

The Congress shall have power to enforce this article by appropriate legislation.

Passed by Congress March 23, 1971.
Ratified June 30, 1971.

AMENDMENT XXVII (PROPOSED)

SECTION 1

Equality of rights under the law shall not be denied or abridged by the United States or by any State on account of sex.

SECTION 2

The Congress shall have the power to enforce, by appropriate legislation, the provisions of this article.

SECTION 3

The amendment shall take effect two years after the date of ratification.

Passed by Congress March 22, 1972.

INDEX

primaries for, 252, 253
and publicity, 178, 179
removal of appointed officials, 344, 345
respect of, 140
role of, 66, 67
and separation of powers, 60
strong presidency, 371
styles of Presidents, 349
symbolism of, 341, 342
treaties and, 356, 357
U.S. Supreme Court justices,
    appointment of, 459–462
veto power of, 359, 360
Vietnam war affecting military
    powers of, 353, 354
wartime emergency powers, 354, 355
White House staff and, 348–350
Presidential systems, 19
Press. *See* News media
Press secretaries, 178
Pressman, J. L., 238
Pressure groups. *See* Interest groups
Presthus, Robert, 432
Primaries
    media covering, 151
    for president, 252, 253
    table of turnout in, 94
    types of, 249
Primary schooling, 146
Priorities, 32
Pritchett, C. Herman, 463, 470
Problems in America, 152–154
Process, politics as, 11, 12
Professional organizations, 278
Professional persons and participation,
    110
Progressive Movement, 62
Progressive party, 231
    and conventions, 249
Prohibition, 118
Property
    and protests, 106
    and voting qualification, 107
Proportional representation primaries,
    252, 254
Protests, 34
    freedom to make, 104–106
    of grievances, 96–98
    peaceful assembly, 69, 284
    restraints on, 105, 106
    and students, 144
    and violence, 34

Protestant National Council of
    Churches, 274
Prothro, J. W., 44, 115
Public defined, 304
Public interest, policy and, 332, 333
Public officials. *See* Leaders
Public opinion polls. *See* Opinion
    surveys
Public policy, 13–16, 131, 132, 303–334
    antipoverty programs, 314–316
    bargaining and formulation of, 325–
        328
    bureaucracy and, 418, 419, 443–446
    coalitions of policymakers, 323–325
    comprehensive approach to
        formulation of, 329–332
    conflicts and, 316, 317
    defined, 303
    formulators of, 305, 306
    gun-control legislation, 311–314
    incremental approach to formulation
        of, 329–332
    information flow and presidential
        policy, 367, 368
    pluralism and, 318–325
    President and, 336
    reciprocity, 329
    redistributing resources, 306, 314–316
    styles of policy formulation, 325–328
    types of, 306
    U.S. Supreme Court and, 467–470,
        480–484
Public Utilities Commission v. *Pollack*,
    462
Publicity
    and decisions of voters, 220
    and presidents, 178
Publicizers of campaigners, 178, 179
Pueschel, J. K., 198

Quincy, Josiah, 4

Racial backgrounds.
    and ideological identifications, 142
    and participation, 115, 116
Racial segregation. *See also* Busing
    courts and, 65, 339, 464–466
    middle-class norms and, 146
    opinion surveys on, 134
    and partisanship, 195, 196
    problems of, 154
    tables on, 135